Praise for *War and Decision*

"The best account to date of how the administration debated, decided, organized, and executed its military responses to the attacks of September 11, 2001. Much of what makes *War and Decision* so compelling is that it is, in effect, a revisionist history. Much to Mr. Feith's credit, however, his book is no apologia, even for those he obviously admires. . . . Indispensable." —Bret Stephens, *Wall Street Journal*

"Extraordinarily frank and persuasive. . . . Our first in-depth look at the inside of the Bush administration's national security top leadership from one who was there. [Feith] should be saluted for getting many materials declassified so that we can have a clearer idea of what was actually going on. . . . He seems to be at pains to relay the arguments of those who had different views fairly and accurately. He concedes some mistakes of his own. And he contradicts much of what has become conventional wisdom about the Iraq war."

—Michael Barone, *U.S. News & World Report*

"If you want to read a serious book about the origins and consequences of the intervention in Iraq in 2003, you owe it to yourself to get hold of a copy of Douglas Feith's *War and Decision*. . . . There is more of value in any chapter of this archive than in any of the ramblings of [Scott] McClellan. . . . I don't know Feith, but I can pay him two further compliments: When you read him on a detail with which you yourself are familiar, he is factually reliable (and it's not often that one can say that, believe me). And his prose style is easy, nonbureaucratic, dry, and sometimes amusing. If a book that was truly informative was called a 'tell-all' by our media, then *War and Decision* would qualify."

—Christopher Hitchens, Slate.com

"Meticulous. . . . A convincing refutation of unfair allegations about the author [and] a balanced analysis of policy debates about Iraq inside the administration. . . . Will be studied for years by journalists, historians, and aspiring political appointees." —Bing West, *National Review*

"Brilliant. . . . [A] controversial and compelling account. . . . Fascinating on many levels. . . . [Belongs on] the necessary shelf of books."

—Hugh Hewitt, *The Hugh Hewitt Show*

"A scholarly, well-documented book. . . . May eventually influence the judgment of history." —Sarah Baxter, *The Sunday Times* (London)

"For anyone seriously interested in the decisions [made] prior to and during the Iraq war, *War and Decision* is a must-read book. . . . Feith provides careful documentation rather than just freewheeling opinions. He explodes many of the journalistic and political myths that have become widely accepted. . . . His judgments are thoughtful—and, for a major player in the process, he is quite objective regarding what went wrong. *War and Decision* will be a treasure trove for the historians—when the current passions have finally cooled."

—James Schlesinger, Director of Central Intelligence, Nixon administration; Secretary of Defense, Nixon and Ford administrations; Secretary of Energy, Carter administration

"This is a very carefully written and serious historical work, and will be required reading for someone who wants a better understanding of why and how we went to war in Iraq. And especially for the Iraq war critics, the book allows one to put strong opinions aside for a moment and learn about the decision process and how it ended up where it did. It's all here. . . . [A] fascinating story and very well told. . . . Extremely well-documented, so well it will become a basic source document about the war. . . . Such refreshing change from this genre of books—those that make sweeping statements or conclusions without any reference or citation of support. . . . Demonstrates—probably better than any other Washington political insider story—how the U.S. national security policy 'process' really works. . . . Mr. Feith is both candid and critical. . . . The best and most objective account to date of the high-level and inside policy dynamics that led to the war in Iraq."

—Daniel Gallington, *Washington Times*

"[Feith] says his goal is to counter the now-common narrative of a reckless administration that twisted intelligence and was bent from the start on war with Saddam Hussein. It's a serious intent, and [*War and Decision*] deserves to be taken seriously.

—Peter Grier, *Christian Science Monitor*

"What's needed now? More memoirs, more data, more information, more testimony. More serious books, like Doug Feith's. More 'this is what I saw' and 'this is what is true.' Feed history."

—Peggy Noonan, *Wall Street Journal*

"Scrupulous in his command of the facts, exacting in his analysis, and lucidly articulate in his writing. . . . Splendid."

—Frank Gaffney, *Washington Times*

"Certain to amaze readers. . . . The most well-documented explanation of how decisions were made. . . . Careful, dispassionate, and massively documented . . . [full of] fascinating detail. . . . Sets a high standard for official memoirs. . . . The press wrote the first draft of the Bush administration and the war on terror, but Feith's book relegates it to the recycling bin."

—Larry Di Rita, NationalReview.com

"As Americans turned on the Iraq war, anti-war forces tried to portray the war as not only a mistake, but the result of a neoconservative coup. . . . In his new memoir, *War and Decision*, Mr. Feith does an admirable job in dispelling this hokum."

—Eli Lake, *New York Sun*

"The fullest and most thoughtful statement of the Pentagon thinking prior to and in the first stages of the Iraq war. Even those . . . who take issue with some of its conclusions will gain a better perspective from reading this book."

—Henry A. Kissinger, National Security Adviser, Nixon administration; Secretary of State, Nixon and Ford administrations

"Douglas Feith has written a model memoir: fair-minded, objective, and without rancor. The fact that the policy to which he contributed was flawed from the outset in no way diminishes the historical importance of this firsthand account."

—Jean Edward Smith, John Marshall Professor of Political Science, Marshall University; author of *FDR*, *Grant*, and *John Marshall: Definer of a Nation*

"One would have expected [Feith to] use the memoir genre to get even. Instead, he is self-critical, even admits to occasional hubris, but, more importantly, also chronicles the contortions and reinventions of so many post–2003/2004 critics of the war. . . . There are also good criticisms of the administration's incompetence in communicating to the public what we were doing in Iraq—and indeed what the war on terror was about and what it was for."

—Victor Davis Hanson, NationalReview.com

"A controversial book. It will certainly anger many readers because it takes a different position than most other accounts on the wisdom of going to war in Iraq, on what mistakes were made, and on who made them. But Feith's is a serious work, well-documented, that presents the best defense to date of the defining policy of the Bush presidency. It is a readable account that deserves to be read, and its argument, debated."

—Robert L. Gallucci, Dean of the Edmund A. Walsh School of Foreign Service, Georgetown University; Assistant Secretary of State for Political-Military Affairs, Clinton administration

Courtesy of the author

About the Author

DOUGLAS J. FEITH was appointed the U.S. Under Secretary of Defense for Policy in 2001, and served until the summer of 2005. Before that, he had worked during the Reagan administration as a Middle East specialist and as Deputy Assistant Secretary of Defense for Negotiations Policy. His articles have been published in the *New York Times*, the *Washington Post*, the *Wall Street Journal*, and elsewhere. Feith is Director for National Security Strategies at the Hudson Institute and is a Belfer Center Adjunct Visiting Scholar at Harvard University's John F. Kennedy School of Government. He lives with his family near Washington, D.C.

WAR AND DECISION

Inside the Pentagon at the Dawn of the War on Terrorism

Douglas J. Feith

HARPER

NEW YORK • LONDON • TORONTO • SYDNEY

HARPER

A hardcover edition of this book was published in 2008 by HarperCollins Publishers.

FIRST HARPER PAPERBACK PUBLISHED 2009.

Designed by Lisa Erb

Library of Congress Cataloging-in-Publication Data is available upon request.

ISBN 978-0-06-137366-4

09 10 11 12 13 NMSG/RRD 10 9 8 7 6 5 4 3 2 1

To my mother, Rose Feith,
to the memory of my father, Dalck Feith, and
to the men and women of the U.S. Armed Forces.

CONTENTS

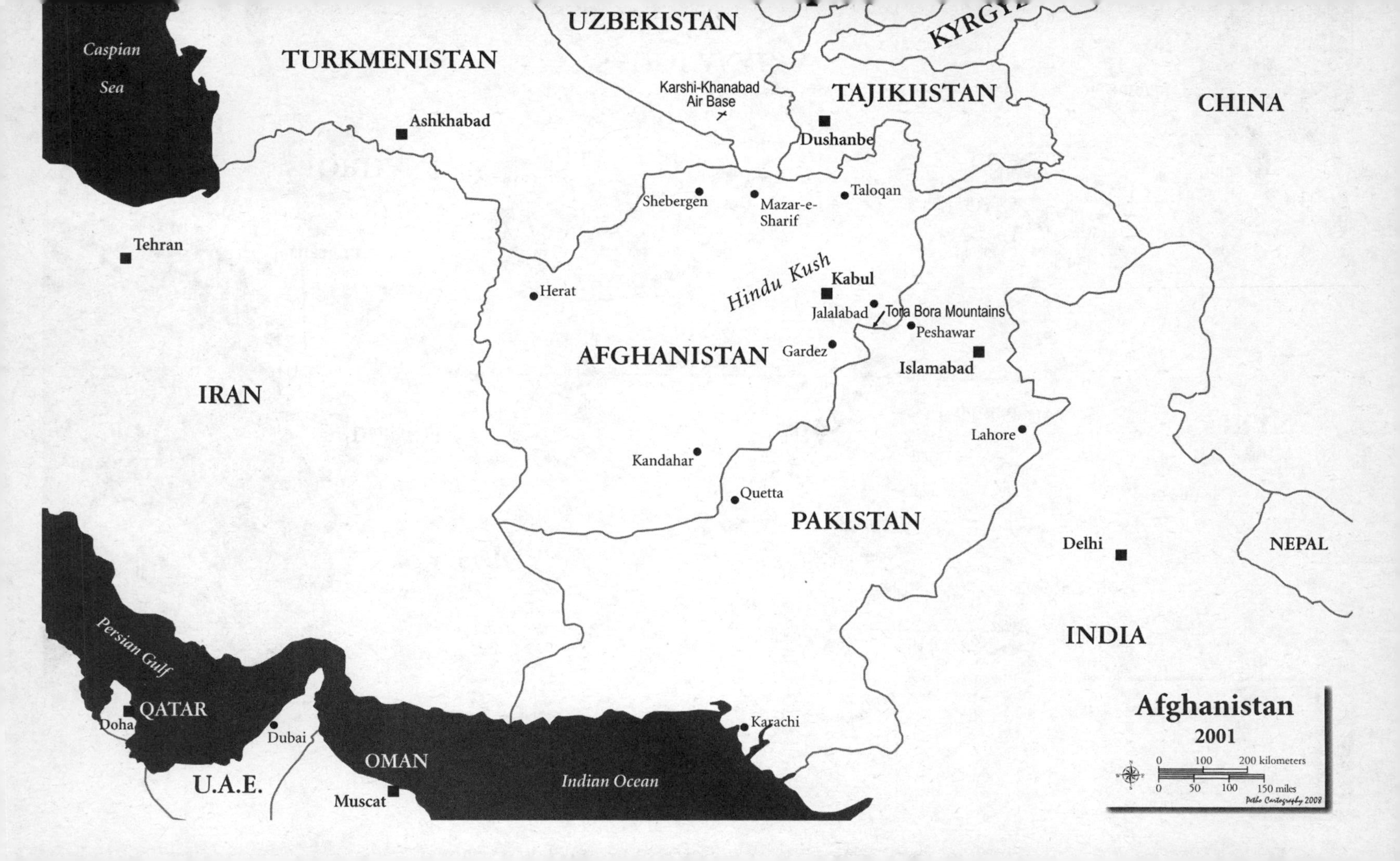
Afghanistan
2001
Caspian Sea
TURKMENISTAN
UZBEKISTAN
KYRGY
TAJIKIISTAN
CHINA
Karshi-Khanabad Air Base
Ashkhabad
Dushanbe
Shebergen
Mazar-e-Sharif
Taloqan
Tehran
Hindu Kush
Kabul
Herat
Jalalabad
Tora Bora Mountains
Peshawar
Gardez
AFGHANISTAN
Islamabad
IRAN
Lahore
Kandahar
Quetta
PAKISTAN
Delhi
NEPAL
INDIA
Persian Gulf
QATAR
Doha
Dubai
Karachi
OMAN
U.A.E.
Indian Ocean
Muscat
0 100 200 kilometers
0 50 100 150 miles
Petho Cartography 2008

Iraq
2003
0 50 100 150 kilometers
0 25 50 75 100 miles
Petho Cartography 2008
TURKEY
Adana
SYRIA
LEBANON
Beirut
Damascus
Mediterranean
Haifa
Tel Aviv
ISRAEL
Amman
Jerusalem
Suez
JORDAN
EGYPT
SAUDI ARABIA
Kurdish Autonomous Region
Mosul
Irbil
Northern No-fly Zone
Sulaimaniya
Kirkuk
NORTHERN OIL FIELDS
Samarra
Balad
IRAQ
Baghdad
Ramadi
Fallujah
Southern No-fly Zone
Tigris
Karbala
Najaf
Euphrates
Shatrah
Nasariyah
Tallil Air Base
RUMAILAH OIL FIELDS
Basra
Umm Qasr
Kermanshah
IRAN
Kuwait City
KUWAIT
Persian Gulf

INTRODUCTION

This memoir is a window into the Bush Administration's decisions—on how to fight the war on terrorism, whether to overthrow the Iraqi regime, and how to deal with post-Saddam Iraq. It does not attempt to persuade the reader that the President decided these issues correctly. I have aimed not to write a polemic, but rather to make a contribution to history, extensively documented and as accurate as one person's account can be.

The war on terrorism, an unconventional conflict, challenges us to answer even the most basic questions: When did the war start? Who is the enemy? Are we winning or losing? How will we know when it is over? Does it make sense to say we are at war with *terrorism*, which is an activity, not an enemy? How can we fight an enemy whose troops are scattered around the world, many of them living in countries with which we are not at war?

These questions can be debated at length from many angles—but 9/11 left little time for elaborate deliberation. Terrorists had attacked Americans on American soil, obliterating the World Trade Center, destroying the west side of the Pentagon, and causing an airliner to crash in Pennsylvania. More than three thousand people had been killed within an hour and a quarter. President George W. Bush and his national security team took action, with one main goal: to prevent another such attack.

I was a member of that team. As Under Secretary of Defense for Policy, I reported to the Secretary of Defense, Donald Rumsfeld, advising him on national security policy and defense strategy. My colleagues in Rumsfeld's wartime inner circle included Deputy Secretary of Defense Paul Wolfowitz and the Chairman and Vice Chairman of the Joint Chiefs of Staff, Generals Richard Myers and Peter Pace.

I headed the Defense Department's Policy organization of approximately fifteen hundred staff members. Its main tasks were, first, to help Rumsfeld develop strategic guidance for the department, including the National Defense Strategy and the instructions the Secretary of Defense issues to his combatant commanders. Second, to manage the department's relations with all foreign countries: The Policy office is sometimes called "the State Department within the Pentagon." And, third, to represent the Office of the Secretary of Defense—that is, the civilian side of the department—in the interagency process for making national security policy. This was the arena of fabled bureaucratic battles between the Defense and State Departments, the subject of voluminous—and occasionally correct—journalistic stories. Those battles are an important part of the history recounted in this book.

The narrative here, particularly on the decision to overthrow Saddam Hussein, is thoroughly at odds with the conventional account provided in recent books and articles on President Bush, terrorism, and Iraq. The now-standard story portrays the President and his supporters in the Administration as militaristic and reckless, closed-minded and ideological, thoughtless at best and even dishonest—and hell-bent on war with Iraq from the Administration's inception.

The record—much of it presented here for the first time—paints a different picture. Historians will find that President Bush and his top advisers wrestled analytically and seriously with difficult problems, many of them without precedent. Officials devised a comprehensive approach to disrupting terrorist networks—targeting terrorist leadership, finances, and movement, and striking at the terrorists' state sponsors. Regarding Iraq, we looked closely at the dangers of war, weighing them against the dangers of leaving Saddam Hussein in power. We heard and considered the arguments of our political opponents and critics, domestic and foreign. We developed sensible plans to deal with a range of contingencies—from humanitarian crises to creation of post-Saddam governmental institutions.

All of this work was done in good faith. And it produced, or contributed to, important good results: most notably, the fact that six years have passed without another major attack within U.S. borders—an accomplishment that looked distinctly unlikely on September 12, 2001.

But on Iraq, in particular, the Administration made some serious errors. Some of these were in its intelligence assessments. Some were in the policy plans and some in the operational plans. Some were in decisions made in Washington in response to events—and some were in decisions made in the field.

This is not to say that every problem the United States has encountered in Iraq is attributable to errors by Bush Administration officials. It is foolish to suppose that any group of officials—even if they were to display extraordinary wisdom, harmony, and attention to detail—could manage a problem-free war. But, in fact, certain actions by Administration officials appear to have caused or aggravated important difficulties, damaging American credibility and otherwise harming the war effort and our national interests. A number of these actions are dissected in this book.

The Iraq challenge predated the 9/11 attack. Throughout the 1990s, Saddam was widely recognized as a danger to his region and to U.S. interests generally. In 1990 he drew us into war by invading Kuwait. In 1991 he accepted a UN-sponsored cease-fire deal, and then spent more than a decade flouting it. In 1998, the United States Congress reacted to Saddam's actions by declaring a policy of "regime change" in Iraq.

The 9/11 attack made the Iraq problem appear more grave and urgent, though not because any officials assumed Iraq was involved in the hijackings. Rather, it was because al Qaida had demonstrated that America's enemies had the opportunity, will, and means to cause devastating harm to our country *without having to defeat us militarily*. With this in mind, U.S. officials reevaluated all major national security threats—and especially the danger that terrorists might acquire weapons of mass destruction. There was intense concern that a hostile state, working with a terrorist group, could precipitate a catastrophic attack against us.

Among critics of the Bush Administration, the conventional view of the Iraq war now discounts all these worries as fear-mongering (a dismissal made easier because Saddam is no longer an active threat to us or his neighbors, and because fears of terrorist attack have diminished since 2001). Critics have argued that U.S. officials manipulated intelligence to induce the President to overthrow Saddam, and to persuade the public to support the war. They insist that officials who made the case for regime change in Iraq did so for ideological or improper reasons—to spread democracy by the sword, or to serve Israel's interests rather than America's.

Among the other key assertions made by these critics are:

- That President Bush and his hawkish advisers came into office intent on launching a war in Iraq and gave no serious consideration to means short of war to deal with the Iraq problem
- That "neocon" officials failed to plan for postwar Iraq, believing that both the war itself and the postwar transition to democracy would be easy
- That Donald Rumsfeld's Defense Department planned to "anoint" Ahmad Chalabi, the Iraqi exile, as the leader of liberated Iraq
- That the State Department had a plan for postwar Iraq, and that Defense officials ignored or discarded that plan

These contentions served the personal and political interests of the officials and journalists who spread them, and they have gained a devoted following. But they will not withstand scrutiny over time.

Readers who have invested time and faith in the current public affairs literature may find it jarring to discover that key Administration figures—Colin Powell, Donald Rumsfeld, Dick Cheney, Condoleezza Rice, Richard Armitage, Paul Wolfowitz, myself, and others—made arguments and advocated policies that run directly counter to the positions usually associated with them. For example:

- It was Pentagon "neocons" who continually urged the President to tone down his democracy rhetoric.
- The most powerful analysis of the downsides of going to war in Iraq came not from the State Department or the CIA, but from Donald Rumsfeld.
- The Pentagon-CIA dispute over the Iraq–al Qaida relationship began with objections by Defense officials about the CIA's politicization of intelligence, not the other way around.
- The work of the State Department's Future of Iraq project on post-Saddam political transition was opposed not by Defense officials, but by Colin Powell and Richard Armitage.
- It was CIA officials who predicted that Iraqis would launch pro-U.S. uprisings after the start of the war.

- It was State Department officials who advocated a multiyear U.S. occupation of Iraq.

As a memoir rather than a history, this work makes no claim to be comprehensive. The stories and topics I discuss here, by and large, are those in which I had a substantial role. This book sheds light on some important decisions by the President, Secretary of Defense, and others, but by no means all such decisions. Writing it has added to my appreciation of Tom Stoppard's play *Rosencrantz and Guildenstern Are Dead*, which wittily retells the Hamlet story from the point of view of two characters who were offstage as key events played out. While I was not as peripheral as those schoolmates of Hamlet, I cannot claim to be an all-seeing narrator—or even an all-comprehending observer of the scenes I witnessed firsthand.

I do, however, offer considerable new information, drawn from the memos and briefings created and exchanged by the President's top advisers. Many of these were papers I drafted for Donald Rumsfeld. I take the reader into meetings of the Deputies and Principals Committees and of the National Security Council, drawing chiefly on the notes I took in those meetings—not on press stories or after-the-fact interviews, in which officials remember (or pretend to remember) what happened months or years before.*

I quote extensively from these written sources, with attention to accuracy and context. Some of the documents I rely on remain wholly or partially classified. But if I have been inaccurate or unfair, I know that people in the government (including members of Congress, who have access to many of the relevant documents) will quickly call me on it. And when the records are eventually declassified, general readers will be able to challenge my interpretations.

Every substantive quotation in the book comes from a conversation or meeting for which I took written notes *at the time*. I have no respect for the now-common practice of authors of nonfiction presenting long passages of dialogue, complete with quotation marks, when all they have to go on is a set of notes that is far short of a transcript.

It has often been remarked that no one ever lost a debate in his own memorandum of conversation: Library shelves sag with self-congratulatory

*All quoted documents are cited in this book, but I have not provided citations to my meeting notes, because I identify the meetings in the text—and the notes are in the National Archives, among my papers or those of Secretary Rumsfeld. I have created a website (www.waranddecision.com) to post most of the unclassified, previously unpublished documents cited here, as well as the cited newspaper and journal items.

volumes of the I-was-surrounded-by-idiots school of memoir writing. I often disagreed with colleagues in the Administration, but I did *not* consider them foolish, even when I thought they were wrong. I have tried to present my bureaucratic rivals and policy opponents—and characterize their arguments—in ways I think they would deem true and in context. On the flip side, I try to deal objectively and even self-critically with arguments and observations put forward by me and those whose views I shared.

Throughout, I have tried to avoid gratuitous judgment and blame-laying. Many of the most significant questions about the campaign against terrorism and the war in Iraq—including why important aspects went wrong and who should be held accountable—cannot be answered authoritatively until a great deal more is known about them.

Critics commonly suggest that every problem is the result of some policy maker's error. But policy making often involves choosing to accept one set of likely problems over another. This book offers an account of recent history from the perspective of a policy official—that is, one whose job it is to deal with history before it occurs. Historical events look different before the fact: Once one knows how a story turns out, it is easy to sift the record for telling comments and actions that can be connected to grand outcomes. But before the fact, we cannot know which potential problem or opportunity might become the hinge of fate.

1
THIS MEANS WAR

The threat of jihadist terrorism was on the list of U.S. government concerns at the start of the Bush Administration in early 2001, but it got less attention than Russia did. As a first order of business, President George W. Bush wanted his new Administration to ensure, if possible, that Russia and the United States would never revive the nuclear tensions of the Cold War.

His Secretary of Defense, Donald Rumsfeld, favored the effort. Over the years, Rumsfeld's view of the relationship between the two countries had been informed by his career as a member of Congress, U.S. Ambassador to NATO, White House Chief of Staff, Secretary of Defense, and corporate executive. The President assigned Rumsfeld a leading role in this Russia project—and so it became my first major assignment when I returned to the government in mid-July 2001 as Under Secretary of Defense for Policy, the top adviser on defense strategy and national security to Rumsfeld and Deputy Secretary of Defense Paul Wolfowitz.

I had worked at the Pentagon before, in the middle years of the Reagan Administration—a bitter period in the Cold War, a time of widespread and well-grounded fear of superpower conflict. A strategic missile fired from the Soviet Union could devastate an American city within seven minutes, and vice versa. Nations around the world watched the Soviet Union and the United States with anxious impotence, knowing that such a nuclear exchange would cause a global disaster.

The Cold War ended well, however, and the world became safer when the Soviet Union died a nonviolent death on Christmas Day in 1991. But Russia retained much of the Soviet Union's nuclear arsenal. Ten years later, President Bush entered office with the goal of making Russia a partner rather than an adversary in security affairs. He viewed Russia with hope because, as he saw it, neither he nor Russian President Vladimir Putin had the zero-sum-game mentality of the Soviet era. President Bush believed he could terminate the 1972 Anti-Ballistic Missile Treaty, build up our missile defenses, and work to enlarge NATO without reviving the Cold War or starting a new arms race.

I was pleased to be joining an Administration that aimed to identify common ground with Russia, dismantle Cold War structures, and change attitudes on both sides. Our success was far from certain. But the benefits—for us, the Russians, and the world—would be considerable if we did succeed.

In pursuit of these goals, on September 11, 2001, I was in Moscow for negotiations at the Russian Defense Ministry. It was my second visit to Russia since taking office less than two months before, part of the initiative to create a new framework for U.S.-Russian relations. But the news from New York that reached us a little before five o'clock that afternoon, Moscow time, forced me and everyone else in the United States to revise our thinking about national priorities.

As thoughtful and careful as we try to be, events have a way of confounding our assumptions. Even wisdom is no proof against surprises. It appreciates the proverb: If you want to hear God laugh, tell him your plans.

My work that day at the Defense Ministry had ended with a joint news conference with my Russian counterpart, General Colonel Yuri Nikolayevich Baluyevsky, an assertive man who sometimes seemed nostalgic for the superpower contention of the bad old days. At the small, ad hoc news conference—known as a "press gaggle"—in the hallway outside the conference room, Baluyevsky and I briefly reviewed the day's discussions. The Russian journalists asked about the Anti-Ballistic Missile Treaty and the prospects for a new nuclear weapons reduction treaty.

After the gaggle, I was heading for the car with Assistant Secretary of Defense J. D. Crouch when a U.S. embassy press officer quietly buttonholed us. He'd just heard, by cell phone, that a plane had hit the World Trade Center.

Skeptical about the news—first reports are almost always wrong—I glanced at Crouch. A cool-headed, intellectual, gentlemanly but tough figure, Crouch had been a university professor and a police SWAT team volunteer officer between tours at the Pentagon. He signaled that he shared my wait-and-see attitude.

Crouch and I kept to our schedule, moving along to an event with English-speaking reporters. When we arrived, minutes later, the embassy press officer told us that a *second* plane had hit the World Trade Center. He handed me a cell phone, and through it I heard CNN broadcast President Bush's first remarks about the attacks, made from an elementary school in Sarasota, Florida. The President said, "Terrorism against our nation will not stand."

The phrase astonished me. This was more than a confirmation that something bad had happened in New York. The President's words clearly echoed those of his father after Saddam Hussein invaded Kuwait in August 1990, as the nation faced the prospect of war in the Persian Gulf.

I did not think this choice of words could have been a coincidence. The first President Bush avoided categorical statements, tending to preserve flexibility rather than invoke fundamental principles. So his unqualified pronouncement that "this *will not stand,* this aggression against Kuwait" was uncharacteristically bold and inflexible—and therefore memorable. When I heard his son use those same words, I commented to Crouch that the President seemed to be talking war. From our location, thousands of miles from Washington, I took the President's words as strategic guidance.

Our conference with the English-language journalists was in a new American-style hotel in Moscow, in a small meeting room full of cameras and boom mikes and reporters with writing pads. Crouch and I were immediately asked about the New York attack, but we had heard nothing then but snippets of news coverage. It was clear that something terrible had happened, but its magnitude was still unclear. The Pentagon had not yet been hit, and the World Trade Center had not yet collapsed.

My main recollection of this press event was the badgering of the *New York Times* reporter, who wanted Crouch and me to agree with him that if airplanes could attack the World Trade Center, it made no sense for the United States to invest in protection against ballistic missiles. I was eager to wrap up the event so that we could learn more about what had happened in New York.

Then a CNN reporter announced to the group that there was "some type of fire at the Pentagon," and the news conference was over.

Eager to return to our posts in Washington as soon as possible, my delegation and I drove to the U.S. embassy, where we tapped the hospitality and communications links of Colonel Kevin Ryan (U.S. Army), the Defense Attaché. Our best source of information, we knew, would be television news; there are far more journalists in the world than intelligence agents. Like the rest of the world, we watched the astounding story unfold. The "fire" at the Pentagon, we learned, had been caused by a third hijacked plane the terrorists had flown into the building. This horrifying news hit us personally. The fifteen hundred people in my organization worked in offices spread throughout the building. Which section of the structure had been destroyed by the hijacked aircraft? Who had been hurt? Had any of the staff been killed? We felt exasperated to be stuck in Moscow—unable to assist and in the dark about the fate of our colleagues at the wounded Pentagon.*

I later learned from Andre Hollis, the head of the Policy organization's counternarcotics operation, that a large fireball had cut through his office. Two members of our staff, Thomas Johnson and Robert Kravinski, had saved themselves by ducking under their desks as the flame swept overhead, incinerating everything it touched. In all, the 9/11 attack took the lives of 189 people working at the Pentagon. By fate's caprice, the people who worked for me were all spared death or severe injury.

The dead at the Pentagon and World Trade Center and on Flight 93 had been murdered simply as symbolic U.S. targets. Americans by the millions felt the loss and risk personally, and in coming days they would express their kinship with the victims by flying American flags and grieving. We mourned them as family.

Sitting in the Defense Attaché's suite in Moscow, there was little I could do to help Rumsfeld at the moment. What I could do was formulate some initial thoughts about our policy going forward. With the President's words in mind, I used the attaché's computer to write Rumsfeld a short memo. This attack, I argued, was more than just a law enforcement matter, and the U.S. government should not feel constrained to limit its response to seeking out the individuals who had planned the attack. Rather, the United States might want to direct blows against the broader network of terrorists. All organizations involved in international terrorism could be considered in partnership with others in that business and held accountable "one for the other," as are partners under the laws of many countries. "In the 19th century," I noted, "when the British Navy suppressed piracy on the high seas and the slave trade, they attacked all vessels engaged in such activities. They did not feel constrained to link any given British attack to any particular crime committed by a pirate or slaver."

Vice Admiral Edmund Giambastiani, Rumsfeld's military assistant,

---

*We would not learn until the following day of the heroism of the passengers on United Airlines Flight 93.

delivered my memo to the Secretary at around noon, Washington time. The Secretary read it right away and told Giambastiani we were thinking along similar lines.

As I set down my thoughts for Rumsfeld, my military assistant worked on getting us home. With ordinary air traffic over the United States shut down, General Joseph Ralston of the U.S. European Command arranged for us to travel back on a KC-135 tanker usually used for aerial refueling of bombers and fighters. Although Russian officials had reacted sympathetically to the attack, and General Baluyevsky had phoned a kind condolence message to us at the embassy, securing Kremlin clearance for a U.S. military plane to retrieve us in Moscow was impossible on such short notice. So early on September 12 we took a commercial flight to Germany, where the KC-135 waited to take us to Andrews Air Force Base, just outside Washington.

The flight turned out to be seminal. By happenstance, it gave a handful of high-level Pentagon civilian and military personnel—including not only our own delegation, but a number of other stranded officials—the chance to compare their views on the nature of the terrorist challenge. Senior officials rarely have a five-hour block of time together to discuss such issues, and this opportunity helped us reach some important conclusions.

It was good fortune to have on the plane Lieutenant General John Abizaid, the head of the Strategy and Plans office of the Chairman of the Joint Chiefs of Staff (a position known in the Pentagon as the "J-5"). Abizaid had been visiting Ukraine on September 11. Of Lebanese Christian descent, Abizaid spoke Arabic and had substantial Middle East experience. He was good to talk and argue with, for he always had ideas and prided himself on speaking up when he disagreed with civilian leaders. He later told me that he thought this trait had gotten him off on the wrong foot with Donald Rumsfeld, but he couldn't have hurt himself too badly: Less than two years later, the Secretary appointed him to succeed General Tommy Franks as Commander of the U.S. Central Command (CENTCOM).

Topping the list of people in my Policy organization who had relevant responsibility and knowledge about terrorism were Peter Rodman, the Assistant Secretary of Defense for International Security Affairs, and William Luti, Rodman's deputy for Near East and South Asia Affairs. Rodman and Luti had been on assignment in Egypt together on September 11, and they joined us in Germany for the ride home.

For hours as we crossed the Atlantic, Abizaid, Rodman, Luti, and I stood together in the middle of the plane discussing what it would mean for the United States to be at war. Even as we deliberated, President Bush confirmed in a late morning statement on September 12 that he viewed the previous day's attack as "war." The KC-135 was not set up for real-time communications, so we didn't learn this until we landed. But the President's initial statement had persuaded us that he was treating the attack as an act of war, not just a crime.

We chewed over some fundamentals. I asked: What should be the main purpose of the U.S. government's immediate action? We agreed that it was neither to secure criminal justice for the perpetrators nor to retaliate, but *to prevent another attack*. The United States should act in self-defense, not for vengeance. This idea was of the greatest importance. It focused our attention on the future; it demanded a strategy for war, rather than mere law enforcement; and it recognized that the enemy was a wide-ranging set of individuals, organizations, and states.

The entire world wanted to know who had perpetrated the attack. Within the Administration and in the news media, speculation had focused immediately on the terrorist network known as al Qaida, because of its history and mode of operation, but we did not yet know who did it. In our airplane discussions, we recognized that identifying the perpetrators was not the same as deciding how to define the enemy. If the proper top priority of U.S. action was to prevent the next attack, after all, then the enemy was not just the particular group responsible for the 9/11 hijackings. It was the wider network of terrorists and their backers that might organize additional, large-scale strikes against the United States—no doubt inspired and energized by the "success" of 9/11.

Bill Luti, like Abizaid, brought a military man's perspective to the meaning of "war" in these peculiar circumstances. As a navy captain with experience as a combat aviator, Luti had been working in Vice President Dick Cheney's office when I hired him away. He retired from the navy to take the job of Deputy Assistant Secretary of Defense. Luti had a PhD in international relations and an irreverent attitude. He could quote extensively from Monty Python movies, and his taste for sarcastic humor would endear him to Rumsfeld. He worked creatively and intensely and drove his office hard, making it productive and influential beyond any other unit in Policy, perhaps in the whole Pentagon.*

Luti noted that politicians often used the term "war" as a metaphor:

---

*When Stephen Hadley became National Security Adviser in 2005, he pulled Luti back to the White House as Director of Defense Policy on the National Security Council staff.

the war on poverty, the war on drugs, the war on crime. For President Bush, he surmised, a war against our terrorist enemies would be more than a metaphor. Luti raised questions about the military's role—questions unlikely to have simple answers in such an extraordinary conflict. There was no precedent in U.S. history for a war against a worldwide "network." Military action might be required to overthrow dangerous regimes that played roles in the terrorist network. Short of invasion, Luti asked, what roles should the U.S. military be expected to play in this war?

Debates about the nature of terrorism, I mentioned, had been under way in foreign policy circles since the late 1960s—and one such debate concerned the nature of these terrorist "networks" and their state sponsors. Peter Rodman was familiar with that literature. He had what our military colleagues referred to as a "fifty-pound brain." Soft-spoken, genteel, and sage, with long experience at the White House and State Department—as a colleague of Henry Kissinger and George Shultz—Rodman had lived much of recent U.S. history and studied much of the rest. He thought well and wrote elegantly. When I was appointed Under Secretary, I had to plead with Rodman to join my team: Given our conflicting views on various issues, he wasn't sure we would work together smoothly. But he took the job after I promised that I would allow him and his memos to get to the Secretary whether or not I agreed with his ideas (a healthy practice I adopted with all my senior staff, down to the level of deputy assistant secretary).

Rodman and I recalled the controversy over Claire Sterling's 1981 book *The Terror Network*, which took the view that many international terrorist groups of the time were operating not as a unified, corporate-style hierarchy but as a network. Sterling's work highlighted the fact that such groups maintained ties among themselves—and that their network served interests of the Soviet Union, which provided them funds, training, explosives, and other support. But she took heat from critics who focused on the local grievances and "root causes" that such groups invoked to explain their actions.

Sterling was not claiming that the terrorist groups in question were simply Soviet fronts. Rather, she argued that such groups could be understood fully only by seeing how they worked with each other and with their state supporters. She would be vindicated as the evidence emerged in the following decades.

With Sterling's perspective in mind, I commented that we needed to know much more about how al Qaida and other jihadists operated as a network. We needed to understand their ideological, financial, and operational connections—to learn what linkages, if any, connected Shiite groups (such as Hezbollah) to Sunni groups (such as al Qaida) and how such groups related to their state sponsors. This would be no easy task: As Abizaid lamented, our intelligence about the enemy was inadequate.

We had to shout to be heard in the tanker's loud, cold, dimly lit belly, but our discussion was energetic and purposeful. We talked about the role governments played in the terrorist network—in particular by offering safe haven, as Afghanistan's Taliban regime did for al Qaida. We would have to take that role into account in identifying the enemy.

Over the years, I commented, some experts had argued for a territorial strategy to combat terrorism. Individual terrorists can be elusive, they warned, but the states providing them haven and support were also responsible for the spread of terrorism, and their fixed, known addresses made them easier to target than the terrorists themselves. A territorial strategy would concentrate on these state supporters, systematically aiming to hobble terrorist groups by cutting off their means of support.

But here was a problem, I said. The U.S. government could not simply define the enemy as a set of terrorist organizations together with states that helped them in one way or another. If we did, we could find ourselves declaring war against all countries that gave safe haven, funds, or ideological and other types of support to terrorists—a list that would include Afghanistan, Cuba, Iran, Iraq, Libya, North Korea, Pakistan, Saudi Arabia, Sudan, and Syria. This was clearly an unrealistic idea.* It further complicated matters that the United States considered some of these states important friends. Moreover, a formal list of terrorist enemy organizations would require continual revision, reflecting the mergers, acquisitions, splits, and name changes that were common among them. We needed a better way to define the enemy, one that would cover all the relevant bases but preserve our flexibility regarding how, when, and against whom we should act.

We did not solve this puzzle on the aircraft. The President eventually dealt with it by coining the term "war on terror," declaring, in effect, that the enemy was not a list of organizations and states but certain inherently evil activities that included both terrorism and state support for terrorism. Though the term was imperfect—many commentators have noted the peculiarity of declaring war against a method of attack—I considered it an intelligent and useful stopgap that acknowledged the unprecedented nature of the challenge represented by 9/11. It avoided the problem of lists,

---

*As of September 11, 2001, the countries formally designated as sponsors of terrorism by the State Department were Cuba, Iran, Iraq, Libya, North Korea, Sudan, and Syria. Among the notable omissions from that list was Afghanistan. Department of State, Office of the Coordinator for Counterterrorism, "Patterns of Global Terrorism (2000)," April 30, 2001, available at: http://www.state.gov/s/ct/rls/crt/2000/2441.htm.

gave the President flexibility, and called attention to differences between us and our enemies on the issue of respect for human life.

One thing we all recognized was that the magnitude of 9/11, and the danger of more terrorist attacks, had driven home the inadequacy of treating terrorism as a law enforcement matter. Law enforcement is mainly an after-the-fact apparatus. Though it helps deter crime, it works mainly to punish, not prevent. No police force is organized and equipped to stop a campaign of sophisticated, internationally supported terrorist attacks. And such attacks cannot be deterred simply by the threat of judicial penalties, however severe. Considering 9/11 an act of war, not just a crime, was a way of recognizing that retaliation would be an insufficient response. We aimed to prevent future attacks—using all instruments of national power, including the military—and doing so would mean targeting a set of actors broader than the individual criminal coconspirators responsible for 9/11.

But how broad should that target set be? This was no easy matter. If we determined that bin Laden was behind the 9/11 operation, should we define the enemy to include only al Qaida and perhaps also its state supporters? Wasn't the United States also threatened by other terrorist groups? Al Qaida is a Sunni Muslim group. Does that mean we should limit our concern to Sunni extremist ideologies? But what about Shiite organizations like Lebanese Hezbollah, which also had formidable capability and much American blood on its hands? Or was it more sensible to focus on violent Islamist extremist groups generally? What about non-Islamist terrorist groups like the Irish Republican Army or the FARC in Colombia? Should we be concerned about state supporters of terrorism generally? What was the threat posed by state supporters of terrorism like Iran, Iraq, and North Korea? They all had ambitions for nuclear and other weapons of mass destruction (WMD); they all had supported terrorist groups and might provide catastrophic capabilities to terrorists in the future. But it was unclear how close those states were, if at all, to al Qaida. Should we include in our definition of the enemy only those states provably and closely linked to al Qaida?

The coinage of the term "war on terror" allowed the Administration to defer naming the enemy while considering these perplexing questions. The threat we faced was not abstract or remote. It was as real as the corpses and debris of 9/11. But in many ways it remained shadowy, defying simple definition. We could not declare neatly that the enemy was a combination of states like the Axis powers in World War II. We could not define the enemy with precision in any short, clear formulation.

What should the United States aim to accomplish in such a war? we asked. The purpose of strategy is to define a goal that can guide the plans and actions of numerous parts of the government, and to ensure unity of effort among those parts.

The President, we realized, would have to set a war aim that was motivational, but also achievable. Preventing the next attack was a sensible immediate mission, I argued, but it could not be a long-term war aim—not least because we assumed 9/11 would be followed by further attacks. We considered naming "eliminating terrorism" as a war aim, but the President could hardly promise that the world would never see another terrorist bomb. On the other hand, the government could aim to damage, curtail, or undermine the terrorists' ability to operate—but that would be setting the bar too low.

We spoke about the lessons of the 1990–91 Gulf War. My colleagues all had vivid memories of the conflict: Rodman had been working in the White House at the time, Luti had flown missions over Iraq during the war, and Abizaid had helped lead stability operations in northern Iraq in the aftermath. The first President Bush had defined his war aim early on as the liberation of Kuwait. On that basis he built an international coalition, and after the coalition expelled Iraq's forces from Kuwait he concluded that his mission was complete. As with all historical what-ifs, it's debatable whether the coalition should have pressed further, seizing the opportunity to get to the root of the Iraq problem. The rape of Kuwait was, after all, only a symptom of the Saddam Hussein pathology. But Bush had set a limited, inflexible war aim, and, together with other considerations, it had constrained him. On the day after 9/11, our team took this lesson from the Gulf War: that the President should not declare a war aim that might later limit his options if and when circumstances developed in unseen ways.

How, then, should we define our goals in this war? Foremost in our minds was the prospect that 9/11 might be succeeded by further large-scale attacks on the United States. That could permanently change the nature of American society, driving the government toward undesirable—even if necessary—protective measures. At stake would be America's essential traits: our civil liberties and the open nature of our society.

It was this insight that ultimately led us to a sound strategic goal for this new war. We could not promise to eliminate terrorism altogether, but we knew we must do more than merely impede terrorism where we could. It would be sensible for U.S. officials to understand their mission as defeating terrorism *as a threat to American freedom and openness*. If we fought the terrorists so effectively that they no longer threatened the nature of our society—isolated future attacks notwithstanding—the United States would have achieved a substantial victory. A war aim defined along those lines would serve the country's strategic interests. It would be flexible, credible, achievable—and important.

Rodman took notes throughout our discussions, and during breaks he returned to his seat to write them up as the germ of what became a strategic concept paper for the war. The plane had one small table, with two narrow seats on either side, and the seating arrangement followed protocol. I sat facing forward, alongside Dov Zakheim, the financial controller of the Defense Department and my fellow Under Secretary of Defense. Across the table were Assistant Secretaries of Defense J. D. Crouch and Peter Rodman. General Abizaid sat farther back. As Rodman drafted his outline, I walked the new pages over to the general for his comments. As he reviewed them, Abizaid commented that any military actions in this new war could have helpful diplomatic effects among our allies—and powerful psychological effects on our enemies.

When Rodman, Luti, Abizaid, and I returned to Washington and joined the ongoing work, we shared these insights at interagency meetings, and they helped shape the government's war aim and strategy. The conversations we had on that September 12 flight contributed to the foundation for our strategy, beginning with the first top-level Pentagon strategic guidance paper for the campaign against terrorism: Rumsfeld's instruction to the Department of Defense, which would guide the combatant commanders as they prepared their war plans.

Less than an hour before landing at Andrews Air Force Base outside Washington, our KC-135 flew over Manhattan. The crew invited me into the cockpit, where Bill Luti joined us. Luti pointed out the F-16s that came to meet us in the air, part of the combat air patrol Rumsfeld had ordered over New York the day before. The pilot rolled our plane slightly, giving us a view of the ground.

On that sunny afternoon, dark smoke covered the southern end of Manhattan Island. The scene, ghastly and sad, intensified my view that playing defense could not be an adequate strategy against terrorism. There were simply too many tall buildings—too many major targets—in New York and across the country for us to protect them by trying to secure each individually. Any such attempt could change life in America radically, and for the worse, requiring measures characteristic of police states. In other words, a defensive approach would not achieve the war aim we had been discussing: preserving the free and open nature of American society.

When we got to Andrews at around 5:00 P.M. on September 12, my superb secretary, Cassandra Bowen Lee, phoned to say that the President would be at the Pentagon at 6:00 P.M. If we could beat the rush-hour traffic, I would be admitted to the meeting. (This President did not welcome latecomers.) My driver, the unstoppable Jarvis Wilkins—a forty-year veteran of the motor pool—turned on his siren and flashing lights and got me to the Pentagon's River Entrance scarcely three minutes before the appointed hour. I hurried past the guards and took the stairs two at a time, instantly tasting the smoke from the crash site on the other side of the building. The stench, bitter in all senses, had spread to every ring and corridor of the Pentagon. This place was a war zone yesterday, I thought as I ran into the conference room with seconds to spare.

At the table with the President were Rumsfeld, Wolfowitz, the Joint Chiefs of Staff, the secretaries of the army, navy, and air force, and the Under Secretaries of Defense. The President, I noticed, had already adopted the tone and attitude of a wartime Commander in Chief. He confined himself to presidential and strategic remarks, avoiding details and extraneous chat. "We believe we are at war and we'll fight it as such. I want us to have the mindset of fighting and winning a war." He wanted the Defense Department, and especially our military leadership, to know that he expected us to present military options that were designed to achieve important results: "We won't just pound sand." He would see to it, he promised, that our men and women in uniform had whatever they needed for the fight, but he also noted that the war would mean casualties. The meeting ended promptly at 6:30 P.M.

In the hours after 9/11, the President had numerous considerations to juggle. There were the big-picture strategic issues—understanding the motives, structures, intentions, and vulnerabilities of our enemies and devising ways to frustrate their plans. These tasks required a global strategy that could not be developed overnight. There was also an urgent domestic responsibility to offer presidential leadership to an outraged country unaccustomed to feeling violated.

This need for reassuring action was a matter that went beyond politics and poll results. If the President did not mount an adequate response, and if the anticipated follow-on terrorist attacks occurred, the government could be seen as violating the social contract—as failing to fulfill its most basic duty, which is to provide security. With smoke still billowing from the ruins of the World Trade Center and the smashed side of the Pentagon, the President's national security team grimly considered the harm that a series of terrorist attacks against our country might do to the unity of our republic, the civil liberties of our people, and the integrity of our Constitution. The President demanded a strategic response, but he also voiced impatience about the time it would take to act.

On Thursday, September 13, the President met with his National Security Council, augmented by Treasury Secretary Paul O'Neill, Attorney General John Ashcroft, FBI Director Bob Mueller, and others. Rumsfeld joined via secure video teleconference (a connection known as SVTC, pronounced "sivvitz"). I accompanied him to the small room where the cameras and monitors were set up, a short walk from the Secretary's office. We were joined there by General Hugh Shelton, the Chairman of the Joint Chiefs of Staff.

Paul Wolfowitz was not present for this conference, but he alerted me in advance that the key issue among the President's top advisers was whether this war would focus on al Qaida in Afghanistan, as the presumed perpetrators of 9/11, or develop into an effort against the jihadist terrorist network globally. In interagency discussions, Rumsfeld and Wolfowitz had been advocating the broader approach; their State Department counterparts urged the narrower approach.

National Security Adviser Condoleezza Rice began the meeting by recapping discussions of the last two days, beginning with what she called "the concept": that the terrorists were a network, and this was a broad war, not a single event. "We're not just going to do something once," she declared. In that meeting, I took Rice's comments to mean that she was on the Rumsfeld-Wolfowitz side of the interagency debate. It was not yet clear whether she was speaking for the President.

In his comments, Secretary of State Colin Powell focused on activities and messages. He reported that different countries were "signing up" to help us, individually and through the United Nations and the Organization of the Islamic Conference. It was important that they knew we were after terrorists, he said, not Arabs or Muslims. We should also get Palestinian-Israeli diplomacy going, he advised, "so we can show we remain engaged."

Powell reported that Deputy Secretary of State Richard Armitage had given Pakistan's President, Pervez Musharraf, a list of seven items the United States wanted, including overflight rights for attacks in Afghanistan, and that Musharraf had approved the list. This caught Rumsfeld by surprise. This was a list with obvious military implications, and he thought he should have been consulted on it. With his microphone turned off, he asked General Shelton and me whether we had cleared the list, or known about it. We gave him the kind of palms-up, never-heard-of-it shrug the military calls a "Pentagon salute."

Rice noted that demands were being prepared for the Taliban. If they did not cooperate promptly, she said, we must make clear that we will go after *them*—not just al Qaida. The President said that he wanted U.S.

action to be complete, and the time frame short. The Taliban might turn over bin Laden to us, he acknowledged, but "that's not good enough." He wanted to know how long it would take for the United States to take action.

President Bush then raised a question about Iraq. Administration officials had been discussing Iraq policy options for months. Saddam was recognized as a serious problem. He was systematically dismantling the elements of the containment strategy devised by the UN Security Council. Having ended the Council's regimen of weapons inspections in 1998, he was corrupting the economic sanctions and campaigning for their complete removal. And his forces were shooting almost every day at the U.S. and British aircraft that patrolled the no-fly zones over northern and southern Iraq. President Bush, of course, wanted to know whether Saddam was implicated in the 9/11 attack or otherwise connected to al Qaida.

The President asked Central Intelligence Agency Director George Tenet whether his agency was looking into possible Iraqi involvement. Tenet replied, "It's a worldwide effort, yes." I couldn't tell whether Tenet meant that the CIA was making a worldwide effort to explore a possible Iraqi connection to 9/11, or that no special effort was being made to look into an Iraqi connection because the CIA was looking all over the world for connections to 9/11.

Treasury Secretary O'Neill reported that he was trying to develop a legal basis for action against terrorist-related financial institutions, but "the lawyers" were slowing him down. Tell the lawyers that we're at war, President Bush instructed, and we're going to get the terrorists' money.

The President was interested in the state of our military preparations. General Shelton reported that the armed forces had an existing plan to attack bin Laden with unmanned Tomahawk cruise missiles that could reach several sites where he was known to stay. General Tommy Franks, the CENTCOM commander, favored a phased approach that would begin by moving more U.S. forces into the Afghanistan region. We had enough force there already for initial action, Franks reported, but we "don't get much bang hitting air defense targets unless we hit them with piloted planes."

Shelton picked up on Franks's point, mentioning the constraints that had been imposed on U.S. military planners in recent years. They had been told to focus on bin Laden rather than the Taliban, and to limit themselves to the unmanned Tomahawk missiles. Now, Shelton argued, we should be considering ground forces and manned B-2 aircraft. In northern Afghanistan—beyond the range of Tomahawks—we could hit targets that would weaken the Taliban in its battles against the Afghan opposition force known as the Northern Alliance.

The President told Shelton to "take all constraints off your planning." He wanted to hit hard, step back, press our demands, and hit again if they were not granted.

President Bush then asked the general about Taliban air defenses, which led Rumsfeld to note how difficult it was to locate command-and-control and other military targets in Afghanistan. The problem with focusing on Afghanistan, he said, was that the country lacked valuable terrorist infrastructure targets. Bin Laden's assets were not buildings but people. Destroying the scant infrastructure in Afghanistan would not cause the kind of pain that was likely to change behavior throughout the terrorists' network, especially by the state supporters. We need to figure out how to fight bin Laden's entire network globally, Rumsfeld insisted, and to impose costs on those who supported that network.

Looking beyond bin Laden and Afghanistan, Rumsfeld mentioned Saddam Hussein's Iraq as a threat to both its region and to the United States. Iraq, he observed, was a state that supported terrorism, and that might someday offer terrorists weapons of mass destruction to use against us.* Unlike Afghanistan, however, Iraq also had substantial infrastructure and military capability. In Iraq, he noted, we could inflict the kind of costly damage that could cause terrorist-supporting regimes around the world to rethink their policies. And we could locate Iraq's assets, including its weapons of mass destruction. No one contradicted this last remark. Supported by the intelligence assessments at the time, it sounded unexceptionable.

President Bush picked up the subject of Iraq, declaring that any U.S. military action there would have to go beyond merely making a statement: It would have to bring about a new government. The United States needed an option that would bring others in the region along with us. I want a plan on what it would take and what it would cost, the President told Rumsfeld and Shelton, who had noted that CENTCOM had some prepackaged strike options for Iraqi targets.

Throughout the discussion, the President concentrated on the second- and third-order effects of military action. He wanted to think through how hitting particular targets could affect the other sectors of the terrorist network. Terrorism could become a bigger problem if you went with a "one-shot wonder," the President mused, referring to the firing of a single U.S. cruise missile. He continued: We'll go after not only bin Laden, but the

---

*Iraq's support for terrorists is detailed in Chapter 6.

places giving him haven. We may have to hurt Afghanistan so severely that everyone takes notice, and we start smoking these guys out of holes. Can we do the Afghanistan and Iraq missions at the same time? he asked. "Yes," Shelton answered.

The conversation then turned to America's allies and their offers of support. Condi Rice called for an interagency committee to compile a list of the support we needed.

It was the National Security Adviser's job to ensure proper coordination among the government agencies. So when she mentioned coordination, Rumsfeld commented that he had never seen the list of demands Armitage had given to Musharraf. Neither Powell nor Rice appeared to give the point much weight. Though he did not pursue the matter, Rumsfeld later made it clear that he considered it more than a simple procedural foul that State, at that moment, was making military-related requests of Musharraf without the Pentagon's input.

The President wrapped up the meeting by directing his team to devise a proper mission, "not a photo op war." I assumed he was referring to the small aerial attacks the United States had launched against targets in Afghanistan and Sudan in 1998, following al Qaida's bombing of the U.S. embassies in Tanzania and Kenya—attacks that murdered 224 people, including twelve Americans, and injured more than four thousand others. The President directed his Principals to expedite their departments' operations. "Get something with a consequence done soon," he told the group. Then, turning to Powell, he said, "It may be time to give the Taliban a heads up." I assumed the President meant an ultimatum.

By way of response, Powell remarked that we were soon going to say we thought bin Laden "did it." Tenet added: "I think the case is there," though he did not elaborate. The Attorney General pointed out that U.S. officials shouldn't feel compelled to prove this as they would a case in court, for we were operating on the basis of intelligence, not legal proof. (It wasn't until November—two months later—that U.S. forces in Afghanistan found a videotape of bin Laden boasting that he had directed the 9/11 attack.)

After the President left the meeting, Rumsfeld engaged Tenet on the problem of identifying worthy targets in Afghanistan. How do we broaden the list? Rumsfeld asked. Tenet suggested that people at the CIA and on General Shelton's staff should work together on this. Rumsfeld asked how to phrase what they should be told to do. Cofer Black, the head of the CIA's Counterterrorism Center, gave a response that jibed with Rumsfeld's thinking: We could coordinate a U.S. military attack with the Northern Alliance in the north. Sending only Tomahawks would be like sending a letter saying, "We surrender." We must have troops on the ground. Otherwise they'll think we're weak. Rumsfeld concurred: We don't want to run the risk of being laughable, he noted. Black remarked that B-52s with conventional ordnance would be almost as good as troops on the ground. Rumsfeld signed off the teleconference and told Shelton to work with CIA on finding "targets that have value."

As I left this meeting, I was struck by several points. Two days after the attacks, I noticed, George Tenet seemed already to have concluded that Usama bin Laden and al Qaida were responsible for 9/11. The speed was impressive, and I wondered how solid the CIA's information was. Second, I noted that the President, Rice, and Rumsfeld were already discussing the war as an effort against not only al Qaida but the terrorists' network broadly conceived, including state supporters of terrorism. So our efforts would have to extend beyond the capture or killing of Usama bin Laden. Finally, I was struck by the general recognition that this would be more than a military operation: It would demand joint action from State, CIA, Treasury, Justice, and many other elements of the U.S. government.

It is in the nature of groundbreaking ideas that they are recognized as obvious almost as soon as they're first expressed. The President's prompt labeling of 9/11 as an act of war came to look unexceptional, even inevitable, but no U.S. President before had applied that concept to a terrorist attack against the United States. The discussion at the September 13 National Security Council meeting suggested that the President's advisers agreed that we were at war. Still, we all had a way to go to understand what kind of war we were in and how the United States should fight it.

In the decades before 9/11, the United States had suffered a series of attacks by terrorist groups. There were bombings of U.S. military personnel at the U.S. Marine barracks in Beirut (1983); a Berlin discotheque (1986); Khobar Towers in Saudi Arabia (1996); and the U.S.S. *Cole* in Aden (2000). Other attacks had targeted civilians, among them the Black September hijackings of civilian airliners (1970); the assassination of U.S. diplomats Cleo Noel and George Curtis Moore in Khartoum (1973); the assassination in Rome of Leamon "Ray" Hunt, the U.S. head of the Sinai peacekeeping force (1984); the assassination attempt against former president George H. W. Bush (1993); the first World Trade Center attack (1993); and the destruction of the U.S. embassies in Kenya and Tanzania (1998).

The decades of academic debate about the nature of terrorism had produced a cacophony of definitions, distinguishing between political motivation and naked nihilism, and between attacks targeting civilians and those targeting the military under various circumstances—on duty, off duty, inside, or outside a combat zone. Though these definitions remain debatable, the term "terrorism" has commonly been applied to each of the anti-American attacks noted above.

The United States, however, had treated these incidents as criminal acts, responding chiefly by sending FBI agents to track down individuals who could be arrested, indicted, and tried for the crimes. Occasionally—for example, after the attacks on the Berlin discotheque (1986) and the east African embassies (1998)—the President had chosen to augment his law enforcement response with a few small-scale aerial attacks in countries thought to have supported the terrorists. Yet these responses stopped far short of declaring war.

President Bush's decision to characterize 9/11 as "war," and to commit America to the fight, was unusual and important. It compelled U.S. officials to rethink the meaning of terrorism. It made us reconsider all our other national security problems in light of this new apprehension of the terrorist threat. Long-standing concerns—weapons of mass destruction in irresponsible hands; threats from the regimes of Iraq, North Korea, Iran, and other so-called rogue states; political instability in the Middle East; narco-trafficking—all took on a new appearance and greater urgency after 9/11.

In that September 13 meeting, the National Security Council took up the challenge of defining the "enemy," as my colleagues and I had done in our airborne discussion, and their thinking jibed to a large extent with ours. I thought the apparent consensus on certain fundamental concepts—including the idea that the enemy functioned as a network comprising terrorist operatives, their organizations, and the states that gave them safe haven, funds, and other resources—boded well for the development of teamwork within the Administration.

It was not clear, however, whether U.S. strategy should concentrate solely or principally on Usama bin Laden and al Qaida, on the assumption that they were behind the 9/11 attacks—or try to hit other elements in the broader terrorist network. Rumsfeld had already developed some thoughts on this question. He saw the terrorist threat from Islamist extremists as a broad-based phenomenon, one that relied on ideologues, financiers, operational planners, commanders, and weapons experts (not all of whom were Islamist or even Muslim) working for groups or governments in many countries on virtually every continent. So a strike against al Qaida in Afghanistan—even if it eliminated bin Laden and denied al Qaida its safe haven there—would not defeat the terrorist threat against us.

If the U.S. government limited its attention to the perpetrators of

9/11, Rumsfeld reasoned, we would not be doing all we could to prevent the next attack, which could come from any quarter of the international terrorist network. If we confined our response to al Qaida's presence in Afghanistan, the terrorists there might simply migrate to other safe havens. Rumsfeld was intent on undoing not just al Qaida's refuge in Afghanistan, but the policies of states around the world that supported or tolerated terrorist groups. He thought our goal should be to make it increasingly difficult for terrorists to find governments willing to support them.

Rumsfeld stressed that the importance of these state supporters went beyond their willingness to provide safe haven. As awful as 9/11 was, he pointed out, it would have been deadlier by orders of magnitude if the attackers had used chemical or (especially) biological or nuclear weapons. Though some terrorist groups might be capable of producing such weapons themselves, a more likely source would be a state supporter. And we knew that the list of leading state supporters of terrorism coincided with the list of so-called rogue states who were notorious for pursuing (and, in the case of Iraq, using) weapons of mass destruction.

The danger of terrorists using such weapons had been recognized for years. In 1995, the Japanese terrorist cult Aum Shinrikyo had manufactured sarin gas and used it to kill people on a Tokyo subway. Yet many analysts discounted this threat, convinced that terrorists were primarily interested not in massive violence, but in political theater. Most terrorism, they reasoned, was intended to create a spectacle—to dramatize the frustrations and aspirations of desperate people in order to win attention and, ultimately, sympathy for their causes. The attacks of the 1970s and '80s supported the conclusion that "terrorists want a lot of people watching and a lot of people listening, but not a lot of people dead."* The terrorists of those decades seemed to content themselves with relatively small-scale violence—assassinations, bus bombings, machine gun attacks at airport ticket counters, and the like. Using weapons of mass destruction,

---

*"While terrorists may kill, by our standards sometimes wantonly, and while they may threaten a lot of people, the objective of terrorism is *not* mass murder," this influential analysis maintained. "A credible threat, a demonstration of the capacity to strike, may be from the terrorists' point of view often preferable to actually carrying out the threatened deed, which may explain why, apart from the technical difficulties involved, terrorists have not done some of the terribly damaging and terrifying things they could do, such as poisoning a city's water supply, spreading chemical or biological agents, or other things that could produce mass casualties." Brian Michael Jenkins, "International Terrorism: A New Mode of Conflict," in David Carlton and Carlo Schaerf (eds.), *International Terrorism and World Security* (London: Croom Helm, 1975), pp. 15–16.

the reasoning went, might forfeit that sympathy irretrievably. This view was commonly held—indeed, it may have been the prevailing theory of terrorism—among Western experts in the era before 9/11.

The obliteration of the World Trade Center and the strike at the Pentagon, however, went far beyond political theater. This was an attack by extremists aiming to kill in large numbers, not to win sympathy. If they should obtain weapons of mass destruction, we had to assume now that they would use them.

This in turn made U.S. officials take a new look at the countries the State Department rather delicately labeled "states of proliferation concern." States such as Iraq, Iran, Libya, North Korea, and Syria were long thought to be contained through deterrence: The United States had the power to strike back decisively against any state that used WMD against us. But one implication of 9/11 was that a hostile state could undermine deterrence by providing WMD to terrorists, who might be able to launch the weapons with no return address.

In the weeks after 9/11, Rumsfeld's repeated public and private references to the "nexus" among terrorists, their state supporters, and WMD, were made with these ideas in mind. Vice President Cheney trumpeted the same theme. They wanted their National Security Council colleagues and the public to appreciate that this strategic problem could not be solved simply by hitting al Qaida or overthrowing the Taliban.

In his first Quadrennial Defense Review, produced largely before 9/11 (and largely before I took office), Rumsfeld's big theme was strategic uncertainty. He argued that our defense establishment must not be organized merely to counter specific threats, for history showed that even our best efforts to collect and analyze intelligence had not improved our poor ability to see the future. The most our government could anticipate with confidence, he warned, were general categories of hostile capability. The U.S. government could not precisely predict which countries would confront us down the road. For decades, we had been surprised time and again by new conflicts and enemies—in Vietnam, in the Persian Gulf, in Bosnia and Kosovo.

With 9/11, we were surprised again. That attack did not mark the start of the war, but it did shock the American people and the world into recognizing that the terrorists had been at war with us for years. This was the kind of strategic surprise that Rumsfeld wanted the Pentagon to understand as a recurring phenomenon in world affairs, and to be strong, nimble, and flexible enough to handle.

Rumsfeld, General Richard B. Myers, and a handful of their National Security Council colleagues were now responsible for advising the President on what to do. President Bush would have to respond—urgently—to the 9/11 attack and the ongoing threat. But the response had to be right on several levels. Everything he and his team did and said would be interpreted by many audiences: the American public, our terrorist enemies, and people around the world who were trying to figure out what this conflict meant for them.

At a moment when our nation overflowed with pain and passion, the government's top national security officials were faced with a challenge of a high order, and forced to confront it dispassionately and farsightedly. We had to review our country's interests and try to understand the nature of the fight we were in. And we had to move quickly from concepts to action.

2
PERSONAL TRAJECTORY

When President Bush nominated me as Under Secretary of Defense for Policy early in his Administration, it was at Donald Rumsfeld's recommendation. But I did not have a long-standing relationship with Rumsfeld. In fact, I first spoke with him when he interviewed me for the position in late February 2001, at the suggestion of some members of Congress and some current and former national security officials with whom I had worked over the years: Senator Jon Kyl, Paul Wolfowitz, Fred Iklé, Richard Perle, Frank Gaffney, and a few others.

Connections among such colleagues are an important feature of the Washington scene. People who work together in government often remain friends, cooperating as private citizens to champion causes and seeking each other out when they return to office. This simple fact overheats the imagination of conspiracy mongers, but such connections are not conspiracies. They are ordinary life.* By the time Rumsfeld invited me to interview, I had spent decades studying, working, and developing relationships in the field of international relations.

Since childhood, history and world affairs have been my favorite subjects. My interest was rooted in fascination with the story of my father, Dalck Feith, who had the misfortune as a young man of living in close touch with grand historical events.

---

*As the saying goes: *I* have friends, *you* have associates, *he* has cronies.

Born in the Polish region of the Austro-Hungarian Empire just before the start of World War I, my father attended *gymnasium* (high school) in the German city of Koenigsberg (now the Russian city of Kaliningrad). Later, in the 1930s, he lived in formerly German Danzig, which the Treaty of Versailles had converted into an international "Free City" to serve as the Baltic Sea outlet of a reconstituted Poland. My father became a sailor, an uncommon occupation for a Jew. As Nazi power grew in Europe, he smuggled endangered Jews off the Continent to Britain. He prepared to remove himself to Palestine, but British authorities were curtailing Jewish immigration, and he did not get a permit. He was captured by the Nazis, who held him for months in solitary confinement and tortured him before he escaped while being transferred to a work camp. Both of his parents, four of his sisters, and all three of his brothers—my grandparents, aunts, and uncles—were murdered in the Holocaust.

A few weeks after the Japanese attack on Pearl Harbor, my father made his way to the United States as a sailor on British and Estonian merchant ships and joined the U.S. Merchant Marine. For nearly four years he carried supplies on the Murmansk Run and in other high-casualty supply operations, losing two ships to torpedoes and one to attack from the air. He was heading across the Pacific to support the invasion of Japan when he learned of the atomic bombs in Hiroshima and Nagasaki. With the war over, his ship turned around. My father left the service and started a new life from scratch in America, which he, like millions of other immigrants, saw as a golden land.

As a child in suburban Philadelphia, I extracted from my father only scraps of information about his life. Trying to make sense of them, I read books on war, diplomacy, politics, and government. What came to interest me especially were the efforts of British leaders to manage the rise of Adolf Hitler through diplomacy. It took no deep analysis to see why diplomacy is usually preferable to war as a way to resolve international conflicts. As Winston Churchill once put it, "Jaw jaw is better than war war." But it was also obvious to me, with hindsight, that nothing short of war could have stopped, let alone reversed, Nazi aggression. This lesson lodged itself in my thoughts when I was a teenager during the debate over the Vietnam War, leading me to question the slogans of the time proclaiming that war is never necessary.

This strain of contradiction did not immediately alter my politics. I was a liberal, very much in line with my parents, who had participated in the American Jewish romance with Franklin Roosevelt. My father and my mother, Rose Feith, admired Harry Truman, disliked Douglas

MacArthur, and assumed that Alger Hiss was innocent. They voted for Adlai Stevenson (twice), John Kennedy, and Lyndon Johnson. We subscribed to the *New York Times* and believed it, and during the Vietnam War our views on the conflict reflected the influence of the *Times*'s editorials. My father proudly contributed to the NAACP, the American Civil Liberties Union, the Democratic Party, and other groups supporting civil rights and free speech.

As I was growing up, there were few identifiable Republicans around me. Among them was John Mulloy, one of my teachers at Philadelphia's Central High School. He taught history from a conservative perspective and stood out at our school as a supporter of the Vietnam War. He assigned us readings from the novels of Soviet dissident author Alexander Solzhenitsyn, passages I remember to this day. My class, mostly liberal like myself, voted Mr. Mulloy "most intelligent teacher," demonstrating an admirable open-mindedness.

As an undergraduate at Harvard College from 1971 to 1975, I studied international relations. Among the hot issues at that time were the U.S. government's attempts to achieve détente with the Soviet Union, and to promote peace through diplomacy between Israel and its Arab neighbors. In both areas I came to distrust the conventional wisdom, with its optimistic assumption that negotiations and treaty relations could produce peace and stability between deadly enemies. The failures of appeasement in the 1930s made me skeptical about the promises of demonstrably bad actors—tyrants, murderers, liars, terrorists, and the like. I believed that history and common sense both warned against relying on international legal agreements to moderate the behavior of totalitarian rulers who were unconstrained by even their own domestic laws.

President Richard Nixon and Soviet premier Leonid Brezhnev advertised détente as a bilateral effort to reduce tensions and limit strategic weapons, pledging not to pursue "marginal advantage" over each other. The policy won Nixon praise from much of the American political spectrum. Given the danger of nuclear war, all sensible people wanted the great powers to try to maintain peace. As I saw it, however, détente suffered from a fatal deficiency: the inaccurate assumption that the two nations had common goals in their dialogue. Americans by and large hoped to achieve peace and stability; Soviet leaders wanted to mislead and exploit the United States to improve their image, restrict our defense programs, obtain trade credits, and otherwise pursue the very "marginal advantage" they claimed to have renounced. Détente, I concluded, was more likely to embolden the Soviet leaders than to moderate their ambitions. I took no pleasure in watching my downbeat analysis confirmed throughout the 1970s and '80s, as the Soviets violated their arms control obligations, offered support to terrorists, and devastated Afghanistan.

When Soviet policies across the globe belied détente, the Nixon Administration found itself making excuses for Kremlin leaders in order to preserve the appearance that détente was a success. I saw it as undignified and bad policy for U.S. officials to offer explanations for Soviet bad actions, rather than pressing Brezhnev to live up to his word.*

The diplomacy of the Arab-Israeli conflict suffered from similar flaws. It was easy to understand why Israelis, despite the lack of Arab encouragement, exhibited a desire for peace. Even in the early 1970s, there was plenty of history to explain why so many Israelis were fed up with war, tired of military service, and eager to free their children from these burdens. But the "peace process," I recognized, suffered from the same lack of mutuality that impaired détente. The Israelis and the Arabs were playing the game with incompatible motives. The Israelis intended to purchase peace and security; their Arab interlocutors were seeking territorial concessions without recognizing—let alone urging their people to accept—Israel's right to exist.

At the end of the 1970s, Egyptian President Anwar Sadat broke the pattern and acknowledged Israel's legitimacy by signing a peace treaty with Israeli Prime Minister Menachem Begin. Yet broader Arab-Israeli peace efforts remained crippled by the lack of a common commitment to peace. Diplomacy, it seemed to me, was unlikely to produce good results if one party saw the talks as a continuation of war by other means.

That cynical diplomacy could make a bad situation worse was hardly an original insight. Even in those days, many students and faculty would acknowledge, if pressed, that it was true. But, in general, they did not want

---

*For example: Asked about the actions of the Soviet Union in connection with the surprise attack launched by its allies, Egypt and Syria, against Israel on Yom Kippur, October 6, 1973, Secretary of State Kissinger replied: "I think everybody is aware that a war of this nature has a possibility of escalating. I think that up to now both sides, the two countries that are most capable of producing a confrontation, that is the U.S. and the Soviet Union, have attempted to behave within limits that would prevent an escalation into such a war. If you compare their conduct in this crisis to their conduct in 1967, one has to say that Soviet behaviour has been less provocative, less incendiary and less geared to military threats than in the previous crisis." Press conference by Secretary of State Henry Kissinger, October 12, 1973, available at http://www.mfa.gov.il/MFA/Foreign+Relations/Israels+Foreign+Relations+since+1947/1947-1974/6+Press+Conference+by+US+Secretary+of+State+Dr+Hen.htm.

to associate with such thinking, lest they appear to prefer conflict to negotiation. Sometimes people were more interested in delivering a message about themselves than in shedding light on the topic.

My doubts about arms control and peace processing helped me land my first job in Washington, D.C. It came my way through Leslie Gelb, the *New York Times* diplomatic correspondent. In 1975, I attended a speech by Gelb at Wellesley College on U.S.-Soviet relations, and afterward I was one of several students asked to join the lecturer for dinner. Over Chinese food, the other students praised détente; I criticized it. "With your views," Gelb told me, "you should be working for Scoop Jackson."

Henry "Scoop" Jackson was a Democratic senator, a national security heavyweight, and the leading critic of President Nixon's détente policies. Gelb said he was friendly with an aide of Jackson's named Richard Perle, and he offered to pass my résumé along to Perle if I was interested in a summer internship in the senator's office. I took Gelb up on his kind offer, and Perle hired me.

Perle operated from a desk at the end of a long, narrow, and crowded room known as the Bunker; this was the office of the Senate Permanent Subcommittee on Investigations, which Jackson chaired. Perle was not even the Subcommittee's senior staffer, but for a Senate aide he was already a singularly influential and publicly prominent figure. As I quickly saw, his meticulous staff work helped Senator Jackson build up extraordinary authority on defense matters. When Nixon Administration officials solicited Senate approval of new arms control agreements with the Soviets, Perle put them through the wringer. And he gave Kissinger fits by inventing and then organizing passage of the famous Jackson Amendment, which tied U.S. trade benefits to Soviet human rights policy.

Unlike many intellectuals, Perle was creative about practical work. He could tell you not only a good way to think about a problem, but a smart way of solving it. Though he had no law degree, he had a lawyer's skill at reading texts. He was succinct and witty in his speech, and his quiet tone of voice increased his effectiveness in debate. He never sounded eager to persuade you of anything. Even his political opponents admitted that he was cultured and likeable. I first saw in Richard Perle something that I saw again in spades with President Ronald Reagan: Personal charm is an invaluable political asset.

Perle befriended talented political allies and helped them in their careers. He showed them attention and loyalty, which bred much loyalty in return. In time, Perle became the hub of an extensive network of successful people.

That summer, rather than relegating me to typical intern chores like photocopying or answering telephones, Perle gave me real work to do. He had me research Senate hearings on Soviet violations of the Strategic Arms Limitations Treaty. I also penned a critique of the newly signed Helsinki Accords, which the Soviets had promoted to legitimate their control of Eastern Europe. (I failed to appreciate the potential importance of the Accords' human rights provisions, which Andrei Sakharov, Anatoly Sharansky, and other champions of freedom later exploited with subversive genius to draw international attention to the Soviet dissident movement.) The more ordinary intern duties also proved educational: Perle, an impresario of intellectual cross-pollination, often asked me to escort his friends around Capitol Hill, including academic luminaries such as Islam scholar Bernard Lewis, defense strategist Albert Wohlstetter, and others.

After that internship, I started law school at Georgetown University. The following summer I volunteered for Admiral Elmo Zumwalt's Senate campaign in Virginia. Zumwalt, a former commander of U.S. naval forces in Vietnam and former Chief of Naval Operations, was running against Harry Byrd, an incumbent from a historic Virginia family. Like his friend Scoop Jackson, Zumwalt was a liberal Democrat who was also hawkish on defense and skeptical of détente.

It is rare for a military service chief to win the general public's attention, but Zumwalt had become a national celebrity—complete with a cover of *Time* and an interview in *Playboy*—for championing civil rights for blacks and eliminating what he called "Mickey Mouse" regulation of sailors' beards, motorcycles, and civilian garb. What made him famous, though, also produced a boatload of enmity for him in conservative navy circles: Virginia was full of retired admirals, and a number of them actively campaigned for his defeat.

Zumwalt lost the election resoundingly. It must have been an unpleasant experience for him, but for me the campaign itself was a treat and a boon. Zumwalt had personal traits I found uplifting to watch at close range: honesty, courage, learning, judgment, love of family, love of country, and kindness. I felt eager to write things for him because he was literate and exacting—and, when satisfied, generous with praise. I happily worked with him on speeches, letters, and policy papers, and we continued to collaborate on writing projects for years after the election.

Zumwalt went out of his way to promote my career, inviting me to dinners with his friends and recommending me for speeches and membership in groups such as the Council on Foreign Relations. From time to time, a newspaper or magazine editor would ask to give the Admiral sole credit for one of our joint articles, and Zumwalt would always push to have my name included.

I bowed out of Zumwalt's campaign briefly to pursue a summer internship at the Arms Control and Disarmament Agency (ACDA). In the era of détente, arms control was a growth industry, and ACDA attracted impressive personnel. Its director was Fred Iklé; his deputy was John Lehman, who met me when I was in college and now pulled me into his agency's summer program. Other up-and-coming officials at ACDA that summer included Carnes Lord, Robert Gallucci, and Paul Wolfowitz, all of whom I got to know during my internship.*

Wolfowitz, like his friend Perle, had strong suits in intelligence and charm. Unlike Perle, he had the air of an academic rather than a political operator. He and I worked together in the summer of 1976 on several projects. One involved a group of Libyan students whom the Libyan Atomic Energy Commission had sponsored to study nuclear physics and engineering in American universities. I remember calling the Federal Bureau of Investigation and asking an agent there whether they knew what the Libyans were up to. "If we had more resources," the agent replied, "first we'd try to find out what the *Soviet* physics students are studying here." When my internship ended, Wolfowitz wrote me a generous letter of recommendation. The letter was like a long pass he threw and then caught himself twenty-five years down the road.

To a young devourer of newspapers like me, the public policy field looked vast and densely populated. In fact, Washington was a small town: For any given subject, just a handful of people were publishing routinely in respected journals. In a field such as Arab-Israeli diplomacy, for example, only a few writers with my slant were placing articles in the *Washington Post* or *Policy Review*; they all knew each other, and they were all known to those who followed the subject closely. When I arrived in Washington and started to get my writings published, I was promptly welcomed by people in the foreign policy community who shared my views. They were eager to enlist me in their projects. That kind of politi-

---

*Fred Iklé became Reagan's Under Secretary of Defense for Policy. John Lehman became Reagan's Secretary of the Navy and recently served on the 9/11 Commission. Carnes Lord worked on the National Security Council staff during the Reagan Administration and then was Vice President Dan Quayle's National Security Adviser. Robert Gallucci had a long career at the State Department and then became Dean of Georgetown University's School of Foreign Service. Wolfowitz's long government career included positions at both State and Defense, and he served as Deputy Secretary of Defense in the George W. Bush Administration and then as President of the World Bank.

cal adoption is a common story in the public policy world, on both the left and the right.

My work for Jackson and Zumwalt attracted the attention of a group of Washington-area businessmen and professionals who were creating a new organization called the Jewish Institute for National Security Affairs (JINSA). They asked me to join as a charter member of the board of directors despite—or perhaps because of—the fact that, at twenty-three, I was less than half the age of almost everyone else involved.

JINSA was formed at a time when Jewish members of Congress, such as Representatives Bella Abzug and Elizabeth Holtzman, were vocal in opposing U.S. defense programs but supported U.S. military aid for Israel. These legislators were caricatured (not entirely unfairly) as arguing that the United States should not have fighter planes, but that those it did have should be given to Israel. JINSA was founded by American Jews who wanted to promote a strong U.S. defense. Its founders, mostly Democrats, favored the muscular policies championed by Scoop Jackson, Admiral Zumwalt, and Ronald Reagan. I helped draft the organization's charter, which had two main goals. The first was drumming up support among Jews for a U.S. policy of peace through strength. The second was promoting appreciation of America's interest in a secure Israel as a strategic ally in the Middle East.

After completing law school in 1978, I became an attorney at a Washington, D.C., law firm. I was determined to keep a hand in foreign policy, so at night I researched and wrote newspaper pieces and journal articles on the subject. When one of my longer pieces was published, a senior partner in the firm confronted me in an elevator. "If you have enough energy at night to write footnoted articles about foreign policy," he said, "you should be billing more hours." It was never clear to me whether he was joking.

One day in 1979, I was in my small office drafting real estate documents when I received a phone call from Fred Iklé, whom I had met only briefly three years before, during my ACDA internship. I could tell he had no recollection of me, but I retained a picture in my mind of him presiding in his grand office, which we interns were wowed to learn had belonged to Dean Acheson during his time as Secretary of State. Iklé said he was helping organize an effort to oppose ratification of SALT II, a U.S.-U.S.S.R. arms control treaty, and some friends had suggested that I might be willing to brief senators and speak publicly on the case against the treaty. I told him I would have to learn a lot more than I then knew, but I was interested, and he agreed to tutor me.

Born in Switzerland, Iklé had a stern manner and proved a demanding tutor. I picked up valuable insights from our work together. I learned about arms control scofflaws throughout the twentieth century. And I learned that not very far beneath the surface of Iklé's formality was an active and appealing sense of humor. Iklé's perspective was unfailingly strategic. He studied history and thought hard and presciently about the future. In the late Eisenhower years, he had foreseen that U.S.-Soviet arms control efforts would founder on unpunished Soviet violations. In the Reagan years, he understood that the militarily formidable Soviet empire had feet of clay and was vulnerable to economic pressure. And in the Clinton years, he anticipated the importance of homeland security. I admired him and he helped me.

In the SALT II debate, our team—which also included Zumwalt and Perle—made the rounds on Capitol Hill, explaining the treaty's pitfalls in front of civic organizations and on television. But it was the Soviets themselves who killed the accord's chances in the Senate when they launched their surprise Christmas-time invasion of Afghanistan in 1979. The treaty was never ratified.

One dividend of the SALT II effort was my introduction to Eugene Rostow, another Democrat of the Scoop Jackson stripe. After a term as Dean of Yale Law School, Rostow had served as Under Secretary of State for Political Affairs in President Lyndon Johnson's Administration. After Jimmy Carter's election in 1976, he helped lead the Committee on the Present Danger, a group of prominent politicians and former officials—Democrats and Republicans alike—who criticized Carter's policies as soft on defense and naïve about the Soviet Union. Among the Committee's targets was the SALT II treaty.

Rostow was for me a fascinating example of how someone could accumulate age, learning, and professional experience without becoming cynical in the slightest. He spoke idealistically about America and its place—that is, its responsibilities—in the world's state system. He took international law seriously; his reflections on that law's sorry history were disappointed but not disrespectful. He admired Woodrow Wilson, and though he never persuaded me to share that admiration, I learned much from Rostow, and we became friends.

After the Iranian revolution of 1979, which caused a new spike in oil prices and new concern about "energy security," I began research on what was then being called the "oil weapon." The term referred to a vague but frightening notion that had emerged during the 1973 Middle East war as the next big thing in world politics. Soon adopted by journalists, politicians, and commentators, it gained currency without really ever taking shape as a coherent idea: No one ever quite explained how oil could be used as a weapon—how one country could wield it to harm another. The term conjured up visions of targeted oil embargoes and gasoline lines, but the more I studied it, the less it made sense to me.

The conventional wisdom about oil and national security in those days ran along these lines: Oil is a unique commodity, not subject to the laws of supply and demand. Oil-exporting countries collect more dollars than they can spend, so, preferring to keep their oil in the ground, they sell it only as a favor to their friends and out of a sense of responsibility to the world economy. If they become unhappy with U.S. foreign policy, however, they can be expected to withhold their favors and sell less oil. Oil exporters might even target specific oil-importing countries for embargo, causing shortages, higher prices, and the dreaded gasoline lines.

This conventional wisdom was an attempt to understand oil as a political problem—without any appreciation of the role played by market forces—and I took issue with it. The importance of a more rigorous economic analysis was emphasized by some academic economists and well-informed businessmen, but their opinions rarely found their way into general-circulation publications. In the course of my research I spoke with several of these critics and found that they generally had no interest in trying to explain elementary economic truths to laymen. So I figured it would be a useful service to learn something of the economics of oil, and then to publicize some basic but uncommon truths about the subject to general audiences.

In a series of articles and speeches, I pointed out that the laws of supply and demand are no more subject to suspension than the law of gravity. No government in history has ever been unable to spend all its revenues—even Saudi Arabia in the boom years of the 1970s. Within five years of the first major oil price spike in 1973, the Saudi government was running a budget deficit. Keeping oil in the ground was a losing proposition when the Saudis could sell it and invest the proceeds. I also challenged the popular notion that oil prices have to rise over time. (Oil price fluctuations over the last quarter century have proved me and my fellow contrarians right.)

My audiences were often surprised to learn that gasoline lines occur only when governments try to control oil prices. Even during the 1973 Middle East war, countries that allowed the market to determine oil prices did not suffer lines; prices rose, if necessary, until the lines went away. When prices rise and fall according to the market, there are neither shortages nor lines.* If the U.S. government keeps the dollar price of oil below market value, the market will extract an additional price from consumers in the form of time spent waiting in lines. This can impose greater hardships on consumers—including the poor, who are often thought to benefit from price controls—than a higher dollar price would.

All in all, I argued, the so-called oil weapon was far less formidable than most Americans feared. Any oil producer that reduced its production would have to take a cut in its own revenues, risking domestic fallout—an especially serious concern in countries like Saudi Arabia that purchased political stability through enormous transfer payments. Moreover, such a reduction in supply could give other producers an opening to sell more. In any case, oil-exporting states cannot target specific importers with production cuts; if the exporters reduce supply, the effect is to drive up prices across the world.

In short, the "oil weapon" was not a grave threat. Rather, it was like a gun in the hands of a man who warns, "Take one more step and I'll blow my brains out all over you."

As I published and talked up my views, one of the people who responded with approval was Richard Allen, a top adviser to presidential candidate Ronald Reagan. When Reagan was elected, Allen became his first National Security Adviser. During the Carter-to-Reagan transition, Allen sounded me out about taking a job somewhere in the new Administration. I expressed interest in working for him at the White House. Perle, Zumwalt, Iklé, and Rostow all weighed in with him on my behalf, and my work during the presidential campaign in helping Zumwalt create an independent pro-Reagan organization ("Democrats and Independents for a New President") helped me get the endorsement of the White House overseers of patronage. So I received a political appointment as the junior member of Allen's three-person Middle East office within the National Security Council staff, with additional responsibility for "energy security."

There is always a degree of tension between political appointees—who make up the President's chosen team—and career government officials. Career people have a professional duty to take direction from the President, but they might not support his policies out of personal conviction. Some career officials, having built up great stores of experience and expertise, develop set opinions and methods that make them resistant to the

*There were no price controls and therefore no gasoline lines in the United States during the 1990–91 Gulf War or the 2005 Hurricane Katrina disaster, for example.

direction of the elected and appointed officials for whom they work. On their side, political appointees—aware that their job tenure is short—often grow impatient with bureaucratic approaches.

The U.S. government is unusual in the extensive use it makes of political appointees. In most of the world's democracies, political appointees occupy only the number one jobs in cabinet ministries; the other jobs are filled by career employees. There are benefits in the American system: Hiring numbers of political appointees gives the President a better chance of securing the energetic cooperation of the bureaucracy. It also introduces a gust of fresh air into officialdom, bringing in voices from around the country, and often from the world of business.

At the same time, as foreign diplomats often point out, the continual shifts in the American system create a lack of continuity from administration to administration. Institutional memory gets lost in the shuffle, and important tasks may get assigned to noncareer people of uneven quality.

Governments populated almost entirely by career officials, however, suffer from their own problems—including insularity, lack of energy, and stale thought. Without a flow of outsiders through the system, government officials operate as if in a hothouse, where every exhalation recirculates.

The degree of tension between political and career officials varies in different parts of the government. In the Pentagon, of course, many of the career employees are in the armed forces. From the time they enter the service, they are taught that military professionals take orders from the National Command Authority—that is, from the President and the Secretary of Defense. Not even top-level generals or admirals expect to be defining national goals or setting policy. They are trained to seek strategic guidance from the nation's top political leadership. In my experience, this made it easier for military officers and political appointees to work together and helped foster cooperation between political and career personnel in the Defense Department.

Elsewhere in the government, career personnel get different training. They do not develop the habit of subordination to presidential authority; rather, they are encouraged to take pride in their own unique insight and expertise regarding the national interest. This inclines them to view the President not as their leader, but as a transient phenomenon whose views are advisory at best. The State Department has had such a reputation for many years. Dean Acheson, who served as President Harry Truman's Secretary of State—and was one of the better political appointees in U.S. history—noted the problem in his memoirs. Lamenting the disagreement "between the bureaucracy and myself over where decisions should be made and command should lie," Acheson observed that the "attitude that presidents and secretaries come and go but the Department goes on forever had led many presidents to distrust and dislike the Department of State." He saw this as one of the "self-inflicted wounds which impaired the standing of the State Department within the Government."

State has unusually potent antibodies against political direction from the White House.* The elite career professionals in the U.S. Foreign Service, the core of our diplomatic corps, are highly educated professionals with extensive cosmopolitan experience, proud of the intellectual nature of their work. They consider it their job to educate the President about U.S. interests in the world; they rarely accept contradiction—even from the President or his National Security Council—without resistance. In his memoirs, Henry Kissinger praised the abilities and hard work of Foreign Service professionals but noted that "the reverse side of their dedication is the conviction that a lifetime of service and study has given them insights that transcend the untrained and shallow-rooted views of political appointees." Kissinger observed: "They will carry out clear-cut instructions with great loyalty, but the typical Foreign Service officer is not easily persuaded that an instruction with which he disagrees is really clear-cut." This caused political appointees to advocate, only half-jokingly, "civilian control" of the Foreign Service—on the model of the Defense Department.

I came into the Reagan Administration along with others who had started their political lives left of center, many of them formerly (or currently) registered Democrats. This group included many of the most active and outspoken supporters of the new president: Eugene Rostow, director of the Arms Control and Disarmament Agency; Richard Perle, Assistant Secretary of Defense; Jeane Kirkpatrick, Reagan's Ambassador to the United Nations; William Bennett, "drug czar" and later Secretary of Education; Elliott Abrams, Assistant Secretary of State; Frank Gaffney, Deputy Assistant Secretary of Defense; and others. These were intellectually prominent people who represented an important new element in American conservative politics. They were not lifelong conservatives. Political commenta-

*Franklin D. Roosevelt also expressed frustration with the State Department: "The Treasury is so large and far-flung and ingrained in its practices that I find it almost impossible to get the action and results I want. . . . But the Treasury is not to be compared with the State Department. You should go through the experience of trying to get any changes in the thinking, policy, and action of the career diplomats and then you'd know what a real problem was." Richard E. Neustadt, *Presidential Power* (New York: Free Press, 1990), p. 37, citing Marriner S. Eccles, *Beckoning Frontiers* (New York: Knopf, 1951), p. 336.

tors distinguished these new conservatives—labeled "neoconservatives" or "neocons"—from the many Reagan Administration political appointees who had grown up on the political right and had always been Republicans. The neocons, in turn, smilingly referred to the lifelong conservatives as "paleocons."

The two groups worked smoothly together, united by a common love for Reagan. The old-guard conservatives considered him a brother, and the neocons claimed him as one of their own, a fellow convert who had begun his political life as a union leader and a Democrat. In the great political and bureaucratic battles of the 1980s, the neocons and the paleocons generally stood on the same side—especially on matters of national security.

The Reagan Administration's outlook was not stodgy, do-nothing, muddle-through, status-quo conservatism. Reagan and his political appointees were ambitious, bordering on radical. They hoped to change the way people thought about large matters like taxes, welfare, and nuclear war. Aiming to transform the federal bureaucracy and remake its policies, they proclaimed a "Reagan revolution," anticipating that many of their goals would be opposed by "the permanent government"—that is, the career officials.

In my areas of responsibility in the Reagan Administration—Middle East policy and energy security—I believed that the president's thinking was consistent with what I knew of Allen's views, which generally aligned with my own. Our ideas were at odds with the long-established views of the State Department. It was not surprising, then, that I got crosswise from the start with the State Department's Near East Affairs bureau. I differed with key officials there on virtually every issue: oil, the Arab-Israeli conflict, Soviet policy in the Middle East, terrorism. When the bureau sent over papers to prepare the President for meetings with foreign leaders, I questioned their analyses—sometimes even their facts—and I occasionally exercised my prerogative as a White House staffer to redo the papers before sending them forward to the President. As a twenty-seven-year-old neophyte in government, I did this with a lack of finesse that produced angry complaints, which State Department officials communicated not to me but to my colleagues and superiors. Today I regret the excess friction I generated in those days, but State's Near East bureau would surely have resented the challenge in any event.

After a few months on the job, it dawned on me that my attitude toward State was wrong. Before coming to the White House, I had criticized the officials in the Near East Affairs bureau in writing, taking issue with their views and performance. Now that I was working in the government alongside them, I saw how skillful they could be in neutralizing their opponents. They cut me out of the paper flow, excluded me from meetings, and otherwise impeded my initiatives. So I decided it was vain—in all senses of the word—to belittle or look down on them, when they were the ones besting me. I needed an attitude adjustment. Instead of merely *acting* as if I respected them, I concluded that they deserved my respect for having important capabilities superior to my own. Even when I fought them about policy, I could appreciate that they were smart, experienced, and tenacious, and often got their way.

The essence of my complaint about the State Department, however, remained the point that Dean Acheson had described disapprovingly: the refusal of officials there to look to the President as their touchstone. They acted as if State were the sole arbiter of our national interests, with no obligation to consult higher leadership. Indeed, when it came to formulating policy, they viewed themselves as the U.S. government. They felt free to draft cables, write memos, and issue statements without regard to any decisions the President might have made to update or otherwise depart from State's standing conception of how the U.S. should conduct itself in the world. For many years, it has been amusing to watch as successive State Department spokesmen maintain that U.S. policies remain constant—even in the face of extraordinary geopolitical change.

At the end of President Reagan's first year in office, Richard Allen was nudged out of his job. Judge William Clark and Robert "Bud" McFarlane were transferred from their positions at State to become the President's new National Security Adviser and deputy. With input from their former colleagues at State, they made various administrative and personnel changes to the National Security Council staff, in the course of which I was transferred to the Pentagon. My friend Richard Perle, the Assistant Secretary of Defense for International Security Policy, recruited me as his special counsel. He reported to Fred Iklé, the Under Secretary of Defense for Policy, and Caspar Weinberger, the Secretary.*

---

*A former CIA official has been quoted in various newspapers and websites asserting falsely that I was fired from the NSC staff in 1982 for "leaking classified data to Israel." The allegation is entirely false but I mention it because it exemplifies the conspiracy theorizing that has become common in the debates over the Iraq war: A simple check would show that this allegation was not raised in my 2001 confirmation hearings. Judge William P. Clark took it upon himself to discredit the claim in a letter to a Montana newspaper, the *Billings Outpost:* "Your article cites a Mr. Cannistraro to the effect that Mr. Feith was fired for wrongdoing from President Reagan's National Security Council in 1982. I was President Reagan's National Security Adviser at the time and I tell you that is untrue. Mr Feith served honorably on my staff and went

A few months later, Secretary of Energy Donald Hodel, citing my record on energy security, invited me to interview for the job of Assistant Secretary of Energy for International Affairs. Because I was only twenty-nine years old, Hodel anticipated difficulties getting the Senate Energy Committee to confirm me unless I first spent some time at the Energy Department as a deputy assistant secretary.

Although Iklé and Perle had supported my moving to Energy to become an Assistant Secretary, they discouraged me from leaving the Pentagon for the lower-level position. "At that price I can keep you here with me," Perle said, and recommended me for the position of Deputy Assistant Secretary of Defense for Negotiations Policy. Secretary Weinberger got Reagan's approval for that appointment in March 1984, and I served in that position until September 1986.

My chief occupation there was multilateral arms control, a field that had few accomplishments other than the Nuclear Non-Proliferation Treaty of 1968. That agreement, despite its abused technology-sharing provisions, helped to slow down, though not completely block, the efforts of various countries to acquire nuclear weapons. During the Reagan Administration, much of what was happening in multilateral arms control diplomacy made no sense. Diplomats were continually dreaming up treaties that were unverifiable and would therefore be ineffective against adversaries of the United States. An adversary could sign on cynically, with the intention of violating its terms, with no risk of penalty even in the unlikely event of discovery.

History is rich with examples of arms treaty violations that incurred no penalties, from the Versailles Treaty of 1919 through the Strategic Arms Limitation Treaty, Anti-Ballistic Missile Treaty, and other arms accords of the 1970s. Yet the proponents of such treaties commanded enormous support in Congress, the press, universities, and the public. They argued that such treaties would make the world more civilized and safe—that they would remedy the instability inherent in arms races. Arms control champions often described a proposed new treaty in exalted language, as the key to peace or the means to safeguard the survival of the planet. They complained that government officials did not take arms control seriously enough. At the same time, they tended to downplay evidence that existing

---

on to serve well at the Pentagon under Secretary Cap Weinberger. . . . It's fine to attack policies you don't support. But it's bad to impugn the character of patriotic public servants on the basis of false information." (Letter to the *Billings Outpost,* September 28, 2005; available at http://newbillingsoutpost.com/news//index.php?option=com_content&task=view&id=17391&Itemid=5.)

treaties—those already on the books—were being violated. In the Reagan years, for example, many individuals who considered themselves supporters of arms control refused to join with Administration officials in making an issue of Soviet violations. Ironically, those of us who called for defending the integrity of the agreements by policing the violations were denounced as opponents of the agreements. In my view, the pattern of turning a blind eye to treaty violations undermined the value of arms control agreements in general. The field became so unhealthy—dominated by diplomatic initiatives that ran counter to U.S. interests as we saw them—that people in my office often described our work as "arms control control."

My negotiations-policy work was gratifying, though I was aware that, with Weinberger, Iklé, and Perle up the chain, U.S. policy in my area of responsibility would likely have turned out as it did regardless of my involvement. On one matter, however, my personal efforts made a difference. The topic was terrorism and the laws of war, which had little visibility during the Reagan Administration. I helped counter an effort by terrorist groups and their state supporters to co-opt the Geneva Conventions, the famous 1949 codification of the laws of war. The arguments I used in the mid-1980s to defend the Conventions resurfaced after 9/11, and helped shape President Bush's decision on the legal status of enemies captured in the war on terrorism.

The issue before President Reagan had been whether the United States should ratify a treaty allowing terrorist groups to qualify for prisoner-of-war status. The treaty, known as Protocol I, contained amendments to the Geneva Conventions. It was the product of several years of negotiations in the mid-1970s, when the Soviet bloc and Arab League countries were working to give greater political status and legal protections to so-called national liberation movements. The protocol was designed to respond to complaints that the Geneva Conventions unfairly discriminated against these national liberation movements. Because national liberation fighters routinely used terrorist tactics, the Geneva Conventions understandably *did* discriminate against them.

The Conventions gave maximum protection to noncombatants—innocent bystanders—and gave the next level of protection to fighters who obey the laws of war. The least protection was given to fighters who did not obey the rules. In this regard, as in many others, the Geneva Conventions were humane and sensible: The Conventions' drafters in the late 1940s had their priorities right. The Conventions created an incentive system to encourage respect for the laws of war and especially to safeguard innocent bystanders. Civilians are endangered when fighters wear civilian clothes, for example, because that makes the fighters indistinguishable from bystanders. So the Conventions provided that captured fighters were entitled to the privileged status of "prisoners of war" only if they met certain conditions, including wearing uniforms and carrying their arms openly. The national liberation groups, whose fighters did not obey those laws, protested that the Geneva Conventions should be amended to entitle their fighters to POW status *even if they concealed their status as fighters.*

The diplomats and lawyers from more than 120 countries who met for years to draft Protocol I devoted much of their time to the particular concerns of the national liberation movements. After considerable debate, the proposed amendment on POW status was approved by a majority vote, over well-argued objections from the U.S. and other Western diplomats. Protocol I called for POW eligibility to be extended to fighters in "armed conflicts in which peoples are fighting against colonial domination and alien occupation and against racist regimes in the exercise of their right of self-determination." Such politicized, subjective language was another reason that my Reagan Administration colleagues and I objected to Protocol I: Warring enemies could never be expected to agree that their conflict revolves around a right of self-determination. It is hard enough to get enemies to obey the law when the standards for deciding whether the Convention applies are purely objective.

Nonetheless, in 1977 U.S. officials, reasoning that the document's various good provisions outweighed the bad provisions, agreed to sign Protocol I. The Joint Chiefs of Staff were uneasy about many elements, but State Department officials prevailed on them to acquiesce in return for an assurance that ratification would not occur until after a thorough military review.

In 1984, almost seven years later, Pentagon lawyers were still working on that review when the matter came to my attention as Deputy Assistant Secretary of Defense. The lawyers had been assuming that the U.S. government was committed to ratifying Protocol I, and that their job was simply to draft reservations to accompany the ratification. I changed the nature of their work. Don't assume anything, I said. Just give Secretary Weinberger your thoughts on whether the United States should ratify the treaty at all.

As the lawyers were reconsidering, I published an article defending the Geneva Conventions and explaining how Protocol I would undermine the Conventions' protection of noncombatants. I saw the Geneva Conventions as a high-water mark of civilization and criticized Protocol I as a move in the wrong direction for humanitarian law. The title of the article was "Law in the Service of Terror: The Strange Case of the Additional Protocol."

Eventually, the Joint Chiefs of Staff recommended against ratification of Protocol I. Among other problems, they cited the language that would have politicized humanitarian law and the harm Protocol I would do to the interests of noncombatants. Meanwhile, President Reagan had appointed a new legal adviser at the State Department, Judge Abraham Sofaer, and he and I were able to bring Weinberger and Secretary of State George Shultz to agreement on the issue. Together with Attorney General Edwin Meese, they jointly recommended that the United States refuse to ratify Protocol I. The President concurred.

In a January 1987 message to the Senate Foreign Relations Committee, President Reagan declared that Protocol I "would undermine humanitarian law and endanger civilians in war." He singled out the provision that would have given POW status as lawful combatants "to irregular forces even if they do not satisfy the traditional requirements to distinguish themselves from the civilian population and otherwise comply with the laws of war," and declared that opposing that provision was a "significant step in defense of traditional humanitarian law and in opposition to the intense efforts of terrorist organizations and their supporters to promote the legitimacy of their aims and practices." He concluded: "The repudiation of Protocol I is one additional step, at the ideological level so important to terrorist organizations, to deny these groups legitimacy as international actors."

The *New York Times* and the *Washington Post*, not usually Reagan supporters, both praised his decision. In an editorial titled "Denied: A Shield for Terrorists," the *New York Times* said that Protocol I created "possible grounds for giving terrorists the legal status of P.O.W.'s," and declared that, if the president had ratified it, "nations might also have read that as legitimizing terrorists." The *Post*'s editorial, "Hijacking the Geneva Conventions," highlighted POW status for terrorists as among the "worst" features of Protocol I. "The Reagan administration has often and rightly been criticized for undercutting treaties negotiated by earlier administrations," it concluded. "But it is right to formally abandon Protocol I. It is doing so, moreover, for the right reason: 'we must not, and need not, give recognition and protection to terrorist groups as a price for progress in humanitarian law.' "

Nearly two decades later, however, these newspapers chose to sing a different tune. The war we are now fighting against terrorist enemies should cause serious people to think rigorously about terrorism and the laws of war. But the controversy over how to treat detainees in that war has instead degenerated into a mess of passion, politics, moral posturing, and name-calling. A sign of how fevered it has become is the contention by some journalists that I inspired disrespect within the military for the Geneva Conventions by publishing "Law in the Service of Terror." These journalists misrepresented the title, on purpose or in error, as a derogatory reference to the Geneva Conventions, when in fact the article defended the Conventions.* The title referred, of course, not to the Geneva Conventions but to the new treaty, Protocol I, which aimed to amend the Conventions to benefit terrorist groups at the expense of noncombatants.

Attempts to correct such sloppy or tendentious journalism are never fully effective.

I served in the Reagan Administration until September 1986, a total of five and a half years, before joining a friend in starting a law firm, which I managed for the next fifteen years. During that period, I was one of a number of former Reagan Administration national security officials who remained active on public policy projects. We functioned as advisers to conservatives in Congress. We wrote articles, gave speeches, and organized academic and think-tank conferences. I personally worked on such issues as

- the 1990–91 Gulf War
- ratification debates on arms control agreements such as the Intermediate Nuclear Forces Treaty, Chemical Weapons Convention, and Comprehensive Test Ban Treaty
- the Oslo peace negotiations between Israel and the Palestine Liberation Organization
- the proposal to station U.S. peacekeepers on the Golan Heights
- the Bosnia war and the Dayton Peace Talks
- missile defense
- the ABM Treaty's legal status after the Soviet Union's demise
- what to do about Saddam Hussein

On many of these projects I worked closely with Jon Kyl, a senator from Arizona who researched national security issues with the intelligent skepticism and rare meticulousness of a Supreme Court litigator, which he had been before entering Congress. Senator Kyl was self-effacing: ready

---

*On May 24, 2004, National Public Radio ran an interview, for example, with Chris Suellentrop from the Internet magazine *Slate* who incorrectly remarked that "This guy, Doug Feith, has, you know, a derisive attitude toward the Geneva Conventions, that he calls it law in the service of terror." Suellentrop added that "it's those kind of things and that kind of attitude that people fear had trickled down" and contributed to the abuse at Iraq's Abu Ghraib prison.

to promote a project's success by letting his colleagues take credit for his work, a trait unusual among senators. He developed a broad and respectful following in the Senate in the fields of defense, intelligence, and foreign affairs, and I gladly served as a member of his brain trust.

Although I chaired a Middle East policy team for Bob Dole's 1996 presidential bid, I was not involved in George W. Bush's campaign. Nevertheless, as soon as the Florida election fiasco was resolved and Bush was declared the president-elect, I began receiving feelers, direct and indirect, from the Defense Department. At first I demurred—until late February 2001, when it was clear that the Administration was establishing an energetic Reaganite national security team that included many of my friends and colleagues.

I had assumed that my next government job would be as an Assistant Secretary, so I was surprised to learn I was being considered for the position of Under Secretary of Defense for Policy. Fred Iklé, who had held the position himself throughout the Reagan Administration, first broached the idea with me. It gave me pause. The job had no geographic boundaries, and there were important areas of the world about which I knew very little. Iklé dismissed my misgivings: "Nobody knows everything," he said. "If Rumsfeld offers you the job, you should take it. But I'm not going to recommend you unless you agree to take it." Paul Wolfowitz, who had already been nominated as Deputy Secretary of Defense (the number two position in the department) called to encourage me to join the team. Soon thereafter I told Iklé that I was willing, and the Pentagon transition office set up an interview for me with Donald Rumsfeld.

For fifteen years, I had been managing attorney at my law firm, where I was comfortable, confident, and not at all eager to leave. I had not sought the Under Secretary job. Even so, at that interview, Rumsfeld managed to flap me almost from his first sentence.

Part of the problem was the way I had been prepped for the meeting. I was warned that Rumsfeld formed impressions of people quickly and didn't change them readily—and that he disliked long-windedness, so I should keep my answers very short. Although I can produce short answers when necessary, I am not usually accused of concision. (After working with Rumsfeld for several years, I would give interviewees different advice. He comments disapprovingly of people he meets who cannot seem to smile or appreciate a joke. It is far better to show a little fire and wit than to answer in a word or two.)

The Secretary's personal office was huge enough to be intimidating, but it was Rumsfeld himself who put me off balance. Having kept a hand in national security matters over the last fifteen years, I was prepared to talk policy with him. Instead, he began by talking bureaucracy: How, he asked, would you reorganize the Policy office?

I had a thought or two about this, but not many, and none that were carefully considered. After all, it had been fifteen years since I'd worked in the Pentagon. Then, as I began floating some tentative thoughts, he stopped me and demanded that I explain the abbreviations I was using. At one point, for instance, I had referred to "ISA." This isn't his first time as Secretary of Defense, I thought. He must know what the International Security Affairs office is. Why is he asking me this?

Whatever his intention, Rumsfeld was doing a good job of tossing me out the window of my own train of thought. Looking back now, I suppose he was mainly interested in seeing if I could right myself amid all his jarring diversions. And, while he probably did know what ISA was, he was training me in how to talk with him: Do not presume—with abbreviations or other information. At the time, though, it was unclear how much of this was interviewing technique and how much was earnest inquiry requiring tedious explanations about the duties of this or that Policy office.

When our scheduled twenty minutes was over, Rumsfeld stood up and dismissed me. I had been so terse that he later wondered out loud to an assistant whether I would have what it took to speak out as the Pentagon's representative in interagency meetings. The interview had gone so badly that I would not have hired me if I were Rumsfeld.

Yet Rumsfeld decided to give me a second chance. Evidently, the discrepancy between his first impression of me and the portrait painted by my colleagues over the years—Wolfowitz, Iklé, Kyl, Perle, and others—persuaded him to ask me back. This time I managed to give him adequate answers; once or twice I even made him laugh. He phoned later that afternoon and offered to recommend me to the President. I accepted his offer, and in April 2001 I received the President's nomination.

It took until July for the Senate to confirm me. The process would normally have been faster, but my confirmation hearing occurred on the very day a senator changed parties, giving the Democrats leadership of the Senate and Democrat Carl Levin of Michigan the chairmanship of the Senate Armed Services Committee. After my nomination was announced, during what are known ironically as courtesy calls, Levin opened our meeting with a blast from both barrels. He told me that he'd "heard" I held extremist views—on arms control and on Arab-Israeli peace. It had long been standard procedure in Washington—on the right and the left—to refer to one's political opponents as extremists, and I had been amply warned to endure the Senate confirmation process with the traditional groveling lack of dignity, so I took Levin's insult in stride. I cited my long list of publications on those and other subjects going back twenty-five years or so, and said that if he could find anything in them that was extreme, I would understand his opposing me.

Levin delayed the confirmation, but he apparently found nothing in all my writings and speeches to warrant opposition. When he finally allowed a Senate floor vote, I was confirmed unanimously. On July 16, 2001, I was sworn in as Under Secretary of Defense for Policy.

From the start, I was plunged into matters involving every region of the world. Policy was working on issues relating to China, where we were managing the ongoing fallout from the aggressive April 2001 Chinese air interception that had caused a collision that forced down a U.S. EP-3 surveillance aircraft; to Colombia, where the Defense Department was providing help in the drug war; and to NATO, which was debating reform and expansion. Other items on the interagency agenda included new treaties on land mines, the international criminal court, the comprehensive nuclear test ban, and missile defense. Inside the Defense Department, my office was reviewing the U.S. nuclear posture, supporting the development of ballistic missile defense, and taking first steps in what was to become a global realignment of our armed forces.

Among the names that occupied our attention in the summer of 2001 was that of Usama bin Laden. In interagency meetings that August we considered the possible use of an armed Predator—an unmanned aerial vehicle—to attack bin Laden, and we reviewed other covert action options to pressure Afghanistan's Taliban government to cut off support for al Qaida. At the time, however, the intelligence community representatives spoke of these matters as important rather than urgent. Without the exigent circumstances of wartime, our interagency meetings on bin Laden, al Qaida, and the Taliban proceeded at the customary petty pace of the government when it deals with thorny issues. The idea of a Predator attack on bin Laden, for example, raised a slew of questions, some major (What are the legal authorities? What rules of engagement should apply? Should the finger on the trigger be military or CIA?) and some minor (Which agency should pay for the operation?).

While I devoted attention to each of these matters, my principal project in those first weeks on the job was the new strategic framework for U.S. relations with Russia. The President and his national security team were determined to remake U.S.-Russian relations, and Defense was working with State on the matter.

Rumsfeld, Wolfowitz, and I spent a great deal of time on the question of how U.S. officials could persuade Russian President Vladimir Putin and his colleagues to encourage cooperation. One approach was to work out what Rumsfeld called "alternative futures"—contrasting visions of the worlds the Russians could choose to inhabit. One choice was the world of the advanced economies. The other was the world of the rogue regimes. In mid-July—just a few days after my confirmation—Rumsfeld sent me a set of his own notes based on our discussions:

> **Discussions with Russia ought not to be stovepiped into segments.**
>
> - **What they want is in the political and economic areas—dignity, respect, standing, and foreign investment to help their economy.**
> - **In the security area, we need to get out of the [Anti-Ballistic Missile] treaty, preferably by mutual agreement.**
> - **If we give them what they want in the political and economic areas, they won't give in the security area unless we keep the three connected, so I intend to keep discussing all three together and I recommend that everyone do so. Our relationship is broad, multifaceted, and not compartmented.**
>
> **Russia can go in several directions—it is their choice.**
>
> - **Russia can consort with Cuba, North Korea, Iran, Iraq—the world's walking wounded—to show that they have a new bloc and try to put pressure on the former Soviet republics to knuckle under. They could turn that nationalistic or implode. If so, Western investors won't invest and their economy will be weak.**
> - **Or Russia can turn to the West, learn from Germany, Japan and Italy after World War II, create an environment that is hospitable to enterprise, demonstrate respect for contracts, the free press, free political and economic systems. If it can be seen as a nation with leadership in literature, math and science [and] a literate workforce . . . investors will come in droves. Their economy will grow, and Russia will have influence on the world stage.**

It is their choice. But if they try both, they will cancel out and Russia will lose.

The United States wants Russia to succeed.

That August, I traveled to Moscow with Rumsfeld to meet with Sergei Ivanov, the Russian Defense Minister. Following his own advice, the Secretary spoke of the big picture. He made his economic point with a memorable aphorism: *Money is a coward.* If Russia makes itself unfree, unstable in its laws and policies, and unfriendly to the United States, he told Ivanov, it should expect foreign investors to flee. His tone was neither bellicose nor condescending; it was matter-of-fact, in the style of a corporate chief executive officer, which Ivanov knew Rumsfeld had been.

At this meeting we also heard from a number of Russian officials, civilian and military. A few sounded open to new thinking about cooperation with us, but it was clear that others still clung to the notions and attitudes of the Communist era and the Cold War. Some Russians did seem to credit our message that Americans no longer viewed them as our enemy. Yet in some cases this was cause for resentment: There were still Russians who saw their country's status in the world—its national dignity—as tied to its role as America's superpower antagonist. To assure them of our goodwill was, strange to say, to demote them.

Ivanov and Rumsfeld agreed that I should return quickly to Russia for follow-up talks. And so it was that I returned to Moscow for the meetings on September 10 and 11, 2001, pursuing the possibility of a new era in international relations.

A new era opened during that visit, to be sure, but it was not the one we anticipated.

3

CHANGE THE WAY WE LIVE, OR CHANGE THE WAY THEY LIVE

Despite the apparent consensus among high-ranking Administration officials about the nature of this new war, there was nothing obvious about what specific measures President Bush should take in responding to 9/11. Though U.S. officials, including CIA Director Tenet, generally believed that al Qaida was behind the attack, that was not yet proven. U.S. officials did not know what larger purposes the attackers had or what follow-up actions they intended. We could not know precisely how 9/11 might inspire or embolden other enemies of the United States.

During the several days after the attack, National Security Adviser Condoleezza Rice and her staff chaired a series of interagency meetings at various levels of the government to discuss how to respond. Should U.S. action extend beyond Afghanistan? Beyond al Qaida? If we should strike Afghanistan, what should be our targets—and our concept of operations?

President Bush needed to decide on a strategy. He scheduled a meeting of his National Security Council for the weekend of September 15–16 at the Camp David presidential retreat in the Maryland mountains near Gettysburg. Secretary Rumsfeld and Deputy Secretary Wolfowitz were the only Defense civilians invited, and I helped them prepare for the discussions.

By then, I had spent enough time with Rumsfeld to know that he would resist starting the Camp David meetings by weighing options for action. When Rumsfeld was faced with a large new issue, he would begin by identifying the major thoughts—the strategic ideas—that should govern our approach. He did not plunge into "What do we do?" until he had satisfied himself on "How should we think about this?" He insisted that all candidate ideas be written down, evaluated for relative importance, and refined with precision ("Above all, precision," he often declaimed theatrically, extending both arms upward to signify ultimate importance). He ridiculed talking about tactics before identifying goals. "If you don't know where you're going, any road will get you there," he often gibed about people who lacked the discipline of strategic thinking. Only after he had pinned down key assumptions and strategic goals was he willing to consider courses of action.

As manager of the interagency process that developed national security policy, National Security Adviser Condoleezza Rice was responsible for coordinating the work and perspectives of the relevant offices in the White House, State Department, Defense Department, CIA, and other agencies, and presenting them to the President. Rice's National Security Council staff made an effort to organize the government's thinking, evaluating possible military, diplomatic, law enforcement, and intelligence action.

Rice's staff had prepared three options for review by the National Security Council. Option 1 was for the United States to attack only al Qaida targets, on the unlikely premise that Taliban leaders would cooperate with us. Option 2 would involve attacks on the Taliban as well as al Qaida, in the event the Taliban would not cooperate. And Rice's staff set out an Option 3 that would include not only attacks on al Qaida and the Taliban, but also action "to eliminate Iraq threat."

As the September 13 National Security Council meeting demonstrated, Iraq was on the minds of many Administration officials—as it had been even before George W. Bush became President. At the time, it was a common assumption among government officials that a global war on terrorism would, at some point, involve some kind of showdown with Iraq—a known sponsor of terrorists who had defied UN sanctions since the mid-1990s and had been launching attacks on U.S. and British air patrols almost daily for more than a year.

This may puzzle readers today—in 2008—because much of the current controversy about the Iraq war has focused on narrow questions such as whether Saddam Hussein supported al Qaida. That question was naturally asked after 9/11, but our deliberations over Iraq were far more extensive than that. By definition, any comprehensive counterterrorism strategy would have to deal with the threats posed by Saddam, as it would have to address threats from any regime that both supported terrorism and sought weapons of mass destruction. In formulating its third option, Rice's staff was raising a narrower question still: whether the President should make action against the Saddam Hussein regime part of the *initial* U.S. response to 9/11.

The Deputies Committee (the highest subcabinet-level committee under the National Security Council) met on September 13 to discuss those options in preparation for the upcoming Camp David meeting. Deputy Secretary of State Richard Armitage declared in favor of Option 2, commenting that it was important to create a "shockwave" that would "disrupt the worldwide network" of the terrorists. Paul Wolfowitz, on the other hand, was unsatisfied with the options Rice's staff had crafted, and endorsed none of them. Rather, he favored having a new paper written for Camp David, one that would clarify that the chief purpose of U.S. military action was not punishing those behind 9/11 but attacking those who might launch the next 9/11.

Wolfowitz warned against focusing narrowly on al Qaida and Afghanistan. The next 9/11, after all, could come from other organizations and places in the global terrorist network. He questioned whether Armitage's preferred option—actions targeting only al Qaida and the Taliban—would be sufficient to create the "shockwave" Armitage was calling for. If we should take hasty action that produced only meager effects, he warned, it could embolden rather than discourage regimes that were assisting our terrorist enemies.

General Myers, then still the Vice Chairman of the Joint Chiefs of Staff, likewise cautioned against haste. If an instant American action appeared reckless, he warned, it could cost the United States support from other countries. Myers observed that our NATO allies were already beginning to "move backwards," demanding "direct evidence" before they would support military operations. He emphasized that U.S. action should be "meaningful" and not just a gesture.

On September 14, the day before Camp David, Rumsfeld laid out his own version of these themes in a Pentagon meeting with General Shelton, me, and a few others. There was pressure on the President to "go soon," he told us, but this created a danger that we might do "something hollow, ineffective, embarrassing." Because our first action would likely be "moderately ineffective," Rumsfeld insisted that the United States should "do something that has three, four, five moves behind it." He wanted our government to plan for a "sustained, broad campaign" that would surprise people and include economic, political, and other moves, not just military action. Reiterating that the threat we faced was from a global terrorist network, not just one organization, he told us: "Don't over-elevate the importance of al Qaida."

I shared Rumsfeld's view. As we saw it, 9/11 did not mean simply that the United States had an al Qaida problem. We had a terrorism problem. A strategic response to 9/11 would have to take account of the threat from other terrorist groups—Jemaah Islamiya in Southeast Asia, Lebanese Hezbollah, various Africa-based groups—and state sponsors beyond Afghanistan, especially those that pursued weapons of mass destruction. We would need to determine what action—military or otherwise—to take against which targets, and on what timetable.

In line with Wolfowitz's suggestion, Rumsfeld decided to send a strategy memo to the President and the other National Security Council participants before the Camp David meeting. His intention was to help frame the discussion of initial U.S. military actions. He asked me to draft the memo, and I wrote it with Peter Rodman—drawing on our discussions with Abizaid and Luti on the flight home two days earlier and on what we had learned since then about the thinking of our bosses and colleagues.

In our paper, Rodman and I memorialized the emerging idea that our enemy in this war was "terrorism against the United States and our interests and state support for that terrorism." We considered identifying the enemy as an ideology and using a term like "radical Islam" or "Islamist extremism." But we were reluctant to do so before the origins of the 9/11 attack were certain, and in any event we did not want to suggest we were at war with Islam. Moreover, we recognized that this enemy was no monolith: There were important differences, even violent antagonisms, among the various terrorist groups and their state supporters. Sunnis were divided from Shiites, for example, and Arabs from Persians. Nevertheless, we argued, the United States must confront " the entire network of states, non-state entities, and organizations that engage in or support terrorism against the United States and our interests, including the states that harbor terrorists. All those organizations and states constitute a threat, jointly and severally. The United States cannot tolerate continued state support for terrorism, regardless of whether a specific tie can be established to the perpetrators of the World Trade Center and Pentagon outrages. The objective is not punishment but prevention and self-defense."

We formulated this war aim to remind people of what the United States had at stake: "We cannot expect to eliminate every terrorist activity but we can realistically aim to prevent terrorism from undermining our way of life and to demonstrate its futility as a weapon of political blackmail against America and our interests." A key goal of the military campaign was to force the terrorists to play defense: If they had to run, hide, and devote their energies to evading our active pursuit, they would have less capability to plan and execute new, large-scale offensive operations.

Rumsfeld directed us to include a cautionary note about coalitions, to put into perspective the State Department's enthusiasm for incorporating as many foreign allies and partners as possible into our military operations. Rumsfeld was in favor of organizing a coalition, but not as an end in itself. He worried that adding coalition partners could jeopardize success if they were not integrated properly into operations. Moreover, if they insisted on political conditions for their participation, they could limit the President's freedom of action to protect the United States. Rumsfeld saw these worries as manageable through careful diplomacy, so long as we stayed sober about coalition building.

Rumsfeld and Wolfowitz also wanted to sketch out the case for acting soon, in one way or another, against the threat from Iraq. Powell and Armitage had been arguing that the U.S. response to 9/11 should focus tightly on Afghanistan and al Qaida. State officials assessed, probably correctly, that our allies and friends abroad would be more comfortable with *retributive* U.S. strikes against the perpetrators of 9/11 than with a global war against Islamist terrorists and their state supporters. A narrowly scoped campaign of punishment would keep U.S. policy more in line with the traditional law enforcement approach to fighting terrorism.

Here we came back to the distinction between punishment and prevention. Rumsfeld, Wolfowitz, and I all thought that U.S. military action should aim chiefly to disrupt those who might be plotting the next big attack against us. Of greatest concern was a terrorist attack using biological or nuclear weapons. We needed actions that would affect the terrorist network as extensively as possible.

Rodman and I proposed in our memo that "the immediate priority targets for initial action" should be al Qaida, the Taliban, and Iraq. Iraq was on this list, we noted, because Saddam Hussein's regime posed a "threat of WMD terrorism," and was systematically undermining the ten-year-old efforts of the United States and the United Nations to counter the dangers of his regime. Among terrorist-supporting states with records of pursuing chemical, biological, and nuclear weapons, only Iraq had been subjected to prolonged, multinational diplomatic pressure, yet Saddam remained defiant and securely in power—and hostile to the United States. The experience of 9/11 sharpened the concern about anti-U.S. terrorism from any quarter, not just al Qaida.

The purpose of a campaign in Iraq, we noted, would be "to destabilize a regime that engages in and supports terrorism, that has weapons of mass destruction and is developing new ones, that attacks U.S. forces almost daily and otherwise threatens vital U.S. interests." Action against Iraq could make it easier to "confront—politically, militarily, or otherwise—other state supporters of terrorism" such as the regimes of Muammar Qadafi in Libya and Bashar al-Assad in Syria, which had a record of backing down under international pressure. We identified Libya and Syria as problems that might be solvable through coercive diplomacy rather than through military action.

At the Camp David strategy sessions, Rumsfeld's remarks generally tracked the ideas in our memo. He left it to Wolfowitz, however, to present the case for action against Saddam Hussein. The President decided to initiate U.S. military action in Afghanistan, but to defer such action against Iraq.

Rodman and I had drafted our paper for the Camp David deliberations not from the viewpoint of the Secretary of Defense but from that of the President. Rumsfeld wanted us to do this with all our strategy papers. He explained that his job was not just running the Defense Department but also advising the President, and it did not help the President to get analyses limited to the concerns of a single department. So when we wrote about issues, we were to do so with a national, government-wide view that would correspond to the President's perspective—an approach that meant commenting on issues within the responsibility of other departments, which frequently caused friction with his colleagues. When he had to choose between staying in his bureaucratic "lane" and giving the President more useful advice, Rumsfeld unapologetically opted for the latter.

At the same time, Rumsfeld was vigilant in protecting the exclusive prerogatives of the only two civilians in the military chain of command—the President and the Secretary of Defense. Other officials saw Rumsfeld (and his subordinates, including myself) as trying to have it both ways—encroaching on other departments' turf, but invoking the sanctity of the chain of command to keep those other departments out of decision making on military operations.

Considered coolly and analytically, Rumsfeld's positions here both made sense: his determination to give the President advice from a presidential perspective was logical and constructive, and his jealous protection of the chain of command served an important national interest and accorded with the law. But personal and bureaucratic resentments do not always yield to cool reason. Sometimes they just fester.

This book is about decisions on national security. To make sense of the story, the reader should know something about the way the government was organized to make those decisions. Here is some basic information—dry, but brief—about the interagency policy-making process.

The ultimate authority for key national security judgments belongs to the President. In 1947, however, the National Security Council was created to advise him. As a matter of law, only four officials are *members* of the **National Security Council**.* During President Bush's first term, these were:

- President George W. Bush
- Vice President Dick Cheney
- Secretary of State Colin Powell
- Secretary of Defense Donald Rumsfeld

Note that the National Security Adviser is not a statutory member of the National Security Council. Nevertheless, the National Security Adviser is in charge of the National Security Council *staff*—a small team of policy analysts. To make matters even more confusing, officials often refer to this NSC *staff* as simply "the NSC."†

Two other officials are designated by law as *advisers* to the National Security Council:

- Chairman of the Joint Chiefs of Staff (General Hugh Shelton, until October 1, 2001, when he was replaced by General Richard B. Myers)
- CIA Director (George Tenet)

As a matter of practice, however, there were several other *regular attendees* at National Security Council meetings:

- National Security Adviser Condoleezza Rice
- Secretary of the Treasury Paul O'Neill

---

*See chart of U.S. government national security organization (Appendix 1).

†Whenever Rumsfeld heard an action of an NSC staffer attributed to "the NSC," he would respond sharply: "The NSC never did that. I'm on the NSC."

- White House Chief of Staff Andrew Card
- White House Counsel Alberto Gonzales

Depending on the subject matter of a meeting, other officials would be invited to attend—for example:

- Attorney General John Ashcroft
- Secretary of Commerce Don Evans
- Federal Bureau of Investigation Director Robert Mueller

At most meetings, these principal attendees were allowed to bring along one subordinate each, known as a "plus one." (At first Wolfowitz served as Rumsfeld's "plus one," but after I became Under Secretary the task increasingly became mine.)

The National Security Council normally met in the Situation Room, as did the lower-level interagency groups described below. The table in the austere main conference chamber seated one person at each end, four on each side, and another fifteen or so in seats against the wood-paneled wall. When the NSC staff designated a meeting as "principals plus one," the main representative of an agency sat at the table and the "plus one" sat behind him against the wall.* The room was so small that a principal leaning back in his tall leather table chair would often bang into the knee of his "plus one."

When the National Security Council met without the President, it was called the **Principals Committee** and was chaired by National Security Adviser Rice. The general rule was that an agency could be represented at meetings of the Principals only by its Secretary or the Deputy Secretary (or counterpart); exceptions were rare.

The highest interagency policy committee below cabinet level was the **Deputies Committee**. As a rule, agencies could be represented there only by a Deputy Secretary or an Under Secretary (or counterpart). Rice's deputy, Stephen Hadley, chaired the Deputies Committee meetings. Over time I became the regular representative of the civilian side of the Defense Department. As Vice Chairman of the Joint Chiefs—beginning on October 1, 2001—General Peter Pace (U.S. Marine Corps) became the regular military representative.

---

*The term "principal" could be confusing, for it was routinely used in two different ways. It primarily referred to cabinet-level officials who attended NSC meetings with the President. But it also was used to refer to the main representative of an agency at *any* interagency meeting, even if the meeting was at the Deputies level or below. When I attended Deputies Committee meetings, for instance, it was usually as the "principal" from the Defense Department.

Below the level of the Deputies Committee, interagency committees had limited subject-matter responsibilities. Those that met at the level of assistant secretaries or deputy assistant secretaries were called **Policy Coordinating Committees** (PCCs). They were generally chaired by members of Rice's staff, as were the "sub-PCCs."

End of tutorial.

Rumsfeld personally wrote a message to his combatant commanders to guide their development of war plans for the counterterrorism campaign. Transmitted through General Shelton on September 19, 2001, the message alerted them that, in reviewing those plans, Rumsfeld would be looking for three objectives:

1. **Targets worldwide, such as UBL Al Qaida cells in regions outside Afghanistan and even outside the Middle East. . . . It will be important to indicate early on that our field of action is much wider than Afghanistan.**
2. **Ground targets that provide opportunities to bring back intelligence that could help us to run down terrorists' networks.**
3. **Opportunities to demonstrate a capability or a boldness that will give pause to terrorists and/or those who harbor terrorists and force them to exercise much greater care, at greater cost or with much greater fear than they otherwise might have.**

The Secretary knew that the commanders had felt constrained by top-down pressure in recent years to design low-risk military options. Believing that the country's political leaders were unwilling to authorize missions dangerous to U.S. forces, the military had limited its recommendations to operations involving such techniques as high-altitude aerial bombardment or the shooting of stand-off weapons, like cruise missiles. Critics bitingly called this the doctrine of "immaculate aggression."

Rumsfeld and his staff worried about the well-being of every American service member. We shared the intense concern that our military men and women inspire in their families whenever combat operations are required. But terrorists had just murdered over three thousand people in the space of an hour and a quarter in New York, Washington, and Pennsylvania. We agreed with President Bush that it would only make our enemies more aggressive if the United States seemed unwilling to pay a price to defend its interests. Our very unwillingness to take casualties would create an extra incentive for our enemies to inflict them. The President had concluded that we could not fight the war on terrorism successfully with such a frame of mind. He underscored this conviction when he stressed the inevitability of U.S. casualties in his Pentagon meeting on September 12. Rumsfeld reinforced that point in this memo.

Rumsfeld directed his commanders to look for ways to divide the Taliban and al Qaida and to aggravate fissures between the Taliban and the Afghan people. He stressed the importance of "WMD targets—including targets that might give evidence of WMD activities." We did not know for sure whether there were any such targets in Afghanistan, but they would be important to find if they existed. He cautioned against "collateral damage that would be used against us from a religious standpoint" and concluded:

> **In short, find targets and opportunities to pressure and otherwise influence the terrorists, their networks and their friends whether state supporters, [non-governmental organizations], other networks or things they value, to root them out, keep them on the move, raise their risks and their costs and cause their friends to begin to fear for their own survival, thus to desert them and/or turn on them.**

In another memo he drafted that day, Rumsfeld expressed concern about support at home and abroad for a war effort that he believed would be protracted and frustrating, yet would depend for its success on the support of a public with an uncertain attention span and limited patience. In a section on "realistic expectations," he anticipated that the campaign would be "a marathon, not a sprint," adding: "[T]he fact that the first, second, or third wave of our efforts does not produce specific people should not come as a surprise. We are patient and determined."

Rumsfeld also wanted the U.S. government to deliver messages to the world that showed an interest in support from our foreign friends. He acknowledged the difficulties they could face in giving that support and recognized that the interests of the United States and our friends would not always mesh on all aspects of this war:

> **The legitimacy of our actions does not depend on how many countries support us. More nearly the opposite is true: the legitimacy of other countries' opinions should be judged by their attitude toward this systematic, uncivilized assault on a free way of life. . . .**
>
> **The coalitions that are being fashioned will not be fixed; rather, they will change and evolve. While most countries are**

concerned about terrorism, and properly so, each country has a somewhat different perspective and different relationships, views and concerns. It should not be surprising that some countries will be supportive of some activities in which the U.S. is engaged, while other countries will not. . . . [S]ome countries will have to conceal or downplay their cooperation with us. That needs to be understood and accepted. . . . [P]eople have fears—fear for themselves, their families and their governments. Therefore, some will be reluctant to join an effort against terrorism or at least some aspects of our efforts. . . .

Soon after 9/11, the President had declared that the war was not directed against Islam. In reiterating that point, Rumsfeld explored the idea that the war on terrorism was, in part, a civil war within the world of Islam:

The Al-Qaida terrorists are extremists whose views are antithetical to those of most Muslims. Their actions threaten the interests of the world's Muslims and are aimed in part at preventing Muslim people from engaging the rest of the world. There are millions of Muslims around the world who we expect to become allies in this struggle.

Rumsfeld concluded his memo with a blandly phrased, but significant, statement about possible changes to America's relationships with other nations:

[A]s we continue to go after terrorism, our activities will have effects in a number of countries. We have to accept that, given the importance of the cause. As a result, relationships and alliances will likely be rearranged over the coming years.

Bureaucrats have been described as people who write memos they don't sign and sign memos they don't write. I have known several top-level government officials who fit that definition—indeed, who did little more than sign memos they didn't write.

Rumsfeld, on the other hand, was a prolific memo writer, happy to sign his own productions. He generated memos of a special type—informal, frugally printed on plain, white copy paper, first draft dictated by himself, sometimes lengthy but often only a few sentences, asking a question or prodding someone for a response to a previous query or assignment—and he turned them out in such profusion that they were called "snowflakes." He tended to phrase them sharply, as he did his comments at Pentagon meetings. Rather than simply ask where project X stood at the moment, he would write: Why is nothing being done on project X? The snowflakes often sent an exasperated, drop-everything-and-get-me-an-answer-immediately message. The blizzard from his office on a typical day could be two dozen; some days it topped one hundred.

As I read his numerous contemplative, demanding, quick-on-the-draw, stimulating, backside-covering, intelligent, and/or disruptive snowflakes, I saw how useful and how irritating they could be to people throughout the Pentagon and the government. To be sure, one had to marvel at their volume and generally high quality. It would have been impressive even if Rumsfeld had had nothing else to do all day but write them. Particularly noteworthy was the high ratio of ideas to words. He was blessed with a mind that naturally produced short, clear declarative sentences.

And he was an avid collector as well as producer of ideas. In his huge office, wherever he held meetings—at his large rectangular conference table, his smaller round table and, for stand-up sessions, next to his stand-up writing desk—Rumsfeld kept small yellow pads handy. When he was out of his office, he would resort to three-by-five cards in an old leather holder in his suit coat. Whenever anyone said anything he deemed noteworthy, Rumsfeld grabbed a pad and scribbled. The worthy note would eventually fall to earth as a snowflake.

It would be petty to allege that Rumsfeld was interested in claiming credit for all the ideas he recorded. Indeed, he deserved credit for his energy and diligence in writing them down and distributing them. But this issue of who invented what idea did cause people to stew about his memos. Once, at an interagency meeting, I and others learned of a bright idea that the head of another government agency was planning to bring forward to the Principals Committee. Soon after, in the course of a hurried exchange, I mentioned to Rumsfeld in a few words that the bright idea was under consideration. I did not go into detail about whose idea it was or where it stood procedurally. Rumsfeld liked the idea and mentioned it in a snowflake to all the members of the Principals Committee before the head of the other agency presented it. I was never able to persuade my interagency colleagues that Rumsfeld here was pure of heart—or to quell their grumbling about plagiarism and glory snatching.

By mid-September, President Bush had made his beliefs clear: As an act of war, 9/11 required a response far beyond the issuance of arrest warrants.

Secretary of State Powell and his deputy, Richard Armitage, spoke of hitting al Qaida and the Taliban with the toughest blows *that could win extensive international support*. Cheney, Rumsfeld, Wolfowitz, and I looked at the matter from a different angle: designing a strategy to prevent another big terrorist attack on the United States. In these early weeks, however, many Administration officials continued to use law enforcement terms like "punishment," "justice," "evidence," and "perpetrators" publicly and in National Security Council discussions. Such long-standing patterns of thought rarely disappear overnight. Even President Bush often resorted to the legalistic phrase "bringing the terrorists to justice," though he would sometimes archly add the more warlike alternative of "bringing justice to the terrorists."

In the interagency debates about the way ahead, the National Security Council Principals would test the President's willingness to break with the standard law enforcement frame of mind. Americans and others instinctively understood that 9/11 was not an ordinary event in the decades-long history of terrorism and counterterrorism. Bush got broad, bipartisan support when he announced that 9/11 meant war. But fighting terrorism strategically was little more than a notion. Having coined the term "war on terror," the President now had to flesh out the idea that international terrorism was more than just a conspiracy of provably guilty individuals.

The 9/11 attack was one of those events in history potent enough to stimulate fresh thought and disturb the complacent. It created an opportunity to give many people—friends and enemies, in the United States and abroad—a new perspective. Rumsfeld, Wolfowitz, and I shared the view that the President had a duty to use his bully pulpit in order to promote awareness of the challenge from terrorist extremists. As we considered options for U.S. action, we asked not only how our actions might directly disrupt enemy operations, but also how they could affect the world's understanding of the nature of this struggle—its geographic scope, the definition of the enemy network, the significance of state supporters of terrorism, and the special dangers of weapons of mass destruction. Whereas Powell stressed the importance of respecting the views of allies and friends abroad, we encouraged the President to act, with due respect, to *shape* those views.

It was typical of Rumsfeld and his team to introduce concepts and principles into policy discussions and consider ways to influence public thinking about strategic matters. And it was typical of his State Department counterpart, Colin Powell, to dismiss such generalities and address policy questions within what he saw as the status quo. The conceptual, intellectually ambitious, strategic talk that Rumsfeld brought into policy debates met with little patience from Powell, who made it clear that he viewed such discussion as so much theory and ideology. Powell presented himself as the practical man of affairs, taking the world as he found it, focused on the here and now, intent on getting organized for the next day's set of meetings on whatever crisis was at hand.

This is not to say that Powell had his feet on the ground and Rumsfeld and his team did not. All the high-level Administration officials understood that we had to operate in the real world—within "the art of the possible," as Bismarck defined politics. But Powell tended to accept his own view of the current lay of the land as defining the art of the possible. Rumsfeld, often joined by Cheney, Rice, and Bush, not only saw the world differently—they were inclined to think that U.S. leadership might be able to alter the landscape, at home or in the world, making more difficult goals attainable.

When Rumsfeld was told, for example, that a certain law required the Defense Department to do business in a less-than-optimal way, he would not simply adjust; he would ask if it made sense to try to get the law changed. Likewise, if the government lacked diplomatic or political support for an action Rumsfeld considered important, his instinct was to clarify the action's strategic goals and use that insight to argue our case to get the support we wanted.

When a pressing issue arose—a possible war, the collapse of a government, preparations for a missile test by a dangerous regime—Powell would come to interagency meetings to discuss the talking points he wanted to use when discussing the matter with his foreign counterparts in the coming days.

Rumsfeld insisted that we formulate our national goals in words—to ensure clarity, precision, discipline within the Administration, and a long-range view. Powell did not conceal his opinion that it was a waste of time to debate abstractions and engage in wordsmithing when action was required—when he had urgent discussions to conduct with foreign ministers from around the world. Powell preferred to think and act as an operator or crisis manager, not as a strategist or innovator.

Rumsfeld was unusually intelligent, but Powell also clearly had an ample intellect. Powell also had—to an extraordinary degree—those qualities that make for what has been called a high "E.Q.," or emotional quotient: the personal traits that allow one to win friends and influence people.

But Powell and Rumsfeld had different frames of mind—a point demonstrated by the approach each took toward his department after 9/11. Rumsfeld created numerous new organizations and offices in the Pentagon, among them the Northern Command, the office of the Under Secretary of Defense for Intelligence, and the office of the Assistant Secretary of Defense for Homeland Defense. He created new forums that allowed (for the first time) the Pentagon's military and civilian senior leadership to meet as a group and with the combatant commanders; redrew the areas of responsibility of the combatant commands; and realigned the U.S. defense posture throughout the world—establishing and shutting down bases and other facilities, revising international agreements, and creating new international military activities and defense forums. (In this Rumsfeld was squarely in line with the President, who created the Department of Homeland Security, the Homeland Security Council, and the Directorate of National Intelligence in this same period.) Powell, however, left the State Department's apparatus of bureaus and foreign missions largely unchanged—complete with major offices devoted to arms control agreements from the Soviet era. When Powell left the Administration in early 2005, one could hardly tell from the State Department's structure that 9/11 had occurred in 2001—or even that the Cold War had ended in 1991.

Perhaps the most telling difference in how the Rumsfeld and Powell teams operated arose from Rumsfeld's passion for documentation and the written word. In his view, the only way to ensure clarity of thinking was to get one's arguments down on paper. Helping Rumsfeld commit his ideas to writing became a major part of my work as Under Secretary. Sometimes my staff or I conceived and drafted items for him; sometimes we just edited memos he drafted. In all events, we put a lot of thinking into writing. This disciplined our work, and it also improved interagency debates and increased our influence.

Powell showed little appreciation for these efforts and made cutting remarks about the stream of Defense Department memos.* State Department professionals did produce many long memos, but these were usually operational discussions of diplomacy, wordy and full of details that fell below the proper purview of the Principals Committee, let alone the President. From Powell on down, State officials generally chose not to challenge strategic or conceptual arguments from Defense, and especially not in writing. As intelligent and persuasive as he was, Powell evidently preferred to forfeit the opportunity to present written strategic arguments

*One morning Rumsfeld saw an article (reprinted in *The Early Bird*, the Pentagon's daily press packet) that cited anonymous State Department sources deprecating and resenting specific memos from Rumsfeld. Seeing this as badmouthing by Powell's staff, Rumsfeld stopped sending memos to Powell through normal channels, delivering them only by hand to Powell personally, so that only he would be accountable for any further grumbling in the press. Nasty comments about Rumsfeld's memos soon subsided; having made his point, Rumsfeld abandoned the practice a few weeks later.

for Bush (and future historians) to weigh against policy papers from Rumsfeld and his staff.

Journalists have depicted Principals Committee and National Security Council meetings as a soap opera of nasty clashes between Powell and Rumsfeld. It is true that there were policy differences between them (and among others at those meetings), but their personal interactions tended to be cordial and their policy differences generally produced no actual clash. When the Secretaries of State and Defense disagreed, each would make his points, but those points rarely banged into each other. Though they were often headed in different directions, Rumsfeld and Powell tended to move on different planes.

President Bush often connected with Rumsfeld—or bumped up against him—on the level of ideas and strategy; the same was true of Cheney and often of Rice. Disagreements among the four of them, which were rarely fundamental, had the effect of polishing or refining their colliding ideas, as debates among generally like-minded people often do. But there was a ships-passing-in-the-dark quality to disagreements between Powell and the others—not just because they differed about philosophy or policy, but because Powell chose to confine his contributions to operational and tactical thoughts.

In the past several years, countless media stories have suggested that Rumsfeld and the "neocons" mysteriously or conspiratorially achieved sway over the President. Defense officials did have influence, but this owed much to a mode of operation that was the opposite of conspiracy: We created a transparent record of the facts and reasoning we used to support our proposals. Bush often complimented Rumsfeld's memos, which addressed him at the level on which he liked to operate—that of strategy, not tactics. They were analytical and mercilessly edited, giving the results of much thought in few words. And they showed confidence that the ideas they contained, when reduced to print on a page, could retain potency and withstand scrutiny over time, unlike arguments that derive their force from the personality of the advocate.

General Tommy Franks arrived at the Pentagon on September 20, 2001, to brief Rumsfeld, Wolfowitz, and the Joint Chiefs of Staff on his war plan for Afghanistan. So far, neither the President nor Rumsfeld had been satisfied with CENTCOM's proposed ideas.

After the session (held in the Joint Chiefs' conference room, known as "the tank"), Rumsfeld called me to his office to help him set down his thoughts about Franks's briefing in a set of "talking points" he could use before the General presented it to the President the next day. (I generally added "suggested" before the term "talking points" because Rumsfeld did not like the implication that his staff was telling him what to say.)

As Rumsfeld voiced his thoughts, I was surprised by his blunt disapproval of Franks's product. It was an early demonstration for me of Rumsfeld's concern for his own credibility and standing. He expected important work by the Defense Department to be done to his own standards, reflecting his personal ideas, editing, and polish. Once he had approved a piece of work, he was ready to call it his own, publicize it in his own statements, and defend it against all critics. But if he had not himself ensured the quality of a project—and in a multi-million-person bureaucracy like the Defense Department there were inevitably many such cases—and the work was not up to his standards, Rumsfeld wanted all relevant audiences to know he was not its author.

In the points he dictated to me, Rumsfeld complimented Franks and his team on trying hard and thinking boldly and creatively. He called them brave officers whose plan entailed serious risks, including the use of ground forces in Afghanistan. But he intended to tell the President: "Even before you hear the plan, I want to state: You will find it disappointing. I did."

This was not Franks's fault, he observed, because CENTCOM was operating with "three key limitations":

1. **Requirement to initiate military strikes within a very short time.**
2. **Focus on al-Qaida in Afghanistan.**
3. **Pitiful lack of intelligence as to potential al-Qaida or Taliban targets.**

These limitations, Rumsfeld said, made it "impossible for Gen. Franks (or anyone) to propose initial military action that comports with the President's concept of a broad and sustained effort against international terrorists and the states that support them." After Franks finished briefing the President, the Secretary planned to review for the President some of the remarks from the session in the tank with the Joint Chiefs, who had also been critical.

In his memoir, *American Soldier*, Franks paints a bitter picture of the September 20 meeting in the tank. He did not want to brief the Chiefs at all, and recalls cursing when General Shelton told him he had to. Franks does not disparage Myers and Pace, but he describes the comments at the meeting of the service chiefs—the military heads of the army, navy, marines, and air force—as so much self-centered, or service-centered, "parochial bullsh–." He accuses the chiefs of failing to appreciate his concept of joint (that is, interservice) warfare—and of imposing on him and Rumsfeld "aimless dialogue, a waste of time that neither the Secretary nor I could spare."

The next day, Franks contends, he met with two of the chiefs—General James Jones of the marines and Admiral Vern Clark of the navy—and told them: "Yesterday in the Tank, you guys came across like a mob of Title Ten motherf—ers, not like the Joint Chiefs of Staff." According to Franks, he then met with Rumsfeld and declared: "We should not allow narrow-minded four-stars to advance their share of the budget at the expense of the mission."

Franks describes Rumsfeld as satisfied with the briefing, and impatient and "visibly annoyed" with the Chiefs' criticisms. But the remarks the Secretary made to me immediately after the meeting, for inclusion in the talking-points memo I drafted that day, demonstrate that Franks had misread Rumsfeld. (None of those points were mine: I had not attended the discussion in the tank and, at that time, I had never met or spoken with Franks, who worked not in the Pentagon but out of CENTCOM's headquarters in Tampa, Florida.)

Rumsfeld's main criticism of Franks's plan was that any effort aimed chiefly at hitting terrorist targets in Afghanistan "will not likely produce impressive results." One reason was that U.S. officials lacked extensive intelligence about Afghanistan—and we doubted the reliability of what we did have.

Rumsfeld and Wolfowitz were doubters by nature. They made a practice of challenging information produced by the bureaucracy. As a lawyer, I appreciated the systematic way they questioned the evidence for propositions made to them, and their sensitivity to the distinction between *evidence* and *proof*. There are many wrong conclusions for which a great deal of evidence exists. Top officials, like judges and scientists, have to decide how much evidence should be required to establish or "prove" a point for a particular purpose. All three of us were familiar with errors the U.S. intelligence community had made in recent decades—about the Soviet economy, Chinese military developments, and North Korean missile programs, to name just a few. So we were particularly skeptical about intelligence products. This was true of factual reports and even truer of analyses.

As my September 20 memo noted, our "knowledge of al-Qaida is sketchy" and we "know little of where they are, what they do." We could not be "confident that Taliban or al-Qaida leadership or forces will be captured or damaged severely."

An important element of Franks's plan was action against a possible chemical weapons facility in Afghanistan. So Wolfowitz suggested including a cautionary tale from the Vietnam War:

> **The greatest risk in Special Forces action is that we may come up empty-handed. Can't count on finding proof of chemical weapons production in the fertilizer factory that is our prime target. During the Vietnam War, we executed a tactically brilliant raid on a suspect POW facility at Sontay, but the intelligence was stale and there were no POWs there when we got there.**

As noted, there was already broad agreement that a less-than-impressive response to 9/11 might embolden the terrorists to strike again. The United States had to find a way to demonstrate a break with past practice and establish that we were willing to go to war to protect ourselves and our freedom.

Rumsfeld thought the President should concentrate on inducing *states* in the terrorism network to decide they would be better off renouncing support for terrorism and pursuit of weapons of mass destruction:

> **If the initial U.S. military action is not confidence-inspiring, it could undermine our entire effort.**
>
> **(1) Bombing for a few days;**
> **(2) not destroying anything of high value (there's nothing of high value in all of Afghanistan);**
> **(3) attacking a suspected chemical weapons facility that may turn out to be a mere commercial factory—none of this reflects the distinctive policies and frame of mind of the George W. Bush Administration. None of this gives substance to the President's pledge of a broad and sustained war against terror and state support for terror.**

A U.S. action in Afghanistan might have the desired formidable effect, Rumsfeld noted, if the United States joined forces with the Afghan Northern Alliance in its war against the Taliban—for example, "by deploying U.S. direct support with Apaches or other capabilities to take out the Taliban's armor capability." The Northern Alliance was a fighting force of Afghans of mostly Tajik and Uzbek ethnicity. Their enemies, the Taliban, were mostly ethnic Pashtuns. Rumsfeld wanted the President to know, however, that such action to help the Northern Alliance would require "more strategic/operational analysis and much better intelligence than I've seen so far."

Rumsfeld questioned the assumption that the United States had to respond to 9/11 with immediate military strikes. One of the ideas outlined in our September 20 memo had been a no-strike option, which would have involved "building up our forces massively, deliberately and ominously in the Middle East—and not just in the Persian Gulf but in the Eastern Mediterranean as well." If the President directed strikes, however, Rumsfeld wanted to reiterate that they should be designed to produce "impressive results," which they might if they hit:

- **Al-Qaida forces and assets in more than one country, including some outside the Middle East. Again we need better intelligence for that.**
- **At least one non-al-Qaida target—e.g., Iraq [and other specified locations].**

Rumsfeld described surprising the enemy as "a crucial operational value." Accordingly, the widespread expectation that the United States would hit Afghanistan "argues for the initial strike to be directed some place else and preferably someplace like South America or Southeast Asia." He continued:

> **The President has stressed that we are not defining our fight narrowly and are not focused only on those directly responsible for the September 11 attacks. . . . It would drive this point home if the initial military strikes hit [targets] in addition to al-Qaida. That is one of the reasons why I still favor an early focus on Iraq as well.**

One of the reasons for including Iraq, we said, was to call attention to the danger of weapons of mass destruction and the fact that key states that support terrorism were also interested in WMD.

Rumsfeld thought he needed another week or so before he could bring the President an option for initial U.S. military actions "as ambitious as the high goals declared by the President." Rather than the current Franks plan, he wanted "a broader plan, better suited to the large task we have to deal with international terrorism."

The 9/11 Commission Report referred to this September 20 memo, noting Rumsfeld's idea of hitting terrorists outside the Middle East, the possibility of an early selection of a non-al-Qaida target like Iraq, and the thought that a U.S. attack in South America or Southeast Asia might surprise the terrorists. David Ignatius of the *Washington Post,* though often a thoughtful commentator, cited the memo contemptuously as evidence that the Bush Administration was not taking bin Laden seriously: "Even after 9/11, some senior Bush officials didn't seem to get it."

We took bin Laden seriously, but we believed that the purposes of U.S. military action after 9/11 went beyond striking at the perpetrators. We felt compelled to choose a more ambitious strategic goal—to prevent further attacks that would kill Americans and compromise our security. And our immediate objectives were to disrupt terrorist operations and generate pressure on terrorism's state supporters. We had little faith—and not enough high-quality evidence—that even successful attacks on the few targets we could identify in Afghanistan would seriously obstruct terrorist operations in the near term.

When presented with war plans, Pentagon civilians have a duty to probe the assumptions of the military commanders who write them. What national purposes should the plan aim to accomplish? If the United States is expected to attack at point X, should we consider attacking at point Y? How directly or indirectly should we engage enemies?

Rumsfeld decided that the first U.S. strikes could serve objectives other than blasting al Qaida's limited infrastructure. They could produce intelligence that would allow us to understand and counter the enemy and create or aggravate fissures in the enemy network. Our strikes could help our foreign friends see that they shared our interest in confronting the jihadists' network. This called for options that might shock that network, perhaps by hitting it where a U.S. response was not expected. We aimed to expose terrorist assets and networks of support in areas other than Afghanistan, calling attention to the conflict's global nature.

On the evening of September 20, President Bush delivered to Congress his first major speech following the 9/11 attack. Reiterating that 9/11 was "an act of war against our country," he identified al Qaida as the organization responsible for the attack, and its members as practitioners of "a fringe form of Islamic extremism." Noting that al Qaida was linked to many other organizations around the world, he said that there are "thousands of these terrorists in more than sixty countries."

Bush touched on our major assumptions. He defined the enemy as a network rather than a single organization: "Our war on terror begins with al Qaeda, but it does not end there."

The war would involve more than military operations, he explained, and would not have a distinct or early end. He announced a strategy of disturbing and dividing the terrorists and driving them onto the defensive.

> **Our response involves far more than instant retaliation and isolated strikes. Americans should not expect one battle, but a lengthy campaign, unlike any other we have ever seen. It may include dramatic strikes, visible on TV, and covert operations, secret even in success. We will starve terrorists of funding, turn them one against another, drive them from place to place, until there is no refuge or no rest.**

In later years, critics would accuse President Bush of promising quick results and full disclosure of U.S. counterterrorist activities, and failing to deliver either one. In fact, in this important speech, the President promised the opposite—and his speech received bipartisan approval.

He ended his speech with a memorable warning to the state sponsors of terror:

> **And we will pursue nations that provide aid or safe haven to terrorism. Every nation, in every region, now has a decision to make. Either you are with us, or you are with the terrorists. From this day forward, any nation that continues to harbor or support terrorism will be regarded by the United States as a hostile regime.**

To the Taliban, President Bush offered an ultimatum—the first application of this emerging Bush doctrine. "By aiding and abetting murder," he said, "the Taliban regime is committing murder." He demanded the closing of terrorist training camps, the delivery to the United States of the al Qaida leaders hiding in Afghanistan, and delivery to appropriate authorities of "every terrorist, and every person in their support structure." He announced: "These demands are not open to negotiation or discussion. The Taliban must act, and act immediately. They will hand over the terrorists, or they will share in their fate."

In that speech, Bush twice used the phrase "way of life." These struck me as his weightiest words. The President noted that our terrorist enemies killed in order to destroy a way of life, and he described the importance of "defeat[ing] terrorism as a threat to our way of life." That formulation of our war aim, I believe, originated with Scooter Libby, the Vice President's

Chief of Staff. It encapsulated my thinking about 9/11's strategic significance, which had taken shape during our in-flight conversation on September 12, and I championed it at Deputies Committee meetings and in extended conversations with Rice's deputy, Stephen Hadley. The phrase called attention to the stakes in the terrorist challenge—the openness, humane liberality, and personal freedom that define our society.

I looked at our new terrorism problem this way: If America were not a liberal democracy, a country that recognizes the worth and political equality of its individual citizens and respects their civil liberties, it would cease to be America. Our country is not so much a land and a people as it is a way of life that embodies an idea—the idea of individual freedom.

Much of what makes Americans happy—our self-governance, economic prosperity, domestic tranquility, and opportunity to better ourselves—derives from the liberal and democratic nature of our society and the degree of mutual trust (sometimes called social capital) that such a society engenders. It is hard to overstate the moral and material benefits rooted in that trust, in our freedom. And this is what terrorism had the potential to undo. Beyond the cost in lives and property, the 9/11 attack—or, rather, our reaction to it—could have far-reaching consequences, especially if it were followed by more such attacks. To protect ourselves physically, we might have to change fundamentally the way we live, sacrificing our society's openness for hoped-for safety.

Because of our historical good fortune, Americans have long enjoyed a high degree of public safety. We have become accustomed to thinking that our civil liberties are not only sacred but unshakeable. But a community's freedom is affected by circumstances. Throughout history, civil liberties have yielded to society's desire for the state to fulfill its fundamental duty of providing security. This has been the case even in America, the "land of the free." Even such an uncompromising champion of liberty as the English philosopher John Stuart Mill bowed to the demands of public safety. Our Constitution and the judges that interpret it often seem to say that our freedoms are absolute, but when danger becomes oppressive, people will recall the quip that the Constitution is not a suicide pact.

In the immediate aftermath of 9/11, fearing another attack, our government acted to eliminate vulnerabilities the hijackers had turned to their advantage. It shut down air travel throughout the U.S. It arrested people for violations of immigration rules that would have been tolerated in less stressful times. It restricted the issuance of visas, limiting not only the freedom of foreigners to travel, but also the freedom of Americans to host them. And it began drafting legislation to allow intelligence and law enforcement agencies to share information more readily.

These steps were considered prudent, indeed necessary, in light of what we knew at the time.* In later years, Bush's political opponents criticized him for undermining American civil liberties by using unusual means to fight terrorist enemies—for example, detaining U.S. and non-U.S. unlawful combatants in U.S. military prisons and conducting domestic surveillance of communications with suspected al Qaida members. I personally worked on some aspects of these issues—though most were outside my area of responsibility—and I saw the President and his advisers wrestling in good faith with hard questions of how to protect our civil liberties to the greatest extent possible, while defending our country from the new threat it faced.

Beyond its human and material costs, terrorism exploits—and therefore endangers—the openness and trust that allow us to enjoy freedom and prosperity. If another 9/11 happened, especially an attack using nuclear or biological weapons, who could doubt that our society would respond by further increasing the powers of the government and inevitably constricting civil liberties? As has happened often in the past, security measures that once seemed outrageous could quickly become routine. And there was a possible ratchet effect worth worrying about: Burdensome security measures aren't always rolled back even after the threat diminishes.

These issues were a major part of my conversations with Hadley, Libby, and my Pentagon and other government colleagues in the days immediately after 9/11. We all recognized the need for a maximum effort to prevent the kinds of further attacks that could transform—perhaps permanently—U.S. society in this way. It was clear that if our strategy were solely or even primarily defensive, it would require wholesale changes in our society—a substantial clamping down, not just at our borders but throughout the country.

The President made this point in his September 20 speech. Noting that we were taking "defensive measures" against terrorism, he announced that Pennsylvania Governor Tom Ridge would serve in a new cabinet-level job to "safeguard our country . . . and respond to any attacks." Bush then observed: "These measures are essential. But the only way to defeat terrorism as a threat to our way of life is to stop it, eliminate it, and destroy it where it grows."

It was an important "but": America, the President was saying, can-

---

*Controversy about these steps remains hot; indeed, it has intensified as we move further away from 9/11 with no new major terrorist attacks on U.S. soil. Legal and political challenges to the U.S. government's post-9/11 security measures have been made in courts and in Congress; some have been upheld in the courts and supported in Congress, others not.

not rely solely on a defensive strategy—not if we hope to preserve our way of life. If all we did to prevent future attacks was beef up homeland security—limiting access to potential targets, searching persons and possessions, resorting perhaps to ethnic profiling and increasing intrusions on individual privacy—we would not be able to maintain our free and open society, "our way of life." To preserve civil liberties, the President had to adopt a strategy of disrupting terrorist networks abroad, where they do much of their planning, recruiting, and training. He had to adopt a strategy of initiative and offense as well as defense. As I saw it, the President decided that, in dealing with the terrorists, he had the choice of changing the way *we* live or changing the way *they* live.

I had been able to do some useful work for Rumsfeld, but in my first two months as Under Secretary, he had kept me and the Policy organization at arm's length. He did not include me, for example, in his operational planning meetings with his commanders. Without that access, I could not do my job properly. I could not know whether my ideas were apt and ripe or merely wasting his time.

With the Defense Department getting on a war footing, I realized that my Policy organization was not contributing as it should. I knew the Secretary well enough to know that if that thought should occur to him, he would not blame himself.

Rumsfeld was not one to feel paralyzed by the absence of advisers. Because of the delays in the White House nomination and Senate confirmation processes for political appointees, he spent the first six months of the Administration with a Policy organization that had no official leadership: no Under Secretary or assistant secretaries and almost no deputy assistant secretaries. Over time he became accustomed to the situation, and he and Wolfowitz handled interagency policy meetings by themselves.

Rumsfeld had known and worked with Wolfowitz for years and was used to relying on him for national security advice. Rumsfeld furthermore had no shortage of ideas of his own in that field. The two men were so well-versed and interested in my area of responsibility—and so self-sufficient—that I sometimes felt I'd entered my job with two Under Secretaries of Defense for Policy above me. This problem was compounded by Rumsfeld's proper concern for secrecy and his management idiosyncrasies. He worked with his military and civilian inner circle by thinking out loud and inviting comments and challenges. In my experience, he did not like to think out loud in large meetings or in front of people he did not know, respect, and trust. He usually insisted on keeping his meetings small, even if this meant barring top-level personnel who had strong arguments for participating. He sometimes excluded even some of his favorite advisers or staff members. This not only helped keep numbers down, but also allowed him to prevent even his intimates (of whom I was not yet one) from presuming they were entitled to any privileges.

Rumsfeld did not advise his staff on how to work with him effectively. He was of the throw-them-in-the-pool-and-see-if-they-swim school of management. If you figured out a way to give him the quality of work he wanted, he would reward you not with a compliment or thanks, but with additional work. He used to joke—and may have believed—that thanks, when given routinely, would "ruin" subordinates. If you could not figure out how to be useful, then he would devise a way to work around you.

Rumsfeld had not brought me in on any of his discussions with Tommy Franks about operational plans. Nor was I included when Rumsfeld met routinely with the Chairman of the Joint Chiefs. I saw that it would take an effort on my part to get the Secretary to admit me into his most sensitive meetings. On the other hand, the burdens on him were increasing, and he needed the sort of help I might be able to provide.

I sounded out both Wolfowitz and Rumsfeld's senior military assistant, Vice Admiral Edmund Giambastiani, about the problem. Military assistants labor at the intersection of substance and process, taking notes at meetings, sometimes speaking up when they can shed light on the subject matter, and always keeping track of their boss's requests or promises. Collectively they are the Defense Department's driveshaft: forcing decisions, getting items on the calendar, and moving urgent matters through the system. During long days together, they develop an intense and intimate comradeship with their principals. They know when the time is right to raise a question with the boss and when the stars are ill-aligned.

Giambastiani operated with finesse, ebullience, and wisdom in the pressure cooker of Rumsfeld's front office. He managed to maintain Pentagon, interagency, and international "situational awareness" (a useful military locution)—and despite that, or perhaps because of it, was always ready for a hearty laugh.

Wolfowitz and Giambastiani explained that my best option was to get myself invited to the "Roundtable" meetings Rumsfeld held each morning with the Deputy, the Chairman, and the Vice Chairman. (No allusion to King Arthur was intended, I was told: The meetings were held at a small circular table just inside Rumsfeld's office.) Roundtable attendance, they said, would remedy for all practical purposes my lack of access to information.

Thinking Roundtable, I dropped in on Rumsfeld for a private chat. He received me standing up and remained standing, his way of saying that this had to be short. I told him I didn't think the Policy organization was serving him as it should. Sensing that I was going to ask for something, he immediately went on the offensive: I don't know that you can move fast enough, he said. I need responses and ideas fast. What I need is a good idea or two lobbed in front of me every day—in front of me, not behind me.

I could do that, I answered, if I were in the relevant meetings, and knew where important projects stood. He said he would think about it. Then, the next day, September 28, he told me to start attending the Roundtable.

The timing was good. A few days later the Pentagon had a new Vice Chairman—Marine General Peter Pace. The connection between my Policy organization and his Joint Staff* was an important element in civil-military relations in the Pentagon. It would strengthen that connection if Pace and I could collaborate as colleagues, but that would be hard to achieve if he were in the Secretary's inner circle and I was not.

My first contact with Pace was on October 1, his first day as the Vice, when I greeted him as he walked into Rumsfeld's office for Roundtable. It fell to me to point out his seat, as if I were an inner-circle member of long standing. Pace made a strong first impression with his articulate talk and beamish affability. We formed a tight professional connection that soon evolved into a delightful friendship.

Pace and I came to spend hours together every day for years—at Roundtable, at interagency Deputies Committee meetings, and at meetings of the Campaign Planning Committee (CAPCOM), a civilian-military body Pace and I created. Soon after 9/11, Rumsfeld had asked how to organize the Pentagon more effectively to fight the war. Stephen Cambone, an experienced Defense Department official whom Rumsfeld particularly admired and appointed as my principal deputy, answered by proposing the establishment of a policy planning committee that I would cochair with the Vice Chairman. Seeing this as a promising way to promote teamwork between Policy and the Joint Staff, I supported the idea—and so did Rumsfeld.

---

*The Joint Staff is the set of intelligence, strategy, operations, logistics, and other military offices in the Pentagon that support the advisory work of the Chairman and the Vice Chairman of the Joint Chiefs. It serves them on the Pentagon's military side much as the Office of the Secretary of Defense (OSD) serves the Secretary and the Deputy on the civilian side.

When Pace became the Vice, he embraced the CAPCOM. He and I devoted a lot of time to it; in periods of intense shared activity, it met every day. At the meetings, we discussed everything from conceptual strategic problems (such as the sequencing of major military operations in the war on terrorism) to ordinary bureaucratic matters (such as why some memo was stuck in an office awaiting a "chop" of approval). The CAPCOM allowed us to eliminate the long-standing but grossly unconstructive practice of the military and civilian sides of the Pentagon each continually sending in to the Secretary's office ideas that other side had not seen and did not approve. The CAPCOM was an important innovation at the Pentagon, although it has received virtually no attention from journalists and commentators.*

As September was ending and President Bush pressed for action, a gap still remained between his conception of a global war against terrorist extremists and CENTCOM's plans. General Franks and his staff had thought about how we could get forces into the Afghanistan theater for military operations of various sorts: aerial bombardment, U.S. ground combat, delivery of humanitarian supplies, the capture-or-kill targeting of enemy leadership, support for anti-Taliban Afghan militias, and combat search and rescue. Franks had briefed on *capabilities*: If our forces received certain types of basing and other support from our foreign friends, we could hit assorted targets and provide necessary supplies. But he did not address Rumsfeld's *strategic* questions—To what end? What were the higher-level purposes of the U.S. military action?

Rumsfeld recognized that Franks would be unable to propose the kinds of strategic ideas his superiors expected until they gave him a clear delineation of their goals. That is what Rumsfeld meant when he referred to the "limitations" that made it impossible for Franks (or anyone else) to propose military action that would satisfy the President's call for a broad effort against international terrorists and their state sponsors. Rumsfeld was responsible for communicating these higher-level strategic purposes to Franks—and, as the papers I have quoted here demonstrate, these strategic ideas were still under discussion.

*A Joint Staff "lessons learned" study in 2005 cited the CAPCOM model as a valuable innovation in civilian-military coordination. My successor as Under Secretary, Eric Edelman, institutionalized CAPCOM as the Policy and Strategy Committee on October 27, 2005.

Paul Wolfowitz made an important contribution by proposing a concept of operations that could serve U.S. strategic purposes in Afghanistan and beyond: U.S. forces should concentrate on supporting Afghanistan's indigenous anti-Taliban militias (an idea Wolfowitz had contributed to Rumsfeld's September 20 memo, which I drafted). In other words, U.S. forces should not take the lead in overthrowing the Taliban, but serve rather in a supporting role, *helping Afghans liberate themselves* from the Taliban. Wolfowitz recorded his thoughts in a September 23 paper for Rumsfeld entitled "Using Special Forces on 'Our Side' of the Line."

Wolfowitz's work on our Afghanistan strategy was one of many examples of what set him apart from the typical Deputy Secretary of Defense. The Deputy Secretary was usually someone with a defense industry or management background, who focused on budget, acquisition, personnel, and management tasks rather than on national security policy. Wolfowitz was a national security expert who had served in high-level positions at State during the Reagan Administration, as Under Secretary of Defense for Policy in the George H. W. Bush Administration, and then as dean of Johns Hopkins University's School of Advanced International Studies.

Wolfowitz's mind worked very differently from Rumsfeld's. For example, Wolfowitz insisted on mastering vast quantities of details on subjects for which he was responsible. Rumsfeld preferred to stay on the level of the big picture, "drilling down" (as he put it) only to check whether his staff knew what they were talking about. And Rumsfeld was thoroughly antisentimental, while Wolfowitz, a bleeding-heart conservative, often spoke of how individuals he knew "felt" about something. One could produce a long list of such distinctions. Despite their contrasting characters and modes of operation and analysis, however, when the two men had a chance to discuss a policy question together, they usually reached the same conclusions.

Given his scope, experience, and ego, it wasn't easy for Wolfowitz to spend four years as second fiddle to so dominant a personality as Rumsfeld, though the Secretary tended to show him considerable deference. Rumsfeld was generally patient with Wolfowitz, and often entirely receptive to his analyses and suggestions.

In this case, the Secretary readily saw the merits of Wolfowitz's proposed concept of operations for Afghanistan. Wolfowitz advocated using our uniquely mobile Army Special Forces—the Green Berets—to make contact with the Afghan Northern Alliance and any other potentially cooperative local forces. The contacts "could be used to exchange information, to bring in key elements of logistical support (including some appropriate weapons) or to provide communications gear." They could allow us to make partners of the Afghan anti-Taliban militias and coordinate U.S. military operations with them.

During much of the civil war in the 1990s (as in the post-Taliban period), Afghanistan had been a patchwork of regions controlled by commanders of local militias, many with their own heavy military equipment. Of the principal commanders or warlords—Ahmad Shah Massoud, Mohammed Fahim Khan, Ismail Khan, Gul Aga Shirzai, and Abdul Rashid Dostum—most had fought as *mujahideen* (holy warriors) against the Soviet army in the 1980s, forcing a Soviet withdrawal in 1989. In the instability that followed, warlords throughout Afghanistan came to play major political roles in their regions. But warlordism was not a standard feature of Afghan history. It provoked popular resentment, which the Islamist extremists of the Taliban movement exploited to seize power in Afghanistan in 1996.

For years, Massoud had been the principal leader of the military opposition to the Taliban under the banner of the Northern Alliance. On September 9, 2001, the Alliance suffered a setback when Massoud was assassinated by al Qaida, the Taliban's strategic ally. But two days later, when al Qaida struck New York and Washington, the Northern Alliance itself acquired a formidable strategic ally, the United States.

Wolfowitz's idea was to use Army Special Forces to turn America's *strategic* alignment of interests with the Northern Alliance into a *military partnership* to overthrow the Taliban. Our Special Forces on the ground could help direct U.S. air attacks, increasing their precision and reducing unintended harm to Afghan people and property. The Special Forces could also direct and help deliver humanitarian aid to where it was most needed. And they could get us better intelligence. The right U.S. ground force could maintain pressure on the Taliban, even if—as Rumsfeld and others worried—initial U.S. aerial bombing of al Qaida and Taliban targets would cause the Taliban little significant damage and no lasting dread.

His proposal, Wolfowitz argued, would minimize the burden and risks for U.S. forces while nonetheless showing that the United States was willing to act boldly and use our own ground forces to achieve a major effect: the overthrow of the Taliban regime. Helping Afghan partners play a stronger leading role against the Taliban would also make it possible to keep the U.S. military presence—our "footprint"—small. We wanted to avoid resembling in any way the heavy-footed force the Soviet Union had imposed on the country in 1979. The Soviets had lost in Afghanistan largely because the fierce and nationalistic Afghans saw them as invaders and destroyers. A small, light U.S. force, working shoulder to shoulder with Afghan fighters, could operate with precision against the al Qaida outsiders and their Taliban collaborators. Such a light force could keep collateral damage from U.S. bombs to a minimum and win local support as a welcome instrument of liberation.

Wolfowitz's list of the strategic benefits of his proposal concluded:

- **It would demonstrate to the American people and to the world that we know how to fight smart;**
- **It allows us to leverage the many elements of opposition to the Arab presence in Afghanistan, to the leadership of Mullah Omar within Taliban and to the Taliban itself;**
- **By improving our ability to manage our internal allies, it helps to reduce the chances that we will have a vacuum inside Afghanistan if the key elements of the Taliban are neutralized;**
- **As it becomes clear that this is part of our strategy, it will help to underscore that we are in for a sustained, but intelligent campaign, countering the impression either that we expect quick results or that we are heading for a long-term occupation of Afghanistan with all of the potentially catastrophic consequences which that entails.**

Franks had envisioned giving some support to anti-Taliban militias in Afghanistan. But he had not given the idea the centrality that Wolfowitz proposed, with all of its potential military and strategic dividends. Wolfowitz discussed these operational concepts with Rumsfeld and me, making a point of bringing General Shelton and General Myers into the deliberations. At the same time, Rumsfeld was daily working on strategic issues—the big thoughts—with Shelton, Myers, and Franks. Common thinking about strategy was beginning to develop among the Defense Department's civilian and military leaders.

But this meeting of minds did not extend to the CIA. The Agency's help was especially important, because CENTCOM believed it could not embed Special Forces with Afghan militias until CIA agents had made face-to-face arrangements with the militia commanders. Franks boasted of his superb working relationship with CIA Director George Tenet and with the resident CIA representatives at CENTCOM's Tampa headquarters. Rumsfeld, too, had created close and cordial ties with Tenet. But there were important disagreements and tensions between the two departments, and they would have lasting consequences.

My own relationship with Tenet was professional and reasonably friendly, but I rarely had the sense that I knew his thinking on whatever subject was under discussion. He had a clipped and colorful way of talking, but his comments tended to be vague or ambiguous, and I found it hard to take notes on them. In any case, he seldom spoke much at National Security Council meetings. Tenet had daily opportunities to talk with President Bush more privately—at the morning intelligence briefings—so I figured he chose not to say much when he was with the President in a bigger crowd such as the National Security Council meetings, which typically included fifteen to twenty people.

For reasons of their own, however, the CIA's Afghanistan experts disagreed with the Defense Department's evolving consensus on goals and strategy for Afghanistan. The CIA officials warned against Wolfowitz's idea of supporting the Northern Alliance, stressing the abiding tensions between Afghanistan's southerners—who were ethnic Pashtuns—and the ethnic Tajiks and Uzbeks of the Northern Alliance. If we decided to help the Northern Alliance against the mainly Pashtun Taliban, they warned, the southerners would see us as anti-Pashtun. The Taliban's base of support was in the south—centered not in Afghanistan's capital, Kabul, but in the main city of the south, Kandahar.

CIA personnel with experience in Pakistan echoed the warnings of Pakistani officials, who tended to favor the Pashtuns, and consistently cautioned against any U.S. actions that would antagonize them. (Many Pakistanis are ethnically Pashtun, as "Pashtunistan" sits astride the Afghan-Pakistani border.) Pakistani officials had in fact helped create the Taliban in the 1990s to protect Pakistan's interests in Afghanistan. And yet, paradoxically, the CIA had fairly good links with the Northern Alliance and virtually none with the Pashtuns in the south.

In meetings with Rumsfeld and his team in early October, CIA experts argued that instead of helping the Northern Alliance overthrow the Taliban—which they claimed would unite the Pashtuns against us—we should exploit Afghan xenophobia by concentrating on fighting the "Arabs," as the Afghans generally called the al Qaida people. The only Taliban targets should be Taliban military units that included al Qaida fighters—or Taliban facilities used by al Qaida. The CIA experts further insisted that we should work to split the Pashtuns—that is, identify southerners who opposed the Taliban and get them to fight.

Milton Bearden, a former CIA operative, published an article in the November/December 2001 *Foreign Affairs* making the same argument that CIA officials had been making in classified government discussions to counter the evolving Defense Department strategy. According to the journal, Bearden "served as CIA station chief in Pakistan from 1986 to 1989" and ran the CIA's "covert action program in support of the Afghan resistance to the Soviet-supported government." Referring to the Defense Department strategy advocated by Rumsfeld and Wolfowitz, Bearden wrote:

> **Some have called for arming and forming an alliance with Afghanistan's now-leaderless Northern Alliance. . . . Already the recipient of military and financial support from Russia and Iran, it seems a logical partner in the U.S. quest to locate and neutralize the bin Laden network and replace the Taliban regime.**
>
> **But that is not a wise course—not simply because of the cold irony of allying ourselves with the Russians in any fight in Afghanistan, but because it is not likely to achieve either goal. It is more than doubtful that the Northern Alliance forces could capture bin Laden and his followers, and there is no reasonable guarantee that they could dislodge the Taliban.**

Bearden held that a partnership with the Northern Alliance would likely cause the Pashtun tribes to coalesce with the Taliban and rekindle a civil war. He asserted that any real military partnership with the Northern Alliance "will backfire."

While it is true that, as of this writing, we have not caught bin Laden himself, Bearden's thesis—the same one the CIA advocated in interagency meetings—was disproved on the ground within weeks. The Northern Alliance did indeed help us kill or capture many of bin Laden's followers. They did decisively and quickly dislodge the Taliban. And our partnership with the Northern Alliance neither pushed the Pashtun tribes into the Taliban's arms nor rekindled a civil war.

The Bearden article was an example of how former intelligence officials became "real-time" public advocates of policies that current intelligence officials were championing in interagency meetings. The interagency deliberations, while still fresh, were properly classified and should not have been leaked.

This leak was an early sign that the CIA was not functioning properly in the interagency process. As far as I know, the offense went unrebuked. This was a problem that grew worse over time. In the aftermath of Saddam Hussein's overthrow, former intelligence officials engaged in open political warfare against President Bush, sharing with selected journalists and congressional staffers up-to-the-minute inside information that was attributed to intelligence community sources.

One CIA official, Michael Scheuer, did not even wait to leave government before attacking the Administration's policies in a book, which he titled *Imperial Hubris: Why the West Is Losing the War on Terror.* Originally published anonymously, Scheuer's volume hit the bookstores a few months before the 2004 presidential election. The CIA had authorized Scheuer to publish the book and to give television interviews about it as an anonymous CIA official, though the agency later changed its position and forbade such interviews. Some weeks later, having retired from the government, Scheuer spoke on the record to the *Washington Post.* Downplaying his own criticism of the Administration, Scheuer gave this remarkable account of the attitude toward Bush that prevailed at the CIA:

> Scheuer said he believes that the agency silenced him after CIA officials realized he was blaming the CIA, not the administration, for mishandling terrorism. "As long as the book was being used to bash the president, they gave me carte blanche to talk to the media," he said. "But this is a story about the failure of the bureaucracy to support policymakers."

The advice the CIA officials gave us in October 2001 was by no means foolish, but we thought their assumptions were off. Rumsfeld asked whether they had the intelligence necessary to ensure an impressive campaign against the targets they were prescribing. We worried that an effort concentrating only on al Qaida and a few Taliban targets would likely do little more than induce the "Arabs" to scatter abroad. If the United States wanted to persuade terrorist-supporting regimes around the world to change their policies, we knew we would have to oust the Taliban regime, not just hit al Qaida.

The CIA's answers did not inspire confidence. CIA officials confessed that their meager ties to Afghans in the south could take months to strengthen—yet the President wanted to initiate military strikes within days. We believed we could begin working with the Northern Alliance almost immediately, for the CIA already had contacts in the north. Were we to hold off action on the ground until the CIA produced an option for us in the south, our military options might be limited to aerial bombing for weeks or months—or we'd have to tell the President we could not initiate operations when he wanted us to.

President Bush resolved this issue in principle when he approved the CENTCOM war plan that called for supporting the Northern Alliance.

But the Defense Department's policy disagreements with the CIA persisted, even after the start of U.S. military operations.

Rumsfeld had spent nearly three weeks crafting a conception of the global war on terrorism. He had analyzed ideas for initial military actions, considered roles for our coalition partners, reviewed CENTCOM's operational plans, heard from Wolfowitz and me, and consulted with General Shelton and General Myers. He had chewed matters over with his fellow National Security Council principals and felt comfortable that he had a proposal for the way ahead that built on the President's instructions. Rumsfeld would record this conception in two documents: a short paper for the President, and a strategic guidance paper for the Defense Department on the "Campaign Against Terrorism."

I wrote the first draft of the paper for the President, which was entitled "Strategic Thoughts." After revising it with Wolfowitz, Abizaid, and Myers, I gave it to Rumsfeld, who edited, signed, and sent it to President Bush on September 30. Collaboration of this kind between the civilian and military sides of the Pentagon became a healthy routine under Rumsfeld and Myers, a remarkable fact of life in the Defense Department. This out-of-the-ordinary story of close civilian-military cooperation at the top levels of the Pentagon was generally overlooked by the news media.

In the "Strategic Thoughts" paper, our main point was that the United States should be focusing on the state actors within the enemy network, which could create a strategic and humanitarian nightmare for us by giving a terrorist group a biological or nuclear weapon that could kill hundreds of thousands of people, perhaps even millions. One way to disrupt terrorist groups was to compel their state sponsors to change policies on terrorism and on weapons of mass destruction. This could be done, we reasoned, through military action against some of the state sponsors, and pressure—short of war—against others. The effectiveness of the diplomatic pressure would hinge to some extent on the success of our military actions.

In some cases, we could get leverage by aiding local opposition groups, rather than sending U.S. forces to take the lead in overthrowing foreign regimes. The regimes that supported terrorism tended to be oppressive domestically as well as aggressive internationally, so there were opposition groups in various countries that we could assist as a way of pressuring the leaders there. The U.S. "strategic theme," Rumsfeld advised the president, should be "aiding local peoples to rid themselves of terrorists and to free themselves of regimes that support terrorism." The United States could set the pattern in Afghanistan by supporting the anti-Taliban and anti-al-Qaida militias:

> **Air strikes against al Qaida and Taliban targets are planned to begin soon. But, especially in the war's initial period, I think US military action should stress:**
>
> - **indirect (through local, non-US forces) action, in coordination with and in support of opposition groups;**
> - **direct use of US forces initially primarily to deliver logistics, intelligence and other support to opposition groups and humanitarian supplies to NGOs and refugees, and subsequently**
> - **on-the-ground action against the terrorists as individuals—leaders and others . . .**

Rumsfeld cautioned that the United States should be restrained on air strikes until we had sufficient intelligence to mandate "impressive (worthwhile) strikes" against al Qaida and other targets. In an especially remarkable passage, he also advised the President that victory in the war on terrorism would require geopolitical changes substantial enough to cause every regime supporting terrorists to worry about its vulnerability:

> **If the war does not significantly change the world's political map, the U.S. will not achieve its aim. There is value in being clear on the order of magnitude of the necessary change. The USG [U.S. government] should envision a goal along these lines:**
>
> - **New regimes in Afghanistan and [some other states] that support terrorism (to strengthen political and military efforts to change policies elsewhere).**
> - **Syria out of Lebanon.**
> - **Dismantlement or destruction of WMD in [key states].**
>
> ———
>
> - **End of many other countries' support or tolerance of terrorism.**

Rumsfeld again raised the idea of deferring military strikes in Afghanistan:

- **It would instead be surprising and impressive if we built our forces up patiently, took some early action outside of Afghanistan, perhaps in multiple locations, and began not exclusively or primarily with military strikes but with train-and-equip activities with local opposition forces and humanitarian aid and intense information operations.**
- **We could thereby:**
  - **Garner actionable intelligence on lucrative targets, which we do not now have.**
  - **Reduce emphasis on images of US killing Moslems from the air.**

  - **Signal that our goal is not merely to damage terrorist-supporting regimes but to threaten their regimes by becoming partners with their opponents.**
  - **Capitalize on our strong suit, which is not finding a few hundred terrorists in caves in Afghanistan, but in the vastness of our military and humanitarian resources, which can strengthen the opposition forces in terrorist-supporting states.**

General Abizaid reacted enthusiastically to these "strategic thoughts" as they circulated in draft form. Perhaps because Abizaid usually fed me criticism of my office's comments on the Middle East and other subjects, Myers made a point of sending me a copy of the message he received from Abizaid: "This is an exceptionally important memo, which gives clear strategic vision. It encourages patience, the nuanced use of power and a way to avoid stumbling into a major conventional war. Recommend that you support this approach." After noting that in the war on terrorism, the United States would need a responsive intelligence "architecture" and an ability to conduct combined military operations with Muslim partner countries, Abizaid added: "The final part of the paper should also emphasize a very strong US push to engage with the Israelis and Palestinians to find a way towards manageable peace." Next to this point, Myers wrote: "Very important aspect."

The idea of helping local people to overthrow such terrorist-sponsoring regimes resonated with President Bush. At a meeting I did not attend, the

President approved the Defense Department plan for Afghanistan, which called for a small U.S. force to destroy al Qaida in Afghanistan while working largely indirectly—through support for the Northern Alliance and other Afghan militias—to overthrow the Taliban regime. The President shared our determination to make this a global war of initiative, one that broke with the standard, backward-looking retaliatory posture the United States had taken in the past against its terrorist enemies. Nevertheless, he did not favor starting with U.S. strikes outside Afghanistan or deferring U.S. military strikes in favor of a troop buildup in the Middle East. He wanted the world to see that the United States was taking military action against those responsible for 9/11.

General Abizaid and I worked together to produce Rumsfeld's first formal, comprehensive instructions to his commanders for the development of "campaign plans against terrorism." Abizaid's J-5 ("Strategic Plans and Policy") directorate took the lead in drafting this "Strategic Guidance," with support from my Policy office. Once again, those of us who flew home together on September 12 were drawing on insights from our in-flight talks. Rumsfeld approved the Strategic Guidance on October 3, 2001, and sent it around the department—to Wolfowitz, the service secretaries, the Chairman of the Joint Chiefs, the Under Secretaries of Defense, the combatant commanders, and others—with the order that "effective immediately, recipients of this memorandum will ensure that campaign plans align with this guidance and address all elements contained therein."

The Guidance began by identifying threats: First, terrorist organizations—including the al Qaida network—that "threaten the US, its people, their interests, territory and way of life." Second, "states that harbor, sponsor, finance, sanction or otherwise support those terrorist organizations." Third, nonstate supporters of terrorism. And fourth, the "capacity of terrorist organizations or their state supporters to acquire, manufacture or use chemical, biological, radiological or nuclear weapons or the means to deliver them."

The strategic objectives stressed the threat that terrorists could use weapons of mass destruction and the requirement to "prevent further attacks against the US or US interests." (See summary chart, reproduced as Figure 1.) It called for Defense Department efforts to "convince or compel" state supporters of terrorism to cut their ties to terrorists, to isolate and weaken such states, and to "disrupt, damage or destroy" their military capacities, including WMD. It also instructed the department, "as directed," to assist other parts of the government to "encourage populations

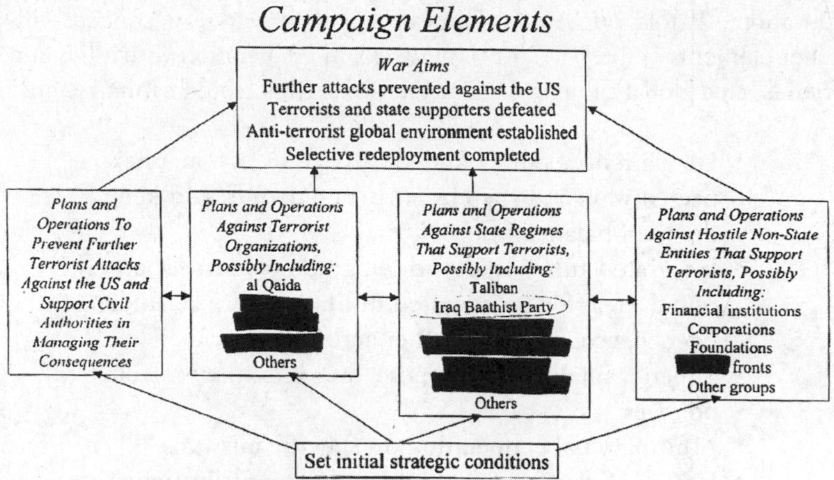

Figure 1. Key points of October 3, 2001, Strategic Guidance for the Defense Department (**redacted for security reasons**)

dominated by terrorist organizations or their supporters to overthrow that domination." This wording made clear that Defense did not have the lead for this particular mission and was not to undertake it unless "directed" to do so.

The Guidance recognized the ideological component of the war on terrorism by making it an objective to "support the creation of an international political environment hostile to terrorism." The concept of a battle of ideas, however, was not highly developed in this October 3 Guidance. Perhaps this was because primary responsibility for that battle lay outside the Defense Department. Perhaps prosecuting it seemed like an abstract and long-term project when the country's main interest was in concrete goals, achievable in the near term. In any event, it would take time for the government, and the country generally, to appreciate that countering the enemies' ideology—through promotion of democratic institutions and otherwise—was of the essence, though it was by no means easy. In later statements of our strategy for the war, we directed more attention to the issue of extremist ideology.

The Guidance set out a "Strategic Concept" of "Multiple Agencies, Multiple Fronts, Multiple Instruments, Multiple Methods and Extended

Duration." It told our Armed Forces to plan to work "in concert with other elements of the US Government and in cooperation with allies and friends" in a global campaign against terrorism that would capitalize on:

- **US patience, power and creativity to act in unexpected ways and thereby surprise enemies and keep them off balance.**
- **Integrated functional and geographic Joint Operational Areas for coordinated military, political, intelligence, economic and other actions.**
- **Superior intelligence, defense, and information technologies. . . .**
- **Multinational cooperation on specific missions.**
- **USG [U.S. government] interagency contributions.**

From the outset, then, Rumsfeld directed the Department of Defense to see the war as an activity undertaken by many U.S. government agencies and many countries. This belies the common criticism that the department was unilateralist. I never heard any Pentagon official say that the war on terrorism could be won solely or even mainly by military means. And I never heard anyone in the Administration contend that the United States should try to fight the war—or the campaigns in Afghanistan or Iraq—alone. The real issues were not whether to have a coalition, or whether the United Nations or NATO should have roles in the war. The issues were what these organizations and our coalition partners were willing and able to do, how quickly, requiring what kind of assistance from us, and what they would ask of us in return.

The stereotype of the military or Pentagon bigwig—reinforced monotonously over decades by the *Washington Post* editorial cartoonist Herblock—was of an aggressive and narrow-minded buffoon who saw every problem in the world as solvable through military action.* In my experience, that image was off the mark. In Rumsfeld's Pentagon, the top military and civilian officials promptly saw the large role that nonmilitary means would play in the war on terrorism. Rumsfeld spoke out loudly and often, including in public, on the importance of financial, diplomatic, law enforcement, information, intelligence, and other operations. In fact, he

---

**Saturday Night Live* produced a variation on this theme in a very funny parody in which the comedian Chris Parnell played me. When this skit first aired on February 22, 2003, my then fifteen-year-old son called me excitedly and, mocking my many other, dull appearances on television, declared: "Now I finally respect you."

was unhappy from the start with the term "war on terrorism," concerned that the word "war" led people to overemphasize the importance of the military instrument in this multidimensional conflict.

The National Security Council agreed quickly that "all instruments of national power" would be required in the coming effort. Yet the war exposed the maddening difficulty of getting the different parts of the U.S. government to work together in joint operations. In general, they lacked experience in such operations and lacked the proper organization, personnel, and contracting policies to carry them out. They did not train for such operations, and had no budget to do so. The Strategic Guidance referred to "integrated functional and geographic Joint Operational Areas for coordinated military, political, intelligence, economic and other actions." But it was easier to pronounce that bureaucratic mouthful than to bring about actual joint work among Defense, State, the Treasury, and other departments of the government.

In a little more than three weeks after 9/11, the Defense Department had helped the President set a course for a war that was ambitious in its scope and unprecedented in its goals. As an element of this, the department had produced from scratch a war plan for Afghanistan.

Franks had digested Rumsfeld's guidance on the strategic purpose of military action against al Qaida and the Taliban, and the prudence of sending a small U.S. force to support anti-Taliban Afghan militias. For all his touchiness and bluster, Franks and his CENTCOM staff dutifully produced a plan worthy of Wolfowitz's hope that we would "fight smart." President Bush approved the plan, which aimed to destroy al Qaida in Afghanistan and overthrow the Taliban regime. We now had to line up operational support from the CIA and, in cooperation with the White House and State Department, obtain access, overflight, and other types of assistance from numerous coalition partners abroad.

Rumsfeld also published throughout the department his strategic guidance for the campaign against terrorism. In response, in the coming weeks, he would receive back proposed war plans from his combatant commanders around the world. They would disappoint the Secretary as thoroughly as Franks's original plan for Afghanistan.

4
STEADY IN AFGHANISTAN

The war in Afghanistan went quickly, but while it lasted it seemed agonizingly and dangerously slow. When the United States was attacked on September 11, 2001, our government had on the shelf no war plan to destroy al Qaida in Afghanistan or to overthrow the Taliban government. Even so, we initiated the war in Afghanistan less than a month later, on October 7. The first major Afghan city, Mazar-e-Sharif, fell to our Northern Alliance allies on November 9. The capital, Kabul, fell on November 13. And the Taliban stronghold of Kandahar fell on December 7. By the end of December 2001, Hamid Karzai had become head of Afghanistan's new provisional government, selected by Afghans at a conference organized by the United Nations and supported by the Bush Administration. In that period, the size of the U.S. force in Afghanistan never exceeded four thousand troops.

A number of players contributed to these accomplishments: U.S. Special Operations Forces, the other U.S. service members involved in the effort (in-theater and at CENTCOM's headquarters), the CIA operators, our coalition partners, and our Afghan allies. The success was also a credit to the strategy that Rumsfeld helped President Bush develop for the Afghanistan campaign:

- Aiming to oust the Taliban regime (not just to hit al Qaida)
- Committing U.S. ground forces

- Using the indirect approach of supporting Afghan militias
- Relying on precision strikes
- Maintaining a small U.S. footprint to avoid problems that the Soviets (and British) had had in Afghanistan

The value of having a strategy is that you don't have to wake up every day and ask yourself basic questions about the best course of action. Well-chosen strategic ideas do not require frequent revision. They help fix your course and guide tactical choices, even as events unfold in unanticipated ways—as events always do.

It may seem obvious that formulating a strategy precisely and adhering to it are fundamental to good statecraft, especially when managing a war. But this doesn't always happen. Some statesmen do not think strategically, and even the most determined may find it difficult to stick with a strategy when the news from the front is bad. Wise wartime leaders review their strategies routinely, judging with prudent steadiness when to modify and when to preserve. But when events seem unfavorable, critics disparage steadiness as pigheadedness—and sometimes they are right. During the war to overthrow the Taliban, President Bush quickly came under harsh attack by those who said he had either no strategy or the wrong one. But the President had considered the major issues. He had a strategy. He was steady, and it paid.

Within hours after 9/11, officials from would-be partner countries—Australia, Britain, Canada, France, Italy, Japan, Norway, Poland, and others—had begun offering the United States help, in the form of aircraft, ships, humanitarian supplies, special forces, and other military personnel. They were impatient to hear if the United States wanted them.

At that moment, however, CENTCOM was scrambling to produce brand-new plans in response to urgent demands from Rumsfeld and the President. Its logisticians were identifying top-priority requirements for access and basing—and transit and overflight authority.* It was impossible for General Franks to decide immediately how, or whether, he could use the support that each new ally might offer. He quickly brought over liaison officers from partner countries and set up a coalition "village" at CENTCOM headquarters in Tampa, Florida. Nevertheless, partner government ministries were soon

*Of particular importance here were three of Afghanistan's neighbors—Pakistan, Uzbekistan, and Tajikistan—and other states in the broader region, such as Oman and Egypt.

calling high-level officials throughout Washington to complain about our government's slow response to their offers.

Everyone on the National Security Council favored a broad coalition for the Afghanistan campaign. So long as the offers of help were useful and not burdened with unacceptable political conditions, Rumsfeld favored accepting them. A broad coalition would demonstrate that the terrorists were enemies of the civilized world, not just of the United States. Also, cooperation often breeds more cooperation, and these activities might make it easier for us to organize future coalition efforts. We had a practical interest, moreover, in spreading the burden. The war on terrorism would benefit all free and open societies, and we believed our democratic friends should be willing to contribute forces or other resources to the effort.

After hearing complaints from several foreign counterparts, National Security Adviser Condoleezza Rice told General Shelton at a September 24 Principals Committee meeting that the Pentagon should stop "slow rolling" the allies. Franks was working the problem with the foreign liaison officers in Tampa, but the high-level protests from overseas kept coming. At the October 1 morning Roundtable, General Myers asked Rumsfeld whether General Abizaid and I should take charge of responding to the foreign offers. After some discussion, the Secretary and Chairman agreed that Franks should continue to handle it, because he was positioned to respond to their requests most precisely, authoritatively, and directly. I agreed. But we turned out to be wrong: The direct military-to-military channel could not solve the problem.

In the end, Franks accepted many of the offers. Britain, Canada, Germany, and Australia each contributed infantry forces and deployed aircraft, naval forces, and special operations units. France provided an aircraft carrier battle group; Japan, fleet refueling ships, naval destroyers, and transport aircraft; Italy, its sole carrier battle group, and a regimental task force, an engineer team, and transport aircraft. More than twenty-five other countries contributed personnel, equipment, or services to the fight. The coalition effort required extraordinary coordination, and CENTCOM worked the logistics intensely. Yet government ministers from various countries continued to complain about CENTCOM's nonresponsiveness. They protested not only through diplomatic channels but also, increasingly, through public statements accusing President Bush of unilateralism, giving grist to critics who were eager to accuse the Bush Administration of insensitivity and a go-it-alone approach to world affairs.

I more than once had to phone Franks and his deputy commander, Marine Lieutenant General Mike DeLong, to alert them that some foreign minister had called Rice or Powell to complain about an unanswered offer. Yet Franks and DeLong usually assured me that they had already accepted the offer or worked out an alternative arrangement with the country in question. Then why, I asked, were we receiving these complaints?

We soon unraveled the mystery: CENTCOM was indeed responding quickly and generally positively to the liaison officers. But the messages often weren't flowing clearly or quickly enough from those officers to the civilian leaders *of their own defense ministries*—and those officials, in turn, sometimes failed to inform their colleagues in their foreign ministry and prime minister's office.

The Afghanistan coalition effort taught us that we couldn't count on reliable communications within the military-civilian operations of our partner countries. We learned to deliver messages to our partners through multiple channels: the coalition liaisons in Tampa *and* our partners' defense attachés, diplomats, and other foreign officials. Defense, State, and the National Security Council staff adapted accordingly. I created a new office for coalition affairs in my Policy organization, and similar offices came into being in the Joint Staff and elsewhere in the U.S. government. The National Security Council staff began holding almost daily interagency meetings on coalition matters.

We hadn't caused the communications problems within our partners' governments, of course, but we eventually found a way to solve them. Meanwhile, though, the Bush Administration's reputation had been damaged. We had been condemned for wanting to fight without our friends' support. The charge was false, but it was repeated widely.

The interest in building a coalition was as strong in the Pentagon as in the State Department and Rumsfeld willingly played a role in the personal diplomacy. Politicians know that eyeball-to-eyeball connections count for a lot, even in foreign relations. Rumsfeld was a politician. He decided he should meet face-to-face with the leaders of key coalition partners before U.S. military action began in Afghanistan.

On the morning of October 2, Admiral Giambastiani walked into my office and interrupted a staff meeting to spring a surprise: The Secretary had decided to leave *that day* on a three-day trip to Saudi Arabia, Oman, Egypt, Uzbekistan, and Turkey. I was to get myself to Andrews Air Force Base to board a large transport plane, a C-32—wheels up at 2100 hours. I was permitted to bring along three people who worked for me—Bill Luti, the Deputy Assistant Secretary of Defense for the Near East and South

Asia; Colonel Ron Yaggi (U.S. Air Force), the senior military assistant for Policy; and Colonel Bob Drumm (U.S. Army), the Gulf States desk officer. If we were late, he'd leave us behind.

Before every stop, our job was to assemble well-conceived, comprehensive but succinct, plain-English background papers for Rumsfeld's review. This was in addition to the "read-aheads" for each planned meeting: These informed the Secretary about his foreign hosts, the issues we should raise, and those they would likely bring up. After each stop, we wrote cables reporting back about each meeting, and shorter, personal communiqués that Rumsfeld would rework and send directly to the President; and there would be a big batch of thank-you notes for him to send to the U.S. ambassadors, defense attachés, and other officials who had given us important assistance. Rumsfeld routinely insisted that all such postmeeting papers be written, polished, and signed by him before the trip ended.

For a typical Rumsfeld foreign trip, the briefing books would take weeks to produce. On this no-notice jaunt, we started working immediately after leaving each new foreign capital: We drafted all the papers for the next capital, reviewed and reworked them with Rumsfeld, and then drafted the reports and papers arising from the past day's meetings. The intensity and pace of this work surpassed anything I had ever experienced. It was hard to believe that Rumsfeld was pushing seventy: We joked that he stayed young by working his staff into premature aging.

Rumsfeld devised a diplomatic approach for this trip that won kudos and cooperation in the foreign capitals we visited. He decided not to ask any of the foreign leaders for anything. Rather, he would give them the courtesy of a substantial consultation. After filling them in on the President's thinking about the war on terrorism and hearing their views, he expressed his understanding that different countries have different circumstances and would therefore contribute to the war in different ways, according to what they were comfortable doing. He would assure the foreign leaders that he would not comment publicly on what any country contributed, letting each characterize its own contributions as it saw fit.

In Saudi Arabia, our hosts said they admired Rumsfeld's approach. They wanted to help us in some practical ways, but they wanted no public discussion of the details. After our talks with Saudi King Fahd and Crown Prince Abdullah, Rumsfeld met with journalists, who pressed him on what precisely he was asking the Saudis to do for us and whether he was satisfied with their response. The Secretary replied truthfully that he had not asked for anything—an answer that pleased the Saudis. They were also appreciative that he refused, as he put it, to "grade" our coalition partners.

Rumsfeld announced that the United States was getting help from many countries, some openly and some in secret, and there was no reason the enemy should be able to learn everything there was to know about the coalition by reading the newspaper. The enemy, he reasoned, should fear the invisible cooperation we were getting.

In Riyadh, we dined at the home of the defense minister, Prince Sultan. I sat next to Prince Saud al-Faisal, the Saudi foreign minister and Rumsfeld's fellow Princeton grad. In a quiet chat over crystal glasses, gilt china, and sweet desserts, the Prince suggested that al Qaida had *not* perpetrated 9/11. Considering the attack's technical sophistication, he called it inconceivable that "cave dwellers" in Afghanistan could have invented, organized, and executed so sophisticated a plan. Very few people—indeed, very few countries—had such capabilities, he mused confidentially. The attack has put America at war with the Muslims, he lamented, so we must ask: What country has an interest in making that happen? He mentioned having read press stories that Israel had warned Jews not to report for work at the World Trade Center on September 11. Of course, he didn't know if those stories were true, he said. But didn't it strain the imagination that a handful of al Qaida members could have pulled off four simultaneous hijackings?

I assumed the prince was trying to provoke me, and as we sat there in his uncle's palace, I saw nothing to be gained from debating weird notions.* I took his unreal line of inquiry as a sign of real distress among Saudi leaders at the fact that nearly all the 9/11 hijackers had been Saudis. As members of al Qaida, they had belonged to an organization intent on destroying the House of Saud. Saudi Arabia's royal officials were facing a problem worse than embarrassment or shame: They were resisting having to admit to themselves that they faced a frightful cancer with no reliable course of treatment.

During the five-country trip, some of our foreign friends made cutting references to ineffectual U.S. reactions to terrorist attacks in the recent past. They wanted to know if the United States was ready now to commit the necessary resources for a significant response—and whether we had the staying power to see the job through even if it meant bearing losses. Rumsfeld communicated our seriousness of purpose, and he helped assuage

---

*The prince was expounding a theory that was launched just days after the attacks and that eventually prompted a rebuttal on the State Department's website, pointing out that the percentage of Jewish victims at the World Trade Center reflected the percentage of Jewish residents of New York City (http://usinfo.state.gov/media/Archive/2005/Jan/14–260933.html).

their concern that the United States would simply perform another round of "we came, we fired cruise missiles, they laughed."

Our most memorable meeting was in Oman with the elegantly berobed Sultan, Qaboos bin Said, who received us on a sweltering afternoon in a large open-sided tent in the middle of the desert. As we Americans melted in our woolen suits, his servants offered us steaming hot drinks. But we received rewards for our discomfort: Qaboos assured us that he would cooperate, making Oman's valuable air bases available for our use.

Qaboos then fascinated us with a strategic exposition on the war's ideological essence. He spoke of a great contest within the Muslim world—between fanatical Islamists, who inspired the terrorists with visions of a restored caliphate, and their opponents. The extremists were driven by their particular vision of a new universal Islamic state that would be heir to the Prophet Mohammed's empire, would follow Muslim law, and would be administered by a *caliph*, Allah's deputy on earth. Qaboos warned us against focusing our attention too narrowly on military objectives, for he thought that the outcome of the war might ultimately be decided in the world of ideas. Rumsfeld and I exchanged a glance to confirm that we had registered the importance of the Sultan's words. When Rumsfeld and I left the tent, he told me to make sure to report those thoughts in his personal note for the President.

There was further coalition diplomacy that needed attention. Accompanied by Bill Luti, I returned from Turkey (our last stop with Rumsfeld) to the Middle East, intending to visit another five countries in the next three days. Jordan's King Abdullah II had already publicly declared solidarity with the United States, and I held successful talks there with the foreign minister and the chairman of Jordan's joint chiefs of staff. They were concerned about threats from Syria and Iraq, and it was in our common interest for the United States to help give them the capability to counter those threats. Unfortunately, while the U.S. Congress generously financed expensive military operations of our own, it usually appropriated only scant funds to help needy foreign partners perform, far less expensively than we could, missions that benefited us both.*

Later that day, in Kuwait, I met with the defense minister and the acting prime minister, Sheikh Sabah al-Sabah. After offering his condolences for 9/11, he spoke at length of his gratitude to America for liberating Kuwait from Saddam Hussein in 1991. As America was with the Kuwaitis in their hour of need, he pledged, the Kuwaitis would be with America now. It is easy to be cynical about diplomatic exchanges; many are mere cant. But his statement was delivered gravely and credibly, and it moved me.

---

*More on this point in Chapters 5 and 16.

That evening, the U.S. Ambassador to Kuwait, Richard Jones, hosted a dinner for me at his home. Among the several Kuwaiti notables in attendance was Sheikh Dr. Mohammed al-Sabah, former ambassador to the United States. Combining wit with engaging suavity, Dr. Mohammed (as everyone called him) declared that 9/11 was going to change the world. Moreover, he expected that, at some point, the United States would take some action against Saddam Hussein as part of the war on terrorism. What he wanted to know was whether we would solve the Saddam problem once and for all this time—or simply pull the tiger's tail and walk away, leaving the beast, now provoked and still capable, to strike out against its neighbors. I could respond only that President George W. Bush took the security of the United States and its friends seriously and that he was not one for half measures. Dr. Mohammed—also clearly sensitive to cant—looked skeptical, but seemed satisfied that I understood his concern.

After the dinner ended, I was called to the chancery for a secure telephone call from Wolfowitz (in Washington) and Franks (in Florida). Tomorrow afternoon, October 7, they told me, we would begin to bomb Afghanistan. They knew I was planning to leave in the morning for Qatar, Bahrain, and the United Arab Emirates, and they asked if I thought I should proceed or cut the trip short. My visits were getting prominent play in the local television and newspapers, they noted, and we agreed that it would be awkward, especially for my hosts, if I were seen to be holding meetings with them as news of the U.S. attack broke. We decided that I would keep my morning appointments in Qatar, but then cancel my final two stops and return home.

So my final meetings on that trip were in Doha the next morning, with Crown Prince Jassim bin Hamad Khalifa al-Thani and with the chief of staff of the armed forces. The two men assured me that Qatar would provide the United States with the military cooperation we wanted. I nevertheless told them that the U.S. government was displeased about the antagonism toward America—and sympathy for terrorists—that routinely aired on al-Jazeerah, the satellite news channel owned by Qatar's royal family. On this, I got nowhere.

Sending my regrets to Bahrain and the United Arab Emirates, I flew back to Washington from Doha as the B-1s, B-2s, B-52s, F-14s, F-15s, F-16s, F-18s, and Tomahawk cruise missiles were beginning to strike targets across Afghanistan.

For weeks, Rumsfeld had been concerned that our initial military action after 9/11 would look puny. If our efforts were "not confidence-inspiring," he feared, we would signal to the world—in particular to state supporters of terrorism—that the United States was still not serious about destroying terrorist networks. Tommy Franks reported reassuringly on the enormous quantities of weapons and the diverse means of delivery that U.S. forces were using. But Rumsfeld did not want to hear of effort, what he called "input," when he was asking about "output," or results. Would the bombing actually accomplish anything? he asked. Would it hurt al Qaida's operational capabilities? Would it cause regimes around the world to reconsider their support for terrorism or for their WMD programs?

Franks reported daily on the Afghanistan war, usually by a secure telephone conference call that I joined along with Rumsfeld, Wolfowitz, Giambastiani, Myers, Pace, and the Secretary's Special Assistant, Lawrence DiRita. Rumsfeld and Myers then summarized Franks's reports for the President at the National Security Council meetings, which took place almost daily. In the first days of the war, Rumsfeld found the reports from Franks less than satisfactory.

Until the late twentieth century, the major problem with any bombing campaign was accuracy. By the time of Afghanistan, however, that problem was largely solved: As the bombing campaigns of Desert Storm in 1991 showcased, U.S. Air Force pilots and Navy aviators, with improved technology and technique, could hit their targets with reasonable reliability—and over the next decade those capabilities improved. What was making Rumsfeld uneasy was that many of the targets we were damaging or destroying in Afghanistan were not very valuable. The bombing wasn't spurring our Afghan partners, who had thousands of soldiers on the ground, to engage the enemy decisively.

Most of our initial targets in Afghanistan were Taliban infrastructure—fixed sites, not movable items like units and equipment deployed for battle. Three days into the bombing campaign, Franks told us that several major Taliban military targets were on the list for that day because they were important for Northern Alliance operations.

Rumsfeld asked how closely we were coordinating our attacks with the Northern Alliance and with anti-Taliban southern tribes. Franks said: "Not too well yet." Franks explained that we wouldn't be able to improve our coordination with the Alliance until we got U.S. Special Operations Forces on the ground, where they could then serve as forward air controllers, managing timing and laser targeting for the bombers overhead. They could also help direct delivery of the humanitarian supplies we were airdropping. But Franks was waiting to send those forces in, he explained, until the CIA could blaze a trail to the Afghans—making personal contact with local leaders, distributing cash, and establishing communications links. "We want to get CIA assessment teams fully on the ground; they're half in and half out. They can use their language skills and learn stuff. CIA says it's working to get them in, but they take time."

The CIA had "nothing going" in the south, Rumsfeld commented. The Secretary spoke calmly, but he was anxious about the danger that the United States might lose credibility through ineffectual action in Afghanistan. As a hedge, he proposed moving against the terrorist network elsewhere. Franks replied that we should be working to block potential safe havens for any al Qaida and Taliban personnel fleeing Afghanistan.

Not everyone viewed the lack of progress against the Taliban on the ground as Rumsfeld did. At recent Deputies Committee meetings, I had heard the fear expressed that the Northern Alliance might rout the Taliban *too quickly*. Zalmay Khalilzad of Condoleezza Rice's staff helpfully brought the issue to the fore. Born in Afghanistan, Khalilzad had come to the United States as a high school student through an educational outreach program in the late 1960s, attended college in Lebanon, and got his PhD from the University of Chicago. After the Soviets invaded Afghanistan in 1979, his family joined him in the United States. He was now serving in the Bush Administration as one of the government's true experts on Afghanistan.

At the October 9, 2001, Deputies Committee meeting, Khalilzad raised the question of where the United States should advise Mohammed Fahim Khan and his men to attack: against Kabul, in western Afghanistan, or elsewhere.

Deputy Secretary of State Armitage, quick on the reply, declared that they should *not* try to take Kabul. The Deputy Director of the CIA, John McLaughlin, reported that CIA people on the ground were "seeking to restrain" the Northern Alliance fighters. If they raised their flag in Kabul, he believed, they could trigger a civil war with the Pashtuns. Though he admitted that the CIA's "contacts in the south are not well-developed," McLaughlin suggested: "Perhaps we can push the Northern Alliance so that if they go to Kabul, they do so together with some key southern tribes, who are Pashtun."

Paul Wolfowitz—who attended quite a few of the Deputies Committee meetings in this early period—answered McLaughlin's comment about the CIA's efforts to restrain the Northern Alliance. Instead of trying to restrain our allies, Wolfowitz suggested, we should find other ways to show that we're not favoring one Afghan group over another. He proposed creating an international force to preserve the neutrality of the capital city (an idea that State would later embrace). He also asked if we could we get some balance among the groups—not by holding the most capable groups back, but by giving them all some incentive to act.

Humanitarian assistance had been a component of the planning from the start, emphasized by both President Bush and Rumsfeld. Regarding incentives, I suggested that we should take care that our humanitarian aid wasn't distributed at cross-purposes with our strategy. We wanted to reward initiative and encourage southerners to fight on our side, but we didn't want our aid appearing to reward unhelpful action, which could happen if we put provisions into the hands of leaders working for the Taliban.

McLaughlin's concern about not alienating the Pashtuns had merit, even though it was presented more as a policy argument than an intelligence assessment. It was useful for the CIA to flag the danger that a north-south civil war could break out in Afghanistan after the Taliban's overthrow. What troubled me was that McLaughlin and his CIA colleagues, along with Armitage, seemed to be assuming that the effort to oust the Taliban would continue through the winter—and this didn't seem to bother them. The CIA wanted more time to create links with the southern tribes. And State liked the idea of having more time to train and equip the Northern Alliance. (At one meeting, Powell called the Northern Alliance a "Fourth World" army and said we should take the winter to get them trained up to the level of a Third World army so they could then take on the Taliban.)

I thought it would be a serious strategic error for the United States to resign itself to an inconclusive, open-ended campaign. If the Northern Alliance failed to advance soon, I thought, we should try to prod them into action before the onset of winter. If that didn't work, we might have to rethink our indirect approach of relying on our Afghan partners to oust the Taliban. It became clear that Rumsfeld, Wolfowitz, Myers, and Pace all shared my belief that we should try to accelerate the fight in Afghanistan, not settle back for a slow winter. At Principals Committee and National Security Council meetings, Vice President Cheney joined Rumsfeld and Myers in supporting a push to achieve results before winter.

When McLaughlin talked about restraining the Northern Alliance at that October 9 Deputies Committee meeting, Wolfowitz leaned over to me and remarked, in a whisper, on how frequently CIA officials made policy arguments. The distinction between intelligence and policy work was something to which Wolfowitz was particularly sensitive. It represents, in essence, the difference between describing a situation and prescribing a way to deal with it. The distinction is not always neat, especially when intelligence personnel speculate about the future. An intelligence official's assessment that a certain course of action will produce great benefits, for example, sounds much the same as a policy official's argument for that same course of action.

Like State and Pentagon policy makers, CIA officials often showed their own policy preferences. Some of us "customers" of the CIA believed that, intentionally or not, the Agency's intelligence reports occasionally reflected a bias for or against certain policies. As a student of intelligence, a walking encyclopedia in some areas of the field, and a severe critic of poor intelligence tradecraft, Wolfowitz was not shy about challenging the quality of intelligence products. He had been doing it since at least the Ford Administration, from inside and outside the government, and I often saw him do so in the George W. Bush Administration. Though he was unfailingly professional and usually even gentle, it was clear from press stories and credible scuttlebutt that intelligence officials had labeled him an enemy.

As Wolfowitz recognized, the CIA's intelligence analysts (like people everywhere) sometimes did unprofessional work, exhibiting bias, sloppy research, faulty assumptions, internal contradictions, unclear writing, or other failings. One basic problem was their practice of basing their assessments almost entirely on information produced through intelligence channels, to the exclusion of commonly available sources or even common sense. That was why some contemporary accounts by academics and journalists of the failures of the Soviet economy, or famine in Mao's China, were closer to reality than the CIA's analyses. Given this historical record, a responsible policy official had no choice but to second-guess intelligence estimates.

Questioning of intelligence analysis produced resentment, however, especially when the questioners were viewed as political opponents. Intelligence officials often seemed to take the position that a critical approach to the intelligence product was somehow illegitimate—that, unlike the work in every other department of government, intelligence analysis could not be subject to review by the consumers of the product. And in defending themselves, intelligence officials sometimes counterattacked by asserting that their critics weren't interested in the truth, but only in manipulating intelligence to support their own policy arguments. (Members of Congress have sometimes echoed those accusations for political reasons.) In the late 1990s the question of potential missile threats to the United States generated this sort of debate, after the Missile Threat Commission—chartered by Congress to investigate the matter—released a report that embarrassed the CIA. The Commission was chaired by Donald Rumsfeld, and Paul Wolfowitz was also a member.

It is one thing for knowledgeable government officials—as intelligence customers—to complain about the quality of intelligence products, and another to try to get those products altered for policy reasons. Rumsfeld, Wolfowitz, and I understood the difference, and we considered it dishonest and harmful for anyone to politicize intelligence—from outside *or within* the intelligence community. We disapproved of policy officials crossing the line between proper questioning of intelligence and corruption of the intelligence. For similar reasons, we also disapproved of *policy advocacy by intelligence officials*. We thought it was wrong for CIA officials to want to preserve the boundary between policy and intelligence only against transgressions from the policy side.

Paul Pillar, a longtime CIA official, exposed the problem, with apparently unintended candor, in a *Foreign Affairs* article he published in 2006 (soon after his retirement from government). He claims that "[t]he intelligence community . . . limits its judgments to what is happening or what might happen overseas, *avoiding policy judgments* about what the United States should do in response." Yet in the same article he also observes, "If the entire body of official intelligence analysis on Iraq had a policy implication, it was to avoid war." Is this a contradiction? "In practice," he writes, the distinction between intelligence and policy judgments is "often blurred, especially because analytic projections may have policy implications even if they are not explicitly stated. But the distinction is still important. . . . [I]t is critical that the intelligence community not advocate policy, *especially not openly*." And what of covert advocacy in the guise of objective analysis? Pillar seems unwilling to condemn it. He implies that intelligence analysts may advocate policy—as long as they do it "not openly."

When I briefed Rumsfeld for the October 11, 2001, Principals Committee meeting on Afghanistan, I suggested that the Principals review the U.S. government's goals. I thought it would be good to clarify, for example, that one key purpose of ousting the Taliban was "to make an example of them" as a state sponsor of terrorism. That would help explain why our operation was urgent: We wanted to disrupt the international terrorist network—to shock the system—as formidably and quickly as possible. Such a decisive achievement could be the key to aborting possible new terrorist attacks against us. It could also buy us time to take other steps—offensive and defensive—to protect the United States. If our only goal was to *punish* the Taliban, however, it would matter far less how swiftly we beat them.

I thought it unrealistic to propose—as Armitage and McLaughlin did—that we should slow down the Northern Alliance while waiting for just the right conditions in Kabul. I suggested to Rumsfeld that he might use the upcoming Principals Committee meeting to warn his colleagues against thinking we could fine-tune the war. The Northern Alliance fighters would have their own ideas about how to proceed. We had influence, but not necessarily control. So it would help to get government-wide agreement on what our goal was *not*: "Creating a stable, post-Taliban Afghanistan is desirable, but not necessarily within the power of the US," I wrote. "The US should not allow concerns about stability to paralyze US efforts to oust the Taliban leadership." Rather, we should "facilitate capture before winter, if possible, of key cities—Mazar-e-Sharif, Herat and Kabul." I drew on the comments of Wolfowitz, Armitage, and McLaughlin at the October 9 Deputies Committee meeting: Anticipating the capture of Kabul by Northern Alliance forces, the United States "should try to arrange for the city to be administered by an international group that will relieve Pashtun fear of domination by Northern Alliance (Tajik-Uzbek) tribes." This international group "may be UN-based or an ad hoc collection of volunteer states such as Turkey, Jordan, Egypt and other NATO states (but not the US)."

I added the phrase "not the US" because Rumsfeld believed that the Kabul mission was one our coalition partners should handle. In his view, the U.S. military had its hands full and should be reserved for operations our partners could not or would not take on. Also, Rumsfeld observed, other states tended to contribute less when we joined a project, shifting a disproportionate share of the burden to Uncle Sam. He later managed to persuade the National Security Council of this view.

Finally, I recommended reassuring the Pashtuns that "nation-building is *not* our key strategic goal." The term "nation-building" had bad baggage. In the 2000 election campaign, Bush had criticized the Clinton Administration for its policies in Bosnia in 1996 and in Kosovo in 1999, which had effectively turned those areas into long-term wards of the international community. Large numbers of U.S. and other outside forces were involved for many years in both places. Civil reconstruction was slow, inadequate, and directed largely by foreigners, not the locals. When Rumsfeld sounded out our European allies about reducing the U.S. presence there, they warned that such a move could bring about wholesale collapse: Years after the U.S. military had helped to save those regions' victimized Muslims, civil government had not yet been established in either place. We did not want the Afghans to think we intended to take the same approach to their country.

A better approach would be to encourage and enable reconstruction by indigenous institutions. This had been my thinking since 1995, when I served as a pro bono legal and policy adviser to the Bosnian Muslims at the Dayton Peace Talks. The focus of my concern at that time was the need to provide adequate policing capacity and police training, so that peacekeeping tasks would not default to foreign military units and impede emerging self-government.

Once the Taliban regime was gone, of course, the United States would have to help put a new Afghan government on a stable footing—not least in order to keep Afghanistan from reverting to its former status as a terrorist safe haven. Rejecting the idea of "nation-building" didn't mean renouncing our responsibility toward post-Taliban Afghanistan. It meant that we intended to play a *supporting* role, with the Afghans in the lead. Rumsfeld often remarked, with disdain, that Americans have saved people from aggression and oppression—only to create debilitating dependencies on external aid. Such dependency was what we wanted to avoid.

We still faced the question in Afghanistan of whether to encourage the Northern Alliance to move against Mazar-e-Sharif in the north or against Kabul in the center-east. But Rumsfeld was not interested in having Washington pick targets. He wanted Franks and Tenet to figure out how to spur friendly Afghan tribes to take action against the enemy. He believed that some Afghan fighters would show more spirit and success than others, and that those were the ones we should concentrate on backing. The challenge wasn't deciding which city we Americans wanted to fall first, but how to motivate our Afghan partners to do something significant—and soon.

The U.S. government had several means to motivate the Afghans: sending messages (often referred to as "information operations," or "IO"), providing air support for Afghan ground operations, and offering money, military materiel, and humanitarian assistance. Regarding IO, Rumsfeld worried that CENTCOM wasn't getting the messages right. The Pentagon had already suffered embarrassment from naming our post-9/11 military action "Operation Infinite Justice": Muslims complained that the phrase was offensive because "infinite justice" belongs only to Allah. (The campaign was quickly renamed Operation Enduring Freedom.) Rumsfeld knew that wrong messages could have strategic consequences. If the U.S.

military produced an offensive or foolish item that appeared on a cable news network or the front page of a newspaper, it could harm us around the world—and not achieve its purpose.

Even before U.S. bombing operations started, Rumsfeld had resolved to supervise the Defense Department's information operations. On September 28, he instructed Franks to clear with me the themes for CENTCOM's radio broadcasts. At the October 1 Roundtable, Rumsfeld told me to review the leaflets that Franks planned to drop by the thousands over Afghanistan. When my staff and I started reviewing those materials, we discovered a few problems. One leaflet used graphics that could be seen as unfriendly to Muslims in general (and not merely to the Taliban). Another would make sense only to people who recognized the World Trade Center towers, which many Afghans might not. And a third leaflet featured a drawing of an Afghan family happily eating from our packages of food—but the father's turban was black. This was a distinctive Taliban symbol recognizable by anyone in Afghanistan. We had the leaflets redone.

Later, when Franks reported that Commando Solo, an airborne broadcasting platform, would soon be transmitting radio messages into Afghanistan, Rumsfeld told him: "I want to see the transcript of the broadcast." Franks, chafing under this supervision, complained repeatedly that "Policy" insisted on clearing his IO material. Discretion being the better part of valor, he chose not to grouse against the Secretary, who—as he knew—was the one doing the insisting.

In the twelve days between the start of Operation Enduring Freedom on October 7 and the insertion of the first dozen U.S. ground troops, Rumsfeld grew increasingly frustrated. The bombing campaign should have been inducing the Afghan fighters on our side to take territory from the Taliban, but it wasn't working. Northern Alliance commanders complained to the press that our air strikes were unimpressive. Franks had promised improvement as soon as he could put some Special Operations Forces "A teams" on the ground with our Afghan partners. Even in tiny numbers, such troops could make a large difference in the effect of our aerial bombing on the ground combat. But the insertion of those Green Beret teams was delayed while Franks waited for the CIA to connect with the Northern Alliance commanders. And the CIA operatives were having logistical problems getting into Afghanistan.

In our morning conference call on October 15, Franks made a string of remarks that vexed the Secretary. To start with, he mentioned that "some say we don't want Kabul to fall yet"—seeming to accept that position as established policy. One could practically hear the chain-of-command alarm bells clanging in Rumsfeld's head. "Who is saying to you that we should not take Kabul?" he asked. Franks answered evasively that CIA people were "discussing the debate as to whether the Northern Alliance wants to move on Kabul." The general's tone made clear that Rumsfeld's frustration with Franks was reciprocated.

Franks said the first detachment of Special Operations Forces—a twelve-man team—would not be inserted for another two days (in fact, they did not enter until October 19). That team would link up with the CIA and with the Northern Alliance's Uzbek commander, Abdul Rashid Dostum. It would take another day before the second twelve-man team entered Afghanistan, and yet another before the third such team came in. Franks mentioned repeatedly that he couldn't insert a Special Operations Forces team before the CIA entered to pave the way. Rumsfeld was galled by this posture: He later declared it inexcusable that the Defense Department couldn't use its numerous and costly forces until the CIA shook some hands.

Soon after that call, Rumsfeld instructed me to begin a review of our Afghanistan strategy, which had assumed that a small number of U.S. forces would support an aggressive Northern Alliance. Should we look at the possibility of sending larger numbers of U.S. ground forces into Afghanistan? He suggested that "we may want to put Special Forces in with *southern* tribes and take over that responsibility from CIA." He was irked that it had not occurred to Franks to make that suggestion. The Secretary also asked me to formulate messages for the United States to deliver to the Afghan tribes. He disapproved of the messages—for example, those urging restraint—that were currently being delivered by the CIA's people on the ground, who were still the only Americans then in the country.

I consulted with Wolfowitz, General Pace, and Lieutenant General Greg Newbold (U.S. Marine Corps), the Joint Staff's director of operations. By a little after 10 P.M. that night we produced a draft paper entitled "Military Strategy in Afghanistan." For the southern tribes, it prescribed three messages: They should join us to balance the influence of the Northern Alliance, we were prepared to give them the same support we were giving in the north, and we were "committed to preserving Kabul as a capital for all Afghans, not one dominated by the Northern Alliance."

For the northern tribes, the key messages were more elaborate. First and foremost, we advised them that it was time to start attacking the Taliban and al Qaida. We would coordinate our air strikes with their ground movements, in addition to providing ammunition, supplies, and food. We also extended more general advice about the conduct of the war:

> **It is crucial that your forces conduct themselves humanely and professionally toward the civilian population. Atrocities will damage your cause. Our support depends on your dealing severely with breaches of professional conduct.**
>
> **. . . [T]he future of Kabul must be decided by a political process and not military action alone. We expect you to declare, as soon as possible, that your goal is not to establish dominion over the entire country, but to get a political process started that will reflect the interests of all the Afghan peoples.**
>
> **We envision some kind of international security arrangement for Kabul. . . . We envision a highly capable peacekeeping force drawn from our allies in Europe, the Muslim world and elsewhere to secure Kabul until stability is achieved.**
>
> **We expect to consult with you on your plans for moving on Kabul. It may be wise to encourage the Taliban to surrender the city without your forces having to invest and occupy it by force, possibly by surrounding the city and introducing a capable peacekeeping force.**

As sensitive as we were to Pashtun views about Kabul, we saw no reason to tell the Northern Alliance to "restrain" themselves when we were trying to get them to start the offensive.

In his comments at interagency meetings, Vice President Cheney had made clear that he shared this sense of urgency about getting decisive results before the winter. But it appeared that neither Powell nor Tenet did, so we decided to explain it in our strategy paper:

- **An early defeat of Taliban/Al Qaida will make it more difficult for them to conduct additional terrorist operations.**
- **Making an example of the Taliban increases our leverage on other state supporters of terrorism.**
- **There will undoubtedly be intense diplomatic activity once winter slows down military operations. That diplomacy should operate against a background of U.S. success.**
- **Success will build U.S. public confidence for action in other theaters.**
- **Early success will maintain the support of key coalition members; protracted fighting may achieve the opposite.**

We also stressed that one goal of our military operations in Afghanistan was to collect intelligence on the ground that might help us disrupt terrorist operations around the world. This was another argument for urgency.

From the National Security Council to the Principals and Deputies Committees down through the lower levels of the U.S. government, the debate over the pacing of the war raged in these early weeks. Matters such as coalition management, humanitarian aid, public affairs, and whether to stop bombing during the Muslim holiday of Ramadan were turned over and over for many hours. After one particularly long Deputies meeting, Abizaid's number two, the witty Major General Michael Dunn (U.S. Air Force), suggested that the war should be called "Operation Infinite Meeting."

The mutual frustration between Rumsfeld and Franks intensified in these first slow weeks of the war. The general seemed to be taking guidance uncritically from his CIA advisers on questions that Rumsfeld thought should be resolved within the chain of command. A CIA Afghanistan expert had suggested early on that our planes should bomb for a few days and then "pause." Franks endorsed the suggestion, until Rumsfeld described it as a whiff of our old failed strategy of "graduated response" in Vietnam. Franks's failure to question the need for a "mother may I" to the CIA before insertion of Green Berets into Afghanistan especially rankled the Secretary, who considered this hesitation a "defect in our capability." And Franks went along with the CIA's Mazar-not-Kabul idea, even though Rumsfeld and Wolfowitz concluded it would be better to push for Mazar *and* Kabul.

Franks could be temperamental, even on a good day. And with no joyful news from the ground in Afghanistan, and Rumsfeld asking every few hours whether we had succeeded yet in getting any military forces into the country, the general lost his composure. On October 17, the promised insertion of the first detachment of Special Operations Forces failed to occur because of bad weather. And then, in that day's conference call, Rumsfeld rebuked Franks about the chain of command: "It's clear to you and everyone that DOD [the Department of Defense] is in charge of the war. You're in charge and I'm in charge and other departments put in ideas, but we make the decisions, right?" "Right," said Franks, sounding chastened. In his book, Franks says that his anger at this time, just before the first team of Special Operations Forces made it in on October 19, finally compelled him to call the Secretary to tell him "it appears that you no longer have confidence in me," and to suggest that he "select another commander."

But Rumsfeld didn't want to fire Franks, any more than he wanted to abandon our strategy. Rather, he wanted his current commander to look for strategic guidance where he was supposed to (namely, to Rumsfeld himself, and not to CIA or State officials), and to see the big picture and think more boldly. The Secretary wanted more creativity and action from Franks in implementing the existing strategy. Rumsfeld was impatient and gruff, but not fickle or flighty. Franks kept his job.

President Bush, meanwhile, asked routinely about U.S. humanitarian operations in Afghanistan. He wanted our shipments of food and other aid to show the Afghans that the United States was well intentioned toward them, even though we were fighting their government.

Joe Collins, the Deputy Assistant Secretary of Defense who tracked such operations, reported that our aid efforts were a mixed bag. Within the first week of Operation Enduring Freedom, CENTCOM had dropped 150,000 daily ration packages, mostly in the Northern Alliance areas. And "unprecedented" coordination was being achieved among State, Defense, and United Nations offices. But we were still not having much luck with creative attempts to "further campaign objectives or better support our friends."

Like most of my Defense Department colleagues, I thought it was obvious that food aid and other types of humanitarian assistance should be distributed so as to support our general effort in Afghanistan. But some officials of the U.S. Agency for International Development (USAID) in the State Department, which played the leading role in distributing our food aid around the world, opposed any suggestion that they be harnessed to serve the Administration's strategic purposes. They argued that their own effectiveness, including their good relations with international nongovernmental organizations, depended on the disinterested nature of their work.

Hadley told the Deputies Committee that the issue was not simple. He said it was a principle with President Bush that "we don't use food as a weapon." We were giving funds for aid to international humanitarian organizations, and they would determine where the need was. It was right for us to ensure that our food was not intercepted by the Taliban, and if Afghan forces were to come over to our side, we would have an interest in provisioning them. But reconciling all these points was a tricky matter, Hadley said. Wolfowitz commented that the Taliban used food as a weapon: They were literally starving the regions of the country where the Northern Alliance had support.

As a legal matter, the chain of command for military operations is straightforward: The President and the Secretary of Defense are the two civilians—the only two—who can issue an order to U.S. military forces. For operations (as opposed to training), the chain runs from the two of them directly to the four-star general or admiral at the top of each combatant command—for example, CENTCOM, Pacific Command, or Special Operations Command. These combatant commanders are responsible for planning and fighting wars—indeed, for planning and executing all military operations, including humanitarian relief and reconstruction. (The officials in the operational chain of command are shown shaded in Figure 2.)

The Chairman of the Joint Chiefs of Staff, the Vice Chairman, and the service chiefs (the top military officers of the army, navy, marine corps, and air force) are not in the chain of command for operations. The Chairman's job is giving military advice to the President, the Secretary of Defense, and the National Security Council—not commanding forces in battle. Rather than run military operations, the service chiefs are responsible for recruiting, training, and equipping.

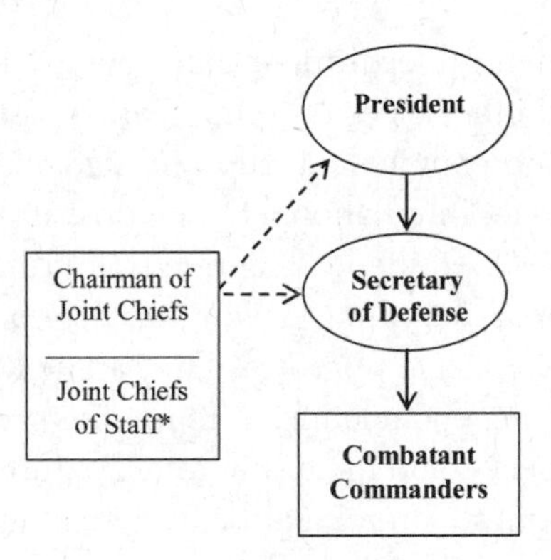

*The **Joint Chiefs of Staff** (JCS) are the Chairman, the Vice Chairman, and the *military chiefs* of each of the four services: Army, Navy, Marines, and Air Force. Each service also has a *civilian head* — the Secretary of the Army, Navy, or Air Force. (Both the Navy and Marine Corps report to the Secretary of the Navy.) None of the JCS, nor any of the service secretaries, is in the chain of command for military operations. (A dotted line reflects an advisory, not reporting, relationship.)

Figure 2. Chain of Command for Military Operations

In thinking through his military advice, the Chairman relies on the Joint Chiefs, who sit as a committee, and on his staff, which is known as the Joint Staff. The Chairman can direct commanders to do planning and provide him with advice, but he cannot order a plan's execution.

No one in the Office of the Secretary of Defense (OSD) below the Secretary is included in the chain of command, not even the Deputy Secretary,* let alone any of the under secretaries. As to military operations, my job—Under Secretary of Defense for Policy—was advisory, not supervisory. The law does not authorize any under secretary to order anyone in any combatant command to do anything. I could affect military planning or operations in two ways: by persuading the Secretary to tell a combatant commander to do something or by selling an idea to someone in a combatant command who buys it voluntarily because he thinks it has merit.

As clear as it is in the law, the term "chain of command" can be misleading. It wrongly suggests that officials at the top of the chain can turn their ideas into action simply by *command*. But a Secretary of Defense who wants his strategic thoughts to take practical shape in military plans must do more than just issue an order. He has to inform, persuade, cultivate, and monitor.

The Secretary of Defense is directly linked to the combatant commanders in the chain of command, and he can communicate directly with them, one-on-one if he wants to. But there is much to be gained by allowing the Chairman and his staff to participate in those interactions and to advise all the parties on substance and style. Rumsfeld made a practice of including either Myers or Pace, or both, in virtually every exchange he had with his commanders.

It is always a tough call whether a civilian boss should *push* or *pull* a military commander in a particular situation. No mathematical formula can tell the Secretary of Defense and the President precisely where strategic supervision ends and improper micromanagement of military operations begins. Rumsfeld wrestled hard with this problem. He was, to be sure, a strong-willed strategist. But his management philosophy, which was respectful of the judgment of the people in-theater, and his instinct for political self-protection, made him disinclined to overrule (if he had failed to shape) the judgments of his operational chief executives.

Rumsfeld had a technique that was generally effective in producing

---

*The deputy secretary can operate in the chain of command when he is serving as acting secretary in the secretary's absence or when the secretary specifically authorizes him to do so. But his status as deputy secretary gives him no intrinsic power to issue a military order.

agreement, though it could be wearing on the commanders. He spent a lot of time discussing concepts with them and often reacted to new proposals—especially war plans—by demanding (in his characteristic fashion) to know the "key assumptions" behind them. For a military planner, a key assumption was an expectation that, if it did not happen, would require a significant change in the plan. In Afghanistan, for example, one key assumption was that the Northern Alliance would seize ground from Taliban and al Qaida forces once the United States provided supplies and air support.

Rumsfeld rejected assumptions that were in the form of precise predictions. He didn't believe anyone could predict the future, no matter how much intelligence was available. As a philosophical conservative, he considered the inevitability of error in human affairs one of the key realities of this world. As imposing as he was in practice, in principle he endorsed intellectual modesty—for himself and others.

Of course, none of this meant that Rumsfeld argued against making plans.* The point of his skepticism was to make sure that our planning accounted for the possibility that important things might happen that none of us had predicted: We should plan to be surprised. That meant planning to maintain broad capabilities, flexible tactics, and an open mind ready to adapt to events as they develop. If a commander talked predictions rather than adaptability and agility, Rumsfeld would correct or "calibrate" him.

Rather than issuing orders, Rumsfeld preferred to massage concepts. A four-star commander (accompanied by his senior planning officers) would visit the Pentagon to present a war plan to the Secretary and the Chairman (joined by a few other senior civilian and military staff, including me). Sometimes the commander himself would present the briefing. "This plan deals with an attack by country X on country Y and, if that happens, our goal would be to defeat the attack," the briefer would begin. Then, as he prepared to leap into his ideas about which forces should deploy, Rumsfeld would interrupt, to ask for a more specific statement of the goal—something less banal than "defeat the attack." Then he would probe the assumptions, firing a series of questions at the briefer. A two-hour block of time slated for a war-plan briefing might be consumed entirely

*Making sensible plans is different from making crystal-ball predictions. Veteran *New York Times* intelligence reporter James Risen misinterprets a comment of mine by missing this distinction. I had asserted that Rumsfeld would have thrown out of his office anyone who pretended to know before the war what postwar Iraq would look like. Risen cites this as evidence that Administration officials failed to do postwar planning and had "convinced ourselves" that no plans were required. (James Risen, *State of War: The Secret History of the CIA and the Bush Administration*, p. 134.) Neither proposition is true, as demonstrated in Chapter 9.

with such discussions. "If you get the assumptions right, a trained ape can do the rest," Rumsfeld would assert with a laugh, no doubt endearing himself to military planners everywhere.

Rumsfeld worked on strategic analysis through a kind of Socratic method of question and answer. He had a way of getting people to offer him back his own ideas, as if they were their own. It was a tour de force of reason and education, not compulsion. But it could be discomfiting for those on the receiving end.

If a commander argued well against an idea from Rumsfeld, the Secretary was willing to be talked out of it. If a commander claimed credit for one of Rumsfeld's own ideas, that was all to the good. It gave the general "ownership": There would be less chance of failure if the officer implementing a proposal had a personal stake in its success. If a commander were told to do something he had not himself proposed, it could hurt both the Secretary and the President in the event of failure. So Rumsfeld rarely gave commands. He asked questions and floated thoughts, made assertions to which he invited challenges, and in general launched an aggressive give-and-take. Rumsfeld did not consider policy ideas sacred. He reexamined his own ideas frequently and would demonstrate this in meetings so that the educational effect would ripple through the Department. This took some getting used to.

One combatant commander, trying to get a war plan approved, was cut short when Rumsfeld launched into an "assumptions drill" that consumed the entire meeting. The result was a refined set of assumptions, but not an approved plan. Some weeks later, the commander flew back to the Pentagon for another try. At the start of this round, the commander waved his refined assumptions slide in front of the Secretary and proposed moving through it quickly: It contained Rumsfeld's own words, meticulously crafted and recorded on his last visit. Rumsfeld held up his hand. I've got to read this, he said. Otherwise, how do I know I didn't put something dumb in here? How do I know that circumstances haven't changed? How do I know I still agree with it? And he meant it. Rumsfeld wanted it known that he saw no humiliation in changing one's assumptions down the road. He also wanted to gauge whether the commander had truly assimilated the assumptions or was just giving them lip service.

These techniques took time. When time was short and communication had to be in writing, Rumsfeld was not always able to get his conceptions and attitudes adopted.

In the first weeks after 9/11, Rumsfeld was impatient to hear how his combatant commanders proposed to take on our enemies. On September 19, General Shelton received a snowflake summarizing the thoughts Rumsfeld wanted to provide to his commanders as they prepared their proposals; on October 3, Rumsfeld followed up with the strategic guidance for the campaign against terrorism. Then it was the commanders' turn to respond.

Apart from the evolving plan for Afghanistan, the commanders' proposals were not what the Secretary was looking for. They said little more than that the U.S. military had superb capabilities to kill targets by air, sea, or ground—especially from the air—and if the CIA gave them "actionable intelligence" on the whereabouts of terrorist training camps, safe houses, vessels, or WMD sites, we could destroy them. The commanders, like Rumsfeld, all knew that this response was far less than the 9/11 attack required. The few targets the commanders proposed, based on existing intelligence, were uncertain and fairly insignificant: a site that might or might not be a terrorist camp, a ship that may or may not be connected to al Qaida. So the typical proposed "way ahead" amounted to waiting for CIA intelligence, planning an air attack (which might take weeks to prepare), and eventually hitting something with a bomb or cruise missile.

Rumsfeld doubted that he could get his *regional* combatant commands—those with geographic areas of responsibility—to adopt a global view of the war. The alternative was to use the Special Operations Command (SOCOM) for worldwide planning and operating, but SOCOM was not set up to handle that mission. So, for the time being, it was necessary to work through the regional commands. At a conference with all of his top commanders in Washington right after 9/11, Rumsfeld had urged them to think globally and "nontraditionally"—and to "think ahead." But it would take more than exhortations to change the frame of mind of large, remote, conservative institutions like the combatant commands.

Rumsfeld shared President Bush's broad concept of the war on terrorism. Indeed, he had helped the President develop it, stressing the worldwide nature of the terrorist threat and warning against focusing too narrowly on Afghanistan and al Qaida. His suggestions about mounting early operations outside Afghanistan, and taking action to address the special danger of terrorists acquiring weapons of mass destruction, reflected the breadth of his view on the matter. But, having promoted his strategic ideas to the President, Rumsfeld lacked recommendations that would make those ideas concrete—a failing that provoked him.

On October 10, Rumsfeld told Myers and Pace that the Defense Department had produced next to nothing in the way of "actionable" suggestions to pressure the terrorists, other than use of cruise missiles and aerial bombs. With copies to Wolfowitz and me, he sent them a snowflake entitled "What Will Be the Military Role in the War on Terrorism," asserting that "something is fundamentally wrong" in a department that was getting a third of a trillion dollars a year, but could not produce a proposal for action.

Was it because the defense establishment "has spent the last decade becoming increasingly risk averse?" Rumsfeld asked. He questioned whether midlevel people were withholding bold ideas because they thought higher-ups would reject them as too risky; were they "dumbing down all proposals other than cruise missiles and bombs?" He said he did not want ideas to be filtered that way: It was his job—and the President's—to make judgments as to risks. Rumsfeld concluded: "You must drive the staffs to solve this problem. I am available to do whatever is necessary to provide the stimulus, incentive or the threats necessary to drive the people responsible for producing actionable ideas."

That was the kind of communication that General Pace called "a spear in the chest." All the Roundtable regulars got accustomed to such shots, though this one was extraordinarily rough. Rumsfeld generally used a more respectful tone with the Chairman and the Vice, and he rarely made a reference like "the last decade," which could be taken as a political slap at the previous Administration. Though Pace had been on the job for only ten days, he took this missile in stride. After some discussion we agreed that, style aside, the Secretary was on to some real problems.

One problem was that the commanders were demanding "actionable intelligence," but the intelligence coming from the CIA wasn't precise enough to be actionable. Instead of just waiting around for the CIA, Pace and I saw that the combatant commanders needed to devise actions that might yield usable intelligence for additional actions. This was the origin of what became known as "expanded maritime interdiction operations." Working with Chuck Allen of the Defense Department General Counsel's office, Michael Mobbs and other Policy officials helped define a mission for U.S. naval forces that aimed not only at seizing terrorist operatives and materiel (including any WMD-related cargoes), but also obtaining information that could become the basis for further counterterrorist operations.

Marshall Billingslea, one of the deputy assistant secretaries on the Policy team, developed this idea into a proposal for *multinational* operations to intercept WMD-related trade. J. D. Crouch and I passed that proposal on to Robert Joseph on Rice's staff, who handed it along to Under Secretary of State John Bolton. It was a seminal contribution to what later evolved into the Proliferation Security Initiative, launched by President Bush in May 2003. Thanks to Bolton's energetic diplomacy, the Proliferation Security Initiative became a success, with more than seventy countries taking part.

That initiative was a nonlegalistic, nonbureaucratic approach to multinational arms control. It produced some fruitful interdictions and made it easier for countries to operate together militarily to nab WMD proliferators. The initiative's greatest coup was the October 2003 diversion to Italy of a German-flagged ship heading to Libya (from Dubai) with a cargo of centrifuges for the production of fissile material for nuclear weapons. That interception appears to have been important in persuading Libya to dismantle its WMD programs. It also helped undo the supply network run by Pakistani scientist A. Q. Khan, which assisted various countries in the clandestine pursuit of nuclear weapons.

When Rumsfeld complained about risk aversion, he was referring (among other things) to the lack of proposals to use ground forces. The intelligence needed to fight terrorists could not be obtained solely, or even mainly, by satellite. We needed human intelligence. We needed to get people into the right locations on the ground. Pace and I used the CAPCOM—the Campaign Planning Committee we cochaired—to connect with SOCOM officers on how to deploy Special Operations Forces, not just for "direct action" against known terrorist targets but also *to obtain intelligence*. The eventual result was a joint Defense Department–CIA effort, initially directed at al Qaida's senior leadership, which contributed to the killing or capture of most of those leaders whose identities were known to our intelligence community. General Myers took the lead in getting Rumsfeld's approval of this effort. He walked Rumsfeld through sticky questions about how to get fast decisions from the Secretary of Defense and the President for action against so-called time-sensitive targets.

Another way around the no-actionable-intelligence barrier was for our combatant commands to consider not just direct action against terrorist targets but also indirect action, relying on foreign security forces. Pace and I helped the combatant commanders develop proposals to enable foreign security forces to attack terrorists locally—by training and equipping them or by providing intelligence, on-the-ground advisers, or other help. Eventually, the commanders, together with CIA colleagues, launched efforts to train, equip, and support foreign forces in Afghanistan, Iraq, Pakistan, the Philippines, Yemen, Georgia, Mali, Kenya, and Saudi Arabia. These initiatives contributed directly and indirectly to important successes. No one can say definitively how much our intelligence, military, or law enforcement efforts helped foreign officials in their operations against terrorists, but countries that were our partners captured an impressive list of terrorist leaders, including:

- Ibn al-Sheikh al-Libi, al Qaida trainer: *captured in Pakistan*
- Abu Zubaidah, senior al Qaida leader: *captured in Pakistan, March 2002*

- Ramzi Binalshibh, 9/11 plot accomplice: *captured in Pakistan, September 2002*
- Abd al-Rahim al-Nashri, al Qaida operations chief: *captured in United Arab Emirates*
- Khalid Sheikh Muhammad, top al Qaida planner, 2000 Millennium plot and 9/11 architect: *captured in Pakistan, March 2003*
- Riduan Isamuddin, a.k.a. Hambali, leader of Jemaah Islamiyah (an al Qaida affiliate): *captured in Thailand, August 2003*
- Ahmad Khalfan Ghailani, connected with 1998 East Africa embassy bombings: *captured in Pakistan, July 2004*
- Abu Faraj al-Libi, al Qaida number three leader: *captured in Pakistan, May 2005*

U.S. partners also killed a number of important terrorist leaders, including:

- Abu Sabaya, leader of the al Qaida–affiliated Abu Sayyaf Group, in the Philippines
- Qaed Salim Sinan al-Harethi, chief al Qaida operative in Yemen, connected with 2000 bombing of the U.S.S. *Cole*, in Yemen
- Yousif Salif Fahad al-Ayeeri, a.k.a. "Swift Sword," al Qaida operative, in Saudi Arabia

---

On a typical day as Under Secretary, even before 9/11, I got up at 4:00 A.M. and spent two hours or so at home reading and writing "action items" and other papers that my staff culled out of my in-box as "hot." I would make it through four to six inches of paper before my Pentagon driver picked me up at a little before 7:00 A.M. for the drive to the office, which gave me twenty-five minutes to devote to reading newspapers. My schedule was chockablock with phone calls and meetings, at the Pentagon or the White House. Spontaneous demands required my appointments secretary, Maggie Souleyret, a genius juggler, to revise my calendar a dozen times each day.

I often put a one-page item in my pocket in the morning, intending to read it when I had three minutes free, and realized at night that the item remained unread because I had not had three minutes free all day. Maggie routinely scheduled members of my staff to ride with me to the White House or even walk with me from the office to the car, so they could get one or two matters resolved in those several minutes. More paperwork occupied the trip home, around 7:00 or 8:00 P.M.

After 9/11, the number of meetings increased—and days off largely disappeared. For the next two years—until the estimable Joyce Rumsfeld pulled the reins in on her husband—I met with the Secretary, the Deputy, or my staff at the Pentagon every weekend, often on both days.

There was no time to read all the current intelligence that came to my office—it sometimes amounted to an inch or two of paper in a single day—let alone background information. The intelligence community's output on terrorism over the years had been mountainous, despite its dearth of "actionable" items. There were daily intelligence items—including many "warning" reports of intercepted "chatter" among terrorist suspects that implied that some kind of event would occur in some (unspecified) place at some (unspecified) time. And there were finished products—short and long information papers on various terrorist groups around the globe, laying out what intelligence analysts thought they knew about their ideologies, organizations, and activities.

Some of this material was illuminating and useful. In any event, it was what we had available. So, a few weeks after 9/11, I asked members of my staff to review all the intelligence paper flow—to look it over and summarize it, and to help me devise counterterrorist strategy and policy recommendations for Rumsfeld. It was a standard request for policy staffers: Extracting strategic insights from intelligence is what policy personnel do every day.

This project evolved into the Policy Counter Terrorism Evaluation Group (PCTEG), which became legendary as the supposed Pentagon "covert intelligence unit" that was alleged to have manipulated intelligence to mislead the President and the public into war in Iraq. I use the word "legendary" literally, because nearly everything said about the PCTEG has been a legend—that is, make-believe. False assertions about the project have been grist for thousands of political speeches and news articles. The legend's proponents usually cite as their sources current or former intelligence officials (often anonymous) who had bureaucratic or policy disagreements with Rumsfeld, Wolfowitz, or me.

The common but untrue storyline about the PCTEG is that I created it because I rejected the CIA's work and wanted to have my own "secret" office, circumventing normal channels, to collect intelligence and focus on proving an al Qaida–Iraq connection to justify a war against Saddam Hussein. According to this line of thinking (as one reporter put it), "Rumsfeld and others considered the unit as a virtual alternative to intelligence analyses provided by the CIA." In *The New Yorker*, the journalist Seymour Hersh garbled his reporting on the PCTEG. As a result, many other writers, who think that reading *The New Yorker* is research, have mixed up the PCTEG with the Office of Special Plans (OSP). The latter office was a different entity and will be examined in a later chapter.

The legend of the PCTEG, however, is so at odds with the facts—a reality so ordinary, benign, and lacking in sex appeal—that the flap over the "intelligence cell" can serve as a cautionary tale for anyone who writes or reads about current events.

As the need for actionable intelligence became more apparent, I determined to get help in reviewing the intelligence that already existed on terrorist networks. A vast quantity of intelligence reporting routinely landed on my desk, including "raw" intelligence reports. Intelligence reporting is intended to help shape policy. It was my responsibility to make use of the reports and for this I needed staff assistance.

I assigned the project to two people in my organization, David Wurmser and Mike Maloof. Wurmser, a quiet, even diffident Middle East scholar with a doctorate from Johns Hopkins University, was an intelligence officer serving in the Naval Reserve. Maloof, a physically imposing, intense man, was a veteran Defense Department professional who had served in both Republican and Democratic administrations. He specialized in analyzing international criminal networks and had worked for years tracking down violators of U.S. export control laws. The review work they did for me was not covert or even secret. They did not collect intelligence. They did not focus only, or even largely, on al Qaida–Iraq connections.

After a few weeks, in December 2001, they produced a fat set of PowerPoint slides, each crammed with information on financial, operational, ideological, or other connections among terrorist groups and their state and nonstate supporters. This information had been developed through a careful reading of the existing intelligence provided by the intelligence agencies. Out of the roughly 150 slides, *only nine* mentioned possible contacts between Iraq and al Qaida. The data in the briefing slides were *all* footnoted to intelligence community reports, not to any information collected independently by my organization or anyone else. Accusations directed at this work have described it as an attempt to circumvent the CIA's analysis. But Wurmser and Maloof did not reject the CIA's work; they used it and cited it throughout their slides.*

---

*The Wurmser-Maloof briefing on international terrorist networks has sometimes been confused with a different, controversial briefing that focused specifically on ties between al Qaida and Iraq, criticizing the CIA. That briefing, which eventually became the subject of a Defense Department Inspector General review, is discussed in Chapter 8.

The Wurmser-Maloof work was professional: carefully researched, organized, and well presented. It helped educate officials about the way terrorists operate as a network of networks. Since its creation in December 2001, the package of slides has been reviewed by various offices in the Administration and in the Congress, including by critics and opponents of the Administration's policies. I know of no one who has ever made a case that the work was bad or was a manipulation of intelligence.

Maloof left the project in December 2001, and Wurmser departed in January for a job at the State Department. Wanting the project to continue, I wrote to the head of the Defense Intelligence Agency, Vice Admiral Tom Wilson, and asked him to lend my Policy organization a few analysts. To reassure him that my request was not open-ended, I specified that I needed the people for a particular project. I defined the scope of the work and gave the project a name: the Policy Counter Terrorism Evaluation Group. I asked for three people. Wilson said he would give me two. I accepted.

No one involved thought of the project as a "secret" of the Policy organization, as a circumvention of the intelligence community, or as a big deal of any kind. It was an ordinary, small-scale, short-lived project and was treated by everyone as such. It served proper purposes within Policy. Had I not asked my staff to help me review the existing intelligence on terrorist networks, critics could justifiably have condemned me for ignoring that material. This project never claimed to publish "intelligence analyses," which are what intelligence agencies publish. Rather, it produced summaries and evaluations of intelligence reports by policy officials. Such work is routine—indeed required—for policy offices.

After the original two staffers departed, the two new, substitute analysts, both Naval Reserve intelligence officers, entered the project in February 2002; one of them stayed only until April. From that point forward, the remaining officer, Chris Carney, a university professor in civilian life, became the PCTEG's sole member. In discussing this once with Senator Carl Levin at a congressional briefing, I said that the PCTEG's true history raised the Zen question: Can you have a one-person "group"? Senator Levin did not find that funny.

So the notorious "covert Pentagon intelligence cell," which some have described as a plot to sideline the CIA, was neither covert nor an intelligence cell. It was simply a very small group of policy officials digesting a mass of intelligence reporting for their boss. It comprised two people, replaced by another two people, who quickly shrank to one. And they never had any contractors working for them. It never occurred to me to replace the CIA with two policy staffers—much less one, though he was good.*

The Secretary had asked Franks on October 22, 2001, to report on his updated plan for Afghanistan for the next thirty days. He wanted him to address what we should do if the CIA failed to produce Afghan partners for us in the south, and what more we could do on the ground if President Bush decided to stop U.S. aerial bombing during Ramadan, beginning November 15. Rumsfeld wanted to ensure that Franks was missing no opportunities to prod our Afghan partners to bolder action. The Secretary was willing to consider changing our strategy, but he wanted to do everything reasonable to make it succeed before proposing that the President switch course to undertake a major U.S. ground operation. The Pentagon leadership agreed that it would be far more advantageous, if feasible, to support the *Afghans* to fight the Taliban.

Two days later, on October 24, there was still no significant ground action by the Northern Alliance. In a National Security Council meeting that day, the President shot a barrage of questions at Rumsfeld and Myers: What is Franks's "winter scenario"? How can we surge our aircraft to help the Afghan opposition forces? How can we use our airpower against cave hideouts, to which some of our enemies have already begun moving? Citing the 1948–49 Berlin Airlift, President Bush wanted to know what a humanitarian effort on that scale would entail. He was pushing Rumsfeld, just as the Secretary was pushing Franks. Whenever Rumsfeld asked his staff if a task had been completed, he disdained the bureaucratic answer "we're working on it"—and he resented having to offer that lame response to the President.

When Franks reported on his updated plan, Rumsfeld judged it a "laundry list" of "unprioritized" things to do. At the October 29 Roundtable meeting, the Secretary started brainstorming on the strategy with Myers. Rumsfeld reiterated that the war on terrorism was broader than Afghanistan. He wanted "visible military action that demonstrates the breadth of the war," something *outside* CENTCOM's area of responsi-

---

*Carney, the last PCTEG-er left standing, stayed on the job until January 2003, when the navy demobilized him. He returned to teaching for a semester. My Near East and South Asia office then brought him back to the Pentagon as a regular civilian employee. He resigned in 2004 to run for office, and was elected as a Democratic congressman from the 10th district of Pennsylvania in November 2006.

bility; "otherwise [we'll be] driven into a narrow focus" on Afghanistan and bin Laden. Rumsfeld favored restating a "broad national strategy" that would aim to persuade states and individuals to drop their support for terrorists. Rumsfeld and Myers agreed that we needed a "strategic influence" effort—engaging in the battle of ideas within the Muslim world regarding Afghanistan and the overall problem of terrorism. He wanted that effort undertaken not just by the Defense Department but by the whole government, guided by the National Security Council.

At this point, Rumsfeld began talking quickly. Regarding the particulars of Afghanistan strategy, he asked: How do we get an important result soon? He tossed out thoughts about combat operations, humanitarian supplies, and diplomatic initiatives. He produced a long list of ideas. Rumsfeld liked generating lists: it helped him think. He could sift through the items and sort them according to importance, urgency, and feasibility. After this burst of thoughts, Myers must have thought that the Secretary was revving a little too fast. He told Rumsfeld "the current tempo is fine; we need patience."

Myers had a strategic outlook; he thought about the long term, took large national interests into account, and considered how actions taken in one area might have nonobvious effects on other areas.* Rumsfeld often accepted Myers's advice; he clearly liked and respected the general. Myers chose to exercise his influence mainly through the Secretary, rather than in interagency forums. He tended to speak a lot more at Rumsfeld's daily Roundtable meetings than in the Situation Room.

But Rumsfeld had little patience, and what little he had was nearly exhausted. He decided he simply could not wait for Franks to produce a satisfactory new plan for Afghanistan. So, at a Roundtable meeting on October 31, Rumsfeld turned to Pace and me and said he wanted us to produce a new strategy paper to address the President's questions. He wanted ways to put U.S. troops into the south quickly to support the tribal leader Hamid Karzai, the CIA's only substantial contact there. He wanted us to propose current objectives—and objectives during Ramadan, during a winter campaign, and during a postwinter campaign. He would reconvene his Roundtable group that afternoon, and he wanted the strategy drafted *within five hours*.

Pace and I swallowed our astonishment and proceeded at a trot

---

*In a formal introduction I once gave for Myers, I noted his classically American virtues: "intelligence without arrogance, patriotism without cant, toughness without brutality, resolution without rigidity, and dignity without vanity." Douglas J. Feith, "Introduction of General Richard B. Myers," "Keeper of the Flame" Annual Dinner of the Center for Security Policy, Washington, D.C., October 2, 2002.

straight from the Roundtable to my office. As Abizaid was away, Pace called Major General Dunn, Abizaid's deputy, to join us. The three of us then closed my office door and started work on the paper for the President. There was no time to staff out this assignment. I sat typing at my classified computer, with the Vice Chairman of the Joint Chiefs of Staff standing behind one shoulder and the Deputy J-5 standing behind the other. We worked in the hectic, manic, but productive fashion of college students completing a group project at the last minute. Dunn and I teased Pace about the predicament of a four-star marine general having to produce a lengthy original composition on a short deadline for a boss who had the critical eye of a persnickety schoolmaster. We marines can do anything, Pace assured us.

Pace was an extraordinary teammate. Despite his uncommon personal and intellectual qualities, he had no pretension—my front-office support staff loved him for fetching his own coffee. He gave intense thought to the responsibilities of senior military service. Pace had memorized his oath as an officer, and when I heard him recite it once in a public speech, I noticed that the words brought emotion to his voice. He had a solemn duty, as he saw it, to remain in the active service as a marine—not to retire—so long as he was allowed to serve. He maintained collegiality with his civilian superiors and colleagues alike, without compromising the independence of his military advice. And he was funny. Once, he ribbed Rumsfeld at a meeting after the Secretary had been overbearing with a briefer. The rest of us laughed and glanced at Rumsfeld to gauge his reaction, and Pace followed up: "I've always believed you should never let a promising career get in the way of a good joke."

Pace, Dunn, and I fulfilled our assignment on time. Our strategy highlighted the virtues of "steadiness" and noted the danger of popular expectations of instantaneous results in Afghanistan. But we also warned of the risk of additional 9/11s, which "could occur any day," and the "pressing strategic requirements for the US to be seen to be building momentum in the war against terrorism." We concluded that "without degenerating into unrealistic impatience, we need to systematically intensify the war efforts, with a greater sense of urgency."

We had two purposes. One was to help organize the government's thinking; the other was to push CENTCOM. We wanted to ensure that Franks was considering all reasonable means to influence the Afghan opposition and others, both in Afghanistan and around the world—through information efforts, force maneuvers, combat operations, and otherwise. To make our push constructive, however, we had to avoid aggravating Franks's sensitivity about whether Rumsfeld still had confidence in him.

We phrased our paper carefully, setting out "illustrative" ideas for intensified U.S. efforts and leaving it to Franks to determine which ideas would actually work. We reviewed how the Afghanistan fighting fit into our global war on terrorism. We set out "broad objectives" for the global war and then proposed a plan with specific actions that Franks could consider immediately for Afghanistan. The actions included: driving the Taliban out of a major city, launching (as President Bush had proposed) a Berlin-airlift-scale humanitarian aid effort, and opening a land bridge to Uzbekistan.

Using some ideas previously floated by Rumsfeld, Wolfowitz, and Myers, we listed additional actions for Afghanistan: planning for "possible deployment of major ground operations, in concert with our allies, and flow forces into region for this purpose"; and establishing a provisional government, either in exile or in a portion of the country.

Pace, Dunn, and I discussed the delicacy of pushing a general who was running an operation. The generals helped me (as they did Rumsfeld) with fine points of judgment: When does a strategic idea get so specific (for example) that it becomes tactical meddling? It is an essential function of the Chairman, the Vice, and their Joint Staff to buffer communications between Pentagon civilians and the combatant commands.

As a matter of principle, Rumsfeld did not want to interfere with Franks's professional military judgments. But deference to such judgments would not excuse his forfeiting the strategic control that is the inalienable responsibility of the only two civilians in the military chain of command. So Rumsfeld pushed Franks—but only sometimes, and always in a measured way. Only later, after he decided to cultivate a personal rapport with Franks, did the Secretary manage to win Franks's voluntary and eager cooperation on almost any matter Rumsfeld signified as important.

As October was ending, the United States finally had the first few dozen U.S. special operators on the ground in northern Afghanistan. Our strategy would now be tested. We would see whether, by playing only a supporting role, we could stimulate and aid our Afghan partners to defeat the enemy and change the government. We would see if we could accomplish a grand result without a massive invasion.

We hoped that we would soon see the impressive results Franks had told us to expect from the linkage of our high-altitude bombers to laser-toting Green Berets on the ground. We wanted our air operations to translate not just into wrecked Taliban infrastructure, but into territory captured by the anti-Taliban tribes. Despite calls by CIA officials to restrain the

Northern Alliance, the Agency's analysts were predicting that, within a month, "most key cities—Kandahar, Herat, Kabul, Jalalabad, Mazar, Taloqan, and Shebergen—will be in tribal hands—our side."

Now Rumsfeld shifted the focus of his impatience. He no longer asked every day whether the Special Operations Forces had made their entry. Now he wanted to know whether the Northern Alliance had begun its offensive. Days passed. Our air operations continued, aimed increasingly at Taliban and al Qaida combat forces. Our funds and supplies were flowing to our Afghan partners. But the Northern Alliance commanders were not yet seizing ground from the enemy.

At the Pentagon we discussed the range of possible explanations. Fahim, Dostum, Ismail Khan, and the other Northern Alliance commanders found themselves outnumbered by the enemy in key areas. They had an understandable desire to build up their forces, receive additional supplies from us, and wait for U.S. airpower to damage Taliban and al Qaida forces further. But how long should we remain patient and understanding of their lack of movement? When and how hard should we push them? It hardly seemed possible that these famous warriors were suffering a lack of courage, but we had no way to know for sure, for none of us had ever had a chance to develop personal familiarity with them. We heard speculation around Washington that some of them may have made deals with the enemy, but we didn't know what to make of the rumor. Afghan history was full of instances where commanders in civil conflicts switched sides. We also wondered whether our new partners might be holding back simply in order to extract more money and materiel from us.

Every strategy is an experiment, and one has to be ready to modify or abandon the hypothesis if real-world results contradict it. We judged, however, that we had crafted this experiment sensibly. The history of British and Soviet military failures in Afghanistan argued against a large U.S. invasion force. We wanted our action to shock state supporters of terrorism into reconsidering any pending operations, and that, too, argued for a small, economical force. Our enemies would know that we retained ample additional capacity to do other missions—whether for the war on terrorism or for other purposes. It made sense to ask ourselves if we were doing everything we should do to impart our own sense of urgency to our Afghan partners. It did not make sense to us to allow impatience to pull the plug on a well-considered strategy that had not yet had a chance to work.

Though we were eager for results, the Pentagon leadership was not surprised that our Afghan partners were showing caution. We had hoped, but not expected, that the Taliban would be ousted immediately. Some journalists and members of Congress, however, commented as if all of us were stunned by the lack of instantaneous victory, a failure that supposedly exposed the bankruptcy of our strategy. They started to ridicule and recriminate. On October 26, the *New York Times* reported that Northern Alliance commanders were disparaging United States airpower. Whereas "they had expected the wrath of the only superpower to be crushing," reporter David Rohde wrote, these commanders were disappointed that our aircraft flew quietly at high altitudes, attacked in small numbers, and struck precisely rather than devastatingly. One compared a typical two-plane U.S. bombing run unfavorably with the attacks launched by the Soviets: "When Soviet troops invaded Afghanistan, 60 airplanes would strike one place, while 100 tanks attacked it." The U.S. bombing, he claimed, was *improving* Taliban morale.*

Peter Jennings of ABC News interviewed Pakistani President Pervez Musharraf and asked if the United States is "possibly facing a quagmire in Afghanistan." Musharraf answered—albeit with diplomatic qualifications—that "it may be a quagmire." The word moved *New York Times* columnist Maureen Dowd to ruminate on the squeamish weakness of the Bush Administration. "Are we quagmiring ourselves again?" she asked. Referring to Afghans "mocking the American airstrikes," she criticized the Administration for "stumbling over scruples against a foe with no scruples." Dowd was outflanking Bush on the right, depicting him as effete, "brought up to believe in Marquess of Queensberry rules," and lacking her own willingness to fight by "the most sordid rules . . . ruthlessly, but also with guile." A Pentagon spokesman "denied we were getting bogged down over there," Dowd wrote, "always a sure sign we're getting bogged down over there."

The *Times* kept the ball rolling with an October 31 front-page piece under the headline "A Military Quagmire Remembered: Afghanistan as Vietnam." The war had started on October 7, not four weeks before.

The *Times* reporter, R. W. Apple Jr., used a device that became a favorite of Administration critics: He invented an unrealistic standard of success that government officials had never set for our efforts and then declared those efforts disappointing for not having met that standard: "Despite the insistence of President Bush and members of his cabinet that all is well, the war in Afghanistan has gone less smoothly than many

---

*While the *New York Times* was reporting that U.S. bombing was small-scale and precise to a fault, the *Guardian*, a prominent British newspaper intensely critical of U.S. policy, was condemning the United States for "carpet bombing." The British editorial declared: "If ever there was a new, Vietnam-style quagmire in the making, Afghanistan must surely be it." "How not to win a war: America is trapped in a B-52 mindset," *The Guardian*, November 2, 2001, p. 21.

had hoped." Many of whom? The "many had hoped" was a straw man so flimsy that even Apple felt compelled to add: "Not that anyone expected a lightning campaign without setbacks; indeed, both Mr. Bush and Mr. Rumsfeld have often said the effort would be long and hard." Apple cited "Senator McCain and some colleagues in both parties" as asserting that airpower alone would not produce victory (as if anyone in the Administration had thought it would) and that a ground effort would be required that "might well involve tens of thousands of troops, hundreds of casualties and many months of effort."*

This *Times* story spawned hundreds of articles in other journals and countless television commentaries on the "quagmire" in Afghanistan. Zbigniew Brzezinski, President Carter's erudite, though sometimes erring, National Security Adviser, told the *Christian Science Monitor*: "When we started out, we were going to smash Al Qaeda and punish the Taliban. Now we seem to be getting engaged in an Afghan civil war, almost as an end in itself. That could be a quagmire."

Brzezinski was wrong, not just about the quagmire, but about the fundamental strategic goal of our attack—which was never to punish the Taliban, but to pressure state supporters of terrorism globally and thereby disrupt terrorist planning and operations. Brzezinski wasn't entirely at fault: His misstatement reflected, at least in part, the Bush Administration's failure to explain our actions clearly to the public. It was an early sign of the public communications problem that would persist for years, with ill consequences of strategic importance—especially later in Iraq.

But the columnists' discussions of quagmire were short-lived. In less than two weeks, Kabul would fall to our side. The critics' lack of prescience was not remarkable; as a famous movie magnate once observed, it's difficult to make forecasts, especially about the future. What deserves remark was their accusatory certitude. *Washington Post* columnist Richard Cohen concluded that Administration officials were dishonest in refusing to admit how badly the war was going. Invoking "quagmire" and Vietnam, he wrote, "We don't expect miracles but we do expect candor." Jacob Heilbrunn commented in his *Los Angeles Times* column: "Despite . . . Rumsfeld's claim that critics are looking for 'instant gratification,' the war effort is in deep trouble. The United States is not headed into a quagmire; it's already in one. The United States is not losing the first round against the

---

*A few days later, *USA Today* reported that a "common scenario" among "experts" envisions "up to 100,000 troops who would move into Afghanistan by spring or summer. . . ." (Andrea Stone and Kirk Spitzer, "Pressure builds on U.S. to begin a ground war," *USA Today*, November 9, 2001, p. 1A).

Taliban; it has already lost it. Soon, a new credibility gap will emerge as the Pentagon attempts to massage the news."

These harsh judgments were quickly exposed as errors. But the later successes on the ground failed to produce a more open-minded or civil style of journalism—let alone any correction for the record.

As I was working and reworking revisions—what Rumsfeld called "iterations"—of our Afghanistan strategy review, Admiral Giambastiani gave a reprise of the surprise travel announcement he had made in early October. A few hours before takeoff, the admiral once again informed me that Rumsfeld had decided to have a busy weekend with me and a few of our colleagues. We were to leave midday on Friday, November 2, for visits to Russia, Tajikistan, Uzbekistan, Pakistan, and India. I shouldn't worry about missing too much office time, though, he said: We would be back in Washington by Monday night, November 5, and could have a full day at the office on Tuesday.

In Russia, we met with the Defense Minister, Sergei Ivanov, and then with Vladimir Putin, the country's president. Putin was so generous with his time that he threw off our ridiculously tight schedule. He spent nearly two hours with us, and he talked—with no one else making a peep—for more than an hour and forty minutes. The Soviets had learned a lot about Afghanistan, and Putin was in a mood to share. He offered his opinions of key players in the country, his military observations, and his take on Afghanistan's neighbors. He touted Russian weapons for the Northern Alliance as far better than other weapons, because its commanders knew the Russian equipment so well. He also spent some time on U.S.-Russian issues—nuclear weapons reductions, missile defense, and the ABM Treaty.

There was a good deal of substance in Putin's monologue. He spoke energetically, indeed compulsively. His style was not that of a Soviet apparatchik, despite his background as a KGB officer; he came across rather as freewheeling and youthful. In part it was his athletic manner that made him seem young, but in part it was his effort to impress Rumsfeld, who was around twenty years his senior—to show him how well-informed and smart he was, how thoroughly in charge he was, how eager Russia was to become our ally in the war on terrorism, how valuable his personal cooperation could be for us. It struck me that Putin looked nervous in that large, high-ceilinged, fancily furnished and gilded room in the Kremlin. He was so eager to cut a figure that he could not switch out of "transmit mode."

As I watched Putin's performance, I thought: 9/11 occurred not two months ago. The United States is engaged in a global war. Here, across the table from him, is the American Secretary of Defense, Bush's key strategist and the man running the combat operations—and Putin is not curious enough or self-disciplined enough to ask Rumsfeld a single question. Putin would have looked more thoroughly in charge, I concluded, had he chosen to hold a proper conversation.

Our meetings in Tajikistan and Uzbekistan were stiff, tightly timed, Soviet-style sessions attended by leaders whose expressions brought to mind a reviewing stand atop Lenin's tomb on a May Day in the bad old days. But Rumsfeld managed some useful dialogue with President Imam Ali Rahmonov and then President Islam Karimov. Each gave us some insights about Afghanistan and al Qaida, and offered us valuable cooperation on access, basing, overflight, intelligence, and other matters.

Before 9/11, Rumsfeld had called attention to Central Asia as a region of strategic importance. Even then he believed that, Taliban-run Afghanistan aside, the United States should find ways to make friends in Central Asia, which included Muslim states that were eager to create links to the West. Some had important economic potential. Their sovereignty and independence were factors in the stability of Asia. They could beneficially influence the security environment in which Russia, China, and other countries were making strategic decisions affecting United States interests. These former Soviet republics had a long way to go to become liberal and democratic. But association with the United States might incline them toward greater freedom, as it had over the years in other countries—for example, South Korea, Taiwan, and El Salvador, not to mention Germany, Italy, and Japan.

Traveling from Uzbekistan to Pakistan in our enormous transport plane, we flew over Afghanistan. Kabul had not yet been liberated, but our air force deemed the country's airspace safe enough for the Secretary of Defense and his party, and we got to glimpse the grand, snow-covered mountains of the Hindu Kush.

As with our three previous stops, when we visited Pakistan and India we had Afghanistan on the top of our agenda, but we kept broader strategic matters in mind, too. No country in the world was of greater importance to our military operations in Afghanistan than Pakistan. Pakistani officials remained somewhat protective of the Taliban, a movement they had helped launch in the chaotic post-Soviet period to protect various interests of Pakistan and the ethnic Pashtuns, whose homeland straddles a large segment of the fourteen-hundred-mile Pakistan-Afghanistan border.

In the hours after 9/11, Bush had sent Richard Armitage to demand that Pervez Musharraf declare whether Pakistan was our friend or our enemy. Musharraf promptly opted for friendship and close partnership with an awesomely enraged America, and renounced the support that Pakistan had been giving the Taliban regime since its inception. Significantly, he even fired the head of his intelligence service, who was closely identified with the Taliban. This partnership was of great practical importance for us: Our personnel, planes, and missiles needed passage through or over Pakistan on the way from the Indian Ocean to Afghanistan (the route through Iranian territory was obviously not an option). Musharraf gave us permission and allowed us to use his facilities to base search-and-rescue teams for our Afghanistan operations. The Afghanistan border area—some of the highest terrain in the world: jagged, frozen, and mountainous—was an obvious potential refuge for bin Laden or our other enemies who might flee Afghanistan. Musharraf promised to try to exert control there, but from time immemorial the region was controlled by local chieftains; Pakistan's central government had never brought it under effective administration, nor had the British authorities in the previous era. It was not clear how hard Musharraf would try to govern the area—or how successful he could be if he tried.

Pakistani security forces were ready to operate against al Qaida, but not yet against Taliban personnel seeking safe haven in Pakistan. Musharraf denounced al Qaida as terrorists, but he would not include in that category the Pakistani extremist groups—especially Jaish-e-Mohammed and Lashkar-e-Taiba—who were infiltrating from Pakistan to India to conduct terrorist raids as part of the long-running conflict over Kashmir. These cross-border operations ran the risk of triggering another war between Pakistan and India, each of whom since 1998 had demonstrated its ability to detonate a nuclear weapon.

Musharraf presented a complex picture to Rumsfeld and the rest of us. He exhibited a well-grounded confidence in his own intellect, and he could be charming. He had come to power as the leader of an army coup against an elected government, but his manner was not that of the stereotypical military dictator. In our meetings, his governmental advisers had a relaxed air and spoke up freely, even interrupting their president at times. Musharraf was forthcoming on the cooperation he felt comfortable in extending. But he was inflexibly resistant to ideas that failed to take full account of what he saw as his domestic constraints.

Rumsfeld understood the delicacy of Musharraf's situation. He saw that we had compelled a great shift in Pakistani policy since 9/11, and that we were pressing Pakistan to shift further on various fronts. Rumsfeld also saw that, if we were zealous and asked for too much too quickly, we could aggravate the risk that Musharraf could get assassinated or overthrown—in favor of people far less amenable regarding terrorism, democracy, and regional peace. We were worried about terrorists or other extremists getting hold of nuclear weapons. The last thing we wanted to see was a nuclear-weapons *state* falling into such hands.

By the time we got to India on Sunday night, most of us were thoroughly wrung out. How many background memos, read-aheads, honor guards, meetings, press conferences, cables, and memos had come and gone since we were in Moscow with Putin on our way to Dushanbe, Tashkent, and Islamabad!—and that was only yesterday morning. We arrived at our hotel in New Delhi around midnight. A little after 1 A.M., running perkily on adrenalin, Rumsfeld thought of something for someone on my staff to add to the talking points for the morning meetings. The Secretary surprised me by banging on my hotel room door to ask where the staffer was. Learning that the fellow had just gone to bed, Rumsfeld slapped the air in front of him and sneered, jokingly, "What a wimp!" Seeing that I was shoeless and on my way to bed myself, he relented: "Okay, we'll do it in the morning."

Our meetings with Indian officials fit within a plan orchestrated by the farsighted U.S. ambassador to India, Robert Blackwill, to use a series of face-to-face encounters to help transform official relations between the United States and India. I had resolved to devote a major personal effort to this initiative before 9/11, indeed before I was confirmed as Under Secretary. As I saw it, we had an opportunity to create a strategic partnership with India. For decades, U.S. officials had tended to look at India primarily in two ways: as part of the India-Pakistan conflict and as a nuclear proliferation problem. But that negative view of India ignored important changes in the world since the Cold War era, when India professed neutrality but tended to side with the Soviet Union. With that superpower's demise, India was looking to improve its ties to the United States, and it was clear to me that Bush, Rumsfeld, and Wolfowitz were in favor of the idea.

In early 2001, before he left the United States to assume his post in New Delhi, I met with Blackwill to discuss India policy. A friend from my time in the Reagan Administration, Blackwill shared with me the conversations he had had with George W. Bush about India, before and after he became President. President Bush, he told me, saw India not chiefly as a problem country, but as a great democratic country on track to become the world's most populous state, a nation with a liberalizing economy that had already made an impressive entry into the information age, and a rising power that could be a natural ally of the United States.

United States and Indian officials were not accustomed to talking together about strategic developments in the world, other than those directly tied to their relations with each other. As Rumsfeld noted in his India meetings, however, the countries shared interests—regarding China, Afghanistan, the Middle East, and missile defense, for example—and we each wanted various kinds of help from the other. As Indian officials plunged eagerly into strategic talks with us, one commented to me that America had unprecedented power in the world and that it was an enviable opportunity for any country to have the ear of the Pentagon.

To begin changing the frame of mind of key institutions in Washington and New Delhi, Blackwill had been pressing U.S. officials to visit India, preferably in quick succession so as to build momentum. The Defense Department was particularly responsive. Rumsfeld's visit in early November was followed two weeks later by a visit from the head of the U.S. Pacific Command, Admiral Dennis Blair. Less than two weeks after that, I led a delegation to India for the bilateral defense forum that I cochaired with Yogendra Narayan, the number two official in the Indian defense ministry. I used that forum to help generate a packed calendar of defense activities, including continual military-to-military exchanges and combined exercises involving all the armed services.

As Rumsfeld and the rest of us flew back home together from India, the news media were still full of quagmire stories and demands for higher U.S. troop levels in Afghanistan. But the Secretary was feeling the elation that he typically allowed himself after such diplomatic exertions. Meanwhile, we glassy-eyed staffers were grinding out the reports and correspondence that had to get approved and dispatched before we landed back at Andrews. I walked forward to the Secretary's private cabin, knocked, entered, and sat down with him for a few minutes to discuss some paperwork. He was relaxed and pleasant, so when I rose to depart, I suggested that he come back with me to the compartment where my staff was sitting and thank them for their prodigious efforts throughout the trip. He paused, tilted his head, and answered deliberately, "What? And ruin them?" The Secretary stayed put.

Our handful of Special Forces embedded in the militia of Northern Alliance General Abdul Rashid Dostum helped persuade him to move against Mazar-e-Sharif in early November. They had spent the two-week "quagmire" period forging teamwork with Dostum's men. The Green Berets provided useful intelligence—for example, alerting us that the key to Dostum's logistics was not diesel fuel but oats, for his forces traveled on horseback, not in armored personnel carriers or even ordinary trucks. Proud of their adaptability, the Special Forces set about learning to ride on the spot. Mike DeLong, CENTCOM's deputy commander, tells the story in his book *Inside CENTCOM:*

> **After a day or two of riding, our troops were terribly saddle sore, to the point of serious disability.**
>
> **To ease the friction, we sent in a hundred jars of Vaseline. But in Afghanistan the dirt is a fine dust and it's everywhere; it lingers in the air and covers you from head to foot. This fine dust collected on the Vaseline; instead of helping, it converted the Vaseline into sandpaper. Now their legs were being cut up. What they really needed were chaps, like cowboys wear. But there wasn't time to measure them for chaps. So we decided on pantyhose. We sent over two hundred pairs. If it worked for Joe Namath in Super Bowl '69, why not for our troops?**
>
> **Lo and behold, it worked like a charm. The pantyhose saved the day.**

Had this tale become public at the time, one could imagine indignant members of Congress calling it an intelligence failure, a planning fiasco, and an example of incompetent Pentagon civilians sending our forces into battle without proper equipment. As that story had a happy ending, it simply offered a homespun vindication of Rumsfeld's defense transformation themes: The unanticipated will happen; don't get overly attached to your own preconceptions; be agile, resourceful, and ready to adapt. American service members had the motivation, training, and ingenuity to function flexibly in the field, as they were continually called upon to do.

According to the classic formula, an attacking force should outnumber by three to one the force defending a fortified position. Dostum sent nine hundred or so men against Mazar-e-Sharif—a force roughly one-tenth the size of the Taliban force entrenched there, not counting their al Qaida allies. But Dostum also had his handful of embedded American Green Berets, and they were linked by laser designators and radios to U.S. aircraft with precision munitions. Defying the classic formula, but with our help, Dostum's force took Mazar on November 9, managed to kill a number of al Qaida fighters, and, in the Afghan way, got the defeated Taliban force to switch sides and join the opposition.

That was a good day. Mazar's fall was a cause for satisfaction and some optimism for Rumsfeld, Wolfowitz, and the rest of us at the Pentagon and at CENTCOM, who had championed the U.S. military partnership with the Northern Alliance and pressed for important results before the winter. New goals now looked readily achievable: opening the land bridge to Uzbekistan, increasing the flow of humanitarian and other supplies into Afghanistan, and building on the momentum to liberate other cities. All of that indeed happened fast.

Another Northern Alliance commander, General Ismail Khan, had been besieging the western city of Herat for weeks, and on Sunday, November 11, he conquered it. Appearing on one of that morning's television news programs, Rumsfeld was asked, "Why don't we want the Northern Alliance to march into Kabul?" It's hard to imagine that question coming from anyone but a reporter with a CIA or State Department source.* Rumsfeld respectfully mentioned President Musharraf's concerns about Pashtun interests in Afghanistan and said we wanted Kabul to become the capital of a broad-based government. When pressed on whether U.S. forces would stand in the way of a Northern Alliance force that was moving to take the city, Rumsfeld said that "we don't have enough forces on the ground to stand in their way," and that the Northern Alliance would make its own decision.

It did. On November 13, together with some anti-Taliban southern Afghan forces, the Northern Alliance entered Kabul and quickly took it over. Rumsfeld and Powell cooperated in getting an international force pulled together to stabilize the city under a mandate from the UN Security Council. Weeks before, Rumsfeld had said that such a force should comprise troops from a number of countries but "not the U.S." That is how it went. The British agreed to take command for an initial period of a few months.

Assistant Secretary of Defense Peter Rodman negotiated the memorandum of agreement between the U.S. Defense Department and Britain, the leader of the new force, which was known as the International Security Assistance Force (ISAF). Rumsfeld insisted that the agreement should set out with precision how ISAF would relate to CENTCOM and what kind of emergency and other help CENTCOM would provide to ISAF under what circumstances. During the negotiation, the British asked for provisions that Rumsfeld judged might interfere with CENTCOM's own mission against Taliban and al Qaida forces. His responses were so tough that Rodman and I thought he might set relations back to around 1812. But we got an agreement that served both sides' interests, and it proved itself in

---

*In an October 29, 2001, paper distributed at a Policy Committee meeting, the CIA said that Northern Alliance commanders, in deference to U.S. concerns about precipitating a political crisis, had said they didn't care to take Kabul. Rumsfeld penned in the margin: "Good grief!"

practice, becoming a model for the agreements we made with other states that succeeded Britain in commanding the ISAF.

Jalalabad surrendered on November 14. That day, the Deputies Committee discussed the Taliban's ongoing loss of control of the country. Anticipating the discussion at an upcoming National Security Council meeting, Stephen Hadley raised the question of how the United States should respond if Taliban leaders offered to surrender and we came under pressure to halt U.S. military operations. Wolfowitz noted that we hadn't yet completed our military mission against the Taliban and al Qaida, so a cease-fire would be premature. Who, he asked, would be in a position to accept a Taliban surrender?

The prospect of the Taliban regime's imminent collapse raised numerous diplomatic and legal questions. When the time came to recognize a new Afghan government, Armitage said, we should seek a Security Council resolution. I suggested that we protect our right to intervene again in self-defense, if terrorists should return to Afghanistan. Armitage reported that State was pushing for an international conference that could lay the foundation for a broad-based Afghan government. Hadley asked if we wanted a provisional government to come into being that could accept surrenders. Pace worried about protecting our military commander's freedom of action to finish his task.

Another matter was the shaping of Afghanistan's post-Taliban leadership. This question received a good deal of interagency attention, but not from Rumsfeld. Experts in the Policy office knew something about Afghan history and key personalities and we sent the Secretary analyses and reports, but he stayed aloof from Afghan domestic politics. U.S. officials, he told me, weren't well suited to try to pick other countries' leaders. When a situation was fluid, as in Afghanistan after the ouster of the Taliban regime, Rumsfeld believed that leaders would emerge by a kind of natural process of interactions among the locals. He seemed to be implying an analogy to the economic marketplace, where the Adam Smithian "invisible hand" raised good products above the rest. Rumsfeld made it a principle that the United States should not try to "pick political winners" (as he put it) in other countries. But this was his personal view, and other officials, especially in other departments and agencies, showed no such restraint. As a result, the Defense Department ultimately had far less influence over such matters than did other parts of the U.S. government.

Though CIA officials had all along advocated our allying with Pashtuns, and not just with northern Afghan tribes, they had difficulty identifying specific Pashtuns to work with us. Eventually they linked up with Hamid Karzai. Born in Kandahar, he led an important clan of a prominent

Pashtun tribe, the one from which kings of Afghanistan had derived since the eighteenth century. The United States equipped him, transported him around the country in helicopters, and arranged for him to play a role in the liberation of Kandahar on December 7. If we were looking for a Pashtun who could credibly claim authority in an Afghanistan that had been freed of Taliban tyranny largely by the northern tribes, said State and CIA officials, Karzai was our best hope.

The State Department recruited the United Nations to organize a conference of Afghan political and tribal leaders to decide how their country would be run in the immediate post-Taliban period. Following on Bush's strategic idea that the United States would liberate but not occupy Afghanistan, we did not want to create a U.S.-led administration in Kabul. For reasons already explained, we also wanted to avoid the kind of "nation-building" arrangement that would have put Afghanistan under UN or multinational control. With help from Zalmay Khalilzad—our government's right man at the right place at the right time—and William Luti of my office, State officials managed to get the UN bureaucracy to work better than usual.

UN officials, led by Algerian diplomat Lakhdar Brahimi, convened the conference in late November in Bonn, Germany. By December 5, the conference participants agreed in writing on a plan, known as the Bonn Process, that kept Afghans responsible for their own governance. The participants—Afghan tribal leaders and other notables—appointed Karzai to head an interim administration of thirty people. The administration's job would be to convene a *loya jirga*, a traditional Afghan tribal council, to establish a broad-based transitional authority within six months. Within the next eighteen months, that new authority was to convene another *loya jirga* to adopt a constitution.

With U.S. approval, the Afghans at Bonn asked the UN Security Council to recruit a multinational force to help with security in Kabul and its environs. The idea was that the Afghan capital should not be patrolled and dominated by the militias of Northern Alliance regional commanders. That could cause the southerners to oppose the new government. The Afghan delegates pledged to withdraw their own militias from those areas where the UN-mandated force deployed. The very next day, the Security Council adopted a resolution blessing the agreement reached at Bonn.

The Bush Administration had given the United Nations an important role and then handled the diplomacy well. This belied the caricature of President Bush as a ham-fisted and reflexively anti-UN unilateralist, but that made little impression on the President's detractors. The launching of the Bonn Process also showed how effective U.S. diplomacy could be when our diplomats energetically directed their formidable skills to promoting the President's policies.

The Bonn conference's selection of Karzai as leader of the interim administration reflected an aspect of international power politics that makes many democracy-minded Americans uneasy: A U.S. endorsement of a foreign figure can in fact confer not only greater status but genuine political attractiveness in the eyes of his compatriots. This is by no means an argument for U.S. officials to try to impose a ruler on a foreign country. But it is worth noting that the Afghans who stayed in Afghanistan during the long period of tyranny and chaos that began with the 1979 Soviet invasion did not refuse to be led by Karzai, although he had chosen to live abroad and ultimately returned as a partner of the Americans who liberated the country.

Every situation has its own circumstances. But it was impressive that the proud and long-suffering Afghan people, who had reasons to distrust foreigners, did not hold Karzai's years of exile or U.S. ties against him. Still, within weeks, U.S. officials working on Iraq policy developed theories about post-Saddam Iraq that not only ignored but contradicted our experience in post-Taliban Afghanistan.

Though President Bush had not identified Usama bin Laden personally as a strategic objective of the Afghanistan campaign, we wanted to capture the al Qaida leader.* Public criticism for the failure to do so has been directed variously at Franks, Rumsfeld, and the President.

CENTCOM knew that the enemy was likely to exploit the forbidding topography of the Tora Bora mountains in southeastern Afghanistan, near the border with Pakistan, by taking refuge in the vast complex of caves there. U.S. airpower targeted that complex throughout the war, and especially heavily in December. Critics have accused Franks of not bringing in enough U.S. ground forces to prevent the Taliban and al Qaida fighters from fleeing into Pakistan. In one of the 2004 presidential election debates, John Kerry said that he, if elected President, "would not take my eye off of the goal: Osama bin Laden" and added: "Unfortunately, he escaped in the mountains of Tora Bora. We had him surrounded. But we didn't use American forces, the best trained in the world, to go kill him. The president relied on Afghan warlords and he outsourced that job too. That's wrong."

*The strategic objective was to prevent terrorist attacks by disrupting their networks, including by targeting their leadership—not to punish the perpetrators of 9/11.

Historians with military expertise and more information than I have will someday make comprehensive, disinterested, nonpoliticized judgments about these criticisms. When they do, they will have to weigh the overall merit of our strategy in Afghanistan, reviewing the benefits we got from keeping our military footprint small and allowing Afghan tribal forces to take the lead while we restricted U.S. forces to a supporting role. They will note the resulting broad support we received from Afghans, who had a history of fiercely resisting foreign forces that were seen as invaders rather than liberators. They will ask if Franks had a realistic option to rush in large numbers of U.S. or coalition ground forces. They will analyze how long it would have taken, and how many thousands (or tens of thousands) of U.S. and coalition troops would have been required to have a reasonable chance of interdicting whatever key al Qaida figures were in Tora Bora. They will also question whether bin Laden was actually there and whether that mountainous terrain could have been "sealed off" in any meaningful sense. They will think through how a large foreign ground force might have antagonized Afghans across the country—how it might have lost us support and possibly triggered a broad-based anti-U.S. insurgency. They will weigh the risks that abandoning our strategy, which had been working successfully, might have destroyed the promising political process launched in Bonn.

The standard criticism—that al Qaida terrorists (and maybe bin Laden himself) escaped because Franks didn't send enough U.S. forces to "seal off" the area—is too simple: It assumes too much and ignores too much. Senator Kerry's reproach of President Bush in the presidential debate was especially odd. The suggestion that the *President* should have told Franks which forces—U.S. or foreign—to use for a particular cordon mission reflects a bizarre conception of the relationship between a President and a wartime military commander. It is hard to imagine any President overriding his general's judgment and ordering him to use American forces to "go kill" bin Laden. A President who would do that needs a new commander.

At the end of December, retired U.S. General Wesley Clark, a former NATO Supreme Allied Commander, was asked on television whether the United States was relying too much on Afghan fighters to help us capture al Qaida leaders at Tora Bora. Though he would later launch a campaign to seek the Democratic Party's nomination to challenge Bush in the 2004 election, Clark's answer on Tora Bora was analytical rather than political:

> **I think that any time you adopt any method of warfare there are always pluses and minuses. . . . [R]elying on the proxies here on the ground . . . got the fight under way quickly.**

> **It brought down the Taliban quickly. It avoided the mistakes of the Soviet Union in putting in a large ground force. If we tried to go in there with several hundred thousand ground troops, we [would] have waited until next summer to have gotten all those troops assembled, moved through Pakistan. Who knows what the impact would have been on Pakistan when we went through?**
>
> **So this was by far the more expedient way to take the fight to the enemy. Is it possible that they weren't as aggressive at the end? Yes, it's possible, but as the president has told us all along, this fight is far from over. There is a long way ahead. And we have got the enemy off balance. We have the initiative, not he. I think the fact that there [have] been no successful attacks on the United States or elsewhere in the world since we started this campaign is a good indication of that.**

General Clark put his finger on an essential part of the U.S. strategy for the "long way ahead" in the war on terrorism: Taking action that forced our enemies off balance and onto the defensive would improve our ability to prevent them from launching future successful attacks. By disrupting Islamist extremist networks—targeting their organizations and their state sponsors using military, diplomatic, intelligence, financial, law enforcement, and other means—we could make it harder for them to communicate, transfer money, train new operatives, and plan new attacks, while increasing our chances of aborting such plans.

By December 2001, the United States had liberated Afghanistan and managed to avoid establishing an occupation government there. The U.S.-led war, and the UN-led political process that followed, were both efficient: Within two months after the start of Operation Enduring Freedom, Hamid Karzai was the head of an interim government with sovereign authority in Afghanistan. Of course, Karzai's authority did not give him actual control. His administration had the right to govern the country, but it would take further efforts to get the warlords and other Afghans to obey the new government. To complete our task in Afghanistan, we would have to help the new interim administration consolidate itself.

The Bush Administration had ideas about how to work with our coalition partners to accomplish this. But some of our bigger ideas proved wrong. And we learned that the U.S. government lacked the tools to promote new leadership in Afghanistan as efficiently as we had removed the old leadership.

Timeline 1. Afghanistan and the War on Terror, September 2001–December 2002

2001	
Sept. 9	Assassination of Ahmed Shah Massoud
Sept. 11	Terrorists strike the United States
Sept. 12	President meets with Joint Chiefs at Pentagon
Sept. 15–16	Camp David meeting of National Security Council
Sept. 20	President addresses Congress
Oct. 7	Beginning of war in Afghanistan
Oct. 19	First entry into Afghanistan of U.S. Special Ops Forces
Oct.–Nov.	American press reports: "quagmire"
Nov. 9	Fall of Mazar-e-Sharif
Nov. 11	Fall of Herat
Nov. 13	Fall of Kabul
Nov. 14	Fall of Jalalabad
Dec. 5	Bonn Process agreement on Afghan interim administration
Dec. 6	UN resolution calls for new government
Dec. 7	Fall of Kandahar
Dec. 22	Karzai government installed
Throughout Dec.	Tora Bora
Dec. 20.	Creation of International Security Assistance Force (ISAF)
2002	
Feb.	Reconstruction Conference
Late April–Early May	Pacha Khan Zadran challenge

5

EASIER TO TOPPLE THAN REBUILD

In 2001 the Bush Administration's task in Afghanistan was to overthrow the Taliban regime and deny al Qaida its safe haven. In 2002 it was to help the Afghan interim administration establish its authority. A reasonably strong Afghan government, based on a new constitution and legitimated through elections, would set back the cause of the Islamist extremists.

President Bush had criticized the "nation-building" approach of the Clinton Administration in the 2000 campaign, and Rumsfeld complained that U.S. officials had made Bosnia and Kosovo dependent rather than self-sustaining countries. We now faced the challenge of reconstructing the Afghan community after regime change—a task the U.S. government was not well organized to carry out. Our armed forces and civilian officials lacked the institutions, authorities, and resources needed for reconstruction work. This problem would bedevil us also in post-Saddam Iraq.

The unusual nature of our fight against the terrorists created a number of institutional challenges. The Administration wrestled with the problem of prisoners captured in the fight: What was their status? Who should be held, and where? What law should govern their treatment? Also difficult was the question of whether and how U.S. armed forces should be used to prevent terrorist attacks within our borders, and how the Defense Department should assist homeland defense.

Another challenging problem was how the U.S. government should organize for the battle of ideas. The ideological element of the struggle was essential, but no office in the U.S. government was well suited to handle it, and no official was appointed to take the lead. Both Rumsfeld and Myers wanted the Defense Department to make an effort on this front, hoping it would complement a vigorous government-wide strategic communications campaign headed by State or the White House. Yet my attempt to fill the gap within the Pentagon would backfire resoundingly, and the Bush Administration never put together a comprehensive strategy to counter ideological support for Islamist extremism.

The UN-sponsored political conference in Bonn had given Hamid Karzai the title of chairman of Afghanistan's interim government. But when he took office in December 2001, his power was meager. Journalists and others belittled him as "the mayor of Kabul, at most." The Bush Administration wanted Karzai to succeed as a *national* leader. We aimed to help him increase his government's authority—but without threatening the position of local Afghan leaders to the point of provoking civil war.

In early 2002, the Bush Administration had two other major goals. The first was to finish the fight against Taliban and al Qaida forces, many of whom had fled across the border into Pakistan. The second was to get international help for Afghanistan's reconstruction.

Being part of an international team would make it easier for the United States to share financial burdens and win diplomatic support. It would also allow us to limit the role of the U.S.-led military coalition: We did not want our troops transformed, in Afghan eyes, into an occupation force. Defense Department officials favored a small U.S. footprint and a light touch to help us maintain Afghan cooperation in the counterterrorism mission.

The Bush Administration helped Karzai in various ways. One of the best services we provided, in my view, was to *withhold* military support at a critical moment.

In the spring of 2002 Karzai faced his first armed challenge from a warlord—a fellow Pashtun named Pacha Khan Zadran. The confrontation agitated and split Bush's national security team, creating heated debate over whether U.S. military forces should intervene on Karzai's behalf. Dramatic reports from the field produced high anxiety among White House, State, and CIA officials—but Rumsfeld made a point of being unflappable and skeptical. He and General Myers insisted on sitting tight, against the urging not only of Powell and Rice but of Cheney, too. Bill Luti and I made Rumsfeld's case in writing, developing the argument that U.S. restraint would give Karzai an opportunity for statesmanship.

Bush went along with Rumsfeld. Karzai rose to the occasion. Pacha

Khan retreated. It was a nonevent of high significance. And it helped put Afghanistan on the road to legitimate government based on nonviolent politics—no small thing.

The drama began when Karzai appointed Pacha Khan to serve as governor of Gardez, a region south of Kabul. When the Gardez *shura* (a council of elders and religious leaders) opposed the appointment, Karzai withdrew it. Pacha Khan's militia responded by setting up roadblocks and firing artillery at the town of Gardez. There were reports of civilians killed by the shells, and the roadblocks were sometimes described as a siege. Pacha Khan proclaimed himself a friend of the United States, denouncing the *shura* as pro-Taliban and declaring that "the Northern Alliance wants to lord over the Pashtun areas forever." He demanded his governorship back and announced that "Karzai has no power." At the end of April 2002, Rumsfeld received the disturbing report that Karzai had threatened Pacha Khan, demanding that he "surrender and leave the area or be annihilated."

Karzai had become chairman of the new national government because he was generally acceptable to the Afghan warlords—in part, because he had no formidable militia of his own, having disbanded the force he led into Kandahar in November 2001. He could not, by himself, attack the warlords militarily. Yet here he was talking of annihilating an opponent.

When Rumsfeld heard the remark, he responded with one of his favorite sayings: "In Chicago we learned that you don't cock it if you're not going to throw it." But what could Karzai throw?

The Afghan Defense Minister, General Mohammed Fahim Khan, had succeeded the assassinated Massoud as head of the Northern Alliance. He was the most powerful warlord in the country. Many of Fahim's armed men remained in the capital after liberating it from the Taliban.* This was one reason his relationship with Karzai was uneasy. Nevertheless, Karzai asked Fahim to provide a couple of thousand fighters to confront Pacha Khan.

Fahim's force was moving toward Gardez on April 29. Stephen Hadley, Rice's deputy, organized a Deputies Committee teleconference to hear from Bush's special envoy in Kabul, Zalmay Khalilzad, and from General Franks. Just before the call, Wolfowitz and I got Rumsfeld's thoughts. He worried that our government might damage its credibility through mixed

*The UN Security Council had authorized the International Security Assistance Force specifically to spare Kabul from relying on warlord militias for security. ISAF was now up and running, with five thousand multinational troops under a British commander—but Fahim's force remained in Kabul.

signals to Karzai; he wanted Karzai clear on what the United States was and was not committed to do. Rumsfeld didn't want coalition forces entangled in fights among Afghan clans. This was one of the key lessons he derived from the British and Soviet experiences in Afghanistan.

Khalilzad came on line with news: The Afghan Interim Authority had just issued an arrest warrant for Pacha Khan. General Pace asked if any Afghans were actually requesting U.S. help. Franks assured us that coalition forces had "not entered the fray." The Defense Department participants knew that Rumsfeld would not tolerate anyone's even hinting at coalition military help, for he had not made a decision to approve any, let alone discussed the matter with the President.

Hadley, Armitage, and CIA Deputy Director John McLaughlin all spoke anxiously about Karzai's vulnerability. In his soft-spoken, professorial manner, McLaughlin argued emphatically for action against Pacha Khan. If Karzai fought and lost, he warned, it would encourage other warlords to defy him. Pace and Franks said it was too early to decide whether action was necessary against Pacha Khan. They suggested we could deal with the problem in stages: First Fahim's forces could remove the roadblocks; then we could let passions cool all around; then we could ask if anyone had to be arrested. McLaughlin listened to the generals' suggestion, but then pressed his own: It would be good to get Pacha removed, he said.

Wolfowitz and I proposed that Khalilzad encourage Karzai to go slow and not to assume he would get military reinforcement from the United States. Wolfowitz summed up Rumsfeld's main concern, that the U.S. should not become "Karzai's enforcer."

In a second teleconference later that day, Khalilzad painted a vivid picture of Karzai's passionate distress. Saying he could not tolerate a warlord acting with impunity as Pacha Khan was doing in Gardez, Karzai had declared he would accept the risk of escalation. He thought he could execute the operation against Pacha Khan on his own—that is, with Fahim's men—but if there were difficulties he would want air support from the U.S.-led coalition. Fahim had expressed interest in consulting with U.S. military officers in Kabul regarding strategy and tactics, and he favored reaching out to Pacha Khan to resolve things politically.

McLaughlin proposed giving Karzai information to help him in the confrontation. Wolfowitz, who could also be emphatic in soft-spoken, professorial tones, pushed back: Passing information at that moment could be interpreted as a signal that the United States favored a military move against Pacha Khan.

Rumsfeld took on his counterparts face-to-face several times that week. Powell and Rice were the most vocal advocates of U.S. military action.

They praised Karzai as central to everything we were trying to accomplish and warned that a successful warlord attack on his government could cause chaos in Afghanistan, help revive the Taliban, and undermine world support for the U.S. war on terrorism. Unlike his deputy McLaughlin, Tenet typically refrained from advocating policy outright, but his comments on Pacha Khan lined him up with Powell and Rice, not Rumsfeld. Cheney shared Tenet's worry. His comments on the matter never matched the intensity of Powell and Rice; I never heard anyone use the expression "hair on fire" about the temperate, deliberate Vice President. But he seconded the argument that we should be ready to use U.S. military force as a safety net for Karzai.

Senior officials at the Pentagon all understood that it would be a bad blow to both the United States and Afghanistan if Karzai lost a showdown with a warlord. But Rumsfeld insisted on placing this episode within a bigger picture: What was at stake was not just whether Karzai won, but what kind of leader he would be.

Our larger, longer-term interest, Rumsfeld asserted, was that Karzai succeed as a respected political figure, not just someone who could squash domestic opponents with a U.S.-supplied hammer. I agreed: Afghanistan needed Karzai to act as a statesman, not a warlord—and certainly not a warlord whose militia was the U.S. military. In Rumsfeld's view, Karzai should learn to operate as the mayor of Chicago did, forging coalitions through consultations, flattery, jobs, and other types of patronage. If a political threat to Karzai should escalate to an armed attack against the entire new Afghan political order, Rumsfeld was ready to direct U.S. forces to protect the Afghan government. But he didn't want America's list of enemies in Afghanistan to include, willy-nilly, any warlord who happened to quarrel with Karzai.

Rumsfeld asked Luti and me to write up his argument. Our paper warned that using American power in internal quarrels created several risks: being "viewed as an invading force," creating "dependency on the U.S.," and "antagoniz[ing] the Afghans." But Rumsfeld's colleagues were more worried that Pacha Khan might knock Karzai out of the box. The usual collegiality of Principals Committee meetings gave way to testiness: Powell and Rice were exasperated to the point of head-shaking and eye-rolling.

Rice was unable to achieve the kind of result she preferred: to resolve interagency disputes at the level of the Principals Committee. Rather than pass along to the President a disagreement in all its naked disharmony, Rice often crafted what she called a "bridging proposal"—an option that borrowed both from Powell's position and from the differing views of

Rumsfeld or Cheney. This was supposed to mollify all the Principals and relieve Bush of having to choose one department's position over another. On issue after issue, Rice worked hard to produce bridging proposals—even though, when Bush was presented with a clear choice among rival views, he showed the ready decisiveness of a confident executive. I never had the impression that Rice was trying to exclude the President from an issue; she consistently showed him loyalty and respect. She just thought of her job as building bridges.

Rice's idea of her role was different from that of the National Security Advisers I had observed in the Reagan Administration. Reagan's National Security Council staff would routinely draft "options papers" for him, presenting the agencies' conflicting views along with their policy prescriptions. Rumsfeld often told me he thought Bush should receive options papers like those done for Reagan. But Rice had her own way of proceeding.*

It was by now clear that President Bush himself would have to resolve the Gardez controversy. With input from the Pentagon team—Rumsfeld, Luti, Rodman, Wolfowitz, and Myers—I drafted a new paper for Rumsfeld to send to his boss. Rumsfeld usually favored understatement, but decided here to frame the issue dramatically:

> **The proper role for US military forces in the Gardez situation is an issue of unusual importance. The position the US takes may be the most significant war-related call to be made since forces were sent into Afghanistan in October, 2001. The issue is whether the Afghan government will be required to take responsibility for its actions—political and military—or whether it will be allowed to become dependent on US forces to stay in power.**

Rumsfeld noted that Karzai commanded only limited armed forces. For the foreseeable future, he would have to be "skillful at bargaining with the local powers-that-be, cajoling and using money, patronage and the like, as necessary, to maintain his position and keep the country united." Rumsfeld thought he should use force against a warlord "only when he can be confident of success on the basis of his own troops."

The proposal to use U.S. forces to guarantee Karzai's success in Gar-

---

*I wondered whether Bush had asked Rice to operate as she did. In the first half year of George W. Bush's second term, Steve Hadley (Rice's deputy) became National Security Adviser when Rice became Secretary of State. Hadley generally preserved the practice of trying to craft "bridging options" for the President.

dez, Rumsfeld admitted, was "a tempting solution," given Karzai's importance. But the Afghan leader and the U.S. government should resist the temptation, Rumsfeld contended:

> **It is not in the interest of the US or Karzai for us to make it easier for Karzai to rely on force, rather than political methods, to resolve problems with regional leaders. That would tend to increase his dependence on US military force to remain in power.**
>
> **It would then become harder and harder for the US to withdraw our forces, without raising the specter that Afghanistan will relapse into internecine warfare if we left.**
>
> **Further, our bolstering Karzai's power with military force risks making him look like our puppet.**
>
> - **If we did so, the US could begin to look like an occupying power, which would impede our ability to accomplish the primary US mission of destroying al-Qaida and the Taliban.**
> - **Moreover, US involvement in what will likely be a series of local conflicts would divert military assets from our primary mission.**

Praising Karzai as "wise and clever," the Secretary added: "He must know clearly . . . that he is responsible for his own decisions regarding the local commanders." Rumsfeld characterized the Gardez conflict as "relatively small in scale" and said that there "may or may not be a dust up." But "US actions with respect to any such fight would set a momentous precedent." Rumsfeld concluded that the United States could either "help Karzai to lead responsibly within his military means" or "train him to rely on the US military to bail him out."

These arguments won the day with the President.

I never saw a memo from Powell answering Rumsfeld's arguments, and it would have been unlike him to write one. It was remarkable how often Rumsfeld gave his colleagues and the President thoughts in writing and how relatively rarely Powell did.

Soon after Rumsfeld prevailed with Bush on the Gardez issue, Karzai rose to the challenge from Pacha Khan. He managed in time to quiet the situation without major fighting, using political skill within his own means. He acted not as Uncle Sam's kid brother, but as the legitimate leader of the new Afghanistan. Pacha Khan, to his credit, stood down. Karzai did not try to ruin his warlord rival and Pacha Khan eventually joined the political process: In the September 2005 national elections, he won a seat in the Afghan parliament. So the worst case did not materialize. U.S. forces did not enmesh themselves in domestic Afghan politics; their role remained limited, and their popularity among Afghans remained high. Karzai had tapped his own reserves of moderation and courage, developing techniques he would use again later in his systematic efforts to constrain other warlords.

Rumsfeld and his allies in the Gardez debate—chiefly, Myers and the President—felt vindicated in their cool and strategic stand. Still, as sound as their analysis was, the tactic had been a gamble. Karzai might have suffered a loss, with disastrous results for U.S. policy. As I saw it, Powell, Rice, Cheney, and Tenet had not been unreasonable to fret about the risk. Their objection would have looked prudent, indeed damning, if fortune had broken against us.

When I was a child, I knew people who made a hobby of military board games in which they played generals moving artillery, infantry, and armor units across maps to fight battles. Avalon Hill, as I recall, was the company that made especially sophisticated games of this kind. I never became an Avalon Hill fan, however, because dice helped determine the outcome of battles. As I saw it, that made the games less true than purely cerebral contests of maneuver such as chess. As a grown-up, I still have no interest in board games, but I have come to see the wisdom of incorporating dice into the play.

There is an old adage: Better to be lucky than smart. In this case, I thought that Rumsfeld and those of us on his side of the debate were both, which is better yet. But it is right to keep in mind the role that fortune can play in world affairs. In our political debates, we often ascribe genius to the people on the winning side of a controversy. Sometimes they deserve the praise. But success is not necessarily proof of having had the better argument.

Entering 2002, the Defense Department had many peas on its knife (as Rumsfeld liked to put it). U.S. forces had unfinished work in Afghanistan. Defense officials were considering ways to meet terrorist threats arising from hostile countries like Iran, Iraq, Libya, North Korea, Sudan, and Syria, and from partner countries like Saudi Arabia and Pakistan. Our soldiers were giving counterterrorism training to security forces in such places as the Philippines, Georgia, Colombia, and Yemen. And CENTCOM's maritime interdiction operations—known as MIO—were making it harder for terrorist groups to use the sea off the Horn of Africa (HOA).*

And, as important as the war on terrorism was, there was much else going on in the world that also required our attention. This book extracts only a few threads from the story of the Bush Administration's national security policy—those relating to Afghanistan, Iraq, and the war on terrorism generally. The reader could get the impression that top officials were focusing only on those matters. But we could devote only a part of our days to war work.

Regulars on the Deputies Committee or National Security Council did not deal only with a particular region, function, or subject matter, but with whatever national security issues arose. Work crossed our desks as a profuse tangle of diverse demands for attention—some important, some merely pressing, some both. On a typical day (January 3, 2002), I drafted, edited, or reviewed papers dealing with:

- Preventing war between India and Pakistan
- Opposing Russian assistance to Iran's nuclear program
- Strengthening Taiwanese military capabilities
- Crafting U.S. counterterrorism policy toward Sudan
- Managing U.S.-Philippines defense relations

Other papers I worked on that day dealt with more detailed matters:

- U.S. military observers for the United Nations mission in Ethiopia and Eritrea
- Coordination of export control policy with Norway and the Netherlands
- The United Kingdom's role in European Union defense talks
- The *despeje* (safe haven) in Colombia
- France's Africa policy

This list does not include the papers on Afghanistan or Iraq for that day, or the various meetings—interagency and intradepartmental—and phone calls.

---

*Because the target of these maritime operations was the top tier of al Qaida, the activity was dubbed "leadership interdiction operations" (LIO). Rumsfeld was asked to review the rules of engagement (ROE). As he was notorious for biting the heads off staffers who talked in abbreviations, we persuaded the courageous Joint Staff briefer to start by explaining that he sought approval of the "HOA MIO LIO ROE."

On another randomly selected day that month (January 28), the corresponding list included planning for continuity of U.S. government operations in the event of a national catastrophe, preparing Rumsfeld for a National Security Council meeting on war-on-terrorism detainees, negotiating offensive arms reductions with Russia, briefing Wolfowitz for a meeting with China's Vice Minister of Foreign Affairs, and managing U.S. relations with Australia, India, NATO, Romania, Saudi Arabia, and South Korea. On the same day, I also briefed Rumsfeld for our meeting that afternoon with Chairman Karzai of Afghanistan.

The lists are diverse, but the topics were all within the field of national security policy. While Rumsfeld and Wolfowitz shared global responsibilities in that field with me, they were also responsible (unlike me) for Defense Department budgeting, acquisitions, personnel and readiness, the overall command of the armed forces, and management of the Department.

The Secretary of Defense—and to some extent the under secretaries—were forced to manage affairs at the level of principle or strategy rather than enter too deeply into details. The calendar was a zero-sum game. Even if we kept our work at a properly strategic level—delegating operational tasks to others—we never had enough time. If we worked inefficiently—got "tangled in the weeds" or failed to delegate responsibility—the issues we ignored would get resolved not by conscious choice but by default: The President's options might change or disappear as policy makers pondered—or dithered. As the saying goes, not to decide is to decide.

Yet top officials cannot simply hurl their concepts and strategies down from Olympus. If they want results, they cannot ignore the details of their subordinates' work. Agency staffs are often more interested in preserving their autonomy than in absorbing new strategic guidance. While high-level officials cannot escape being second-guessed by journalists, legislators, historians, and others, many officials at lower levels manage to keep their work out of the public eye and beyond close supervision, even by their own bosses. So it can be a challenge for senior officials to ensure that their subordinates pay attention and perform—that they understand the strategic guidance, execute it, test its effectiveness, and report back on results. History provides many cases where strategies adopted in a nation's capital were ignored in the field.

President Bush knew that strategic success in Afghanistan required more than overthrowing the Taliban. If reconstruction failed, Afghanistan could once more become a safe haven for al Qaida or other terrorists. America's reputation for effective action would suffer, and other countries would be less willing to cooperate with us. If reconstruction succeeded, however, in producing a reasonably stable and friendly representative government, our interests would be served not only in Afghanistan but globally. Such success could stimulate support for political reforms throughout the Muslim world. It could help counter the appeal of extremist ideologies that motivated our terrorist enemies.

President Bush acknowledged in an April 2002 speech that rebuilding Afghan national institutions would be difficult: "[T]he history of military conflict in Afghanistan . . . [has] been one of initial success, followed by long years of floundering and ultimate failure. We're not going to repeat that mistake." Throughout 2002, in interagency meetings at all levels, Administration officials debated the best ways to promote peace and stability in the new, post-Taliban Afghanistan.

Rumsfeld was determined not to do "nation-building" as the United States typically did it in the 1990s. Rumsfeld wanted the United States to help the Afghans build their *own* nation, not to commit to building it for them. If the dad never lets go of his kid's bicycle seat, he warned, the kid will become a forty-year-old man who can't ride a bicycle. (This was the logic, of course, behind Rumsfeld's insistence that Karzai handle the warlord challenge without U.S. forces.)

Rumsfeld also took issue with the term "reconstruction." He pointed out that our aid would be building many things from scratch, not rebuilding them. Afghanistan, after all, was among the most wretched countries in the world—poorer even than most states in sub-Saharan Africa. It had been pummeled by the Soviet invasion, civil disorder, and Taliban oppression—and for the past four years, moreover, blasted by drought.

Afghanistan lacked roads and other essentials of economic life. It needed a hand in setting up government ministries, a police force, and a justice system. It required help to revive its agriculture and to eradicate the illegal trade in narcotics, which threatened to corrupt and engulf the entire country. Afghanistan's only major source of revenue, in fact, was poppies grown for heroin.

So the United States provided Afghanistan with economic aid. We built the road between Kabul and Kandahar. We took the lead in training and equipping the new Afghan army, and also, eventually, the new police and border security forces. The top Bush Administration officials all agreed that providing such assistance was the right thing to do. But we found time and again that we lacked tools to do reconstruction work quickly or efficiently.

When Chairman Karzai visited us at the Pentagon on January 28,

2002, Rumsfeld asked about Afghan attitudes toward a new army. Karzai expounded on the importance of the army's having a "national character"—with a unified command, troops from all regions of the country, and commanders who do not function as regional warlords.

Mohammed Fahim Khan, Karzai's defense minister, had drawn up a plan to create a national army and delivered it to Secretary Powell. Rumsfeld asked about Fahim's plan, and we were impressed to find that Karzai knew of it and approved it—a sign that Afghanistan's "interagency" process was working. Karzai said that Afghanistan needed around $10 million to get the army going—for uniforms, training, and the like. As soon as the tax system was up and running, Afghanistan would be able to pay army salaries, Karzai assured us, but it was important to get the army established quickly so it could begin to go after al Qaida and defend the country.

Rumsfeld asked Franks to "scrub" (that is, polish) Fahim's plan. Some Afghans, we had heard, envisioned the new army as simply a large agglomeration of warlord militias, paid for with foreign cash. Rumsfeld wanted none of that. He asked for a CENTCOM assessment: What kind of military force did Afghanistan need? What missions should it have—should it provide border security, for example, or should that be left to the Interior Ministry? What size force was needed? Should members of warlord militias be recruited into the new army? How could that be done without sowing seeds of factionalism? What is the best way to handle ethnic integration within units? We knew that a poorly organized army could aggravate ethnic divisions in the country. If done right, however, it could become the national institution that Karzai spoke about, one that would transcend ethnic and regional loyalties.

Rumsfeld worried about affordability. He opposed creating a larger army than the Afghans could sustain over time with their own funds. Foreign aid would not last indefinitely: It was difficult to raise, and most donors contributed in kind rather than in cash. Countries willing to give cash commonly insisted, with sanctimonious impracticality, that their donations not be used for military-related purposes. If Afghan officials created a large military and then ran out of cash to pay it, the resulting unhappiness in the ranks could destabilize the country. A related concern was how to control aid funds to guard against misuse or theft.

Within a few weeks, CENTCOM developed a plan to begin to train and equip the new Afghan army. To start, Franks said, they would need $4 million. As the Pentagon at this time was spending several hundreds of millions of dollars every month on Operation Enduring Freedom, this was a modest sum—a "rounding error," in that arch Pentagon phrase. Nonetheless, to make the money available, the Department's legal and financial personnel had to devise a complex ad hoc arrangement, because training and equipping foreign military forces was normally a job for State, not Defense.

It took a squadron of lawyers, accountants, policy people, and military officers many weeks of meetings to solve the financing problem. Because there was no appropriation allowing the Defense Department to perform the train-and-equip mission as such, the solution was to list all the specific tasks involved in the mission and find an existing appropriation to fit each of them. Congress had not foreseen that a mission of this kind—though tiny in financial terms—might be the key to winding down our own enormously expensive military effort in Afghanistan.*

Three different "pots of money"—funds created by different laws—were tapped to cover the several aspects of the train-and-equip plan. Combatant commander initiative funds (capped for this project at $860,000) could be used for bedding, cots, and local transportation, but not for building firing ranges. The emergency and extraordinary expense authority of the Secretary of Defense (not to exceed $950,000) could be used for infrastructure development, but not to buy uniforms. Presidential drawdown authority (not to exceed $2 million) was available for uniforms, trainer per diems, and airlift. And so it went. Each pot of money had its own accounting requirements. The different types of funds had different rules on when spending required a notification to Congress and whether it required an assurance of one type or another from the recipient country. And those rules could not be waived on account of war.

Lining up the spending authorities was an administrative nightmare that consumed many weeks. Waiting for funding and managing the paperwork exasperated our forces in-theater. The task of quickly creating an army from scratch for a newly liberated country—afflicted by political instability and ongoing violence—was a hard enough assignment without having to maneuver through the legal intricacies of a hodgepodge funding apparatus.

Our commanders in Afghanistan were ready to launch a number of tasks—efficient, strategically valuable initiatives—for which they lacked legal authority. They were eager to implement my office's suggestion to

---

*My office prepared legislation to give the Defense Department the authority and funds to carry out similar train-and-equip missions. It took a major effort to overcome objections from Deputy Secretary of State Richard Armitage and State's protectors in Congress. The objections were essentially nonsubstantive—they were efforts to retain for State the exclusive authority to perform such missions—even in cases where the scale of the mission was beyond the capability of State.

offer small financial rewards (from a few hundred to a few thousand dollars) for information or other cooperation. And they wanted to be able to pay out small amounts of cash in support of their missions—for example, to have a well dug in a village. Sometimes it became important to buy items for partners—such as night-vision or communications equipment for Afghan or Pakistani forces—to allow them to attack terrorist enemies where we could not. But our laws either prohibited such spending altogether or required us to use ordinary acquisition procedures designed for peacetime, procedures that were slow, cumbersome, and subject to legal challenges that could delay purchases for months. Meanwhile, our forces were trying to win a war.

Our national security legislation told us, in effect, that if our commanders wanted to use our own forces to conduct combat, they could go right ahead. But if they wanted to use noncombat means or to encourage our partners to take action instead of us, then they were out of luck. Put another way, the law did not allow us to use money as a weapon of war, though money could sometimes be more effective than munitions—and far less costly in U.S. dollars and blood. General Pace often commented on the maddening irony that our military officers could fire off hundreds of millions of dollars' worth of munitions and put at risk billions of dollars of equipment—as well as the lives of our service men and women—but they lacked the authority to disburse a few thousand dollars that might be the difference between an operation's success and failure.

Other than begging for international aid, the only way Karzai could raise cash for the government was by collecting customs duties—and at first his government was too weak to exercise control of the borders. This meant he could not secure the country against drug traffickers or Taliban or al Qaida terrorists. Warlords took their own areas' customs duties for themselves. If the central government remained weak, we feared that Afghanistan might fall back into the kind of warlordism that had plagued the country (and proved so exploitable by the Taliban) in the mid-1990s.

But in the half dozen years since he came to power, Karzai has succeeded in extending his government's writ through democratic institutions: an enlightened constitution, a democratic political process, and a multiparty election in which men and women voted in large numbers throughout the country. As President, Karzai took constitutional command of a new U.S.-trained Afghan army that performed reasonably well against opponents of the new democratic order. He revived Afghan schools, allowing girls to receive the education that was denied them by the Taliban. He strengthened ties between his government and ours, as the United States retained high popularity among the Afghan people.

And, miraculous to say, he systematically clipped the wings of the warlords, stripping them over time of their military equipment, fighters, and warlord political power, while opening paths for them to assume official roles in the new Afghanistan. Karzai reduced the warlordism problem—at least for the time being—more than even most optimists thought possible.

Afghanistan was a failed state under the Taliban, and today it remains debilitated from a quarter century of disasters. There is no guarantee that it will not again someday fall backward. But the United States, with the discipline of a smart strategy, helped Karzai give the Afghan people a chance to achieve a degree of unity, order, peace, and freedom. Karzai became more than the mayor of Kabul. Though his government's authority remains incomplete, he became the President of Afghanistan—in both law and fact.

The effort to get the new Afghan government on its feet was of concern to more than the United States. UN officials had done good work in crafting the Afghan Interim Authority and in planning the Bonn Conference, with Zalmay Khalilzad and other U.S. officials. The UN Security Council blessed the resulting Afghan political process and authorized the International Security Assistance Force for Kabul. All this was accomplished harmoniously. And there was no interference with our coalition's military operations against al Qaida and the Taliban.

At a United Nations-sponsored series of donors' conferences for Afghanistan, in early 2002, U.S. officials helped to develop a multilateral strategy for Afghan reconstruction that the Bush Administration embraced. The strategy's big idea was to divide Afghanistan's main requirements into categories and assign each to a "lead nation." Other countries could make contributions supporting the lead nations. The British, for example, agreed to lead the fight against the narcotics trade. The Germans took on the job of training Afghanistan's police. The Italians promised to organize Afghanistan's judicial system. To help eliminate warlordism, United Nations officials would run what was known as a "DDR" program to disarm ("D") and demobilize ("D") warlord militias and reintegrate ("R") their men into civilian life. The Japanese undertook to pay for DDR. In addition to continuing to lead the coalition's fight against al Qaida and the remaining Taliban, the Americans committed to train Afghanistan's new army.

This "lead nation" strategy produced mixed results, but overall it was a failure. The United States moved in fits and starts to create the new army, eventually bringing a capable force into being. And the DDR program, though it took a while, went reasonably well, to the credit of the UN professionals and the Japanese: Nearly all the warlord militias' heavy equipment was collected into cantons. Much was destroyed or made inoperable and the rest was either incorporated into the new Afghan army or put under guard. Most members of the militias were demobilized. Some were absorbed as individuals into the new Afghan military or police forces, and some found other jobs in or out of the government.

But the lead-nation efforts of the British, Germans, and Italians were disappointing. The British performed as energetic, courageous, and valuable allies in Afghanistan in a number of areas, including counterterrorism operations and the ISAF. But as lead nation in the counternarcotics effort, they failed to invest the necessary resources. Having undertaken to train Afghanistan's special counternarcotics police, for instance, the British did not send enough trainers even by their own count. (They did have an excuse—their trainers were special operations forces, busy at the time doing higher-priority tasks, including combat against al Qaida and the Taliban.)The British also failed to send in enough trucks and helicopters for operations against the drug lords. Such equipment was in short supply in their own national arsenal, and they did not find other countries willing to chip in. So they asked us in the Pentagon for equipment, as if the United States was not contributing heavily already in Afghanistan. The British even requested cash from us to buy helicopters. We were not inclined to provide cash (and could not have done so without new legislation), but we did help out with some leased aircraft.

The Germans, too, performed poorly in their assigned task: police training, where they should have excelled. Like the British, they were participating usefully in ISAF and in coalition combat operations.* But Afghanistan needed a comprehensive, nationwide police capability, including patrol officers, leaders, personnel with special skills (like forensics and bomb disposal), trainers, and functioning links between the field offices and the Interior Ministry. It was especially urgent to get some cops onto the street with at least minimal training. At the April 2002 multinational Afghanistan aid conference, Germany was proud to assume the role of lead nation for Afghan police training, but it then focused its efforts

---

*At a meeting in my office, Germany's Ambassador to the United States, Wolfgang Ischinger, made the wistful (if practiced) comment that this was the first time in more than a hundred years that his country's soldiers were actually fighting on the right side of a war.

on the narrowly conceived, long-term task of educating senior officers in multiyear courses—ignoring almost all of Afghanistan's immediate police-related needs.

I urged my State Department colleagues to press Germany to step up to its full responsibilities, but either the Germans resisted our arguments or State did not press them very hard. No other country came forward to take up the slack. In time, the United States wound up shouldering the expense and burden of helping the Afghans create police capabilities. This was not how an international team effort should have worked—but it was not unusual either.

As lead nation for reconstruction of the Afghan judiciary, Italy made the underperforming Germans look good. Italian military forces sacrificed and performed impressively in multiple roles in Afghanistan. But Italy barely lifted a finger to fulfill its judicial reconstruction responsibilities. Without a judicial system, Afghanistan would lack basic law and order and the means to fight its narcotics traffickers. It would not be able to build political stability or a substantial economy.

For well over a year the Italians failed to send to Afghanistan a team of experts; in fact, they did not send a single person. When I raised the problem with Italy's Defense Minister, Antonio Martino—as thoughtful and reliable an ally as one could hope for—he said he would try to help, but judicial matters were not handled by his ministry. So here, too, we turned to our State Department colleagues for help in pressing the Italian government to do its duty. For a long time—years—our complaints produced little action.

State Department officials generally resisted suggestions to pressure Afghan aid donors publicly or privately. They explained that it's often difficult to obtain pledges for multilateral aid projects. If those who are willing to pledge are later embarrassed by American complaints about their subpar performance, they may stop contributing altogether. Our diplomats generally took the view that if another country failed to deliver on an important promise, the United States should simply serve as the default provider.

This became clear early on when a State Department official at a Deputies Committee meeting proposed spending more than $20 million for Afghan police training. It had taken substantial work to identify U.S. funds available to help us train the Afghan army, a commitment we had already undertaken. And we all knew that the U.S. government would need funds to do other important and costly reconstruction tasks in Afghanistan. When I questioned State's $20 million–plus proposal, on the grounds that police training was Germany's obligation, the State official responded that Germany wasn't going to do it, so that was that.

Even before the failures of the lead-nation strategy for Afghanistan became clear, the standard problems of multilateral aid were well known: Only a few countries pledge. The total amount pledged is inadequate. Countries attach unrealistic or in any case unhelpful conditions to their pledges. They pay their pledges slowly, sometimes incompletely, and sometimes not at all. Moreover, the help that donors provide is not guided by a common strategy. There is no one in charge of coordinating the delivery of the help—serving as "general contractor" for the effort. As a result, the different donors often get crosswise, negating one another's efforts.

These problems were not an argument against trying to line up multilateral support for Afghanistan. But we kept them in mind both to maintain realistic expectations and to head off or mitigate whatever problems we could.

In December 2001, when the United Nations had called on countries to contribute forces to ISAF for security in Kabul, the Pentagon leadership was pleased. Rumsfeld saw ISAF as a way to attract more international help for Afghanistan than it was already receiving, and we had been early supporters of the idea.

Rumsfeld thought ISAF had certain features that could appeal to potential donors. It was created by a UN Security Council resolution. It had a limited, peacekeeping (that is, noncombat) mission. It would receive help from the United States, though American troops would not become part of ISAF. This last restriction was important to Rumsfeld. He reasoned that ISAF's contributors would have less incentive to support the effort if they believed the Americans would join the force and the United States would therefore likely be willing to cover any shortfalls.

Rumsfeld agreed, however, to have U.S. forces provide various types of help to the ISAF, such as rapid-reaction rescue if the ISAF found itself *in extremis*. CENTCOM entered into a formal agreement with ISAF to provide such help.

The British had consented to have one of their generals command ISAF for the first six months, until mid-2002. Under their leadership, ISAF was launched respectably, though it was short on resources and hampered by restrictions—known as "caveats"—that some countries had built into the rules of engagement for their troops. Some of these caveats tied forces down to their garrisons, meaning they could not perform patrols. Other caveats prohibited troops from using force except in the most extreme circumstances of self-defense—effectively ordering them to run away when faced with danger. The more restrictive the caveats, the less valuable ISAF would be—and the greater the risk that CENTCOM would get a call to bail it out. In the coming months, U.S. officials prodded the participating countries to accept certain changes that would help make ISAF a success.

Rumsfeld asked often how ISAF was coming along, and we wondered about its prospects. Would ISAF develop the standard problems of multilateral aid, failing to get the resources and the freedom of action it needed? Then, a suggestion came out of UN headquarters that raised the stakes for the fledgling force. The idea was that ISAF, under UN leadership, should expand beyond Kabul and take charge of security in several other large Afghanistan cities. Soon afterward, critics of the Bush Administration started calling for ISAF expansion. The Pentagon in particular was blamed for opposing it.

Assistant Secretary of Defense Peter Rodman passed along to Rumsfeld a State Department report that it was Lakhdar Brahimi, the special envoy to Afghanistan of UN Secretary-General Kofi Annan, who "has been toying with the idea of a UN-led force (4500 strong) to deploy in 5–6 places outside of Kabul as a substitute for ISAF." A few days later, Rodman reported that the idea for expanding ISAF had not been fully developed and Annan had now declared it "off the table." Annan himself apparently recognized how hard it would be to raise and sustain such a force.

Rumsfeld resented that the Pentagon was blamed for opposing ISAF expansion when the Pentagon—meaning Rumsfeld—would have been delighted if other countries contributed enough new resources to ISAF to allow it to operate outside Kabul. On April 10, 2002, he asked me at Roundtable why people thought the Administration—Defense officials in particular—opposed ISAF expansion. I ventured that our political opponents, who portrayed us as mindless opponents of "multilateralism," probably just assumed we did. He responded that the Defense Department shouldn't oppose ISAF expansion "if others want to provide men and money."

It soon became clear, however, that our critics wanted the United States to support the expansion *by providing U.S. forces and funds to make it possible.* This reflected the very frame of mind that Rumsfeld warned against: the Yankee can-do, fill-every-vacuum hyperactivity that deprives other countries of incentives to pull their weight in multilateral projects. If the United States wanted to increase security in an area of Afghanistan using U.S. soldiers and money, we could do it through the multinational coalition we were already leading. One of ISAF's key purposes was to allow others in the world to help the new Afghanistan. Rumsfeld did not favor reflagging U.S. operations—having our soldiers perform a mission and calling it an ISAF rather than a coalition effort—simply to make ISAF look robust. He told me he wanted ISAF to be useful, look successful, and take on more responsibility if it could, but as a serious partner, not functioning on the cheap. We were by no means mindless opponents of multilateralism. But we did not support mindless multilateralism either.

It was not only our military commanders who needed to be able to use noncombat means in the war on terrorism. Civilian agencies of our government, especially the State Department, had key roles to play in such fields as reconstruction and stability operations and countering extremist ideology. But State had no office responsible for such operations. State had a "public diplomacy" office, but no battle-of-ideas strategy for the whole government. It was not leading an interagency effort to fight that battle—and had not requested or received the funds to do so.

There was a grotesque imbalance between the funds Defense had for the war on terrorism and those appropriated to State to fight the ideological battle. The Secretary of Defense made more noise about this gap than the Secretary of State. It was Rumsfeld who time and again commented that it was far more expensive to capture or kill terrorists than to prevent young people from becoming murderous enemies to begin with.* To fund its efforts to counter jihadist extremism, State received less than one-five-thousandth of the amount that Congress appropriated annually to Defense.

At the time of the 9/11 attack, the U.S. government was not set up to fight this new war flexibly and well. Our institutions and laws did not provide adequate resources for efforts to counter enemy ideology. And the bureaucracy was underequipped and poorly organized for strategically important stability and reconstruction operations.

The latter problem had hindered our government for decades. Our institutions and laws have not allowed us to conduct such operations efficiently—not after World War II, or in Vietnam, Somalia, Haiti, Bosnia, Kosovo, or anywhere else. It was a problem in Afghanistan, and it would become one in Iraq.

The Bush Administration began to address the problem institution-

---

*Secretary of Defense Robert Gates focused on this issue in a recent speech:

Funding for nonmilitary foreign affairs programs has increased since 2001, but it remains disproportionately small relative to what we spend on the military and to the importance of such capabilities. . . . What is clear to me is that there is a need for a dramatic increase in spending on the civilian instruments of national security—diplomacy, strategic communications, foreign assistance, civic action, and economic reconstruction and development.

Robert M. Gates, Landon Lecture, Kansas State University, November 26, 2007, available at http://www.defenselink.mil/speeches/speech.aspx?speechid=1199.

ally. It obtained from Congress greater flexibility for military commanders. It got new laws enacted to increase Defense Department train-and-equip authority and to launch the President's Global Peace Operations Initiative. And it created a new stabilization and reconstruction office in the State Department. But more needs to be done.

By December 2001, U.S. forces in Afghanistan had begun to hold prisoners—Taliban and al Qaida fighters, either captured by our soldiers or turned over by the Northern Alliance. CENTCOM was eager for the Pentagon to establish an out-of-theater institution to take on the burden of detention and the responsibility of interrogation.

To prevent the next 9/11, U.S. officials needed intelligence on the organizations and plans of jihadist terrorists, and the most promising source of intelligence was the terrorists already captured. In a conventional war, there are many ways to obtain information on enemy strengths, weaknesses, and strategy. During the Cold War, U.S. spy satellites could monitor the Soviet Union's western military districts for signs that armored divisions were readying to deploy. But terrorist activity presents few "signatures" for detection by technical means. The key to discovering terrorist locations, capabilities, and designs was human intelligence. And until U.S. intelligence could penetrate terrorist networks, this meant capturing and questioning individual terrorists who had that knowledge.

These were enemy fighters caught on the battlefield, not criminal defendants: The legal basis for holding them was their role as part of an enemy force at war with the United States. The purposes of detention were interrogation and—as with German or Japanese prisoners of war in World War II—keeping them off the battlefield while the war continued. If the U.S. government wanted to *punish* them, it would have to prosecute them under criminal statutes—and presumption of innocence and other procedural protections would apply. But enemy fighters detained during a war have not usually been prosecuted for crimes, and their detention is not for punishment. They are held simply to keep them from returning to the battlefield.

One of the first questions that arose was where to house several hundred CENTCOM detainees. The facility would have to be reasonably remote, to make escape or terrorist attack difficult. And government lawyers argued that a facility on non-U.S.-owned territory would likely not be subject to habeas corpus petitions by the detainees.* President Bush

---

*The U.S. Supreme Court eventually held that detainees have habeus corpus rights even if held at Guantanemo Bay, Cuba. See *Hamdi v. Rumsfeld,* 542 U.S. 507 (2004).

ultimately selected the U.S. naval base at Guantanamo Bay, Cuba, as the best available location.

Rumsfeld was displeased to have the Defense Department take on the detention mission and protested the idea repeatedly. But he knew that intelligence from these detainees could help save lives. We could not count on any other country to perform the mission—and no other agency of the U.S. government was ready to do it. So Rumsfeld accepted the task, though he told his staff from the outset that the responsibility would be a source of more trouble and more criticism than anyone could predict. It proved every bit as bad as he anticipated.

In the first months of 2002, the U.S. Southern Command prepared a plan for the construction of the Guantanamo detention facility. General Pace presented the plan to Rumsfeld at a meeting I attended. It showed a facility to house more than two thousand prisoners. Rumsfeld objected that this was far too large. Complaining that he didn't want to be the "world's jailer," he explained how bureaucracy worked. The United States, he insisted, should not be holding anyone we did not absolutely need to hold. But if we built a prison for two thousand people, the military "system" could be expected to fill it. Rumsfeld wanted to have limited holding capacity, so that commanders would feel pressure to release anyone they did not have strong reasons to detain.

Pace found himself the man in the middle over the next few weeks, as Rumsfeld issued repeated orders to the Southern Command to cut back its construction plans. A frustrated CENTCOM was unable to hand off its detainee burden until Pace finally obtained Rumsfeld's approval of a new Guantanamo plan, to house approximately four hundred detainees.

Aside from the size of the facility, which was an internal Defense Department matter, another major issue was the legal status of these prisoners—a matter that ultimately rested with the President. Early interagency discussions among lawyers clarified that the 1949 Geneva Conventions on the laws of war applied to conflicts between "High Contracting Parties" to the Conventions—and al Qaida was *not* such a party. I heard no one argue that the Conventions, as a matter of law, applied to America's new conflict with al Qaida, or that they governed U.S. detention of the al Qaida prisoners taken in Afghanistan or anywhere else. (Iraq, on the other hand, was a party to the Geneva Conventions. Accordingly, I never heard any U.S. official question the fact that the Conventions applied to Iraqi detainees.)

Taliban prisoners were another matter, however. In attacking the Taliban, the coalition was fighting a war against Afghanistan, which *was* a party to the Geneva Conventions. Nevertheless, some lawyers at the Justice Department, White House, and Pentagon believed that the United States should not apply the Conventions to its conflict with the Taliban. Their rationale was that Afghanistan was a failed state, not a normal sovereign country: The Taliban should be deemed an armed gang engaged in a civil war, and not a proper government.

The President scheduled a meeting with his National Security Council on February 4, 2002, to discuss detainees in Afghanistan. The issues were: first, whether the Geneva Conventions applied to the U.S. war with the Taliban; and, second, what standard of treatment U.S. forces should apply to Taliban prisoners. Rumsfeld asked me to review the subject with him. Drawing on my work on the Conventions during the Reagan Administration, I viewed this issue as an important matter of principle.

When I arrived in Rumsfeld's reception area a few minutes before our meeting, General Myers was already there. The United States, he told me sharply, should not be looking for a way to "weasel out" of applying the Conventions. As a rule, Myers was congenial and even-tempered, but now he spoke with an extraordinary intensity. In our six months working together, it was the first time I glimpsed the fighter-pilot steel beneath the general's good-natured manner. As an assistant beckoned us into Rumsfeld's office, Myers turned and pointed his finger at me. "I want you to know," he warned, "I feel very strongly about this, and if Rumsfeld"—I noted the unprecedented omission of the Secretary's title—"doesn't defend the Geneva Conventions, I'll contradict him in front of the President!"

As we walked together into the Secretary's office, I had only a moment to reply that I agreed with him. The answer clearly surprised him. I had a reputation as a critic of various arms control and other treaties, and he must have assumed I would knock the Geneva Conventions too. But I supported treaties that I believed served the national interest, and Geneva qualified.

Rumsfeld met us in front of his desk, and we talked standing up. He must have read Myers's body language as aggressive, because he immediately went on offense—hitting the general with a battery of legal and historical questions about the Geneva Conventions. Rumsfeld wasn't arguing either for or against applying the Conventions to the war on terrorism. He just seemed determined to neutralize whatever push Myers had planned on the subject.

With this preliminary head-butting out of the way, I intervened to field Rumsfeld's prosecutorial interrogatories. The question for the upcoming National Security Council meeting was phrased in terms of whether the United States should or should not "apply" the Geneva Conventions. Given that Rumsfeld liked to cite the U.S. Constitution and often lectured his subordinates on scrupulous obedience to the law, I got his attention by pointing out that *the Conventions were a treaty in force*. Therefore, under the Constitution, they had the same status as a statute. They were not a mere recommendation, like a UN General Assembly resolution, but part of the "supreme Law of the Land." Compliance was *mandatory*, not optional.

I argued that the Geneva Conventions were law that served U.S. interests—and especially the interests of our military. Rumsfeld knew I was no uncritical admirer of U.S. treaties, so he listened rather patiently. Myers reinforced the point about our military's interests: We teach our service members to respect the Geneva Conventions, as the "gold standard"—a key part of our military culture.

I walked Rumsfeld through the options being presented to the President. Because the war on terrorism was an unprecedented conflict, with features not squarely addressed in the Conventions, the President faced difficult problems of interpretation. I supported Myers's view that our government should not be striving to "weasel out" of acknowledging that the Conventions applied to the war in Afghanistan. Rather, the President should interpret the Conventions so as to promote worldwide respect for them. Even if the lawyers insist that the Conventions did not clearly govern the Taliban *as a matter of law*, the President (I recommended) should nevertheless apply them *as a matter of policy*, pending further study.

My presentation to Rumsfeld also highlighted a point that many people, inside and outside the government, failed to grasp: Deciding that the Conventions governed the war with the Taliban was not the same thing as deciding that Taliban detainees were entitled to prisoner-of-war (POW) status. The Conventions grant such status *only* to those fighters who operate overtly, who respect the interests of noncombatants by wearing recognizable uniforms and carrying arms openly, who fight under a chain of command, and who obey the laws of war. The Conventions distinguish in effect between lawful and unlawful combatants (without using those labels)—and they establish POW privileges as a kind of incentive, a reward for operating as lawful combatants. The Taliban fighters did not operate overtly or obey the laws of war. U.S. Taliban detainees therefore were not legally entitled to POW status, even though the Conventions governed our conflict with the Afghan regime.

Rumsfeld said he wanted me to come to the February 4 National Security Council meeting to present these points. I wrote up some talking points for Rumsfeld, Myers, and me, which Myers was happy to approve. That paper emphasized the Defense Department's interest in the Conventions, summarized as follows. (I focused on the Third Geneva Convention, as most relevant.)

- **The Convention is a good treaty.**
- **One could quibble about details, but the Convention is a sensible document that requires its parties to treat prisoners of war the way we want our captured military personnel treated.**
- **U.S. armed forces are trained to treat captured enemy forces according to the Convention.**
- **This training is an essential element of U.S. military culture. It is morally important, crucial to U.S. morale.**
- **It is also practically important, for it makes U.S. forces the gold standard in the world, facilitating our winning cooperation from other countries.**

Our own armed forces would be more likely to get the benefits of the Convention if it were "applied universally," I argued. It would be "highly dangerous if countries make application of Convention hinge on subjective or moral judgments as to the quality or decency of the enemy's government"—and it would be dangerous, therefore, to claim that the Convention does not apply because the Taliban are "the illegitimate government of a 'failed state.' " Countries typically view their enemies as gangs of criminals. If officials had to certify an enemy as a "legitimate government" to apply the Convention, few countries would ever do so.

I contended that a "pro-Convention" position, on the other hand, would reinforce U.S. moral arguments in the war on terrorism:

- **The essence of the Convention is the distinction between soldiers and civilians (i.e., between combatants and noncombatants).**
- **Terrorists are reprehensible precisely because they negate that distinction, by purposefully targeting civilians.**
- **The Convention aims to protect civilians by requiring soldiers to wear uniforms and otherwise distinguish themselves from civilians.**
- **The Convention creates an incentive system for good behavior. The key incentive is that soldiers who play by the rules get POW status if they are captured.**

I recommended that our government stress "[h]umane treatment for all detainees," and that al Qaida as well as Taliban personnel should receive the treatment they are entitled to under the Convention—or that they would be entitled to, if the Convention governed our conflict with them.

As none of the detainees qualified legally for prisoner-of-war status, I believed that humane treatment was the proper standard for *all* of them—

whether or not they had been captured in a war governed by the Convention. Even if the President were unwilling to conclude that the Convention governed our fight against the Taliban, I recommended that he make the following declaration: Although U.S. officials have not yet resolved the question of whether we are legally required to do so, the United States would give *all* detainees the status that they would be entitled to under the Convention—in other words, humane treatment.

At the February 4 meeting, Rice began the discussion with this same point. She observed that the legal question of the Convention's applicability was "not of practical effect" because we would in all events treat all detainees "in accordance with the principles of the Geneva Convention." Rumsfeld asked me to make my case. I did—with Myers's reinforcement.

Attorney General John Ashcroft said that the main problem with applying the Geneva Convention is that it could preclude effective interrogations. I assumed he was referring to the rule that a detainee *who is entitled to prisoner-of-war status* cannot lawfully even be cajoled—let alone pressured—into answering questions. It would violate the Convention, for example, to tell a prisoner that he would get a special benefit or treat if he answered a particular question. As I saw it, this was not a problem. The Taliban detainees did not qualify for prisoner-of-war status—even if the President were to decide that the Convention applied to them.

Ashcroft then explained the legal theory for declaring that the Convention did *not* apply to our war with the Taliban. The theory rested on characterizing the Taliban regime as a less-than-legitimate government. He argued that the United States could say that the Taliban and al Qaida are a "coalition of pirates," so our war was not an international conflict governed by the Convention. As I saw it, Ashcroft was making the type of mistake that was common when lawyers operated at the intersection of legal and policy considerations. He identified his mission as supporting maximum freedom of action for his client, the President. In doing so, however, he gave inadequate weight to the broader policy implications of making the government appear disrespectful of the Geneva Conventions.

But President Bush had apparently absorbed our reasoning: With two brief questions, he punctured the illegitimate-Taliban-government theory. "Would you apply the Convention to Iraq?" he asked the Attorney General. "Yes," Ashcroft responded. "But you can say that Saddam is a pirate too," the President remarked. That ended the argument. The Justice Department's theory clearly went too far.

The President resolved the matter well. On February 7, 2002, White House press secretary Ari Fleischer announced the President's position on the Third Geneva Convention. President Bush had determined that the

Convention governed the U.S. conflict with the Taliban in Afghanistan, but it did not govern our worldwide conflict with al Qaida. He decided that U.S.-held Taliban detainees were not entitled to prisoner-of-war status because they did not meet the conditions set in the Convention—but they would receive humane treatment. The al Qaida detainees would also receive humane treatment. Fleischer's announcement concluded: "The Convention remains as important today as it was the day it was signed, and the United States is proud of its fifty-year history in compliance with the Convention."

Rumsfeld's unease in being put in charge of detainee operations was well grounded. The responsibility would bring with it a series of serious problems. The Pentagon's leadership appreciated the importance of honoring the Geneva Conventions, but issues arose time and again that required the very difficult balancing of weighty but competing interests: on interrogation methods,* on transferring detainees to their home countries, and on whether to prosecute individuals as criminals or simply continue to hold them as enemy combatants. And, apart from the policy dilemmas, there was the potential for abusive treatment that would materialize so disgustingly at Abu Ghraib. Despite Rumsfeld's astute forebodings about becoming the world's jailer, he was not able to head the problems off.

Among the key changes we made at Defense in response to 9/11 were the creation of the Colorado-based Northern Command in late 2002 to serve as the department's military organization for homeland defense, and the establishment, a few months later, of a Pentagon-based counterpart civilian organization: the office of the Assistant Secretary of Defense for Homeland Defense.

That Assistant Secretary reported to me. The job's first incumbent was a former Democratic three-term congressman from Pennsylvania, Paul McHale, who looked more like an owlish lawyer than a Marine Corps

---

*Al Qaida personnel had been trained to resist standard questioning techniques, and some of these detainees were believed to have important intelligence. The Southern Command therefore requested permission to try some techniques that went beyond the Army Field Manual but were still within the bounds of U.S. and international law—for example, requiring detainees to stand for up to four hours at a time while being questioned. When some military department lawyers questioned the legality of those additional techniques, Rumsfeld revoked his approval and asked for a Department-wide legal review. The review produced a report in April 2003 that unanimously endorsed some of the techniques and reported disagreement on others. Rumsfeld authorized the unanimously endorsed techniques and rejected *all* of the legally contested ones.

warrior, though he was both. His office helped plan security for major events like the Salt Lake City Olympic Games and the summit meeting of the eight heads of the world's industrialized powers. It linked Defense to the Homeland Security Department and to state and local officials. And it produced the department's homeland defense strategy.

One of McHale's more complex duties was a post-9/11 reconsideration of how U.S. military forces should operate to protect the United States within our borders. Their missions and rules of engagement necessarily differed in a domestic setting. Deciding when and how military forces should operate at home was a delicate matter of democratic statecraft.

The Departments of Justice and of Homeland Security shared the main responsibilities for preventing terrorism within the United States. Rumsfeld complained that there was too little public discussion of the way terrorism-related duties were assigned in our government. If another major terrorist attack occurred, Rumsfeld expected that Congress, and perhaps the President, would insist on our military's taking on key tasks at home—perhaps airport security, border security, and other counterterrorist operations on American soil. The Defense Department could be held responsible for preventive action against domestic threats that our military forces—for long-standing, sound, civil-liberties-related reasons—were not set up to undertake.

In a healthy, free society, domestic security is the job of law enforcement and other civilian officials, who are schooled to operate within constitutional constraints. The military's attention, by and large, is directed outward. Rumsfeld wanted McHale to push civilian officials across the country—federal, state, and local—to help ensure that they could play their proper role in securing the homeland. At the same time, the Secretary recognized that American citizens, paying nearly a half trillion dollars a year for our armed forces, would expect those forces to contribute substantially to homeland defense. McHale's job was to help get the balance right, and his combination of military, legal, and congressional perspectives suited him well for the task.

I saw it as admirable that the Pentagon's leadership was worried about what would happen if a series of terrorist attacks seemed to turn our country into a war zone. What if such attacks convinced the American public that their security could be ensured only by sacrificing important freedoms in favor of an increased military presence at home? This was one of the more profound dangers that terrorism posed to our way of life. It underlined the importance of disrupting and attacking terrorist networks abroad and beefing up at home the capabilities of police, intelligence, and other nonmilitary security institutions.

In his January 29, 2002, State of the Union address President Bush elaborated on points he had made a few months earlier, in his September 20, 2001, address to Congress. In that short period of time, his Administration had engineered the overthrow of the Taliban regime, the expulsion of al Qaida from its Afghan safe haven, and the creation of an Afghan interim authority under Karzai. Reiterating that the war on terrorism was a global fight that would not end quickly, the President focused special attention on those state supporters of terrorism with records of pursuing (or using) chemical, biological, and nuclear weapons. (Given the later controversy about prewar intelligence on Iraq, it's worth noting that Bush spoke accurately about Iraq's WMD programs. He did not refer to the WMD *stockpiles* that U.S. intelligence officials were incorrectly predicting we would find in Iraq.)

At the end of the speech, Bush touched on what he described as universal aspirations for "liberty and justice" and declared that "we will demonstrate that the forces of terror cannot stop the momentum of freedom." With these comments, he was recognizing that the war was about more than just capturing and killing terrorists; it was also about people's aspirations and thoughts about justice. But this was little more than an allusion to what we in the Pentagon called the "battle of ideas" in the war on terrorism. I thought the subject deserved more prominence and more careful discussion—a deficiency that reflected the relatively scant attention the Administration gave to the ideological aspect of the war.

Rumsfeld, Wolfowitz, Myers, Pace, and I often discussed the crucial importance of information and influence operations—a subject we raised also in interagency meetings. Rumsfeld was critical of any discussion that overemphasized the military dimension and understated the significance of our enemies' beliefs, ambitions, and ideological frame of mind. Ideas were an important element in recruiting young people into their ranks.

At Defense, the more we thought about our strategy for the war, the clearer it became that ideas—information, influence, ideology—could contribute decisively to our ultimate success, even more than military, intelligence, or police actions could. In this, our thinking heeded the warnings of the Sultan of Oman, who had shared his insights into Islamist extremism with Rumsfeld and me during our memorable October visit to his tent. But the Defense Department did not have the lead in this field. I agreed with Rumsfeld and Wolfowitz that someone at State or perhaps the White House should seize the responsibility of designing a government-wide campaign to use all available tools to undermine the appeal of our enemies' extremism. There was recent, and honorable, precedent: During the Cold War, many U.S. officials understood the centrality of ideological warfare, and they organized and marshaled resources to conduct it. The war on terrorism gave the U.S. government an urgent interest in doing that again.

There were numerous interagency meetings on how we should fight the ideological part of the war, but these discussions produced little valuable action. Colleagues from State would show off glossy brochures depicting happy Muslims practicing their religion and living comfortably in the United States. The discussions were devoted to refining the points we wanted to make to the Muslim world: *This is not a war against Islam. America is good to its Muslim citizens. U.S. military forces have fought on behalf of Muslims in the Gulf War, Somalia, Bosnia, Kosovo, and Afghanistan, all in the last dozen years.*

Those messages were true, and State officials wanted to get them into a form in which they could be circulated successfully. And it was important to polish the language so that our diplomats wouldn't confuse terms like "Islamic" (a reference to the religion) and "Islamist" (a reference to a political viewpoint or movement). But in my view, writing up themes for official talking points didn't get to the heart of the matter.

At these meetings, I argued that the dialogue of greatest strategic importance was not the one between America and the Muslim world, but the one *within* the Muslim world. The key question wasn't what U.S. officials should say, but what we could do to encourage Muslims to speak openly against the extremists' views and to make extremist ideology less attractive.

Immediately after 9/11, President Bush had emphasized in his public statements and inside the government that the United States was in no way at war with the religion of Islam. The extremist ideology we were fighting was that of an international network—in the nature of a political movement—that selectively used Islamic ideas and vocabulary to put itself at war, not only with all non-Muslims, but with virtually all Muslims, too.

Extremists like Usama bin Laden draw on Islamic literature and religious concepts, including the duty to wage *jihad* ("holy struggle," a term the extremists interpret in a militant fashion) and the requirement to kill apostates. They use these elements to brew an intense, resentful, accusatory, and violent ideology with the power to intoxicate and exhilarate Muslims in numerous countries and in various social and economic conditions.

What these extremists preach transcends even the program of Islamists, who promote a political Islam emphasizing that a proper life can be lived only if Muslims exercise political control over their communities and apply *sharia* (Muslim law). Some scholars term the violent extremists "jihadists" to distinguish them from the political Islamists. These jihadists insist that each Muslim has a personal duty to fight to establish proper Muslim government in this world by killing Islam's enemies. They define these enemies as the current political leadership throughout the Muslim world, whom they condemn to death for apostasy, as well as the non-Muslims they deem opponents of Islam, especially Jews and Americans.

The jihadists' writings make a special point of condemning democracy. Democracy's foundation stone is the sovereignty of the citizenry, which the extremists view as an attack on their most basic article of faith: the sovereignty of God.

In the days after 9/11, Rumsfeld and Myers returned time and again to the subject of strategic communications and influence operations, often referring back to the Sultan's ideas. Consulting over weeks with Wolfowitz, Pace, and my Policy organization colleagues, I considered ways that the Administration could organize such a campaign.

It was clear that our government needed, first of all, a better understanding of the ideological battlefield: Who were (or might become) the most influential voices in the Muslim world to oppose jihadist violence? We needed a strategy that would help us find the clerics, journalists, educators, and politicians throughout the Muslim world—from Jordan to Pakistan to Indonesia—who are opposed to terrorist violence, and to find ways to amplify these moderate voices. We should help them to find money and to improve their ability to communicate their messages, through print, broadcast, and the Internet.

This was an opportunity for our government to cooperate with the private sector. Universities, charitable foundations, humanitarian groups, and other nongovernmental organizations could serve the national interest by promoting moderation in the Muslim world. They could promote humane education, sound economic policies, and political reform in key countries, with more credibility and flexibility than our government could. The 9/11 attack had produced a sense of community across America, and we assumed that private groups would be willing to talk with us and become part of an international campaign against suicide bombings and other terrorism. The key would be to make clear that the government had no intention to control those groups' actions or compromise their independence.

The strategy would also have to counter the proponents of terrorist violence who preached that it was permissible and even obligatory for good Muslims. This might mean interdicting their funding. It might involve police or intelligence activity. Or it could involve an information operation—for example, publicizing truthful information about personal corruption.

The strategy would require many parts, public and private, U.S. and foreign. But no one took charge of this project for the U.S. government. State did not strategize a government-wide campaign or assemble a team, preferring to focus on such public-diplomacy activity as distributing U.S. government messages to Muslim audiences abroad. Hence, the glossy brochures.

Evidently, neither Powell nor Armitage saw the philosophical dimension of the war as particularly important. This was consistent with their general lack of interest in what they called "ideology." As jealous as Powell and Armitage always were of their department's "turf," they chose to forgo this important interagency project that State should have captained and failed to use the turf they so vigorously protected.

State Department officials would often comment on these issues by arguing that nothing of importance could be done to push back against jihadist extremism until we resolved terrorism's "root causes"—defined as economic despair and the Arab-Israeli conflict. Leading students of terrorism doubt that those are in fact root causes of jihadist violence, pointing out that Muslim terrorists are not often drawn from the ranks of the poor, and that the Palestinian issue was for many years marginal to al Qaida propaganda.* As I saw it, curing poverty and solving the Arab-Israeli conflict were worthy goals even aside from the war on terrorism, and the U.S. government would pursue them in any event. But in practice such talk of "root causes" tended to produce paralysis rather than motivate action against terrorist extremist ideology.†

Paralysis was not what was called for in the weeks and months following 9/11. Victory for us in the longer term would require fighting the ideas that our enemies used to recruit and indoctrinate new terrorists. So it was

---

*"The leadership and the largest cluster of the jihad . . . come principally from the upper and middle class. . . . [A]bout three-fourths of global Salafi mujahedin were solidly upper or middle class, refuting the argument that terrorism arises from poverty." Marc Sageman, *Understanding Terrorist Networks* (Philadelphia: University of Pennsylvania Press, 2004), pp. 73–74.

On the Palestine issue in al Qaida literature, see Usama bin Laden, "Declaration of War against the Americans Occupying the Land of the Two Holy Places," originally published in *al-Quds al-Arabi* (London), August 23, 1999; available at: http://www.pbs.org/newshour/terrorism/international/fatwa_1996.html.

†In interagency meetings, I got the impression that State officials sometimes pushed the root-causes argument as an ironic way of twitting the President for not plunging personally into Middle East peace diplomacy as Clinton and Carter had done.

unconstructive, to say the least, to give up on fighting terrorist ideology until we had cured world poverty or solved the Palestine problem—goals we could hardly count on reaching soon, if ever.

Rather than leave such an important task neglected, I made an effort within my Pentagon office to fill the gap by creating a new organization that became known as the Office of Strategic Influence. Its brief history is a case study in turf warfare, showing how bureaucratic infighting of little apparent significance can cause substantial and enduring harm to the national interest.

Because Rumsfeld and Myers assigned such high importance to information and influence, I knew I would need some people to work full-time on these matters. The Pentagon's Public Affairs office could not handle every aspect of the communications effort: Its main mission was reactive, fielding questions and getting answers for (generally U.S.-based) journalists. Similarly, the State Department's Public Diplomacy office was responsible for public affairs and related work directed at foreign audiences. Neither office was equipped to promote initiatives to fight jihadist ideology—for example, programs to improve other countries' schools, or increasing the audience for moderate Muslim leaders. A proper information or influence strategy would include some public affairs and public diplomacy work, but also go well beyond it.

In late October 2001, I organized my new information-policy team within the office of Robert Andrews, the (acting) Assistant Secretary of Defense, who already had responsibility for overseeing "psy-op" (the military's psychological operations to influence enemy attitudes and actions). The Office of Strategic Influence (OSI), as it was titled, had several purposes: First, to develop strategies against jihadist ideology. Second, to coordinate information-related work of the Defense Department—civilian and military.* And third, to represent the Policy organization in interagency meetings on information policy. I recruited Air Force Brigadier General Simon P. "Pete" Worden to run the new organization. A rocket scientist,

*Many Defense offices had responsibilities regarding means of communication, such as allocating funds to buy radio and television transmitters for the combatant commands or investing in jamming technologies. Many other offices worked on messages—public affairs items for the American people, support for State's public diplomacy efforts, CENTCOM's "psychological operations" broadcasts (to encourage surrender by Taliban forces, for example), and CENTCOM's public-service-type leaflets (to warn Afghan civilians to stay clear of unexploded ordnance, for example).

Worden brought to the task a creative intellect, technical know-how, and drive.

From the outset, however, OSI found itself at loggerheads with Victoria "Torie" Clarke, Assistant Secretary of Defense for Public Affairs. Clarke insisted that her office was in charge of all "outreach" by the Defense Department, and she complained that OSI was encroaching on her office's duties. She insisted that OSI's plans be sent to her for approval, which she sometimes withheld, without suggesting a way to resolve the impasse. Although I agreed to coordinate all of OSI's projects with her, she was not mollified.

Clarke also raised a more fundamental objection: OSI was supposed to give policy guidance not only to military personnel engaged in information operations and "psy-op," but also to public affairs officers. Clarke feared that putting both of these information-related responsibilities into one Policy office ran the risk of damaging her office's credibility. Though she often stated her case antagonistically, I thought she had a point.

A debate over how to organize the Department's information-related offices had been brewing since long before OSI and 9/11. Policy officials wanted, sensibly, to coordinate work among the offices in order to prevent Defense's many information-related efforts from undercutting one another because the right hand was unaware of what the left hand was doing. On the other hand, Clarke and her fellow public affairs officers wanted, reasonably, to maximize their credibility by insulating themselves from other activities of the Department—especially military activities relating to psychological operations and military deception of the enemy. I thought it was possible to find a way to balance these concerns.

Rumsfeld was pleased that OSI was up and running quickly, though we were still trying to refine its charter to satisfy Clarke and others. Five days after OSI was established Rumsfeld approved its first project, and about a week later he visited OSI's offices and approved the concept for its first major information campaign.

One example of OSI's creative thinking was a project to give the Pakistani government technology that could improve public education in regions where extremist religious schools (*madrassas*) were dominant. Worden considered providing inexpensive satellite radios for remote regions. He envisioned creating kiosks featuring "Internet in a box," a laptop computer to give local populations access to language lessons, literature, and news media from throughout the world.* These initiatives would serve

---

*In late 2006, the *New York Times* reported that a not-for-profit U.S. organization had entered into an agreement with the government of Libya to provide that country's

the strategic purpose of helping Pakistan's government educate its people for productivity in the world's economy. This was not a matter of public affairs or public diplomacy. It was a way to use communication technology to oppose the influence of jihadist groups.

In early 2002, I was hoping to resolve Clarke's concerns about OSI. But the charter for the office was still in draft when OSI took what turned out to be a fatal hit on the front page of the *New York Times.* A February 19 article, citing unnamed "military officials," claimed that the "Pentagon is developing plans to provide news items, *possibly even false ones,* to foreign media organizations as part of a new effort to influence public sentiment and policy makers in both friendly and unfriendly countries." The story continued: "The plans, which have not received final approval from the Bush administration, have stirred opposition among some Pentagon officials who say they might undermine the credibility of information . . . [from] the Department's public affairs officers." After recounting the story of OSI's creation, the *Times* quoted unnamed Pentagon officials as saying that "General Worden envisions a broad mission ranging from 'black' campaigns that use disinformation and other covert activities to 'white' public affairs that rely on truthful news releases." Unnamed senior officials were said to have questioned whether OSI's mission "is too broad and possibly even illegal."*

The accusations that OSI contemplated spreading false news items and disinformation were untrue. But in the asymmetric warfare of bureaucratic leaking, officials who talk to journalists "on background" have a decisive advantage over officials who have to reply on the record.

The *Times* story became a sensation. Journalists and editorial writers around the world instantly turned it into fodder for their front and editorial

---

1.2 million schoolchildren "a wireless-connected laptop that will cost about $100." General Worden had developed a variant of that idea in late 2001 as one of his office's first initiatives. See John Markoff, "U.S. Group Reaches Deal to Provide Laptops to All Libyan Schoolchildren," *New York Times,* October 11, 2006, p. A14.

*The *Times* article asserted that "administration officials worried that the United States was losing support in the Islamic world after American warplanes began bombing Afghanistan in October [2001]" and that those concerns "spurred the creation" of OSI. The *Times* highlighted General Myers's interest in having the Pentagon "broaden its efforts to influence foreign audiences." Myers told the *Times* what he had repeatedly said in Roundtable meetings: "Perhaps the most challenging piece of this is putting together what we call a strategic influence campaign quickly and with the right emphasis. That's everything from psychological operations to the public affairs piece to coordinating partners in this effort with us." James Dao and Eric Schmitt, "A Nation Challenged: Hearts and Minds; Pentagon Readies Efforts to Sway Sentiment Abroad," *New York Times,* February 19, 2002, p. A1.

pages and radio and television shows. As it reverberated, the accusations against OSI were often embellished. The tawdry recklessness of this inflationary process led to comments like those of cable television talk show host Chris Matthews, who announced: "The Pentagon has created a new Office of Strategic Influence which plans to put out false news stories to the world's newspapers. This plan, *worthy of Joseph Goebbels* . . ." Goebbels, of course, was the Nazi propaganda chief in the 1930s and '40s.

Note how Matthews took the *Times*'s lead sentence—that the Pentagon was "developing plans to provide [to foreign media] news items, *possibly* even false ones"—and turned it into a flat-out assertion that OSI "plans to put out false news stories." Even the *Times*'s milder words were wrong, but what Matthews said was chutzpah on stilts. "Possibly" was an important qualifier in the *Times* article, so Matthews had to know he was misstating the report. In invoking Goebbels he was making a Goebbels-like attack of his own.

Worden flatly refuted the essence of the story—OSI's alleged intention to put out false information to mislead journalists and the public. I considered issuing an immediate denial to try to nip the scandal early, but I knew that a hasty statement ran the risk of aggravating the problem. The accusations required my office to prove a negative—to confirm that *no one* in OSI had ever proposed lying or disinformation. If I went on the record before marshaling all the facts, a reporter might produce a memo or briefing slide I had never seen, suggesting that someone at some level in OSI had in fact considered lying to the press. The Department then would be damned for lying about lying.

I met with my staff on the best way to proceed. We agreed that I should ask for Defense Department attorneys to do an official review of OSI's files. We rushed to define the assignment, persuade the General Counsel's office to do it, and submit all the relevant documents. The lawyers wrote up their findings. It was a frustrating process: A toxic, anonymous accusation could be made in the blink of an eye, creating outrage around the world—but it took weeks to do the meticulous work needed for an unqualified denial.

That work was eventually completed, and the results vindicated OSI entirely. In response to questions from Senator Carl Levin, Chairman of the Armed Services Committee, the Office of the General Counsel reported that its attorneys had reviewed all documents pertaining to all of OSI's campaigns, operations, and programs that had been submitted for senior-level review and approval, and found no evidence to support the *Times*'s allegations. "None of these proposals mentions the word 'disinformation'. Moreover, none of these proposals includes language that suggests, directly or indirectly that [OSI] had engaged in, was planning to engage in, or was seeking approval to engage in disinformation activities." They also reviewed the documents *internal* to OSI that "were never staffed for further review." One of these, they found, did use the word "disinformation"—but in the context of "controlling or denying an enemy his ability to carry out his [*the enemy's*] disinformation activities." In short, the report concluded, "There is no reference, direct or indirect, to any U.S. disinformation effort."

But all the while the lawyers were combing through those files, thousands of press stories were spreading the accusations. Television commentary accused us of being Nazis, providing grist for political cartoonists and late-night television hosts.

Rumsfeld had affirmed, the day after the *Times* story, "The Pentagon is not issuing disinformation to the foreign press or any press." And at a meeting with a group of journalists, I pledged: "We have an enormous stake in our credibility and we're going to preserve it. . . . We are not going to have Defense Department officials lying to the public, neither the foreign public, nor the domestic public, nor to the press." But neither Rumsfeld nor I could offer a point-blank denial of the OSI accusations until the lawyers finished their review. Meanwhile, the President was hit with questions about OSI while traveling overseas. He was displeased to have to defend his honesty.

At the height of the story, I had a several-day trip overseas. On my return, Rumsfeld and I met alone in his office. The Pentagon and White House public affairs offices were reporting that the OSI furor was intensifying, and the Secretary wanted to know how we were going to put an end to the story. Leaning on his stand-up desk and squeezing a special ball he often used to exercise his grip, Rumsfeld asked if I could assure him that no one in Policy had done what the press charged. At that point, I could give only incomplete assurances: I knew of no one who had planned any operations involving lying or disinformation. I had never authorized any such plans. But it would be days before the lawyers could confirm that no one in my office did what the unnamed "Pentagon officials" told the *Times*. I reminded Rumsfeld of Mark Twain's remark that lies could get halfway round the world while the truth was still tying its shoes.

Wise as Twain's insight was, there was no consolation in it. The Secretary scowled as he ran through a series of questions: Could OSI ever dig out from under this heap of garbage that had fallen on it? It was supposed to be in the information business, where its credibility would be essential. Could it ever be credible again?

I had already reviewed these questions with my staff, and I had answers. OSI's mission was important, its work first-rate, the accusations against it scurrilous. Moreover, it was galling to reward underhanded bureaucratic attacks—to reward officials who had planted the false story that OSI was planning to give journalists false stories. But OSI was clearly beyond repair. Rumsfeld did not order me to shut down OSI, but it was clear what he wanted done. I told him I would shut it down that day, February 26, 2002.

I gave the bad news to General Worden. Naturally, he and his OSI colleagues resented the decision and were angry about the untruths. We all saw the irony that an office formed to plan information operations had been blown away by a disinformation operation. Concentrating on foreign enemies, OSI hadn't protected its back from other Pentagon officials.

Several people from OSI asserted that it must have been Torie Clarke who had provided the original accusations to the *Times*, but they gave no proof. They noted that when the news media frenzy was under way, she must have realized that the Public Affairs office's failure to respond forcibly to these demonstrably false allegations would pour gasoline on the fire. These same points appeared in several articles—in *U.S. News and World Report*, the magazine *Insight* (owned by the *Washington Times*), and *The New Republic*—arguing that Clarke was behind OSI's demise. I do not know who gave the original false story to the *New York Times*. I never obtained enough information to resolve the mystery.

I do know that the OSI affair damaged me and the Policy organization. For the first time, we drew intense attention from the world's news media. The attention was negative to the point of vilification, and no one ever mounted an effective defense for us—not even ourselves. Political opponents of the Administration took note. The scandal, in effect, hung a "kick me" sign on us. I paid too little attention to this at the time, as I came to realize when those initial bad press stories spawned more bad press stories.

Whoever was behind the original *New York Times* piece may have considered it a standard episode in the government's turf wars. But it had a costly and enduring effect, helping to craft a false image of the Pentagon—and by extension the Bush Administration—as a knowing trafficker in misinformation.

The OSI affair damaged our government's prosecution of the war on terrorism. Some of the office's coordination functions were picked up by other Pentagon offices, but no one took responsibility for producing a comprehensive information or influence campaign for the war on terrorism—neither in the Defense Department nor anywhere else within the U.S. government. The government never recovered from the dishonest smearing of OSI.

Rumsfeld and Myers continued to complain that the Administration was not putting the necessary resources, energy, or even thought into the ideological battle. On two or three occasions I proposed putting together a team composed of Policy, Public Affairs, and other officials to address these complaints. Each time, however, mention of the OSI affair was enough to stymie the effort. The chilling effect of the OSI scandal had a long half-life.

In President Bush's second term, Condoleezza Rice, then the Secretary of State, hired President Bush's communications adviser, Karen Hughes, as Under Secretary of State for Public Diplomacy, giving her the counterterrorism battle-of-ideas portfolio. But State's approach, in line with Hughes's title, focused chiefly on public diplomacy. The need for a broader strategy remained unaddressed.

Despite the untimely death of OSI, I wanted my Administration colleagues to stay active in fighting the battle of ideas. I assumed that the OSI debacle would make officials even more reluctant to take on the jihadists' ideology. Some argued against viewing the war on terrorism as ideological. They believed al Qaida was not so much an enemy of America or of Western liberal democracy as of American foreign policy. That was in line with the argument that nothing important could be achieved in the battle of ideas until the Arab-Israeli conflict had been resolved. Many officials simply had no interest in ideological warfare: They considered it impractical to try to influence the way millions of people thought.

But the last two hundred years have seen a number of successful international ideological campaigns—from struggles against the slave trade and dueling in the eighteenth and nineteenth centuries to the confrontations with fascism and communism in the twentieth century. I did not agree that terrorist violence was the inevitable expression of the frustrations of poor or politically desperate people. After all, a terrorist leader had a tough job to indoctrinate young people to overcome their natural human aversion to killing children and to destroying ordinary people going about their daily business—let alone to blowing themselves up. I saw the difficulties of indoctrination as one of our enemies' key vulnerabilities.

In April 2002, a few weeks after OSI's demise, I laid out my thoughts on the subject in a speech (circulated in advance to State, White House, and Pentagon colleagues):

[W]e frequently hear that suicide bombing is the product of the combination of poverty and hopelessness.

. . . We assume that only a person ensnared in deep despair could do such a thing.

This diagnosis implies its own solution—that the world should address what is called the "root causes of terrorism," the poverty and political hopelessness that many people imagine are the traits and motives of the suicide bombers. This diagnosis, however, doesn't jibe with actual experience. . . .

When we look at the records of the suicide bombers, we see that many aren't drawn from the poor. . . .

Indeed, as we learn from a recent *New York Times* interview with Hamas leaders in Gaza, what characterizes the suicide bombers—and especially the old men who send them off on their missions—is rather hope than despair.

First of all, the bombers cherish a perverse form of religious hope. The promise of eternity in paradise is a tenet of many faiths, a noble incentive and consolation to millions of people. It's as cynical as it is sinister that leaders of al Qaida, Hezbollah, Hamas and other groups convince young people that eternity in paradise is available as a reward for the murder of innocents.

Second, there is the bomber's hope of earthly glory and reward—praise as a hero from political leaders and honor for one's parents and a $25,000 check to the bomber's family from Saddam Hussein. . . .

Third, there is the homicide bomber's political hope. . . .

***

This suggests a strategic course for us: attack the sources of these malignant hopes.

***

[W]e must ensure that terrorism is not seen as a winning strategy. This is today's immediate challenge: For example, we have to make it understood that the Palestinian homicide bombers are harming, not helping, their political cause.

Peace can be achieved when the conditions are right: and the most important condition is the state of peoples' minds. Thus, we must take seriously the incitement to hatred that creates the intellectual atmosphere in which terrorism can flourish. If we seek the "root cause" of terrorism, this is where we'll find it.

Timeline 2. Iraq: 1968–2001

1968

July	Baathist takeover of Iraqi government

1979

July	Saddam Hussein becomes president; purge of Baath leadership

1980

Sept.	Iraq invades Iran, beginning Iran-Iraq War

1988

Feb.–Sept.	Anfal campaign against Iraqi Kurds
Mar.	Gassing of Halabja
Aug.	End of Iran-Iraq War

1990

Aug.	Iraq invades Kuwait

1991

Jan.–Mar.	Operation Desert Storm
March	Massacre of Shiites
Apr.	UN Resolutions 687, 688 (sanctions)

1993

Apr.	Assassination attempt on former President Bush

1994

Oct.	Iraqi forces mobilize again to invade Kuwait

1995

Aug.	Defection of Hussein Kamil, son-in-law of Saddam

1996

Dec.	Oil-for-Food program begins

1998

Aug.	Saddam announces suspension of UN inspections
Oct.	Iraq Liberation Act becomes U.S. law
Dec.	UNSCOM withdraws its staff from Iraq
Dec.	Operation Desert Fox (U.S. bombing of Iraq)

1999

Dec.	UN creates UNMOVIC, but unable to restart inspections or monitoring

1999–2002

	Iraq fires on U.S./U.K. patrol aircraft (almost daily)

6
WHY IRAQ?

Why did President Bush decide to overthrow Saddam Hussein?

In short, it was to end a range of threats. No other contemporary leader—and few in history—had a record of aggression to match Saddam's. He had started major wars of conquest. He had brutalized his citizens and killed them in enormous numbers. He had given aid and support to terrorists. And, in violation of treaty obligations,* he had not only pursued mass-destruction weapons, but used them, on his foreign enemies and on his own citizens.

The problem of Saddam Hussein predated 9/11. It had become a principal U.S. preoccupation when he seized Kuwait in 1990. Saddam survived the Gulf War, and Iraq remained a danger throughout the 1990s—one the UN Security Council had tried to contain by imposing economic sanctions and weapons inspections. In August 1998 Saddam generated a crisis by shutting down the UN weapons inspections. Two months later, the U.S. Congress—concerned that the Iraqi threat was growing, while the

---

*Saddam had violated the Nuclear Non-Proliferation Treaty (available at the UN Disarmament website: http://disarmament.un.org/wmd/npt/npttext.html) and the Biological and Toxin Weapons Convention (available at http://www.opbw.org). The cease-fire agreement that ended the Gulf War was not a treaty, strictly speaking, but a multilateral settlement created through UN Security Council Resolutions.

world's resolve to "contain" Saddam was weakening—passed the Iraq Liberation Act, which called for regime change in Baghdad:

> **It should be the policy of the United States to support efforts to remove the regime headed by Saddam Hussein from power in Iraq and to promote the emergence of a democratic government to replace that regime.**

President Clinton signed the Iraq Liberation Act into law. Democratic Senators Carl Levin (Michigan), Tom Daschle (North Dakota), John Kerry (Massachusetts), and others had sent a letter to President Clinton urging that he "take necessary actions (including, if appropriate, air and missile strikes on suspect Iraqi sites) to respond effectively to the threat posed by Iraq's refusal to end its weapons of mass destruction programs." In an October 1998 speech, Levin declared:

> **It is my sincere hope that Saddam Hussein, when faced with the credible threat of the use of force, will comply with the relevant UN Security Council Resolutions. But, I believe that we must carefully consider other actions, including, if necessary, the use of force to destroy suspect sites if compliance is not achieved.**

The "containment" strategy continued to deteriorate, prompting news media warnings. A *Washington Post* editorial declared that no problem "is more dangerous—or more urgent—than the situation in Iraq":

> **Over the last year, Mr. Clinton and his team quietly avoided dealing with, or calling attention to, the almost complete unraveling of a decade's efforts to isolate the regime of Saddam Hussein and prevent it from rebuilding its weapons of mass destruction.**

The *New York Times* sounded similar alarms. "Even a few more weeks free of inspections might allow Mr. Hussein to revive construction of a biological, chemical or nuclear weapon," one *Times* editorial said. Another pointed out: "The Security Council is wobbly, with Russia and France eager to ease inspections and sanctions." Yet another warned that any "approach to Iraq that depends on Security Council unity is destined to be weak."

Then came 9/11, which focused Americans' attention on our vulnerabilities and reduced the government's tolerance for dangers to national security. It caused U.S. officials to rethink *all* serious threats—whether or not they were directly linked to the attack or to al Qaida. Important as the Iraq problem had been beforehand, it looked graver and more urgent after 9/11, for reasons that are worth exploring.

Today, the ongoing controversy about the Iraq war has skewed memories. It may be hard (or inconvenient) for politicians and others to recall accurately what they were thinking and saying before the war began. Soon after Saddam's overthrow in 2003, some war critics began to contend not only that the war was unnecessary, but that Saddam had never been a significant problem for the United States—regarding terrorism, WMD, or any other matter. They claimed that serious concern about him was the peculiarity of a small band of ideologues—"neocons," without reason or honesty—who used manipulation and deception to spread their anxiety to good, sincere people.

But there is an ample record on the Iraq issue and it tells a different story.

Saddam Hussein dominated Iraq for three decades. His megalomaniacal passions and erratic brutality became policies for Iraq, atrocities for its people, and crises for the world.

Saddam entered politics as a would-be assassin at the age of twenty-one in 1958, acting for the Baath Party, whose ideology—a mix of socialist and Arab nationalist views—was inspired by the European Fascist movements of the 1930s. Members of Saddam's Sunni Arab family ran the party, which overthrew the Iraqi government in 1963, but they were quickly ousted. The Baathists retook the government in their second coup d'étât in 1968 and held power until Saddam's overthrow in April 2003.

In July 1979, at the age of forty-two, Saddam succeeded his cousin as President of Iraq, and promptly began a bloody purge of the Baath Party. At a meeting of hundreds of party officials, he identified people sitting before him as traitors and had them removed dramatically from the room and marched off for execution. Those who remained, doubtless seized by mingled relief and terror, shouted cheers and praise for their new President. In a stroke of strategically inspired sadism, Saddam required a number of the cheering survivors—cabinet-level government and high-ranking party officials—to participate personally in the firing squads for their purged party colleagues.

Saddam created complex mechanisms to supervise, suborn, intimidate, torture, and murder his own people. And he kept records of this work. After his overthrow, U.S. officials collected some of these records—videos made by Saddam's security services—onto a sickening DVD. When a copy arrived at my Pentagon office, I could bear watching it for no more than a few minutes. One segment was a series of home-movie-quality scenes of prisoners, arms bound behind them, being walked across the flat roofs of two- or three-story buildings. Each man in turn was thrown off the roof and the camera caught his crushing impact with the ground. Another segment showed a member of Saddam's security forces accused of some kind of dereliction. His punishment was to have his arms broken with a heavy stick in front of a group of his fellow officers. One of those fellow officers, identified as a close friend of the accused and looking very distressed, was ordered to break the bones. The video shows him doing it.

In 1980, a little more than a year after becoming President of Iraq, Saddam invaded Iran, starting an eight-year war that killed an estimated one million people. This was his attempt to take advantage of the Iranian revolution of 1978–79, which had overthrown the Shah, Reza Pahlavi, and installed Ayatollah Ruhollah Khomeini as Iran's Supreme Leader. Saddam aimed to exploit his neighbor's political turmoil and discourage Iraq's Shiites from attempting their own revolution. He killed important Iraqi Shiite leaders and kept his domestic enemies in check, but he did not defeat Iran. In the course of this war, Saddam used chemical weapons against Iran—becoming the first person in history to employ nerve gas on the battlefield.*

Near the end of the Iran-Iraq War, Saddam launched attacks against his own Kurdish population in northern Iraq. The attacks depopulated large areas of Iraqi Kurdistan, along the Iranian border, by razing approximately two thousand villages and expelling an estimated 150,000 people from their homes. A UN special reporter concluded that tens of thousands of Kurds "disappeared" in these attacks, which Saddam designated the "Anfal" campaign—meaning "booty" or spoils of war. One human rights organization estimated the number of dead at 70,000 to 150,000. Another put it at more than 100,000. Human Rights Watch estimated that 50,000 to 100,000 noncombatants died or disappeared in the Anfal campaign.

The Anfal campaign's most notorious event was the March 1988 attack on the Iraqi Kurdish town of Halabja. Saddam hit the town with a combination of weapons of mass destruction: mustard gas and the nerve gases sarin, tabun, and VX. Wire services around the world published

---

*The chemical weapons used in World War I were mustard and chlorine gas, not nerve gas.

heartbreaking photos of the victims: Kurdish women in colorful dresses struck dead in the town's streets, sprawling beside the babies who had been in their arms when the gases killed them on the spot. An estimated five thousand Kurds died during Anfal before the Iran-Iraq War came to its nonglorious, negotiated end in 1988.

Astoundingly, it was only two years later that Saddam started another war—the Gulf War—by attempting to incorporate the neighboring nation of Kuwait as Iraq's nineteenth province. On August 2, 1990, he invaded Kuwait, prompting the United States to organize an international coalition in response. In early 1991, the coalition's forces expelled the Iraqis from Kuwait in Operation Desert Storm. As Saddam's troops withdrew, they set fire to more than a thousand Kuwaiti oil wells and caused 250 million gallons of oil to pour into the Persian Gulf. Created for the specific purpose of liberating Kuwait, the coalition did not destroy the retreating Iraqi army or move against Baghdad to overthrow the Saddam Hussein regime.

Saddam interpreted the coalition's restraint as a historic victory for Iraq over the United States. Saddam touted his successful deterrence of the U.S.-led coalition as "the mother of all battles," celebrating it in frequent references to his ministers, generals, and the Iraqi public. A notable U.S.-government-sponsored study of intelligence gathered after Saddam's overthrow concluded:

> **In the 1991 Gulf War, the Americans had appeared on the brink of destroying much of Iraq's military, including the Republican Guard, but then inexplicably stopped—for fear of casualties, in Saddam's view.**
>
> ---
>
> **In his recorded conversations with senior staff, he constantly reminded them of the source for his confidence. Had he not by force of his own extraordinary will led Iraq to its great victory in the Iran-Iraq War? Was he not responsible for designing the successful invasion of Kuwait? Had he not stood up to the Americans and won the "Mother of All Battles?"**
>
> ---
>
> **Even Operation Desert Storm (1991) failed to impress Saddam. [He believed] that America had spent an inordinately long time bombarding Iraq from one end of the country to the other before they were finally willing to commit ground forces. Once American ground troops were committed, American irresolution allowed the bulk of the elite Republican Guard forces to escape; left the oil exporting city of Basra unoccupied;**

and, most critically, failed to do anything that threatened the regime's survival.

So Saddam emerged from the Gulf War with a strong, if perverse, sense of accomplishment. Retaining his army, he felt free to continue endangering his enemies, foreign and domestic.

To mitigate that danger, the UN Security Council adopted a resolution in April 1991 ordering Iraq to destroy its chemical and biological weapons and long-range missiles and stop pursuing nuclear weapons. That resolution created the UN Special Commission on Iraq (UNSCOM) to monitor Iraqi disarmament; it demanded that Iraq renounce terrorism; and it reaffirmed economic sanctions against Iraq. The sanctions banned all commerce other than for humanitarian needs (mainly food and medicine).

Soon after the coalition forces liberated Kuwait, the Shiites in southern Iraq challenged the Baathist regime's authority. Saddam crushed them, using a fleet of helicopters as gunships.* Tens of thousands were killed and their cultural heritage destroyed. One hundred fifty thousand people then lost their homes when Saddam drained the famous marshes at the mouth of the Euphrates and Tigris rivers, the ecological foundation of the millennia-old culture of the "marsh Arabs." In a coordinated effort, the Kurdish population in northern Iraq also launched a resistance campaign, also unsuccessful.

The Security Council promptly adopted another resolution, directing Iraq to cease oppressing its own civilians. To protect terrorized Iraqi Kurds and to enable U.S. reconnaissance flights to monitor disarmament, Britain, France, and the United States established a "no-fly zone" over northern Iraq. With security and other help provided by the United States and other outside powers, the Kurds achieved a substantial degree of autonomy in northern Iraq. Although they remained part of Iraq, they governed themselves and were not under Saddam's day-to-day control. A year later, a similar no-fly zone was established in the south to protect the Shiites.

For Saddam, terror was an ordinary means of exercising political power. He used it domestically and abroad. In 1993, his Iraqi Intelligence

---

*In the course of negotiating the Gulf War cease-fire, the U.S. commander, General Norman Schwarzkopf, made a goodwill gesture to his Iraqi military counterparts by allowing them to fly helicopters in the south. The Iraqis used them as gunships to kill Shiite civilians. Schwarzkopf later said that Saddam's generals tricked him. See Rick Atkinson, *Crusade* (New York: Houghton Mifflin, 1993), pp. 489–490. See also General H. Norman Schwarzkopf with Peter Petre, *It Doesn't Take a Hero* (New York: Bantam Books, 1992), pp. 488–489.

Service tried, without success, to kill George H. W. Bush in Kuwait with a car bomb.

Saddam also maintained connections to foreign terrorists. To some he gave refuge. Others he allowed to operate from Iraqi territory. He trained thousands of foreign terrorists in Iraqi facilities and provided them political support and funds. The CIA reported in September 2002 that "Iraq continues to be a safehaven, transit point, or operational node for groups and individuals who direct violence against the United States, Israel, and other allies. Iraq has a long history of supporting terrorism." Unlike its assessment of Iraq's WMD, this CIA assessment of Iraq's support for terrorism was reinforced by postwar discoveries (discussed below). He also promoted terrorism indirectly, with cash rewards for the families of Palestinian suicide bombers.

Among the terrorists whom Saddam harbored in Iraq were:

- Abu Nidal, the Palestinian terrorist who targeted cafes, hotels, and, most notoriously, the ticket counters at the airports in Rome and Vienna, killing hundreds, including many Americans
- Abu Abbas, who led the takeover of the *Achille Lauro* cruise ship in 1985, during which he murdered Leon Klinghoffer, an elderly American
- Abu Musab al-Zarqawi, an al Qaida associate before Operation Iraqi Freedom, who swore allegiance to Usama bin Laden after Saddam's overthrow and became the leader of al Qaida in Iraq

The terrorist groups that Saddam allowed to operate bases or other facilities in Iraq were:

- Mujahedin-e Khalq
- Kurdistan Workers Party (PKK)
- Abu Nidal Organization
- Palestine Liberation Front
- Popular Front for the Liberation of Palestine
- Arab Liberation Front (ALF)

Documents captured during the war provide evidence that Iraq also took an active role in training terrorists. The regime's paramilitary organization, the Fedayeen Saddam, opened camps in 1994 to teach paramilitary skills to thousands of volunteers each year. In later years, according to one official Iraqi document captured by U.S. forces after Saddam's overthrow, the Fedayeen Saddam brought Arab volunteers from Egypt, Palestine,

Jordan, the Gulf, and Syria to those camps for training. (Where the volunteers went after their training remains unclear.) This terrorist training was supported by the Iraqi Intelligence Service, which not only directed Iraq's ongoing bioweapons work but also operated "covert laboratories to research and test various chemicals and poisons"—suggesting a potential connection between terrorist operations and biochemical programs.

In 1994, Saddam mobilized his army near Kuwait again, threatening another invasion. The UN Security Council responded with a condemnatory resolution demanding that Iraq not "enhance its military capability in southern Iraq." In order to implement the resolution, the United States and Britain then declared a military "no-drive zone" in the area of southern Iraq's no-fly zone.

Meanwhile, the UN WMD inspectors were surprised to find that Iraq's nuclear weapons program was substantially more advanced than they (and Western intelligence officials in general) had thought before the Gulf War. The inspectors were surprised again in August 1995, when Saddam's son-in-law, Hussein Kamil, the head of Iraq's WMD programs, defected from Iraq. As a result of the defection, the inspectors came to learn about important Iraqi weapons activity that they had missed in their own inspections. In July 1995, UNSCOM reported, "Iraq, for the first time, acknowledged that it had had an offensive BW [biological weapons] programme but still denied any weaponization." The following month, however, after Hussein Kamil's defection, "Iraq admitted that it had weaponized BW agents and deployed biological weapons for combat use."

At the same time, the Iraqi regime acknowledged that its biological weapons scientists were experimenting with camel pox—a substance, relatively safe to handle, that could allow them to learn how to produce and use a smallpox weapon. Years later, after Saddam's overthrow, the American-British-Australian Iraq Survey Group (ISG) investigated Iraq's WMD history. The ISG's American head, Charles Duelfer, confirmed that "Iraq's interest in camel pox and its inclusion in the viral BW program have led ISG to assess that camel pox R&D was a surrogate for smallpox research. . . ."

Duelfer reported that the Iraqi regime had been working to develop smallpox weapons *before* Desert Storm—and that, after Desert Storm, in response to the start of UN weapons inspections, Saddam modified his WMD programs:

> **With an eye to the future and aiming to preserve some measure of its BW capability, Baghdad in the years immediately after Desert Storm sought to save what it could of its BW infrastruc-**

> **ture, hide evidence of the program, and dispose of its existing weapons stocks. . . . the Regime sought to continue a covert BW development effort under the cover of civilian research.**

The Duelfer Report said that the Iraqi regime's confessions about its biological weapons work showed that "Saddam was willing to risk an element of Iraq's WMD program in a bid to gain economic and sanctions relief." Getting out from under sanctions was by this time "an overarching Regime objective."

After the 1995 disclosures, the Iraqi regime claimed to have destroyed its biological weapons program and materiel—although it did not do so under UNSCOM supervision, as required by the Security Council. The Iraq Survey Group later found that the regime had preserved some so-called "dual-use" biological facilities that had a civilian function but could also be used for military production. Also, Saddam initiated new, *covert* biological weapons work, which he located within his intelligence apparatus. As Duelfer reported:

> **With the bulk of Iraq's BW program in ruins, Iraq after 1996 continued small-scale BW-related efforts with the only remaining asset at Baghdad's disposal—the know-how of the small band of BW scientists and technicians who carried out further work under the auspices of the Iraqi Intelligence Service.**

Astonishingly, Hussein Kamil returned to Iraq in February 1996, lured by a promise of pardon from his father-in-law. Could anyone possibly have been surprised when he was promptly killed? According to the Duelfer Report, he was shot by family members determined to redeem their tribal honor. Saddam professed innocence: "When I pardon, I mean it."

Because northern Iraq enjoyed U.S.-led military protection and was not under Saddam's control, the region served as a base for anti-Saddam groups, some of which had relationships with the U.S. government. One of these groups was the Iraqi National Congress (INC), run by Ahmad Chalabi. The INC had a dual nature: It functioned as an independent voice of the Iraqi democratic opposition. But it also served as an umbrella organization that included several Iraqi exile and Kurdish groups. Those other groups were not only members of the INC but also its rivals.

Chalabi—a secular, U.S.-educated Iraqi businessman and banker—became a central figure in the story of the U.S. invasion and occupation of Iraq, but not because he shaped or implemented U.S. policy. It was, rather, because of the suspicion and antagonism he excited in key parts of the U.S. national security establishment, as well as within the Arab world. That suspicion would in the end derail the U.S. government's preparations and plans for Iraq's political transition.

Chalabi favored ousting Iraq's Baathist regime through a popular uprising. He said that such an uprising could draw on the desire for freedom among the Iraqi people, and especially among the country's Kurds and Shiites (approximately 80 percent of the population) who suffered particular oppression at the hands of the Sunni-dominated Baath Party. Chalabi advocated replacing the Saddam Hussein regime with a democratic government. Neither of these positions found favor among the Arab governments, who feared the effects in the region of both Shiite political power and democratic reform.

The INC's chief rival among the opposition groups was the Jordan-based Iraqi National Accord (INA), an organization committed to different principles. The INA was headed by Iyad Allawi, a medical doctor who, like Chalabi, was a secular Muslim from a prominent Shiite family. But Allawi had entered Iraq's political sphere as a Baathist. After he fell out with Saddam and fled to Britain, he founded (with Saudi help) the INA, a group whose membership was largely Sunni. It included many former Baath Party officials, some drawn from the higher ranks of Saddam's army.

Allawi's goal was a military-led overthrow of Saddam: "We think that any uprising should have as its very center the armed forces." This approach, he contended, would safeguard stability: "We don't preach civil war. On the contrary, we preach controlled, coordinated military uprising supported by the people that would not allow itself to go into acts of revenge or chaos." Despite the differences between Allawi and Chalabi, the INA was (except for a period in the mid-1990s) a member group of the INC.

The CIA had its own reasons for opposing Chalabi. In 1995 and 1996, the Iraqi oppositionists clashed with one another and, ineffectually, with the Iraqi military, leading to recriminations between the oppositionists and U.S. officials. Chalabi denounced the CIA for incompetence—gaining a respectful audience with members of Congress and other current and former U.S. officials, but burning his bridges with the CIA.

The CIA had first approached Chalabi in May 1991, soon after the Gulf War, and after several years of cooperation the CIA presented him an award "in recognition of his distinguished service in facilitating a [1994] cease-fire agreement between two warring Kurdish groups in northern Iraq." But Chalabi saw himself as "the leader of a political process and not a U.S. intelligence asset." He insisted on being free to cultivate support on Capitol Hill and elsewhere in Washington. His relationship with the CIA also suffered from "squabbles within the CIA about which Iraqi opposition members to support"—disputes that mirrored the rivalries within the Iraqi opposition.

These "squabbles" affected important events on the ground in Iraq. In March 1995, the opposition groups in the north were planning a low-level insurrection, designed to recruit allies from disaffected Iraqi military units. Chalabi worked alongside a friendly CIA representative to build support in the region for the action, including support from Iranian officials. The CIA's own communications, however, were not timely and clear, and when White House officials learned of the opposition plans there was "a firestorm in the National Security Council." On the very day the action was to occur, the U.S. government sent a strong, negative message to the Iraqi opposition. The oppositionists decided to proceed anyway. The action failed. Although some CIA officials thought it produced some positive results, it also produced "[a]nimosity toward Chalabi from some groups in the CIA," who campaigned actively against him. The September 2006 report of the Senate Intelligence Committee teases apart the strands of this hostility to Chalabi. It notes that the CIA in 1998 had given three reasons for "reassess[ing] our relationship with Chalabi": that he had entered into the plan unilaterally, that he hadn't consulted on it with the CIA, and that he claimed the U.S. supported the uprising. But the Intelligence Committee's report found that all those CIA reasons were false: "Chalabi *did not* enter the plan unilaterally," he "*did* consult CIA from the beginning," and "the CIA representative's role . . . *did* signal to the opposition that the plan had U.S. support." But this refutation was late in coming, and by then the CIA's mistaken reassessment had hardened into a hostility toward the INC that spread within the U.S. government.

In March 1996, a year after the abortive rebellion, the CIA supported a different anti-Saddam operation that made use of its military contacts. Chalabi obtained a meeting with CIA Director John Deutch and (Chalabi later told the committee) warned him that Saddam had uncovered this new plan. In late August, Saddam routed the oppositionists, a calamity for thousands of them—and a humiliation for the CIA reminiscent of the 1961 Bay of Pigs fiasco.* U.S. intelligence officials rescued more than five thousand Iraqis from Iraq. "[I]ntelligence capabilities and assets

---

*An ABC news report included the following:

> [ABC reporter] Chris Bury: The American loss was compounded when Iraqi armor moved into Irbil, near the center of a five-year-old CIA operation aimed at toppling Saddam. As many as 100 Kurds associated with the Iraqi National Congress, funded by the CIA, reportedly have been executed by Iraqi secret

were exposed. . . . Saddam arrested hundreds of Iraqi soldiers and executed many of them, including [one] CIA asset's three children." Out of this painful history, the CIA and Chalabi developed a mutual hatred that would affect U.S. policy before and after Saddam's overthrow.

Time after time, whenever Saddam confronted those who would contain him, he showed that he had more stomach than his opponents did. The UN economic sanctions on Iraq began unraveling as soon as they were created. It was an open secret that Saddam cheated on the sanctions by smuggling oil through neighboring states. And he stimulated criticism of the sanctions through the strategic placement of lucrative contracts with companies from France, Russia, and elsewhere.

After U.S.-led coalition forces expelled Saddam's army from Kuwait in 1991, the United Nations put sanctions on Iraq that included a general ban on all trade, including Iraqi oil exports. There was a narrow exception to allow Iraq to buy humanitarian supplies.

In February 1996, the UN Security Council negotiated the Oil-for-Food (OFF) Program with Iraq. The program permitted Iraq to resume selling its oil, with sales revenues to go into a UN-administered account, to be disbursed only for permissible items. Yet Saddam quickly took advantage of the United Nations' maladministration to subvert the OFF program. He was able to seize control of billions of dollars' worth of oil sales revenues, which he used to buy diplomatic support, and to import banned items, including militarily relevant goods. Charles Duelfer, head of the Iraq Survey Group, described the pattern of abuse:

> **Over time, sanctions had steadily weakened to the point where Iraq, in 2000–2001, was confidently designing missiles around components that could only be obtained outside sanctions. Moreover, illicit revenues grew to quite substantial levels dur-**

---

police, who stripped this building of files, computers, communications equipment and any chance of threatening Saddam.

Graham Fuller, former CIA National Intelligence Council: It's a real tragedy, both on the political and human level, because thousands of people have been killed and the very infrastructure, I think of this very important Iraqi National Congress, which is really the main vehicle for our political opposition to Saddam, political and military opposition, looks like it has received—I don't want to say fatal—but a very, very heavy blow.

Nightline, ABC News, September 10, 1996 (transcript #3992-1.)

ing the same period, and it is instructive to see how and where the Regime allocated these funds.

Duelfer testified in Congress that "Baghdad exploited the mechanism for executing the Oil-for-Food program to give individuals and countries an economic stake in ending sanctions." The Duelfer Report underlined the success of this ploy, pointing out that "sitting members of the Security Council were actively violating resolutions passed by the Security Council":

> **The Regime quickly came to see that OFF [the Oil-for-Food program] could be corrupted to acquire foreign exchange both to further undermine sanctions and to provide the means to enhance dual-use infrastructure and potential WMD-related development.**
>
> **By 2000–2001, Saddam had managed to mitigate many of the effects of sanctions and undermine their international support. Iraq was within striking distance of a de facto end to the sanctions regime, both in terms of oil exports and the trade embargo, by the end of 1999.**

Many opponents of the sanctions argued that the economic squeeze on Iraq was hurting ordinary Iraqis, which was true. This was a serious problem, but ordinary people become unintended victims whenever a country is subjected to international economic sanctions. Rogue regimes—those that threaten the world's peace and security—force responsible states to choose among evils. Economic sanctions are supposed to serve as a means, short of war, to pressure dangerous regimes to change their policies. But sanctions are a blunt instrument at best. Though one can try to design sanctions to avoid unnecessary harm, they inevitably aggravate misery for the ordinary people in the sanctioned country. The problem is that scruples against the blunt instrument of economic sanctions can drive countries to the even blunter instrument of war.

The sanctions against Iraq were weakly crafted, poorly administered, corrupted by Saddam (and by UN officials), and disrespected by countries they were supposed to constrain. Nevertheless, they made it harder for Iraq to do international business. While they did not stop Saddam from buying military articles abroad, they crimped his military supply lines. Saddam and others criticized the sanctions as draconian and strove to dilute them. And in the meantime the sanctions served another important, if cynical, purpose: They allowed governments that did not know what to do about Saddam (or that were on his side) to claim falsely—knowingly or otherwise—that Saddam was "in a box."

Much the same could be said of the UNSCOM weapons inspections. The Security Council designed them defectively and Saddam undermined them systematically. Though some of the inspectors were admirably professional and courageous, the overall inspection regime was never rigorous. It prevented the inspectors from conducting effective no-notice tours, so that the Iraqi regime could clean house before an inspection, and it allowed Iraqi officials to escort the inspectors. According to Hans Blix, the head of UN inspections, "inspectors' video tapes showed how files were moved and documents burned while the inspectors were forced to wait." Saddam's intelligence agencies may have had access to the inspectors' plans; in 1999, the UNSCOM Final Report noted delicately that "Iraq has attempted to defeat the principle of no-notice inspection by working assiduously to track and predict the Commission's inspection activities."

Furthermore, Saddam brazenly violated his obligations to cooperate with the inspections. He excluded UNSCOM from his enormous palace complexes, which were large enough to conceal all manner of proscribed materials, and barred individual inspectors who seemed too determined or thorough in their work. Saddam worked around the inspection regime by switching from single-use military production facilities to dual-use facilities that could produce civilian and military products—a tactic that would give him "deniability" when it came to questionable facilities.

Soon after the Gulf War, UNSCOM had uncovered Iraq's large investments in developing and making chemical, biological, and nuclear weapons. But Saddam was determined to prevent the inspectors from knowing what he possessed or the status of his programs, and throughout the 1990s he stymied UNSCOM's attempts to track the results of those investments—the personnel, technology, and materiel. The UNSCOM inspections evidently irritated Saddam, but his efforts made it impossible for the inspectors to expose any clandestine Iraqi production of banned weapons or missiles. Saddam's ability to conceal was far greater than the inspectors' ability to discover.

By early 1998, two of the main elements of the Security Council's containment strategy for Iraq—economic sanctions and weapons inspections—were coming undone. Saddam appeared to be wearing down the resolve of the UN and the world at large. The Clinton Administration supported the UN containment strategy, but critics of the strategy noted that if Saddam had ever actually been "in a box," he was well on his way out by now.

On January 26, 1998, a Washington, D.C., think tank called the Project for the New American Century published an open letter to President Clinton signed by eighteen individuals, mostly former U.S. national security officials, declaring that the "current American policy toward Iraq is not succeeding." Observing that " 'containment' of Saddam Hussein has been steadily eroding over the past several months," the signers said that the United States could no longer rely on its Gulf War coalition "to continue to uphold the sanctions or to punish Saddam when he blocks or evades UN inspections." They warned:

> **Our ability to ensure that Saddam Hussein is not producing weapons of mass destruction, therefore, has substantially diminished. Even if full inspections were eventually to resume, which now seems highly unlikely, experience has shown that it is difficult if not impossible to monitor Iraq's chemical and biological weapons production. . . . [I]n the not-too-distant future we will be unable to determine with any reasonable level of confidence whether Iraq does or does not possess such weapons. . . .**
>
> **The only acceptable strategy is one that eliminates the possibility that Iraq will be able to use or threaten to use weapons of mass destruction. In the near term, this means a willingness to undertake military action as diplomacy is clearly failing. In the long term, it means removing Saddam Hussein and his regime from power.**

The list of the eighteen signers of this letter included a number of individuals—Richard Armitage, Paula Dobriansky, Donald Rumsfeld, and Robert Zoellick, among others—who were not "neocon" by any definition.

A few weeks later, on February 19, most of those eighteen people joined more than two dozen others in signing another open letter to President Clinton. Sponsored by a bipartisan group called the Committee for Peace and Security in the Gulf, this letter reiterated the call for "a determined program to change the regime in Baghdad":

> **For years, the United States has tried to remove Saddam by encouraging coups and internal conspiracies. These attempts have all failed. Saddam is more wily, brutal and conspiratorial than any likely conspiracy the United States might mobilize against him. Saddam must be overpowered; he will not be brought down by a coup d'état. But Saddam has an Achilles'**

> **heel: lacking popular support, he rules by terror. The same brutality which makes it unlikely that any coups or conspiracies can succeed, makes him hated by his own people and the rank and file of his military. Iraq today is ripe for a broad-based insurrection.**

I was among the signers of this February 19 letter. The forty people who subscribed to it included liberal Democrats as well as conservative Republicans. The list was headed by former Democratic Congressman Steve Solarz and former Assistant Secretary of Defense Richard Perle, who cochaired the sponsoring group.

Throughout 1998, concern about Saddam and the inadequacy of the containment strategy grew among Republicans and Democrats. In September, a bipartisan group of members of Congress drafted a law declaring that U.S. policy should be "to remove the regime headed by Saddam Hussein from power." They wanted President Clinton to help Iraqi democratic opposition organizations—exile groups and Kurdish groups living in the mostly autonomous region of northern Iraq. The legislation authorized Clinton to provide the oppositionists with $97 million worth of military education and training. One of its leading Senate proponents was Senator Robert Kerrey (D-Nebraska), who described the measure as a "clear commitment" to a U.S. policy of regime change:

> **This bill is a statement that America refuses to coexist with a regime which has used chemical weapons on its own citizens and on neighboring countries, which has invaded its neighbors twice without provocation, which has still not accounted for its atrocities committed in Kuwait, which has fired ballistic missiles into the cities of three of its neighbors, which is attempting to develop nuclear and biological weapons, and which has brutalized and terrorized its own citizens for thirty years. *I don't see how any democratic country could accept the existence of such a regime, but this bill says America will not.* I will be an even prouder American when the refusal, and commitment to materially help the Iraqi resistance, are U.S. policy.**

The legislation passed with bipartisan support. The House approved it by a vote of 360 to 38 and the Senate did so unanimously. On October 31, 1998, as he signed it into law as the Iraq Liberation Act of 1998, President Clinton stated:

> **The United States favors an Iraq that offers its people freedom at home. I categorically reject arguments that this is unattainable due to Iraq's history or its ethnic or sectarian make-up. Iraqis deserve and desire freedom like everyone else. The United States looks forward to a democratically supported regime. . . .**
>
> **My Administration has pursued, and will continue to pursue, these objectives through active application of all relevant United Nations Security Council resolutions. The evidence is overwhelming that such changes will not happen under the current Iraq leadership.**

The INC's Ahmad Chalabi championed the measure on Capitol Hill. I don't remember when I first met him, but it was likely during that effort. He spoke thoughtfully, in articulate and idiomatic English, about Saddam's threats and crimes and the goal of a free and democratic Iraq. He capitalized on the respect his organization had won in the Congress for working well with diverse Iraqi democratic oppositionists. Chalabi had his detractors in Washington, especially at the CIA, but at this point he still had strong bipartisan support on Capitol Hill.

Saddam himself helped spur enactment of the Iraq Liberation Act when he decided in August 1998 to end Iraq's cooperation with UN weapons inspections. He closed the door on both UNSCOM and the International Atomic Energy Agency, the UN body that inspects nuclear facilities under the Nuclear Non-Proliferation Treaty. Declaring Iraq's action "unacceptable," the UN Security Council adopted a resolution of condemnation on September 9, 1998. It adopted another such resolution two months later, on November 5. Saddam shrugged off the condemnations and continued to refuse to cooperate.

In mid-December 1998, President Clinton responded with seventy hours of bombings and cruise missile strikes on Iraq. The campaign, dubbed Operation Desert Fox, did not move Saddam. As it got under way, members of Congress, including liberal Democrats, spoke out on the perils of Saddam's WMD ambitions. Representative Nancy Pelosi (D-California), for example, declared: "Saddam Hussein has been engaged in the development of weapons of mass destruction technology which is a threat to countries in the region and he has made a mockery of the weapons inspection process."

A year later, the UN Security Council adopted yet another resolution, putting UNSCOM out of its misery and replacing it with a new organization called the United Nations Monitoring Verification and Inspection

Commission (UNMOVIC). UNMOVIC was designed to appease Saddam and induce him to admit inspectors again by burying his quarrel with UNSCOM. Yet UNMOVIC failed to get support from Saddam's friends on the UN Security Council—China, France, and Russia—and for years Saddam refused to cooperate with this agency as well.

In 1999, some months after Operation Desert Fox, Saddam began firing antiaircraft artillery and missiles at the U.S. and British aircraft flying daily patrols over Iraq's northern and southern no-fly zones. He soon intensified the shooting, capitalizing on his other victories: the termination of the weapons inspections and the erosion of support for economic sanctions. Saddam's attempts to shoot down U.S. and British patrol aircraft were a clever type of aggression, with a rich actual and potential payoff for Iraq and apparently no major downside. They allowed Saddam to embarrass his enemies, impress Iraqis and the world with his defiance, and poke another hole in the tissue of measures that were supposed to keep him contained. Neither Britain nor the United States reacted strongly to this challenge. And neither drew much interest or thanks for the dangerous and costly effort involved in enforcing the zones. Another element of the containment strategy had been compromised by Saddam's defiance.

The collapse of the weapons inspections; the corruption, circumvention, and undermining of the economic and import controls; and the challenge to the no-fly-zone patrols—all tended to undo the Security Council's containment policy for Iraq, the most important UN peacekeeping initiative of the 1990s. Governments and observers around the world debated how to respond—but few argued that the Iraqi regime's threat to peace and order was insignificant. Saddam was far from a spent force. And he was acting as if time were on his side. By the time the Bush Administration was preparing to take office, the incoming officials knew they would soon have to shore up the Clinton Administration's policy of containment, or replace it.

On the eve of the January 2001 inauguration of George W. Bush, the British Broadcasting Company published a biographical piece about Saddam. It is noteworthy for its insights about Saddam's self-assurance and his grim hold on the Iraqis:

> **Gulf states and Western countries alike have come to realise that his grip is stronger than it seems—and stronger by far than his grasp of reality often appears to be.**
>
> **He insists that the 1991 Gulf War, which he famously described as the Mother-of-All-Battles, ended in victory for Iraq.**

By the same token, Saddam boasts that Iraq can shrug off any Western military attack. The Iraqi people have no choice but to nod in agreement.

So it will go on until the moment comes for bombastic slogans to be replaced by a succinct epitaph to one of the most infamous dictators of the century. For the overwhelming majority of Iraqis, that moment cannot come too soon.

Soon after President Bush came into office in 2001, his Administration began to debate Iraq policy options. Between my April nomination and my appointment as Under Secretary in mid-July, I was kept generally informed of this interagency work, and after my confirmation I participated directly in the discussions.

Before 9/11, the Iraq debates rarely involved the Principals. At the Deputies level, however, the Administration reviewed in depth the existing devices for pressuring Saddam's regime: economic sanctions, WMD inspections, and the no-fly zones in northern and southern Iraq. All the national security officials viewed Saddam as a problem, but there were important differences among us: first, concerning containment versus regime change, and, second, concerning whether "regime change" should mean merely a coup against Saddam Hussein or a more thorough removal of the Baathist government. Furthermore, there was the question of whether to continue the American and British no-fly zone patrols in light of the virtually daily attacks against our aircraft.

A compelling consideration for some of us was the U.S. interest in maintaining international respect for the legally binding "decisions" of the UN Security Council on international peace and security. One did not have to be a proponent of world government—or even an admirer of the UN's work—to appreciate the danger of allowing the Security Council to be exposed as ineffectual, as was the League of Nations in the 1930s. It was the Security Council, after all, that had designed the 1991 cease-fire arrangements in hopes of containing Saddam Hussein. By 2001, as UNMOVIC head Hans Blix later noted, containment was weakening: "The inspectors were gone. The sanctions were condemned by a broad range of world opinion and in any case they had become less painful, and were eroding."

This breakdown of the UN cease-fire provisions was disturbing, and not just because of the specific dangers of the Saddam Hussein regime. The UN's ten-year effort to contain Iraq amounted to a major experiment in international relations. It tested whether the world had an effective way of protecting itself against a repeat-offense aggressor without having to invade his country to oust him from power. After all, having expelled Iraq's invasion forces from Kuwait in 1991, the coalition might have proceeded to overthrow Saddam's regime, in the interests of regional peace and security. Instead, with U.S. support, the Security Council undertook to impose effective constraints on Iraq's ability to threaten the peace again.

In a hopeful sign of cooperation (made possible by the end of the Cold War), all of the Security Council's permanent members supported the constraints, welcoming the prospect of developing ways to deal with such regimes other than by ignoring their threats or overthrowing them in a war. Given our unique military capabilities and leadership role, no country had a greater interest than the United States did in finding new means to handle such threats. Publicly and privately, President George W. Bush stressed the importance of upholding the integrity of the resolutions on which the Security Council built its containment strategy.

By violating the sixteen Security Council resolutions adopted to contain him, Saddam was exposing a paradox: Any means short of war would be worthless unless Security Council members were willing to enforce them—*through war if necessary*. The stakes in the Council's confrontation with Iraq had implications far beyond Iraq.

There is more than one way of seeing any international problem. Some U.S. officials looked on the Iraqi Baathist regime not so much as an aggressive tyrannical disturber of the peace but as a force for order. At Deputies Committee meetings on Iraq, John McLaughlin and his CIA colleagues often stressed the value of stability. They argued that if Saddam were to be ousted, he should be replaced by another Baathist military strongman—someone who would preserve Sunni authoritarian predominance in Iraq. Many CIA papers before 9/11 therefore argued for ousting Saddam by coup rather than by the wholesale removal of the Baathist regime.

Stability and continuity were themes identified with Iyad Allawi and his Iraqi National Accord (composed largely of former Baathists, including senior military officers), for whom CIA officials had particular admiration. Unlike Chalabi, Allawi tended to extol order rather than democracy. He argued that the Sunni-dominated Baathist military was the key to keeping Iraq under control after Saddam's overthrow. Though himself a secular Shiite, Allawi (and his Sunni followers) shared the outlook of the Sunni Arab royalty in Saudi Arabia and throughout the region. Neither democracy nor political power in the hands of Shiites was a comfortable prospect for the region's political elites, however much they hated and feared Saddam.

The Sunni-Shiite division within Islam dates from the seventh century A.D., when the question arose of who should succeed Mohammed after the Prophet's death. The community of believers split into two camps, with the Shiites insisting that the Prophet's successors had to be members of his family. The majority (Sunni) view was that they did not. Over the centuries the split hardened into a sort of ethnic divide, with distinctive modes of worship and other cultural differences. The divide spawned severe and sometimes violent antagonism. Within the Middle East, the Shiites are a small minority—but they are the majority in Iran (whose ethnic makeup is predominantly Persian) and Iraq (which is predominantly Arab).

The advice we got from the region's Arab rulers—none of whom was Shiite—was that the Iraqi Shiites would serve the interests of the anti-American, theocratic regime of Iran. They stressed that the main Iraqi Shiite organizations (the Supreme Council for the Islamic Revolution in Iraq—SCIRI—and the Dawa Party) had long depended on Iran's theocrats for funds, materiel, refuge, and other support.* These warnings tended to ignore or understate the importance of such Shiite leaders in Iraq as Grand Ayatollah Ali al-Sistani, who opposed the Iranian model of clerical government and who, after Saddam's ouster, would prove an influential advocate for a unified Iraq with a nontheocratic, indeed democratic, government.†

Like personnel at State and other U.S. agencies, CIA officials often adopted the views of the elites in the foreign countries where they served. In our interagency meetings, they routinely made arguments that favored the interests of Sunni Arabs over those of Iraq's Shiite Arabs (and the Kurds). I shared the CIA's concern about the turmoil that would follow Saddam's overthrow, but I believed it was shortsighted to view the status quo as orderly and stable. The problem with their warnings about Iraq was that they tended to focus only on the problems of regime change,

---

*The Iranian regime and the Iraqi Shiite organizations it aided had a common enemy in Saddam, but there were important differences between the Iranians and the Iraqis—including the historical enmity between Persians and Arabs. If the Baathist regime were overthrown in Iraq and the Iraqi Shiites achieved political power, they were at least as likely to become dangerous rivals of the Iranian clerical rulers of Iran as their cats-paws.

†Another important Shiite leader also urged national unity: Grand Ayatollah Mohammed Esagh al-Fayyadh warned people not to "politicize religion" by using mosques for sectarian purposes. ("Iraq cleric seeks religious separation," AP News, September 7, 2008, available at http://abcnews.go.com/International/wireStory?id=3574585.)

ignoring the dangers of leaving Saddam in power. *Any* course of action President Bush might adopt on Iraq would involve problems. Like most government officials, however, CIA analysts had little to say about the risks of inaction.

When one government office proposes an initiative, the other agencies typically point out how it might go wrong. Officials tend to prefer the predictability of the status quo. Or they resist new ideas cooked up by others ("not invented here"). And there is less personal risk in offering a caution than in supporting a proposal that may or may not succeed.

The CIA's warnings about a sweeping regime change in Iraq had weight, but their contribution to the Iraq debate amounted to a case for leaving Saddam in power. When pressed, CIA officials were quick to mention—as they had over the past decade—the possibility of a coup against Saddam by Iraqi senior military officers. But *no practical coup option actually existed.* Though the U.S. government (through the CIA) had been trying to bring one about, the effort was in vain: Saddam uncovered at least 150 percent of all plots against him. He was far more effective at destroying his opponents than the CIA had been in enabling them.

Even if the coup option were feasible, the risks were substantial. It could leave us with a worse situation than we had. A new Iraqi regime, even if it retained its predecessor's Baathist ideology and aggressive ambitions, could expect a generous honeymoon from a world relieved to be rid of Saddam and happy to suspend the remaining international pressures—and this new regime might react by exploiting that opening with new dangerous behavior of its own. We referred to that possibility as "Saddamism without Saddam."

Nor was it clear that a coup would guarantee a more stable post-Saddam Iraq. There were some serious what-ifs.

Suppose we could bring about Saddam's replacement by Iraqis who would preserve Sunni control—the most likely candidates, given their predominance in the Baathist regime. Even aside from whether the American people would tolerate their government's installing a new dictatorship in Iraq, the deck would be stacked against that new regime. The Kurds and the Shia are 80 to 85 percent of the Iraqi population. What if one or both of those groups seized the opportunity to rebel? What would be America's responsibility and response? In the hope of achieving stability, could we support the dictatorship in crushing a rebellion for majority rule? It was not America's proudest moment when we watched Saddam crush the Shiites after Desert Storm in 1991. Now we would be standing by in favor of leaders we had helped install.

The coup option would thus require either a huge leap of faith—or a complete abandonment of principles. And the likelihood of a successful coup was in any case extremely slim. The more one thought about it, the more the CIA's warnings about post-Saddam instability looked like an incomplete argument for leaving Saddam in power, rather than a broad-gauge effort to help the President evaluate and manage the whole range of our national security concerns.

In Deputies Committee meetings on Iraq in early 2001, Paul Wolfowitz and Scooter Libby had been the principal voices favoring action to counter the threats posed by Saddam Hussein and his regime. Beyond these considerations, we were also concerned for the safety of our no-fly zone patrols, and for the Security Council's ability to enforce its containment measures.

Deputy Secretary of State Richard Armitage did not deny these threats and concerns, but he tended to downplay them. CIA Deputy Director John McLaughlin generally weighed in on Armitage's side of the debates. Wolfowitz and Libby stressed that Saddam was not being contained effectively. Wolfowitz insisted that the Iraqi regime was a problem that wasn't going away, and that could become harder to handle over time. Iraq already had large sums of cash, and would have far more, without constraints, if and when economic sanctions ended. Saddam considered himself aggrieved, especially by the United States, and remained vengeful and violent. He was a threat to Kuwait, Saudi Arabia, Jordan, Israel, and other states in the region against which he had grudges.

Saddam also remained secretive about his WMD programs. Having used such weapons internationally and even domestically to produce what he considered successful results, it was reasonable to worry that he would use them again, or threaten to do so. We knew he was harboring and training terrorists, Iraqi and non-Iraqi—though we had little detailed information on the scope and intent of this activity—and we knew he was encouraging anti-Israel extremism with his offers of rewards to the families of suicide bombers and other measures, doing his best to block movement toward a negotiated Palestinian-Israeli peace.

Unless we found ways to constrain him and undermine his regime, in short, Saddam would become more threatening and influential in the coming years, in his region and beyond. And as that happened, America would become less able to win cooperation from countries known to be subject, through intimidation or bribery, to Saddam's influence.

Wolfowitz proposed developing a strategy for regime change that would not necessarily entail a U.S. invasion. He outlined a few strategic goals for consideration:

- Win cooperation from other countries, building on the sixteen UN Security Council resolutions on Iraq since the Gulf War
- Strengthen the Iraqi democratic opposition, improving their military capabilities through U.S. training
- Help the opposition economically by, among other means, excluding from the UN's sanctions those areas in Iraq (in the Kurdish north) not under Saddam's control

Either the United States could take the initiative and try to advance our interests in Iraq on our own schedule, Wolfowitz concluded, or Saddam would act first—for example, by shooting down a U.S. military airplane—and force us to react.

While CIA officials debated with Wolfowitz and Libby about the best form of regime change, State Department officials argued for muddling through with variations on the containment policies of the 1990s.

A few years earlier, Armitage had signed the open letters advocating regime change in Iraq prepared by the Project for the New American Century and the Committee for Peace and Security in the Gulf. As Colin Powell's deputy, however, he advocated containment rather than regime change.*

Armitage was a colorful character. A hulking bodybuilder with a foghorn voice, he cultivated the persona of a stereotypical longshoreman union enforcer. He was cocky, brusque, and contemptuous, but there were aspects of his background one had to admire. He graduated from the U.S. Naval Academy and did multiple combat tours in Vietnam. He worked as a U.S. Senate aide and served in Ronald Reagan's Pentagon.

---

*Armitage and Wolfowitz had worked closely for several years during the Reagan Administration, when they occupied counterpart positions at Defense and State respectively (dealing with East Asian affairs). Wolfowitz expressed surprise and frustration early in the Bush Administration when Armitage was unwilling to meet with him, formally or informally. Armitage's new coolness appeared to be connected to job-related resentments: Wolfowitz told me that Powell had asked him to take the job of UN ambassador, but Wolfowitz turned it down to serve as Rumsfeld's Deputy Secretary—thereby blocking Armitage from the Pentagon post. Powell would have had an especially favorable bureaucratic situation if he had headed State while his best friend, Armitage, was the number two at Defense.

After doing special diplomatic missions for President George H. W. Bush, he had run a business consulting firm. Armitage talked fast and favored earthy, and occasionally crude, vocabulary. In the time I spent with him in the White House Situation Room, his most salient traits were his devotion to his close friend Colin Powell and his passionate protection of State Department bureaucratic prerogatives.

Armitage tended to come to Deputies Committee meetings with positions rather than analyses. The positions were Powell's, which were generally those championed by State's career officials. Armitage staked out his ground aggressively and defended it forcefully, but he was less effective in explaining his views, let alone persuading others of their merits.

Powell and Armitage were promoting what they called "smart sanctions" as the way to reinvigorate the Security Council's flagging containment effort. The original UN sanctions of 1991 had barred Saddam from selling oil. The Oil-for-Food program of 1996 cleared the way for him to sell oil, so long as he used the resulting revenues only for specifically *permitted* items (notably food and medicine). The idea of smart sanctions was to retreat an additional step, to allow Saddam to use his oil revenues to buy any items that the UN did not specifically *prohibit*.

These sanctions would be "smart," their proponents claimed, because they would cover a shorter, more precisely defined list of items. But Wolfowitz and others responded that smart sanctions looked like another victory for Saddam in wearing down the Security Council. Defense officials brought forward detailed, technical objections, citing specific items Iraq would now be allowed to buy—for example, heavy trucks that could be used as military tank transporters—and questioning the process the United Nations would use for approving Iraqi transactions. But the main problem with the smart sanctions initiative was that it would not help to counter the challenge we faced from Iraq.

When Powell or Armitage were asked what they intended to accomplish with smart sanctions, they gave a tactical, not strategic, reply: Smart sanctions, they said, would allow us to preserve the sanctions regime. Narrower sanctions would win the United States greater cooperation at the United Nations. Such points were fine as far as they went, but in our view they were secondary issues. Would smart sanctions help in some significant way to contain the threat posed by Saddam Hussein? Would they disarm him, or prevent him from rebuilding his WMD capabilities? Would they undermine Saddam's grip on power in Iraq?

I saw Powell's smart sanctions initiative as a way to *seem to* be addressing a problem without doing anything difficult or risky—or effective. Powell spoke of making the sanctions as tough as possible. At the Defense Department, we wanted them to be as tough *as they needed to be* to limit Saddam's ability to threaten other countries.

In late spring of 2001—before I joined the Administration—Condoleezza Rice's staff produced a proposal on "freeing the Iraqi people." It was an effort to bridge the various divides within the Administration on Iraq. The paper proposed extending immediate military assistance to Iraqi oppositionists, using the authority that remained untapped in the Iraq Liberation Act of 1998. A possible next step would be arming the oppositionists so they could eventually undertake operations to damage Saddam's regime and undermine its authority. A third possible step was action against the Iraqi regime by American forces.

On June 22, 2001, the Deputies met to discuss Iraq. They spent some time on the proposal from Rice's staff, deciding to include "lethal training" of the opposition in the first set of measures for our new Iraq policy.* Most of the meeting, however, dealt with Iraq's northern and southern no-fly zones. The key question was how the United States and the United Kingdom should respond to Iraq's attacks against their patrol planes. U.S. practice had been to try to bomb the specific Iraqi radars and artillery pieces being used in the attacks against us. But our retaliatory strikes often missed the highly mobile radars and artillery, and those that were hit were easily replaced, leaving Iraq's antiaircraft capability largely unaffected. Rumsfeld, Wolfowitz, and our military leadership were asking whether the benefits and costs of the no-fly-zone mission—flying the patrols, getting shot at, and retaliating—netted out on the plus side.

That June 22 meeting took place before I was confirmed as Under Secretary. Another Deputies Committee meeting was scheduled for July 13, and though I was still three days away from receiving my formal appointment from the President, I was able to attend as Paul Wolfowitz's "plus one." It was a solemn thrill to enter the famous Situation Room in the basement of the White House West Wing. As Condoleezza Rice's deputy, Steve Hadley took his seat at the head of the table, where the President sits during National Security Council meetings. As always, on Hadley's left was Armitage, representing State; on his right was Wolfowitz, representing Defense.

The meeting returned to the issue of the no-fly zones, which Hadley

---

*The term "lethal training," of course, means training for lethal operations—not training lethal to the trainee.

wanted to put on the agenda of the next Principals Committee meeting. Wolfowitz argued that if we wanted to hit the Iraqis for shooting at us, we should go after targets that would hurt them seriously. We should aim to induce Saddam to stop shooting at us, or in any event, weaken him significantly. Hadley agreed, saying that we should make clear to the public that our strikes were intended to reduce Iraqi military capabilities in the areas under the no-fly zones, to protect Kuwait in the south and the Kurds in the north.

The talk of targeting discomfited General Myers, at that time still the Vice Chairman of the Joint Chiefs. Myers believed that the Principals shouldn't be in the business of selecting targets, that discussing "desired degree of damage" was a matter for the military. Policy makers could properly talk about destroying targets that the Iraqi regime held dear, he argued, but they shouldn't get into tactics. Hadley did not dispute Myers in principle, but he observed that the Deputies had to inform their bosses whether the strikes proposed were really likely to do substantial or strategic damage to Saddam.

Myers also stressed the importance of mounting effective diplomacy and public affairs initiatives, in the interest of getting support from Saudi Arabia, Turkey, and other key partners. If a new U.S. strategy undermined that support, he warned, we would be in trouble when we next needed their help. Myers was clearly comfortable addressing strategic political-military considerations, even as he warned his colleagues not to violate the sphere of professional military judgment.

Armitage questioned whether this was a "smart time" to raise the issue of Iraq with the President, given that the Palestinian-Israeli peace process was not going anywhere and our position with the Gulf states "stinks." (This hinted at the common diplomatic complaint that President Bush was not involved enough personally in Palestinian-Israeli diplomacy.) If things were quiet on the Palestinian issue, Armitage said, the United States could then make Saddam our top priority.

Wolfowitz replied that weakening Saddam could serve our goals in the Palestinian-Israeli peace process, as Saddam was opposing Palestinian compromise and encouraging Palestinians to become anti-Israel suicide bombers. Armitage shot back that, under current circumstances, if we took steps to weaken Saddam, we would be accused of acting for Israel.

This was a strange twist: In presenting his case for action against Saddam based on U.S. security needs, Wolfowitz had mentioned Israel only as one of several concerned neighbors of Iraq. Armitage then cited Israel—specifically, the Israeli-Palestinian impasse—in arguing *against* Wolfowitz's case, regardless of U.S. security. When Wolfowitz replied that his proposal might actually further Arab-Israeli peace, Armitage complained that we could be accused of helping Israel if we confronted Saddam, an ally of the Palestinian extremists.

At this point, Libby spoke up. A short and lean man, Libby was intellectually acute, quiet-voiced, cautious in his remarks, and often silent throughout meetings—in every way the opposite of Armitage. In response to Armitage's suggestion that Iraq should be kept off the President's agenda for the present, Libby noted that the President had asked for a paper on Iraq a long time ago. We should submit one, he noted, and ask him to decide in principle on an approach, even if he decides not to take action right now.

The Deputies returned to the issues of regime change and support for opposition groups. Hadley's staff had prepared a paper on the subject for the upcoming Principals meeting, but Hadley was dissatisfied with it, calling it more of an action plan than a strategy. What was needed, he said, was a review of the fundamentals: What should the United States be trying to accomplish in Iraq? When Armitage questioned whether we should still be using the term "regime change," Wolfowitz said he, too, had concerns about the term, because it implied that the United States was intent on effecting the change by itself. He thought that our strategy should focus on supporting all reasonable efforts by Iraqis to free *themselves* from Saddam's tyranny.

Building on his theme of finding nonwar options for Iraq, Wolfowitz suggested creating a coordinating mechanism between the U.S. government and the Iraqi opposition. He also proposed an approach he had long favored—that the United States could recognize a provisional government of free Iraq, which would allow us to escape from the "stupid argument" that the UN's economic sanctions must apply even to those areas of Iraq (the Kurdish region in the north) that were not under Saddam's control.

Wolfowitz knew that the Turks would intensely oppose singling out northern Iraq for special international status, for fear of putting that region on a path toward independent Kurdish statehood. (Turkey has its own sizeable Kurdish minority.) So he suggested trying to create a second autonomous area along Iraq's southern border with Kuwait. These two Iraqi areas not under Saddam's control might then combine politically to form a "Free Iraq." With international diplomatic recognition, this new entity might then gain legal possession of the billions of dollars of Iraqi government assets that had been frozen in various countries since Saddam's 1990 invasion of Kuwait. And if those areas could be enlarged, under U.S. protection, to encompass Iraq's oil fields, Saddam's regime might become vulnerable to overthrow by increasingly strong domestic forces.

The purpose of this Deputies discussion was to prepare the Principals to present Iraq policy options to the President. But Armitage made it clear that Powell was not eager for the Principals Committee to discuss these issues—or to develop any policy options for Iraq. Powell preferred not to do anything new on Iraq policy other than put smart sanctions in place, so keeping the issue away from the President was fine with him.

I knew that Rumsfeld believed the status quo was not serving U.S. interests—and that the situation would worsen over time if Bush did not determine a proper U.S. strategy for dealing with Saddam Hussein. In any event, regardless of whether Bush would support his position or Powell's—or neither—Rumsfeld insisted he wanted to learn what the President thought. Rumsfeld's attitude toward the President matched the position Libby expressed at this July 13 Deputies Committee meeting: On important subjects of dispute within the Administration, top officials should seek the President's guidance, rather than trying to get their own way by keeping the President out of the picture.

Rumsfeld urged Rice to schedule a Principals meeting on Iraq in preparation for a National Security Council discussion with the President. Not content to rely on the Deputies to set the agenda for his discussions with his colleagues and the President, he began writing down some of his own provocative thoughts on the matter, drafting a snowflake and asking Wolfowitz and me to revise it.

In the meantime, Wolfowitz and I had been preparing a memo reporting to Rumsfeld on the Deputies' discussions on Iraq. We received his snowflake just as we were finishing up our own memo, which we sent him on July 26. In our memo, we sought Rumsfeld's approval for the positions we had been advancing with the other Deputies. We proposed changing our no-fly zone enforcement "from tit-for-tat responses to attacks on strategic targets that weaken Saddam's rule," and ending the "logjam" on support for the Iraqi opposition. We noted that some of our Arab friends criticized what they called "pinprick U.S. responses" to Iraqi provocations. They found it nerve-racking when the United States bombed Iraq in a way that heightened tensions without actually diminishing Saddam's ability to retaliate against his enemies.

Referring to Armitage's point about holding off on tough action on Iraq because Arab-Israeli diplomacy was stagnating, we advised Rumsfeld that the Administration's hesitancy in recent weeks had been, in part, "due to a fear that, with the Israeli-Palestinian impasse in such a raw state, strong U.S. action against Iraq was too risky." But we answered that U.S. weakness in the face of Saddam's aggressiveness "undercuts our leverage in the region on *everything*, including in the Israeli-Palestinian diplomacy."

After finishing our memo on the Deputies meeting, I gave Rumsfeld our comments on his draft snowflake on Iraq. The next day, July 27, Rumsfeld signed it out to Rice, Powell, and Cheney. After reviewing recent history, he argued in the memo that sanctions were proving insufficient to compel Saddam to change his policies and were getting weaker: "[Saddam] undid the UN inspections in the 1990s and is working now to further undo the sanctions and the no-fly zones. He appears to believe he is getting stronger." On the no-fly zones, Rumsfeld pointed to a shoot-down of a U.S. or U.K. plane as "an increasingly likely danger," and argued that the recent ground-to-air attacks demonstrated:

- **a greater degree of Iraqi aggressiveness; and, even more important,**
- **what appears to be significantly improved Iraqi air defense capability, coupled with a reduction in U.S. ability to know what they are doing—partly because of their improved fiber-optic linkages.**

If some important U.S. interest were being accomplished by the flights, Rumsfeld asserted, it was worth the risk of a shoot-down—but "[i]f not, it isn't." One option was to launch "a fairly significant U.S. strike against Iraq's fiber-optic links, radars, SAM [surface-to-air missile] sites and perhaps some asymmetrical strategic assets that would impose a more-than-tit-for-tat cost on Saddam for his endangerment of our pilots." But hitting some of those targets would create dramatic television pictures, inevitably producing accusations that we were killing civilians and public criticism from our Arab friends in the region (whatever encouragement they might offer in private).

Another option was to "seek to limit the risk to coalition aircraft by cutting back on the number and/or locations of patrols." But limiting our air activity, including our bombing of Iraqi military assets in the no-fly zones, would allow Iraq to strengthen its air defenses. That would lead to further pressure to limit or stop our patrol flights.

In all events, Rumsfeld noted, the no-fly zones were only a slice of the Iraq problem: "It is the broader subject of Iraq that merits the attention of the Administration." Though others in the government should be able to propose "more nuanced options," he said, he wanted to launch the discussion among Principals by presenting a set of options (which ranged from passive to radical):

- **The U.S. can roll up its tents and end the no-fly zones before someone is killed or captured. We can try to figure out a way to keep an eye on Saddam Hussein's aggressiveness against his neighbors from a distance. We can publicly acknowledge that sanctions don't work over extended periods and stop the pretense of having a policy that is keeping Saddam "in the box," when we know he has crawled a good distance out of the box and is currently doing the things that will ultimately be harmful to his neighbors in the region and to U.S. interests—namely developing WMD and the means to deliver them and increasing his strength at home and in the region month-by-month. Within a few years the U.S. will undoubtedly have to confront a Saddam armed with nuclear weapons.**
- **A second option would be to go to our moderate Arab friends, have a reappraisal, and see whether they are willing to engage in a more robust policy. We would have to assert strong leadership and convince them that we will see the project through and not leave them later to face a provoked, but still incumbent, Saddam. The risks of a serious regime change policy must be weighed against the certainty of the danger of an increasingly bold and nuclear-armed Saddam in the near future.**
- **A third possibility perhaps is to take a crack at initiating contact with Saddam Hussein. He has his own interests. It may be that, for whatever reason, at his stage in life he might prefer to not have the hostility of the United States and the West and might be willing to make some accommodation.**

A dialogue with Saddam would be "an astonishing departure" for the U.S. government, Rumsfeld wrote, noting that he had met with Saddam when he worked for President Reagan in the mid-1980s. Starting a dialogue would "win praise from certain quarters," Rumsfeld thought, "but might cause friends, especially those in the region, to question our strength, steadiness and judgment." And "the likelihood of Saddam making and respecting an acceptable accommodation of our interests over a long period may be small." Rumsfeld argued that there "ought to be a way for the U.S. to not be at loggerheads with both of the two most powerful nations in the Gulf—Iran and Iraq," given that they "do not like each other" and "are firing at each other." He added: "The particularly unfortunate circumstances of Iraq being governed by Saddam and Iran being governed by the clerics have suspended the standard rule that 'my enemy's enemy is my friend.' "

It might appear that Rumsfeld had inserted the idea of a dialogue with Saddam merely as a straw man—a throwaway option, included to create the false appearance of choice. (It was a standard joke that State Department papers always had the same three options: [1] Suffer in silence; [2] do some diplomacy; [3] nuclear war. State would boldly support the second option.) But that's not how Rumsfeld's mind worked. Floating such a suggestion—to talk with Saddam to explore a mutual accommodation—was characteristic of Rumsfeld's approach to problem solving. Despite a common misperception, Rumsfeld was not closed-minded or ideological. Indeed, he was actively anti-ideological: All ideas, theories, and preconceptions were open to continual examination and challenge. It was clear to him that approaching Saddam was a bad idea, and he signaled as much in his memo, confident that others would agree. But he wanted the Principals and the president to *think the idea through*. That way, if they rejected it, they would do so affirmatively and know why.

This continual process of evaluation was the most significant feature of Rumsfeld's mind—though many failed to recognize it, perhaps because they could not see past his intimidating personality. As we weighed the many questions surrounding Iraq, the secretary always wanted a comprehensive menu of ideas, each of them rigorously formulated and considered, so that he could say in good conscience that he had presented the president with the full range of options.

As of late summer 2001, neither Rumsfeld nor the President had decided on what U.S. policy toward Iraq should be. Rumsfeld (as I knew from my earliest meetings with him) regarded war with Saddam as a last resort. But it was not clear that we had an effective alternative.

7

RISKS OF ACTION AND INACTION

The Bush Administration found it difficult in its early months to agree on a course of action toward the Saddam Hussein regime. Iraq demanded attention—if only because, as Rumsfeld often pointed out, it was the only place in the world at the time where U.S. forces (the aircraft patrolling the northern and southern no-fly zones) were routinely under hostile fire. Officials debated the magnitude, nature, and urgency of the Iraq threat—and the best ways to respond.

The debate occurred mainly at the level of the Deputies and below—in preparation for eventual discussion at the National Security Council. In arguing for the status quo policy of containment, State and CIA officials tended to depict the threats from Saddam as remote, confined to his region, and unlikely to materialize in the near future. Saddam gave support to terrorists, but was the U.S. a likely target? He was (thought to be) pursuing nuclear weapons, but how many years would it take him to acquire them? U.S. intelligence officials believed that Saddam had both chemical weapons (CW) and biological weapons (BW), but how worrisome was that for us? After all, Saddam did not have intercontinental-range missiles. In any case, did the United States have any good options against him?

When the 9/11 hijackers struck, President Bush and his National Security Council had not yet resolved any of these issues. The attack required Administration officials to take a new look at *all* national security dangers—including Iraq. It gave us a new apprehension of America's vulnerability. Dangers that had seemed remote or manageable now looked closer and more distressing. President Bush's national security team had to reconsider how willing the United States should be to abide threats—or how active it should be to end them.

For more than thirty years before 9/11, most Americans had accepted the common view of terrorist attacks as a means various political groups used to gain international attention for their causes, not a way to wreak destruction for its own sake. Some terrorists proclaimed far-reaching goals: the elimination of Israel; the overthrow of governments or social systems in Rhodesia, South Africa, and elsewhere. But their operations themselves were relatively small-scale—assassinations, bus bombings, machine gun attacks at airport ticket counters, and the like—and not designed to produce mass destruction. Accordingly, the terrorists showed little if any interest in chemical, biological, or nuclear weapons, which might forfeit public goodwill irretrievably.

The 9/11 attack was a new phenomenon, and not just because it hit Americans on American soil. It was not an act of political theater; rather, it was the first successful case of terrorism of mass destruction.* Though the al Qaida hijackers killed only—only!—around three thousand people, one had to assume that the terrorists would have been glad to kill all thirty thousand people who worked at the World Trade Center, and even multiples of that number.

This was why keeping weapons of mass destruction out of the hands of terrorists became, suddenly and inevitably, a far more pressing and higher-order concern than it had been before. It concentrated the minds of U.S. officials on the threat from states that both coveted WMD and supported terrorists.

Iraq was such a state. Its singular history of aggression, and its defiance of the world's many efforts to constrain it, made Iraq stand out even among such other WMD-coveting, terrorist-supporting states as Iran and North Korea.

After 9/11, President Bush promptly asked the obvious questions: Was Iraq tied to the attack, or to al Qaida? CIA officials never reported

---

*There had been two unsuccessful previous attempts at mass murder of Americans: the 1993 World Trade Center bombing (intended to demolish one or both towers, during working hours); and a 1995 plot to bomb twelve U.S. passenger jumbo jets in flight.

a substantial tie between Iraq and 9/11. Nor did they quickly produce an authoritative report on what they knew of the interactions of al Qaida and the Iraqi regime over the years. When the President decided at Camp David that our first military operation in the war on terrorism should target al Qaida and the Taliban in Afghanistan, the question of action against Saddam Hussein was deferred.

Still, our concerns about Iraq intensified after 9/11—but not because anyone thought Saddam had actually conspired in the 9/11 attack. No one I know of believed Saddam was part of the 9/11 plot; we had no substantial reason to believe he was. Nor did we have any intelligence that Iraq was plotting specific operations with al Qaida or any other terrorist group. Rather, the concern reflected our general recognition of the dangers posed by Saddam's regime—and Saddam's hostility to the United States.*

Given Saddam's record, it appeared highly likely that, if left in power, he would soon slip out from under the UN sanctions and eventually take aggressive action—perhaps a new assault on Kuwait—that would once again bring him into conflict with the United States. If, by then, Iraq had made strides in developing its biological or nuclear weapons, U.S. officials would be facing a serious problem—and asking how we had allowed this terrible situation to develop.

Possession of WMD could put Saddam in a position to deter the United States from interfering. He could further complicate our calculations by cooperating with terrorists who could present us with additional types of threats: His long history of dealing with terrorists and terrorist organizations opened the possibility that he would work with al Qaida or another such group.

After Saddam's fall, investigators confirmed that Iraqi intelligence had assisted the regime's paramilitary organization with terrorist training—and that the Fedayeen Saddam were training Iraqi and Arab volunteers by the thousands in Iraq. In analyzing possible scenarios, U.S. officials worried that Iraq might give terrorists poison gas, or an anthrax or smallpox weapon—or eventually, perhaps, a nuclear device. Putting such capabilities in the hands of terrorists would change the world's security picture and could intimidate countries—perhaps including the United States—into

*Saddam Hussein was the only international figure, other than Usama bin Laden, to praise the attacks of 9/11. And U.S. troops would later discover two dramatic murals—one installed in Iraqi army headquarters—celebrating the airplane attacks on the World Trade Center.

accommodating Saddam, even if the weapons were never actually used to kill anyone.

After 9/11, Americans asked what we might possibly have done to prevent the catastrophe. Officials searched their own souls for answers. This was well before the 9/11 Commission hearings made famous the reproach that some officials had failed the American people by not "connecting the dots" soon enough about terrorist threats. It was proper to examine whether our government had been vigilant, far-sighted, and active enough in defense of the nation. But it was more urgent to ask what dots we should connect *now*, after 9/11, to defend the nation from this point forward. The expectation of further major terrorist attacks remained widespread.

Just a few weeks before 9/11, a prestigious team of private organizations had reported on a political-military exercise they conducted that simulated the effects of a smallpox attack in the United States. The report, entitled "Dark Winter," received high-level attention within the U.S. government, both because the players included such eminent individuals as former Senator Sam Nunn (D-Georgia) and because the lessons from the exercise were so horrifying.* Even before 9/11, Scooter Libby talked often about "Dark Winter," noting that Vice President Cheney considered it a particularly significant study.

The exercise scenario was set in the near future, in December 2002. It posited outbreaks of smallpox—a contagious, disfiguring, and fatal disease—in Pennsylvania, Georgia, and Oklahoma. Participants in the exercise were unable to identify the source of the biological agent, but suspected Iraq because of its history of biological weapons development.

As the exercise unfolded, the disease quickly exhausted the U.S. government's vaccine supplies. Governors in the affected areas ordered National Guard units to try to keep out refugees from infected neighboring states. Other countries banned U.S. air traffic. Though the scenario was imaginary, real-life experts in contagious disease made projections of how the smallpox infection would spread. Three thousand cases of smallpox by mid-December would increase tenfold by early January, they projected, and tenfold again by mid-January. By early February, the study concluded, *three million people would be infected, including one million deaths*.

---

*Other participants included Frank Keating, former Governor of Oklahoma; David Gergen, former presidential adviser; James Woolsey, former CIA Director; John White, former Deputy Secretary of Defense; General John Tilelli (U.S. Army, retired); Frank Wisner, former Under Secretary of Defense for Policy; William Sessions, former FBI Director.

In their June 2001 report, the participants in the "Dark Winter" exercise drew the following lessons:

1. **A BW attack on America with a contagious pathogen could potentially cripple the country.**
   - ***Noncontagious pathogens similarly crippling.***
2. **A local BW attack quickly becomes a national and global crisis.**
3. **Government responses will pose enormous challenges to civil liberties.**
   - ***The less prepared we are, the more threats there will be to civil liberties.***
4. **America lacks the resource stockpiles required for appropriate response.**
   - ***This includes vaccines and antibiotics, and a means of effective distribution.***
5. **Forcible constraints on citizens may likely be the only tools available when vaccine stocks are depleted.**
6. **Today we are ill equipped to prevent the dire consequences of a BW attack.**

The participants' report did much to make the problem vivid, including graphics on the horrifying effects of the disease.

Naturally, as officials worried about new attacks after 9/11, memories of the "Dark Winter" exercise kept the danger of smallpox and other biological agents at the front of our minds. We wondered: What would President Bush tell the American people if a "Dark Winter"–type attack occurred, and if the biological weapons agent were traced to Iraq? After an attack of that kind, the effects of which would dwarf those of 9/11, how would President Bush explain why he had failed to "connect the dots" and head it off? Could he tell the American people that we didn't know that Saddam was hostile? Or aggressive? Or had worked with biological weapons? Or had supported terrorist groups? Could President Bush excuse himself by claiming he thought that Saddam was "in a box," "contained," or otherwise lacked the ability to hurt us in this way? Could the President say there was no need to worry about Saddam, given that Iraqi officials appeared not to have conspired in the 9/11 attack? The President could not honestly say any of those things.

We knew Saddam's weapons scientists had been researching smallpox, plague, and other biological agents. We knew he had used nerve, mustard, and other poison gases against civilians. We knew he had no scruples about working with terrorists—that he had harbored, financed, trained, and encouraged leaders and operatives from various terrorist groups over the years, and that he had publicly commended the success of the 9/11 attacks. We knew that Saddam was not so "contained" as to lack the resources to hurt us. And we knew he was dangerous to us whether or not Iraq was linked to al Qaida.

This knowledge was *not* secret. It was *not* available only from intelligence sources. Anyone who read newspapers, watched television news, or read history books had the essential facts.

In a small meeting in his office on September 29, 2001, Rumsfeld asked General Myers (just two days away from becoming Chairman of the Joint Chiefs) to begin preparing military options for Iraq. The Secretary identified two objectives. One of these related to weapons of mass destruction: Rumsfeld asked for a CENTCOM plan to find the weapons, clean them out and destroy them, and find the people who had manned the WMD programs. The other objective was regime change—and for this task Rumsfeld asked that the options include one that would take only one or two months and 250,000 troops, not necessarily all from the United States.

Operation Enduring Freedom would begin in Afghanistan on October 7, and the combatant commanders were beginning to offer their ideas for action in the broader war on terrorism. But Rumsfeld was also faced with the possibility that Saddam might provoke a conflict by shooting down a no-fly-zone patrol plane, invading the autonomous region of northern Iraq, or attacking us in some other way. Meanwhile, envelopes containing anthrax arrived by ordinary mail at one of the U.S. Senate office buildings and at the offices of journalists, including Tom Brokaw of NBC News in New York. The anthrax powder was immediately sent off for analysis to try to determine who might have manufactured it—and among the suspects was Iraq, given that UNSCOM inspectors had confirmed that Iraqi weapons technicians had done work on anthrax.

Rumsfeld wanted our government, as much as possible, to *control* its dealings with the Iraqi regime, not just to react to Saddam's actions. Toward this end, he asked me to evaluate what actions we might take to neutralize Iraq's WMD threat, or the terrorism threat, or both.

I responded with a paper that (according to our normal practice) reflected the thinking of the Defense Department policy leadership generally. It drew on Rumsfeld's own ideas, along with input from Wolfowitz and from my staff—in particular Peter Rodman, his deputy Peter Flory, William Luti, and Abram Shulsky. And we met several times with General Peter Pace and members of the Joint Staff to brainstorm about the problem. Those civilian-military meetings tended to combine concepts with practical, operational proposals; they were always usefully informal, with lots of questions and opinions being voiced without regard to rank.

The resulting paper, delivered to Rumsfeld on November 8, offered ideas on actions *short of war* that the United States could take to pressure Saddam and increase our leverage against him. One thought was to use Iraqi opposition groups to cultivate contacts inside Iraq. The hope was that, in the event of U.S. military action, our forces would not have to wait for links to be forged on the ground, as we had had to do in Afghanistan. Other ideas for consideration included helping bolster the autonomy of northern Iraq and creating in the south a "no go" zone for Iraqi military forces—also, encouraging Iraqis to defect north or south to work for a change in regime, and using the Iraq Liberation Act to aid the Iraqi National Congress (INC) in serving as an umbrella organization for Iraqi democratic opposition groups.

I suggested in this paper that we assume that the Iraqi regime had penetrated the INC—a reasonable guess given the pervasiveness of Iraqi intelligence and the failure of past coup attempts. U.S. aid, I proposed, should therefore go for activities like propaganda inside Iraq and humanitarian relief that might not be harmed greatly if they were discovered by Saddam's agents.

Later, in November 2001—as Northern Alliance forces, with U.S. help, were capturing Afghanistan's main cities one after another—Rumsfeld worked to produce an up-to-date war plan for Iraq. This did not reflect a decision by him or the President to attack Saddam. Commanders routinely develop war plans to support policy making when there is no present intention to go to war. President Bush recognized he needed to develop his Iraq policy. As part of a comprehensive review of U.S. policy toward terrorist organizations and their supporters, it was important that he understand his military options.

Roughly two weeks later, Rumsfeld prepared strategic guidance for General Franks for a new war plan for Iraq. In a series of meetings, Wolfowitz, Myers, Pace, and I worked out a set of ideas for Rumsfeld to use when he met with Franks on November 27 to discuss the Iraq war plan.

Rumsfeld wanted the plan to present a range of options for the President to consider, not a binary choice between doing nothing and launching a massive U.S. invasion. He decided, therefore, to consider the problem in terms of "slices"—goals, targets, or pressure points. He wanted proposed ways to handle each of these slices that would serve broader U.S. interests in the war on terrorism.

In the larger war, Rumsfeld said, the chief strategic danger was that an extremist group could obtain a biological or nuclear weapon. Saddam's record on WMD and terrorism made us worry that Iraq might be the supplier. So the Iraq campaign, he concluded, should "focus on WMD." It should do everything possible to prevent Iraq from providing WMD to terrorists for use against the United States. The Secretary wanted to present the President with options that were short of regime change but could still reduce the WMD danger to some extent—for example, by attacking WMD sites and missile sites and seizing Saddam's economic assets. These options might create momentum for regime change, either by Iraqis or by U.S. and coalition forces, without committing the President to overthrow Saddam.

With little time to write up our ideas for Rumsfeld to use with General Franks, I gave the Secretary a set of rough notes reflecting earlier discussions among his team. It listed a few "slices" relating to WMD and missiles, oil-producing areas, and Republican Guard units. Rumsfeld penned in some additional options and objectives:

- **regime change**
- **SF [U.S. Special Forces] on the ground in north—coordinate with Kurds**
- **protection for provisional government**
- **seize W. [western] desert**
- **deployment of ground forces...**
- **cut off Baghdad**

Rumsfeld's additions reflected the broad range of ideas he was already considering: from fostering a "provisional government" to developing an autonomous north-south entity that would leave Baghdad isolated—cut off—from the rest of the country in military and other ways.

One of my notes for Rumsfeld included the phrase: "Surprise, speed, shock and risk." Rumsfeld penned in "Momentum for regime change." Rumsfeld suggested: "Start military action before moving into place all the forces that would be required in the worst case." One worry was that Saddam might order terrorist attacks in the United States by cells he may already have created in the United States, or by other affiliated groups. With this in mind, Rumsfeld wanted Franks to think of ways to cut off the Iraqi leadership as early as possible from any means of communicating with the wider world. And even though the Secretary expected cooperation from partner countries, he said that we should plan for the possibility that we might have to go without substantial support from them.

As a reminder of our strategic objectives in Iraq—beyond the military overthrow of the regime—I urged that we plan early for Iraq's political reconstruction: "Unlike in Afghanistan, important to have ideas in advance about who would rule afterwards." Rumsfeld's marginal notes showed that he was already thinking about an Iraqi provisional government and its security requirements.

Rumsfeld intended Franks to make a first cut at a plan—a "rough concept, not complete execution-level planning"—and come back to talk it over with him. The Secretary jotted down some additional points: He noted the danger that Saddam might move suddenly to crush the Kurds. He wanted to talk with Franks on managing the military coalition. He had questions on how the Defense Department might provide support—logistics or intelligence, for example—to WMD inspectors. And he wrote that the U.S. government needed to formulate a "declaratory policy"—a policy statement that we could communicate either publicly or privately to Saddam and other relevant Iraqi civilian or military officials, designed to reduce the risk that Saddam might use chemical or biological weapons against us.

Some commentators have claimed that President Bush was hell-bent on deposing Saddam Hussein, either before 9/11 or immediately after. That was not the impression I had. Members of the National Security Council and other senior officials spent many hours evaluating and debating options for dealing with Iraq. Our understanding was that President Bush wanted his advisers to devise every sensible way to resolve our Iraq problems short of war. At the Deputies level, we had grappled for months with whether regime change in Iraq was a necessary goal of U.S. policy—and, if so, whether it might be achievable without war.

Common explanations of how the Bush Administration resolved on military action against Iraq have generally followed one of a few different storylines.

One line of argument is that "they" lied the United States into war. Sometimes the "they" in question has included the President. Sometimes it has referred only to lower-level officials, including myself, who have been accused of willfully misrepresenting Iraq's WMD programs or support for terrorism to get the President and his National Security Council to make war against Saddam. Critics have sometimes asserted *both* that Bush lied to the public and that he was lied to by his subordinates, though those propositions contradict each other.

The assertion that officials lied about the war's rationale is false. In the many thousands of official comments on the matter, there were some sloppy formulations, ill-chosen phrases, and outright errors. Officials also cited intelligence reports about Iraqi WMD that later proved faulty. But misstatements and other mistakes are not lies. As documents quoted throughout this book make clear, U.S. officials believed that Iraq had chemical and biological weapons stockpiles—as Republican and Democratic voices in the government had generally agreed since the mid-1990s.

A second explanation—questioning no one's honesty—has been that the war's rationale hinged on intelligence about WMD that turned out to be false. Although inaccurate intelligence was indeed a factor in the Administration's thinking, the reasoning that drove the Administration to overthrow Saddam had a broader base than the bad WMD intelligence.

Which brings us to the third explanation of why we went to war against Saddam: The President had an honest, well-grounded rationale, one that was not undermined by our failure to find WMD stockpiles in Iraq. I believe this was the case.

As the year 2002 began, President Bush made it clear that his Administration should be focused on preventing another major terrorist attack. At the Pentagon, we asked ourselves if we were doing everything possible to keep our enemies on the defensive, to disrupt their networks, to pressure the states supporting terrorism to change their policies, and to preclude, if possible, terrorists from gaining access to weapons of mass destruction.

For years, Islamist extremists had been murdering ordinary people as stepping-stones to their theocratic utopia. They operated within a worldwide movement and had constructed a network with nodes on many continents. Rumsfeld urged the government to take seriously the word "global" in the phrase "global war on terrorism." Although there was much work left to be done in Afghanistan, he pushed for a comprehensive strategy designed to counter threats not just from Afghanistan. Our responsibility was to pursue al Qaida terrorists around the world—as well as terrorists from other significant groups. And we had to devise strategies to handle each of the key states in the global terrorist network, especially those with nuclear, biological, or chemical weapons ambitions.

Bush often said that the United States would prosecute the global war on terrorism with "all instruments of national power"—including diplomatic, intelligence, financial, and law enforcement means, not just military power. Administration officials weighed which combination of means was best suited for each part of the enemy network. General Pace and I led an effort within the Pentagon to analyze which state supporters of terrorism might be manageable through diplomacy or other nonmilitary means, and which might require the President to use military means, though not necessarily to launch a war.

Ultimately, President Bush concluded that he had to remove Saddam's regime from power by war. In my judgment, his moment of decision came in December 2002, when the Iraqi regime made its unsatisfactory WMD declaration to the United Nations. From that point forward, it seemed to me, the only way Saddam Hussein could have prevented war was by recognizing the inevitability of defeat and relinquishing power.

It bears repeating that the United States was still engaged in a conflict with Iraq that dated back more than a decade. Saddam never renounced his "claim" to Kuwait, and he never resigned himself to the terms of the 1991 cease-fire, which he violated as best he could. He had worked systematically to dismantle the Security Council's containment measures. Having ended the weapons inspections, he was now on track to defeat the UN economic sanctions, with the help of France, Russia, and other friends. By 2002, much of the world had grown weary of keeping Iraq under sanctions. The economic restrictions (including the Oil-for-Food arrangement) impinged on many countries—not just Iraq but its potential customers and suppliers, too.

Removing even these weakened sanctions would have been a signal victory for Iraq. It would have strengthened Saddam politically, while increasing the resources he could use to increase Iraqi military capabilities, including WMD. (After Saddam's fall, the Iraq Survey Group found that he intended to reinvigorate his efforts to produce nuclear, biological, and chemical weapons and long-range missiles after the sanctions were removed—and had taken pains to preserve Iraq's ability to do so.)

Meanwhile, the United States and Britain had to decide whether it was wise to continue enforcing the no-fly zones over Iraq, with Iraq shooting at the patrol aircraft almost every day. Ending those flights would further embolden Saddam, while severely frightening the Kurds, the Shiites in southern Iraq, and the Kuwaitis. Yet if the flights continued, it would be only a matter of time before Iraq was once again engaged in a violent clash with the United States. And if the patrols didn't lead to conflict, some new aggression—against Kuwait or some other target—was likely to do so. That would give Saddam a chance to intimidate and hurt the United States—perhaps through cooperation with terrorists, and possibly through the brandishing, use, or transfer of biological or other catastrophic weapons.

President Bush ultimately decided that the risks of getting drawn into a renewed war on Saddam's terms were unacceptable. Weighing America's vulnerabilities against Saddam's record of aggression, he decided that it would be too dangerous to allow Saddam to choose the time and place of his next war with us.

Deciding how to keep the United States secure is a large responsibility. President Bush approached the task with a sense of peril heightened by the 9/11 catastrophe. He reviewed the ways that the United States and others had tried to counter the Iraqi threat over the last decade: diplomatic protests, Security Council resolutions, weapons inspections, economic sanctions, no-fly zones, no-drive zones, and limited military strikes. We had attempted every reasonable means short of war. War would be risky; no one could know in advance the duration or cost of such a conflict. But leaving Saddam in power would be risky, too. Reasonable people differed then, and differ now, on whether war was the right choice.

Concern about biological-weapons terrorism was an important part of the rationale for overthrowing Saddam, once it became clear that we had exhausted all other means of disarming him. But wasn't that rationale undermined by the Iraq Survey Group's failure to find the expected WMD stockpiles in Iraq? No—because, as we'll see, the Administration's rationale did not depend solely on concern about weapons of mass destruction, much less on whether Saddam had WMD stockpiles on hand. Yet many people believed, then and now, that it did hinge on the existence of stockpiles—and this became a disastrous credibility problem for the Bush Administration.

The reports we had from U.S. intelligence officials on Iraqi WMD painted essentially the same picture that those officials had presented to the Clinton Administration. The CIA declared that Saddam had chemical and biological weapons stockpiles. The stockpiles catalogued by the UN weapons inspectors in 1999 were still unaccounted for, and were therefore presumed to exist. The UN inspectors' final report in 1999 noted, among other troubling points, that Iraq's "virus studies" focused on camel pox—the smallpox surrogate—and that "the rationale for this work was not given."

The CIA also reported to policy makers that Saddam could have a nuclear weapon within "several months to a year" if he could get the necessary plutonium or enriched uranium from outside Iraq, as opposed to trying to produce his own fissile material domestically. The possibility of Iraq's importing fissile material could not be dismissed, given that Saddam had billions of dollars' worth of oil revenues—and other countries, such as North Korea, had fissile material but were severely short of cash.

But the rationale for war did not actually stand or fall on the accuracy of CIA and UNSCOM assessments of Iraq's WMD stockpiles. The danger was that Saddam might someday soon provide terrorists with WMD—biological weapons, for example. Our concern was not simply that he might do so out of stockpiles he kept on hand, for we knew Iraq could produce biological weapons within a matter of weeks in the dual-use facilities he maintained for this purpose. Administration officials didn't feel comfortable guessing whether production of WMD or a transfer of WMD to terrorists was "imminent." We knew our intelligence wasn't reliable, precise, or timely enough to allow us to count on seeing such activity before it occurred—or even promptly after.

Now, in 2008, we realize the CIA was wrong when it said we would find substantial chemical and biological weapons stockpiles in Iraq. So the question is: How might President Bush and others in the Administration have changed their thinking if they had believed there were no stockpiles? History is not a controlled experiment; we can only guess what might have changed *if the U.S. government knew then what we know now about Iraq's weapons programs.*

Imagine, for a moment, that the CIA's agents had reported that Saddam had destroyed his WMD stockpiles. The question then would be: How readily could he produce significant amounts of chemical or biological materiel? The accurate answer was that Saddam had retained the personnel and the facilities required for the task—and the intention to reinvigorate his programs. Production could begin within a few weeks of a decision to go forward.

Like my government colleagues generally, I believed the CIA's assessment that Saddam had chemical and biological stockpiles, not just programs. That intelligence was consistent with assessments from the Administrations of George H. W. Bush and Bill Clinton, and from foreign intelligence organizations and UN inspectors. But I knew that the existence of WMD *programs* was far more important than the question of stockpiles.

I had first worked on chemical and biological weapons issues during the Reagan Administration, and in the course of that work I learned that a country bent on using such weapons could have ready biological or chemical weapons capabilities without maintaining stockpiles. Countries—like Iraq—with fertilizer or insecticide factories could make nerve gas or other chemical weapons easily, if they were so inclined. Given what UN inspectors said publicly as late as 1999 about Iraq's biological weapons work, we didn't need secret intelligence to realize that Iraq could produce small but militarily significant stockpiles of biological weapons agents in its medical and pharmaceutical laboratories—rapidly, at any time.

On January 25, 1999, the UN weapons inspection organization issued a clear warning: "[I]t needs to be recognised that Iraq possesses an industrial capability and knowledge base, through which biological warfare agents could be produced quickly and in volume, if the Government of Iraq decided to do so." And in an *unclassified* report to Congress published in August 2000, the CIA stated: "We assess that since the suspension of UN inspections in December of 1998, Baghdad has had the capability to reinitiate both its CW and BW programs within a few weeks to months, but without an inspection monitoring program, it is difficult to determine if Iraq has done so." In a follow-up report, the CIA wrote:

> **In 1995, Iraq admitted to having an offensive BW program and submitted the first in a series of Full, Final, and Complete Disclosures (FFCDs) that were supposed to reveal the full scope of its BW program. According to UNSCOM, these disclosures are incomplete and filled with inaccuracies. Since the full scope and nature of Iraq's BW program was not verified,** *UNSCOM* ***assessed that Iraq continues to maintain a knowledge base and industrial infrastructure that could be used to produce quickly a large amount of BW agents at any time, if needed.***

After Saddam's overthrow, Charles Duelfer, who supervised the Iraq Survey Group (ISG), confirmed much of what U.S. officials knew or suspected about the Iraqi programs before the war. His comprehensive report on the ISG's findings noted how quickly and easily Saddam could have reconstituted an Iraqi biological weapons arsenal:

> **[B]etween 1991 and 1996 Iraq possessed an expanding BW agent production capability. From 1996 to OIF [Operation Iraqi Freedom], Iraq still possessed small but significant dual-use facilities capable of conversion to small-scale BW agent production. ISG has found no evidence that Iraq used this capability for BW production.**

The Duelfer Report cited examples of dual-use facilities such as one run by Samarra Drug Industries, which had "fixed assets that could be converted for BW agent production within 4 to 5 weeks after the decision to do so." And it noted that Saddam could break quickly out of the constraints imposed on Iraq's BW program after the Gulf War: "[T]he movable assets at the Al Dawrah FMDV Plant could provide the core of an alternative break-out capability at any other suitable site in Iraq, perhaps within 2 to 3 weeks after the decision to do so."

According to the report, the Iraq Survey Group also found that Saddam's primary interest was getting Iraq out from under the economic sanctions—and to accomplish this he needed to *appear to* comply with the UN's disarmament demands. But this didn't stop Saddam from trying to preserve his investment in biological warfare:

> **. . . BW capability is technically the easiest WMD to attain. Although equipment and facilities were destroyed under UN supervision in 1996, Iraq retained technical BW know-how through the scientists that were involved in the former program. . . .**
>
> ***ISG judges that in 1991 and 1992, Iraq appears to have destroyed its undeclared stocks of BW weapons and probably destroyed remaining holdings of bulk BW agent. However ISG lacks evidence to document complete destruction. Iraq retained some BW-related seed stocks until their discovery after Operation Iraqi Freedom (OIF).***
>
> ---
>
> ***The destruction of the BW infrastructure in the mid-1990s halted Iraq's BW activities, with the exception of its efforts to preserve intellectual know-how, the Regime's most valuable asset.* BW programs are primarily the product of trained innovative scientific minds. Extensive scientific laboratories and vast industrial complexes are unnecessary. A handful of dedicated, bright scientists, supported by dexterous, intelligent, and experienced technicians working with simple but effective equipment, materials, and animals in a secure environment can accomplish most of what is required to lay the foundations of a BW program.**

After the war, the Iraq Survey Group failed to find evidence to support two of the intelligence community's key prewar assessments: that Iraq was maintaining substantial chemical and biological weapons stockpiles, and that Iraq's nuclear program was active rather than dormant. In sum, the Iraq Survey Group confirmed Saddam's *intention* and *capability* to produce biological and chemical weapons. But the stockpiles themselves were not found.

In its review of such prewar intelligence failures, the Silberman-Robb Commission criticized the CIA, and the intelligence community in general, for flawed tradecraft. Those failings raise the question of whether policy officials were skeptical enough about the intelligence—whether we challenged the CIA vigorously enough—and if not, why not. The errors created an enormous credibility problem for the United States, because Administration officials, for reasons we'll explore further, chose to make the stockpiles—and the intelligence about the stockpiles—part of the case for war.

The decision to feature the CIA's badly crafted assessments of Iraqi WMD stockpiles this way was unfortunate, because the existence of those stockpiles was *not* a cornerstone of our rationale for going to war. But the differences between the actual strategic rationale for the action against Saddam and the public presentation were not lies or misrepresentations. They reflected mistakes in judgment about how best to focus the presentation both at the United Nations (whose support we sought for resolutions approving action against Saddam) and to the American people. By presenting the case for the war poorly, the Administration hurt more than its own credibility; it jeopardized the success of the war effort itself.

This error by the Administration was more than a mere public relations problem. When leaders decide that war is necessary, communicating their reasoning—showing "a decent respect for the opinion of mankind," as Thomas Jefferson put it—is a critical element of strategy and statecraft. The Administration's public statements were the basis on which the American people and their representatives in Congress supported the war. The flaws in that presentation inevitably affect the public's willingness to continue to support the war, at times when patience is required and confidence in victory is shaken.

8

DISCORD IN WASHINGTON

Soon after 9/11, General Pace and I did an analysis of the global terrorist network. The Campaign Planning Committee we cochaired—the CAPCOM—examined groups in the network, including al Qaida, other jihadists, and non-Muslim terrorists. We considered the roles played by states that provided them safe haven, funds, intelligence, training, and weapons. We worried especially about the possibility that terrorists could obtain biological or nuclear weapons from such a state.

The United States needed a way to deal with each of these states, especially those with WMD ambitions. General Pace and I developed a grid that arrayed the problem states with a list of possible actions from diplomatic measures through U.S. economic pressure and multinational sanctions—to blockade, limited strikes, and regime change by military force. The grid summarized the pros and cons of each action for each problem state, noting where persuasion might work and where compulsion might be necessary.

The grid was not a plan, but it helped to organize our ideas on how to get these states to end their support for terrorism and to drop their pursuit of WMD. Our Policy and Joint Staff analysts drew on intelligence and other information to assess the gravity of the threats in each case. We considered the nature of each regime, its history, and its vulnerabilities. We discussed the importance, urgency, and difficulty of possible U.S. military operations. And we reviewed the available nonmilitary means for each situation.

For some states, we concluded, diplomacy might suffice. Libya and Syria, for example, had curtailed support for terrorism in response to international pressure in the past. Other regimes appeared more difficult. The three hardest cases, we believed, would be Iraq, Iran, and North Korea. Our evaluation was intended to assist Rumsfeld as he reviewed contingencies and policy options. Although we did not share the work outside the Defense Department, others around the government were doing similar analysis and reaching some of the same conclusions.

In his January 29, 2002, State of the Union address, President Bush introduced the term "axis of evil" to describe Iraq, Iran, and North Korea. I do not know what—if any—interagency deliberations considered labeling those countries that way, but it was a seminal formulation.

In his State of the Union speech, President Bush explained:

> **Some of these regimes have been pretty quiet since September the eleventh. But we know their true nature. North Korea is a regime arming with missiles and weapons of mass destruction, while starving its citizens.**
>
> **Iran aggressively pursues these weapons and exports terror, while an unelected few repress the Iranian people's hope for freedom.**
>
> **Iraq continues to flaunt its hostility toward America and to support terror. The Iraqi regime has plotted to develop anthrax, and nerve gas, and nuclear weapons for over a decade. This is a regime that has already used poison gas to murder thousands of its own citizens—leaving the bodies of mothers huddled over their dead children. This is a regime that agreed to international inspections—then kicked out the inspectors. This is a regime that has something to hide from the civilized world.**
>
> **States like these, and their terrorist allies, constitute an axis of evil, arming to threaten the peace of the world.**

President Bush described these regimes as "a grave and growing danger" because they sought weapons of mass destruction and "could provide these arms to terrorists, giving them the means to match their hatred." Putting the world on notice that "America will do what is necessary to ensure our nation's security," he declared:

> **We'll be deliberate, yet time is not on our side. I will not wait on events, while dangers gather. I will not stand by, as peril draws closer and closer. The United States of America will not**

permit the world's most dangerous regimes to threaten us with the world's most destructive weapons.

Each of the "axis" states had earned its designation, and our strategy would have to take account of each. But there were important differences among them.

The North Korean regime had a history of surprising, violent, inhumane behavior, including a series of terrorist-style attacks, kidnappings, and assassinations of South Korean officials in the mid-1980s. It had a million-man army with enough conventional artillery deployed in the southern mountains to devastate South Korea's capital, Seoul. North Korea had renounced nuclear weapons when it signed the Nuclear Non-Proliferation Treaty in 1985, but it continued to develop those weapons anyway. In 1993, North Korea announced its intention to withdraw from that treaty, claiming its nuclear program was for electrical power, not weapons.

U.S. officials wanted North Korea to remain a party to the treaty and to stop violating it—to abandon its nuclear weapons work altogether. In October 1994, soon after the death of its longtime leader Kim Il Sung, North Korea signed a deal with the United States in which it made or reaffirmed a number of denuclearization promises. In the deal, which became known as the Agreed Framework, North Korea agreed to end production of fissile material in return for a promise from the United States to give the new North Korean regime—headed by Kim Jung Il, the son of Kim Il Sung—nuclear power plants that would not be usable for weapons purposes.

Despite the Agreed Framework, however, U.S. intelligence detected evidence of ongoing violations. In October 2002 State Department officials raised the matter with North Korean officials, who said that they were indeed enriching uranium. In January 2003, North Korea withdrew from the Nuclear Non-Proliferation Treaty.

Officials of the Kim Jung Il regime boasted that they had manufactured several nuclear weapons. The U.S. intelligence community credited their claim, and reported that North Korea also had large stocks of chemical weapons. Aware that the U.S.-Soviet Anti-Ballistic Missile (ABM) Treaty prohibited the United States from building defenses against intercontinental ballistic missiles,* North Korea had invested heavily in developing

---

*President Bush directed U.S. withdrawal from the Anti-Ballistic Missile (ABM) Treaty in 2002 because he wanted to build strategic missile defenses. Unlike North Korea's actions in defying the Nuclear Non-Proliferation Treaty, our withdrawal

such missiles. In early 2002, it was working on building a nuclear-capable missile of intercontinental range.

The regime, meanwhile, had impoverished the country to the point of mass starvation. With Kim increasingly desperate for cash, U.S. officials worried that he might sell fissile material or entire nuclear weapons. The possible buyers in the market included not only Iran and Iraq—which had ample cash—but also al Qaida or another well-financed terrorist group that was willing to take some risk. Such an exchange would be a provocative and risky proposition for seller and buyer alike, but all the parties involved were known for some degree of risk taking.

Iran was not as far along in nuclear weapons development as North Korea. U.S. intelligence analysts assessed that Iran did not yet possess such weapons, but that it was working to produce fissile material and developing long-range missiles that could deliver nuclear weapons to Europe—and eventually to the United States. U.S. officials feared that Iran might be able to shorten its timeline by buying nuclear weapons, missiles, or their components from North Korea or another outside source.

The Iranian regime adhered to a revolutionary Islamist ideology, which it aggressively promoted abroad—for instance, with Hezbollah, the Shiite terrorist organization that Iran created, armed, and funded. Based in southern Lebanon, Hezbollah had debuted on the world stage by destroying the U.S. Marines barracks in Beirut, Lebanon, in 1983, killing 241 American service members. Up until 9/11, Hezbollah had killed more Americans than any other terrorist group.

As one of the world's leading exporters of oil, Iran had wealth, even though its people lived poorly. The country's clerical leaders had made a hash of Iran's economy ever since they came to power during the revolution of 1978–79 that overthrew the Shah of Iran. Unlike North Koreans, Iranians had open communication with the outside world, including Internet access, and many spoke out against the personal corruption of the ruling clerics. The Ira-

---

did not violate the ABM Treaty but indeed conformed with the treaty's withdrawal provision. As a legal matter, it may not even have been necessary for the United States to withdraw: The ABM Treaty was a two-party international political agreement between the United States and the Soviet Union, and in December 1991 the Soviet Union had ceased to exist. In the late 1990s, my law firm colleague George Miron and I did a legal analysis concluding that the treaty lapsed automatically when the Soviet Union died. See George Miron, "Did the ABM Treaty of 1972 Remain in Force After the USSR Ceased to Exist in December 1991 and Did It Become a Treaty Between the United States and the Russian Federation," *American University International Law Review*, Vol. 17, No. 2 (2002), p. 189. See also the Miron-Feith memorandum, reprinted in Hearings before the U.S. Senate, Committee on Foreign Relations, 106th Congress 106–339 (May 25, 1999), p. 231.

nian regime looked unpopular and perhaps brittle: It might, in time, be swept away through domestic political upheaval, independent of U.S. pressure.

As hostile and dangerous as the North Korean and Iranian regimes were, Saddam Hussein was in a class by himself as a mass murderer and initiator of aggressive wars. As President Bush declared in his State of the Union speech, the Iraqi regime posed a potential for "catastrophic" harm to the United States. But what chiefly distinguished Iraq from the other two members of the "axis of evil" was that, over the last ten years, the United States had exhausted virtually every means short of war to end the danger from the Iraqi regime. In the coming months, the President would do what was necessary to eliminate the qualifier "virtually."

When it came to North Korea and Iran, President Bush could *not* say that the United States had run the string on diplomacy, economic pressure, UN actions, or military operations short of war, such as blockade or limited strikes. Also, our alliance with South Korea was a complicating factor, for the South Korean government would not have supported military action against Kim Jung Il's regime. And, in both North Korea and Iran, there were possibilities that the regime might collapse or be toppled by domestic opponents without U.S. military intervention. There appeared no realistic prospect of that in Iraq.

War is an extremity, as President Bush clearly understood. His policy was to try all reasonable means other than war for dealing with North Korea and Iran. But when he considered Iraq, he saw that such means had already been tried comprehensively, and without success, for a decade. A stack of UN Security Council resolutions—sixteen of them adopted from 1991 to 1999—all violated by Saddam, testified to the failure of diplomatic solutions to the Saddam Hussein problem.

President Bush's duty was to protect the United States and its interests from Saddam's revanchist hatreds, intense violence, defiance of the world, ambitions to procure WMD, and opportunities to use terrorists to cause us unattributable harm. Saddam's record made it impossible to dismiss the danger as theoretical or remote. Nor could we expect the situation to improve over time. The sanctions were crumbling, and we anticipated that at some point Saddam would reenergize his programs to produce catastrophic weapons. In the months after 9/11, President Bush and his national security team were asking themselves whether it would be responsible to leave Saddam Hussein in power.

In principle, the United States sympathized with freedom-loving opponents of dictatorial regimes everywhere. But over the decades, the United

States tended to increase its support for pro-democracy activists when our national security was directly at stake.

President Bush liked to discuss this point from the opposite perspective—by proclaiming that he supported struggles for freedom not only because it was good for America, but also because it served higher purposes. Referring to "the non-negotiable demands of human dignity: the rule of law; limits on the power of the state; respect for women; private property; free speech; equal justice; and religious tolerance," he ended his 2002 State of the Union speech with the declaration:

> **America will take the side of brave men and women who advocate these values around the world, including the Islamic world, because we have a greater objective than eliminating threats and containing resentment. We seek a just and peaceful world beyond the war on terror.**

In the same speech, however, he said: "Our first priority must always be the security of our nation."

Much has been written about the George W. Bush Administration's attitude toward promoting democracy. A key question is how it differed from the so-called "realist" school, represented by former officials such as Brent Scowcroft and James Baker, which deemphasized the importance in world affairs of whether states are organized internally as democracies, dictatorships, or something in between.

I do not doubt that President Bush meant what he said when he spoke high-mindedly of his policies and the unselfish, humanitarian benefits he hoped to achieve. But to my knowledge—and contrary to what his critics have charged—he never argued, in public or private, that the United States should go to war *in order to* spread democracy. While he was willing to conclude that the United States might have to go to war in self-defense, I never heard him say that we should do so simply or primarily to help a foreign pro-democracy movement oust a dictator.

Neocons, including myself, were commonly accused of wanting to spread democracy by the sword. But I saw no evidence of that—and as to me personally, it was untrue. In my view, the reason to go to war with Iraq was self-defense. If that necessity drove us to war, the fighting might open the way for a new democracy to arise (as it did with Germany, Italy, and Japan after World War II). If that new democracy developed successfully, the United States, as well as the Iraqi people, would benefit. But it's one thing to try to ensure that your defeated enemy becomes a democracy after the war comes to an end, and quite another to *initiate* a war for that purpose.

The spread of democratic institutions around the globe in the twentieth century served U.S. national interests. Americans enjoyed greater security and greater freedom as more and more countries came to respect what President Bush called the "demands of human dignity." And the experience of the twentieth century suggests that war is less likely between democratic states than between states that are not both democratic.

Moreover, history demonstrates that our domestic civil liberties are safer in a world where freedom and democracy are spreading rather than shrinking. When Americans have sensed that enemies are gaining ground abroad, we have tended to curtail liberty at home. Fears about anarchism and Bolshevism after World War I—after Lenin took power in Russia—gave rise to antisedition legislation and the so-called Palmer raids. When both Hitler and Stalin rode high in the months after the Nazi-Soviet Pact of 1939, Congress passed the Smith Act, which made it a crime to advocate the violent overthrow of the U.S. government. And the extension of Communist rule to Eastern Europe and elsewhere after World War II helped give rise to McCarthyism.

America's interest in the growth of democratic institutions abroad increased after 9/11, as we realized that such institutions could contribute to undermining the appeal of jihadist extremism. Even so, promoting democracy was only one of several important considerations we weighed in developing U.S. national security policy after the attack.

I did not think that a U.S. president could properly decide to go to war just to spread democracy, in the absence of a threat requiring self-defense. I did not see democracy promotion as trumping every other national security consideration. Moreover, not all countries are equally ready for democratic reforms. Democracy requires certain building blocks to be in place: legal or political institutions, including an independent judiciary, a free press, and multiple centers of power that can check and balance one another; and cultural institutions, such as the habits of resolving disputes through compromise and of accepting decisions by majority vote.*

President Bush said many times that human beings naturally crave freedom, and I think he was correct. But not every society has the institutions necessary for democracy to thrive: the rule of law, limits on the power of the state, respect for women, private property, free speech, equal justice, and religious tolerance. (This is the list President Bush gave in the above

---

*These cultural institutions are rooted in liberal philosophical principles: the political equality of each individual, regardless of race, religion, or sex; and the distinction between areas of life that are private and those that can properly be governed by man-made laws. A society that sees all spheres of life as governed exclusively by religious dictates cannot have popular self-government.

quotation, which showed that he did *not* assume that democracy could quickly be established everywhere.)

Despite the formidable difficulties of promoting democracy, however, I disagreed with the assertion that it was impossible to launch democratic institutions in the Arab or Muslim worlds. Twentieth-century history offers quite a few examples of democracy's growth, over time, in lands that hardly seemed rich with democratic potential. Consider what someone with a so-called "realist" outlook might have said in 1946, about the idea that Germany and Japan, with their autocratic politics and militaristic cultures, could become within a few decades democratic, stable, and largely pacifistic.

It is easy to sound sage being negative. But the United States had much to gain from democratic political reform in the Muslim world, just as we had gained a great deal from such reform in Germany and Japan. It was by no means certain that Muslims or Arabs could build the kind of free political institutions that other peoples from diverse cultures created for themselves over the last century—including, notably, Muslim Turks—but it could not prudently be dismissed as impossible.

The self-styled "realists" have a theory that U.S. interests are unaffected by whether other countries in the world have totalitarian governments and hostile philosophies. That theory is hard to square with recent history. When communist ideology collapsed in the Soviet empire in the late 1980s, almost all the Warsaw Pact states shed that ideology—and instantly ceased to be enemies of the United States. Within a few years, they became our NATO allies. The notion that the national interests of those countries were somehow "objectively" determined—unrelated to whether their leaders were communists or democrats—is unrealistic, in my view. To assume, on the basis of "realist" theory, that the United States had no interest in whether Saddam's regime would be replaced by democratic government or a Baathist dictatorship would have been ideological closed-mindedness rather than pragmatic policy making.

Critics have accused the Administration of going to war in Iraq for the sake of a political experiment in Arab democratization. But the primary decision the President faced was not whether democracy could or should flourish in Iraq, but whether the United States could live with the risk that Saddam Hussein might one day threaten to attack us, directly or through terrorists, with biological or other catastrophic weapons. If we decided we had to remove Saddam from power, the *next* decision was whether the United States should try to help the Iraqis build democratic institutions—or accept the possibility that Saddam might be replaced by another military dictator. Given the options, President Bush decided that the interests and principles of the United States required us to try to promote democracy.

Rumsfeld and Wolfowitz assessed the circumstances in Iraq similarly. We often discussed the importance of balancing U.S. interests in promoting democracy abroad with our other interests. We sometimes disagreed on how much weight to give the various interests, but none of us insisted that democracy promotion necessarily took precedence over all other U.S. interests. Commentators from the "realist" school accused the neocons of being ideological rather than pragmatic on this issue. But the weighing process I have described was the pragmatic and realistic approach.

In early 2002, Rice's deputy Steve Hadley organized twice-weekly Deputies meetings specifically to discuss Iraq policy. The meetings, held in the White House Situation Room, were known as Deputies Lunches. These meetings were unusual in several respects. Hadley strictly restricted attendance. Whereas twenty to twenty-five people—representing eight to ten offices—would crowd into the Situation Room for an ordinary Deputies Committee meeting, these lunches included only Hadley, Armitage, Under Secretary of State Marc Grossman, Wolfowitz, myself, General Pace (or Lieutenant General George Casey), Scooter Libby, Deputy CIA Director John McLaughlin, and a single NSC staffer.* No others were allowed.

The forum was "close hold"—not simply in that the discussions were classified, but in that the participants were asked to keep secret, even within the government, the very fact that we were meeting regularly on Iraq. Unlike those for ordinary Deputies' meetings, the papers for the Deputies Lunches were distributed in special channels. Such secrecy was unusual, as was the fact that the existence of these lunches did not leak to the press at the time.

The extra secrecy, Hadley explained, would allow us to discuss controversial Iraq matters openly, without having to worry how every word might be spun on a cable news network later in the day. Though in general I consider our government overly secretive, in this case Hadley had a point. Serious, candid, skeptical discussions of controversial national security issues would have been impossible if participants could not count on a reasonable degree of confidentiality.

The Deputies Lunches were unusual also because—at least at first—they included food service in the Situation Room. For the first few weeks, the staff of the White House Mess laid a cloth on the conference table

---

*At first, the additional NSC staff member was General Wayne Downing, the counterterrorism coordinator, who left the Administration in the summer of 2002. He was succeeded by Zalmay Khalilzad and later by Frank Miller.

and set it, rather elegantly, with each person's order (charged to our individual accounts). The scene represented a civilized, old-world incongruity in our scrambling, gobble-a-bite-in-ten-minutes-if-you-have-time-to-eat-at-all lives. But after a few weeks, Pace commented that we often wasted five minutes or so waiting for the table to be set after the previous meeting ended, so we agreed to dispense with the lunch service. The meetings continued to be called Deputies Lunches anyway.

The discussions there differed from interagency Iraq meetings before 9/11, when there had been much debate about regime change versus containment. After 9/11, top Administration officials all accepted—or at least none openly disputed—that Iraq must be disarmed of WMD: Its chemical, biological, and nuclear weapons programs must be ended and dismantled verifiably, and not reconstituted. And no one argued that disarmament could be achieved without regime change.

As the Administration weighed the case for military action, we analyzed the difficulties and possible drawbacks. But, as the policy papers and meeting notes from this post-9/11 period show, the starting point for all the agencies was recognition that Saddam was a threat. No one in any top-level interagency meeting disputed that Saddam had dangerous WMD programs and connections to terrorist groups. No one asserted that the risks of leaving Saddam in power were manageable through diplomacy and therefore, on balance, acceptable. And no one argued that Saddam could be removed from power without military action.

In Congress, likewise, there was a widespread acknowledgment of the dangers he posed, and wide, bipartisan endorsement of the general rationale for regime change in Iraq. Even a Democrat like Senator Kent Conrad (D-North Dakota), who opposed the authorization for military action in Iraq, pointed to the following "clear and unassailable" facts:

> **Saddam Hussein is a menace to the whole region of the Middle East and a vicious tyrant who harms and oppresses his own people. He has waged war against neighboring nations, and he has attacked the people of his own country. He has acquired chemical and biological weapons. He is attempting to acquire nuclear weapons and the means to deliver those weapons using ballistic missiles.**
>
> **There is no question that Saddam Hussein is ignoring the will of the United Nations and that he has not honored the agreements he made following the Gulf War. Saddam Hussein is a dangerous force in the world.**

Senator Charles Schumer (D-New York) declared:

Saddam Hussein is an evil man, a dictator who oppresses his people and flouts the mandate of the international community. While this behavior is reprehensible, it is Hussein's vigorous pursuit of biological, chemical and nuclear weapons, and his present and potential future support for terrorist acts and organizations, that make him a terrible danger to the people of the United States.

Senator Hillary Clinton (D-New York) made similar arguments:

I believe the facts that have brought us to this fateful vote are not in doubt. Saddam Hussein is a tyrant who has tortured and killed his own people, even his own family members, to maintain his iron grip on power. He used chemical weapons on Iraqi Kurds and on Iranians, killing over 20,000 people. . . . It is clear, however, that if left unchecked, Saddam Hussein will continue to increase his capability to wage biological and chemical warfare and will keep trying to develop nuclear weapons. Should he succeed in that endeavor, he could alter the political and security landscape of the Middle East which, as we know all too well, affects American security. This much is undisputed.

Through most of 2002, in fact, the Iraq matter that was most hotly disputed within the U.S. government was not *whether* Saddam Hussein should be overthrown, but what (if anything) should be done to lay the groundwork for a new Iraqi government.

One of Steve Hadley's tasks was to sort out the tangle of relationships—positive and negative—between the Bush Administration and the various Iraqi anti-Saddam groups. There were five main opposition groups.

The Iraqi National Congress (INC) was the opposition group (and umbrella organization) headed by Ahmad Chalabi, who (as we've seen) enjoyed extensive contacts in Washington—and who was the target of bitter enmity from the CIA and, increasingly, the State Department. Richard Armitage and key officials in State's Near East bureau spoke out strongly against Chalabi, as did a number of CIA officials. Ever since the mid-1990s, when Chalabi condemned the agency for incompetence, CIA officials had talked of him with anger, even hatred. They produced an amazing volume of reports written to make him look ill informed, ill motivated, unskillful, and untrustworthy. For example, after the Jordanian government indicted Chalabi for financial malfeasance following the 1990–91 Gulf War (convicting him in absentia in a military court), State and CIA officials would report these charges at face value, omitting to note that Jordan's King Hussein received substantial aid from Iraq and had sided with Saddam Hussein in the Gulf War—and Chalabi was Saddam's most prominent Iraqi opponent. Although (or because) we supported a broad-based, nonmilitary Iraqi government, Defense Department officials were disparaged at State and CIA as supporters of Chalabi.

The CIA favored Iyad Allawi and his Iraqi National Accord (INA), the group formed by former Sunni, Baathist military officers who had fallen out with Saddam. The INA said it favored democracy for Iraq, but its leaders, supported by Sunni-controlled Arab governments, wanted the country's Sunni-controlled military to continue to play a key political role in Iraq. How that squared with the INA's proclaimed support for democracy was unclear.

The two main Kurdish groups—the Kurdish Democratic Party (KDP), headed by Massoud Barzani, and the Patriotic Union of Kurdistan (PUK), headed by Jalal Talabani—were not just opposition parties: They already governed pieces of Iraq. Each controlled a region in the north that had enjoyed substantial autonomy and freedom since the 1990–91 Gulf War, when the United States began providing them aid and protection.

The fifth of these groups was the Supreme Council for the Islamic Revolution in Iraq (SCIRI), a Shiite organization that was viewed with suspicion throughout the U.S. government. Iran had been instrumental in its founding and provided it with funds, training, and other support. Though SCIRI claimed to support democracy for Iraq, we wondered whether it would evolve, post Saddam, into a loyal Iraqi-Arab political party, or would function as an Iranian surrogate. The Bush Administration treated SCIRI as a responsible, pro-democratic party, but retained the concern that it might prove to be a cat's-paw of the Iranian regime.

SCIRI's record since Saddam's overthrow has been mixed. It has played a leading role in advancing Iraq's democratic political process—drafting the constitution, forming electoral lists, organizing the balloting, campaigning, and sending representatives to help run ministries and serve in the parliament. At the same time, it has not always respected the government's authority—refusing, for example, to disband its militia, known as the Badr Corps.

The U.S. Congress had recognized the INC as a coordinating body for all the Iraqi opposition groups, including under its umbrella the other four groups—INA, KDP, PUK, and SCIRI—together with some smaller anti-

Table 1. U.S. Partners in Iraqi Opposition

Group	*Leader*	*Constituency (location)*	*Note*
Constitutional Monarchy Party	Sherif Ali	Supporters of Hashemites (exile)	
Iraqi National Accord (INA)	Iyad Allawi	Mainly Sunni, supported by Arab states (exile)	Favored by CIA
Iraqi National Congress (INC)	Ahmad Chalabi	Umbrella organization (exile)	Alienated CIA and State Department in 1990s
Kurdish Democratic Party (KDP)	Massoud Barzani	Kurds (northern Iraq)	Kurdish region governing body
Patriotic Union of Kurdistan (PUK)	Jalal Talabani	Kurds (northern Iraq)	Kurdish region governing body
Supreme Council for the Islamic Revolution in Iraq (SCIRI)	Abdulaziz el-Hakim	Shia (exile)	Supported by Iran
Iraqi Christian organizations	Various	Christians (exile)	

Saddam parties.* The anti-Saddam opposition groups were sometimes collectively called "exiles," although the Kurdish groups continued to reside in Iraq, so they were not exiles. As a shorthand, Administration officials coined the term "externals" to refer to the whole set. Their membership was difficult to estimate. The leaders of the exile groups resided mostly in Europe, and the members were scattered throughout Europe and the Middle East.

Hadley saw a useful role for the Iraqi opposition leaders as potential U.S. partners: to promote an Iraqi government that would not oppress its own people or threaten others, to build international support for action against Saddam, and to contribute to U.S. intelligence on Iraq. However, the Administration's policy differences relating to Iraq soon emerged in bitter disagreements over the role of the Iraqi externals, and particularly the role of the INC. Hadley was by no means a pro-INC partisan, but it exasperated him that anti-Chalabi maneuvering was impeding sensible cooperation with the Iraqi opposition.

For Rumsfeld, it was a consistent principle that U.S. officials should not try to pick specific leaders for other countries. That principle governed Rumsfeld's attitude toward Afghanistan as well as Iraq. But State and CIA officials tended not to share this principle, and did not even recognize that Rumsfeld was applying it. To them, Rumsfeld's insistence that the U.S. government should not discriminate for or against *any* of the friendly, pro-democratic groups was seen merely as camouflage for a campaign to "anoint Chalabi." The officials hostile to Chalabi viewed others who did not share their hostility as dangerous, pro-Chalabi partisans.

In January 2002, Libby proposed organizing a political conference where the various external groups could show solidarity in favor of a free Iraq—publicizing Saddam's brutalization of the Iraqi people and reaffirming the admirable political principles they had formulated at conferences during the 1990s. Armitage opposed the idea, citing a list of administrative questions: Who among the Iraqis would take the lead in organizing the conference? Where could it be held? How would it be run? Eventually it became clear that he was concerned about the possibility that the INC would play the lead role and thus make Chalabi look good. Libby then announced that State should let "a thousand flowers bloom"—let all the externals participate equally—adding that he had no interest at all in giving Chalabi any advantages. In that case, Armitage responded, State can get the conference organized by April. Hadley urged convening the conference as

*These smaller parties included Iraqi Christian groups as well as the Constitutional Monarchy Party of Sherif Ali, claiming the throne of the Hashemites (overthrown in 1958).

soon as possible to increase the chances of an effective post-Saddam government. But the planning process dragged on for weeks. Despite Libby's pitch for nondiscrimination, State officials proposed excluding the INC altogether. Finally, at the March 22, 2002, Deputies Lunch, Hadley got Armitage to commit to inviting Chalabi and the INC. The conference was then planned for June in the Netherlands, at the Hague.

But State officials (and their outside contractor) squabbled with INC personnel, aggravating relations with the INC, so that finally, on April 23, Armitage informed the Deputies that he'd had to fire the contractor because of all the bickering. He then proposed, with evident embarrassment, to slip the conference date to August or September. Hadley, normally even-tempered, responded with annoyance. "Earlier is better," he said. Any decision to push the date off, he said, would have to be reviewed by the Principals.

It wasn't easy to exhaust Hadley's patience, but the State-CIA campaign against Chalabi and the INC did it. Each of the anti-Saddam groups had personal and philosophical complaints against the others, and with "regime change" becoming a real possibility, the anti-Saddam organizations began serious jockeying for U.S. favor, each of them looking to gain advantage over its rivals. Eventually—with encouragement from State and CIA officials—the INA, KDP, PUK, and SCIRI declared themselves the "Group of Four": They would operate independently of the INC in order to win points with the U.S. powers that be (although they all remained formally under the INC's umbrella). State gave an account of the Group of Four in a March 26, 2002, paper that reflected (but never acknowledged) State's role in encouraging this development. That paper, distributed at a Deputies Lunch, described Chalabi as "autocratic," criticizing him for his "efforts to dominate" and unwillingness "to work cooperatively with others." It praised Allawi and the INA for favoring "pluralistic democratic government" and for "good working relationships" with Saudi Arabia and others, and "good relations with a variety of Shi'a clerics and tribalists."

Meanwhile, Armitage informed the Deputies that he wanted to cut off U.S. financial support to the INC. For several years, beginning in the Clinton presidency, State had provided it support, under the Iraq Liberation Act of 1998, totaling around $15 million. This funding went to support general INC activities—political, economic, humanitarian, and other work to bring about political transition in Iraq—and also the Information Collection Program, through which the INC gave the U.S. government access to information regarding Iraq.* (Other Iraqi oppo-

*The Information Collection Program attracted its own allegations, though without supporting evidence. A widely aired charge was that the INC was providing faulty

sition groups had their own connections to various parts of the U.S. government.)

In early 2001, State's Near East bureau got the department's inspector general to review the INC's finances. His report, issued in September 2001, found no corruption. It stated that "improvements in accountability" were needed, and that not all the applicable regulations and agreements had been complied with. Noting that the INC's officials "generally agreed with our observations," the report offered recommendations to resolve the problems. In March 2002, State's Near East bureau again clashed with the INC over funding-related allegations, and when State withheld promised monies, the INC was unable to pay the rent for its Washington office. At Deputies Lunches, Armitage spoke contemptuously of Chalabi, asserting that the man did not deserve to be trusted. He proposed ending not only general support for the INC but also the Information Collection Program.

Hadley remained doubtful about the allegations against Chalabi. He said that it served U.S. interests to work with all the opposition groups, and not to favor or shun any that accepted basic democratic principles and our general hopes for a free Iraq. He said he didn't want the INC bankrupted, and he called for an end to the campaigning against the INC and Chalabi. The President was considering whether war with Iraq was necessary, Hadley argued; we needed all the intelligence we could get. Even before we learned just how sparse the CIA's on-the-ground efforts in Iraq were at that time, all the Deputies understood that we needed a lot more information about what was happening in that tightly controlled country. Hadley judged that it made no sense to terminate the Information Collection Program unless there was a strong reason to do so—and mere bookkeeping issues hardly sufficed.

At the April 23 Deputies Lunch, Armitage relented grudgingly. He

---

intelligence, which contributed to the decision to go to war in Iraq. The Senate Select Intelligence Committee, in its investigation of the relationship between the INC and the intelligence community, cited the 2002 conclusion of the National Intelligence Council: "The written material provided to the Intelligence Community (IC) by the Iraqi National Congress contains little of current intelligence value" (*SSCI Report on Chalabi Group*, p. 36). The *SSCI Report* further noted, regarding the interviewed sources provided by the INC, that those interviews "were not used as the primary basis for any of the key judgments about Iraq's weapons of mass destruction capabilities" (ibid., p. 39). For the most part, the INC-provided information lacked sourcing detail and was therefore viewed as unverified rather than erroneous (ibid., pp. 40–49).

promised that State would not force the INC to shut down its local office, but he said he would not continue funding the INC beyond that.

A few months later, State's inspector general published a follow-up report on the INC's accounting mechanisms, reporting "significant steps" to implement his earlier recommendations. He criticized State for squeezing the INC financially, which had made it impossible for the organization to satisfy some of those recommendations. He said the INC's "level of compliance" made it no longer necessary to preserve the restrictions he had recommended earlier. The INC was far from perfect, but its relentless foes at State emerged from this skirmish with egg on their faces.

Looking back on the interagency decision-making process, I am struck by its lack of clarity. On issue after issue, where there were disagreements they were not brought to the surface to be presented to the President for decision. Rather, basic disagreements were allowed to remain unresolved—as long as a degree of consensus could be produced on immediate next steps.

Powell came to be seen by some commentators as opposing regime change or war. But he never actually stated such opposition. Officials from State (as from all the agencies) warned that war could cause instability and other problems. But that was not the same as contending that Saddam should be left in power. (Indeed, although Rumsfeld did not oppose the war, he compiled what was arguably the Administration's most comprehensive list of warnings of calamities a war might cause—a list reviewed in Chapter 10.) When called upon to develop briefings and talking points for use outside our government to explain the rationale for regime change and for war, State officials did so, over and over again.

Similarly, although George Tenet implies in his memoir that he was a dissenter on the war—or at least a skeptic—he too refrained at the time from any comments or questions that clearly challenged the premises of the Administration's case for war. Neither he nor his agency contradicted President Bush's key points: Saddam's record of aggression and hostility to the United States, Saddam's support for various terrorists, his tyrannical oppression of Iraq, his history of developing and using weapons of mass destruction—indeed, the CIA maintained that Iraq still held stockpiles—and Saddam's firm grip on power.

The lack of dissent from Powell and Tenet did not mean there was harmony within the Administration about Iraq, even at the upper reaches.

There was not, by any means. Top officials disagreed and argued—but not about the fundamentals. The contending camps on the National Security Council did not divide as prowar and antiwar. Rather, there were those (chiefly, the President, Cheney, Rumsfeld, and Rice) who developed the conviction that removing Saddam from power was necessary, even if it required war. And there were the others (Powell first and foremost) who went along with the President's Iraq policy halfheartedly at most. Through comments and body language, the latter group signaled lack of commitment, but they did not champion an alternative strategy. Media accounts that describe Powell as "dovish" suggest, wrongly, that he advocated a solution other than war. Rather, Powell became the leader of the neither-fish-nor-fowl faction. While acknowledging that the Iraqi regime was dangerous, Powell tended to downplay the degree and urgency of the threat. He caused disagreements in the Situation Room by proposing tactical measures—for example, reviving United Nations inspections of Iraq—that could impede the President's evolving strategy of regime change. But he did not propose a different solution to the Iraq problem.

It bears emphasis: Powell did not say that regime change was wrong, let alone map out a different way to protect American interests. He never declared that the dangers of trying to oust Saddam were graver than those of leaving him in power. He did not argue that containment was an adequate policy. Whether on purpose or not, Powell put himself in a position where, if the war went well, he could say he supported it, and if not, he could point to his warnings as proof that he was a prescient dove. It would have been more helpful, and more forthright, if he had openly challenged the President's conclusions in his meetings with the President.

Richard Armitage confirmed to *New York Times* reporter Michael Gordon and former Marine Corps Lieutenant General Bernard Trainor, the coauthors of *Cobra II*, that he and Powell did not oppose going to war against Saddam:

> **"Powell and I did not object to the prospect of taking out Saddam Hussein, but we had real questions about timing," Armitage recalled. "Neither the secretary nor I can tell when the president made his mind up to go. The secretary thought he had the president in a good place. A good place meant we would consolidate Afghanistan, work vigorously with the allies to get as many people on board, and then go. The thinking I had in mind was January 2005—win the election and then that would be a good time to begin the attack."**

These were revealing comments. Like Powell, Armitage shared the common view that Saddam threatened U.S. interests, that he had active WMD programs and chemical and biological weapons stockpiles. Armitage said he approved "taking out Saddam Hussein" by "attack." In other words, he saw Saddam's regime as *a danger grave and pressing enough to justify war.* But he told Gordon and Trainor—though he never said so at a Deputies Committee meeting—that the President should have waited until *after the 2004 presidential election* to act on this threat. Armitage, in effect, wanted to gamble on whether the United States would actually remove the danger. There was no guarantee that President Bush would win reelection, and it was even less certain that the President's Democratic opponent would overthrow Saddam if he won. It was a strange position: Armitage seems to have concluded that war was necessary to protect our country, but he favored rolling the dice on whether to take the necessary action. I wondered whether he was devious or merely confused.

It was during the run-up to the Gulf War in 1990–91, after Saddam had invaded Kuwait, that Colin Powell had earned his reputation as a "reluctant warrior." As used by *Washington Post* reporter Rick Atkinson, in his book on the Gulf War, the term was ironic and not flattering. He painted Powell as a man who hedged his bets, not a fully invested member of the President's team. But the term could also be taken without irony as a political win-win for Powell. It allowed him (and his many admirers) to emphasize either the warrior part or the reluctant part, depending on the circumstances and the audience. Powell reprised his role as reluctant warrior in the George W. Bush Administration.

In his book *Plan of Attack*, the journalist Bob Woodward recounts how Powell met with President Bush for two hours in the summer of 2002. Neither Cheney nor Rumsfeld was present, and Powell was able to unburden himself to the President, warning how difficult an Iraq war could be. Woodward provides a lengthy report of both the meeting and his own on-the-record discussion about it with President Bush. According to Woodward, Powell spelled out for the President the "downsides" of the war. Powell stressed that the United States could not act unilaterally; we would need allies. The President asked what he should do. Powell replied that he should consider using the United Nations as the vehicle for our diplomacy in order to "internationalize" the problem. The Secretary of State did not argue for leaving Saddam in power. "Powell felt that he had left nothing unsaid," Woodward wrote, adding:

> **The Reluctant Warrior was urging restraint, but he had not tossed his heart on the table. He had not said, Don't do it.**

> Taken together the points of his argument could have been mustered to reach that conclusion. Powell half felt that, but he had learned during 35 years in the Army, and elsewhere, that he had to play to the boss and talk about method. It was paramount to talk only within the confines of the preliminary goals set by the boss. Perhaps he had been too timid.

This is presumably the same conversation Powell referred to in remarks at a conference in Aspen, Colorado, in 2007, but by then he was offering a somewhat different account:

> The former American secretary of state Colin Powell has revealed that he spent 2½ hours vainly trying to persuade President George W Bush not to invade Iraq and believes today's conflict cannot be resolved by US forces.
>
> "I tried to avoid this war," Powell said at the Aspen Ideas Festival in Colorado. "I took him through the consequences of going into an Arab country and becoming the occupiers."

Woodward later asked the President about Powell's warning that the United States would "own" Iraq:

> "And my reaction to that is, is that my job is to secure America," the president said. . . ."My frame of mind is focused on what I told you—the solemn duty to protect America."
>
> I [Woodward] sat there somewhat non-plussed as the president discussed the issues of freedom and security, which were very much beside the points Powell had made. "And he's talking tactics though," I began to ask.
>
> "That's his job," Bush answered, "to be tactical. My job is to be strategic."

In fact, America would have been better served if the Secretary of State had provided strategic rather than just tactical advice. Clearly aware of the distinction, President Bush may have thought that, too, but he had no interest in sounding negative about Powell in discussions with journalists.

What if Powell, after 9/11, had actually made the case to President Bush against overthrowing Saddam? He might have persuaded the President. Or, Powell himself might have been persuaded by others on the National Security Council, in which case he could have led the State

Department in wholehearted support for the President's policy. When united, the U.S. government is far more effective in winning international cooperation. Or, a third possibility, Powell might have remained at odds with the President and, given the importance of the war issue, resigned. In all events, there would have been a helpful debate.

None of these outcomes occurred. Instead, as the State Department's leader, Powell blew an uncertain trumpet. U.S. diplomacy on Iraq lacked consistency, conviction, energy, or creativity. Between President Bush's September 2002 speech on Iraq to the United Nations and the start of Operation Iraqi Freedom in March 2003, two of our key NATO allies, France and Germany—both members of the United Nations Security Council at the time—refused to support the United States on Iraq. This was an important problem for us, one of our principal difficulties at the United Nations. Yet Powell in that period gave no speeches in France or Germany. Indeed, he did not visit either country. He traveled to Western Europe during those months only once and briefly, to attend the World Economic Forum in Davos, Switzerland.

Under these circumstances, it was not surprising that the United States lost ground at the United Nations in the months before the war. But this outcome was especially frustrating, given that Powell had prevailed upon the President to make the United Nations the main arena for our Iraq diplomacy. It was a fateful choice.

Though he tended not to offer affirmative strategic ideas of his own, Powell was often influential regarding specific courses of action. He operated skillfully within the interagency system run by Rice.

That system, in key respects, was a legacy of the Administration of President George H. W. Bush. The senior Mr. Bush, while Ronald Reagan's Vice President, had disapproved of the bureaucratic warfare between Caspar Weinberger's Pentagon and George Shultz's State Department. Many issues there became deadlocked in contentious meetings and had to be elevated to President Reagan for decision. When George H. W. Bush became President, he insisted on an interagency process that minimized such disputes. He got it, largely by allowing Secretary of State James Baker a more dominant role than Secretaries of State had played throughout most of the Reagan Administration.

Condoleezza Rice had served her apprenticeship, as it were, on the first President Bush's National Security Council staff. It was there, I assume, that she developed her belief that interagency disagreements are a symptom of dysfunction rather than useful debate. After becoming National Security Adviser, she often commented that if the differing views of National Security

Council members could not be resolved through combining elements of each—if the President were required to choose one member's policy option over another's—that would represent a failure on her part.

Though Rice worked to spare the President having to decide between clear-cut, mutually exclusive options, none of his top advisers exercised the kind of dominance that James Baker did when he was Secretary of State. Rather, Rice relied on her practice of bridging or blending key elements of the views of several interagency players—an approach that tended to paper over, rather than resolve, important differences of opinion. Her pursuit of harmony came, at times, at the expense of coherence.

Regarding Iraq, the interagency process made it easier for Powell and Armitage to affect Administration policy through passivity and delaying tactics. When Cabinet consensus was required to bring forward a particular proposal to the President (for example, the proposal to convene a political conference of Iraqi oppositionists), it was easy for State officials to block the initiative for weeks or months—without having to explain themselves to the President. The interagency process reinforced the bureaucracy's innate bias in favor of inaction. Sometimes that bias works benignly, but in the case of Iraq, I believe, it caused problems that hurt the war effort.

As Powell, Tenet, and their deputies helped develop Administration policy on Iraqi regime change, some lower-level State and CIA officials were voicing more or less open opposition to the policy. But they did not propose an alternative approach either. They presumably felt safe in bucking the President on Iraq because high-level State and CIA officials were so frequently being cited (anonymously) in news stories, leaking their criticisms of the President, his supporters, and his policy to gain public support for their own views. Many of the leaks were misleading or simply inaccurate, reflecting either misinformation or dishonesty. Reinforced by on-the-record commentaries by former diplomats and former intelligence officials, the stream of leaks eventually congealed into the elaborate, false narrative summarized by the slogan "Bush lied, people died," which played a role in the 2004 presidential election campaign and beyond.

The term "leak" refers generally to the unauthorized publication of secret information. What I am discussing here, however—the dozens of negative stories attributed to State and CIA officials during the George W. Bush Administration—were not leaks in that sense. Rather, they were policy arguments conducted through the press, with no opportunity for direct rebuttal, no referee, and little regard for accurate information. I am not sure if it makes sense to call a false story a leak. When officials incorrectly described meetings and wrongly attributed views (to "neocons" or others), they were pretending to leak, but were actually just fabricating.

Rumsfeld would have given no quarter to any subordinate of his who operated that way. On at least half a dozen occasions I saw him lecture his staff about maintaining peace within the Administration. He said it was disloyal and harmful to the President to squabble needlessly or excessively with interagency colleagues. And he warned severely against giving journalists accounts of confidential interagency deliberations. I don't believe that Rumsfeld ever leaked classified information or provided a reporter with any kind of unauthorized account of a meeting with the President or his fellow Principals. Doing so would have violated his personal code, which he talked about, at rare relaxed moments, with the intense earnestness of the Eagle Scout he had been as a boy. Some Boy Scout traits—and not just his use of "good golly" and "darn"—survived in him, despite all his hardheaded sophistication. As a rule, Rumsfeld did not even give "background" interviews to journalists, a convention that would have allowed them to quote him as an unnamed source. When he spoke to them, he did so on the record.*

I shared Rumsfeld's scrupulousness about leaking and keeping meetings confidential. I rarely spoke to journalists (which was a mistake on my part) and almost never gave them material "on background." Early on in my tenure as Under Secretary, when I was quoted in a news article as an unnamed "Pentagon official," Rumsfeld mentioned the quotation disapprovingly, assuming that whoever provided it did so without authorization. He would have had no problem with it if it had been attributed to me. That taught me a lesson about talking "on background."

I passed along to my subordinates Rumsfeld's warnings about leaks, and his other "now hear this" announcements for the staff. People in my office sometimes made satirical remarks about colleagues from other agencies, but if they crossed the line into disrespect, I reminded them of Rumsfeld's admonitions about harmony and loyalty. Recalling my experience during the Reagan Administration, I said it was a mistake to think they could work collegially with people they insulted, even if those people were not hearing the insults. I told them they should speak even in internal Pentagon meetings as if our State and CIA colleagues were present in the room.

I knew this advice sounded Pollyannaish, but it served the govern-

*Rumsfeld not only told journalists to quote him by name, but also recorded his news media interviews and had them transcribed. After the reporter's story was published, Rumsfeld would post the transcript of the interview on the DOD website, allowing the public to compare what the Secretary said to what the reporter chose to use.

ment's interests to maintain civility and honesty. On the other hand, I now see more clearly the intense animus behind the systematic leaking and "backgrounding" that undermined President Bush and others who supported him. Our failure—as targets—to heed the attack, to protest it, and to fight back, was a form of unilateral disarmament that did not serve the interests of the President, the country, or truth.

Peter Rodman, the Assistant Secretary of Defense for International Security Affairs, believed that the various Iraqi exile groups should be encouraged to coordinate their efforts in advance of Saddam's overthrow. In a May 9, 2002, paper for Rumsfeld, he advocated "organizing the democratic opposition groups . . . into a real political-military force," in order to "avoid a political vacuum" in Iraq.

Rumsfeld praised Rodman's work, and on July 1 he forwarded it in the form of a memo to his fellow Principals—Cheney, Powell, Tenet, and Rice. This idea of cooperating with the "democratic opposition groups" became the starting point for a series of Defense Department proposals to prepare for post-Saddam governance of Iraq. Although he opposed trying to choose another country's leader, Rumsfeld favored helping to establish political principles for Iraq's reconstruction. He thought the U.S. government should organize a group of responsible Iraqis in the hope that, when the time came, they might steer Iraq toward creating a broad-based, representative government. Laying the groundwork for a political process would be crucial to a timely transfer of authority to Iraqis, to avoid a prolonged occupation government.

Rodman was concerned that State and CIA tended to accentuate the negative about Iraqi "externals" as a group, even though these were the only partners available for planning to reconstitute the Iraqi government. Armitage and McLaughlin claimed that the externals would be resented in Iraq as lacking "legitimacy." It was evident, however, that their underlying concern was that if the externals had an important role in post-Saddam Iraq, it would open the way to an important role for the detested Chalabi.

It was never clear how anyone in our government could pretend to know the particular opinions of the internals—to gauge fine points of the thinking of people living in Iraq's frightened, insular society. But State and CIA officials insisted that the "internals" would oppose the "externals": that they would reject leadership from Iraqis who had chosen to live abroad rather than to share the misery of life under Saddam. State and the CIA produced an enormous body of analysis arguing that one of the great divides in post-Saddam Iraqi politics would be between externals and internals. Even before events in Iraq refuted that argument there were reasons to doubt the claim. Hamid Karzai, after all, could fairly be described as an external whom the Afghan internals accepted without questioning his legitimacy.

State and CIA representatives were cool to any initiative to mobilize the Iraqi opposition. Armitage flaunted his lack of enthusiasm for an opposition political conference. And he rejected suggestions to work with the opposition to organize a provisional government for Iraq, either before regime change or immediately after. This negative attitude toward the opposition seriously impeded the Administration's prewar planning in general.

State was determined to prevent the externals from capitalizing on their political "head start" over the internals. But without a head start, there would be *no* Iraqi leadership to take on a governing role. (No one was arguing any longer that the Baathist government should stay in place with a replacement dictator at the top.) And without an Iraqi government to take power swiftly after Saddam's ouster, we would have to create a government of occupation, run by the United States or perhaps the United Nations. State officials accordingly drafted a proposal for a "transitional civil authority" to serve as an occupation government, to ensure that the externals did not take over. The strongest argument against such a strategy was that a long-term occupation was likely to produce widespread resentment and perhaps violent resistance. At times, State officials acknowledged that danger, but they never reconciled it with their plan for a transitional civil authority.

Without arguing for promoting Chalabi or the INC, Rumsfeld urged, in his July 1 memo to the other Principals (drawing on Rodman's work), that *all* the friendly, democratic opposition groups be organized into a cooperative body, and he cited historical parallels. In 1943–44, Roosevelt and Churchill "had plans for an Allied Military Government for *postwar France*," based on the theory that the Free French under Charles de Gaulle—the exiled French general—did not truly represent the French people.

> **Had FDR and Churchill actually imposed an occupation government, the Communist-dominated resistance would have been the only significant political force on the ground in the country. The Gaullists would have been neutered, and the Communists would have ruled the countryside.**
>
> **DeGaulle, in power from 1944–47, was able to expand his own political movement and effectively neutralize the Communists.**

Rumsfeld pointed out that, inside Iraq, there were "undesirable opposition elements" with "presumably some support around the country." Organizing the groups that shared our broad principles and goals would be essential to preempt these undesirables and "avoid a chaotic post-Saddam free-for-all." Referring to State's "transitional civil authority" proposal, Rumsfeld warned: "An international presence, or interim international 'commission', would not be an adequate substitute for helping friendly indigenous forces establish their political and military authority quickly on the ground."

Ahmad Chalabi was a complex figure. He could achieve prodigies of consensus building, but his high-handedness could drive large numbers of people to unite against him. He had admirers, and he had outright enemies. He was more than a personality; in the bitter debate about the war, he became a symbol of the case for U.S. military action to overthrow Saddam.

Antagonism toward him grew into a phenomenon. U.S. officials at odds with the Administration's Iraq policies damned and fought Chalabi as if he were President Bush's surrogate or the source of the Bush doctrine. Chalabi's enemies in the U.S. government detested him with much greater intensity than his friends supported him. They attacked him far more persistently than his friends defended him. (This will be obvious to any historian who comprehensively reviews the record. Perhaps they will come to understand all the reasons. I do not.)

Anti-Chalabi officials—those intent on blocking him from ever exercising political power in Iraq—found it useful to claim to the press that their bureaucratic rivals (notably Rumsfeld, Wolfowitz, and I) were trying to "anoint" Chalabi as leader of Iraq after Saddam. Citing State Department sources, Seymour Hersh asserted in a May 2002 *New Yorker* article, "A dispute over Chalabi's potential usefulness preoccupies the bureaucracy, as the civilian leadership in the Pentagon continues to insist that *only the I.N.C. can lead the opposition*." The allegation has survived to the present: In his memoir, George Tenet described the DOD proposals for post-Saddam Iraq as "thinly veiled efforts to put Chalabi in charge."

However often the story is repeated, it was and remains incorrect. I never advocated that the United States should select Iraq's leader, and I never heard Wolfowitz argue for favoring a particular Iraqi leader, whether Chalabi or anyone else. We knew Rumsfeld would not tolerate any of his subordinates playing such a game.

I assume that some of these unnamed "official sources" knew that the allegation was bogus. But it served their purpose, keeping Chalabi (and the Defense Department) on the defensive. Some who spread the allegation probably took it at face value; it was asserted so often that many came to accept it. But the claim was false as to Rumsfeld, Wolfowitz, and me, and I know of no official for whom it was true. We declared this orally and in writing, publicly and in confidential government meetings. I do not know what might exist in the file cabinets of every official in the Defense Department, but of the thousands of pages of material that senior Defense Department officials wrote for interagency meetings on post-Saddam Iraqi governance, I know of *not one* supporting this charge. Even in informal meetings and conversations, I never heard anyone at the Defense Department make an argument or suggest a plan for putting Chalabi into power in Iraq. We believed the U.S. interest was in a stable Iraqi government that would respect key principles of international peace and human rights—not in selecting particular leaders for Iraq.

As with any conspiracy theory, however, those who clung to the belief that we plotted to anoint Chalabi were not impressed by logic, evidence, or counterargument. Denials were dismissed as evidence that the plotters wanted to conceal their actual plans. It is significant, however, that the two individuals who led the U.S. effort to create political structures for post-Saddam Iraq have never claimed that they were asked to "anoint" or favor Chalabi. General Jay Garner, the head of the Office of Reconstruction and Humanitarian Assistance, was the coalition's civil administrator, with responsibility for developing an Iraqi interim authority. Ambassador L. Paul Bremer, who succeeded General Tommy Franks as the head of the Coalition Provisional Authority, took over this responsibility from Garner. It would have been impossible to pursue any political agenda in post-Saddam Iraq without bringing either Garner or Bremer on board. Yet neither of them has reported receiving encouragement, let alone instructions, to give Chalabi any advantages—and both of them are on record as having opposed the idea. In response to an interviewer's questions about Chalabi and the other Iraqi external leaders, Garner responded, "I never saw a plan to take any one of those guys and stick him up as a president or a leader of Iraq. . . . When I first took over the job, Doug Feith took me through the pluses and minuses of every one of the opposition leaders." That neither Garner nor Bremer was ever asked to help Chalabi, let alone "anoint" him as leader of Iraq, should dispose of the allegation that the Pentagon's leadership team was working on a pro-Chalabi plot. If Garner and Bremer were not in on such a plot—and never saw one—then there was none.

State nevertheless wrote many papers premised on the assertion that there were plans or plots within our government to impose Chalabi on Iraq. The "anoint Chalabi" mythology was a symptom of State's negative attitude toward Rumsfeld and his team—but it also helped shape that attitude. The tenor of this one-sided hostility is suggested by this comment attributed to a State official, referring to civilian Defense officials: "It's the return of the right-wing crazies, crawling their way back."

Even when State's papers didn't mention Chalabi by name, they warned again and again that U.S. officials should not allow the externals to play a major role in post-Saddam Iraqi politics. One such paper, a State Department analysis of the Iraqi opposition, was distributed at the June 6, 2002, Deputies Lunch. The U.S. government, it argued, should "not rely on any Iraqi émigré grouping to carry a heavy load. . . ." Warning that "external players alone cannot form a credible provisional government," it cautioned against forming a provisional government "before regime change allows access to internal constituencies." None of the groups (it asserted) "have real constituencies, or credibility," except for those of the Kurds, "who are circumscribed by ethnic issues from playing [a] leading role on [the] larger Iraq scene." This last claim would turn out to be as incorrect as the general thesis that Iraqi internals would reject leadership by the externals.*

This State paper listed more than a half a dozen "problems in working with the opposition," including the externals' internecine quarrels—what State called the "food-fight factor"—and the danger that cooperating with the externals would alienate "Iraqis inside." But, at the same time, it acknowledged the possible benefits we had been discussing at Deputies Lunches: "Iraqi émigrés can help advance U.S. goals. . . . [T]hey can present a vision for Iraq, provide experts for pre-liberation working groups, investigate war crimes, promote vision of U.S. action as liberation vs. invasion, [and] be [a] vehicle for Iraqi exiles to feel they're contributing to liberating their country." Evidently State officials felt constrained to heed Hadley's oft-repeated message: The President wanted U.S. officials to find ways to work with the Iraqi opposition without playing favorites. But our diplomats generally remained unenthusiastic.

Steve Hadley worked hard to overcome State and CIA efforts at obstruction, and by June I was able to get my State counterpart, Under Secretary Marc Grossman, to help organize a meeting of State, Defense, and CIA representatives with leaders of *all* the main Iraqi external groups. If Grossman and I cochaired a meeting, Rodman had suggested, this coop-

---

*Iraq's first elected president, its foreign minister, and its top military officer were all Kurds (as noted in Chapter 15).

erative activity could foster and demonstrate harmony both among the groups and among the U.S. agencies. That meeting could spur the groups to move forward together—in particular, to hold the political conference the Deputies had been asking State to help organize for so many months.

Grossman readily accepted the idea of the cochaired meeting. Unlike Armitage, he did not reflexively oppose any idea originating at the Pentagon. A career diplomat who had been Director General of the Foreign Service and served as U.S. Ambassador to Turkey, Grossman showed love and loyalty toward the State Department. But when he represented State at interagency meetings, the quality of his contributions could put the department in a strange light. The papers prepared at State for these meetings were generally far less persuasive than the remarks made by Grossman himself, who was articulate and pithy. Before forwarding a State proposal to the Principals Committee, Hadley would usually ask State to rewrite it—not only to incorporate comments from other agencies, but also to accommodate Grossman's own remarks. It was as if Grossman had commented on the work of some *other* agency's staff.

Grossman and I set a date in early August for our meeting with the Iraqis. In spite of some bumps along the way (State officials, for example, persisted in belittling Chalabi by referring to the opposition as the "Group of Four, plus the INC"), work on the meeting proceeded fairly smoothly. The Iraqis were receptive to our invitation, mentioning appreciatively that it came jointly from State and Defense. They took that as an unusual display of unity—and a sign that President Bush must be getting serious about action against Saddam.

Political work wasn't the only way the externals could assist the U.S. policy of regime change in Iraq. They could also carry out intelligence, humanitarian, and other projects in Iraq. In the event of war, their language skills and knowledge of the country and people could be invaluable to our forces—both during the fight and in the aftermath. (The lack of reliable interpreters would develop into a serious problem in the field for U.S. military and civilian personnel alike. It became clear that what we needed was not merely individuals who spoke both languages, but *people we knew well enough to trust*.) With proper preparation, the externals could assist coalition troops in combat. An Iraqi force trained by us could then play an important role in training Iraqi police and military units. And after the Baathist regime's ouster, the externals could help us vet Iraqi candidates for key jobs in the new Iraq.

If the externals were going to have a substantial role in liberating their country, we needed to train and equip them. The Iraq Liberation Act of 1998 had authorized the President to do that by drawing down funding from Defense Department resources, to a total of $97 million. President Clinton had authorized using only $5 million, and my office wanted to tap some of the remaining funds.

Wolfowitz believed that training the Iraqi externals could have strategic importance extending well beyond Iraq. This aligned with his recommendation for Afghanistan, that the United States overthrow the Taliban by supporting local Afghan antiregime forces—a strategy of liberation rather than occupation. Wolfowitz spoke often of the importance of helping foreigners promote freedom in their own countries against antidemocratic, anti-U.S. regimes. I shared his view that U.S. national security could benefit from such help. The regimes around the world that worried us most—Iraq, Iran, and North Korea, for starters—were not only endangering peace and threatening U.S. interests, but also oppressing their own people. Those regimes were widely hated by their own citizens, a vulnerability we might be able to exploit.* Supporting local opposition forces could possibly be a more effective way to pressure the regimes than diplomacy alone—whether those opponents were in exile (like many in the Iraqi opposition) or based in the country (like the Iraqi Kurds, or Afghanistan's Northern Alliance forces).

Although Wolfowitz had been championing the military training of Iraqi externals since the 1990s, it was hard to get any such initiative off the ground. In a March 15, 2002, meeting, he told me that CIA's John McLaughlin opposed any Defense Department work in this area. Hadley, on the other hand, favored it. To get a green light from the President, Hadley would have to work the matter through the Deputies and Principals Committees—and for that he needed a written proposal. Wolfowitz asked me to draft it.

The Policy organization's Office of Near East and South Asian Affairs, run by Bill Luti, developed the concept, seeking advice from other agencies: It estimated the number of trainee candidates (from all the opposition groups), proposed a process for screening them, and identified possible training sites in Europe and the Middle East. General Wayne Downing (U.S. Army, retired), Deputy National Security Adviser for counterterror-

*Rumsfeld, Wolfowitz, and I had also made the case that a strategy of supporting local, antiregime forces in Afghanistan and elsewhere could also strengthen our diplomacy with problem regimes (such as Syria, Libya, and Sudan), causing them to reconsider their policies on terrorism and weapons of mass destruction. These regimes might become more accommodating if they feared we would otherwise actively support their domestic opponents.

ism and the former commander of the Special Operations Command, worked with Luti on the proposal.

We brought our training recommendation to the Principals in May. Arguing that starting the program at that time would be too risky, Powell persuaded his colleagues to defer it. There were fears (notably at CENTCOM) that initiating training of Iraqi externals could provoke Saddam, who might lash out violently before U.S. military forces were ready to respond.

Throughout the spring of 2002, Iraq-related contingencies were debated at a series of interagency meetings: What should we do if Saddam attacked the Kurds? Or if Iraqi forces downed a U.S. or U.K. plane patrolling the northern or southern no-fly zone? Or if they fired a missile at another state, or if Saddam were overthrown in a military coup? Concerns about such emergencies—which were increasingly likely as we turned up the heat on Saddam—helped spur General Franks to create what he called his "running start" option for the Iraq war plan. Instead of assuming that the U.S. could choose the timing of our military action, the running start would allow us to act more quickly in response to events—to initiate military action against Iraq, if necessary, even before the full contingent of U.S. forces arrived in-theater.

In our interagency discussions, we recognized both the perils of an untimely provocation of Saddam and the merits of training the externals. There were dangers in pressuring Saddam, but there were dangers also in forgoing pressure. In the national security field, risks attend every proposed act and omission. The gravest part of the President's job—the essence of strategic decision making—is deciding *which* risks the country should run at any given time. As Dean Acheson wrote: "At the top there are no easy choices. All are between evils, the consequences of which are hard to judge."

The decision to postpone training of the externals did not prevent all forms of cooperation. The externals could continue to provide us with intelligence from inside Iraq, for example. Their information was a mixed bag, combining accurate and inaccurate reports that had to be sifted and reviewed critically—typical of any human intelligence program. But, as Hadley observed, we needed as much intelligence about Iraq as we could get.

We knew the CIA's coverage of Iraq was spotty, though it wasn't until after Saddam's ouster that we learned how pathetically scant its sources in Iraq were. Before Operation Iraqi Freedom began, for example, the CIA did not have a single dedicated, unilateral source there devoted to WMD-related matters. The Silberman-Robb Commission eventually judged that "[w]e had precious little human intelligence, and virtually no useful signals intelligence on a target [i.e., Iraq] that was one of the United States' top intelligence priorities."

I recall no intelligence official ever confessing the inadequacy of the intelligence sources to the Deputies Committee at the time. On the contrary, many intelligence reports suggested that the CIA had substantial knowledge of what was happening inside Iraq. The CIA published confidently worded assessments not only about Iraqi WMD, but also about the Iraqi public's *favorable* views of the Iraqi police, and *unfavorable* views of the "legitimacy" of the Iraqi externals. CIA officials also claimed to know that Iraqi officials, on ideological grounds, would not cooperate with al Qaida. CIA officials made much of this last point. They argued that Iraqi regime leaders, as members of the secular Baath Party, would not cooperate with the Islamist extremists of al Qaida—a presupposition that would later produce an imbroglio.

Some of us thought the CIA overstated its noncooperation argument. History, we pointed out, was full of examples of regimes that forged strategic alliances despite serious ideological differences. After all, the Nazis and the Soviets, who had conflicting ideologies, entered into secret strategic cooperation in August 1939. Saddam and al Qaida had interests in common, we noted: They shared hostility toward the United States and the declared intention to expel our forces from the Middle East. CIA analysts never convincingly countered our objections.

Like al Qaida, the Iraqi regime had shown tactical flexibility in the service of its strategic goals. Saddam embraced Islam and Muslim symbols when it suited his purposes: In January 1991, he added to the Iraqi flag the Koranic verse "Allah is the Greatest," styled in his own handwriting. And he used a top lieutenant, Ibrahim al-Duri, who had a reputation as a devout Muslim, to cultivate links with Islamist groups. As I saw it, shaping U.S. counterterrorism policy around the CIA's hypothesis of noncooperation would not be responsible.

The most outspoken advocate of the noncooperation theory was Paul Pillar, the CIA's National Intelligence Officer for the Middle East from 2000 to 2005. Pillar was a critic of President Bush's Iraq policy, a point he made known even while at the CIA, and his theory supported his policy views. In the fall of 2005, soon after he left government service, Pillar denounced the Administration in a *Foreign Affairs* article (quoted more fully in Chapter 4).The CIA's work on the Iraq–al Qaida issue suggested that intelligence officials were not open to information inconsistent with Pillar's theory.

The nature of the problem became clearer when the CIA was given the opportunity to interview al Qaida–related terrorists in northern Iraq. On March 25, 2002, *The New Yorker* published an article by Jeffrey Goldberg on the Kurds. Goldberg had traveled to northern Iraq, spending time in the area governed by Jalal Talabani's Patriotic Union of Kurdistan (PUK). PUK officials escorted Goldberg to visit a prison in Sulaimaniya, where they were holding members of Ansar al-Islam, a religious extremist group of Kurds and Arabs who had trained in al Qaida camps in Afghanistan. The Ansar prisoners were accused of colluding with the Iraqi regime. According to Goldberg, the charges were that

> **Ansar al-Islam received funds directly from Al Qaeda; that the intelligence service of Saddam Hussein has joint control, with Al Qaeda operatives, over Ansar al-Islam; that Saddam Hussein hosted a senior leader of Al Qaeda in Baghdad in 1992; that a number of Al Qaeda members fleeing Afghanistan have been secretly brought into territory controlled by Ansar al-Islam and that Iraqi intelligence agents smuggled conventional weapons, and possibly even chemical and biological weapons, into Afghanistan.**

If true, the *New Yorker* article noted, these charges "mean that the relationship between Saddam's regime and Al Qaeda is far closer than previously thought."

The PUK intelligence director told the reporter that "he hoped I would carry this information to American intelligence officials," because the "F.B.I. and the C.I.A. haven't come out [here] yet." The director's deputy added, "Americans are going to Somalia, the Philippines, I don't know where else, to look for terrorists. But this is the field, here." (In response, a CIA spokesperson issued a standard refusal to comment.) Goldberg quotes James Woolsey, the former CIA Director, on the situation: "It would be a real shame if the C.I.A.'s substantial institutional hostility to Iraqi democratic resistance groups was keeping it from learning about Saddam's ties to Al Qaeda in northern Iraq."

This stunning passage required an explanation from the CIA. At a Deputies Lunch soon after its publication, Wolfowitz brought it to the group's attention and asked McLaughlin why the CIA had not accepted the PUK's offer to debrief the prisoners. Appearing pained, McLaughlin said he didn't have an answer, but that he would look into the matter.

For weeks and months, Wolfowitz used the Deputies Lunches to urge McLaughlin to have the CIA interview the Ansar prisoners. How could the agency justify its lack of curiosity to talk with al Qaida–affiliated terrorists, Wolfowitz asked, when they claimed they were receiving funds and other cooperation from Saddam's regime? Wolfowitz mastered his exasperation, managing not to raise his voice, but he was as persistent in pressing the question as McLaughlin was in stonewalling. The CIA never provided a reasonable explanation. After a while, it seemed to me, McLaughlin must have gotten indigestion at the mere thought of another Deputies Lunch.

Although he also asked Rumsfeld to raise the matter with Tenet, Wolfowitz got nowhere on the Ansar prisoners until the summer. Then, on June 27, 2002, McLaughlin announced at a Deputies Lunch that the CIA would interrogate the prisoners—but "only if the Principals OK'd it." Wolfowitz shook his head, leaned toward me, and whispered: "As if the Agency asks for the Principals' okay whenever it wants to talk to someone." In July, the CIA finally sent operatives to the PUK to talk to the Ansar prisoners. The debriefings yielded many reports of cooperation between Iraq and Ansar, reports that were assessed as credible and important by the CIA's own analysts.

More recent public information suggests that the CIA in fact had very few American personnel at all in Iraq. But all the while that Wolfowitz, Rumsfeld, and others were pressing to have the prisoners debriefed, the CIA did not reveal to the Deputies this embarrassing lack of resources.

In dragging their feet on interviewing the Ansar prisoners, CIA officials were ignoring—and actually refusing to investigate—possible Iraq–al Qaida connections. That was one way to protect their position that those connections could not exist, but it was not a proper way. News stories cited assertions by "senior intelligence officials" that there was no evidence of such connections—creating the impression that diligent efforts had been made to uncover such evidence.

I considered Saddam a serious danger, whether or not there were significant or operational ties between him and al Qaida.* I never found

*A presentation prepared by my office in September 2002 concluded with this item:

> Don't we need a link to 9/11?
> No: This isn't about revenge or retaliation, but about self-defense. A link to 9/11 would just emphasize what we already know—that the current Iraqi regime is extremely hostile to us and is willing to cooperate with international terrorism.

"Presentation: The Case for Action," September 12, 2002.

much comfort in the CIA's theory that secular Baathists would not want to cooperate with religious extremists, even if it were correct. If, for ideological reasons, Saddam preferred to team with *secular* terrorists—of the Abu Nidal stripe, for example—there was no shortage of them. And if he wanted someday to work with al Qaida he might have options for cooperation, with or without any prior relationship.

Events following Saddam's overthrow proved that even hard-core Baathists, under the right circumstances, would make common cause with Islamist extremists. The insurgency's Baathist leadership included Saddam (until his capture in December 2003) and Ibrahim al-Duri. The jihadist leader was Abu Musab al-Zarqawi, until he was killed by U.S. forces in June 2006. The strategic alliance between their two camps was a key element in the insurgency. A similar alliance, however, might have developed even if Saddam had remained in power. The CIA officials had overstated the Baathist-jihadist divide—as they overstated or erred about other political and military matters before the Iraq war.

Political controversy about Iraq in 2002 was intense enough to test the professionalism of officials throughout the intelligence community. Some failed the test by allowing their views on policy or politics to interfere with their intelligence analysis. That harmed the quality of the intelligence. And it hurt relations between the intelligence community and policy makers, undermining trust and confidence between them.

Intelligence analysts should operate without fear or favor. Their work should be nonpolitical: the raw information marshaled with care, the analysis rigorous. They should not filter intelligence or trim it to suit their *own* policy views, preconceptions, theories, or prejudices—*or those of any policy maker either*. That intelligence officials were shading their reporting to suit their theories was bad enough. The situation became worse, however, when CIA officials reacted to criticism by going on the offensive, using the press to accuse their critics of pressuring them to give support to the President's policies. The actual story is quite different.

I did not personally undertake a detailed examination of the intelligence about the Iraq–al Qaida relationship, but I understood why Wolfowitz thought it worth his while. He made an issue of the close-mindedness of CIA officials on this question and, in the fall of 2002, he asked several Defense Department officials to stay on top of the intelligence reporting on the relationship. This ad hoc team—a few people from my office and his—helped Wolfowitz develop questions on the subject, which he then posed to the CIA officials who provided his daily intelligence briefings.

Skeptical questioning of this kind is one of the best uses of the daily intelligence briefings. But some commentators argued that Wolfowitz's questions, simply because they were critical and persistent, showed that Defense Department policy makers wanted to corrupt the intelligence and distort it to suit their purposes. The Senate Intelligence Committee investigated that charge, as did the Silberman-Robb Commission. Each group concluded, in its own unanimous, bipartisan report, that the accusation was entirely without merit. Yet some journalists, former intelligence officials, and members of Congress persist in asserting it.

In the story of the policy-versus-intelligence disagreements about Iraq and al Qaida, a key subplot began when a staffer in my organization asked a question of an intelligence official. His unexpected reply gave rise to whistle-blowing about the way the intelligence community was filtering its own intelligence information. The resulting critique of the CIA's work on the Iraq–al Qaida relationship would become the subject of bureaucratic and political attacks, but the Pentagon team's criticism of the CIA was proper.

The Policy staffer, Christina Shelton, had been a career intelligence analyst for two decades, with ten years' experience in counterintelligence. The Defense Intelligence Agency (DIA) had lent her to my organization to work as a policy official. Her job was to support a project on Special Access Programs, a set of highly classified, technological military capabilities. For years, these programs were so secret that they were sometimes concealed even from key planners in the combatant commands—and therefore not incorporated into war plans! This was a classic Pentagon absurdity I hoped to cure. My office initiated a project to analyze the requirements of the combatant commands and bring the Special Access Programs to the attention of the appropriate commanders, and Shelton assisted that project.

In the aftermath of 9/11, Shelton was reviewing intelligence on terrorist networks when she came across a noteworthy analysis from 1998—a finished CIA assessment, not a raw report—relating to the activities of the Iraqi intelligence service. Though she had not been directed from above to investigate Iraq's support of terrorism, she decided on her own to do some digging. From the CIA she obtained the material underlying that 1998 analysis. That material included reports, dating back to 1996, of linkages between al Qaida and the Iraqi government. It puzzled her that those CIA reports were not featured in the intelligence assessments currently being produced. Some of the reports were ignored; others were mentioned but dismissed offhandedly. Shelton asked some officials at DIA why this was so.

The answer she received took her aback. One official told her that citing those reports of Iraq–al Qaida connections "would be playing into the hands of people like Wolfowitz." Shelton considered this a disturbingly unprofessional comment and promptly wrote a memo recounting the exchange. Officials in my office later provided that memo to the Senate Intelligence Committee, and to other congressional committees that requested our documents on pre-Iraq-war intelligence.

Shelton decided to take a closer look at the intelligence community's work on the al Qaida–Iraq relationship. Her work did not produce a competing intelligence assessment, but rather a critique of the intelligence officials' analytic work. Her main point was that the analysts were not properly taking into account all the relevant information they had. She criticized intelligence officials for shading and filtering information to defend their own preconceptions and policy preferences, which they did not always reveal to their customers.

CIA analysts would shade their information, Shelton complained, through the use of "spin" language. For example, when the CIA produced or obtained reports that *supported* its analysts' thinking, the agency often described the reports as "credible" without necessarily explaining why. When reports *contradicted* its analysts' theories, however, the CIA commonly described them as "unconfirmed"—though they were no more lacking in corroboration than the reports described simply as "credible." Shelton reproached the CIA for using such nonrigorous, prejudicial terminology.

She also pointed out that intelligence officials filtered their data—for example, by ignoring reports that were inconsistent with their theory that the Iraqi regime's secular ideology precluded cooperation with al Qaida religious fanatics. Shelton wasn't arguing that the ignored reports were necessarily credible or true, *but that they should not simply be ignored.* They were part of the record. If the CIA wanted to discount them, it should cite them and explain why it considered them unimportant. Like scientists or scholars, she argued, intelligence and policy officials alike should take into account as much relevant information as possible. If the information failed to support their theories, they should think about modifying the theories. They should not simply obscure the inconvenient data behind a veil of disparaging adjectives. There should be standards for the use of evaluative terms like "credible" and "unconfirmed."

As Shelton developed her critique, she joined forces with others in the Pentagon who were analyzing al Qaida–Iraq contacts. For a high-level policy official, Wolfowitz knew the intelligence on the subject in extraordinary detail. He had an astute special assistant, James Thomas, who studied the subject and helped him generate new questions. Chris Carney (who was by mid-April 2002 the sole remaining member of the Policy Counter Terrorism Evaluation Group) had also acquired knowledge about al Qaida and Iraq in the course of his review of linkages among terrorist groups and their state supporters. Work by Shelton, Thomas, and Carney was merged on this matter.*

I met Shelton in June 2002, when her boss, Deputy Under Secretary of Defense Kenneth deGraffenreid, told me that someone in his office was challenging the CIA's work on al Qaida and Iraq and provided me with Shelton's critique. It impressed me as a sophisticated, well-reasoned argument. It cited intelligence reports that, if credible, raised serious concerns: For the past decade, according to the cited CIA documents, Iraqi intelligence officials had been meeting with senior al Qaida personnel and providing al Qaida with support, including safe haven, travel documents, and training in sophisticated explosives.

I had not studied the mass of detailed intelligence reports and assessments that Shelton and her colleagues were reviewing and criticizing, so I didn't know if their critique was substantively correct. But it was obviously well organized and logically argued. Wolfowitz shared my favorable opinion of the critique, and we recommended that Rumsfeld hear it. When the Secretary received the briefing on August 8, 2002, he reacted as I had. After some general compliments, he made a disclaimer: He had no way of judging if the briefers' criticisms were valid, but the material was compelling. Though it challenged the CIA's work, Rumsfeld was confident that Tenet would view the briefing as constructive. He directed me to call Tenet and arrange to bring it to him.

On August 15, Shelton and Carney briefed Tenet and twenty-five or so of his colleagues at CIA headquarters. DeGraffenreid and I accompanied them, along with Admiral Lowell Jacoby, the head of DIA. (James Thomas was not present.) On the way there, DeGraffenreid, Shelton, Carney, and I discussed the risk that our CIA colleagues might react badly, even angrily, to being criticized. They might denigrate the briefing as an attempt by policy officials to pressure or politicize intelligence analysts. We agreed to conduct the briefing in such a way that no one could honestly make that claim.

Accordingly, I introduced the briefing with decidedly nonthreatening remarks. There were many ways to look at the information available on contacts between al Qaida and Iraq, I said. While the briefing put forward thoughts that took issue with CIA assessments, the critique was by no means definitive. It was intended simply to raise questions and provoke

---

*Shelton and James Thomas consolidated their work in a briefing that combined an oral presentation, given mainly by Shelton, with briefing slides drafted principally by Thomas.

thought, not dictate any conclusions. I made clear that we recognized the difference between proper feedback from consumers of intelligence in the policy community and an improper attempt to influence intelligence to serve a policy purpose.

Shelton and Carney spoke well. They dealt diplomatically with the delicate subject of intelligence analysts' filtering and shading information to vindicate their own preconceptions. When the briefing was over, there was little feedback from the CIA attendees. Tenet took me back to his office and complimented the briefing as useful, adding that he had "issues" on this subject with some of his people. His remark suggested he was sympathetic to the presentation. I didn't know precisely what he meant by "issues," but I decided it was best not to try to probe into Tenet's relationships with his own staff. He thanked me for bringing the briefing to him and suggested that "our experts should get together to follow up."

The experts had their follow-up session on August 20. I heard it went well. The Defense Department representatives got to say their piece, and the atmosphere was described as reasonably collegial.

The following month, the CIA issued a report entitled *Iraqi Support for Terrorism* that gave somewhat greater prominence to its own formerly overlooked reporting, identifying Iraq as an "operational node" in the network of international terrorism. The conclusions of that report were summarized by the Senate Intelligence Committee:

> **Iraq continues to be a safehaven, transit point, or operational node for groups and individuals who direct violence against the United States, Israel, and other allies. Iraq has a long history of supporting terrorism. During the last four decades, it has altered its targets to reflect changing priorities and goals. It continues to harbor and sustain a number of smaller anti-Israel terrorist groups and to actively encourage violence against Israel. Regarding the Iraq-al-Qaida relationship, reporting from sources of varying reliability points to a number of contacts, incidents of training, and discussions of Iraqi safehaven for Usama bin Ladin and his organization dating from the early 1990s.**

The Defense Department acted properly when it shared its critique with the CIA, and the CIA performed properly when it issued a more complete report reflecting the information in its own files.

Word naturally got around the government that Tenet and his group of CIA officials had received the Defense Department briefing. At least twice in late August, in meetings attended by McLaughlin and others, Hadley mentioned to me that he wanted to hear the critique himself. I had no problem with that, and McLaughlin voiced no objection. Hadley's staff made the arrangements through Wolfowitz's office rather than mine—I had given my staff standing orders to respond to requests from Wolfowitz as if they came from me—and the briefing occurred on September 16.

Pentagon Policy personnel briefed colleagues at the White House on various matters almost every day, and this presentation by Shelton and her colleagues was handled as a routine matter. I learned in due course that Hadley and Scooter Libby had heard the briefing, but I don't think I discussed it with Hadley or Libby until more than a year had passed. By then, its purported significance had achieved absurd proportions through magnification by conspiracy-minded journalists and politicians.

Some intelligence officials evidently did resent the criticism in the briefing. News stories cited anonymous intelligence officials accusing the Pentagon and the Vice President's office of trying to politicize the intelligence. The stories didn't explain the actual nature of the criticism from the Pentagon—which was simply that intelligence officials should not manipulate assessments to bolster their own theories and policy preferences. Shelton and her colleagues were not trying to bias intelligence assessments; they were trying to eliminate the bias already there.* But that was not the picture painted by the news media, or by the unnamed intelligence officials who fed them the story.

The relationship between the Iraqi regime and al Qaeda—like the question of Iraq's WMD programs—became a high-profile issue within the debate over Iraq, especially in retrospect. Shelton and her team made a persuasive case that some CIA analysts had allowed their views to distort their presentation of the available reporting. I saw the importance of objecting to poor intelligence tradecraft, though I did not attach great significance to the issue of ties between Iraq and al Qaida. In my view, there were other, more compelling reasons for the President to worry about Iraq; Saddam was a serious threat, no matter how one interpreted the years of murky contacts between Iraqi intelligence and al Qaida.

But for some journalists and politicians, the combination of the al Qaida issue with a DOD-CIA dispute was irresistibly intriguing. In time, the briefing by Shelton and her colleagues would become the focus of an accusation that Defense officials were trying to pressure the CIA to alter

---

*Chris Carney, as it happens, was a Democrat, elected to Congress in 2006. He was by no means promoting a political agenda in his professional work on the CIA's Iraq–al Qaida analysis.

its conclusions on what was sometimes depicted as *the* central issue in the debate over the Iraq war. This accusation, like other elements of the anti-war conventional wisdom, has proven impervious to repeated disproof.

Senators Jay Rockefeller (D-West Virginia) and Carl Levin (D-Michigan) scrutinized the Iraq–al Qaida briefing as part of the Senate Intelligence Committee's investigation of pre-Iraq-war intelligence. In July 2004, the committee published a unanimous report concluding that policy makers did *not* pressure intelligence officials to politicize the intelligence. The committee interviewed hundreds of intelligence officials and advertised for officials who had stories about pressure to come forward. *It found not a single case of untoward pressure.* The committee reported that it "was not presented with any evidence that intelligence analysts changed their judgments as a result of political pressure, altered or produced intelligence products to conform with Administration policy, or that anyone even attempted to coerce, influence or pressure analysts to do so." The bipartisan and unanimous conclusion was that "none of the analysts or other people interviewed by the Committee said that they were pressured to change their conclusions related to Iraq's links to terrorism." The committee found also that Shelton and her Defense Department colleagues behaved professionally—and that their work had beneficial effects:

> **In some cases, those interviewed stated that the questions had forced them to go back and review the intelligence reporting, and that during this exercise they came across information they had overlooked in initial readings. The Committee found that this process—the policymakers probing questions—*actually improved the Central Intelligence Agency's (CIA) products.***

In short, the briefing served the constructive purpose we had intended.

The Silberman-Robb Commission, too, looked into the briefing, and in March 2005 it also concluded that policy officials had made no effort to politicize Iraq intelligence. The commission approved of the kind of criticism Shelton and her colleagues offered—vigorous, challenging give-and-take between intelligence officials and their customers—and said there should be *more* such interaction: "We conclude that good-faith efforts by intelligence consumers to understand the bases for analytic judgments, far from constituting 'politicization' are entirely legitimate."

Despite the findings of these two bipartisan bodies, however, the controversy didn't end. In September 2005, Senator Levin (of the Senate Intelligence Committee) pressed for the Defense Department Inspector General to reinvestigate the issue. The Committee asked for an official decision on whether the briefing had been illegal, improper, or inappropriate. The result was a Defense Department Inspector General finding that there had been *nothing illegal or improper* in the Pentagon briefing, and that we had not misled Congress. Nevertheless, Acting Inspector General Thomas Gimble managed to give some satisfaction to Senator Levin by saying that the briefers acted "inappropriately" when they made their presentation to White House personnel: It was inappropriate, he said, for policy officials to present material that could have been misconstrued as an intelligence briefing.

Hadley and Libby both knew that the briefers worked in my office; they could not have mistaken them for intelligence officials. (Gimble amazed a Senate committee by admitting that he had not interviewed either Hadley or Libby on this matter.) Moreover, the briefing was expressly presented as a *criticism* of the intelligence community, not an intelligence community product. One of the briefing slides was labeled: "Fundamental Problems With How the Intelligence Community Is Assessing Information." Gimble had no basis to say the briefing was seen, or could have been seen, as an intelligence activity.

Gimble's main conclusion was that criticism of intelligence is an intelligence activity—and therefore inappropriate for policy officials. I believe that is a misguided notion, and it is the opposite of the conclusions reached by the Senate Intelligence Committee and the Silberman-Robb Commission. I answered Gimble in an article in the *Washington Post*:

> **The recent inspector general's report argues that policy officials "undercut" the CIA by pointing out " 'fundamental problems' with the way the Intelligence Community was assessing information" on the issue of Iraq-al-Qaeda relations—even though Gimble last week said at a Senate hearing: "Again, I need to just remind everyone, we didn't make an assessment on the validity of either side of this issue." He labeled the Pentagon briefing "inappropriate" not because of any errors in it but because he viewed it as an "intelligence activity" that "varied" from "the intelligence community consensus." The Pentagon officials told the IG, however, that the briefing was a policy activity—a critique of an intelligence product.**
>
> **If this report hadn't become part of a political battle, Gimble's position would be scoffed at across the political spectrum. Sensible people recognize the importance of vigorous questioning of intelligence by the CIA's "customers." In bipartisan, unanimous reports on Iraq intelligence, both the Senate intel-**

ligence committee and the Silberman-Robb WMD commission called for more such questioning.

Though he admitted that he hadn't assessed the validity of the Pentagon's criticism of the CIA, Gimble questioned the Defense briefing's accuracy simply on the grounds that the briefers disagreed with the CIA's conclusions. In my *Washington Post* article, I pointed out the circularity of Gimble's reasoning:

> **In his report, Gimble wrote that the Pentagon briefing was not the "most accurate analysis of intelligence." This has been taken to suggest it was false or deceptive. But [Gimble] said he meant only that the briefing was at "variance with the consensus of the Intelligence Community." Of course it was at variance! It was a critique. That's why it was prepared in the first place.**

In *U.S. News and World Report,* the historian and commentator Michael Barone summed up the illogic of Gimble's criticism of the Pentagon briefing:

> **The idea that presidential appointees are obliged to treat intelligence community consensus as holy writ, not to be questioned or criticized, is loony. The fact that the same people who are criticizing George W. Bush and his appointees for accepting the intelligence community consensus that Saddam Hussein had weapons of mass destruction are also criticizing an appointee for questioning the intelligence community consensus on another point beggars belief.**

More than a year after the briefing was presented to Rumsfeld, Tenet, Hadley, and Libby, the Senate Intelligence Committee asked me some questions about it. One of the questions was: What were the old intelligence reports that Shelton had believed were being ignored or downplayed by the intelligence analysts? My answers included a list of the reports, prepared by my staff, with short summaries and some observations about them.

In November 2003, this list became the subject of a cover story in the *Weekly Standard* that incorrectly depicted it as my "case" for claiming a close connection between Iraq and al Qaida. That supported the magazine's own editorial position, but in fact the list was no such thing.

Rather, it was simply a set of references to the intelligence community's own papers on the Iraq–al Qaida relationship that cast doubt on the CIA's views. It was not a "case" at all, much less an argument that an "operational" relationship existed between Iraq and al Qaida. I had sent the list to the Senate Intelligence Committee not because I was advocating anything, but to comply with a request from the committee.

Journalists and others have since written articles and books about this list, referring to it either as the "Iraq-al Qaida Annex" or the "Feith Memo." Some say it was part of an effort to manipulate intelligence to induce the President to go to war. It was not. Before the *Weekly Standard* story, the list had been sent only to the Senate Intelligence Committee. As far as I know, it had never been sent to anyone else outside my office. And it was sent to the Intelligence Committee approximately five months *after* Saddam had been overthrown.

Like the head of any organization, the President of the United States needs good advice, sharpened by free, rigorous debate among his counselors. After the debate is over, however, he needs the whole government to work as a team to carry out his decisions. It is not easy to square these two interests. It takes effort, skill, and a lot of cooperation all around to ensure, first, that proposals are subjected to tough-minded, skeptical challenge, and then that all parts of the Administration move from debate to unified action.

This ideal of government coordination—lively debate leading to solid teamwork—was not achieved in the Bush Administration. State and CIA personnel refused to function as active members of the President's team.

How does a top-level adviser, such as the Secretary of State or Defense, implement policies he opposed in debate? This is usually not a problem. The President ordinarily gets loyalty and deference from his top officials. They know that their job is not to *be* the President, but to advise him. High-ranking officials often find themselves executing decisions they would have made differently if they were President. If they disagree with the President on an issue they consider a matter of principle and conscience, they can resign.

Iraq policy making in the Bush Administration after 9/11 did not conform to this pattern. Various senior State and CIA officials—including some at the highest levels—did not support the President's analyses and policies. For their own reasons, however, they were unwilling to challenge them openly in interagency discussions or to offer alternatives.

I don't think the problem was that the President discouraged challenges. He routinely allowed his thoughts to be questioned. He could more justly be faulted for an excessive tolerance of indiscipline, even of disloyalty, from his own officials. The government would have benefited from deeper and more skeptical discussions about strategy within the confidential forums of the interagency process. Instead of arguing their positions boldly within the Administration, however, some leading officials chose to air their dissent outside. They supplied journalists and former officials with a stream of mutually reinforcing stories—full of inaccuracies—designed to make the President and his supporters look unreasonable. Articles citing anonymous State and CIA officials' critiques of the Administration became a fixture of the public discussion of Iraq. These negative news-story sound bites did not improve the quality of the Administration's decision making, as proper interagency exchanges might have done. They did not help the Administration win necessary support from foreign partners; on the contrary, they signaled that our own government was divided on the issue. And they did not facilitate teamwork—the energetic, unified, government-wide action the President needed to implement his decisions.

President Bush did not receive the benefit of active debate on the fundamentals of his strategy. Nor did he get harmony in its execution. Key national security officials remained reluctant to endorse policies even after the President had resolved on them. At that point, they might either have pitched into the government's efforts wholeheartedly or stepped aside, allowing the President to appoint officials who would carry out his decisions with vigorous good faith. But even as they retained their reluctance, they retained their high-ranking positions.

9

IRAQ PLANNING—THE WHO AND WHY

By the summer of 2002, the Deputies' discussions on Iraq dealt less with whether the United States should press for regime change and more with how to bring it about. The policy did not necessarily mandate war, but it called, at a minimum, for a credible *threat* of war. President Bush decided to confront Iraq in a public speech in early September.

In the mid-1990s, the Security Council had been able to make Saddam bow to its will on weapons inspections and back off from again threatening Kuwait, thanks to military pressure from a U.S.-led coalition. Now, in August 2002, U.S. officials were working once again to generate pressure on Saddam, organizing a new coalition capable of deposing his regime on short notice. We hoped, though we knew it was unlikely, that this new coalition might be able to force Saddam's hand without actually going to war.

The Administration's planning dealt with war preparations, war fighting, and postwar reconstruction. Interagency teams discussed how to enlist foreign support for regime change—including how to arrange access, basing, and overflight rights for military operations. Other teams worked to ensure Iraq's food supplies in the event the World Food Program could not operate in a war zone. Officials analyzed how to deal with terrorist detainees, enemy prisoners of war, and regime leaders charged with atrocities. CENTCOM was responsible for developing operational plans for post-conflict security and civil-military operations. The State Department was responsible for soliciting ideas on political and economic reconstruction from scores of Iraqi expatriates, an activity known as the Future of Iraq Project.

The planning documents written by officials in Washington were, as a rule, general, conceptual, strategic, and short. They were referred to as *policy plans.* Steve Hadley and the Deputies Committee orchestrated this Washington work, coordinating input from an elaborate set of interagency groups. In contrast, the *operational plans* were voluminous and minutely detailed—the kind of documents that matched the tail numbers of cargo aircraft with specific containers of supplies. These operational plans were drafted by military officers at CENTCOM in Florida who reported to General Franks, who in turn received guidance from Rumsfeld (either directly or through General Myers).

The common accusation that the Administration neglected to conduct postwar planning for Iraq is wrong. Especially during the 2004 presidential campaign, critics often claimed that the Pentagon's civilian leaders believed no such planning was required—that Administration officials naively accepted assurances from Iraqi exiles that liberation would be joyous and trouble-free. The criticism is not only inaccurate, it makes no sense. Joy at liberation, to whatever extent it might occur, could not possibly turn Iraq into a problem-free country after thirty years of Baathist tyranny.

The sensible questions to raise about the Administration's prewar work are these: In all the planning efforts, did the government fail to anticipate major problems that would emerge? Did it have good plans for the problems that it anticipated and encountered? Did it implement its plans well?

The answers are not simple. Some serious problems were anticipated: sectarian violence, a power vacuum, severe disorder. Some other serious problems—including large numbers of refugees pouring across Iraq's borders, mass hunger, and environmental disasters—were averted, in large part because of Franks's war plans, which focused on speed in order to diminish their likelihood.

But the crippling disorder we call the insurgency was *not* anticipated with any precision, by either intelligence analysts or policy officials. Whether by plan or improvisation, the Baathists—in cooperation with the jihadists—managed to organize, recruit, and finance a highly damaging quasi-military campaign.* Across the board, Administration officials

*The insurgency was never a grassroots resistance, and in time it turned large areas against al Qaida.

thought that postwar reconstruction would take place *post*—that is, after—the war. That turned out to be a major error.

The Joint Staff's Strategic Plans and Policy directorate (J-5) was now headed by Lieutenant General George Casey (U.S. Army), who had taken over from General Abizaid. On July 10, 2002, Casey created an interagency group to coordinate planning on Iraq work: to mesh the policy concepts being developed in Washington with the detailed operational planning under way at CENTCOM, and to support CENTCOM "before, during, and after" a war. He dubbed the new group the Iraq Political-Military Cell and appointed Joint Staff officers to direct it. The cell included officials from State, CIA, the National Security Council staff, the Vice President's office, and my Policy organization.

Much of the planning work in Washington focused on the post-Saddam period. The Iraq Political-Military Cell's charter highlighted such postwar issues as coalition force requirements, infrastructure, humanitarian action, transition plans for an "interim commission" or provisional government, and how to achieve "acceptance" from Iraqi externals and internals. The group's security planning tasks included protecting oil fields and creating a new Iraqi police force, a new military, and a new intelligence agency.

Franklin Miller (of Rice's staff) urged that this Joint Staff–led cell should be connected more tightly to the White House. Hadley had recently included Miller in the Deputies Lunches as executive secretary, to keep track of assignments and prod offices around the government for plans and papers. A career civil servant with extensive Pentagon experience, Miller enjoyed running projects. He could be immodest, even aggressive, and often reached directly into civilian and military offices at the Pentagon rather than going through channels—asking questions, and giving what some took to be orders, in a way that flouted the chain of command and therefore irritated Rumsfeld. But overall I thought he made a positive contribution.

When Miller proposed creating (and chairing) an Executive Steering Group to direct the Iraq Political-Military Cell, I discussed the proposal with Pace and Casey, and we agreed it was a good idea. On August 12, 2002, Miller convened the group, including representatives from the White House, State, CIA, and Defense. It met several times a week from that point on, becoming a key forum for Iraq planning. It coordinated projects and got them approved by the Deputies, the Principals, and the President. Over time, other interagency planning efforts tucked in under the Executive Steering Group, including the Humanitarian Reconstruction Group, the Energy Infrastructure Working Group, and the Coalition Working Group.

The creation of the Iraq Political-Military Cell and its Executive Steering Group made Iraq policy planning more routine and inclusive. Now that the President was preparing to put Iraq front and center on the world's agenda, Rice and Hadley no longer limited Iraq planning so tightly to the Principals, key Deputies, and a few others. I welcomed the new arrangements, hoping they might promote stronger teamwork within the U.S. government. Perhaps State, CIA, and the rest of the government would set aside old differences and work to build an international coalition intimidating enough to make war unnecessary.

The teamwork did not develop, however. Nor were the old divides transcended. One of the principal divides was—again—how to deal with the Iraqi external opposition groups, and in particular with Ahmad Chalabi and his Iraqi National Congress.

Richard Armitage had decided (as we have seen) to shut down the Information Collection Program, the arrangement by which the INC provided U.S. intelligence officials with access to documents and human intelligence sources. At the July 25 Deputies Lunch, however, Steve Hadley reported that he had achieved an agreement among Armitage, Wolfowitz, and McLaughlin: State would transfer the program to the Defense Intelligence Agency (DIA). This was the Defense Department's intelligence office, established to collect and analyze information of interest to military commanders. The DIA reported to the Secretary of Defense, but not to me: My office was not in the intelligence collection business, formally or informally. Although journalists and others have claimed that my office served as "Chalabi's handler," and that we ran the INC's Information Collection Program, that was never the case.

At that same July 25 Deputies Lunch, Armitage distributed two short papers on the governance of Iraq after Saddam's overthrow. The papers showed that State was torn between conflicting aims: wanting to allow the *Iraqis* to rule themselves, and wanting *Americans* to rule Iraq long enough to ensure that the externals would not become the leadership.

The first paper, entitled "Diplomatic Plan for the Day After," warned of the danger of America's being painted as an "occupying power." The result "would likely be delegitimized government; instability; . . . and possibly terrorist acts—against U.S. forces."My office agreed, which was why we consistently promoted liberation rather than occupation as the basic theme of the Administration's strategy for Iraq.

Armitage's other paper, however, went off in another direction. It said there "must be no doubt who has international executive authority in Iraq"—namely, a U.S.-led "Transitional Civil Authority." State proposed that authority as the alternative to an Iraqi-led government for post-Saddam Iraq.

In this second paper, State alluded to the recent history of Afghanistan. When the Taliban regime fell, the diplomacy known as the Bonn Process produced immediate Afghan self-rule, without any period of occupation. Armitage argued, however, that Bonn should *not* serve as a model for Iraq—because the externals had more "weight" in Afghanistan than in Iraq. This was a momentous conclusion to reach on the basis of a vague metaphor—without supporting evidence:

> **[A Bonn conference] to get agreement on an internal leadership won't work for Iraq as for Afghanistan, [where] the weight of real leadership was external to the country. . . . [The balance in Iraq] was weighted much more to inside.**

The paper emphasized that it was "crucial not to appear to disenfranchise those internal constituencies," which meant the United States would have to play an "overt leadership role" and "take time to develop credible, democratic Iraqi leadership." The U.S-led transitional civil authority should therefore transfer power to the Iraqis only "gradually"—and we should expect a "*multi-year transitional period* to build democratic institutions."

Armitage also insisted that oil revenues be kept out of Iraqi hands. And finally, in a slap at the Defense Department's proposed plan for military training of Iraqi externals, he declared he was against creating an "army" for the Iraqi political opposition.

In short, this second Armitage paper proposed a U.S.-led administration for postwar Iraq—one that sounded a lot like the foreign "occupying power" that its companion State paper had, wisely, warned against, as likely to provoke instability and anti-U.S. terrorist attacks. Determined to keep the Iraqi externals from political power, Armitage showed no recognition of this inconsistency. Passion against the externals appeared to be muddling the thought of officials at both State and CIA.

State officials would in time write many more memos promoting the transitional civil authority concept. The memos tended to be vague about how long the period of non-Iraqi transitional rule would last, though (as Armitage had acknowledged) the authority would have to remain in place for years to accomplish its purpose. Even champions of the authority had to admit that Iraqis would resent being ruled for a long time by foreigners. State officials were never quite able to reconcile their recognition of that danger with their support for deferring Iraqi self-rule for a "multi-year transitional period."

This fundamental contradiction would impede the Administration's efforts to prepare for postwar Iraq. In the end, it spawned a fourteen-month U.S.-run occupation government—an avoidable disaster that fueled the insurgency and retarded postwar Iraq's political development.

In light of the insurgency, it is remarkable that key U.S. officials believed that the Iraqi externals were the chief danger the United States had to guard against in post-Saddam Iraq. Yet the main idea behind the transitional civil authority was precisely to guard against the externals dominating the post-Saddam political scene in Iraq. Why should that have been a goal of U.S. policy at all? When challenged on this point, top State and CIA officials responded that the leaders of the external groups were not skilled enough and, moreover, lacked legitimacy.

Rumsfeld, Wolfowitz, and I considered State's view presumptuous and dangerous. We did not see what right or interest the United States had in serving as Iraq's occupier for an extended period just because some U.S. officials labeled the external leaders illegitimate. What exactly did "illegitimate" mean? If the term simply equated to "unelected," then anyone governing Iraq at that moment would be illegitimate—not least the Americans who ran the occupation government. If the term referred to the leaders' popularity, ability to win votes, and respect for the law, then legitimacy could not be determined immediately. We would have to see how well the leaders did at the polls and whether they respected the results.

Supporters of the transitional civil authority approach, however, dismissed our questions and objections by claiming that we in the Pentagon wanted to put Iraqis in charge of their own government *simply to help Chalabi gain power.* The strange implication was that if it were not for this interest in promoting our own candidate, we would favor a long U.S. occupation of Iraq. But neither Rumsfeld nor any of his top advisers was, in fact, plotting to put Chalabi in power, and in no event could we ignore the obvious danger that keeping Iraq under protracted occupation could detonate nationalist outrage and produce a rebellion.

Given President Bush's commitment to "liberation, not occupation," it was not surprising that he refused to embrace State's concept of the transitional civil authority. As we'll see, he set the idea aside just before the Iraq war started, when he approved the Iraqi Interim Authority plan developed by my office.

The day after this Deputies Lunch, on July 26, 2002, Luti briefed Joint Staff officers on his proposal for military training of Iraqi oppositionists, hoping that the Principals would revisit their May decision to defer that effort. CENTCOM needed guidance from Washington to develop ways to use opposition forces in the war plan. Such forces could help provide local political leadership (or assist Iraqi officials in doing so). They could secure lines of communication, sort and secure enemy prisoners of war, and assume command of any defecting Iraqi units. Most important, Luti argued, they could serve as knowledgeable intermediaries, helping to:

- **advise senior coalition leaders**
- **form Iraq [intelligence] fusion cell**
- **provide interpreters**
- **provide scouts for combat units**
- **contract for indigenous logistics support**

Luti contended that a fifteen-hundred- to two-thousand-man Iraqi force could help CENTCOM perform civil-military operations during and after a war. General Franks could organize the force into units of military police, capable of vetting and commanding Iraq's civilian police and generally contributing to law and order after Saddam's removal. Knowing that CENTCOM's leadership already opposed giving Iraqi externals a combat role, Luti did not propose such a role for them. His briefing recommended that Rumsfeld present our proposal to the Principals Committee and that the Secretary ask General Myers to draft a military plan that "turns this from a concept into action."

Before Luti's briefing went to Rumsfeld, Myers reviewed the slides. He penned a marginal note that he favored a decision to direct CENTCOM to do this training even more quickly than Luti proposed—and that it should create "a plan B that uses the opposition more aggressively than in this paper." Luti and I were pleased by the Chairman's enthusiasm. CENTCOM, however, did not share that enthusiasm.

On August 9, in a conference room on "Mahogany Row"—the executive suite on the seventh floor of the State Department—Mark Grossman and I finally took a big step toward the long-delayed Iraqi opposition political conference: We cohosted a meeting with Iraqi opposition leaders. Also present were members of our staffs and representatives of the CIA, including some Iraq specialists well known as friends or antagonists of the various Iraqi groups. The presence of the full range of competing players on a single U.S. delegation, in dialogue with all the major Iraqi groups, was intended as a message in itself.

We assured the Iraqis that President Bush was committed to removing

Saddam Hussein and his regime, though not necessarily by war, and this meeting signified our seriousness of purpose. We asked the Iraqis to cooperate with us and to coalesce, as we in the Administration were doing.

Grossman and I told our guests that we saw them as the future leaders of a free Iraq. I don't know whether Grossman was just being polite, but I believed that these men might actually become important figures in the democratic politics of post-Saddam Iraq. We turned out to be more correct than we knew—far more correct than those who disparaged the Iraqi externals as incapable of obtaining democratic support. Sitting across the conference table from us were a number of the future leaders—appointed and elected—of the new Iraq, including:

- President Jalal Talabani (elected and reelected)
- Prime Minister Iyad Allawi (appointed in June 2004, served until April 2005; later elected twice to parliament as the leader of a significant political party)
- Deputy Prime Minister Ahmad Chalabi (elected in January 2005 elections)
- Foreign Minister Hoshyar Zebari (appointed by the Iraqi Governing Council in September 2003, reappointed after both elections in 2005)
- Abdulaziz el-Hakim, the leader of Iraq's main predominantly Shia political party

This list belies the influential CIA theory—one might call it a prejudice—that the externals would be incapable of winning electoral support inside Iraq.

Now was the time, Grossman and I said, for supporters of Iraqi liberation to focus on principles roundly shared, not on political differences. We urged the Iraqis to work with us to convene a political conference—building on the Iraqi opposition conferences held in the 1990s—where they, along with a large number of their fellow externals, could endorse such principles. Such a conference might lay the foundation for post-Saddam political reconstruction and could demonstrate the existence of a responsible alternative to the Saddam Hussein regime. Over several months, Iraqis could—cooperatively—hammer out constitutional principles for a new era.

In the process, they would be developing a political culture of compromise, practicing as a group the kinds of negotiation and mutual accommodation that underpin successful democratic government. Playing by the rules, splitting differences and accepting the will of the majority are habits we Westerners tend to take for granted, as incorporated into our thinking and action from childhood. But Iraq had no rule of law: Its winner-take-all politics had nothing to do with a culture of compromise. A political conference would allow the Iraqis to engage in give-and-take on such fundamental matters as individual rights, federalism, and the role of religion, and these democratic practices might be carried forward into the politics of liberated Iraq.*

Promoting teamwork and productivity among the opposition leaders—and doing so *early*—would be far better than trying to put the political pieces together after Saddam's ouster had created a political maelstrom in Iraq. Scooter Libby, Paul Wolfowitz, and I had been making that point in Deputies Lunches over the past eight months. Such advance work, we argued, would also allow U.S. officials to assess these leaders' philosophies and characters, and their leadership skills and executive abilities. To promote a healthy post-Saddam Iraqi political system, we argued, U.S. officials should seize the opportunity to create rapport and develop mutual trust, as appropriate.

Grossman assured the Iraqis that State would help organize the political conference quickly. After our meeting, an Iraqi delegation spokesman told journalists that the conference would occur within a few weeks, in September. And yet the delays continued: The political conference, which Libby had originally proposed in January 2002 and Armitage had promised for April, was finally organized by State in *December.*

The delay of almost a year in holding the political conference looks especially damaging in light of the later experience of the post-Saddam Coalition Provisional Authority (CPA). When the CPA's head, Ambassador L. Paul Bremer III, set aside the Administration's plan to transfer substantial political power early to the Iraqis, he did so on the grounds that he had not seen the Iraqis demonstrate teamwork and productivity. These deficiencies would have been mitigated—and perhaps remedied—with eight or ten months of intense political cooperation.

During the August 9 meeting, Colin Powell dropped in to greet the Iraqis and offer a general word of encouragement. The next day, Rumsfeld received them at the Pentagon and Cheney spoke with them from Wyoming by videoconference. All three echoed the points that Grossman and I had communicated. The Iraqis commented to the press that they

---

*As we will see, a few months of intensive work under Bremer's tutelage did result in important compromises—unfortunately, much later in the process of political reconstruction.

were impressed: first, by the clear message they had received of President Bush's determination to bring an end to tyranny in Iraq and, second, by the united stand of the officials from across the U.S. government.

With all this Iraq-related activity under way, it was time for the President to refine his formulation of what we aimed to achieve. The Deputies got to work drafting an up-to-date paper on goals and strategy.

Defense Department officials saw the Saddam Hussein problem as an element of the U.S. war on terrorism—as the Joint Staff made clear in its June 2002 Political-Military Strategic Plan for Iraq. That plan referred back to the October 3, 2001, Strategic Guidance for the Defense Department that Abizaid and I had drafted, which framed the war on terrorism as a confrontation with state and nonstate supporters of terrorist groups, as well as the terrorist groups themselves. That guidance focused attention on those states that both supported terrorism *and* aspired to weapons of mass destruction. In its June 2002 plan, the Joint Staff said that the U.S. objective in Iraq should be not only to end the threat from the Saddam Hussein regime, but to help us "convince or compel other countries to renounce WMD and support to terrorism."

As the Deputies worked on formulating U.S. goals and strategy, I contributed a summary of the four main problems with the Iraqi regime, using a mnemonic: "WMD and the three Ts"—*terrorism*, *threats* to neighbors, and *tyranny*. In my view, the tyrannical nature of Saddam's rule was not merely a problem for Iraq's Kurds and Shiites. Tyranny meant that there were no domestic checks or balances to curb Saddam's ambition and aggression. The risks of wild behavior tend to be greater with autocratic rulers than with governments that distribute power among large bureaucracies. Moreover, it was hard to learn what was going on inside an oppressive dictatorship. That limited the usefulness of diplomacy: Agreements are difficult to verify in a closed and terrified society. All of this meant that Saddam was a threat not simply because he supported terrorism or pursued WMD, or both, but for an array of reasons relating to his record and his intentions, traits, and capabilities.

Rice's staff contributed a paper called "Liberation Strategy for Iraq," circulated for discussion at the August 6 Principals Committee meeting. The paper reflected Rice's own strong support for democracy promotion in the Middle East and her support for working with *all* the friendly Iraqi opposition groups. At the same time, the paper followed Rice's practice of blending or bridging conflicting ideas: Although it supported a strategy of "liberation, not occupation," it also incorporated the State/CIA idea of a U.S.-led administration of Iraq, designed to prevent the externals from alienating internals. The paper thus embodied the same contradictions we had encountered in Armitage's two July 25 papers.

Rumsfeld bristled as he read the first few sentences of Rice's Liberation Strategy paper. This was the wrong way, he said, to start an analysis of why the U.S. might have to go to war: A U.S. strategy paper should open with a statement of *U.S. interests*. This paper, however, began by stating how regime change would help the Iraqi people and the Middle East:

> **When we move to bring about a change of regime in Iraq, we would want:**
>
> - **The Iraqi population to believe that they will be enfranchised politically and better off economically as a consequence of U.S. actions.**
> - **To create a democratic, unified Iraq that can be a model of good governance for the region and a strategic partner of the United States, and to describe the U.S. effort as a struggle for the Iraqi people. Such an Iraq would have [a] transforming effect on the region.**
> - **We do not want the world to view U.S. actions in Iraq as a new colonial occupation. . . .**
>
> **The sum of these concerns is for a U.S. regime change operation to be perceived as a liberation of the Iraqi people by the U.S. as opposed to a hostile, exploitive occupation.**

Rumsfeld and I concurred with the paper's emphasis on liberation, not occupation. Iraq belonged to the Iraqis, and so the U.S. should emphasize that point—rather than acting as if we owned the place or planned to run it. But much in the paper was inconsistent with the idea of Iraqis being allowed to run their own affairs after Saddam's removal.

The statement that the United States aimed to create democracy in Iraq struck both Rumsfeld and me as off base. The proper way to think about this, we believed, was that the Iraqis would have to *create their own democracy*; the United States should not undertake to do it for them. Democracy in Iraq, if it were possible, would be highly desirable. But we wanted President Bush to clarify that the measure of success of his regime change policy would be whether we ended the dangers posed by Iraq—WMD, support for terrorism, threats against neighbors, and tyranny. If the United States accomplished that, we would have achieved a hugely valuable victory—even if the Iraqis were slow (or unable) to build a stable democracy.

I commented to Rumsfeld that Rice's emphatic language about promoting democracy reflected the intensity of the President's commitment to the idea. But that was not a reason, we agreed, to say that America's success depended on whether Iraq became a model democracy. It would be dangerous to measure the success of our war effort against an accomplishment that was beyond our ability to guarantee. We also saw strategic, political, and even legal drawbacks to the notion that the United States was considering war not for self-defense but for the purpose of implanting democracy in Iraq.

There was another big problem with the Liberation Strategy paper that flowed from its emphasis on creating democracy. Despite its strong language about avoiding *even the appearance* of a U.S. occupation, it adopted Armitage's argument that the United States would have to run Iraq "for many years"—even though this risked our being seen as "a new colonial occupation":

> **[T]he one option for regime change which gives the most confidence in achieving U.S. objectives is the employment of U.S. forces to accomplish regime change, *staying in significant numbers for many years to assist in a U.S.-led administration of the country.***
>
> . . .
>
> **As we take these steps, there is a risk that Iraqis, Arabs, Moslems, and even some others might perceive U.S. actions as a new colonial occupation. . . .**

Once again, key U.S. officials ensnared themselves in this inconsistency. They were so preoccupied with the need to block the externals from playing too large a political role that they lost sight of their own stated goal, which was to avoid a prolonged post-Saddam occupation. While Rice's paper was far more positive about the externals than Armitage's had been, it nevertheless made a point of our having to guard against "using" them too much, lest that antagonize the internals. The paper warned: "The scope and pace of the use of oppositionists would need to be weighed against the danger of alienating internal elites. . . ."

Having blended Armitage's line into her paper, Rice wound up offering confusing advice: The United States should avoid an occupation, but should set up a U.S.-led administration anyway, even though that could cause people to "perceive U.S. actions as a new colonial occupation." All this self-contradiction was driven by the notion that the internals would be unwilling to vote for externals—a premise that eventually was proven false by the Iraqi elections.*

Rice's paper was discussed in the Principals Committee on August 9. Rumsfeld, calling the paper "non-rigorous," said it needed to be rewritten. On the issue of democratic government for Iraq, Rumsfeld cautioned that "we shouldn't pretend we can create it." U.S. officials, moreover, should not suggest that we had "a precise political template that we're going to impose" on the Iraqis. Cheney did not argue that the United States should specify precisely what kind of institutions or laws another country should have, but he said "we should make it clear that we are intent on major democratic change." Rice added that "we shouldn't shy from using the term 'democracy,'" and she directed Hadley to have the Deputies rework the document. This was the kind of conceptual discussion that Powell tended to let pass without comment, and my notes record no comment from him.

I had a standing invitation to ride with Rumsfeld to and from White House meetings, and I often took him up on it, welcoming the opportunity for discussion. (Carpooling with Rumsfeld also saved me a few valuable minutes per trip, because his specially secured official car did not have to stop to be sniffed by bomb dogs at the White House gate.) On the way to the White House, Rumsfeld usually read papers (often those from my office about the meeting we were heading to). On the ride back to the Pentagon, however, he tended to relax. He would ask for my impression of the meeting and wanted to know when he had missed a chance to make a point, or had flubbed an answer that now required follow-up. I found these seven-minute conversations a useful way to raise large ideas for further discussion later.

After the Principals Committee meeting on August 9, I told Rumsfeld that his comments about democracy had sounded negative. They could be taken as denying or belittling America's interest in seeing a democratic government arise in Iraq after Saddam's demise. He said he understood full well that a democratic Iraq would be a good thing. It could serve our interests in the Middle East and help counter the appeal of the extremism that fueled terrorism.

But there was a danger in making simplistic references to democracy.

---

*See Chapter 15.

Democracy is complex; it is a lot more than just organizing an election. We both worried that loose talk about democracy might lead foreigners to think we intended to impose an American model on them. Our democratic system worked well for us, but it might be altogether wrong for people in different geographies, with different histories, cultures, and other circumstances.

This got us onto the subject of Edmund Burke, the eighteenth-century British politician and philosopher, whose writings had made a lasting impression on me in college. Burke warned against labeling one's own political ideas "universal" and then expecting them to apply to foreign nations. His *Reflections on the Revolution in France* observed that healthy political institutions have an organic quality: They grow naturally in the local environment. They cannot be imposed, whether from the outside or by arrogant local reformers—like the revolutionaries of Burke's day who thought they could remake French society "rationally," in defiance of deeply rooted local customs, beliefs, and social structures. All of which supported Rumsfeld's view that U.S. officials should refrain from suggesting that we would push Iraq to copy American political models. Burke's main message, I said, was a call for humility, for recognition of the limits of our intelligence—in all senses of the term. Iraqi self-government and freedom, if they were to be achieved, would look different from ours. This was not an argument against helping Iraqis who aspired to build some kind of democracy in the post-Saddam period. It was a reminder to think and talk about the subject with proper respect for the difficulty of the task and the time it would require.

Rather than talk simplistically of creating democracy, we concluded, U.S. officials should think of creating *democratic institutions*, calling attention to the building blocks of democracy and freedom: the rule of law (that is, law that constrains not just ordinary citizens, but also the highest officials); the decentralization of power; an independent judiciary; a free press; and private property.*

Rumsfeld often warned against the common error of describing democracy as the ready product of a quick election. In places that lacked a proper foundation for democratic institutions, elections could bring to power parties that opposed democracy and would refuse to submit to future

---

*President Bush was already inclined to talk of democracy as a set of concepts, as we saw in his January 2002 State of the Union speech. Iraq or any other country that might hope to achieve political freedom would have to adopt such concepts for itself in ways that suited its own circumstances.

elections—a phenomenon often referred to, with grim irony, as "one man, one vote, once."*

A few days later, on August 14, Rice circulated to the Principals a new paper called "Iraq: Goals, Objectives, Strategy," which had been drafted by interagency committees and reviewed by the Deputies. Shorter and more coherent than the Liberation Strategy paper, it began with a section called "U.S. Goal":

Free Iraq in order to:

- **Eliminate Iraqi weapons of mass destruction (WMD), their means of delivery and associate programs, to prevent Iraq from breaking out of containment and become a more dangerous threat to the region and beyond;**
- **End Iraqi threats to its neighbors;**
- **Stop the Iraqi government's tyrannizing of its own population;**
- **Cut Iraqi links to and sponsorship of international terrorism;**
- **Maintain Iraq's unity and territorial integrity; and**
- **Liberate the Iraqi people from tyranny and assist them in creating a society based on moderation, pluralism, and democracy.**

The language on democracy was still ambitious, in my view. But declaring that the U.S. aimed to *assist Iraqis* to create a society *based on democracy* was more modest and sensible than promising outright that the United States would create democracy in Iraq.

My office proposed in writing to get the word "democracy" changed to "rule of law," but we did not succeed. The Administration was not fully taking to heart Rumsfeld's cautions against overpromising on democracy in Iraq. But in its short section on strategy, the paper called for setting up a post-Saddam government that "encourages the building of democratic institutions." Rice's staff must have blended the phrase "democratic institutions" into the mix as a sop to the Pentagon, but there was no actual

*For example, the Algerian election of 1991 was won by a party philosophically committed to antidemocratic principles. The 2006 parliamentary elections won by Hamas in the Palestinian Authority territory is another example.

meeting of the minds across the National Security Council on how to formulate our objectives for the post-Saddam Iraqi government.

Nevertheless, the principals approved this August 14 version of "Iraq: Goals, Objectives, Strategy," as did the President later that month. The purpose of such a statement of goals was to foster consistency among planners throughout the U.S. government. And indeed, when General Myers conveyed guidance for the Iraq war plan to General Franks, he always started by reciting these goals, as approved by the President. When CENTCOM officers drafted briefings on their war plan, they routinely included a statement of those goals and a reference to the National Security Council document. This was the essence of the civilian leadership's broad instruction to the military commands.

War plans are made not at the Pentagon, but by military officers at the relevant combatant commands. For Iraq, this command was CENTCOM. The President and the Secretary of Defense—the only civilians in the military chain of command—tell the combatant commander what plans to prepare, for what purposes, and with what policy assumptions.

Rumsfeld gave strategic guidance on Iraq to General Franks over a period of months, always after consulting with either General Myers or General Pace (or both), and having at least one of them participate in the conversation or written communication with Franks. Rumsfeld understood that it served his own interests, substantively and politically, to keep Myers and Pace "in the loop," and they were pleased with the connection. It gave them formidable influence, and it helped them fulfill their key duty—to provide well-informed, intelligent military advice to the Secretary of Defense, the President, and the National Security Council.

Although I sometimes gave input to Rumsfeld on war plans, I was not always called in on his communications with his commanders. When Franks briefed his war plans to Rumsfeld, Myers's staff sometimes got a look at the PowerPoint slides a few hours in advance—unlike the civilian officials. Wolfowitz and I would get our first look at those briefings in the meeting when Franks presented them to Rumsfeld. Even when a briefing lasted three or four hours, time was always tight, and I generally hesitated to ask questions of my own.

Through his body language at these long sessions—and especially in his profane (if humorous) grumblings on leaving Rumsfeld's office—Franks made it clear that he didn't enjoy fielding lots of questions. Though he was very deferential to Rumsfeld, and moderately so to Wolfowitz,

Myers, and Pace, when I asked a question Franks tended to give it short shrift. If Rumsfeld signaled an interest, however, Franks would make a point of complimenting the question; if Rumsfeld seemed neutral, Franks took it as license to brush the question aside.

The first time I asked how the war plan would change if Saddam used poison gas against U.S. troops, Franks was dismissive. "We'll defeat him" was all he said. But we're planning to defeat him anyway, I answered, and *something* should change if he "slimes" our troops; otherwise, Saddam—or anyone else, for that matter—wouldn't be deterred from using chemical weapons again.* But Rumsfeld appeared ready to move to another subject, and Franks merely rolled his eyes.

I knew Rumsfeld would appreciate the importance of this point when he was ready to focus on it. When Franks returned to Washington for a war plan briefing session,† we circled back to the issue. This time, it was Rumsfeld who nudged Franks into thinking about the deterrence problem. (I had meanwhile arranged for J. D. Crouch and Keith Payne to brief the Secretary on their impressive analysis of WMD deterrence.) "Shouldn't it make a difference for Iraq" if it hits us with WMD? Rumsfeld asked. This time, Franks said it was a "good question"—and CENTCOM developed a proper response.

I could understand that Franks didn't want to feel subjected to a slew of Pentagon civilian "bosses," so I often gave my ideas to Rumsfeld or Pace to be passed to Franks without reference to me. Sometimes, however, Rumsfeld would direct me to raise a matter with Franks, who would then conclude, reasonably enough, that Rumsfeld lacked conviction about the idea. That was what happened with my office's plan for training Iraqi exiles to take part in CENTCOM's invasion and reconstruction operations.

In standard fashion, Franks had divided his Iraq war plan into four phases:

- Phase I—preparations for a possible invasion
- Phase II—"shaping the battle space," beginning with the start of air operations
- Phase III—decisive offensive operations and major combat operations, including "complete regime removal"
- Phase IV—posthostilities stabilization and reconstruction.

---

*All senior U.S. government and military officials believed that Iraq had CW battlefield capability—as did Saddam's own military commanders. See Kevin M. Woods, et al., *Iraqi Perspectives Project*, p. 92.

†On October 18, 2002.

My organization worked in the area of strategy rather than military operations or tactics, and our function was to help formulate policies, not implement them. Detailed operational planning was handled by the military or civilian organizations responsible for executing those plans in the field (CENTCOM, for example, or State's Agency for International Development). So Rumsfeld did not look to me or the Policy organization for advice on Phase II or Phase III issues, such as command structure, force levels, or deciding which service—marines or army—to use for which tasks. These were matters he (and sometimes Wolfowitz) would resolve exclusively with Franks, Myers, and Pace.

Franks's Iraq briefings to Rumsfeld concentrated on Phase III of the war plan—major combat operations—and Rumsfeld would often raise issues of his own. (In a December 2 meeting, for example, Rumsfeld asked Franks to ensure that Saddam's communications were cut off immediately upon our invasion, so that his regime could issue no messages to its troops, to terrorist cells, or to the public.) Only rarely did I raise questions about such operations. My attention was mainly on Phase IV, the post-major-combat period, which involved strategic issues on which Rumsfeld welcomed my advice.

My Policy colleagues and I were constantly raising issues with CENTCOM relating to the transition period: how to shape our military operations to show that we aimed to liberate Iraq, not occupy it; de-Baathification; vetting Iraqis for official jobs; and how to address law-and-order problems, in the political vacuum following Saddam's overthrow. But, as we now know, General Franks gave far less attention to Phase IV planning than to planning major combat operations. Indeed, Franks would later signal his relative lack of interest in Phase IV operations by announcing his resignation approximately six weeks after his forces took Baghdad. In a revealing remark, he has written that he saw my questions at his briefings as rarely having relevance to his operational concerns.

My personal dealings with Franks were generally congenial, despite the impatience he showed me in his briefing sessions with Rumsfeld. We chatted comfortably and had laughs together in the Secretary's reception room while waiting for meetings to begin. I did not take his occasional snappishness as a significant affront: He had weighty responsibilities, and it was obvious that he felt a lot of intellectual stress in his exchanges with Rumsfeld. And it was not only with me that he showed irritation about questions, as we saw in his encounters with the Joint Chiefs of Staff before the start of Operation Enduring Freedom. At the time, I regarded his impatience about my comments as a sign of his single-minded focus on getting guidance from Rumsfeld. I now understand it as a symptom of his disinclination to deal with the challenges of post-Saddam Iraq.

The Iraq Political-Military Cell (run by the Joint Staff) was not always successful in coordinating between Washington policy makers and CENTCOM. In an October 2002 briefing, for example, the cell presented a well-thought-through account of key postwar issues. Their top two prescriptions were clear, even emphatic: *Secure the postwar environment* and *immediately promote civil order.* Several months later, however, we were still trying to concentrate CENTCOM's attention on these issues. I learned much later that the Joint Staff had been uneasy about the lack of attention Franks was devoting to Phase IV, and they nudged him repeatedly during the year leading up to Operation Iraqi Freedom. On July 9, 2002, Myers issued a planning order to Franks addressing "civil affairs" or "CA"—that is, U.S. military personnel working with Iraqi civilians to provide governmental and other basic services in liberated areas. The order pushed Franks to begin to give his attention to planning for such operations:

> **CA Guidance. CA considerations should be included in all phases of this operation. Planning will include interagency coordination. Post-operations planning will be initiated *as early as possible* in the planning process.**

Again, on September 6, 2002, after reviewing a "Hybrid Start" plan developed by CENTCOM, the Joint Staff's Strategic Plans and Policy directorate took CENTCOM to task for not grasping the usefulness of Iraqi opposition groups:

> **The role of opposition groups, especially in strategic command and control, is not adequately addressed. May impact on setting conditions for long-term stability and broad-based government post-Saddam, both are US strategic and strategic military objectives.**

A few weeks later, the Joint Staff held a seminar called "Prominent Hammer II" to analyze resources and risks relating to Iraq. The seminar identified a need for a new task force headquarters, specifically to help CENTCOM plan for "complex Phase IV requirements." And as late as December 19, 2002, General Myers directed Franks once again to "refine planning for Phase IV operations." (Myers finally received the Phase IV plans for review in March, just days before the war started.)

Myers's December 19 instruction was conveyed in a planning order, a formal directive from the Chairman of the Joint Chiefs. In this order, Myers reiterated that Franks would be responsible for the military governance of Iraq. The administration that would "initially govern Iraq" after Saddam's ouster would be a "largely civil organization," with "support and advice from liberated Iraqis," and would initially "be assisted by a US-led Combined Joint Task Force (CJTF) responsible for the military aspects of post-war requirements." Myers specified that the civil organization* and the CJTF would *both work for Franks.* There was no ambiguity here: Franks would be responsible for all aspects of governing Iraq. Myers pushed Franks again:

> **The military will play a pivotal role in setting the conditions for accomplishment of strategic objectives for post-war Iraq. To ensure rapid success during the transition to Phase IV post hostilities operations, detailed coordination must begin to integrate interagency efforts *at the earliest opportunity.***

In briefings with Rumsfeld, Franks claimed to be on top of his Phase IV responsibilities. Nevertheless, Myers and Rumsfeld eventually concluded that they had to ask Admiral Giambastiani (then heading the Joint Forces Command) to help General Franks with Phase IV planning. On January 10, 2003, Rumsfeld directed Giambastiani to create a Joint Task Force to support CENTCOM's postwar planning efforts.

On the civilian side of the Pentagon, as of the summer of 2002 the Policy organization had only two staffers devoted full-time to Iraq. This absurd understaffing was rectified with the creation of the team that became known as the Office of Special Plans.

Over the course of that summer, as the President moved toward challenging Iraq in the United Nations, the Iraq-related workload in Policy became overwhelming. In August, William Luti and I received permission to hire an additional dozen or so people for the Near East and South Asia Affairs office, which Luti headed. The extra personnel allowed Luti to cre-

*This was the operation that became the Office of Reconstruction and Humanitarian Assistance.

ate separate divisions in his office: South Asia, North Africa and the Middle East, and the northern Persian Gulf. The northern Gulf division created a problem of perceptions. The President was emphasizing his desire for a diplomatic solution to the Iraq problem, but various journalists interpreted his intensified attention to Iraq as a sign that he had decided on war. Hadley had warned Administration officials not to aggravate this problem, and Luti and I anticipated a flap if news media reported that the Pentagon was creating a new Iraq office. So we gave this new division the nondescript name "Special Plans." But the Office of Special Plans was nothing more than a standard geographic office within the Policy organization, with the same kinds of responsibilities that every other geographic office in Policy had. It was simply the office of Northern Gulf Affairs—and indeed, after Saddam was overthrown, that became its name.

Although the name "Special Plans" was intended to *avert* overheated speculation, the two words eventually were taken by conspiracy theorists to imply deep and nefarious motives. Some reporters depicted the office as an intelligence operation or "cell" set up to compete with the CIA's Iraq bureau, or to manipulate intelligence to make the case for war.* This was nonsense. I addressed the issue in a letter to Senator John Warner (Chair of the Senate Armed Services Committee): OSP was "a policy planning group" and a "consumer, rather than producer, of intelligence." But the mythology about the Office of Special Plans became more elaborate over time, and it would prove especially useful those who claimed that the President "lied" America into war.

Rumsfeld often complained that the Iraq problem had so much baggage from a dozen years of debate that it was difficult to get people to think clearly about it. No sooner was the issue broached in public or in government meetings than recriminations and quarrels began: about what was done or left undone in the Gulf War; about President Clinton's foreign policy; about Chalabi and the Iraqi externals. Rumsfeld wanted to find a way to analyze the essence of our Iraq problem without getting entangled in the secondary questions. He asked for a conceptual or generic approach to thinking about the risks that arose out of the nexus of terrorist groups, their state supporters, and weapons of mass destruction.

Meanwhile, I told Rumsfeld about an informal talk I had recently

---

*Two journalists who reported accurately on OSP were James Risen of the *New York Times* and Dana Priest of the *Washington Post.* Others were content to repeat the distorted account that Seymour Hersh had published in *The New Yorker.*

given to a private group that included a number of former U.S. officials. My talk addressed critics of the Administration who were anxious about what they saw as President Bush's unchecked power to overthrow foreign governments. I said we should be respectful of those critics, given the traditional American opposition in principle to unchecked power. In an August 17 snowflake, Rumsfeld asked me to write up that argument, too.

I combined these assignments in a short paper entitled "Sovereignty and Anticipatory Self-Defense."* The paper framed the problem as follows: U.S. officials should heed concerns about whether there are proper checks and balances on the use of U.S. military force in the world. Those concerns can be seen as having philosophical roots in the American Revolution against British abuses and usurpations of power, and they have practical importance today. If U.S. citizens and our friends and partners around the world view us as misusing our military power, they could decide to withhold their support—political, diplomatic, military, and otherwise.

Some critics called for U.S. power to be checked more directly by requiring the United States to obtain UN approval before launching military action, but in my view that was an unworkable notion. It would push beyond the requirements of international law and impede the President's constitutional duty to defend our country. Nor would it serve the practical need to maintain peace and stability in a world with lawless regimes headed by the likes of Saddam Hussein, Kim Jung Il, and the Iranian theocrats. I argued that the President's power was, in fact, checked in various ways:

> **The President's strategy of preemptive action, or, as it might be called, "anticipatory self-defense," has important implications for the way we view international relations. It modifies the traditional view of sovereignty. According to that view, states, unless constrained by customary international law or by agreements to which they have consented, have the sovereign right to do whatever they want within their own borders. A corollary is that a state may take military action against another state only when the latter launches an aggression across an international border.**
>
> **In general, the United States supports traditional concepts**

---

*Rumsfeld directed that my paper be sent to Rice, who then distributed it to Cheney, Powell, General Myers, and Tenet (and to White House Chief of Staff Andrew Card and Presidential Counsel Alberto Gonzales) as background for the August 27, 2002, Principals Committee meeting on Iraq. She also sent copies to all the Deputies.

of sovereignty; indeed, in most cases, we insist on them. Our key political values—democratic self-government and the protection of individual rights—can be safeguarded only if the U.S. remains a sovereign state. . . .

Despite the importance we attach to sovereignty, we recognize that circumstances require certain narrow but important exceptions. For example, many states now tend to regard certain human rights conventions as applying even to states that are not signatories. But the most compelling reason *for making an exception to the traditional concept of sovereignty is the danger posed by weapons of mass destruction.* There is simply no way, for example, that the civilized world could allow a state that has repeatedly behaved recklessly and aggressively to prepare to use smallpox as a weapon.

. . . In the pre-missile era, one had the option to build defenses that could *prevent* that power from doing one harm. After missiles came on the scene, one could still attempt to *deter* the power from doing harm by threatening to retaliate. Finally, before development of weapons of mass destruction, one might be able to *extract compensation* for any harm done.

These approaches are no longer adequate. A hostile power may be able to deliver weapons *covertly* or in other ways that bypass existing defenses. A hostile power may be able to use terrorist groups to deliver weapons in an unattributable, and hence undeterrable, manner. A hostile power may be able to inflict such massive damage that no adequate compensation would be possible. These considerations lead inevitably to a doctrine of anticipatory self-defense.

Nevertheless, this doctrine is unsettling to many people, and for good reason. It appears to authorize the unchecked use of military power against any country that the U.S. President dislikes or suspects. Americans can easily sympathize with this concern. The fear of unchecked power resonates deeply in the American political tradition—if there was one thing our Founding Fathers feared, it was the idea of unchecked political power. The U.S. Constitution was therefore constructed as a system of checks and balances.

U.S. government leaders also understand that anticipatory self-defense appears to introduce a certain instability and unpredictability into the international system. But the source of that problem is the proliferation of weapons of mass destruction, of which the doctrine of anticipatory self-defense is the inevitable result.

Even given a doctrine of anticipatory self-defense, American power is far from being unchecked. First of all, there are the internal checks inherent in our political system. The existence of two relatively equal centers of power—the President and the Congress—makes it likely that American military power will be exercised in a deliberate manner. In addition, the large role played in the policy process by the media and other nongovernmental actors (such as think tanks and private political groups) also imposes a check on American military power. The openness of the American political process also means that it is much more subject to influences from abroad. Foreigners can join in the debate, either directly, or indirectly, and capitalize on their ability to influence Americans by their arguments.

American military power is also subject to external checks. The U.S. needs allies to operate in the world—it needs access to bases, overflight rights, etc. There is a price to be paid if U.S. actions are at odds with the civilized world's view of proper behavior in the world. The U.S. respects the views of responsible states and recognizes that valuable cooperation with them is theirs to grant or withhold in their own sovereign judgment.

Finally, American military power is checked by the beliefs of American political leaders. Despite the current complaints from many corners of the world, a fair-minded observer would have to admit that no country with a preponderance of military power similar to that enjoyed by the U.S. today has ever acted with such restraint and respect for the rights of others.

In assessing U.S. behavior, one has also to consider the possible alternatives. Would a powerful supra-national authority, if one could be created, be more restrained in its use of power? Might it not become an even greater threat to the sovereignty of nations? Alternatively, if the ability of the U.S. to use power in its own self-defense were to be checked by a requirement for international approval of some kind (for example, from the United Nations) would respect for the rights of other states around the world be more secure or less? If the U.S. were severely constrained in the world, wouldn't that mean that regional powers would be freer to attack their neighbors, as Iraq invaded Kuwait? If the threat of U.S. action against states that develop and use WMD were to disappear, would the rights of others

be safer? Would there be less or more incentive for additional countries to acquire WMD? Wouldn't peaceful countries be faced with a greater threat from hostile neighbors?

My paper ended with this string of questions. I realized that it did not provide an answer that would satisfy the Administration's critics; I did not find it completely satisfying myself. Americans and foreigners alike might prefer more checks and balances on the President of the United States. But the President had his duty to protect his country. And I could propose no additional checks and balances that would better protect our country, or better serve our interest in international peace and security.

In a few days, U.S. officials would be commemorating the first anniversary of 9/11. We were aware of a major accomplishment: The United States had made it through the year without another successful terrorist attack on our soil. We could not be sure how various measures had contributed to this success. But the FBI, Treasury, CIA, local police departments, and other arms of the government—together with the U.S. Armed Forces—were actively engaged in penetrating terrorist networks, denying them resources, and impeding their operations. We knew we were making life more difficult for terrorist groups than before 9/11. Terrorists were now obliged to work at playing defense.

Nevertheless, whenever anyone proposed that the Administration take credit for the absence of a second attack, the suggestion was rejected. President Bush and his National Security Council were aware that another attack could occur at any moment. Al Qaida had a history of requiring two or three years of planning and preparation between major operations. Jihadist extremists remained determined to pursue their apocalyptic visions. There were still regimes in power in the world that supported terrorists and aspired to catastrophic weapons.

No top-level U.S. officials thought we were out of the woods yet. On the contrary, we saw that terrorist groups and their state supporters were adapting to the world's new security situation, operating without a safe haven in Afghanistan and under the intensified scrutiny of intelligence and police officials. The chief danger remained—that terrorists someday might get their hands on a nuclear bomb or biological weapons and carry out an attack that would make 9/11 look small. As the first anniversary of 9/11 approached, President Bush was determined to reduce that danger—and he saw Iraq as an element of it.

10
UNITED NATIONS BOUND

Tony Blair and Colin Powell had serious reasons for urging President Bush to bring the Iraq question to the United Nations. Saddam was a problem not just for the United States but for the world in general, as the Security Council's long series of resolutions demonstrated. Also, it would be easier for the United States to line up military coalition partners if we had support for our policy at the United Nations.

But there were also good reasons *not* to make the United Nations our main diplomatic arena on Iraq policy. The organization was an unfriendly forum for the United States, as Powell acknowledged by calling the United Nations a "mosh pit" and a "quagmire" in meetings with President Bush. Cheney and Rumsfeld were concerned that officials and diplomats at the United Nations, given the organization's special interest in WMD inspections, would ignore other important aspects of the Iraqi threat.

The Security Council had created UNSCOM in 1991 to perform WMD inspections in Iraq. After Saddam effectively expelled the UNSCOM inspectors in 1998, the Council created a new, and weaker, inspection agency to replace it: the UN Monitoring Verification and Inspection Commission (UNMOVIC). UNMOVIC sat idle ever since—nearly four years—waiting for Saddam to allow its inspectors in.

Worries about UN diplomacy were well founded. The debate there did tend to obscure the complexity of the Saddam Hussein problem—his record of aggression, deception, defiance of the Security Council, mass murder at home and abroad, and training and financing of terrorists—in favor of a narrow focus on WMD. Indeed, UN diplomats were inclined to see the Iraq problem primarily as a question of how to revive the UN inspection process. President Bush had asked whether the Iraqi regime was too dangerous to leave in power. This was a bigger question than whether Saddam was willing to allow UN inspectors to return.

Some of us voiced the worry that if Saddam readmitted UN inspectors, he might be able to shift the burden of proof in the court of public opinion from himself to the inspectors. Uncertainties about Iraq's WMD programs and its dangerous capabilities and intentions would then get resolved in Saddam's favor unless the inspectors could uncover prohibited items. Did it make sense to give Saddam the benefit of such doubts? At the Pentagon, we thought not. At State, however, Powell and Armitage made the revival of weapons inspections the main goal of our Iraq diplomacy.

When it originally launched UNSCOM, the Security Council noted that Saddam could subvert the inspections by hiding weapons. The inspectors could confirm cooperation on disarmament, but lacked the ability to ferret out hidden contraband in a large country like Iraq. The Council imposed on Iraq the burden of proving that it had rid itself of the prohibited programs and items. In its final 1999 report, UNSCOM stressed that its "primary assumption" was that "Iraq would willingly and fully cooperate with the Commission," and it "postulated 'monitoring friendly' policies and behaviour by Iraq." In other words, if Iraq chose to *cheat*, the inspectors could not be expected to prove it. By 2002, as the UNMOVIC monitors waited in vain for Iraq to open its doors, it was apparent that Iraq's policies were not "monitoring friendly."*

At the May 7, 2002, Deputies Lunch, we took up the question of U.S. policy toward UNMOVIC. Three options were debated:

1. Support starting UNMOVIC inspections of Iraq.
2. Don't support starting the inspections.
3. Insist on bolstering UNMOVIC's authority as a precondition to starting the inspections.

Bolstering UNMOVIC by giving it authority to conduct unrestricted inspections would make Saddam even less inclined than before to allow

---

*In theory, if the inspectors came close to uncovering contraband, and Saddam acted to thwart them, that could trigger international outrage. But history offered many cases of weapons inspectors being thwarted—by Iraq, North Korea, Iran, the Soviet Union, and others—with no significant international reaction.

the inspectors in. But even with more authority, UNMOVIC could not win the inevitable cat-and-mouse game with Saddam. Iraq was simply too large and tightly controlled, and important weapons capabilities were too easy to conceal.

Armitage nevertheless spoke up in favor of the third option. Let's not reject UNMOVIC, he advised, because that will "upset people." Better to beef it up and let Saddam be the one to reject it. To me, that approach seemed an unwise gamble. It might do some good if Saddam quickly rejected the beefed-up UNMOVIC, but it could be harmful otherwise.

At a recent Principals Committee meeting, I recalled, George Tenet had sensibly warned that the United States risked losing cooperation from the Kurds if they thought we were counting on the United Nations to constrain Saddam. From their own experience (and that of Bosnia and other unhappy victims), the Kurds had learned not to rely on the United Nations to shield them against brutality. I mentioned Tenet's warning: If we were trying to persuade the Iraqi people and others of U.S. seriousness of purpose, I argued, we shouldn't make ourselves look frivolous by suggesting that UN inspectors—even under a strengthened UNMOVIC—could neutralize the Iraqi threat.

Furthermore, Saddam might *not* reject the beefed-up UNMOVIC. In that case, I argued, the United Nations could find itself conducting open-ended inspections, while Saddam would get the benefit of looking cooperative—even if we had little confidence that Iraq had actually rid itself of the banned weapons and programs. We could get drawn into endless and fruitless inspections. Scooter Libby agreed, phrasing the point pithily: The ultimate goal of U.S. policy was to disarm Iraq, not inspect it.*

The Deputies did not reach a consensus on new inspections. President Bush ultimately sided with State on the issue, agreeing to support initiation of UNMOVIC inspections. Through the summer and fall of 2002, the Deputies Committee debated how to strengthen UNMOVIC's authority and give it "unrestricted access."

The U.S. Ambassador to the United Nations, John Negroponte, would negotiate the details of UNMOVIC's new authority. The Deputies worked for weeks on an instructions cable for him. All agreed that he should speak positively about UNMOVIC: If given "unrestricted access" (which our cable defined in detail), the inspections could serve useful purposes. I proposed that the United States clarify that *UNMOVIC by itself could not counter the Iraqi WMD threat.* My point was the same one

---

*Rice apparently liked Libby's line: She used it on June 18, 2002, while meeting with Hans Blix of UNMOVIC.

Libby had made: that there was more at issue than getting Iraq to agree to new inspections. The Deputies finally approved a draft cable, but Powell refused to transmit it because he opposed the clarification I had recommended. Powell evidently wanted to leave open the possibility that the United States might take the inspectors' return as a satisfactory solution to the Iraq problem.

I urged Rumsfeld to address this matter. In a memo to the Principals, dated August 6, Rumsfeld highlighted the risks of a bad inspections arrangement. He reiterated that inspections should "not be considered an end in themselves, but rather the means to an end"—the end being Iraq's actual WMD disarmament:

> **The obstacles to achieving that end have grown during the past four years during which no inspections took place in Iraq. We must keep our eye on the ball and ensure that the circumstances under which inspections resume, if they do, are such as to facilitate total Iraqi WMD disarmament, as required by [UN Security Council Resolution] 687.**
>
> **The U.S. must make a public statement of this position as soon as possible. This is necessary to prevent confusion and to preempt the move that Saddam . . . may be preparing to cut an unsatisfactory deal with the UN on inspections.**

Rice's staff drew on these points for a paper entitled "Declaratory Policy on UN WMD Inspections in Iraq," distributed two days later. Rice evidently shared Rumsfeld's worries:

> **The goal of the United States is to guarantee the verifiable elimination of Iraq's WMD. Elimination is called for by the UN mandate, and is the only way to protect the national security of the United States. . . .**
>
> **The essential issue is disarmament by Iraq, not inspections by the UN. Under [UN Security Council Resolution] 687, Iraq is obliged to disarm itself of all WMD. The Iraqi regime has succeeded in shifting the burden from itself to the UN. Most of the world now believes that the UN has the burden of proving Iraq's noncompliance with its obligation to disarm. In fact, Iraq has the burden of proving its compliance with its UN obligations.**

At the heart of the U.S. problem with Iraq was uncertainty. Even if new inspections occurred, we would not learn for sure what was happening with Iraq's WMD programs and stockpiles. After all, Saddam was capable of prodigious denial and deception. Discussing "burden of proof" was a way of highlighting that important uncertainties would remain no matter what UNMOVIC accomplished.

President Bush would have to make his national security decisions despite those uncertainties. He would have to choose which set of risks he preferred to run. Every possible course of action—including doing nothing—had its perils.

Although his political opponents had labeled him a unilateralist from the outset of his Administration*—or perhaps for that reason—President Bush chose to work the Iraq problem through the United Nations. In late August, President Bush decided to make Iraq the subject of his annual speech to the UN General Assembly. That speech, scheduled for September 12, would lay the foundation for U.S. diplomacy on Iraq.

The U.S. plan to end the Iraqi danger, preferably without war, required us to mount a credible threat of imminent military action. If Iraqis saw they faced such a threat, various possibilities might open up: a successful coup or popular insurrection, or even Saddam's abdication and exile. Or we might lead a multinational force to oust his regime.

We wanted a great deal of cooperation from partner countries. We were especially eager to secure access, basing, and overflight rights from Iraq's neighbors—Kuwait, Saudi Arabia, Qatar, Jordan, and Turkey—but they had grounds for reluctance. Could the United States assure them that, when the confrontation ended, the Iraqi regime would be gone? The Kuwaiti diplomat, Dr. Mohammed, made the point back in October 2001: The U.S. must not pull the tiger's tail and then leave him in place, ready to strike his neighbors. An unequivocal promise of regime change would be essential to building our coalition among Iraq's immediate neighbors.

At the same time, however, President Bush planned to emphasize at the United Nations that he was trying to resolve the Iraq problem *without war*. State officials argued, no doubt correctly, that he would win more support at the United Nations if he spoke more of his desire for a peaceful outcome than of the possibility of military action to change Iraq's regime.

The goals of regime change and avoiding war were not necessarily inconsistent. They were reconciled in the Administration's "ultimatum strategy," which called for a coalition military buildup to persuade Sad-

---

*Even before 9/11, critics often cited Bush's position on such issues as the Kyoto Treaty and the International Criminal Court as evidence of unilateralism.

dam that he had only two options: Face a war with us that would result in his death or imprisonment, or avert war by leaving Iraq with his sons and a small number of his top lieutenants to enjoy amnesty in permanent exile. It never seemed likely that Saddam would bow to the ultimatum, but President Bush took seriously his duty to exhaust all reasonable means short of war. The Defense Department also took this responsibility seriously: As late as March 2003, my office was working on an "action plan" for the ultimatum strategy, including a list of the candidate countries for asylum and a draft UN resolution.

In August, Rice's staff (with input from around the government) drafted a plan entitled "Ultimatum to Saddam Hussein and the Iraqi Regime." Hadley presented it to the Deputies for review on August 30. The rationale for regime change was set out comprehensively. Going beyond the CIA assessment that Saddam had stockpiles of chemical and biological weapons, it encompassed four broad issues: Iraq's WMD capability and infrastructure, its support for terrorism, its threats to neighbors, and its tyrannical nature. (Again, the rationale followed the formula I had nicknamed "WMD and the Three Ts.")

The paper went on to say that the only way to achieve all the war's purposes was "through a pluralistic, democratic, representative government." I thought this phrase was overstated, like the "create democracy" language in Rice's earlier "Liberation Strategy" paper. Though encouraging freedom abroad could serve U.S. interests, I argued that we should be clear that we were not starting a war to spread democracy.

Months later, I had an occasion to clarify this democracy point on the public record in an interview I gave to Nicholas Lemann for *The New Yorker.* Ousting the Saddam Hussein regime, I told Lemann, would open a potentially valuable opportunity to promote democratic institutions in Iraq and throughout the Middle East—but creating that opportunity was *not* a reason to go to war. Lemann asked me "whether the United States, if it goes to war, would be doing so partly because it wants to change the Middle East as a whole." I replied: "Would anybody be thinking about using military power in Iraq in order to do a political experiment in Iraq in the hope that it would have positive political spillover effects throughout the region? The answer is no."

The paper from Rice's office was just one of the many memos and briefings distributed to help organize discussions at high-level interagency meetings. Rice and Rumsfeld and their staffs were probably the most prolific sources of such papers. Powell, General Myers, and others also made written contributions from time to time. Sometimes the Principals as a group approved a text, but Principals Committee meetings did not always produce a formal decision either to endorse or to revise papers under discussion.* Occasionally, the submitting office would claim that its paper had been "approved" at a Principals meeting, suggesting that it had been adopted as policy—but other offices viewed the same paper as merely a draft for discussion.

President Bush had already committed his Administration to changing the regime in Iraq; at the same time, he had pledged to avoid war if at all possible. Though the ultimatum strategy was a logical way to square these commitments, there was clearly tension between them. Some of the countries whose support we sought were opposed to war in Iraq no matter what happened. They were reluctant to cooperate in generating pressure on Saddam, fearing that such measures would not cow him and would create momentum for war. Others—especially Iraq's neighbors and the Iraqi Kurds—needed certainty that Saddam's regime would be gone at the end of the day. For them, our resort to the United Nations was worrisome: If the Security Council (as was likely) refused to endorse a war for regime change, they feared that President Bush might settle for some new UN inspection arrangement.

The dilemmas of U.S. diplomacy on Iraq were the main topic at the "quad talks" I attended on September 3 and 4, 2002—part of a longstanding series of meetings among top-level policy officials in the defense ministries of Britain, France, Germany, and the United States. I opened the meetings by commenting that "U.S. policy in the war on terrorism is not based on vengeance or retaliation, but . . . on the requirements of self-defense." (Quotations here come from the report I sent back to Rumsfeld at the time.) In explaining our focus on Saddam Hussein, I cited Iraq's general history of aggression, hostility to the United States, pursuit of WMD, and cooperation with terrorist groups. I also stressed that the question of an Iraqi role in 9/11 "is not (repeat: not) of the essence." I explained: "The US cannot count on being able to defend against or deter the use of . . . Iraqi weapons, especially given the danger that they could be provided by Iraq to terrorists who could give Iraq deniability." Moreover, I said, it "does not

*Ideally, Principals meetings should have a formal wrap-up, summarizing what had been agreed and what issues remained open for later resolution. In practice, the written summaries of conclusions of interagency meetings—of the Deputies, Principals, and National Security Council—were very general, stating little more than the topics that had been discussed.

serve the interests of peace and world order for Iraq to use sovereignty as a screen behind which it can develop, unhindered, biological and nuclear weapons."

My British counterpart, Simon Webb, highly regarded throughout the Pentagon, mentioned the importance his Prime Minister ascribed to the United Nations. But he warned, "[w]e should guard against speaking of the UN as a necessary source of legitimacy for action against Iraq." Addressing the "burden of proof" question, he argued that we should not require "clear evidence" of WMD, for it would be perverse if we imposed on ourselves a standard that rewarded Saddam's concealment efforts—especially given that Iraq had shut down the UNSCOM inspectors in 1998.

The French defense ministry was represented by Marc Perrin de Brichambaut, an appealing person of formidable intellect and diplomatic finesse worthy of a government far more honorable than the one then in office in France. The United Nations, he said, could help with *political legitimation* for military action against Iraq, but its role is not to provide *legal authority*, for "states do not need UN approval to act in their own self-defense." De Brichambaut explained that France wanted to see the United States act jointly with its allies, some of whom may not want to send combat troops to Iraq but would be willing to help in other ways, such as lightening the burdens on the United States in Afghanistan, the Balkans, or elsewhere.

In contrast, the remarks of Walter Stuetzle, the State Secretary of the German Ministry of Defense, were cold and stern. Pointedly responding to our British colleague, he called for production of clear evidence of WMD, which he said existed for Iraqi chemical weapons but not for biological weapons. He stressed the need to use the "moral authority" of the UN and its expertise in international law and security. The German Chancellor had gone on record opposing the U.S. government's position on Iraq; Stuetzle kept faith with his Chancellor.

When I returned home from Berlin, I gave Rumsfeld some thoughts on designing a useful role for the United Nations. The United States should not allow the United Nations "to give the Iraqi regime 'one more chance' to satisfy Iraq's obligations regarding WMD." That would contradict the logic of our case against Iraq: "The Iraqi regime (1) cannot be trusted under any circumstances and (2) will pose an unacceptable WMD danger so long as it remains in power." Nevertheless, the Security Council could be helpful by adopting a resolution reviewing Iraq's record on WMD and the three Ts (including its violations of previous resolutions) and condemning Iraq for those violations. Alluding to a standard Rumsfeld theme, I wrote: "The proponents of such a resolution should frame their diplomacy so that the resolution is presented not as a test of the legitimacy of U.S.-led efforts to defend the US and the world against Iraqi WMD, but as a test of the UN's willingness to uphold its own principles."

The new UN resolution might " 'decide' that the leaders of the Iraqi regime will not be prosecuted for their past crimes in any international forum and will be allowed to enjoy amnesty if they yield authority and leave Iraq to spare their country a war." The idea of promising amnesty, of course, raised difficult questions of justice and morality that were discussed and analyzed in interagency meetings. The prevailing view was that avoiding war would justify granting amnesty, even to as bloody a character as Saddam.

The Administration's policy of building military pressure to support a threat of imminent action against the Iraqi regime involved some serious risks. U.S. officials worried that Saddam might respond by striking out in a last-ditch effort, perhaps with an apocalyptic biological weapons attack. My office reasoned along these lines: "Saddam is likely to believe that he cannot physically survive regime change. Unless we can, and are willing to, offer him some *credible* hope of comfortable survival, he may figure he has little to lose by using WMD, *once he believes his downfall is imminent.* In any case, he may not be interested in exile, if that means living quietly under conditions of virtual house arrest." Accordingly, we recommended:

- **We should aim to delay Saddam's recognition of the *imminence* of his downfall for as long as possible.**
- **Saddam appears to believe that he is good at political maneuvering, and that he can outmaneuver us, despite our intentions.**
- **Thus, our goal should be to convince him that he has more time to maneuver than he actually does.**
- **When the end comes, it must come quicker than he imagines.**
- **In addition, we should try to persuade those who would have to carry out his orders to use WMD not to do so.**

The possibility of a last-ditch WMD attack also received attention in the public debate. In a much-discussed *Wall Street Journal* op-ed article published on August 15, 2002, former National Security Adviser Brent Scowcroft cited the threat of such an attack as an argument *against* going to war with Saddam. If the United States invaded Iraq, he warned, "Saddam would be likely to conclude he had nothing left to lose, leading him to unleash whatever weapons of mass destruction he possesses." On the other hand, Scowcroft downplayed the danger of WMD blackmail by Saddam, on the grounds that threatening to use these weapons would open Saddam to a devastating U.S. response.

But catastrophic weapons in Iraq's hands were a threat not just because Saddam might decide one fine day to use them to hit the United States. A likelier problem was that they would affect our willingness to defend U.S. interests. After Saddam invaded Kuwait in 1991, the U.S. Senate approved the first President Bush's decision to go to war by only a five-vote margin. If Saddam had had a nuclear weapon at that time, would Congress have voted differently?

If Saddam were to invade Kuwait again—or attack Saudi Arabia or Jordan, for example—Iraq's WMD would become an argument for not opposing that aggression. Saddam would not have to threaten us expressly; blackmail would inhere in the situation. Especially worrisome was the possibility that Saddam might attack us by providing a weapon to a terrorist group, and so manage to avoid detection and retaliation. (Recall the unsuccessful effort to discover who was responsible for the anthrax used in the September 2001 attacks against the U.S. Senate and other offices—a mystery still unsolved today.)

In his *Wall Street Journal* article, Scowcroft claimed that the United States was not "an object of [Saddam's] aggression." Even if true, this was beside the point. Saddam might even prefer to leave us alone. The issue was whether Iraq's WMD capabilities would compel us to leave *him* alone—free to attack Americans and our friends and interests, as he had done more than once in recent years.

It seemed ironic that Scowcroft, of all people, would argue for leaving Saddam in power on the grounds that the United States was not "an object of his aggression." After all, it was during Scowcroft's term as National Security Adviser that we got into a war with Iraq in 1990–91—when we were even less the object of Saddam's aggression. We fought the Gulf War because the first President Bush concluded we couldn't let Saddam get away with stealing a whole country, especially one with enormous economic resources. It was like arguing that the Chicago police had no reason to worry about Al Capone because they weren't the object of his aggression: Capone would have been happy to leave them alone if they had left him alone.

Scowcroft argued for new weapons inspections in Iraq, saying that the United States should be "pressing" the UN Security Council to insist on such inspections. If Saddam refused, his rejection could provide the "persuasive casus belli" that we lacked. "Compelling evidence that Saddam *had acquired* nuclear-weapons capability" could likewise provide a proper cause for war, Scowcroft argued. That is to say, the United States would have good grounds for war if we waited until *after* Saddam acquired nuclear weapons. President Bush considered that too risky. Anyway, according to the logic of Scowcroft's article, if we waited there would be a stronger argument against clashing with Saddam, lest the dictator "unleash" the very nuclear weapons our previous restraint had allowed him to acquire.

In his speech to the UN General Assembly, President Bush had to thread several needles. He had to start the buildup of military pressure on Iraq, while being careful to avoid making war appear either inevitable or imminent. He had to signal that Saddam's regime was doomed, while declaring that a peaceful outcome was both possible and preferred. And he had to invite the United Nations to play the central role in resolving the problem, while preserving America's freedom of action to ensure our defense.

I always felt some tension in watching a speech by the President, because we in the Pentagon did not necessarily know in advance what he would say. Although presidential speeches on national security were important policy statements, they were produced not through Deputies, Principals, and National Security Council meetings, but by the President's speechwriters, in coordination with the National Security Adviser and other White House officials. Rice usually sent Rumsfeld a draft of a presidential speech for comment a few days (or occasionally a few hours) before it was scheduled for delivery. Rumsfeld usually gave the draft to Wolfowitz and me, and we would give him our comments to pass back to Rice. Sometimes I recognized the ideas in the draft speech from policy papers. Sometimes, however, the ideas had not been discussed in interagency meetings; they may have been developed by the President, Rice, or another official—or they may have originated with the speechwriters themselves. The speechwriters sometimes heeded our comments, especially factual corrections, but they often resisted suggestions about themes or presentation. When it came to crafting the President's public statements—often his most important articulations of policy—even the most productive interagency policy discussions amounted to little more than suggestions to the speechwriters, that they could either take or leave.

President Bush delivered his Iraq speech before the General Assembly on September 12, 2002, one day after the anniversary of 9/11. He described the dangers of the world's new political landscape as shaped by 9/11. He cited the risk that an "outlaw regime" might supply terrorists "with the technologies to kill on a massive scale." He identified Saddam's Iraq as "one place" where we found the gravest international dangers "in their most lethal and aggressive forms, exactly the kind of aggressive threat the United Nations was born to confront." (Apparently with North Korea and Iran in mind, the President did not say that Iraq was *the* one place.)

The President recalled the deal Saddam had made with the United Nations in 1991, to end active hostilities after Iraq's expulsion from Kuwait. Saddam had promised to renounce weapons of mass destruction, sever his ties to terrorist groups, and end his repression of the Iraqi people. It was Saddam who was obliged to prove to the United Nations that he was living up to his word:

> **To suspend hostilities, to spare himself, Iraq's dictator accepted a series of commitments. The terms were clear, to him and to all. And he agreed to prove he is complying with every one of those obligations. He has proven instead only his contempt for the United Nations, and for all his pledges.**

The President wanted the United Nations to exert leadership, but he insisted that action to counter Saddam was necessary:

> **My nation will work with the UN Security Council to meet our common challenge. If Iraq's regime defies us again, the world must move deliberately, decisively to hold Iraq to account. We will work with the UN Security Council for the necessary resolutions. But the purposes of the United States should not be doubted. The Security Council resolutions will be enforced . . . or action will be unavoidable. And a regime that has lost its legitimacy will also lose its power.**

Bush exhorted the United Nations to uphold its own resolutions and assert its authority. "We want the United Nations to be effective . . . and successful," he added. If the United Nations proved unable to enforce its resolutions, the President was saying, it would compel the United States to take action. The result would be regime change in Iraq. Notably, however, he stopped short of declaring that the *only* acceptable resolution was regime change.

The President warned:

> **Events can turn in one of two ways: If we fail to act in the face of danger, the people of Iraq will continue to live in brutal submission. The regime will have new power to bully and dominate and conquer its neighbors, condemning the Middle East to more**

years of bloodshed and fear. The regime will remain unstable, with little hope of freedom, and isolated from the progress of our times. With every step the Iraqi regime takes toward gaining and deploying the most terrible weapons, our own options to confront that regime will narrow. And if an emboldened regime were to supply these weapons to terrorist allies, then the attacks of September the eleventh would be a prelude to far greater horrors.

In describing the threat from Iraq, President Bush spoke of Saddam's record of aggressive war and "grave violations of human rights," and of the shelter and support Iraq gave to "terrorist organizations that direct violence against Iran, Israel, and Western governments." He observed that Saddam's regime targeted Iraqi dissidents abroad for murder and tried to assassinate the Kuwaiti emir and "a former American President." Moreover, "al Qaeda terrorists escaped from Afghanistan and are known to be in Iraq." Contrary to later claims by many commentators, President Bush did not build his case against Saddam exclusively on assertions that Iraq possessed stockpiles of weapons of mass destruction.

Not even the portion of his case that dealt with weapons of mass destruction focused only on stockpiles. A single line in his speech noted that UN inspections "revealed that Iraq likely maintains stockpiles of VX, mustard and other chemical agents." In the same sentence, the President went on to speak of Iraq's presumed capabilities: UN inspections also revealed that the Iraqi regime "is rebuilding and expanding facilities capable of producing chemical weapons."

President Bush spoke of Iraq's WMD *capabilities* and *programs*. He cited Iraq's history of using such weapons against Iran and the Kurds and its confrontations with UN weapons inspectors throughout the 1990s. Emphasizing the burden-of-proof point, he recalled:

In 1991, the Iraqi regime agreed to destroy and stop developing all weapons of mass destruction and long-range missiles, *and to prove to the world it has done so* by complying with rigorous inspections. Iraq has broken every aspect of this fundamental pledge.

By lying to the inspectors, interfering with their work, and ultimately shutting them down altogether, Saddam had created disturbing uncertainties. President Bush explained how he viewed these uncertainties:

We know that Saddam Hussein pursued weapons of mass murder even when inspectors were in his country. Are we to assume

that he stopped when they left? The history, the logic, and the facts lead to one conclusion: Saddam Hussein's regime is a grave and gathering danger. To suggest otherwise is to hope against the evidence. To assume this regime's good faith is to bet the lives of millions and the peace of the world in a reckless gamble. And this is a risk we must not take.

President Bush was later accused of making reckless allegations about Saddam's WMD and even of dishonesty, but all of his arguments were well within the bounds of what was generally believed not only by intelligence and policy officials in the United States, but also at the United Nations and around the world at that time. The President was dealing with a true dilemma: How should he resolve serious doubts and fears relating to Saddam? Saddam had previously stockpiled chemical and biological weapons (as confirmed by UNSCOM) and had used WMD more than once. Saddam had long wanted to end the UN economic sanctions, and he could have done so at any time by satisfying the inspectors. What grounds did we have—in fact or logic—to believe that Saddam had ended his proscribed weapons programs, even though he refused to allow the UN to verify his compliance?

In this speech, President Bush listed the actions "we now expect of the Iraqi regime." The items went well beyond weapons inspections. They included the many unfulfilled demands from the sixteen Iraq-related resolutions the Security Council had adopted since the Gulf War. The President set out this list in five paragraphs, each beginning "If the Iraqi regime wishes peace, it will . . ." Throughout the Administration, officials later parsed this section of the speech to understand exactly what the President was saying about regime change. If Iraq complied with all the requirements—renouncing his support for terrorism, pursuit of WMD, repression of the Iraqi people, etc.—then, President Bush said (rather murkily), that such a shift in and of itself could represent a transformation of the Iraqi regime—one that might be tantamount to regime change:

If all these steps are taken, it will signal a new openness and accountability in Iraq. And it could open the prospect of the United Nations helping to build a government that represents all Iraqis—a government based on respect for human rights, economic liberty, and internationally supervised elections.

What was clear was that the President was purposefully being unclear. He needed to assure some audiences that this confrontation would end with a new regime in Baghdad. At the same time, he wanted to suggest that the problem was solvable without war. He evidently calculated this was not the time or place to reveal that he planned to give the Iraqi leadership an ultimatum—voluntary exile or overthrow by force. So he decided to fudge his language, implying that regime change was inevitable, but not quite saying so.

Press coverage of this speech was detailed and largely positive. The *Los Angeles Times* described it as "a relatively conservative case based on widely accepted intelligence findings." All the major American newspapers accurately represented the President's case as broadly based on the full record of Iraq's defiance of UN resolutions—not limited to the issue of proscribed weapons. The *Washington Post* noted that the speech included "a recitation of past U.N. resolutions ordering Baghdad to end its weapons programs, [to] stop repressing its own people and to end threats against its neighbors and all support for terrorists." None of the coverage interpreted the speech as focusing exclusively on Iraq's weapons programs, much less weapons stockpiles. That piece of revisionism would come later.

In the weeks after his speech, President Bush turned his Administration's efforts toward drafting a new resolution on Iraq and building support for it at the Security Council. Throughout the fall of 2002, Administration officials labored on the draft, debating which points to include and exclude. We hoped that the resolution would strengthen our hand with Saddam, but we saw the risk that a badly crafted resolution could tie our hands.

On October 5, Rumsfeld sent the President a memo specifying that the usefulness of a new resolution would be *political*, not legal. The United States did not actually need new Security Council authorization to use "all necessary means" against Saddam, Rumsfeld wrote, because we already had two strong legal bases for military action against Saddam. We had the right of self-defense, as recognized in Article 51 of the United Nations Charter. And we had the right to respond to Saddam's multiple material breaches of the post–Gulf War Security Council resolutions that had formed the basis for our cease-fire with Iraq in 1991.

As we began formulating a new resolution, however, opponents of U.S. policy—led by the French—sought to use it to derail our Iraq strategy. They wanted the new resolution to condemn Iraqi bad behavior, but then require a *second* resolution before we could use military force. That would allow the countries on the Security Council to vote both ways on the issue—first in favor of a toughly worded condemnation, and then against effective action.

Rumsfeld acknowledged in his memo that a new resolution could serve a useful purpose by helping us recruit members for our military coalition. But he warned that "anything that says or implies that there will be a second resolution" could be harmful: Some countries—especially Iraq's neighbors—might be afraid to join the coalition if there were a chance the Security Council would fail to approve the second resolution.

The United States and Britain worked together on a draft resolution that both Bush and Blair could support. One key element was the requirement that Iraq publish a new, formal declaration of its current WMD facilities and materiel. In a follow-up memo to the President, Rumsfeld argued that the U.S.-British draft should specify that a false declaration by Iraq "is by itself a material breach"—yet *another* breach—of the Gulf War cease-fire resolutions. Rumsfeld mapped out the pitfalls of our United Nations diplomatic strategy: "[T]he purpose of entering into UN negotiations was to test the UN's seriousness regarding Iraqi WMD, not to indulge a fantasy that we could design an inspection regime that will allow us to score a quick checkmate against Saddam Hussein against his will."

A few days after the President's UN speech, Iraq had announced that it would allow UN inspectors back into Iraq for the first time since 1998—though they were not admitted until November. But the prospect of new inspections was a mixed blessing at best. Rumsfeld's follow-up memo observed that Iraq "has had more than half a decade to improve its denial-and-deception techniques"—and, moreover, "UNMOVIC today is a notably weaker organization" than its predecessor, UNSCOM. He proposed measures to bolster UNMOVIC, warning against getting trapped in "an endless inspection game" that would produce no definitive answers about Iraq's WMD capabilities.

At the October 15 Principals Committee meeting, George Tenet reiterated that the CIA did not have "a smoking gun today—a site that we know will produce a smoking gun." Though CIA officials lacked specific data on *where* Saddam's chemical or biological weapons were located, they said they were certain, from multiple sources of information, that Saddam possessed such weapons.

Powell reported at that meeting that the United States had been trying to arrange for a single resolution that would include "all necessary means" language, to compel Saddam to cooperate with UNMOVIC and to disarm Iraq of WMD. The French, however, were insisting there would have to be a second resolution before the United States (or anyone else) could take enforcement action. Powell observed, with resignation, that pressure was growing—even from the British—to require a second resolution. Rice countered that President Bush had said that U.S. action could not be conditioned on a second resolution, noting that this was a "red line for the President." Substituting for Rumsfeld at the meeting, Wolfowitz said that the proposed second-resolution language "does the opposite of what's required" because it "would tell Saddam Hussein that the Russians and French will work to save him." He concluded: "There are worse things than having our . . . draft defeated or vetoed by France."

Even though they were crossing President Bush's "red line," Powell was inclined to go along with the French and the Russians. Responding as if Wolfowitz had attacked the United Nations as such, Powell remarked: "Showing the UN to be irrelevant is not in our long-term interest." Although the United States had dozens of countries supporting our position on Iraq, Powell took the view that proceeding without French support would amount to U.S. unilateralism. "Going it alone with a couple of like-minded nations" would not be good, Powell said. Given that the British and Italians, as well as most of Iraq's neighbors (and other important partners) were with us, I couldn't understand Powell's contention that, because there was not unanimity on the Security Council, we would be "going it alone."

Powell advocated presenting the best resolution we could get the French, Russians, and other permanent Security Council members to endorse. A more effective negotiating posture, it seemed to me, would have been to start with a statement of U.S. requirements, in the expectation that other countries would be willing to compromise to keep us in the negotiation. Weeks earlier (as Rumsfeld noted in his October 14 memo), the President had set a guideline that the "US goal at the UN is *not* to get merely the best resolution possible, but to achieve a resolution that actually meets the standards appropriate to the threat and to the goal of achieving disarmament."

Nevertheless, when push came to shove, President Bush deferred to Powell. The result of the Administration's efforts at the United Nations was a resolution that specified no consequences for Iraq—beyond holding a further Security Council meeting—if it should fail to comply.

In October 2002, Rumsfeld spent a great deal of time on the question of how post-Saddam Iraq should be managed. After several weeks of discussion with Wolfowitz, Myers, Pace, and me, he concluded that a single U.S. official should be responsible for the full range of reconstruction tasks—political, economic, and security. Those tasks depended on one another. As we had seen in Bosnia in the 1990s, even if the military completed its security-related missions, it would not be able to pack up and depart unless civil institutions were also up and running. Rumsfeld wanted to ensure that whoever headed civil reconstruction in Iraq had the same incentives as he had to complete the job.

Assisted by the Joint Staff and my own staff, I wrote a briefing for President Bush with recommendations on organizing the post-Saddam administration of Iraq, using the terms "unity of leadership" and "unity of effort" to refer to Rumsfeld's concept. After the Secretary approved it, I presented the briefing at a National Security Council meeting on October 15. The key recommendation was to put a single cabinet official in charge of all the tasks necessary to complete our military mission. This could avert the standard finger-pointing exercise—State officials asserting that economic development was impossible until the military created security, and Defense officials claiming that security was unachievable until State created economic opportunities to get idle young men off the street.

If the President agreed with this unity-of-leadership idea, I said, the single official would have to be the Secretary of Defense. No one else could take charge of security, because no one else had the legal authority to command our armed forces.

Some State officials later complained that the decision to put Rumsfeld in charge of post-Saddam reconstruction usurped a traditional State Department role. At the meetings where the matter was discussed, however, Colin Powell never offered a word of doubt or challenge. On the contrary, after I made my presentation on the unity-of-leadership approach, Powell nodded and remarked, "That makes sense." There was no disagreement at senior levels over who should lead the post-Saddam reconstruction effort. But unity of leadership would prove difficult to maintain in practice.

Another management issue was the need to appoint someone to take charge of the government's civilian planning for Iraq—including postwar planning. This idea had been raised and dropped several times since mid-2002. When the idea of appointing an "Iraq coordinator" came up at the June 27 Deputies Lunch, Armitage argued successfully for delay.

On two or three occasions that summer, I urged Rumsfeld to designate a person to head a postwar planning office. That person could set up the office and begin integrating the plans that had been developed around the government over several months. Rumsfeld asked me for a job specification and a list of candidates. I provided them, but even after I gave him a second list a few weeks later, he did not report back to me on his choice of candidate. On October 18, at a meeting with Franks, Rumsfeld at last told me to set up a postwar planning office, though he had not yet picked a candidate to run it. Soon afterward, however, he reversed this order without explanation.

Much later, I learned from Hadley that President Bush had worried that setting up a postwar planning office at that moment would undercut his diplomacy. At a moment when he was trying to reassure world leaders that he hoped to avoid war, he didn't want to have to explain why the Pentagon was creating a new organization to run Iraq after Saddam was overthrown. The benefits of getting a centralized postwar planning effort under way were obvious, but the President had many interests to balance. Though I had pressed to get the office created, I could not argue that the costs of delay outweighed the diplomatic risks that concerned the President.

The war planning intensified as the fall progressed. Rumsfeld met often with General Franks, usually together with Myers, Pace, Wolfowitz, and me. At an October 18 briefing session, Rumsfeld returned to his theme that the Administration needed an information plan. He wanted Defense and other departments to coordinate with the White House in a professional, systematic effort to explain our Iraq policy to the Congress, news media, and the public. Rumsfeld banged this drum often—including at meetings of the Principals Committee and the National Security Council. The President also commented continually that the Administration should improve its strategic communications. But no effort was ever organized that satisfied the President, Rumsfeld, or the other top officials.

Rumsfeld also raised the fundamental question of how the new Iraqi leadership would arise after Saddam's overthrow. "What is the *loya jirga* process for Iraq?" the Secretary asked, referring to the tribal council that had launched Afghanistan's political reconstruction. No one offered Rumsfeld a detailed answer at that October 18 meeting. Franks responded with a warning that jibed with Rumsfeld's thinking: "Don't separate security from reconstruction."

Franks was aware of our unity-of-effort presentation for the President, and more than once he had heard Rumsfeld remark that recent U.S. reconstruction efforts—in the Balkans, Afghanistan, and elsewhere—had suffered because they were divided among officials in unrelated bureaucracies. In Bosnia, for example, security tasks and civil reconstruction were managed through different lines of authority. In Afghanistan, each major element of reconstruction—military training, police training, creating a judiciary, combating narcotics, eliminating militias—had been assigned to a different "lead nation."

Once he overthrew Saddam Hussein's regime, Franks would become responsible for governing Iraq. Rumsfeld had been clear that he did not want that responsibility fragmented and distributed among separate chains of command. The Secretary anticipated that, at some point, President Bush might appoint a civilian administrator for Iraq, to assist (or perhaps relieve) Franks regarding some of the governance tasks. As Franks well understood, Rumsfeld nevertheless intended to retain personal responsibility for the whole range of Iraqi reconstruction tasks. Franks's comment endorsed Rumsfeld's thinking on unity of effort.

Franks's comment counters an anecdote in Bob Woodward's book *State of Denial:* Franks (Woodward says) came away happy from one of these meetings greatly relieved that Rumsfeld was assigning him responsibility *only for security* in the post-Saddam period. According to Woodward, Franks believed that Rumsfeld had separated security from all the other reconstruction tasks—and had assigned the latter *to my Policy organization.* Franks's operations director purportedly greeted this news by saying, "We don't own the reconstruction stuff. We just dodged a big bullet."

But my Policy organization did analysis and gave advice on policy planning. We didn't plan operations in Iraq or anywhere else. Operational planning was the responsibility of the same organization that would be carrying out those operations. Otherwise, when problems inevitably arose, the planners would blame the operators (and vice versa). My Policy office had *no one* stationed in the Middle East to carry out operations. On the other hand, Franks headed an operational command that would have *hundreds of thousands* of men and women in-theater; moreover, he had thousands of operational planners in his headquarters. The notion that Rumsfeld would take responsibility for postwar planning or operations away from the CENTCOM commander before the war—and give it to his Pentagon-based policy adviser—is ludicrous. Though he should have known better, Woodward must have judged the story credible because so many other journalists had misreported that my office was "in charge" of the government's postwar work in Iraq. But it didn't happen, and Franks patently didn't think it happened.

At the same meeting, Rumsfeld asked Franks for his thoughts on post-Saddam reconstruction: How was CENTCOM going to work with coalition partners, other U.S. government agencies, and the Iraqi external groups? Also, how did Franks intend to link up with the Joint Task Force that General Myers's staff had recommended CENTCOM create for postwar planning? This was another necessary nudge, for Franks had not yet moved on the September recommendation to set up a Joint Task Force.

Rumsfeld was uneasy about the way Administration officials talked about our goals in Iraq. One of "Rumsfeld's Rules" was "Underpromise and overdeliver." He disapproved of imprecise—let alone grandiose—rhetoric about democracy, and warned that U.S. officials should take care in describing our standards for success in Iraq. In an October 28 meeting with Franks, Pace, and me, Rumsfeld asked me to "work on how to define victory." Rumsfeld wanted the U.S. mission circumscribed. Iraq belonged to the Iraqis, not to us, he said repeatedly; Iraqis would have to take the lead in creating their own new, free governmental institutions. He told me to avoid a definition of victory that was not achievable in the near term. He didn't want a definition that hinged on seizing or killing Saddam personally or locating all of his weapons of mass destruction. Nor did he want a definition that hinged on the Iraqis creating a stable democracy, which might not occur for many years.

At the same meeting, we touched on the subject of what the military calls "endstates." I posed a fundamental question—"When Saddam is ousted, who is the authority in Iraq?"—and ventured my own answer: The responsibility for administering the country would fall to our military. This point reflected my constant concern that Franks, while focusing on major combat operations, was showing relatively little interest in his duty to establish order and run Iraq after Saddam's overthrow. It was crucial that CENTCOM work with officials in Washington on plans for reconstruction and political transition in Iraq.

Responding to prodding by Rumsfeld, Rice's staff circulated a revised version of the Administration's "goals and objectives for Iraq." The language was refined to take account of arguments Defense officials had been making in interagency meetings since the President approved the first version in August. Instead of defining the U.S. goal as "a society based on moderation, pluralism, and democracy," this improved version, dated October 29, set out a more limited aim: an Iraq that "encourages the building of democratic institutions." The new version dropped the phrase "establish a broad-based democratic government" and substituted a more realistic formula: "establishes an interim administration in Iraq that prepares for the transition to an elected Iraqi government as quickly as practicable."

Rumsfeld welcomed these revisions. Keeping the Administration's strategic formulations precise and down-to-earth, however, was a job that never ended.

Discussions about information warfare recalled the propaganda battles of the Cold War. The Soviets were remarkably successful, especially in tailoring messages to various specific audiences. It is easier, of course, to tailor one's messages if truth is not a concern. But it is possible to be truthful and straightforward in explaining one's positions and still account for the listeners' diverse points of view.

Working at the Pentagon during the Reagan Administration, I had a hand in the ideological battles of the Cold War, representing the department in interagency meetings on public diplomacy. Especially on arms control, the Soviets achieved formidable credibility and appeal, despite the gross unattractiveness of Soviet life. If the wooden communists of the Brezhnev regime could show suppleness and subtlety in their information operations, one could only wonder, and despair, at the rigidity of the strategic communications of the George W. Bush Administration.

Communism may have doomed itself by misunderstanding human nature, but while it lasted, its Soviet propagandists were savvy about how to win a worldwide audience. They showed this in the early 1980s with their campaign for a "nuclear freeze," an initiative that sounded evenhanded but would have secured a significant Soviet advantage in intermediate-range missiles in Europe. The freeze campaign was built on the insight that people cherish a variety of identities: Americans, for example, may identify themselves as Catholics, or medical doctors, or Hispanics, or women, or environmentalists. The Soviets therefore tailored their message to reach specific groups—religious, professional, ethnic, and political—in Europe and America. The arguments they used for these diverse publics differed and sometimes contradicted one another, but they shared a conclusion: Support the nuclear freeze.

Reagan Administration officials countered Soviet propaganda energetically. The Reagan White House encouraged *all* its officials, not just those at the cabinet level, to tailor messages to our various audiences. When addressing lawyers' groups, for example, we offered legal analysis. In academic settings, we would explain our thinking in greater depth than in television broadcasts.

The George W. Bush Administration, however, took a different approach to strategic communications. Its key concept was to "discipline the message." White House officials did not generally encourage subcabinet officials to do speeches, interviews, or op-eds in support of our Iraq policy or our war on terrorism strategy. They chose to rely almost entirely on the President, Vice President, Powell, Rumsfeld, and Rice. That made it easier to keep official pronouncements "on message," but it also meant writing off important audiences—including journalists, academics, and intellectuals—that could not be satisfied with generalizations delivered at a distance.

I gave public speeches infrequently—perhaps one every four to six weeks, mostly in Washington.* On one occasion I drafted a talk about U.S. counterterrorism strategy including some new ways to explain Administration policy. Although we were not required to clear our speeches in advance, I sent the draft to Steve Hadley for review. Hadley said that, although he liked the speech, Rice had misgivings *in principle* about introducing new arguments. "Under secretaries are not supposed to be inventing arguments," she told him, and suggested that I should make my points by quoting from President Bush's speeches.

The President's political and communications advisers had considerable talents. They organized President Bush's successful reelection campaign in 2004, after all. But they never managed to organize sophisticated information efforts to support our national security policies, either abroad or at home.† Part of the problem was that the President tolerated the anemic efforts of the State Department—not to mention the steady stream of anti-Administration leaks from unnamed State and CIA officials. But a deeper problem was that no one at the White House took the initiative to strategize a well-resourced, creative campaign of ideas on a scale commensurate with the stakes in the war on terrorism. We wondered how the President's team could be so skillful, even brilliant, in political campaigning, yet so poor in using information to serve national security purposes.

The inadequacy of the Administration's strategic communications was obvious to all. My Pentagon and Situation Room meeting notes show literally hundreds of comments from 2001 forward—by the President, Cheney, Rice, Rumsfeld, Myers, Pace, Abizaid, and others—calling for better public diplomacy and public relations. Countless papers were written on the subject. Offices were created for the purpose at the White House and at State, and many meetings were held. But the Administration never managed to convey information and ideas to journalists, academics, diplomats, and members of Congress nearly as effectively as its opponents did—even though many of the opponents' arguments were distorted or downright false.

Of course, the Administration's problems with domestic or world public opinion were not entirely or even largely the result of poor "public rela-

---

*Rumsfeld did not like his Roundtable regulars to travel when he was at the Pentagon. He preferred to keep us available to meet with him in person.

†One of the better products the White House communications office produced was a presentation of the case against Saddam (White House, "A Decade of Deception and Defiance," April 2003, available at http://www.whitehouse.gov/infocus/iraq/decade/book.html).

tions." They owed a great deal to our setbacks in Iraq, controversial policy decisions, and other substantive grounds for criticism. But the failure to present its case and to correct misstatements by its critics left the Administration open to every attack on its competence and credibility. As events in Iraq grew disappointing and then distressing, that failure became strategically significant, eroding the congressional and public support President Bush needed to sustain the war effort in Iraq and elsewhere.

The CIA was responsible for evaluating information on Iraq's capabilities and intentions. In the weeks after President Bush's UN speech, it produced important statements on Iraq's links to terrorists and its WMD programs. On October 7, 2002, CIA Director George Tenet released an unclassified letter addressed to the Chairman of the Senate Intelligence Committee, Bob Graham (D-Florida), summarizing the current intelligence reporting on Iraq's relationship with al Qaida.

The Tenet letter drew on months of effort by the intelligence community. The CIA, he declared, had "solid" and "credible" information on the relationship, which had been developing for years in spite of their philosophical differences:

> **Our understanding of the relationship between Iraq and al-Qa'ida is evolving and is based on sources of varying reliability. Some of the information we have received comes from detainees, including some of high rank.**
>
> - ***We have solid reporting of senior level contacts between Iraq and al-Qa'ida going back a decade.***
> - **Credible information indicates that Iraq and al-Qa'ida have discussed safe haven and reciprocal non-aggression.**
> - **Since Operation Enduring Freedom, *we have solid evidence of the presence in Iraq of al-Qa'ida members, including some that have been in Baghdad.***
> - ***We have credible reporting that al-Qa'ida leaders sought contacts in Iraq who could help them acquire WMD capabilities. The reporting also stated that Iraq has provided training to al-Qa'ida members in the areas of poisons and gases and making conventional bombs.***
> - **Iraq's increasing support to extremist Palestinians,**

> **coupled with growing indications of a relationship with al-Qa'ida, suggest that *Baghdad's links to terrorists will increase, even absent US military action.***

This authoritative statement by Tenet went a long way toward correcting the problems that Christina Shelton and others had criticized in their own briefing, which would later become so controversial. Tenet's letter in effect vindicated those criticisms.

Tenet's assertion that the CIA had multiple and credible reports of Iraqi–al Qaida links forged over many years did not suggest, of course, that Iraq had conspired with al Qaida in the 9/11 attack.* Though some argued that Tenet's letter understated the Iraq–al Qaida relationship, I wasn't interested in further belaboring the point. The critical fact, as I saw it, was that President Bush had grounds for concern that Saddam might work with terrorists—whether al Qaida or any other group—to hurt the United States, especially by providing them with mass-destruction weapons.

After months of controversy over the issue, I welcomed Tenet's summation of the available intelligence, which appeared more clear and objective than previous characterizations from the CIA. Coming as it did from the Agency's director, I took it as the intelligence community's definitive statement on the subject. I never challenged Tenet's conclusions publicly or privately: From the day it was published, everything I said about Iraq–al Qaida connections was grounded in that letter's findings.† I believe that was true also of Rumsfeld, President Bush, and most other high-level Administration officials.

After Saddam's overthrow, critics implied that the Iraq–al Qaida relationship was a major reason for the war. That was not true. Before Operation Iraqi Freedom began, Administration officials made thousands of statements to journalists and public audiences on the rationale for the

---

*The Czech intelligence report of a spring 2001 meeting in Prague between one of the future 9/11 hijackers and an Iraqi intelligence official eventually became a focus of controversy. The CIA, over time, concluded that the meeting likely did not occur, although Czech intelligence stood by the report. Even if it occurred, however, the meeting would not by itself prove that Iraq was involved in the 9/11 plot.

†It was only from press accounts that I learned I was supposed to have been engaged personally in a battle with the CIA over this letter. The *New York Times* reported this, for example, in an article by Jason DeParle, "Faculty's Chilly Reception for Ex-Pentagon Official," *New York Times*, May 25, 2006, p. A20. (I was unable to correct the record: The *Times* did not publish my letter to the editor.)

war. The Iraq–al Qaida connection was a minor part of that discourse—as it was a minor, indeed insignificant, part of the confidential discussions within the government.

The 9/11 Commission Report, published in the summer of 2004, muddied the issue by asserting that there was no "collaborative operational relationship" between Iraq and al Qaida—implying that someone in the Administration had claimed that such a relationship existed. As far as I know, no one ever did. Making matters worse, many commentators slipped quickly and sloppily from the phrase "no *collaborative operational* relationship" to "*no relationship*"—possibly influenced by the news headlines that simplified the issue.

In any case, it was unclear what the commissioners meant by the term "collaborative operational." Would they use that term, for example, to describe the relationship between the Taliban and the 9/11 attack? The Taliban gave al Qaida safe haven. Did that link Taliban leaders "operationally" to the attack? Iraqi intelligence had trained thousands of non-Iraqi terrorists. If some al Qaida members were among them (a detail we are unlikely ever to know), would that training amount to an "operational" relationship? I could not figure out why the 9/11 Commission introduced the term "collaborative operational" into the debate. The absence of an "operational" relationship would not necessarily mean that a state supporter of terrorists was not dangerous, or that it should be permitted to continue providing safe haven and training to terrorist organizations.

Inevitably, opponents of the Administration wove the wildly overstated Iraq–al Qaida issue into their allegation that "Bush lied" to take the United States into war. Some claimed that I insisted that an Iraq–al Qaida relationship existed, in the face of CIA conclusions to the contrary.* The Tenet letter refutes that claim, in the public record.

President Bush, in meetings with his National Security Council, was

---

*See Eric Schmitt, "Senior Official Behind Many of the Pentagon's Most Contentious Policies Is Stepping Down," *New York Times*, January 27, 2005, p. A11, which states: "Last fall, Senator Carl Levin of Michigan, the ranking Democrat on the Armed Services Committee, said that Mr. Feith had repeatedly described the ties between Iraq and Al Qaeda as far more significant and extensive than United States intelligence agencies had." I did *not* make such an assertion, and the CIA's position was *not* that there was no evidence of an Iraq–al Qaeda relationship—as the Tenet letter made clear. The latter point was muddied, however, by statements such as this one by John McLaughlin, former Deputy Director of the CIA: "We said at some point in the timeframe that we had no evidence linking Iraq to Al Qaeda and to those attacks." Interview with John McLaughlin, *Frontline*, PBS, January 11, 2006, transcript available at http://www.pbs.org/wgbh/pages/frontline/darkside/interviews/mclaughlin.html.

concerned not about historical debates over sketchy intelligence on a decade's worth of Iraq–al Qaida interactions, but about the danger Iraq was currently posing. He made it clear, at those meetings, that his primary concern was preventing another big terrorist attack on the United States. Saddam's brutality, aggression, hostility to the United States, pursuit of catastrophic weapons, and *undisputed* ties to various terrorist groups provided ample grounds for those worries—whether or not one attached significance to whatever past or present connections Iraq had with al Qaida.

Less than a week after Tenet presented his unclassified letter on the Iraq–al Qaida relationship, the CIA released the National Intelligence Estimate (NIE) of October 2002—its long-awaited classified report on Iraq's banned weapons programs. The key judgments included the following passages:

> **We judge that we are seeing only a portion of Iraq's WMD efforts, owing to Baghdad's vigorous denial and deception efforts. . . .**
>
> **Iraq has largely rebuilt missile and biological weapons facilities damaged during Operation Desert Fox and *has expanded its chemical and biological infrastructure* under the cover of civilian production. . . .**
>
> **If Baghdad acquires sufficient fissile material from abroad it could make a nuclear weapon *within several months* to a year. Without such material from abroad, Iraq probably would not be able to make a weapon until 2007 to 2009. . . .**
>
> **Although we have little specific information on Iraq's CW stockpile, Saddam probably has stocked at least 100 metric tons (MT) and possibly as much as 500 MT of CW agents—much of it added in the last year. . . .**
>
> **We judge that all key aspects—R&D, production, and weaponization—of Iraq's offensive BW program are active and that most elements are larger and more advanced than they were before the Gulf war.**
>
> **We judge Iraq has some lethal and incapacitating BW agents and is capable of quickly producing and weaponizing a variety of such agents, including anthrax, for delivery by bombs, missiles, aerial sprayers, and covert operatives.**
>
> **Baghdad has established a large-scale, redundant, and concealed BW agent production capability.**
>
> **Baghdad has mobile facilities for producing bacterial and toxin BW agents; these facilities can evade detection and are**

highly survivable. Within three to six months these units probably could produce an amount of agent equal to the total that Iraq produced in the years prior to the Gulf war.

These findings were consistent with what UNSCOM reported in the 1990s. When Saddam forced UNSCOM to abandon its mission in 1998, the inspectors' final report listed large quantities of chemical and biological weapons material that Iraq had not shown to be destroyed. In his September 12 speech to the UN, President Bush said it was unreasonable to believe that Saddam had quietly performed the required dismantlement and destruction *after* stopping the inspections. It was indeed unreasonable to believe that—though it may have been true.

Where was the NIE correct and where was it incorrect? When inspectors from the CIA-led Iraq Survey Group (ISG) entered the country after Saddam's overthrow, they found a "far from permissive" environment, with "threats and attacks" against their own teams and against Iraqi personnel, and evidence of ongoing "dispersal and destruction of material and documentation related to weapons programs." As the official Duelfer Report made clear, the Iraq Survey Group failed to find evidence to support two of the intelligence community's key prewar assessments: that Iraq was maintaining substantial chemical and biological weapons *stockpiles*, and that Iraq's nuclear weapons program was *active* rather than dormant. But—in spite of Iraq's systematic efforts at concealment—the inspectors found ample evidence of Saddam's ability to resume these weapons programs, once Saddam had succeeded in getting the sanctions lifted.

The Duelfer Report (presenting the findings of the Iraq Survey Group) gives this snapshot:

- **[A]fter 1996 Iraq still had a significant dual-use capability—some declared [to the UN inspectors]—readily useful for BW if the Regime chose to use it to pursue a BW [biological weapons] program. Moreover, Iraq still possessed its most important BW asset, the scientific know-how of its BW cadre.**
- **Saddam wanted to recreate Iraq's WMD capability—which was essentially destroyed in 1991—after sanctions were removed and Iraq's economy stabilized, but probably with a different mix of capabilities to that which previously existed. Saddam aspired to develop a nuclear capability in an incremental fashion, irrespective of international pressure and the resulting economic risks.**

- **ISG judges that Iraq maintained the expertise and equipment necessary for R&D of bacteria, fungi, viruses, and toxins that could be used as BW agents up until Operation Iraqi Freedom (OIF) in March 2003. . . . A definitive conclusion is impossible, but, based on the available evidence, *ISG concludes that Iraq intended to develop smallpox and possibly other viral pathogens . . . as potential BW weapons.***

In other words, the Iraq Survey Group team concluded that Saddam had retained the ability to produce chemical and biological weapons rapidly (within a month or two). In the 1990s he had shut down factories dedicated solely to making such weapons, replacing them with *"dual-use" facilities* capable of producing both civilian products and chemical or biological weapons. That gave him deniability if inspections ever started up again, as Saddam evidently expected they would. The Iraq Survey Group also found that Saddam had the *intention* to revive Iraq's chemical and biological weapons programs once the sanctions were ended. He had preserved the necessary teams of technicians, who would be the key to reviving the programs quickly. The Iraq Survey Group also reported on a connection between Iraq's active chemical weapons research and the Iraqi intelligence agency:

ISG uncovered information that the Iraqi Intelligence Service (IIS) maintained throughout 1991 to 2003 a set of undeclared covert laboratories to research and test various chemicals and poisons, primarily for intelligence operations.

Similarly, the inspectors reported the Iraqi regime's intention to restart the nuclear weapons program, which it had suspended:

Nevertheless, after 1991, Saddam did express his intent to retain the intellectual capital developed during the Iraqi Nuclear Program. Senior Iraqis—several from the Regime's inner circle—told ISG [Iraq Survey Group] they assumed Saddam would restart a nuclear program once UN sanctions ended.

Several former senior regime officials also contended that nuclear weapons would have been important—if not central—components of Saddam's future WMD force.

Accordingly, the regime prevented scientists from the former nuclear weapons program from leaving either their jobs or Iraq. They were also kept actively working:

> **Saddam directed a large budget increase for IAEC [Iraqi Atomic Energy Commission] and increased salaries tenfold from 2001 to 2003. He also directed the head of the IAEC to keep nuclear scientists together, instituted new laws and regulations to increase privileges for IAEC scientists and invested in numerous new projects.**

The Iraq Survey Group did not assess the probable time period necessary to produce a nuclear weapon. Whatever that period, it would be cut substantially if Iraq obtained fissile material from an outside supplier, such as North Korea, rather than trying to produce the fissile material itself. The CIA had provided an estimate that Iraq would require less than a year to produce a nuclear device using imported fissile material: "If Baghdad acquires sufficient fissile material from abroad it could make a nuclear weapon within several months to a year." That estimate is consistent with more recent research by a Harvard expert on nuclear terrorism, who concluded that a terrorist group with some expertise, and with imported fissile material, could produce a nuclear bomb in less than a year.

Up until the start of Operation Iraqi Freedom, Iraq was importing other prohibited material and equipment (but not fissile material, as far as we know) from a number of outside suppliers, including North Korea. The Iraq Survey Group confirmed in detail the Administration's prewar concerns about Iraq's illicit procurement of weapons and missile components, noting that Saddam's international suppliers "shifted in the 1998 time-period from former-Soviet and Arab states to some of the world's leading powers, including members of the UNSC [UN Security Council]." Iraq, moreover, had ample financial resources (thanks to diverted Oil-for-Food funds). The possibility that Saddam would acquire fissile material from one or another of its suppliers was a serious and compelling concern.

For many readers, this information about Iraq's "dual-use" production plants, illicit importation of weapons components, and cadres of WMD experts may come as a surprise. The public's impression of the Duelfer Report on these matters was shaped by news media headlines to the effect that "nothing was found." Those headlines were misleading (one might even say fundamentally false), because the ISG found substantial WMD capabilities in Iraq, including personnel, materiel, facilities, and intentions—but not the stockpiles of the weapons themselves.

This is not to deny the gravity of the intelligence errors. It was a serious mistake for the CIA to assert that it would find chemical and biological weapons stockpiles and an actively running nuclear weapons program in Iraq. It was proper for the President, Congress, and others to ask why Administration officials did not challenge the CIA's conclusion more aggressively.

The short answer is that the CIA's findings on Iraqi weapons stockpiles were *believable.* Saddam had killed thousands of Iranians and Iraqi Kurds using chemical weapons during the 1980s. In March 1991, he used chemical weapons "to help put down a Shi'a rebellion" in southern Iraq. After the Gulf War, cease-fire arrangements required Saddam to destroy his WMD programs and to demonstrate he had done so, but he acted as if he were retaining them: impeding the UN inspectors' work, giving them false information, blocking their movement, and eventually causing them to walk out altogether. Even after the Security Council replaced UNSCOM with the weaker UNMOVIC, and promised to reward cooperation by lifting sanctions, Saddam refused to cooperate. Given Saddam's intense interest in ending the sanctions, it was sensible to assume that Iraq *appeared* to have retained its proscribed weapons because it *actually* had retained them. Citing the Iraq Survey Group report, the Silberman-Robb report provides this concise account of the intelligence quandary:

> **Iraq's decision to abandon its unconventional weapons programs while simultaneously hiding this decision was, at the very least, a counterintuitive one. And given the nature of the regime, the Intelligence Community can hardly be blamed for not penetrating Saddam's decisionmaking process. In this light, it is worth noting that Saddam's fellow Arabs (including, evidently, his senior military leadership as well as many of the rest of the world's intelligence agencies and most inspectors) also thought he had retained his weapons programs. . . .**

In private conversations that were intercepted by U.S. intelligence, Iraqi officials spoke as if Saddam continued to possess WMD. Even Iraqi generals believed he did. In the fall of 2002, the Iraqi military conducted exercises in chemical protective gear—but not because they thought the U.S.-led coalition was going to use chemical weapons. Every serious intelligence agency in the world—including those of our European allies, Russia, and others—believed that Iraq had WMD. UN officials believed it. And, of course, the CIA believed it. If Saddam had destroyed his stockpiles, we assumed he would have been able to show proof. As UNMOVIC's Hans Blix commented: "[P]roducing mustard gas is not like producing marmalade. You keep track of how much you make and what happens to it."

In the end, there are only three possible explanations for the failure to find the WMD materiel that had been catalogued in detail by UNSCOM. Saddam might have destroyed it, he might have hidden it in Iraq, or he might have transferred it out of Iraq. To this day, we do not know for sure which explanation is correct.* The Iraq Survey Group concluded that Saddam "probably" destroyed his biological weapons:

> **ISG judges that in 1991 and 1992, Iraq *appears* to have destroyed its undeclared stocks of BW weapons and *probably* destroyed remaining holdings of bulk BW agent. However ISG *lacks evidence to document complete destruction.* Iraq retained some BW-related seed stocks *until their discovery after Operation Iraqi Freedom* (OIF).**

One hopes that someday the world will get to the bottom of this. As wrong as it was for the October 2002 National Intelligence Estimate to declare categorically that Iraq had chemical and biological weapons, it was also wrong for journalists, legislators, and others to assert that U.S. weapons investigators "found nothing" in Iraq. The Iraq Survey Group confirmed that President Bush had grounds for viewing Iraq's WMD capabilities as a compelling threat. The CIA's unsupportable statements about Iraqi stockpiles and WMD activity did not justify critics in making unsupportable pronouncements of their own, to the effect that Saddam had no WMD ambitions or capabilities.

If Saddam had nothing to hide, why did he defy the UN inspectors and keep Iraq under the hated sanctions? Why did he risk a U.S. military attack to overthrow him? After Saddam's overthrow, some answers began to emerge from months of interviews that U.S. officials conducted in Iraq with captured former high-ranking Iraqi civilian and military leaders, including Saddam himself, Foreign Minister Tariq Aziz, Ali Hassan "Chemical Ali" al-Majid, and others. The answers provide a window on the weird perceptions of the Iraqi tyrant.

Saddam, it seems, didn't want to store WMD that UN inspectors might find if they should ever return to Iraq. Yet he was intent on *appear-*

---

*Lieutenant General James R. Clapper, head of the National Geospatial-Intelligence Agency during the Iraq war, has been quoted as suggesting that some material had been transferred to Syria: "[S]atellite imagery showing a heavy flow of traffic from Iraq into Syria, just before the American invasion in March, led him to believe that illicit weapons material 'unquestionably' had been moved out of Iraq." Douglas Jehl, "The Struggle for Iraq: Weapons Search; Iraqis Removed Arms Material, U.S. Aide Says," *New York Times*, October 29, 2003.

ing to have such weapons in order to frighten Iran and the Iraqi Kurds and Shia, the enemies he had attacked with WMD in the past, and whom he considered the primary threats to his rule. As for the risk that pretending to possess WMD might provoke the United States, Saddam discounted it because he considered the United States a paper tiger. Though Americans, in his assessment, might bluster about regime change, they would prove unwilling to take the heavy casualties he thought would be inevitable in an invasion of Iraq (and especially in a march to Baghdad).

This bizarre jumble of self-delusions and too-clever-by-half machinations helps to explain Iraq's policy on WMD. But this is an explanation that our intelligence agencies could not have obtained before Saddam's overthrow, and that would certainly have met with disbelief if they had. Imagine trying to argue before the war that Saddam was only pretending to have stockpiles, even though he had in fact destroyed them—and that Saddam was doing this because he feared Iran but not the United States.

In its review of the prewar intelligence failures, the Silberman-Robb Commission criticized the CIA, and the intelligence community in general, for flawed tradecraft. Contrary to the allegations of Administration critics, however, the bipartisan commission also concluded, unanimously, that there was no evidence of political pressure on intelligence analysts, stating that not a single instance of improper pressure occurred. Almost a year earlier the Senate Intelligence Committee, also bipartisan, had reached the same unanimous conclusion: The intelligence errors were not politically motivated or directed.

Nor were those errors an essential part of the Administration's rationale for regime change. Suppose that President Bush had made the public case for war entirely accurately, in light of all that we learned afterward about Iraqi WMD programs. He would have presented the case essentially as he did—but without using the CIA's incorrect assessment about stockpiles. He would have said that Saddam still *intended* to produce WMD and had preserved the ability to make chemical and biological weapons *within a few weeks*.

In 2002, the idea of U.S.-led military action to overthrow Saddam had broad support across the United States, including in the Congress. Would those who supported the war have failed to support it because Saddam was three or five weeks—or even twenty weeks—away from having the chemical and biological weapons we thought he had? Would anyone concerned about Saddam's obtaining nuclear weapons have been comforted to hear that he had simply put his enrichment program on hold, even though Iraq might still *import* fissile material and produce a nuclear weapon in less than twelve months? Saddam had the technicians and scientists necessary to produce a nuclear bomb—and he retained the intention to do so after economic sanctions were lifted.

The prewar intelligence errors were serious and costly. It is not making light of them to reject the common claim that people who supported the war would not have done so if they had known the truth about the WMD. A clear picture of what we found in Iraq refutes the notion that Administration officials had to overstate the facts about Iraqi WMD in order to make the case for war. The CIA's errors, though sloppy, were evidently made in good faith. And, though the erroneous claims made their way into the Administration's public and private discussions of the Iraqi threat, they did not significantly bolster the case for action against Saddam beyond what the facts, as we learned them later, would have done if correctly presented.

Rumsfeld resolved to give the President a comprehensive list of possible calamities in the event of military action against Iraq. The decision on war was pending, and Rumsfeld, of course, would be associated with it. Weighing risks had naturally been part of the policy-making and planning processes on Iraq all along, but Rumsfeld thought it would be valuable to review all together the major problems we could anticipate, to get them in writing and air them with the President and the National Security Council—well before irrevocable decisions were made. No one asked him to do this, but an exercise of this kind was an important check on the assumptions underlying our planning.*

Rumsfeld had shown me a version of this list back in August, and I had given him some written comments in response. Now, in mid-October, Rumsfeld called a "drop everything" meeting with Wolfowitz, Myers, Pace, and me. As we sat down at his office conference table, Rumsfeld handed each of us the draft of his list of possible problems and disasters, which had been substantially revised since the August version. Highlighting roughly twenty items, it made for grim reading.

After letting the four of us absorb it for a minute or two, the Secretary asked us to sharpen the list, add to it, or otherwise improve it. We spent more than two hours in intense discussion reworking the paper. To relieve some of the tension inherent in the task, I began referring to the memo as the "Parade of Horribles." By the time we finished with our revisions, it had grown by another ten items or so.

*Rumsfeld noted at the end of the memo that it would have been possible, of course, to write a similar memo listing the dangers involved in leaving Saddam in power.

The ultimate version of the Parade of Horribles memo was dated October 15, 2002. Its key political warnings can be summarized as follows:

- The United States might fail to win support from the United Nations and from important other countries, which could make it harder to get international cooperation on Iraq and other issues in the future. We might fail here by not properly answering the question: If the United States preempts in one country, will it do so in other countries, too?
- The war could trigger problems throughout the region: It could widen into an Arab-Israeli war; Syria and Iran could help our enemies in Iraq; Turkey could intervene on its own; friendly governments in the region could become destabilized.
- The United States could become so absorbed in its Iraq effort that we pay inadequate attention to other serious problems—including other proliferation and terrorism problems. Other countries in the Middle East and elsewhere might try to exploit our preoccupation to do things harmful to us and our friends.
- The war could cause more harm and entail greater costs than expected, including possibly a disruption in oil supplies to world markets.
- Post-Saddam stabilization and reconstruction efforts by the United States could take not two to four years, but eight to ten years, absorbing U.S. leadership, military, and financial resources.
- Terrorist networks could improve their recruiting and fund-raising as a result of our being depicted as anti-Muslim.
- Iraq could experience ethnic strife among Kurds, Sunnis, and Shia.

Most of these dangers, Rumsfeld noted, would become more likely and more severe with a longer war, underlining the tactical importance of speed and surprise.* This was one of the factors arguing for a smaller force.

---

*Speed and surprise did indeed prove important: Our troops found that Iraq's bridges and oil fields had been prepared for demolition—but the wiring had fortunately not been completed.

In addition, the memo included these three notable items:

- "US could fail to find WMD on the ground in Iraq and be unpersuasive to the world."
- "World reaction against preemption or 'anticipatory self-defense' could inhibit US ability to engage [in cooperation with other countries] in the future."
- "US could fail to manage post-Saddam Hussein Iraq successfully, with the result that it could fracture into two or three pieces, to the detriment of the Middle East. . . ."

This was a serious and disturbing memo. The concerns it listed included military, diplomatic, and economic matters. The list was more wide-ranging and hard-hitting than any warning I saw from State or the CIA—even though their leaders are widely viewed as the Administration's voices of caution on the war. Even so, this memo did not anticipate post-regime violence of the type that we have encountered in the insurgency—an effort organized, financed, and directed largely by former Baathist officials, in strategic alliance with al Qaida fighters and other foreign "holy warriors."

Rumsfeld distributed the Parade of Horribles memo at a National Security Council meeting and discussed the items one by one. (That meeting was "principals only"—I was not present.)

One of the standard accusations made against the Pentagon's leadership (and other Administration officials who supported the President's war policy) was that we "cherry-picked" intelligence. The term implies that we tried to manipulate the President by highlighting bits of information that argued for war while obscuring or hiding other material. The fact is that Pentagon officials were not in a position to cherry-pick. We did not control the flow of intelligence to the President; he received it daily, directly, and voluminously from the CIA.

But, more important, Rumsfeld and his team did not operate that way. The Parade of Horribles memo was typical of how we viewed our responsibility to advise the President. Had we worried that our views required protection from inconvenient facts, we would not have embraced those views in the first place. Our strategy in interagency debates was to put forward our own ideas *together with countervailing thoughts.* We often heard the comment that we set out the case against our own ideas more compellingly than our opponents did. We figured if we showed how our analysis withstood strong criticism, we could be more effective—not to mention more honorable—than if we tried to keep the President in the dark about relevant facts or analyses. Our approach, as reflected in this important memo, was precisely the reverse of cherry-picking.

Beyond its influence on the rest of the Administration, the work on this list helped guide our own Iraq planning efforts. For example, when the Joint Staff briefed the Principals Committee two months before the war, its presentation of "Some Potential Post-War Challenges" mapped more than a dozen issues of concern, many of them rooted in Rumsfeld's memo. In particular, the list of dangers sharpened our appreciation of the value of tactical surprise and of maximizing the speed of major combat operations. A number of the potential calamities—humanitarian crises, Saddam's destruction of Iraq's oil fields, regional instability, and terrorism by Iraqi agents against the United States, for example—were likelier to happen, and to be more severe, if the fighting to overthrow Saddam were prolonged.

The fact that we anticipated various problems, of course, did not mean the Defense Department or the Administration could avert them all. Even the best planning cannot ensure a problem-free war. Nevertheless, it's fair to ask whether the department and the Administration took the exercise seriously enough and performed all the practical follow-up work that was called for. This is a subject that deserves comprehensive review, building on the several "lessons learned" studies that have already been done by the Joint Staff, the Joint Forces Command, and other military organizations.

On November 8, 2002, the Security Council unanimously adopted Resolution 1441, its seventeenth resolution on Iraq since the Gulf War. The resolution noted that Saddam was still violating previous resolutions, and deplored, in particular, Iraq's failure to disclose its programs for WMD and long-range missiles. Characterizing the Iraqi violations as "threats . . . to international peace and security," the Council declared that it was "determined to ensure full and immediate compliance by Iraq."

Even though the condemnatory rhetoric was tough, Resolution 1441 was not an authorization for war. Rather, it gave Saddam "a final opportunity" to cooperate in a new inspection regime to avert war. The resolution, in essence, gave Saddam an option to wipe the slate clean.

Resolution 1441 noted that the 1991 Gulf War cease-fire had been contingent on Saddam's complying with the postwar resolutions. Saddam's "material breach" of that condition added to the U.S. legal justification for military action. But the resolution's new "final opportunity" provision meant that Saddam's violations over the last dozen years could *not* now be cited as justifying war—if Saddam agreed to enter into a new disarmament scheme.

The first big step for Iraq was to come in thirty days. On December 7, 2002, it would have to declare all aspects of its proscribed weapons programs. An incomplete or false declaration would "constitute a further material breach of Iraq's obligations." Resolution 1441 required Iraq to give the international inspectors immediate and unlimited access for searches and interviews. It spelled out the inspectors' powers. If Saddam were not truthful and cooperative, the inspectors were to report the problem to the Security Council, which would then convene "to consider the situation and the need for full compliance with all of the relevant Council resolutions in order to secure international peace and security." Saddam now had a way to avert war and remain in power. The key was cooperating with the weapons inspectors enough to head off a credible accusation that Iraq was in "material breach" of this new resolution.

Resolution 1441 was silent on who would judge whether a new material breach had occurred; neither UNMOVIC, the IAEA, nor the Security Council was assigned the decision. President Bush refused to make America's right to self-defense conditional on approval by international civil servants or by the Security Council, which was subject to the veto power of China, France, and Russia.

The United States had not insisted that Resolution 1441 expressly authorize military operations against Iraq. As Rumsfeld wrote to President Bush on October 5, we did not need an "all means necessary" provision, and we didn't want to imply that we did. President Bush consented to a second Security Council meeting to "consider the situation" after UNMOVIC and IAEA reported, but he blocked France's effort to require an additional resolution before military action against Iraq could begin.

Resolution 1441 was a peculiar way station. Administration officials praised its strong rhetoric and congratulated themselves on the unanimous vote in the Security Council. Determined to win broad international support for his Iraq policy, President Bush greeted this resolution as a sign of progress. But Resolution 1441 distorted public discourse on the Iraq issue, focusing the debate narrowly on WMD disclosures and inspections—and therefore on whether the inspectors would find contraband stockpiles. And it ignored the logic of the rationale for regime change—that Saddam's record of aggression was so long and so bloody as to be irredeemable. The resolution gave Saddam an opportunity to start a WMD hide-and-seek game of indefinite duration. If he played the game better than the United Nations officials did, we worried, Saddam now had a chance to preserve both his regime and his WMD capabilities.

With Resolution 1441, our diplomatic tactics were putting our strategy at risk. The Iraqi regime had been offered a final opportunity to prove it could be trusted. UNMOVIC and IAEA had been asked to start inspections, though it was unclear when they would finish: If the Iraqi regime withheld full cooperation, who would declare the inspections over? The Security Council had resolved to reconvene on Iraq when the inspection reports were in, and France and Russia were poised to veto any measure that would serve American interests.

The broader strategy was to confront Saddam with an ultimate choice between exile or defeat, but Resolution 1441 now afforded him substantial room for maneuver. We feared he would use it to remain in power.

11
LOSING GROUND ON THE DIPLOMATIC FRONT

If Iraq's weapons declaration of December 7, 2002, had satisfied Hans Blix, Operation Iraqi Freedom might never have begun. Blix (the head of UNMOVIC) was intent on averting war, but the Iraqi information did not reveal enough to allow him to call it acceptable. Though the declaration was twelve thousand pages long, it consisted largely of recycled reports that UN inspectors had found inadequate in prior years. Saddam was evidently determined to keep the world guessing about his WMD capabilities.

Resolution 1441 had created the risk that Saddam could appear cooperative, by readmitting the UN inspectors even while continuing to conceal prohibited weapons programs. Saddam could have provided a more forthcoming declaration and given the inspectors just enough cooperation to win upbeat reports from the inspection agencies—without actually dismantling his weapons programs.

What we didn't know—until after his overthrow—was that Saddam did not consider it a top priority to head off U.S. military action, because he didn't take our military preparations seriously. The United States has a history of presenting, inadvertently, a misleading impression of decadence and timidity. Much like Kaiser Wilhelm II, General Tojo, and Adolf Hitler, Saddam apparently underestimated America's willingness to fight fiercely when provoked.

Saddam's preoccupation with his local enemies (the Iraqi Kurds and Shiites) and his regional enemies (the Iranians) appears to have distorted his view of the wider world. While he recognized that he had problems at the United Nations, he counted on French and Russian officials to help him there, whether or not he entered wholeheartedly into the new inspection arrangements. Saddam calculated, fatally, that he could best hold all his various enemies at bay by hiding the facts about his weapons programs, including information that might have forestalled U.S. military action.

Blix asked for seven weeks—until January 27, 2003—for UNMOVIC to examine the voluminous Iraqi declaration, though it was obvious immediately to Blix and other experts that the Iraqi documentation was not the complete and accurate accounting demanded by the Security Council.* The Bush Administration accepted Blix's timetable because it allowed us time to deliberate on a diplomatic response—and to send more forces to the Gulf region to carry out CENTCOM's war plan, if it came to that.

A key debate within the Administration concerned when and how we should declare this weapons declaration a "material breach" of Iraq's obligations to the Security Council. The declaration effectively rejected the "final opportunity" offered by Resolution 1441: Instead of wiping the slate clean of the many Iraqi breaches of the 1991 Gulf War cease-fire conditions, Saddam's unsatisfactory declaration added yet another breach to his record. But this presented President Bush and his top advisers with a tricky decision. If they publicly declared Saddam to be in breach, would it mean that war was imminent? Or, if this new show of defiance by Saddam did *not* trigger war, what consequences should it produce? And, down the road, what future events might force military action to disarm Iraq?

On December 18, ten days after Saddam's declaration, President Bush discussed it with his National Security Council. Powell led off, reporting that Blix saw gaps in the Iraqi documents. All the Security Council members "recognize there are problems with the declaration," Powell reported, though the British did not want to call it a material breach. "I have no problem calling it a material breach," Powell announced, without explaining why, or what that would signify. Half-stating, half-asking, President Bush responded, "It's clear that Saddam is not cooperating." "That's right," Powell confirmed. The President took this as a grave judgment, and his face showed it. "That's a significant statement," he said. "It means it's the beginning of the end for the guy."

Powell chose not to dwell on that large thought. He brought the meeting straight down to a question of diplomatic maneuvers at the United

---

*Blix reported to the Security Council on December 19 that, based on a "preliminary examination," the declaration "had not provided material or evidence that solved any of the unresolved disarmament issues." Blix, *Disarming Iraq*, p. 108.

Nations, offering thoughts on what UNMOVIC could do in the coming weeks, pending Blix's January 27 report to the Security Council. It could audit Saddam's declaration in detail, Powell suggested. Then he mentioned another option—that UNMOVIC could identify Iraqi WMD personnel and insist on interviewing them outside Iraq, an idea Wolfowitz had been promoting. But Powell really did not take Wolfowitz's idea seriously, as he showed by remarking that UNMOVIC could not "abduct" the Iraqis for interviews.

In speaking of "abduction," Powell was echoing Blix, who had opposed interviewing Iraqis outside their country. Wolfowitz had made the commonsense point that no Iraqis would feel free to reveal any secrets if they or their families remained within reach of the regime. Nor could any Iraqi risk *requesting* to be interviewed outside the country. The UN inspectors needed the power to demand such interviews.* Powell's comment annoyed Rumsfeld. At a later break in the discussion, Rumsfeld said: "Talk of abduction is rubbish because Saddam has an obligation to produce the people for outside interviews." President Bush promptly agreed: "Absolutely."

Powell proposed that, soon after Blix delivered UNMOVIC's formal verdict on January 27, 2003, the United States should make its case to the Security Council that Saddam was not cooperating. (This suggestion evolved into Powell's famous presentation to the United Nations on Iraqi WMD on February 5, 2003.) The United States could then ask the Security Council for another resolution. Resolution 1441 had implied that we might try for a second resolution before any military action against Iraq, but it did not require us to get one. Powell was now advocating that we seek a second resolution.

The Vice President was clearly uneasy with Powell's talk of a second resolution. As a legal matter, the United States did not need another resolution from the Security Council to authorize action against the Iraq threat, and Cheney did not want to imply that we did. Instead, Cheney moved the discussion to the issue of what circumstance might trigger the war. If the United States took military action against Iraq, the war could be under-

---

*Given the practical impossibility of randomly searching or spot-checking a country as large as Iraq, a key to effective inspections was obtaining information from knowledgeable Iraqis. To obtain cooperation, however, the UN inspectors would have to identify the relevant Iraqi personnel and demand that they (and their families) be transferred to UN custody outside Iraq, *without seeking their consent.* There were obviously grave practical problems with this idea. The underlying problem was that Saddam's tyranny was so pervasive and vicious that it precluded useful interviews by the inspectors. Again, inspections were meaningless unless the Iraqi government had a radical change of heart and created a truly cooperative environment.

stood as having either a unilateral or a multilateral legal foundation. The *unilateral* legal basis was America's right to act in self-defense to protect its own interests against the dangers posed by Saddam. The *multilateral* principle was the right of members of the United Nations to uphold the 1991 cease-fire provisions designed by the Security Council. The words "material breach" were essential to this multilateral basis for military action. As we have seen, Resolution 1441 purposely left open the questions of *who* would decide whether Iraq had committed a new material breach, and whether military action was therefore justified.

The Vice President proposed that we call Saddam's declaration a material breach right away—not waiting for Blix to announce his own view. America's stakes in the confrontation with Iraq were so large that Cheney opposed leaving the question to any foreign or international official to decide. Like the President, he clearly considered "material breach" a term of importance. Cheney aligned with Powell on wanting to label the declaration a material breach immediately, but unlike Powell he emphasized the importance of preserving U.S. freedom of action.

Rumsfeld disagreed with Powell and Cheney on quickly calling the Iraqi declaration a material breach. He worried that we would drain the words of significance and hurt our credibility if we invoked the term and then responded merely by calling for another round of UN inspections. I knew he had given these issues hours of thought, discussing them in meetings that included me and two other Policy officials (Rodman and Luti), together with Wolfowitz, Myers, and Pace.

"The term 'material breach' is big," Rumsfeld warned, and we should not use it "unless we are sure of it and we're ready to do something about it." He added: "I'd be cautious about having our words differ from our actions." If we delayed using the term, perhaps until Blix reported in late January, that would allow us time to increase international cooperation (especially in the region) and to send in more forces, refine our planning, and shore up support from the American people.

Powell made clear in the course of the meeting that he favored an immediate announcement of material breach *precisely* to drain the term of its practical importance. He argued that we could not avoid using it because "today's newspapers focus on whether the U.S. will call the declaration a material breach." Powell suggested saying that Saddam's declaration "looks like a material breach," based on Blix's initial assessment, but he argued that "we don't need to trumpet it." (Powell talked to reporters continually, so it was no surprise when a news story appeared that "compelled" him to do something he wanted to do anyway.)

For the President, this was not an issue of how to respond to press inquiries. He pushed Powell: "The question is, is war inevitable after you say 'material breach'?" Powell answered that he thought not, explaining that in any event the United States would have to wait several weeks before Blix's January 27 report.

At National Security Council meetings, the President generally did not talk at length. This time, however, he was more voluble. He turned to Powell: "So war is not inevitable, according to your view." President Bush paused and then stated: "I think war is inevitable." As I recorded this in my notes, it registered that I had never heard the President say that before. I heard it as a momentous comment.

The President picked up on Rumsfeld's point: As soon as we use the words "material breach," he said, the world will expect a serious, prompt U.S. response. Knowing that General Franks preferred not to start offensive operations right away, President Bush worried that "if we escalate the rhetoric, the war drums will beat too soon." The "worst thing," he warned, would be "to declare a 'material breach' and then have to protest that we're not going to war."

President Bush urged everyone to "keep the burden of proof on Saddam." The weapons declaration told us that Iraq was not cooperating in this "final opportunity" to disarm, he observed, and it would be useful to have Saddam continue to make that fact clear to the world. But no matter how openly Saddam refused to work with UNMOVIC, President Bush warned, we should not expect the world to demand action against Saddam: *"That won't happen."*

I took the President's comment as an allusion not just to people who actually opposed war to overthrow Saddam, but also to the various politicians—abroad and at home—who hoped to have it both ways on Iraq. We knew there were officials abroad, like some American political figures, who had reasons to favor Saddam's removal by force but who also had an interest in not appearing to support the war. Confident that President Bush would take action anyway, such officials could silently welcome U.S. military action while preserving their own ability to criticize or condemn it.

Rumsfeld, who was familiar with the interagency work done in the summer on the ultimatum strategy, said the United States could give Saddam "an ultimatum to leave to avoid war." Over the next few days, he recommended, we should say only that Saddam is "beginning to confirm our worst fears, but avoid the term 'material breach.'" Considering the term important and wanting to preserve its potency, Rumsfeld concluded that our "rhetoric should coincide with our determination to go." Yet Powell stood firm: "We should say Saddam failed the test and this is a material breach."

In the weeks since Resolution 1441 was adopted, the implications of the anticipated Iraqi declaration had been discussed and debated throughout Washington. Administration officials viewed the declaration as a sign of how well our efforts to pressure Saddam had worked—of whether he was ready to bow to the Security Council. If so, he could avoid war. If he remained in breach, however, the President's determination was clear: to eliminate the Iraqi threat by force. President Bush wondered, at this National Security Council meeting, whether we had made our reasoning clear to the American people and the world. He foresaw "a debate on whether this is enough to go to war," and he asked the table: "What would you say: Does this mean war?"

The Secretary of State answered, it did not. *"I'd like to take the currency out of the term 'material breach,'* " Powell announced. State had circulated a paper for approval at this December 18 meeting that proposed announcing at the Security Council on the following day that the United States "has decided that this material breach is *not* a sufficient casus belli for us at this time."

This was an amazing comment, given that it had been U.S. policy for months to use our UN diplomacy and the Security Council resolutions—old and new—to intensify pressure on Saddam. If this pressure proved inadequate, there was no hope of ensuring Iraq's disarmament without war. Yet now Powell was saying that he wanted us to declare Saddam's newest—and arguably ultimate—defiance of the Security Council to be a nonevent. If he did not want to use "material breach" to increase pressure on Saddam, why use the term at all? What strategy was Powell pursuing? What was he trying to accomplish?

After Powell's peculiar statement, the President returned to the question of how the world would view our position. "We've got to be sure of ourselves when we say we're going to war," he observed, warning that we had to "get our case solid." Rumsfeld concurred: We needed to "get our position in writing."

The President then reminded everyone in the room that the point of the December 7 declaration was to test whether Saddam would accept the "final opportunity" for peace that the Security Council had offered him. "We've got what we need now," President Bush summed up, "to show America that Saddam won't disarm himself."

The *New York Times* reported in some detail on this debate about the term "material breach." After the National Security Council meeting (it wrote), some officials began considering a blander term, "material omission," as "less likely to precipitate immediate war." Powell and other officials stressed that "the United States would continue to work through the United Nations and support the weapons inspections under way in Iraq." U.S. officials were trying to determine whether other members of the UN Security Council "would be antagonized" if the United States asserted that Iraq was in material breach of Resolution 1441.

The *Times* account reported that "American diplomats determined that there was little support for treating the flaws in the declaration as sufficient grounds to trigger the clauses in Resolution 1441 . . . that could result in a declaration of war," and that U.S. officials "increasingly regarded the shortcomings of the Iraqi declaration as so obvious that Iraq's defiance of the Council would become clear without Washington's having to insist too heavily on it."

Powell was evidently unpersuaded by the National Security Council discussion. In a press conference the following day, he offered an assessment of the Iraqi declaration's inadequacies—using the very language that Rumsfeld and the President himself had argued against:

> **Iraq's response is a catalogue of recycled information and flagrant omissions. It should be obvious that the pattern of systematic holes and gaps in Iraq's declaration is not the result of accidents or editing oversights or technical mistakes. These are material omissions that, in our view, *constitute another material breach.***

Having declared Saddam to be in breach, Powell then called simply for an audit of the Iraqi declaration, supported by "interviews with scientists and other witnesses outside of Iraq" and by intensified inspections inside Iraq. He pledged that the United States would continue international consultations on "how to compel compliance by Iraq with the will of the international community."

Journalists posed some skeptical questions. One observed that Powell had made a point of using the expression "material breach" and then asked if Powell was "in fact, devaluing the expression?"

Effectively confirming that he was, Powell replied, "I think, perhaps, too much has been made of the term." Powell categorized Saddam's rejection of this "final opportunity" for peace as merely the latest in a long string of Iraqi violations of Security Council resolutions: "I don't think we are devaluing the term [material breach]. I think we are using the term to make it clear to the world that, once again, we have a breach on the part of Iraq with respect to its obligations and therefore the spots have not changed." Powell concluded on a more ominous note, however, warning that if "Iraq continues its pattern of non-cooperation, its pattern of deception, its pattern of dissembling, its pattern of lying," then "we're not going to find a peaceful solution to this problem."

The *New York Times* story and Powell's public remarks about "material breach" were ill omens. They showed that the Bush Administration was uncertain about the significance of Saddam's dishonest declaration. They failed to clarify the relationship between Saddam's unwillingness to cooperate and the inspectors' inability to prove Iraqi disarmament. And they reflected a lack of discipline within the President's team. None of this made for optimally effective diplomacy on the Iraq issue. At this important moment, the United States was losing, not gaining, ground at the Security Council.

On November 27, 2002, for the first time since 1998, Saddam allowed UN inspectors back into Iraq. But it was an open question whether Iraq had yet made the strategic decision to cooperate on disarmament. As postwar assessments confirmed, the pressure of Resolution 1441—even buttressed by the buildup of U.S.-led coalition forces—did *not* accomplish our fundamental goal: to compel Saddam to eliminate his WMD programs altogether.

What results could we expect from the UN inspections? For months, my office had analyzed the good and the harm that could come from new inspections. Inspections could help confirm disarmament done in obvious good faith—as they had over the years in South Africa, Ukraine, Kazakhstan, and elsewhere. If the Iraqi regime remained secretive, on the other hand, UN inspectors would not be able to prove or disprove its disarmament claims. The inspectors could catalogue items presented to them, but they could not be expected to ferret out proscribed weapons, facilities, or materiel. Thus, my office warned, "inspections make no sense if Iraq has not made the strategic decision to rid itself of WMD."

There were obvious problems when it came to interpreting the results of inspections in a noncooperative country. If the inspectors discovered incriminating material, the public might feel reassured that inspections were "working"—even though the material found would signify that the country was trying to hide something. And conversely, if the inspections failed to uncover anything, the public might conclude that the inspections were unnecessary—discounting the possibility that the incriminating material had simply been successfully hidden. In the case of Iraq, the inspectors were being asked to do a task they could not accomplish: to get to the bottom of the Iraqi WMD mystery. Suppose they failed to find the material that UNSCOM had previously catalogued. Should that be taken as evidence that it had been destroyed, or as evidence that it was being concealed?

As President Bush pointed out, shortly before the Iraqi declaration, there was little reason to expect cooperation from Saddam or his regime. In a public statement on December 2, the President referred to Iraq's daily attacks on U.S. and U.K. aircraft patrolling the Iraqi no-fly zones and to its complaints about its disarmament obligations: "A regime that fires upon American and British pilots is not taking the path of compliance. A regime that sends letters filled with protests and falsehoods is not taking the path of compliance."

As 2002 came to a close, we considered other ways to make Saddam realize we were serious in demanding the elimination of the Iraqi WMD threat. If UNMOVIC would insist on out-of-country interviews of his WMD personnel, we thought, it could signal toughness while still implying that Saddam could retain his position in Iraq if he carried out the necessary disarmament. If that failed, President Bush could choose the moment to issue his formal ultimatum: Depart Iraq with your family and top officials or face capture and death. The underlying idea was to try everything reasonable to solve the Iraq problem, short of war. We know now that we were trying to square a circle. Rational efforts to influence Saddam were fruitless.

For a dozen years, the United States had supported the Security Council's containment policies for Iraq. They were intended to show strength and resolve and to make it unnecessary to overthrow the Saddam Hussein regime by force. For Saddam, though, our containment policies had signified *the reluctance of the United States to go to war,* despite his many provocations: the massacres of Iraqi Shiites in 1991; the attempted assassination of former President Bush in 1993; the expulsion of weapons inspectors in 1998; and the ongoing no-fly-zone attacks. We were dealing with an enemy who made diplomacy ineffective because he would not take our demands and warnings seriously.

Saddam plainly did not understand the effect of 9/11 on American perceptions and will. He misread U.S. policy, and he remained unenlightened by those subordinates who understood Americans better—no doubt, because he frightened bad news away.

American politicians often accuse one another of being unrealistic. Critics commonly say that U.S. Presidents listen only to information they want to hear—that they blind themselves to unpleasant realities and surround themselves with yes-men. All of this may be true in some cases, and to some extent. But it would be frivolous to compare the paralyzing fear, self-censorship, absurd dishonesty, and closed-mindedness of the Saddam Hussein regime with anything that exists in the government of the United States or of any other free country. Saddam's advisers lived in a state of physical terror. They knew that other officials (and sometimes their families) had been tortured and killed for displeasing the dictator. Anyone trying to understand Saddam through analogies to American politics is sure to be wildly off the mark.

The dysfunctions of tyranny ultimately defeated the Bush Administration's strategy of trying to resolve the Iraqi WMD issue through pressure on Saddam. The Iraqi dictator refused to believe that the United States would overthrow him. His lack of realism canceled out whatever pressure on him we tried to generate.

Following Iraq's inadequate weapons declaration, President Bush had told his National Security Council that war was "inevitable." It now became possible to create a central postwar planning office for the U.S. government.

I had been pushing for such an office for months, sending Rumsfeld lists of possible candidates to head the office—former state governors, retired generals, and others. Rumsfeld's hands were tied, however, because of President Bush's reluctance to be seen planning to manage postwar Iraq while our diplomacy was still aiming to avert war.

It may seem odd for the President to have worried about setting up a postwar planning office, when CENTCOM had thousands of people working on a war plan. War planning, however, is a routine matter in military organizations around the world, and it isn't taken to mean that the President necessarily intends to go to war. But advance planning to reconstruct a country after a war is not routine. The President knew that creating a new office, with a new director, to consolidate the Administration's previously low-key, decentralized efforts on Iraqi reconstruction would be seen around the world as an unusual step—and a sign that war was likely and imminent. Now, however, the President was beyond that worry. He was confident that his good faith and Saddam's bad faith were clearly established.

In late December, Rumsfeld asked me to move forward on drafting the charter for the new office. He had not yet nominated a candidate to the President to launch and head it, but he wanted the foundation laid. Because the office would need people and resources from around the government, not just from Defense, I asked Steve Hadley to draft the charter with me.

As chairman of the Deputies Committee, which ran the government-wide policy-planning effort for Iraq (outside of CENTCOM's planning), Hadley said that the new office should not reinvent the work that had already been done. Officials from State, Defense, the White House, and elsewhere had produced plans on a wide array of subjects, including food distribution, suppression of oil field fires, care of refugees, post-Saddam governance, reform of Iraqi security institutions, and prosecution of former regime figures. This work had been supervised either by the Executive Steering Group, chaired by Franklin Miller of Rice's staff, or by the Iraq Political-Military Cell, led by military officers on General Myers's staff.

The job of the new postwar planning office would be to tie together the existing plans, identify gaps, and fill them. It would organize a team to help CENTCOM carry out the plans, including some of the officials who created those plans—and arrange for that team to deploy to Iraq. Hadley suggested that we envision it as "an expeditionary office." We agreed that its charter should be set out in a National Security Presidential Directive, the government's most formal internal statement of policy, so that the President could order all agencies to support the new office.

Hadley and I did not always agree, but he was always open to argument and I often found his reasoning persuasive. He was steady, good-humored, thoughtful, and never an egotist. Our work writing the directive went smoothly, and Hadley circulated our draft for approval by all the relevant agencies.

Meanwhile, Rumsfeld had been compiling lists of candidates to run the postwar planning office. In early January 2003, he called me down to his office and said he had a good person in mind for the job: retired Army Lieutenant General Jay Garner, with whom he had served in the 1990s on the Space Commission. Garner had experience in Iraq, having helped with reconstruction in the Kurdish region after Desert Storm. (I do not know what process Rumsfeld used—and with whom he consulted—in deciding to ask Garner to serve.) Rumsfeld asked me to call Garner and press him to take the job—stressing that it wouldn't last long, because soon after Saddam's overthrow the President would be sending someone with a political or diplomatic background to become the senior U.S. civilian in the country.

I phoned Garner, introduced myself, and told him that his friend Don Rumsfeld wanted him to return to government service. We discussed the nature of the new office, and I noted that he would report straight to the Secretary (not to me). When I mentioned that he could count on being relieved fairly soon, once the President appointed a former political leader or diplomat, Garner self-deprecatingly said he understood that the President would want "a person of stature." I laughed and protested that *he*, of course, was a person of stature. I explained Rumsfeld's view that the job would at first require mainly organizational talents, such as Garner possessed, and later would require someone with a background in political negotiation. After a day or two, Garner agreed to create and head the new postwar planning office.

President Bush signed the charter for the office on January 20, 2003. The operation became known as ORHA—the Office of Reconstruction and Humanitarian Assistance. Its role has so often been misreported that it is worth a few sentences to get it straight.

As mentioned, General Franks was working under orders that he would be in charge of Iraq after he overthrew the regime. He would be responsible for all basic official functions and for creating new governmental institutions. ORHA's purpose was to serve as a team of expert assistants for Franks—an organized set of civilians to help him fulfill his post-Saddam duties. The ORHA staff would include officials who had been working on postwar planning in Washington over the last year or so. Their various agencies would assign them temporarily to the new office at the Pentagon; and, a few weeks later, the whole group would deploy to Kuwait, where they would prepare to move into Iraq as soon as circumstances permitted.

In the weeks before the war began, ORHA had between a hundred and two hundred people. It was a small office, created in late January 2003 for a war that was to begin in mid-March. Although Garner reported directly to Rumsfeld while at the Pentagon, he and his team would become part of CENTCOM as soon as they deployed to Kuwait. Franks put ORHA under Lieutenant General David McKiernan, CENTCOM's land component commander.

In his book *My Year in Iraq*, L. Paul Bremer explained ORHA incorrectly. Before the Iraq ground war started, he wrote, "responsibility for 'post-hostility operations' had been removed from General Tommy Franks and assigned to the Pentagon's new Office of Reconstruction and Humanitarian Assistance, ORHA." But that was not the case. Rumsfeld would never have considered taking the responsibility for postwar operations away from Franks and his huge CENTCOM organization. ORHA was created to become part of CENTCOM and to help it in Phase IV planning and operations, not to supplant it in any way.

Everyone knew it would be difficult for ORHA to play even this limited role. There was only a short time to get this ad hoc group of civilians to work together as a team. Interagency teamwork is a challenge under the best of circumstances, not least because different team members have different bosses, loyalties, and incentives. It was a famously arduous task to get members of the army, for example, to work jointly with members of the air force. It took half a century after World War II to achieve even relatively low levels of interservice "jointness" among U.S. military personnel. Promoting interagency civilian jointness would be harder, and getting the new ORHA civilian staff to mesh smoothly with our military forces in-theater would be harder still.

This was a problem that had burdened U.S. government stability and reconstruction operations throughout the twentieth century. It was not one that could be solved quickly. ORHA might have been somewhat more capable if it had been created in October rather than January, but probably not much. It would have been a great deal better if the U.S. government had created ORHA ten, twenty, or thirty years ago—for reconstruction efforts in Vietnam, or Haiti, or Bosnia, or Kosovo. For decades, our efforts to rebuild war-ravaged countries have suffered from the lack of a standing capability in this field. In case after case, we simply made do, and we did that again in Iraq.

Rumsfeld thought it would help to put ORHA in the hands of former generals, who knew how combatant commands worked. They had the management and leadership skills to create ORHA quickly, and they might be able to integrate the new office into CENTCOM without excessive friction. It was a sensible idea, given that the U.S. government lacked permanent institutions for large-scale, complex stability and reconstruction operations. But it was not a success.

Even with decades of military service, General Jay Garner found it difficult during his time at ORHA to obtain the support he needed from CENTCOM. I was surprised to receive several calls from him, while he was still based in Kuwait, asking for my help in obtaining needed transport or equipment. As a civilian Pentagon official, I was not in a position to resolve such matters. Rumsfeld, who—at least technically—was entitled to instruct Franks on how to use his resources, wasn't about to start micromanaging the deployment of trucks. The hoped-for integration between ORHA and CENTCOM never happened on the ground. Each of the organizations always referred to the other as "them."

The Administration was now in agreement: The United States would make a formal presentation on the Iraqi threat at the UN Security Council, to be delivered perhaps by the U.S. Ambassador to the United Nations. The task of preparing the case fell to the CIA. Deputy Director John McLaughlin wrote a draft presentation. He came to Rumsfeld's office and walked several of us through the presentation, focusing exclusively on weapons of mass destruction. The Secretary said little during the meeting, but after McLaughlin and his CIA colleagues left,

Rumsfeld told Wolfowitz and me that the presentation struck him as surprisingly thin—not at all compelling.

Given the (literally) thousands of intelligence reports we had all seen on WMD and other Iraqi threats, we asked one another why McLaughlin's briefing was so weak. Did the CIA lack solid intelligence, or had McLaughlin simply not pulled it together effectively? We still weren't aware of how few sources the CIA had on Iraq and how sparse its information was—disabilities that became known to policy officials and the rest of the world only after Saddam's overthrow, when the Senate Intelligence Committee and the Silberman-Robb Commission undertook their investigations of Iraq-related intelligence mistakes on WMD.*

In its 2005 report, the Commission said that the intelligence community had "erred in failing to highlight its overwhelming reliance on [a single source] for its BW [biological weapons] assessments":

> **The presentation of the material as attributable to 'multiple sensitive sources,' however, gave the impression that the support for the BW assessments was more broadly based than was in fact the case. A more accurate presentation would have allowed senior officials to see just how narrow the evidentiary base for the judgments on Iraq's BW programs actually was.**

In the name of protecting sources and methods, the CIA and other intelligence agencies did not allow policy makers much information about the number of agents they had operating in an area, or the nature or degree of confirmation they had for particular reports or assessments. As a result, our ability to judge the soundness of their conclusions was severely limited.

Rumsfeld asked me to sketch out a better way to present the CIA's material. I worked on this with my staff, but our effort came to naught when the President decided that Powell should make the case at the United Nations. The Secretary of State took personal charge of the preparations, working on the speech in collaboration with Tenet and Rice. Defense officials were not part of the process.

Cheney and his staff, supported by Wolfowitz and other Defense officials, urged Powell to balance his presentation fairly evenly among three

---

*The CIA's errors on WMD were effectively the opposite of those on the Iraq–al Qaida links. Whereas CIA analysts downplayed and even ignored evidence pointing to the possibility of past or future cooperation with al Qaida, they tended to overstate the evidence pointing to ongoing WMD production.

topics: *terrorism, human rights,* and *weapons of mass destruction.* Powell, however, chose to talk mainly about WMD. He referred admiringly to Adlai Stevenson's 1962 appearance before the Security Council, where shocking reconnaissance photos were used to prove the recent Soviet deployments of missiles in Cuba. Powell thought he could produce an Adlai Stevenson effect by revealing detailed intelligence information. This was a mistake that would have far-reaching consequences.

It bears recalling that in the October 15, 2002, Parade of Horribles memo, Rumsfeld noted the risk that we might not find WMD in Iraq. Powell might have shown similar caution. He did not have to focus so dramatically on specific CIA findings on WMD. He could have chosen to discuss the broad range of threats Saddam posed, setting out the general historical basis for our concerns about those threats. Instead, the case he made relied heavily on intelligence-based particulars—leaving us open to devastating attacks if those particulars turned out to be wrong.

Even as Powell was preparing his remarks, Hans Blix delivered his report on the inspections program and the Iraqi WMD declaration. "Iraq appears not to have come to a genuine acceptance—not even today—of the disarmament which was demanded of it and which it needs to carry out to win the confidence of the world and to live in peace," the UNMOVIC director told the Security Council on January 27, 2003. While noting that Iraq was cooperating in some areas, Blix criticized the weapons declaration: "Regrettably, the [declaration] does not seem to contain any new evidence that would eliminate the questions or reduce their number." He went on to cite particular discoveries by UNMOVIC, including chemical rocket warheads, prohibited types of missiles, and indications of undeclared work on chemical and biological weapons. The *New York Times* called the Blix report "a grim 15-page catalogue."

As Blix put it, Iraq had continually rejected the Security Council's demand for "declare and verify" and "too often turned it into a game of 'hide and seek.' " That game kept anyone from knowing what weapons Iraq had. Blix understood that the key question now was how to deal with the resulting uncertainties. He said that the Iraqis "are fond of saying that there are no proscribed items and if no evidence is presented to the contrary they should have the benefit of the doubt." UNMOVIC presumed neither that there were proscribed items and activities in Iraq, nor that there were not. It was up to Iraq to provide evidence and "full transparency," Blix commented.

On the day Blix released his report, Powell effectively addressed this burden-of-proof issue at a news conference: "The issue is not how much more time the inspectors need to search in the dark. It is how much more time Iraq should be given to turn on the light and to come clean. . . . Iraq's time for choosing peaceful disarmament is fast coming to an end."

On February 5, two months after Iraq's weapons declaration, Colin Powell made his memorable presentation to the UN Security Council on the threat from the Saddam Hussein regime. Using audio- and videotape as well as slides, Powell spoke to the Council for almost an hour and a half, describing Iraq's biological, chemical, nuclear weapon, and missile programs, and its links to terrorism. Sitting right behind Powell, prominently onscreen in the live television broadcast, was CIA Director George Tenet, who had collaborated with Powell on the presentation. Powell's speech drew on the Blix report, supplemented with materials provided by the CIA. (Britain's Foreign Minister, Jack Straw, supported Powell with formal remarks at the same session, declaring, "There is only one possible conclusion to all of this, which is that Iraq is in further material breach as set out in UNSCR 1441.")

In his UN speech, Powell reminded listeners of Iraq's burden of proof: "This Council placed the burden on Iraq to comply and disarm, and not on the inspectors to find that which Iraq has gone out of its way to conceal for so long. Inspectors are inspectors; they are not detectives." He elaborated on why Iraq had the duty to prove its disarmament and why uncertainties caused by Iraqi bad faith should not be allowed to work in Saddam's favor:

> **When [the inspectors] searched the home of an Iraqi nuclear scientist, they uncovered roughly 2,000 pages of documents. . . . Some of the material is classified and related to Iraq's nuclear program.**
>
> **Tell me, answer me: Are the inspectors to search the house of every government official, every Ba'ath Party member and every scientist in the country to find the truth, to get the information they need to satisfy the demands of our Council?**

Powell complained that Saddam was concealing munitions as well as documents:

> **At this ballistic missile facility, again, two days before inspections began, five large cargo trucks appeared, along with a truck-mounted crane, to move missiles.**
>
> **We saw this kind of housecleaning at close to 30 sites. Days**

after this activity, the vehicles and the equipment that I've just highlighted disappear and the site returns to patterns of normalcy. We don't know precisely what Iraq was moving, but the inspectors already knew about these sites so Iraq knew that they would be coming.

Saddam's WMD declaration had failed to account for biological weapons material that UN inspectors in the 1990s had identified. Powell pointed out that Iraq declared 8,500 liters of anthrax, although "UNSCOM estimates that Saddam Hussein could have produced 25,000 liters," and that "Saddam Hussein has not verifiably accounted for even one teaspoonful of this deadly material." The key point, Powell insisted, was that the "Iraqis have never accounted for all of the biological weapons they admitted they had and we know they had."

Powell's explanation of the Iraqi threat did extend beyond the issue of WMD stockpiles—indeed, beyond the issue of WMD generally. He cited Iraq's aggressions against neighboring states, Saddam's record of support for terrorists, and the tyrannical nature of the Iraqi regime. "Nothing points more clearly to Saddam Hussein's dangerous intentions and the threat he poses to all of us than his calculated cruelty to his own citizens and to his neighbors," Powell told the Council. Powell's speech gave a picture of the challenge President Bush faced in the high-tension period following 9/11—the need to decide what our country should do about the Saddam Hussein regime. This required weighing problems of various kinds—not only the uncertainties of war, but also the risks of leaving Saddam in power, defiant, resentful, ambitious, aggressive, and capable, even as international support faded for the surviving elements of the containment strategy.

It was possible, therefore, for a careful listener to appreciate that there was a broad rationale for military action. Like President Bush's September 12, 2002, speech to the UN General Assembly, Powell's presentation explained the Iraqi threat, discussed uncertainty and risk, and reviewed the attempts that had been made over a dozen years to handle the danger without resort to war. But the time he spent on these points was brief compared with his extensive comments regarding WMD. And he was speaking at the Security Council, where the center of attention was UNMOVIC and its weapons inspections. On the whole, then, Powell's UN speech gave disproportionate weight to the WMD issue.

Nonetheless, Powell's argument for countering the Iraqi threat did not depend entirely on the bad intelligence. His speech contained enough accurate material that he could have organized it into a serious argument for military action even without reference to any of the information that turned out to be wrong or unproven. (Indeed, none of the points cited above have been discredited.)

Some members of Congress and others who initially supported the war said later that they would not have done so "had we known then what we know now." But much of the rationale for the war—much of what Powell told the Security Council—was supported by information we know now was *correct,* concerning his bloody record, his dangerous intentions, his credible threats, and his ability to hurt the United States. The Security Council's long-standing strategy to contain him was disintegrating, and the world showed no inclination to shore up that strategy enough to make it effective.

President Bush faced a difficult timing calculation. The antiaircraft attacks on U.S. and British patrols might produce a crisis at any point. And in general, Saddam could be expected to get stronger over time, more assertive in his region, and more capable with weapons of mass destruction. If he should someday force a confrontation (by attacking Kuwait, for example), did it made sense for the United States to postpone that fight? How would President Bush justify having allowed Saddam to acquire substantial nuclear or biological weapons, instead of ending the Iraqi threat before the WMD problem matured?

This was a problem President Clinton had called attention to, in the less intense era before 9/11:

> **Now, let's imagine the future. What if he [Saddam] fails to comply [with the UN Security Council], and we fail to act, or we take some ambiguous third route which gives him yet more opportunities to develop this program of weapons of mass destruction and continue to press for the release of the sanctions and continue to ignore the solemn commitments that he made?**
>
> **Well, he will conclude that the international community has lost its will. He will then conclude that he can go right on and do more to rebuild an arsenal of devastating destruction.**
>
> **And some day, some way, I guarantee you, he'll use the arsenal. And I think every one of you who's really worked on this for any length of time believes that, too.**

Finally, even if time were not on our side in *strategic* terms, is it possible that we would have gained an advantage in the *diplomatic* arena by delaying action (as some commentators have argued)? It is a difficult matter to judge. But in the months from December 2002 to March 2003, the U.S. diplomatic position was eroding rather than gaining strength.

As Powell established in his UN speech, the United States was unwilling to give Iraq the benefit of the doubts that Saddam had created through defiance of the Security Council. By violating the Council's resolutions, shutting down UNSCOM's inspections, attacking the U.S. and British aircraft patrolling the no-fly zones, undermining the economic sanctions and pressuring Council members to eliminate them altogether, Saddam was challenging the United Nations. The Council's credibility was at stake—and it was not just Administration officials who understood the gravity of this matter.

Senator Joseph Biden of Delaware, the ranking Democrat on the Senate Foreign Relations Committee, argued that the Bush Administration should take military action against Iraq, but not in the name of preempting Iraqi threats. Rather, Biden insisted, the war should be understood as an enforcement action to protect the standing of the Security Council—specifically, to uphold the cease-fire that the Council arranged after Desert Storm and that Saddam had violated. In a Senate speech on January 28, 2003, Biden said he would choose to act "even if we do not get world support." He reasoned as follows:

> **Saddam is in material breach of the latest UN resolution. Yesterday's damning report by the UN inspectors makes clear again Saddam's contempt for the world and it has vindicated the President's decision last fall to go to the UN. The legitimacy of the Security Council is at stake, as well as the integrity of the UN. So if Saddam does not give up those weapons of mass destruction and the Security Council does not call for the use of force, *I think we have little option but to act with a larger group of willing nations, if possible, and alone if we must.***

Biden called on President Bush to state that "we are not acting on a doctrine of preemption, if we act" but rather "are acting to enforce a UN resolution that is the equivalent of a peace treaty which is being violated by the signatory of that treaty." He insisted: "We have a right to do that and it is the world's problem."

In the more than four years since coalition forces overthrew Saddam, it has become common for war critics to assert that he never posed much of a threat to the United States or to the world at large. Members of Congress—often those interested in obscuring their records of support for the war—have claimed they were somehow misled by Administration officials who advocated war against Saddam. Congress, however, received the same information that the CIA provided to top Administration officials. Moreover, the essential points in the CIA's threat assessments of Iraq were the same during the Bush Administration as they were in 1998, when Congress passed (390–23 in the House, and unanimously in the Senate) the Iraq Liberation Act, which President Clinton signed into law. That act called for *regime change*.

This is why a number of leading Democratic Party figures, no less than Administration officials, spoke out emphatically on the threat posed by Saddam Hussein, especially after 9/11. On September 23, 2002, former Vice President Al Gore warned that "Iraq's search for weapons of mass destruction has proven impossible to deter and we should assume that it will continue for as long as Saddam is in power." Two weeks later, Senator John Kerry asserted: "I will be voting to give the President of the United States the authority to use force—if necessary—to disarm Saddam Hussein because I believe that a deadly arsenal of weapons of mass destruction in his hands is a real and grave threat to our security."

Senator Jay Rockefeller, then the ranking Democrat on the Senate Intelligence Committee, declared, "We must eliminate that threat now, before it is too late." He went on to analyze the problem of "imminence":

> **There has been some debate over how "imminent" a threat Iraq poses. I do believe that Iraq poses an imminent threat, but I also believe that after September 11, that question is increasingly outdated. It is in the nature of these weapons, and the way they are targeted against civilian populations, that documented capability and demonstrated intent may be the only warning we get. To insist on further evidence could put some of our fellow Americans at risk. Can we afford to take that chance? We cannot!**
>
> ---
>
> **Saddam Hussein represents a grave threat to the United States, and I have concluded we must use force to deal with him if all other means fail.**

A year later, however, Rockefeller reversed himself, contending that the question of "imminence" was not outdated—indeed, it was essential. "I just think it's extraordinary," he said, "that a decision was made to go to war, and that we were told by our highest policymakers that there was, you know, an imminent threat." But Rockefeller was right the first time, when he criticized the notion that we could *know* of an attack's imminence. At what point (for example) did the 9/11 attacks become "imminent"?

When asked in the summer of 2004 why he had supported the Iraq war, former President Bill Clinton chose not to slide into revisionism. Rather, he recalled the frame of mind common in the United States in the period between 9/11 and Operation Iraqi Freedom. He reflected with empathy on President Bush's duty to defend the country in the face of disturbing risks of uncertain dimensions:

> **After 9/11, let's be fair here, if you had been President, you'd think, Well, this fellow bin Laden just turned these three airplanes full of fuel into weapons of mass destruction, right? . . . Well, my first responsibility now is to try everything possible to make sure that this terrorist network and other terrorist networks cannot reach chemical and biological weapons or small amounts of fissile material. I've got to do that.**
>
> **That's why I supported the Iraq thing. There was a lot of stuff unaccounted for. So I thought the President had an absolute responsibility to go to the UN and say, "Look, guys, after 9/11, you have got to demand that Saddam Hussein lets us finish the inspection process." You couldn't responsibly ignore [the possibility that] a tyrant had these stocks. I never really thought he'd [use them]. What I was far more worried about was that he'd sell this stuff or give it away. . . . When you're the President, and your country has just been through what we had, you want everything to be accounted for.**

By the time of Colin Powell's speech, then, there was substantial momentum for war with Iraq. The preceding five months had seen dramatic steps in that direction, starting with President Bush's September speech to the UN General Assembly. Yet that same five-month period also saw some political and diplomatic missteps by the Administration that would ultimately deprive the President of the broad support he sought for the war effort.

In October 2002 (less than four weeks after his UN General Assembly speech) President Bush had won a vote in Congress supporting military action against Iraq. The resolution authorized the President to use the U.S. Armed Forces to:

1. **Defend the national security of the United States against the continuing threat posed by Iraq**
2. **Enforce all relevant United Nations Security Council resolutions regarding Iraq**

In the Senate, more than half the Democrats voted to authorize war. In the House, eighty-one Democrats joined nearly all the Republicans in the majority of 296 to 133. Having won a respectably broad base of support at home, President Bush now hoped to do the same internationally. Powell persuaded President Bush to use the United Nations as the main vehicle for U.S. diplomacy on Iraq.

The diplomatic strategy began well. The President's September 12 speech got good reviews from many diplomats as well as editorial writers. The Security Council adopted Resolution 1441, which contained some strong language. Although the United States agreed to compromises to win the Council's unanimous support, Saddam failed to exploit the openings we had allowed him.

But the Administration's UN diplomacy ultimately proved disappointing. Support abroad for the U.S. position on Iraq was stronger in the immediate aftermath of the President's General Assembly speech than it was six months later, when the war started. The main sign of our diplomatic failure was our inability to get a second Security Council resolution. Although we didn't need the resolution, Powell insisted on trying to secure one, but his efforts fell short when France dug in its heels and threatened a veto. The end result was that the U.S.-led coalition started Operation Iraqi Freedom under a cloud—the refusal of the Security Council to approve new authorization-of-force language—amid the contention of a debate that was now focused narrowly on the issues of WMD stockpiles and inspections.

President Bush had urged the United Nations to recognize that Saddam's defiance of the Security Council challenged the effectiveness of the institution itself, as a force for international peace and stability. If the Security Council had acted boldly in demanding Iraq's compliance with its obligations, it would have bolstered the UN's ability to address other threats to international peace—such as the nuclear weapons programs of Iran and North Korea. But the Administration's diplomacy was not up to the task of enlisting international support. The shortfall would impair not only our war effort, but also the chances of preserving the long-term effectiveness of the United Nations.

12

FINAL PREPARATIONS FOR WAR AND ITS AFTERMATH

In the first weeks of 2003, President Bush was moving toward his formal decision on war. At the Pentagon and CENTCOM, planning activity intensified. As General Franks worked the war plan with Rumsfeld, General Myers, and the Joint Chiefs of Staff, Steve Hadley, who chaired the Deputies Committee, directed the interagency planning process on Iraq. The array of new special committees created in the summer of 2002—the Iraq Political-Military Cell, the Executive Steering Group, and several others—remained active, and they were joined by new interagency teams created to develop plans for relief and reconstruction.* General Peter Pace and I held Campaign Planning Committee meetings more or less daily to ensure teamwork between the Joint Staff and the Policy organization on Iraq and other subjects.

---

*The Iraq Political-Military Cell, run by the Joint Staff, linked Washington's work to that of CENTCOM. The Executive Steering Group, chaired by the NSC staff, supervised and channeled the nonmilitary planning, through the Deputies and Principals Committees to the National Security Council and the President. There were also specialized interagency working groups preparing plans for humanitarian and reconstruction operations, energy infrastructure, and coalition coordination. A new interagency team was made responsible for ten sectors: Health, Education, Water/Sanitation, Electricity, Shelter, Transportation, Governance and the Rule of Law, Agriculture and Rural Development, Telecommunications, and Economic and Fiscal Policy.

The goal of all this planning, of course, was to anticipate problems and devise ways to avoid or manage them. We drew on Rumsfeld's October "Parade of Horribles" memo, adding new lists of possible challenges, pitfalls, and disasters.

The Iraq planning we did in Washington generally involved strategic or policy issues: whether to recognize an Iraqi provisional government; how to preserve Iraq's territorial integrity; how to deter WMD use against coalition forces. But we sometimes also addressed operational matters. The line between policy and operations work was not always obvious and usually did not matter.

On one occasion, however, the distinction did matter—as I understood too late. This occurred when my office developed advice for CENTCOM on maintaining civil order in post-Saddam Iraq.

It was clear that Saddam's overthrow would convulse Iraq. The Baath Party's rule had been severe, its reach pervasive; we knew its removal would leave a large hole in the fabric of Iraqi society. Beyond the challenges of filling the need for governmental power, we worried about social upheaval and large-scale violence. In our planning papers, we warned of violence between Shia and Sunnis, between Arabs and Kurds, and between poor and rich in the cities—all of which might be aggravated by Iraq's neighbors.

Rumsfeld and Myers had directed Franks to plan for the restoration of civil order in the aftermath of Saddam's overthrow. A December 19, 2002, modification of the war-planning order told Franks to "conduct planning for the transition of operations in Iraq from decisive combat through the post-hostilities restoration of Iraq." Franks was instructed to plan "for the disarming, demobilizing, and re-shaping of the Iraqi military to a force capable of defending Iraq, accountable to civilian authority and not a threat to Iraqi citizens or regional states," and to identify forces required to provide security throughout Iraq and to defend against external threats and "the threat of internal groups hostile to US and coalition forces."

I took particular interest in this portion of CENTCOM's order because of an experience I had had in 1995, when, as a private citizen, I spent nearly a week at Wright-Patterson Air Force Base informally advising the Bosnian Muslims at the Dayton peace talks.*

During much of my time at Dayton, I tried to persuade U.S. and European officials to assign constabulary forces to handle key stabilization tasks in Bosnia. Even though the peace accords assumed that such tasks

---

*The Clinton Administration had gathered the Bosnian Muslims, Serbs, and Croats for the Dayton talks—in an effort to end the war launched by the Serbs to prevent

would be performed, the diplomatic sponsors had no intention of deploying police units to do them. I saw this "force gap" as a major obstacle to securing peace in Bosnia. In a November 1995 memo to various U.S. officials, I argued that Bosnia's need for police forces "cannot be met by local manpower." The situation called for forces committed "to protecting returning refugees, deterring attacks against other civilians and securing the election process." If external forces weren't doing the job, "there is danger that outrages or provocations will create pressure for [foreign military peacekeepers] to perform the necessary police functions"—but those military peacekeepers were "not well-suited to the task and both the U.S. Joint Chiefs of Staff and [NATO] have made it clear that they do not want [those peacekeepers] succumbing to 'mission creep.'"

The officials I spoke with at Dayton generally agreed that a couple of thousand constabulary forces would be better than ten times that number of additional *military* peacekeepers. But they explained that neither the United States nor the Europeans had such police forces available to send to Bosnia.

Eight years later, this Dayton experience came to mind as I heard Franks brief the evolving versions of his Iraq war plan. I asked a member of my staff, Christopher Lamb,* to prepare a paper on constabulary forces and the establishment of civil order after Saddam's overthrow. A thoughtful analyst, with technical skill and experience directly relevant to the task, Lamb worked with me to produce a fourteen-page analysis and proposal

---

Bosnian independence. U.S. Assistant Secretary of State Richard Holbrooke invited former Assistant Secretary of Defense Richard Perle and me (as Perle's former deputy) to help the Bosnian Muslims develop their responses to various proposals, in particular regarding the international stabilization force. (Perle and I had been outspoken supporters of the Bosnian Muslims during the grim period when Serb forces were pushing past ineffectual UN peacekeepers and massacring Muslim civilians by the thousands.)

Perle spent two or three days in Dayton; I stayed nearly a week. We saw the Muslims as victims not only of their direct murderers, but of the wrongheaded policies and cowardice of their fellow Europeans, the UN, and, for quite a while, the U.S. government. We had criticized the George H. W. Bush and Clinton Administrations on Bosnia, especially for their arms embargo policy, which deprived Bosnian Muslims of the means to defend themselves as the Serbs attacked them. But we supported the Clinton Administration's peace efforts, so we wanted to help Holbrooke succeed. See, generally, Richard Holbrooke, *To End a War* (New York: Random House, 1998).

*Lamb worked on Bosnia policy in the mid-1990s; I had first met him in that connection. Now he was a Deputy Assistant Secretary of Defense, overseeing war plans for my Policy organization.

for CENTCOM on the challenges of "maintaining public order" in Iraq. The resulting paper contained an unusual amount of planning detail for a Policy office product, reflecting the topic's importance and our concern that CENTCOM had not fully addressed the matter in its operational plans.

Our starting point was the CIA's assessment that the Iraqi police force would continue to function after Saddam's ouster. Most Iraqi policemen would remain on the job, the CIA projected, because they were professional and not viewed by Iraqis as an instrument of Baathist repression. In the run-up to the war, CIA officials made this case in several papers and briefed it to the Deputies Committee at least twice. CENTCOM planners relied on the CIA's assessment in calculating troop levels for the Iraq war, assuming that large numbers of Iraqi police would be available to maintain public order after regime change.

The notion that the police in a blood-soaked police state would enjoy a popular reputation for professionalism sounded wrong to me. I knew that Wolfowitz and Libby shared my skepticism, but we had no hard information contradicting the CIA on the point. My office did not challenge the CIA assessment head-on; rather, we hoped CENTCOM planners would view the CIA assessment critically. To persuade those planners to listen to us, we first tried to establish some common ground.

Accordingly, we began our public order proposal by observing that a force of tens of thousands of Iraqi police could "be of assistance" after Saddam's ouster—"if it is properly coopted." At the same time, we stressed that the U.S. government had "scant intelligence" on the Iraqi National Civil Police, and we questioned whether CENTCOM would be able to use those police when the time came.

With a relatively small invasion force, we suggested, CENTCOM had good reason to *try* to use the Iraqi police. We proposed ways to increase chances for cooperation, urging that U.S. forces dedicate personnel for a "Quick Reaction Force to quell disorder in physically unoccupied areas" and give that force "high priority for scarce Civil Affairs, Linguist, PSYOP [psychological operations], Military Police, Non-lethal Weapons, and mobility capabilities." Finally, we questioned whether CENTCOM was adequately addressing public order issues in its information operations and public affairs plans.

We warned about rioting, looting, sectarian fights, and other types of civil disorder, which could undermine military success:

- **Historically, the U.S. has struggled with reestablishing and maintaining public order and safety during and after military**

> **operations. Civil disturbances, looting, and ethnic violence have marred operations in the past.**
> - **Acts of disorder and civil disobedience increase humanitarian assistance requirements, expose U.S. forces to greater risk, and ultimately detract from the success of the operation. . . .**

These dangers were so great, we stated, that we could "win the war but lose the peace."

In his paper, Lamb expressed concern that "maintaining order in Iraq may suffer from lack of detailed planning." The lack of cooperation between CENTCOM and its reconstruction arm was increasingly troubling: ORHA was expecting Franks to provide forces for maintaining order, but CENTCOM "believes these forces have other priorities." Lamb and I supported ORHA's position:

> **Currently the fundamental planning assumption about maintaining order is that swift combat operations will limit large civil disturbances, [but] the same assumption was made in Operation JUST CAUSE in Panama and proved wrong; massive civil disorder began almost immediately.**

In Iraq, we foresaw "some degree of civil disorder—ranging from common lawlessness to ethnic/religious reprisals to regime-generated acts that cause major disorder and harm." We pointed out that the ultimate goal of the coalition's operations was to create "an Iraqi state that respects the rule of law." We advised CENTCOM that success would rest "not only on the successful maintenance of civil order during Phases II and III" (the preparatory and major-combat phases of the war plan), but also on a rapid transition to Phase IV (the posthostilities period) and success in reconstruction. We identified three tiers of civil disturbance and the challenges they posed:

> - **"Contain public disorder at minimum levels."**
> - **"Containing public disorder that exceeds the National Civil Police's capability."**
> - **"Containing mass disturbances that exceed the [Quick Reaction Force's] capability."**

Our proposal gave guidance for each tier.

Critics have accused my office of assuming that post-Saddam Iraq would be happy and peaceful, and therefore of neglecting plans to deal with civil disorder. Some critics have charged that we were seduced by

At President Bush's first post-9/11 meeting in the Pentagon, on September 12, 2001, he declared, "We believe we are at war and we'll fight it as such." As the meeting ends, Secretary of Defense Donald Rumsfeld is seen at right, with Franklin Miller (of Rice's staff) and Deputy Secretary of Defense Paul Wolfowitz. In the background are members of the Joint Chiefs of Staff: Generals Jim Jones, John Jumper, Richard Myers (obscured), and Hugh Shelton (obscured), and Admiral Vern Clark. *(Courtesy of the Department of Defense)*

With National Security Adviser Condoleezza Rice, Secretary of State Colin Powell, and Deputy Secretary of Defense Paul Wolfowitz. Rice tried—not always successfully—to create interagency harmony by blending the policy positions of State and Defense. *(AP Photos/Charles Dharapak)*

With Rumsfeld, his military assistant Vice Admiral Edmund Giambastiani (in black jacket), and Deputy Assistant Secretary of Defense Bill Luti (in background)—en route to Saudi Arabia, October 2001. *(David Hume Kennerly/Getty Images)*

At a memorable October 2001 meeting in the Omani desert, Sultan Qaboos bin Said offered incisive observations about ideological conflict within the Muslim world. *(AP Photo/Salim Al Hashli)*

Meeting Russian President Vladimir Putin in November 2001. As our host in the early days of the war in Afghanistan, Putin was eager to impress—but not to listen. *(Courtesy of the Department of Defense)*

With Hamid Karzai in January 2002. Later that year, an Afghan *loya jirga* would make him interim president of post-Taliban Afghanistan. In the background are Paul Wolfowitz and General Richard Myers. *(Robert D. Ward/courtesy of the Department of Defense)*

Taking questions at the U.S. embassy in Kabul, September 2002. After the Taliban's overthrow, the United States maintained an embassy in the capital (under heavy security) but—unlike in Iraq—it did not establish an occupation government. *(REUTERS/Romeo Ranoco RR)*

CIA Director George Tenet with Colin Powell, following Powell's presentation to the United Nations Security Council, February 5, 2003. Although Powell's speech presented a broad rationale for action against Iraq, it emphasized the CIA's intelligence on WMD stockpiles—undermining the Administration's credibility when those stockpiles could not be found. *(REUTERS/Mike Segar GMH)*

At an Iraq war briefing at the Pentagon with Paul Wolfowitz and Vice President Cheney on April 8, 2003, the day before the liberation of Baghdad. Behind Cheney are (from right to left): I. Lewis "Scooter" Libby, the vice president's chief of staff; Ryan Henry, my principal deputy; Paul McHale, the Assistant Secretary of Defense for Homeland Defense. Behind them is Bill Luti, then Deputy Under Secretary of

With Ambassador L. Paul Bremer, whom President Bush appointed to lead civilian reconstruction efforts in Iraq in May 2003. Some of Bremer's key decisions have been criticized unfairly. Nevertheless, his decision to set aside the Iraqi Interim Authority plan in favor of a protracted occupation contributed to the difficulties we faced in Iraq. *(Lauren Haber)*

On my first trip to Iraq, August 2003. In east Baghdad, with the temperature over 130 degrees, a U.S. Army Reserve soldier (facing the camera, in sunglasses) describes how he arranged to provide fresh water for a neighborhood that had never had running water or electricity. That conversation helped inspire my proposal to President Bush to create a U.S. civilian reserve corps. *(Lauren Haber)*

Members of Iraq's Governing Council meet in central Baghdad, Sunday, July 13, 2003. Bottom row: Samir Shakir Mahmoud, Ahmad Chalabi, Naseer al-Chaderchi, Adnan Pachachi, Mohammed Bahr al-Ulloum, Massoud Barzani, Jalal Talabani, Abdulaziz al-Hakim, and Ibrahim al-Jaafari. Middle row: Sondul Chapouk, Aquila al-Hashimi, Younadem Kana, Salaheddine Bahaaeddin, Mahmoud Othman, Hamid Majid Moussa, Ghazi Mashal Ajil al-Yawar, and Mohsen Abdel Hamid. Top row: Raja Habib al-Khuzaai, Iyad Allawi, Wael Abdul Latif, Mouwafak al-Rabii, Dara Noor Alzin, Abdel-Karim Mahoud al-Mohammedawi, and Ezzedine Salim. *(MARWAN NAAMANI/AFP/Getty Images)*

By August 2003 a new Baghdad City Council was operating, and I addressed the Council during my visit. The members expressed gratitude for liberation, but also complaints about deteriorating security and the lack [illegible]ssential services. *(Lauren Haber)*

General Peter Pace and Rumsfeld at a press conference in the difficult month of April 2004. Pace and I spent hours together almost every day, including as co-chairs of the CAPCOM—the Campaign Planning Committee—which integrated work of my Policy office and of the Joint Staff. It was a model of close, candid, and constructive civil-military relations. *(REUTERS/Jonathan Ernst)*

Talking with the president in the Oval Office, just before I briefed the National Security Council on the Global War on Terrorism strategy on May 25, 2004. That briefing evolved into the National Military Strategic Plan for the War on Terrorism, and eventually into a new National Security Presidential Directive. *(White House Photo)*

Ahmad Chalabi's predictions that Iraqis would rejoice when liberated from Saddam's tyranny. On each of these points, the critics are mistaken.

Our assumptions tended to be conservative, not optimistic. And we proposed detailed strategies to respond to possibly severe civil disorder. We did think that Iraqis in general would be pleased to be rid of Saddam—but we never assumed that that alone would ensure order. We worried that the CIA was being overly optimistic in expecting the "professionals" who made up the Iraqi police to remain on the job after regime change.

After Saddam's overthrow, our military learned quickly—and so reported—that the Iraqi police were generally viewed as thugs, not respected professionals. By and large, they were neither willing nor able to stay on in their jobs and maintain law and order. Libby, Wolfowitz, and others challenged CIA officials on this subject, but the CIA stuck to its positive assessment of the Iraqi police. CENTCOM relied on that assessment in making its plans to handle looting, rioting, and civil disorder after regime change. Learning the truth about the Iraqi police should not have been so difficult. It did not require an exquisite penetration of Saddam's inner circle. That our intelligence officials got this important matter so wrong was a sign of how limited their knowledge of Iraq was—and how ready they were to dismiss challenges from policy makers in favor of their own confident opinions.

Because our public-order policy proposal presented ideas that were basically operational—"how-to" thoughts, not strategic policy challenges—we delivered it to CENTCOM, which was responsible for ensuring civil order in Iraq, rather than to Rumsfeld.*

We passed the proposal through two channels. First, a military officer on Lamb's staff gave it directly to a planner he knew in CENTCOM's operations directorate. Knowing that Franks was easily annoyed with advice from Washington, we thought a low-key delivery of the proposal might give it a better chance of acceptance. Our second channel was the Joint Staff. At the CAPCOM, I gave a copy of the proposal to General Pace for delivery to Franks, who received suggestions more tolerantly from Myers and Pace than from civilians.

Evidently, CENTCOM did not adopt the recommendations. After Saddam's overthrow, civil disturbances did indeed become a major problem. No one can say what our proposal, if implemented, would have

*The general topic of police forces did come up in top-level meetings. My office wrote discussion points for Rumsfeld for a National Security Council that included the observation: "The sooner we get international police in Iraq, the better." (Office of the Secretary of Defense, "Megabrief IV Talking Paper," February 26, 2003.)

accomplished. In retrospect, however, I wonder whether we could have focused the general's thinking more effectively on the problem of civil disorder if I had given our plan to Rumsfeld and he had personally handed it to Franks as guidance. CENTCOM might have been better prepared to counter the looting and violence that erupted after it ousted Saddam.

When journalists criticized our troops for not suppressing the looting, Rumsfeld tried to give Franks some cover by making light of the rioting. "Stuff happens," he told the Pentagon press corps. It was not his finest moment, and I wished I had made more of our analysis on the importance of maintaining public order.

Administration officials were similarly concerned about the future of Iraq's army. We planned for the army in post-Saddam Iraq to help with both security and reconstruction. But we knew it would be a challenge to remake that army into an institution suitable for the new Iraq.

On January 21, 2003, Bill Luti's office outlined a plan for "rebuilding the Iraqi military." Luti expected that the decision on "reforming vs. creating a new army" would hinge on how the war was fought, how it ended, and "what happens to the Iraqi military in the process."

CIA officials had told CENTCOM that Iraqi military units might defect to our side once the war started. (Unfortunately, this was another intelligence disappointment.) If Iraqi military leaders did indeed "play a positive role," Luti wrote, then "more of the existing military structure will survive the conflict" and the United States would focus on reforming the Iraqi army and reducing its size. He noted that a "formal surrender by a high-ranking military officer" might help prevent disintegration of the Iraqi military, but that desertions might reduce its size. If whole units were simply to "disappear," on the other hand, then "U.S. emphasis might be on creating a new army."

Luti's plan envisioned eliminating Saddam's secret police and elite military units, such as the Special Republican Guards and the Fedayeen Saddam. Some personnel would be prosecuted for human rights abuses, while others would "retrain in various civilian skills" because "employment is crucial to averting crime and terrorism."

There was nothing ideological or harsh in Luti's proposal. It recognized the desirability of preserving the civilian police, the general intelligence service, and regular army and even some Republican Guard personnel, "after vetting." Luti's idea was to use the Iraqi army ("troops may be used for reconstruction projects"), but he sensibly foresaw that our plan might have to change because our key assumption—that the army would remain intact—might turn out to be wrong.

A few weeks later, Jay Garner produced his own plan for the Iraqi army, which resembled Luti's in essential respects. Garner proposed using the Iraqi army to do reconstruction work, on the assumption that the force would stay largely intact. He intended to reform and "downsize" the Iraqi military into "an apolitical force, subordinate to civilian control." When Garner presented his plan to the Deputies Committee, he was encouraged to use the army as a type of "civilian conservation corps" for reconstruction after Saddam's removal.

Rice wanted the President briefed on Garner's plan at the March 10, 2003, National Security Council meeting. Garner and his ORHA colleagues wrote the slides for the briefing, which stressed that "Iraq is one of the most heavily militarized & armed societies in the world" and that "disarming, demobilizing and re-integrating the current forces & re-shaping the new military will not be a simple or short-term program."

Garner specified that his plan depended on "how much of the Iraqi armed forces and security services will remain intact on cessation of hostilities." Meanwhile, he expected to dismantle Saddam's paramilitary forces (including the Baath Party militia and the Fedayeen Saddam) and the Special Republican Guard. He said he would also eliminate the regular Republican Guard, but retain "some mid ranking/junior officers and some enlisted personnel" for the new army. And he proposed using the regular army as a "national reconstruction force" while beginning "massive demobilization of excess personnel."

Rumsfeld told me to brief Garner's plan at the National Security Council meeting, using Garner's slides. When I made the presentation to President Bush, I highlighted considerations for and against preserving the army. The main arguments for keeping it were its assets—organization, infrastructure, discipline, skilled personnel, and vehicles—and the likelihood that we would need the army for reconstruction work. Moreover, there was the question of what we would otherwise do with the soldiers; putting large numbers of armed men out of work and onto the street would clearly create a problem.

At the same time, however, there were serious arguments in favor of dismantling the army and building a new one from the ground up. Saddam's force was grotesquely organized. It had more than eleven thousand general officers, for example, compared with fewer than eight hundred in the entire U.S. armed forces (though the U.S. military was much larger). Physical abuse by the mainly Sunni officers of the mainly Shiite conscripts was habitual. And the army was corrupt and generally detested among Iraqis for its history of domestic murder, destruction of villages, and political repression. A radical overhaul would be required once Saddam's regime was ousted, and it was far from certain that anyone could actually reform so sick and malformed an institution and give it a professional culture suitable for a new, free Iraq.

Netting out these pros and cons, it seemed to me, was a close call. But Rumsfeld decided to accept Garner's recommendation to preserve the Iraqi army, try to reform it, and plan to use it for reconstruction. That proposal was what I put forward to the President. No one at that National Security Council meeting in early March spoke against the recommendation, and the President approved Garner's plan.

As it happened, the Iraqi military did not stay intact through the war. Much of it was destroyed in the fighting, and much of the rest of it disintegrated. For that reason, when L. Paul Bremer was about to leave Washington for Baghdad to take over the Coalition Provisional Authority in May 2003, he argued that it made more sense to build a new Iraqi army than to try to reassemble and reform the old one. That argument—and how it carried the day—will be recounted in Chapter 14.

We knew that our coalition forces could achieve military victory—that is, the overthrow of the regime. Strategic victory, however, was a larger and more challenging goal that would require us not just to fight against Iraqis, but to work with them to help create a new government, one that would no longer threaten its neighbors, support terrorism, tyrannize its people, or pursue weapons of mass destruction.

There was no controversy among the Deputies and Principals that the U.S. aim was to liberate, not occupy, Iraq. Papers from all the agencies—State, Defense, CIA, and NSC staff—endorsed the principle of liberation, warning that, if Americans were seen as occupiers, we would be inviting guerilla warfare, terrorism, and political instability. "Liberation, not occupation" was the President's own guiding principle, and Rice referred to the concept in all her Iraq policy papers for the top-level interagency meetings.

My Pentagon colleagues and I made the liberation concept central to our Iraq efforts. We judged policy proposals according to whether they would help the United States communicate that it had no intention to dominate Iraq, much less steal its oil. We never tired of remarking that Iraq belonged to the Iraqis and not to us. As much as possible, we wanted to be seen as helping Iraqis rid *themselves* of the Saddam Hussein regime.

The way to implement this policy would be to enter into a working partnership with some Iraqis before the war began. The only Iraqis available to work with us, of course, were the externals—the Kurds in northern Iraq and the exiles abroad. My office looked for ways to get Iraqi externals involved in the liberation of their country. We proposed that they serve as advisers to our war planners and encouraged the U.S. intelligence community to seek information from all the external groups. We developed plans to train Iraqi externals so they could play a useful and visible role in the coalition's combat operations and, later, during reconstruction. Both President Bush and Rumsfeld spoke in favor of a nondiscrimination policy toward all the friendly Iraqi opposition groups.

In our view, the key to avoiding a long military occupation of Iraq lay in developing our confidence in a number of Iraqi political leaders who shared our basic principles and who were ready to assume leadership after Saddam was gone. We had long pushed for a political conference, where Iraqis from all the democratic groups could hammer out constitutional principles for a new Iraq. We had developed a proposal for an Iraqi provisional government, one the United States could recognize soon after Saddam's ouster or perhaps even before. And we argued for putting substantial governmental authority into Iraqi hands as quickly as possible after regime change.

In testimony to the Senate Foreign Relations Committee on February 11, 2003, I listed some ways Iraqis "might play a progressively greater role in administering the country":

- **An Iraqi consultative council could be formed to advise the U.S./coalition authorities.**
- **A judicial council could undertake to advise the authorities on the necessary revisions to Iraq's legal structure and statutes to institute the rule of law and to protect individual rights.**
- **A constitutional commission could be created to draft a new constitution and submit it to the Iraqi people for ratification.**
- **Major Iraqi governmental institutions—such as the central government ministries—could remain in place and perform the key functions of government after the vetting of the top personnel to remove any who might be tainted with the crimes and excesses of the current regime.**
- **Town and district elections could be held soon after liberation to involve Iraqis in governing at the local level.**

And yet, despite this apparent consensus on "liberation, not occupation," every practical proposal to build up the capacity or responsibility of the Iraqi externals would founder, time and again. State and CIA officials routinely opposed, delayed, or mismanaged cooperation with the externals, whether on political, intelligence, or military matters. Intentionally or not, their actions ensured that if Saddam were overthrown, the United States would have to control Iraq—that is, run an occupation government—for quite a while.

Powell and Armitage showed less concern about getting responsibility transferred from Americans to Iraqis than about keeping it out of the hands of the externals. Armitage had argued since at least the early summer of 2002 that the United States would have to run Iraq for a "multi-year transitional period" so that U.S. officials could cultivate a different, "credible" Iraqi leadership. Though the President never endorsed that approach, its adherents were persistent.

Armitage had made a point of his lack of regard for the Iraqi externals when Scooter Libby recommended in January 2002 that State organize a political conference of Iraqi oppositionists. In spite of prodding to get the conference under way, State—in a classic bureaucratic slow roll—managed to delay the agreed-on conference until December. And Armitage's campaign to terminate State's contract with the Iraqi National Congress for the Information Collection Program nearly succeeded, before Steve Hadley arranged to transfer the program to Defense.

CIA officials were at least as antagonistic to the Iraqi externals as was Armitage. For months, they had ignored the invitation of the Patriotic Union of Kurdistan to debrief prisoners (including al Qaeda affiliates) being held in a PUK prison in autonomous northern Iraq. They produced a steady stream of field reports, daily briefs, and longer analyses that impugned the externals' reliability and truthfulness, asserting that they had no "legitimacy" in Iraq and predicting that they would have no political support in the post-Saddam era. These papers belittled the externals in general and Ahmad Chalabi in particular.

These State and CIA officials had staked out a rigid position that lacked substantiation, but their views had far-reaching effects. Although they often failed to carry the day in the Principals Committee or with the President, they influenced decisions in the field. Disdain for the externals became an important factor in the policies of L. Paul Bremer, the civilian head of reconstruction in Iraq. Reflecting the influence of their State and CIA advisers at headquarters, General Franks and his deputy, Lieutenant General Michael DeLong (USMC), spoke dismissively of the Iraqi oppositionists, remarking that giving them military training was a waste of time.

Senior State and CIA advisers are regularly assigned to assist the combatant commands, working daily, shoulder to shoulder, with the military planners. Each combatant command is served by a senior State Department political adviser, or POLAD, and a senior CIA intelligence liaison. These officials understandably exercise a great deal of influence—especially on political-military issues, about which military officers may have little background and no strong views of their own. (In contrast, members of the Office of the Secretary of Defense or the Joint Staff are not normally resident at combatant command headquarters.)

The four-star officers who headed each combatant command valued their opportunities for personal discussion with the Secretary of Defense and the Chairman of the Joint Chiefs, but those discussions were occasional and limited in time and scope. A more detailed discussion of day-to-day operations might have been possible at the staff level, but there was no routine, day-to-day relationship between the staffs at the combatant commands and at the Pentagon.

Rumsfeld properly guarded the chain of command. Ongoing discussions between the combatant commands and the Pentagon at the staff level would have opened up the possibility of reporting and instructions that bypassed the top levels of civilian and military command—practices that both the combatant commanders and Rumsfeld would have opposed. In contrast, as the commanders saw it, the staff-level channels connecting the commands to State and the CIA were helpful without restricting autonomy. When General Pace and I floated proposals to assign Joint Staff or Pentagon civilian personnel to work full-time at the combatant commands, the commanders generally balked.* We get direction from the Secretary of Defense, they replied, but we don't want political commissars at our headquarters.

The makeup of the interagency teams at the combatant commands helps explain why CENTCOM's thinking on contested issues—training exiles, involving Iraqis in our war plans, setting up a provisional

---

*This was important because high-level commanders routinely developed strategic and political-military ideas on their own and directly translated them into military operations. But the ideas of one combatant commander did not necessarily mesh with those of another: CENTCOM views on the role of Turkey in our Iraq policy, for example, did not always jibe with those of our European Command. Another question was whether the combatant commanders were acting under effective civilian control. The Secretary of Defense was the only person who could harmonize strategic concepts across the Defense Department, but even as imposing a Secretary of Defense as Rumsfeld didn't always find this easy.

government—often clashed with the views of the Pentagon leadership. Rumsfeld wasn't shy about imparting his thinking to his commanders, but no Secretary of Defense could contribute daily war-planning guidance—or influence military officers' attitudes—as persistently or effectively as the resident State and CIA advisers with whom those officers were in continuous collaboration.

On countless occasions, State and CIA officials declared that the Iraqi externals lacked "legitimacy" and would therefore have no substantial political support in Iraq after regime change. It is hard to overstate how important this idea was in shaping thinking about post-Saddam Iraq at State, the CIA, and CENTCOM. Someday a serious study may examine how the notion of a great rift between externals and internals took hold within key departments of the U.S. government. Part of the answer must have been the animus some officials felt toward Chalabi. Another part may have been the influence of the Arab leaders throughout the Gulf region, all of them Sunnis and none of whom governed a democracy.

In general, the Sunni elite throughout the region hated the prospect of Shiite political power in Iraq—and, even worse, Shiite power confirmed through democracy. Chalabi and most of the externals advocated Iraqi regime change and democracy (which would mean Shiite predominance in a country that was 60 percent Shiite Arab). That alone ensured that the region's Arab leaders would be hostile toward the externals. They feared and disliked Saddam, but would have preferred to see him replaced by another Sunni general: no Shiite ascendancy, no experiment in democracy.

In January 2003, the Administration was trying to decide whether to encourage the Iraqi externals to form a provisional government as an alternative to a U.S. military occupation. Taking a lesson from our success in Afghanistan, where the United States avoided a military occupation by recognizing a provisional government headed by the Afghan "external" Hamid Karzai, I asked Bill Luti's office to write up the pros and cons of an Iraqi provisional government. That briefing began by noting that the U.S.-led coalition *military force* was to take "initial responsibility" for:

- **Providing security, law, and order**
- **Securing WMD sites**
- **Eliminating terrorist infrastructure**
- **Providing emergency humanitarian relief**

The coalition would install a "Civil Administration" to deal with humanitarian, economic, and civil affairs. To maintain "unity of leadership," both the military force and the Civil Administration would report to the Secretary of Defense through General Franks.

We pointed out that current U.S. policy "has been opposed to creation of a provisional government" for a number of reasons: to avoid interference with a U.S.-led administration; to postpone power struggles among Iraqi groups until several key institutions—an improved economy, a free press, rule of law, and "civil society"—were in place; and to avoid the "perception that [the] U.S. is 'imposing' a government of expatriates." I considered this last concern—pressed most often by State officials—to be valid, but I thought we should avoid the perception of imposing *any* kind of government on Iraq, not just a government of expatriates.

A memo from my staff argued this point directly:

> **We disagree with the State Department's assertion that the external opposition should be treated any differently than newly-liberated Iraqis.**
>
> - **Many external opposition groups have demonstrated their connections to those inside Iraq.**
> - **Establishment of quotas . . . goes against principles of one-man, one-vote, and perpetuates artificial division.**
>
> **External opposition figures who return to Iraq should be treated as full Iraqis and allowed to participate fully in any structures.**

Rumsfeld and his advisers looked for ways to address this whole set of concerns. We thought we could reduce at least some of them if a new Iraqi government—but one with *less than full sovereign authority*—were to come into being right after Saddam's overthrow. Initially it could allocate responsibilities between itself and the coalition, perhaps under an arrangement approved by the UN Security Council. The new Iraqi leaders would then become fully empowered after they had demonstrated a degree of competence, honesty, and ability to win cooperation from other Iraqis.

Rumsfeld considered it particularly important that Iraqi politicians prove themselves in administering certain areas of responsibility before they get independent control over Iraq's formidable military and economic assets. Accordingly, he favored thinking of the initial political arrangement after Saddam's overthrow as an Iraqi provisional *authority* rather than a provisional government.

Through Luti's briefing, we set out the arguments in favor of an authority of this kind: It could help legitimate the coalition's role in governing postwar Iraq, make it easier for us to deal with the United Nations, and improve chances that the new Iraqi leadership would be good for the Iraqi people and friendly to the United States. If we hoped to have such an authority when we needed it, we would have to lay the foundation before the war.

Yet the United States would not get the advantages we sought if the provisional authority were merely an American "puppet." The best approach, we argued, would be to enable Iraqis to run their own country, to show them respect, to encourage them to manage projects (even if they proved less efficient than Americans would be), and above all to avoid doing anything that needlessly validated the accusation that the United States wanted to control Iraq, dominate it, steal its resources, colonize it, and deny the Iraqis freedom.

Our key point was that promptly recognizing an Iraqi authority would help the United States avoid having to maintain an occupation government. An Iraqi authority could "enable Iraqis friendly to us to increase their domestic political standing." We did not want to act as occupiers and thereby "enable those hostile to us to play the 'nationalist' card effectively." If we failed to put Iraqis in charge of their own affairs, we worried that "Iranian-backed and Islamist groups may seek to challenge violently the U.S. presence in order to build nationalist credentials." (Moqtada al-Sadr and his anti-American militia and movement would become, in later years, the sorry vindication of this worry.)

There would be dangers in either extreme—a hands-off approach or a heavy-handed one. If we did not help good people fill the power vacuum after Saddam's overthrow, others would press forward. We also worried that a coup, perhaps in response to international military pressure, might result in the "catastrophic success" scenario we called "Saddamism without Saddam": a threatening regime that would no longer be subject to existing UN sanctions.

Our analysis did not persuade the Administration as a whole to support creation of a *prewar* Iraqi provisional government or authority. But the idea of an Iraqi authority that would make a power-allocation arrangement with our military coalition after Saddam's overthrow did win support within the National Security Council. It evolved into the plan for the Iraqi Interim Authority, which my office drafted, Powell and Armitage tried to delay, President Bush approved, Jay Garner began to implement, and L. Paul Bremer buried.

One of the better resources for Administration officials working on the structure of a post-Saddam Iraqi government was the "Final Report on the Transition to Democracy in Iraq," produced in November 2002 by a group of Iraqi Americans who met under the auspices of the State Department–led Future of Iraq Project. This 102-page paper set out steps for moving from a transitional authority to a transitional government that would produce a permanent constitution and hold national elections for a permanent government. It looked at historical precedents for transitional governments, referring to the Bonn Process for Afghanistan and the government set up by Charles de Gaulle in Paris in 1944. It identified the elements of a bill of rights as well as the necessary executive, legislative, and judicial bodies for the transitional period. The report contained thoughtful discussions of transitional law and justice; democratization and civil society; and reform of the army, of "the law and order structure," and of the judicial system.

The group of Iraqi externals who produced the report was informally headed by the scholar Kanan Makiya, author of *Republic of Fear* and *Cruelty and Silence.* Makiya advised many Administration officials on constitutional and political considerations for post-Saddam Iraq—at State, the White House, and the Pentagon, including my Policy office.

The Future of Iraq Project, which started in the spring of 2002, comprised more than a dozen working groups, mainly of Iraqi Americans. Each addressed its own topic—Democratic Principles, Water, Agriculture, Defense Policy, or Oil, for example. Most of the groups produced a report on reforms in Iraq that might become possible after Saddam was ousted. Though State ran the project, officials from other agencies (including my office) participated, and the reports were shared around the government. This project was State's main connection to the community of Iraqi externals.

Numerous news articles and books have presented a distorted history of the Future of Iraq Project, claiming that it produced a plan for administering postwar Iraq and that the Pentagon's civilian leaders, who were supposedly hostile to the project for ideological and bureaucratic reasons, ordered Jay Garner and ORHA to ignore it. John Kerry used that story in the 2004 presidential debates, and it eventually became so well-established a piece of conventional wisdom that journalists and members of Congress could invoke it without feeling obliged to cite sources or seek confirmation.

The story is false: untrue in all respects. First of all, I was not hostile to the project, nor were the other Pentagon senior leaders, as far as I know. I encouraged people from my office to participate, and we thought the project produced some valuable work.

The "Transition to Democracy" report was one of the project's more important products. Its main observations and recommendations actually aligned more closely with my office's thinking than with the views of Powell and Armitage. For example, calling for creation of an Iraqi provisional authority before Saddam was overthrown, the report said: "To prevent disarray and a repeat of 1991, a temporary Iraqi authority of some sort . . . must be on the ground and capable of operating as soon as the regime begins to disintegrate. Preparations for this eventuality must be made in advance, before the fall of the regime." My office sympathized with that idea; Powell and Armitage did not, and they were instrumental in persuading the President to oppose it. Similarly, the report said that it was "paramount that many thousands of Iraqis, currently in exile, begin training for law and order duties to be undertaken jointly with US troops in the immediate aftermath of a change in regime." My office supported such training; Armitage did not.

Second, the Future of Iraq Project did not produce a plan. It produced concept papers. Bremer makes this point in his book, citing Ambassador Ryan Crocker (of his own staff), who had served as Deputy Assistant Secretary in the State Department bureau responsible for the Future of Iraq Project. Bremer writes:

> **Sometime after arriving in Baghdad, I read press reports about a State Department study on the future of Iraq, claiming that it provided a full plan for postconflict activities in the country. Crocker had been deeply involved in the study, so I asked him if it provided a practical "plan" for postwar Iraq. "Not at all," he told me. Its purpose was to engage Iraqi-Americans thinking about their country's future after Saddam was ousted. "It was never intended as a postwar plan," Crocker noted. When I eventually had a chance to read the fifteen volume study, I agreed.**

The purpose of a plan is to give direction. The Future of Iraq reports, in contrast, often just examined and weighed ideas. The reports sometimes stated a view and then competing views, without attempting to reconcile or choose between them. In my opinion, the main value of such reports was to record the thinking of some knowledgeable people. It is no insult to say that they were not a plan, when they were never intended to be one.

There was another problem with calling the Future of Iraq reports a State Department plan: They were not actually State Department reports. They were the product of Iraqi externals: the Iraqi Americans in the working groups. No one ever refined or adopted them, as representing State Department policy; State's role in the project was simply to host the committees. Ryan Crocker confirmed this when we met in my Pentagon office in early 2005: He emphasized that not even State's Near East bureau (let alone the State Department) had adopted the Future of Iraq papers. Although State shared the reports around the government, no State official ever presented them to the Deputies, Principals, or National Security Council as a State Department proposal or plan for postwar Iraq.

Why, then, have so many news stories and books talked about a State Department plan that the Pentagon rejected? As far as I can tell, the reason relates to a personal rejection inflicted on the project's director.

The Future of Iraq Project was directed by a State official named Thomas Warrick. He made himself a partisan in the factional quarrels among the Iraqi Americans who worked on the project, and word got back that he spoke harshly against Cheney, Wolfowitz, and others in the Administration whose views he opposed.

I recall hearing about one particularly unpleasant incident just after it occurred. When Paul Wolfowitz went to visit with a group of Iraqi Americans in Dearborn, Michigan (on February 23, 2003), he learned that Warrick had urged them to stay away from the Wolfowitz meeting, threatening to exclude them from the Future of Iraq Project. Wolfowitz told me this with disgust on his return to the Pentagon. I had never met Warrick, though I had heard about his quarrels with Pentagon and White House officials and with several Iraqi Americans. Some people on my staff and a few Iraqi American acquaintances of mine said Warrick lacked judgment, that he indulged his personal likes and dislikes without regard for Administration policy. The Dearborn episode supported those criticisms.

Later in February, when Jay Garner was seeking personnel, Warrick got himself recruited to a position in ORHA. I heard Wolfowitz inform Rumsfeld about Warrick. I don't know if anyone else spoke with Rumsfeld about him, but Rumsfeld himself later told me that he urged Garner to un-hire Warrick. Garner did so.

But keeping Warrick out of ORHA wasn't the same thing as tossing out the work of the Future of Iraq Project. Rumsfeld did the former; no one did the latter. Neither Rumsfeld, Wolfowitz, nor I ever told Garner to ignore the project. Warrick had been a problem, but what of it? The work wasn't his—in fact, he didn't even agree with all of it. On the subject of a provisional authority, for example, we knew he lined up with Powell and Armitage, rather than with the theme of the "Transition to Democracy" paper. We didn't equate Warrick with the work, and we knew the Future of Iraq reports contained useful material.

In general, ORHA did not shun State Department people or their work. Garner's top political adviser in ORHA was Ambassador Crocker, who had overseen the Future of Iraq Project at State; Rumsfeld supported his appointment. When we talked in 2005, Crocker said it was crazy that anyone would think ORHA officials had ignored the project, or were ordered to ignore it, given that he himself served as Garner's chief adviser on many of the matters the project addressed. Rather, ORHA openly made use of the work of the Future of Iraq Project: When ORHA produced its briefing on justice and law enforcement, for instance, it cited the Future of Iraq Project paper "Transitional Justice" as one of its key sources.

But the false story that the Pentagon had trashed the Future of Iraq Project's work has become magnified in political debates. The fact is that the project didn't play an important role in the prewar period—not because Defense officials despised it or killed it, but because its reports remained simply *concept papers*. State officials never developed them further—never turned them into plans, or even briefings or memos. In order to do so, they would have had to overcome the fundamental conflict between the project's endorsement of an Iraqi provisional government and the Powell-Armitage view, which favored an extended period of non-Iraqi rule. The detailed recommendations contained in the "Transition to Democracy" report were specifically formulated as advice to an Iraqi provisional authority, which was expected to assume substantial power right after Saddam's overthrow. When the Administration's plan for an Iraqi Interim Authority was scuttled, most of the report's recommendations lost their relevance.

Besides the Future of Iraq Project, the main forum where the externals deliberated as a body was the long-delayed political conference of the Iraqi opposition, which finally met in London in December 2002. The delegates saw this conference as the continuation of a political process that had begun with the opposition gathering in Salahuddin (in northern Iraq) in 1992 and that was revived in the August 2002 meetings that Grossman and I cochaired.

Organizing the London conference was a joint project of the Iraqi externals and the Bush Administration. The idea was to devise a broadly supported political transition for Iraq that would mesh with the U.S. plan for regime change. After delaying the conference for nearly a year, Armitage then tried to exclude Chalabi's Iraqi National Congress, until Steve Hadley told him not to discriminate against any of the prodemocracy opposition groups.*

The three-day conference opened on December 14, with more than 340 delegates attending. They represented a range of opposition groups, including all those who had participated in the August 2002 Washington meeting.† The delegates were diverse ethnically, religiously, and politically, and differed sharply among themselves on many issues. They were able, however, to pull together to agree on a political statement, to appoint a sixty-five-person leadership council, and to decide that the council would meet again in the autonomous region of northern Iraq within a few weeks.

It was clear that certain basic questions would vex the politics of post-Saddam Iraq:

- Ethnic and sectarian discrimination
- The role of Islam—in particular, Muslim religious law as a source of legislation
- Federalism and how the Kurdish regions would relate to the central government
- Oil policy and the United Nations Oil-for-Food program
- Remedying Saddam's "Arabization" policies in Kirkuk and other cities

Each of these issues was debated heatedly at the conference, but on each the delegates succeeded in drafting a resolution that won general endorsement.

The conference also adopted a resolution rejecting "all forms such as occupation, internal or external military rule, external mandate and

---

*At a preparatory meeting a few weeks before the London conference, Chalabi himself caused problems—risking further delay—by insisting that the INC serve as the conference host. Hadley instructed Bill Luti (who was leading the U.S. contingent at the planning meeting) to deny Chalabi's request. Luti handled the matter with toughness and finesse, persuading Chalabi to drop his ill-considered demand.

†As described in Chapter 8, these included the Constitutional Monarch Party, Iraqi National Accord, Iraqi National Congress, Kurdish Democratic Party, Patriotic Union of Kurdistan, and Supreme Council for the Islamic Revolution in Iraq.

regional interference." All of the opposition groups supported this resolution. A complicated game was going on here. The terms "occupation" and "external military rule" referred to the United States; "external mandate" referred to the United Nations. The State Department had long been promoting a transitional civil authority that would run Iraq, perhaps for several years, in the period between U.S. military rule and Iraqi self-rule. State's papers on the subject consistently kept open the question of whether that authority would be led by the United States or the UN. This resolution came down squarely against both variations of State's transitional civil authority idea.

None of the groups believed it could keep or win political support among Iraqis if it countenanced either occupation or trusteeship for Iraq. At the same time, it was commonly thought that if the United States overthrew Saddam and then quickly handed power back to the Iraqis, the "Karzai" of Iraq—the appointed first leader—would be Ahmad Chalabi. That prospect was strongly opposed by the leaders of Saudi Arabia, Jordan, and the region's other Arab states as well as by some top U.S. officials (especially at State and CIA, where the views of the Arab states were especially influential). Though none of the externals could publicly support a U.S. occupation of Iraq, some of them who opposed Chalabi advised their friends in the U.S. government that after overthrowing Saddam, the United States should hold on to power long enough to ensure that Chalabi could be blocked.

Chalabi was widely believed to be a thoroughly dominant figure among the externals, with an iron hold on the Pentagon's loyalty. According to that view, the only way to block him from taking over Iraq after Saddam was for (non-Pentagon) U.S. officials to build up the *internals*, over time, as leaders who could beat him in elections. This view turned out to be wrong. Chalabi did not have an iron hold on the Pentagon's loyalty. And it wasn't an assertion of political leadership by internals that blocked him from taking over the leadership of Iraq. Rather, it was a combination of other factors, including damaging accusations by U.S. officials and electoral miscalculations by Chalabi himself.

The conference delegates knew that the principles and words approved in London would become the foundation for the work of future Iraqi political meetings, including the meetings in liberated Iraq designed to launch the new Iraqi government (or authority) and produce a new Iraqi constitution. That was, in fact, the case. The December 2002 statement was echoed in the words adopted at the opposition leadership council meeting in northern Iraq two months later. Those words, in turn, became the basis for the declaration of principles approved at the first political meeting of Iraqis on newly liberated territory, which took place in April 2003 in Nasiriyah. And when the representatives of the Iraqi Governing Council met to draft the interim constitution in the winter of 2003–04, they were able to take down from the shelf, as it were, principles that had already become reasonably well established in free Iraqi politics.

How much faster and better might the Iraqi political process have progressed after Saddam's ouster if the London conference had been convened in April 2002—with two or more follow-up conferences (rather than just one)? If U.S. officials hadn't been preoccupied by the incorrect speculation that the externals would be rejected politically by the internals, could we have built a better foundation for Iraqi self-government? Might we have become more knowledgeable about key personalities and key issues and more inclined to trust the Iraqis earlier to run their own affairs? Might we have avoided keeping the Coalition Provisional Authority for over a year as an occupation government? Might we actually have served as liberators rather than occupiers in Iraq—and fundamentally changed the history of post-Saddam Iraq?

These questions have no provable answers, but they're hard to ignore, given the unhappy history of the U.S. occupation of Iraq. As Winston Churchill put it in his history of the First World War, "The terrible 'Ifs' accumulate."

One important step in the "liberation, not occupation" strategy, in my view, was training Iraqi expatriates to work with coalition forces to overthrow Saddam's regime. Bill Luti and I had briefed the idea of a "free Iraqi force" to the Deputies and Principals in the spring of 2002. On May 26, however, the Principals had decided to shelve the idea, out of concern that it might provoke Saddam into aggressive action before U.S. forces were well positioned to respond.

In July 2002 Luti produced an updated briefing, which he called an "action plan," on training and equipping an Iraqi opposition force. When the Joint Staff passed it to General Myers for review, he wrote on it that CENTCOM should indeed train Iraqi oppositionists—even more quickly than Luti's briefing proposed—and should devise "a plan B that uses the opposition more aggressively than in this paper." This was constructive criticism, and Luti and I were pleased that Myers endorsed the strategic value of working with the Iraqi opposition.

A trained force of free Iraqis could help us remedy a number of war-planning deficiencies. Operational planners, like policy planners, never know enough about their theater of operations, and this was clearly the case with Iraq. Militarily trained Iraqis could add greatly to CENTCOM's understanding of Iraq—everything from how its military operates to the location of cultural sites to the nature of its sectarian and ethnic problems. Iraqi oppositionists could serve as interpreters, scouts, and guides and help coalition forces interact with the population. They could advise U.S. officials, civilian and military, who had to vet Iraqis for jobs in the new government. Our success in post-Saddam Iraq might hinge on finding responsible Iraqis reasonably quickly to help administer the country. Where else could the coalition turn for assistance and advice?

Luti and I argued that training a few thousand Iraqis could help us before, during, and after a war. We stressed the importance of becoming familiar with the trainees' characters, abilities, leadership qualities, and even political philosophies. If and when the time came to reform the Iraqi army and police, for example, we knew we would need the ideas and efforts of Iraqis we knew to be capable and trustworthy.

Beyond these operational benefits, there would be strategic value in publicizing a partnership between the coalition and a trained body of free Iraqis. A public diplomacy campaign about that partnership—featuring, among other things, videos of free Iraqis drilling as a unit under an Iraqi flag and voicing their hopes to contribute to their country's liberation—might help counter Iraqi fears that our intention was to occupy their country, exploit their resources, and run their lives.

But these potential benefits failed to impress General Franks. CENTCOM showed no interest in working with a free Iraqi force. Part of the explanation may be the Yankee can-do attitude typical of U.S. military and civilian officials—the view that whatever needs to be done, we Americans can do it ourselves faster, better, and more easily than if we have to rely on foreigners, especially if we have to train them. So they should stand aside, even in their own country, and let us handle the project the American way.

CENTCOM planners also worried about our troops' security. They rightly focused on the risk of sabotage. We shared their concern—which explained why we asked the Defense Intelligence Agency to sift the list of potential recruits so extensively. But we knew that CENTCOM could not achieve strategic victory if it refused to trust Iraqis altogether.

Franks's resistance to giving Iraqis a role in liberating their own country also reflected the influence of CENTCOM's State and CIA advisers, who generally opposed the idea of a free Iraqi force. One diplomat at State actually referred to the training as "fomenting treason"—as if rebellion against tyrannical dictatorship were offensive to American principles. In his memoir, CIA Director George Tenet writes that, as early as the fall of 2002, CIA officers suggested to Defense officials that they "scrap the idea of a fighting force of Iraqi exiles." Some CIA personnel objected in general to a training program that would be *overt* and run by the *military*—rather than covert and run by them. But the main argument that State and CIA officials made against the program was simply that it was a mistake to work so closely with the externals.

Though the program had energetic backing from top members of his Pentagon team—Wolfowitz, General Myers, Luti, and me—Rumsfeld did not support it consistently. As Luti and I developed the training concept and discussed the pros and cons with him throughout the summer of 2002, Rumsfeld said he wanted to press ahead. He emphasized especially the public diplomacy benefits he foresaw from an open partnership with Iraqis willing to fight to free their homeland. We then obtained input from the various agencies of the government and a green light from the Principals Committee, despite the lack of support at State and the CIA.

But then came the news stories, citing State and CIA sources, that depicted the training program as a stalking horse for Chalabi—echoing the widely touted allegations that Rumsfeld and his team were intent on anointing Chalabi as Iraq's leader after Saddam. Rumsfeld resented those allegations, which were untrue and came with no supporting evidence. But the criticism may have made him reluctant to push Franks on the issue of opposition training: Rumsfeld went out of his way to avoid even appearing to help Chalabi, much less favoring him over other externals.

In the fall, Rumsfeld asked me to update Franks on the training program, which I did at one of the war plan review sessions in Rumsfeld's office. Luti was with me. Franks listened and appeared to accept our analysis. Then, when the meeting broke up and Rumsfeld had walked away from the conference table, Franks walked around to where Luti and I were standing. He leaned over me LBJ-style and delivered into my face the unforgettable remark: "Doug, I don't have time for this f—king bulls—." I answered that it would have been better if Franks had shared his thoughts with the Secretary.

I later told Rumsfeld the gist of Franks's comment. But Rumsfeld never made the training program a personal project—and Franks felt free to handle the matter by his own lights.

To put together a force of a few thousand men, the Administration would need to obtain and vet lists of nominees, marshal the volunteers, and transport them to the training center (which Hungary had allowed us to establish on a military base there, after some persuasion from State). The recruits would then receive several weeks of training, geared to the roles and missions CENTCOM defined under general policy guidance from Washington. For the program to work, we all had important tasks to perform—the Iraqi opposition groups, the State Department, the U.S. intelligence community, CENTCOM, and my office. None performed well; by the start of the war, only seventy-three (!) members of the Free Iraqi Forces were available to contribute to CENTCOM's war operations.

Almost everything that could go wrong did. One reason recruitment was poor was that CENTCOM made clear from the outset that it would assign the Free Iraqi Forces only "support" missions—no combat—and there would be no separate Iraqi unit. Nor would we train the Iraqis to use rifles, only sidearms. The Iraqis' work—as interpreters, advisers, and liaisons—would be valuable, but those roles were less than inspirational. To the Iraqi expatriate community, it was clear that the U.S. military would be, at best, a reluctant partner of the Free Iraqi Forces.

My office was responsible for collecting names of potential recruits from the various Iraqi opposition groups, but the groups promised more than they could deliver. When challenged, they complained about the pay, which, to be sure, was low. Most of the potential recruits were working men with families to support. But, as some U.S. officials asked scornfully, was it admirable for an expatriate community to fail to rally—*for financial reasons*—to bring freedom to their country?

Some of the larger pools of potential recruits came from countries that announced they would not allow their residents to join the Free Iraqi Forces. When Canada and other countries declared such a prohibition, we asked State to persuade them to reverse it. State did not succeed.

The Principals Committee approved the idea of training Free Iraqi Forces in August 2002, but the President didn't sign the necessary funding authorization until December 9. The Defense Department didn't get Rumsfeld's signature on an "execute order" for the program until December 28. The order directed that training begin on February 1, 2003—just seven weeks before the war would start.

The one thing that went well was the training itself. The Iraqi recruits benefited from a program well run by the commander, Major General David Barno (U.S. Army), who afterward became the commander of coalition forces in Afghanistan.

At the February 14, 2003, National Security Council meeting, I briefed President Bush on the status of the Free Iraqi Forces program. The opposition had nominated more than 5,000 men. Invitations went out to

625 fully vetted nominees and 1,809 partially vetted nominees. The vetting process was continuing, but as of February 1 only fifty-five volunteers had begun training in Hungary. But there was no substantial discussion of the poor showing and little real interest in the program around the table. Many of the agencies represented there bore some of the blame. Some of the officials, who had long opposed the program, had no interest in making a fuss to push it forward.

In all, the failure to train large numbers of Free Iraqi Forces was a wasted opportunity and a setback to the strategic idea of "liberation, not occupation." Looking back, who can doubt that we would have been better off with thousands—or even a few hundred—of Iraqis trained by us, known to us, and ready to help with the building of new Iraqi institutions after Saddam's overthrow? They might have contributed, first and foremost, to the leadership of the new Iraqi military and police forces. Perhaps they would have won special credibility from having played an honorable role in the military campaign to free their country from the Saddam Hussein regime.*

Even if one did not recognize in advance the value of the Free Iraqi Forces, it should have been obvious in retrospect. But Franks, in his book, shows no sign of appreciating the lost opportunity; indeed, he fails to mention the Free Iraqi Forces at all. And Franks's deputy, Lieutenant General Michael DeLong, disparages the idea in his own book as "another Wolfowitz-recommended venture that turned out to be a waste of time and energy for us." George Tenet likewise writes contemptuously of the idea of training Iraqi security forces in advance of the war. Both DeLong and Tenet claim that the failure of the Free Iraqi Forces program vindicated their opposition to it. Neither reflected on how such a program might have succeeded had they, like Myers, appreciated the ways our military operations—during and after the war—would have benefited from a proud Iraqi face.

The Free Iraqi Forces program fizzled largely due to interagency discord of the kind that confounded the President's Iraq policy from the outset of the Administration. An important element of that discord was the tension

*In a "Lessons Learned" briefing on the Free Iraqi Forces effort, General Myers's staff noted that the "limited number that did participate proved valuable in obtaining surrenders from Iraqi combatants" and made other contributions. If substantial numbers had been achieved, the Free Iraqi Forces "could have proven an invaluable asset to the Combatant Commander during armed conflict." (Joint Staff J5 directorate briefing on "Lessons Learned—Issue to Improve," June 30, 2006.)

between State and Defense, which began to build even before 9/11. It became worse over time, in part because basic differences—such as the dispute over the Iraqi externals—were papered over again and again, and never actually resolved.

Of all the Iraq-related quarrels between State and Defense, none produced more toxic antagonism at the top levels of State than the fight in February 2003 over certain senior jobs at ORHA. Strange to say, the Iraq matter that elicited State's fiercest response was not the question of whether to go to war—or any other strategy or policy issue—but a personnel action.

One of Jay Garner's more difficult tasks was recruiting officials to join ORHA. He needed people who had relevant skills and were willing to be detailed away from their home agencies to deploy to Baghdad. And he needed them right away. President Bush urged all government departments to contribute good people to ORHA. State, to its credit, provided many. Defense was not as responsive. My office, in particular, had a rather small staff for Iraq work,* and we did not provide lots of people to ORHA. By late February, Garner later said, he had between seventy and one hundred people staffing his new operation.

In developing his reconstruction plan, Garner decided that ORHA should supply a senior adviser for each of the main departments in Iraq's new government. These Senior Ministry Advisers would be key figures in the U.S. reconstruction effort. Rumsfeld had told Garner to move boldly in organizing ORHA, and, accordingly, Garner arranged to fill almost all the Senior Ministry Adviser positions with State officials, including a number of former ambassadors. He did that on his own initiative; the date for the start of the war was still uncertain, and he wanted to put his organization together before events overtook him.

In late February 2003, Garner reported on the hiring of the Senior Ministry Advisers at a meeting where the Secretary was receiving a series of briefings from a string of people who were crowding his large conference room. Rumsfeld was more impatient than usual: By then he knew that the war would start in less than a month.

When Garner's turn came, he gave Rumsfeld a printout of a briefing slide showing perhaps two dozen boxes. Each box had the name of an Iraqi ministry and the name of the prospective Senior Ministry Adviser, together with that person's home agency. Rumsfeld moved his finger down

*The Office of Special Plans was created in late summer 2002, within the Near East and South Asia Affairs office, increasing the number of staffers devoted to Iraq work from two to around twenty.

and across the page, reading out the labels: "State, State, State, AID, AID, State." ("AID" is the abbreviation of the Agency for International Development.) Rumsfeld asked, "AID is part of the State Department, isn't it?" The answer was yes. Rumsfeld shook his head. He saw what had happened. Garner needed people, and when State proved a willing source, Garner readily used them to fill his requirements.

Rumsfeld said nothing disparaging about State. He did say that he understood from Garner the importance of the Senior Ministry Advisers, some of whom might effectively run the ministries in the critical period immediately after Saddam was ousted. And some of those ministries would be crucial to our success—Defense, Interior, Foreign Affairs, Planning, and Oil, for example. Time was running short; but even so, Rumsfeld told Garner, he couldn't approve people for these key adviser jobs without a proper analysis and process. He expected Garner to identify the main skills needed for the key jobs and to present Rumsfeld with several candidates for each. He wanted to try, quickly, to find the best candidates in the United States, not just the best ones in the U.S. government. He gave the example of Walter Slocombe—Under Secretary of Defense for Policy in the Clinton Administration—as a strong candidate for the Defense Ministry Adviser, even though he was no longer in the government.

Rumsfeld then crossed out eight or nine of the names on Garner's slide—the ones for the most important ministries. I don't think the Secretary knew any of the individuals named; it was not personal. He wanted options. He told Garner to come back to him later with key qualifications and candidates for those positions.

The Secretary's rejection created havoc at State. Officials there took it as the grossest of insults that Rumsfeld would toss that group of senior diplomats overboard. Steve Hadley called to tell me that Powell was enraged beyond anything that anyone had seen before.

I had been only a spectator in this drama, but Hadley asked me to help clean up the mess. We reviewed what had happened. Rumsfeld clearly thought—to use a Pentagon expression—that Garner had gotten out in front of his own headlights. I told Hadley, however, that Garner had been doing what Rumsfeld asked him to do: to put ORHA together in a hurry, without bothering with the standard procedural niceties. At the same time, I didn't think it was unreasonable for Rumsfeld to want a voice in selecting the key Senior Ministry Advisers. He felt those decisions should be made with some rigor. We all might regret it someday if ORHA simply hired some senior diplomats who happened to be between assignments.

Finally, I told Hadley, I understood Powell's unhappiness. State had come through with personnel for ORHA, agreeing to send people into an uncertain, possibly dangerous, situation. These nominees had consulted with their families and begun making arrangements to go abroad. And now Rumsfeld had pulled the plug on them, without ceremony, without any expression of gratitude or even a "sorry we jerked you around."

Hadley set up a meeting to discuss the matter in the Situation Room, inviting Marc Grossman and me, among others. Hadley asked me to explain what Rumsfeld was doing. I had gotten out no more than a sentence or two when Grossman stood up and walked out of the room in protest, saying over his shoulder something like "I'm not going to listen to this." That ended the meeting.

Hadley later called and said that Grossman blamed me for Rumsfeld's decision to cross off those State Department names. Grossman pointed out that I had asked State to detail people to ORHA, which was true, and said it was "dishonest" that those State officials were dropped. Neither Hadley nor I understood what Grossman thought was dishonest, but he declared (according to Hadley) that he would never talk to me again. This wasn't even a case of shooting the messenger: State had learned about Rumsfeld's action immediately, and not from me. I hadn't even *been* the messenger.

Eventually, Hadley persuaded Grossman to take a call from me. I assured him that I sympathized with the State officials who'd been bumped. They were willing to do a tough job and deserved better treatment. I told him I thought everyone involved had acted in good faith, but that the whole situation would have benefited from more courtesy and patience and levelheadedness.

Grossman was willing to repair relations with me to the point that he no longer stormed out of meetings when I spoke. But the Senior Ministry Advisers incident was no mere transient fit of pique. It infuriated Powell, Armitage, Grossman, and many others at State. It further damaged the already strained relationship between State and Defense. And its effects never quite wore off, certainly not as long as either Powell or Rumsfeld remained in his job.

In the weeks that followed, it became more common for newspaper stories to quote anonymous senior State officials, denouncing "pissant," "pencil-necked" Pentagon officials—phraseology characteristic of Richard Armitage. Journalists suddenly flooded my office with requests for comment on stories attributed to "senior State officials" that made untrue allegations about the work of Rumsfeld and the "neocons."* Attacks of this

---

*Powell himself was quoted by journalist Bob Woodward as calling my policy operation a "Gestapo office." This astonished me. I had what I thought was a cordial relationship with Powell going back over twenty years, and he knew that my father was

kind had been emanating from State since the beginning of President Bush's term, but the blowup over the Senior Ministry Advisers took the warfare to a new level. The damage it caused was not confined to the Pentagon. The President suffered politically, and U.S. policies lost support abroad.

The actual history of the Administration's prewar work on Iraq is not the commonly reported tale of starry-eyed assumptions, lack of planning, and good doves versus bad hawks. In fact, it is a story of grave strategic dilemmas; conservative, though by no means flawless, assumptions; some sound planning; and substantial discord, with the discord sometimes killing or undermining the plans.

Much of the discord had roots in disagreements about working with the Iraqi externals. The prevailing view at State and CIA anticipated a major external-internal rift in Iraq; it was not preposterous—but it was wrong. It delayed for months the Administration's policy decision on post-Saddam governance. It hamstrung all the Administration's major initiatives to work with Iraqis before the war and to transfer authority to Iraqis

---

a Holocaust survivor. The day the *Washington Post* first reported this comment (see William Hamilton, "Bush Began to Plan War Three Months After 9/11; Book Says President Called Secrecy Vital," *Washington Post*, April 17, 2004, p. A1), Rumsfeld spoke about it by phone with Powell and then informed me: "I told Powell that I thought he [Powell] was better than that. Powell said he did not recall ever having said it. I said: In that case deny it; otherwise apologize. So we'll see what he does." Later that day, I was called out of a briefing I was giving to take a call from Powell. He said (according to the notes I made during the call): "I don't know where Woodward got the comment that was used about you, about the Gestapo. You and I have had our agreements and disagreements over the years—we've known each other a long time. I want you to know that I think the comment is inappropriate. It's distasteful. I don't recall having said it. But once it's in a book, it's out there. I'll do what I can to address it. I hope I get asked a question in public about it." The next day, Powell sent me a handwritten note repeating his phone comments almost verbatim and adding: "I will do everything I can to erase this despicable characterization." But when a journalist asked him about the Gestapo comment, Powell answered only that he did not recall having made it and that it was "out of place." See Colin Powell interview on APTV with Barry Schweid and George Gedda, April 19, 2004, available at http://www.state.gov/secretary/former/powell/remarks/31588.htm.

This unpleasant story is worth recounting only to illustrate the remarkable (though unreciprocated) animus that top-level State Department officials had toward Rumsfeld and his team—and the way State officials influenced public perceptions through the news media. No one at the Pentagon, as far as I know, ever counterattacked in response to the Gestapo smear.

quickly after Saddam's overthrow. And in the end, disdain for the externals at State and CIA made it impossible to implement the President's strategic idea that the United States should act in Iraq as a liberator and not an occupier.

Were the problems that developed in Iraq inevitable? Could they have been foreseen—and, if so, were they sufficient reason to leave Saddam in power? Or were some of them avoidable if we had developed different strategies or implemented our strategies better?

Historians face a mountain of terrible ifs.

13
SADDAM'S REGIME FALLS

On March 17, 2003, President Bush extended his formal ultimatum to Saddam Hussein. In a television broadcast from the White House, he announced that Saddam could avoid war under one condition: if he and his sons left Iraq within forty-eight hours.

That ultimatum was the truly final opportunity in a long line of "final" opportunities for Saddam Hussein that stretched back to April 1991, when the UN Security Council established a regimen of weapons inspections, economic sanctions, and other measures, as the alternative to overthrowing his regime. As President Bush observed, however, in the last dozen years "peaceful efforts to disarm the Iraqi regime have failed again and again—because we are not dealing with peaceful men." He announced that "the decades of deceit and cruelty have now reached an end," and that if Saddam and his sons did not accept this final offer, their refusal "will result in military conflict, commenced at a time of our choosing." The President also reaffirmed that the rationale for the war was to eliminate the threat posed by the Iraqi regime:

> **We are now acting because the risks of inaction would be far greater. In one year, or five years, the power of Iraq to inflict harm on all free nations would be multiplied many times over. With these capabilities, Saddam Hussein and his terrorist allies could choose the moment of deadly conflict when they are**

strongest. We choose to meet that threat now, where it arises, before it can appear suddenly in our skies and cities.

In acting against this threat, the President said, the United States would also work "to advance liberty" in the Middle East. But he made this point only briefly, at the end of the quarter-hour broadcast, and immediately reiterated his main theme of defense: "Free nations have a duty to defend our people by uniting against the violent."

The President was usefully distinguishing between the war's goal—defending our people against threats—and the over-and-above opportunity it might create to promote democracy in Iraq. Rumsfeld, with my assistance, had urged the President to keep this distinction sharp. If U.S. forces overthrew Saddam's regime, President Bush would surely work to get a democratic government established in Iraq—and it was prudent to try. But creating democracy was not a primary reason to go to war, and it was dangerous to suggest that it was—especially because we might not be able to achieve it.

To no one's surprise, Saddam showed no interest in the offer of exile. Operation Iraqi Freedom began sometime after 3:00 A.M. on March 20, Baghdad time, with an air strike on Dora Farms, a site in the Baghdad region where the CIA thought (erroneously, as it turned out) that Saddam was meeting with his top lieutenants. Within hours Special Operations Forces entered Iraq from the south and the west, followed quickly by an air campaign and a ground invasion by a force of American and British soldiers and marines entering Iraq through Kuwait.

In their war plan meetings, Franks and Rumsfeld agreed on the importance of achieving surprise in the opening phase of the war. Rumsfeld believed that some of his gravest concerns about the war—including humanitarian disasters, the destabilization of friendly governments in the region, and terrorist attacks—were likelier to materialize if we had to fight a long war to oust Saddam. Surprise could help shorten the war, Franks emphasized: He liked to quip that "speed kills."

The prevailing view among intelligence and policy officials was that we could *not* achieve strategic surprise; after all, it was assumed that Saddam knew we were coming. Franks focused on *tactical* surprise—shocking the Iraqis as to when, where, and how our forces would strike. CENTCOM developed several ideas. One was to use ground forces right from the start. We later learned that this stratagem worked: Assuming we would fight the same way we had in 1991, senior Iraqi military officers interrogated after Saddam's overthrow said they "believed Coalition efforts would open with a sustained air campaign possibly followed weeks later by ground operations"; it was "a shock to many of them when the coalition offensive began with a simultaneous air and ground attack."

Franks also hoped to surprise Saddam by starting the war with fewer troops in the theater than Saddam would expect. This was a principal argument he made for launching the war with a relatively small force.*

Rumsfeld saw the issue of force levels as an operational matter, not a policy question. He did not look to my office for technical military judgments—and the size of a force needed for a given mission was such a judgment. But I was often present when Rumsfeld discussed the issue with Franks, Myers, and Pace, and I heard them develop the rationale for what was called the "light footprint."

I think Rumsfeld influenced Franks's thinking on the issue of force levels. Especially in the early stages of working on the Iraq war plan, Rumsfeld reminded Franks of the large excess of men and equipment that had been sent to the theater for Desert Storm in 1990–91. As the Secretary pointed out, five hundred thousand troops were used in Desert Storm, and close to ninety percent of the munitions shipped for that operation was later returned to the United States still packed in its original boxes. That particular application of the overwhelming-force concept had proven remarkably wasteful. Moreover, both the U.S. military and the Iraqi military were smaller than they had been in the early 1990s.

Nonetheless, the Iraq war plan CENTCOM had on the shelf when 9/11 occurred called for more than half a million U.S. troops. The Secretary worried that there could be serious strategic as well as financial costs if Franks used a much larger force than was necessary. Among these costs was the risk of weakening deterrence against aggression in other theaters around the world. With all the uncertainties and demands facing our military after 9/11, Rumsfeld wanted CENTCOM to question the standard everything-but-the-kitchen-sink approach to war planning and think through what was actually required to do the job.

The new approach CENTCOM evolved was to start the attack with a force of approximately 150,000 troops, with additional troops "in the pipeline"—en route or readying to deploy to the theater. Never afraid of a mixed metaphor, Franks devised what he called on-ramps and off-ramps for the troops in the pipeline, to give himself flexibility to increase or decrease the number of forces in Iraq for Phase III (major combat) or Phase IV (reconstruction and stabilization), depending on how the war was going.

It was obvious to everyone who sat in regularly on Franks's briefings of

---

*Franks also argued that the time required to assemble a large (and highly visible) force would eliminate any possibility of surprise. See Franks, *American Soldier*, p. 349.

Rumsfeld and Myers (including, of course, Franks himself) that he would receive Rumsfeld's consent for such additional troops if asked. Although the Secretary was famous for his willingness to challenge everyone's thinking and planning, he tended to defer to his field commanders on operational decisions. Operators "on the ground" saw things that were invisible to officials "back home," he often said, and they needed to be able to act quickly, so they shouldn't be micromanaged from Washington.

Rumsfeld was also attuned to the political risks of overriding judgments by commanders, especially on matters within their professional military competence. If a Secretary of Defense insisted that a military operation be run with greater risk than the combatant commander considered prudent, there would be aggravated hell to pay for both the Secretary and the President if the operation went badly.

Various civilian and military officials have charged that Rumsfeld ignored his top generals in insisting on a light footprint. From what I saw, that was false. Some of his generals now say they favored a heavier force, but *the* top general for Operation Iraqi Freedom was Tommy Franks. He was the person who rejected the arguments for increasing our footprint. The heavier-force proponents appear not to have pressed their case at the time: As General Myers later testified before the Senate Armed Services Committee, "There was never a push inside the Joint Chiefs of Staff for more forces." If the generals who favored a heavier force had persuaded Franks, there would have been a heavier force.

Franks originally intended to create a vise that could close on the Iraqi regime from north and south. In the south, the coalition's forces did roll into Iraq, seize the city of Basra and the southern oil fields, and pursue multiple lines of attack northward toward Baghdad. Overall, they moved with amazing speed. The operation that began on March 19 succeeded in taking Baghdad and toppling the regime by April 9.

The vise, however, lacked its second piece: the U.S. 4th Infantry Division (ID), which Franks had planned to send into northern Iraq through Turkey. The Turkish government had told us it favored allowing transit for the division, but on March 1, 2003, the Turkish parliament failed by a narrow margin to confirm the approval.

U.S. officials had been trying to obtain the Turks' cooperation since the previous summer. Our military briefed the Turkish general staff on the Iraq war plan. Remembering that Turkey had paid a large price as a result of the 1990–91 Gulf War—not only financially but also in accepting hundreds of thousands of Kurdish refugees—the Administration assembled a large aid package. Turkish officials feared threats to their own territorial integrity if Iraq were to fracture along ethnic lines and if the Kurdish part, just across Turkey's border, were to move toward independence. The U.S. government reassured Turkish officials that we respected their strategic interests in Iraq and told them we shared their concern that regional instability could result from Iraq's disintegration. And we promised Turkey an important voice in the coalition's post-Saddam reconstruction policy.

Leading the effort to win Turkish cooperation were Marc Grossman—who, years before becoming Powell's Under Secretary for Political Affairs, had served as a well-regarded U.S. ambassador in Ankara—and Paul Wolfowitz, an outspoken friend of Turkey. It didn't make their job easier that the Turkish government was, for the first time ever, in the hands of a recently elected Islamist political party. That party, in power for only four months, did not share the pro-American tradition of Turkey's other leading parties—and key Turkish officials were novices who lacked experience in working issues in the Turkish legislative assembly.

When the Turkish parliament failed to approve passage of the 4th ID through Turkey into northern Iraq, Franks decided to make lemonade out of the lemon. The troops of the 4th ID were aboard ships in the Mediterranean Sea; the Turkey roadblock would force Franks to divert them through the Suez Canal and on to Kuwait by sea. Franks predicted that Saddam would wrongly assume we'd be unable to start the war before the 4th ID was in position to enter Iraq, and we could exploit his mistake. Franks decided to keep the division afloat in the Mediterranean, misleading Saddam about the war's start date and keeping him guessing about whether the 4th ID would enter from the south or perhaps eventually from Turkey.

Turkey's leaders professed to be as amazed as we were when the deal they made with Grossman and Wolfowitz failed to win parliamentary blessing. The disappointment caused embarrassment all around. There were surely grounds for asking whether the Bush Administration's diplomacy had been organized properly. One key question was why Powell himself had not made a greater personal effort: He had made some phone calls on the matter but had not taken the time to visit Turkey. Given that the problem involved winning over a large group of parliamentarians, Powell's prestige and charm might have made the difference.

Despite Franks's adaptation of the war plan, this diplomatic fiasco had negative operational effects, as some commentators have noted. Since no large force marched on Baghdad *from the north*, all the heavy fighting in Iraq occurred in Baghdad and south of the capital—in predominantly Shiite areas. The so-called Sunni Triangle did not see major combat. The historian Victor Davis Hanson has asked: "To what degree did the inability of the 4th Infantry division to head south from Turkey mean not merely that the Sunni Triangle was not immediately attacked but that it never really became a theater of war whose Iraqi combatants would learn the hard wages of fighting Americans?" Hanson suggests that the lack of major combat in the Sunni Triangle may have left in place a major impediment to postwar success for the coalition: "Given the rapid American victory and the directive to avoid killing not merely civilians but enemy soldiers as well, was there, perhaps, an inescapable Catch-22 in Iraq—as if an enemy humiliated and fleeing, but never really conquered, could ever make an easy subject for radical reconstruction?"

Though Turkey disappointed us on our main request, other countries responded well to our appeal for support. A few (Australia, the Czech Republic, the United Kingdom) contributed combat forces. Some (including Canada, Denmark, Netherlands, Poland, Romania, and Slovakia) provided combat support or combat service support. Others gave us access, basing, and overflight rights. Some of these helpful countries were eager to be identified openly as coalition members; others had reasons not to want a public association with the war. Following Rumsfeld's approach in October 2001, we allowed each country to characterize its relationship with the coalition as it saw fit. The list of coalition members publicly acknowledged by the State Department eventually ran to thirty countries. Some commentators would continue to characterize Operation Iraqi Freedom as "unilateralist," but that was untrue—and unjust to the dozens of countries that incurred serious risk and expense to contribute valuably to the war.

It took even less time to overthrow the Iraqi regime (twenty-one days) than to oust the Taliban (two months). As in Afghanistan, though, there was a moment when the military campaign appeared to be stuck, and, as in Afghanistan, critics eagerly declared a "quagmire." Some, amazingly, invoked the ghosts of the battle of Stalingrad in World War II, which lasted nearly six months and was among the bloodiest in history. The sandstorm that slowed the advance toward Baghdad blew for three days, from March 24 until March 27.

It was during that sandstorm that we saw the first indications of how a ready contingent of trained Iraqi forces could have helped our side. A shortage of embedded interpreters impaired the coalition military efforts from the start. During those three days, Lieutenant General John Abizaid, CENTCOM's forward-deployed deputy commander, complained that coalition forces in Iraq were not seeing Shiite uprisings against the regime. Before the war, Abizaid recalled, the CIA—not, in this case, Vice President Cheney or any optimistic neocons—had predicted that we would see helpful uprisings among newly emboldened Iraqis after the invasion began. But the Shiites apparently retained too strong a memory of the period after the Gulf War, when they rebelled with U.S. encouragement—only to be crushed savagely by Saddam's forces as the United States stood by.

Some CENTCOM leaders eventually began focusing on how our war effort could benefit from Iraqis playing a visible role in the liberation of their country. Abizaid, who had always been more receptive to this argument than most at CENTCOM, now began pushing two ideas my Policy organization had long favored: an Iraqi opposition force to fight alongside the coalition; and an Iraqi political conference on newly liberated soil (a successful effort, discussed later in this chapter).

On March 26, Abizaid surprised Chris Straub of my Near East and South Asia Affairs office with a phone call asking for advice on how to spur a Shiite uprising. Abizaid said he considered it urgent to "put an Iraqi face" on the campaign to oust Saddam. Straub was a good person to ask. His credentials included twenty-two years in the U.S. Army, where he was a Middle East Foreign Area Officer. Later, on the staff of Senator Bob Kerrey (D-Nebraska), Straub immersed himself in Iraq issues and came to know many of the leading externals. While working in the Policy organization at the Pentagon, Straub helped develop the concept of operations for the Free Iraqi Forces.

At that point, Ahmad Chalabi was hoping to put together his own unit of Iraqi oppositionists to enter the fight in the south. Abizaid told me he shared the CIA's distrust of Chalabi and doubted that Chalabi's group, the Iraqi National Congress (INC), could produce a substantial group of fighters. Straub said that Wolfowitz favored Chalabi's offer. Abizaid said he would discuss it with CENTCOM's liaison to the INC, an army colonel named Ted Seel.

Seel was new in his job. In the weeks before the war, Wolfowitz had pressed General Franks to appoint liaison officers to the several democratic opposition groups present in northern Iraq. Franks resisted, disdaining the INC (and the Iraqi externals generally) in line with advice from his CIA and State advisers. On March 3, General Pace called Franks on the matter. He later updated me: "Tom has no problem assigning liaisons . . . to the [Kurdish oppositionist groups] but does not want to assign anyone to the INC. He said the INC does not have a military component like the Kurdish parties." Eventually, after some back and forth with Wolfowitz, Franks relented, and Seel was selected for the INC assignment.

When Abizaid spoke with Seel on March 27, he asked how many men Chalabi could recruit for an operation in the south. Chalabi thought he could get a thousand, though Seel told Abizaid the real number was probably closer to seven hundred.

Abizaid was eager to secure that "Iraqi face" for the coalition, and such a large unit of U.S.-trained Free Iraqi Forces would have been ideal. On the advice of the CIA, however, Franks had scoffed at training Iraqi oppositionists and helped cripple the program. Now, in late March, with fighting under way and the coalition's momentum at risk, Abizaid was scrambling to assemble an Iraqi opposition force, and he was willing to use these untrained INC fighters if Chalabi could deliver them. Using arguments similar to those Bill Luti and I had advanced in the fall of 2002, he made the case to Franks.

Not surprisingly, Abizaid proved more persuasive with Franks than we had been. At the March 31 Principals Committee meeting, Rumsfeld announced that Franks "wants to move quickly to put an Iraqi face on our efforts in Iraq." George Tenet advised against taking quick action to team with the externals: "There are concerns about outsiders being imposed on the insiders." Tenet's comment implied that he had information about the "concerns" of the Iraqi public, but he offered no supporting details. Rumsfeld countered: "That will be a concern any time you put any idea forward" that might affect the politics of post-Saddam Iraq.

Franks approved Abizaid's proposal to fly Chalabi's several hundred men to the south. Seel turned out to be reasonably close on the numbers: Chalabi mustered a force of six hundred–plus Iraqis, many of whom had been in exile in Iran. These were men the INC had hoped to send to Hungary for the Free Iraqi Forces training program, if Chalabi had been able to extract them from Iran in time. Though the expatriates had missed out on the U.S. training, Franks and Abizaid thought they could be helpful. They came to be referred to as the Free Iraqi Fighting Force—the FIFF—to distinguish them from the handful of Free Iraqi Forces (FIF).

After he talked with Seel, Abizaid did not update Straub on this operation. If I recall correctly, my office heard about CENTCOM's plan for the Chalabi force only when it came up in top-level interagency discussions. Speaking by video, Franks informed the National Security Council of CENTCOM's plan to fly the Iraqi expatriate force from northern into southern Iraq. That was also the first time Franklin Miller of Rice's staff had heard of the plan. As chair of the Executive Steering Group, which managed interagency Iraq planning, Miller was unhappy to be caught by surprise on this matter. After the meeting, he called Luti to demand an explanation, but until that moment Luti had never heard of Franks's plan. Promising to look into the matter, Luti dispatched a member of his staff to speak to Seel, who told him what Franks and Abizaid had in mind.

It is noteworthy that Abizaid's initial phone call came as a surprise to Straub, that Franks's announcement of the Iraqi force deployment surprised Miller, and that Miller's inquiry surprised Straub's boss, Luti. These surprises refute the claims that Pentagon neocons invented this scheme to deploy the Iraqi force and rammed it down CENTCOM's throat—a further fictional subplot in the anoint-Chalabi myth.

The credibility of an essentially false story can get a big boost from a kernel of truth—and that was the case here. There was indeed a point on which Paul Wolfowitz clashed with Abizaid. As CENTCOM was transporting the six hundred or so Iraqi fighters to southern Iraq, I was later told, Chalabi insisted on accompanying his men and participating in the fight. Abizaid said no on the grounds that giving a special role to one of the oppositionists would entangle CENTCOM in Iraqi politics. Chalabi replied that his men would not go unless he went with them.

Abizaid called Wolfowitz for guidance. If the expatriate force had a serious mission to perform, Wolfowitz said, it wouldn't be sensible to jeopardize it simply to exclude Chalabi. Abizaid argued that taking Chalabi along would look bad—as if CENTCOM were favoring Chalabi politically. Wolfowitz replied that the bulk of the men had been recruited by Chalabi, who was part of the force, and it was just as much playing politics to exclude him as to include him.

CENTCOM officers then generated a list of objections. Some specifically opposed Chalabi's participation in the operation. Some used the occasion to renew their old objections to any Iraqi expatriate operation, even though CENTCOM's own General Abizaid had launched the idea. There were objections that CENTCOM could not guarantee Chalabi's personal safety, that CENTCOM should not show favoritism to any opposition leader, and that the Kurds objected to the operation altogether. Other government agencies also raised their voices to object.

In a memo to Wolfowitz, Luti answered these objections in writing. He said the Pentagon was "committed to working with any Iraqis willing to fight for their country" and willing to contribute to our military effort. His office had not recruited potential Iraqi freedom fighters only from the INC, but had "made extensive efforts to recruit from all eligible groups." At Wolfowitz's request, Luti then sounded out the Kurdish leaders. They supported deploying the Iraqi freedom fighters to the south, though for political reasons they would have preferred that Chalabi stay behind.

Wolfowitz told Abizaid not to exclude Chalabi. CENTCOM allowed Chalabi to deploy with his men, but Abizaid was unhappy about it. The matter was not brought to Rumsfeld for decision.

Through this improvisation with the Iraqi force, Abizaid was sensibly trying to remedy the war plan's lack of "an Iraqi face." But it was a bad moment for such improvisation. The commanders inside Iraq had their hands full. They did not properly grasp Abizaid's intent. They were unclear on what the Iraqi fighters were supposed to do. And they had questions about who was promoting the initiative—Abizaid? Franks and Abizaid? Pentagon civilians?—and why.

When the Iraqi fighters arrived at Tallil Air Base, just below Nasiriyah in southern Iraq, no one had prepared plans for using them or made proper arrangements to feed and accommodate them. Chalabi seized the opportunity to drive into Nasiriyah, where he drew a large crowd who cheered and chanted celebratory slogans. Some of the Iraqi fighters did useful and courageous work in the town of Shatrah on April 11, and they helped protect pilgrims on April 15 during the grand Arbaeen Shiite pilgrimage to Karbala.* But they were underemployed and neglected: At one point early on, they were left for many hours in desert heat without water. We heard reports that their discipline was poor and that they were getting supplies for themselves through looting.

George Tenet, General Michael DeLong, and other longtime opponents of creating an Iraqi oppositionist force cited those reports of looting as proof that such a force was a bad idea and that Chalabi's INC deserved the poor treatment CENTCOM gave it. But it seems reasonable to ask whether the Iraqi fighters might have refrained from such conduct if they had been adequately supplied—at least with some water!—and employed as Abizaid envisioned. A properly trained FIF team could have been integrated more readily into the ground operation, especially if its role had been thought through in advance. Indeed, this ad hoc Iraqi force's performance did improve after it was assigned U.S. Special Operations Forces as trainers and mentors; in time, it would become the 36th commando battalion of the Iraqi Civil Defense Corps, which performed respectably in combat in support of the new Iraqi government.

The failure of the Free Iraqi Forces program was costly. If a large number of free Iraqi fighters had been trained and integrated into CENTCOM commanders' thinking months before the war started, CENTCOM might have been able to use them, as Abizaid had hoped, during that sandstorm late in March. Throwing the Iraqis into the fight at the last minute seemed like a worthwhile gamble, but it didn't produce major results on the

*The Arbaeen pilgrimage to Karbala is one of the major annual events in Shiite Islam. That it occurred in mid-April 2003 was due to the coalition's liberation of Iraq: It was the first time in three decades that the Shiites were free to perform the pilgrimage.

ground. Its grandest effect was to appear to confirm the false suspicion that top Pentagon civilians aspired to make Chalabi the leader of Iraq.*

It was clear that liberating Iraq would require a strategy with a political as well as a military component. For months, my Pentagon colleagues and I had proposed working with the externals to lay a foundation for governance of post-Saddam Iraq. State and CIA officials resisted, warning against allowing Iraqi externals to structure the new government—warnings that were worded generally, but were clearly directed chiefly against Chalabi.

In telling the Pentagon not to impose a political leader on Iraq, State and CIA were pushing on the proverbial open door. Rumsfeld and his team repeatedly made clear that we were interested not in playing favorites, but in ensuring the quality of Iraq's post-Saddam government—and in helping all Iraqis who shared our key principles regarding peace, terrorism, and human rights. If the externals failed to make substantial political progress before Saddam's overthrow, Iraqis might be—or appear to be—unready to assume authority when the time came. The result could be a political vacuum, a situation that could play into the hands of foreign and domestic extremists and unfriendly neighbors—and suck the United States into the long-term role of an occupying power.

Rumsfeld remained convinced that the United States should hand authority to the Iraqis as quickly as possible after Saddam's overthrow. He didn't believe the CIA's speculation that the externals wouldn't be considered legitimate by the internals. Legitimacy, he argued, was no abstract philosophical matter; it was a practical question of acceptance. If the new Iraqi leaders performed well as government officials, they would be accepted; if not, not. The interim leaders could help inspire cooperation, he pointed out, by emphasizing that the initial post-Saddam political arrangements were merely provisional—and that the Iraqi electorate could change its leadership peacefully in short order.

As much as he disliked the idea of a U.S. occupation government, however, Rumsfeld didn't want to be reckless about putting Iraq into the hands of relatively unknown leaders who might prove grossly incompetent, corrupt, or abusive of their new authority. This was a bigger problem

*In a television interview for PBS's *Frontline*, for example, a journalist tried to get former ORHA Director Jay Garner to confirm that CENTCOM's use of the expatriate force "was a plan to move Chalabi in to start up a government." Garner said he did not believe that. Interview with General Jay Garner, *Frontline*, PBS, July 17, 2003, available at http://www-c.pbs.org/wgbh/pages/frontline/shows/truth/interviews/garner.html.

in Iraq than in Afghanistan, because Iraq had a substantial army and enormous oil resources. (This was a key reason the Afghan model of an immediate interim-provisional-government was not adopted for Iraq.) Rumsfeld wanted to strike the balance between promptly recognizing a new, free Iraqi government and performing due diligence on the initial leadership.

The State Department had other ideas. With its low opinion of these Iraqi leaders, State proposed creating a transitional civil authority to govern Iraq *for a multiyear period,* perhaps under UN auspices—a plan designed to keep power out of the externals' hands until a new Iraqi *internal* leadership could come into being. This approach was directly opposed to the Pentagon's, which focused on how to get control of post-Saddam Iraq *into* the hands of Iraqis, not how to keep it *out* of their hands. In any case, putting Iraq under some kind of United Nations trusteeship seemed unrealistic and undesirable: it was unlikely to appeal to the Iraqis, many of whom felt the UN had been ineffective in protecting them from Saddam, it seemed far beyond what the UN would be willing or able to take on, and it could present possibilities for corruption even beyond the notorious Oil-for-Food program.*

My office worked on plans to move directly from a brief U.S. military occupation to Iraqi self-rule. One plan was for an Iraqi provisional government. Before the war, having heard the idea opposed by Powell and Tenet and also, for different reasons, by Rumsfeld, President Bush decided against it. In February 2003, the President's Special Envoy, Zalmay Khalilzad, had conveyed the President's decision to the Iraqi opposition leaders at the Salahuddin (northern Iraq) political conference. He told them that the United States intended instead to put in place a transitional civil authority after Saddam's removal, which would mean non-Iraqi rule for a substantial but undefined period. The Iraqis complained publicly about this U.S. policy, referring to the resolution they had adopted at the December conference that rejected "occupation," "internal or external military rule," and "external mandate."

I continued to work with my staff to develop new ways to avoid a prolonged U.S. occupation of Iraq while addressing the concerns that Powell, Tenet, Rumsfeld, and others expressed about the legitimacy, competency, and honesty of the Iraqi leaders who would succeed Saddam. To square the circle, my office developed the proposal for the Iraqi Interim Authority (IIA).

---

*The UN had an office in Iraq to assist in the post-Saddam reconstruction, but after that office was bombed in a terror attack in August 2003—killing its director, Ambassador Sergio Vieira de Mello—Secretary-General Kofi Annan pulled UN personnel out of Iraq.

The IIA plan was designed to share governmental power in Iraq through a formal agreement between Iraqi leaders and the U.S.-led military coalition. Together, they could form the transitional civil authority that would pave the way to full Iraqi self-rule. The core of the leadership group would be the Iraqi Leadership Council selected at the February 2003 political conference in Salahuddin. They would be responsible for quickly expanding their number to include internals, as soon as internals became available for service after Saddam's ouster. The resulting group of leaders would exercise independent or sovereign authority over some Iraqi ministries right from the start; then, as they proved their management and political abilities, their authority would extend to the remainder of the ministries. The UN Security Council could be brought in to endorse the IIA arrangement and to provide technical assistance and other support for reconstruction—but not to run it.

The IIA concept would allow Iraqis to exercise substantial authority promptly after Saddam's overthrow and allow the United States to avoid maintaining an occupation government. But Iraqis would not immediately control all of the country's military and economic assets. By managing a number of the national ministries, the new leaders could prove themselves—to the Iraqi people and to us. Once they did so, they could take on the rest of the ministries and the United States could responsibly recognize the IIA as the new, fully empowered government of Iraq.

In developing the IIA concept, of course, we had in mind our recent experience in Afghanistan, where the United States immediately recognized an interim government of Afghans and never became an occupying power. Despite the obvious differences, the Afghanistan case offered some lessons worth heeding.

The IIA plan specifically took into account the concerns about legitimacy: it would not give authority across the board to Iraqis right away, but it would not hoard all power in American hands either; it did not empower only externals, but it did not treat the externals as illegitimate; it built on the leadership group selected by the prewar Iraqi political conferences, but it required that group to expand itself to include internals; and it did not favor Chalabi or the Iraqi National Congress over the other externals; rather, it provided neutrally that Iraqis would select their own officers.

The Principals Committee took up the IIA idea as a concept (not yet a detailed plan) at meetings on March 1 and March 7, 2003. Powell, Armitage, and Tenet were absent at the first of these meetings; the Defense civilians included Rumsfeld, Wolfowitz, and me. National Security Adviser Rice highlighted the key point of the IIA: that some ministries would come under Iraqi control right away, while others "would be held for a while" by the U.S.-led coalition. Wolfowitz suggested moving the Foreign Ministry quickly into Iraqi hands so that they could "occupy the UN seat and run embassies." When Deputy CIA Director John McLaughlin seconded Wolfowitz's suggestion, Vice President Cheney commented, "The sooner we turn things over to the Iraqis the better."

Rice sounded out the Principals on what role the United Nations should play in relation to the IIA. Cheney warned that UN officials might try to choose Iraq's leaders; President Bush had insisted that Iraqis should select their own leaders. It would be hard to achieve the President's strategic objectives, the Vice President commented, if the United Nations were wrestling the United States for control of the "steering wheel." In response, Rice said we would want to recruit other countries to work with us as partners—including to help "pay the bill"—and said they would need UN "cover" if they were going to cooperate. Cheney did not disagree.

Acknowledging my role in developing the IIA concept, Rice directed that the Defense Department would take the lead on working IIA issues. "It's critical to do an IIA early," she concluded. "Let's move quickly from principles to procedures."

My staff and I fleshed out the IIA concept in papers we wrote for the Principals' March 7 meeting. We proposed that the United States "recognize the IIA as *the legitimate governmental authority of Iraq*, pending the Iraqi people's ratification of a new constitution and election of a new government." In return, the IIA would agree to give the coalition freedom of action to eliminate Iraqi WMD and terrorist infrastructure.

The IIA was to consult with the coalition on how to run the Iraqi ministries (and would gradually assume control over all of them, one by one). Its key task would be organizing the constitutional commission and elections, resulting in a fully formed government that would put the IIA out of business. At this point in early March, we envisioned an IIA executive council of twenty-one persons, who would elect a chairman from among their number. U.S. officials would not "anoint," or even appoint, the chairman. In part to contradict the "anoint Chalabi" conspiracy theories—which we knew could hurt us in Iraq, not just in Washington—we proposed that the IIA chairman be *ineligible for elected office* for seven years after ratification of the new constitution. Even so, various Administration officials continued to assert that the IIA was designed to make Chalabi the new leader of Iraq.

Regarding the council's membership, we decided to tackle head-on the antiexternals antagonism prevailing at State and the CIA. If at all possible, we said, the United States should secure the consensus of the six-member Iraqi Leadership Council in appointing the interim leaders. We proposed reserving nearly half the council seats for internals. But the majority should be allocated to externals—referred to as "Free Iraqis"—because they would be "better positioned to understand concepts of democracy than are those who do not have exposure outside Iraq." All council members would have to subscribe to basic principles regarding human rights and representative government.

In our draft proposed agreement between the United States and the IIA, we detailed the IIA's responsibilities. These focused mainly on addressing the problems that had motivated U.S. interest in regime change in Iraq: Saddam's threats of international aggression, support for terrorists, and pursuit of weapons of mass destruction—and the tyrannical nature of Saddam's regime. The IIA was designed to prevent those problems from resurfacing in postwar Iraq.

We divided Iraq's ministries into categories. The IIA would appoint interim senior officials for some—for example, Foreign Affairs, Religious Affairs, Justice, and Agriculture. For other ministries, the IIA appointments would be subject to coalition consent—for example, Health, Trade, Education, Planning, and Industry and Minerals. In this early post-Saddam period, the United States would have the authority to appoint top officials for the ministries of Defense, Finance, Interior, and Oil—sensitive responsibilities to be reassigned with great care.

State officials responded to our draft proposal with a paper of their own, which they circulated for the March 7 Principals Committee meeting. They called for the United Nations to select the members of the IIA council and asserted, as usual, that the Free Iraqis (other than the Kurds) had "questionable legitimacy." The State paper opposed selecting members of the IIA council until after we removed the Iraqi regime—an approach that I thought would needlessly give away a useful option in our contingency planning. If an IIA council could be constituted before the war, it would be ready to invite coalition forces into Iraq if a prewar coup against Saddam took place (or, for that matter, if Saddam accepted exile). That would help avoid the "Saddamism without Saddam" scenario, in which the dictator might be replaced by a fellow Baathist with aggressive ambitions like his own—and one who could win a "honeymoon" from the United Nations.

I presented the Defense Department's IIA proposal to the Principals at the March 7 meeting. As soon as I finished, Armitage said, "Don't rush. We'll sacrifice legitimacy." "Legitimacy" had become a buzzword freighted with all of State's negative views of the externals. Cheney clearly was not sympathetic to Armitage's point. Nor did he approve of State's resistance to laying groundwork for the post-Saddam governance of Iraq. He countered that we "can't leave the government to chance." Rumsfeld likewise bristled at Armitage's use of the word, reiterating that the IIA would be a temporary body, and that "*how well it works will determine its legitimacy.*"

But Armitage continued to press for delay in creating an Iraqi authority. He insisted that we should take two or three months to consult with all Iraqis before we appoint an IIA. Rice was surprised that Armitage would argue for keeping all power in U.S. hands for that long. "Does it have to take two or three months?" she wondered. Cheney, too, was incredulous. Referring to that initial period of exclusive American authority, he asked Armitage, "So you wouldn't have an IIA at all?"

Here we were, two weeks before the start of the war, and Armitage was pushing for a delay of several months in creating an interim *authority*, not even a government, to take control of Iraq after the war. In July 2002, Armitage had first called for a "multi-year transitional period" before the United States should permit Iraqi self-rule, asserting that it would take that long for a "credible" Iraqi leadership to arise. Now, with the war upon us, Armitage was apparently willing to revise his calculations, but even this shorter timetable did not go over well with the Principals.

Had Armitage put his cards on the table at this March 7 meeting and argued for the multiyear U.S.-led occupation he had initially proposed, the issue could have been debated in a straightforward fashion and resolved. Armitage presumably anticipated that the President would go against him, so he gave the Principals Committee the impression that he and Powell now envisioned empowering Iraqi political leaders within three months after Saddam's removal.*

At the same meeting, CIA Deputy Director John McLaughlin proposed criteria for IIA council members. The CIA, he said, had concluded that the United States should "exclude representatives of current Iraqi political parties"—in other words, the externals—from the council. (McLaughlin allowed an exception for the Kurds, because they were "insiders.") No one else, however, voiced support for an external-free IIA.

Apparently uneasy about the drift of the remarks from Armitage and McLaughlin, the Vice President posed a general question to the group, "Do we agree that we need an [Iraqi] interim authority?" Rice quickly answered, "Yes."

Three days later, on March 10, I briefed the IIA concept to the President at a National Security Council meeting, explaining that the alternative to a prolonged U.S. occupation was to put authority back into Iraqi

*When L. Paul Bremer was appointed the head of the Coalition Provisional Authority, as we'll see, State leaders made clear that they opposed any early transfer of independent authority to the Iraqis.

hands as soon as possible. If the United States were to retain all governmental power in Iraq after we overthrew Saddam, I warned, we would be criticized for "military rule" and have a hard time winning support in Iraq, the United Nations, or the world in general.* We would create a power vacuum that Iran and others would exploit. And the people of Iraq would have no "productive outlet for Iraqi nationalism."

The IIA was designed to balance a number of interests, I told the President—specifically, to "maintain sufficient U.S. control over the process of reconstruction while preserving the legitimacy of our presence and the *bona fides* of cooperative Iraqis." I then reviewed the ideas we had for selecting externals and internals to serve in the IIA. Finally, I raised questions about timing: When should the IIA be established? And when should U.S. officials begin discussing the concept with others? I proposed we consult immediately with the Free Iraqi Leadership Council and our key allies and discuss the concept publicly.

This interagency debate on the pros and cons of the IIA was intended to set the course of Iraqi political reconstruction after Saddam. The President would in fact approve the IIA as our way forward in Iraq. Yet the IIA plan has received almost no attention in the memoirs of insiders published to date about the Iraq war. Tenet seems to be referring to the proposal when he criticizes the Defense Department "approach," but he never actually mentions the IIA plan. Instead, he presents his own inaccurate version of the thinking of "Pentagon civilians," supported by an invented quotation:

> **The vice president and Pentagon civilians, however, advocated a very different approach. Rather than risking an open-ended political process that Americans could influence but not control, they wanted to be able to limit the Iraqis' power and handpick those Iraqis who would participate. . . . Doug Feith clearly stated his belief that it would not be necessary for the Iraqi exiles to legitimize themselves: "We can legitimize them," he said, through our economic assistance and the good governance the U.S. would provide. They never understood that, fundamentally, political control depends on the consent of the governed.**

---

*A point we did not make—and one the CIA should have emphasized—was that bin Laden's fatwa expressed outrage at "the presence of the Americans in the Arab Peninsula" as a "pre-planned military occupation." An occupation policy would, of course, bolster his position. See [Usama bin Laden], "Declaration of War against the Americans Occupying the Land of the Two Holy Places," published in *Al Quds al Arabi*, August 1996, available at http://www.pbs.org/newshour/terrorism/international/fatwa_1996.html.

Tenet implies here that there was some alternative proposal on the table for an "open-ended political process that Americans could influence but not control." But the alternative actually under consideration was State's transitional civil authority idea, which would have *maximized* American control by installing an open-ended occupation government. He also fails to acknowledge that, in the politics of post-Saddam Iraq, the issue of the exiles' legitimacy proved to be of no great significance.

At this March 10 meeting, President Bush approved the IIA concept I presented. The meeting's official summary of conclusions, an unusually detailed memorandum, specified that the President endorsed the key points in my presentation (paraphrased here):

- The IIA should be formed "as soon as possible after liberation" and include internals, Kurds, and exiles.
- We were to ensure that internals were "fully represented," which could be done by convening a political conference on liberated Iraqi territory.
- The United States should allocate responsibilities with the IIA by agreement.
- The IIA "would serve only in the interim, until a more fully representative government can be established through elections."
- The United States and IIA should work together on appointing ministry officials* and the United States should transfer each ministry to full Iraqi control as soon as possible.
- We should sponsor a UN Security Council resolution that would authorize the IIA and otherwise support Iraqi reconstruction after Saddam's overthrow.

The next day, in a "backgrounder" paper for the news media, my office explained the rationale for the IIA. "The Coalition does not intend to leave a mess behind after liberating Iraq," we declared; we had a commitment to stay and complete the mission. At the same time, however, "Iraq belongs to the Iraqis, not to any foreigners": We also had a commitment to leave. The IIA would *not*, we stressed, be a U.S. military occupation government of Iraq. Rather, it would be:

---

*The National Security Council briefing referenced here was similar to the one I gave at the March 7, 2003, Principals Committee meeting (detailed above).

- **An Iraqi "government in formation," that will exercise increasing authority to run governmental institutions in Iraq**
- **A means for Iraqis to participate immediately in the economic and political reconstruction of their country**
- **A productive outlet for Iraqi nationalism**
- **An arena in which the Iraqi people can begin the process of building democratic institutions**

Rice asked me to work with Zalmay Khalilzad to inform Iraqi oppositionist leaders of President Bush's decision to support the IIA. Khalilzad—who worked for Rice on the National Security Council staff besides serving as the President's Special Envoy to the Iraqi opposition—was assigned to call Iyad Allawi and Adnan Pachachi, the former Iraqi Foreign Minister. At Rice's direction, I telephoned the Kurdish leaders Massoud Barzani and Jalal Talabani, Sherif Ali of the Constitutional Monarchy Movement, and Ahmad Chalabi. This was a diplomatic job, normally one for State officials to perform, but Rice chose not to assign it to State, presumably because Powell and Armitage had so consistently opposed the IIA.

My office was also given the responsibility for turning the IIA concept into an action plan. We did so, and reviewed the detailed plan with other agencies, preparing to brief it to the Principals before asking the President for approval.

The Bush Administration has often been condemned for thinking it would be easy to set up a democratic government in post-Saddam Iraq. But the discussions in which I participated reflected no such thinking. We saw serious difficulties in encouraging democracy in a country with no history of democratic practice. Iraq lacked key institutional and cultural building blocks. The history of democratic progress elsewhere in the world suggested that Iraq might be able to overcome these problems, but they were clearly large and complex. President Bush believed that after eliminating the threat from Saddam's regime, it would be necessary to confront those challenges and put Iraq on the path to democracy—as the United States had done, with great mutual benefit, for other former enemy countries throughout the twentieth century.

My office pointed out the tensions and paradoxes involved in promoting democracy in Iraq. The effort required Iraqi leadership, but there were not many Iraqis who were actually familiar with democratic practice. The United States could not force democracy on Iraq; it is a contradiction in terms to think that one country can force another to practice government by, of, and for the people. But we saw that Iraq would need outside help. Without a reasonably strong guiding hand from the United States, Iraq might not even get launched in the direction of limited government and rule of law.

It would have been naïve to assume that democracy would arise spontaneously in Iraq if we simply left the country to its own devices. In Afghanistan, the United States and other foreign actors (including the United Nations) had played an important role in shaping the country's government and leadership. The results were proving popular with the Afghan people—though the Afghans probably wouldn't have been able to produce them "democratically" on their own. Our best chance of promoting representative, responsible government in Iraq, I thought, was to maximize the influence of those Iraqis who had experienced life in democratic societies, thought seriously about cultivating democracy in Iraq, and participated in democratic give-and-take in the various Iraqi opposition political conferences over the last dozen years or so.

For a March 31 Principals Committee meeting, Rumsfeld sent Cheney, Powell, Tenet, Rice, and the other Principals a set of thoughts that explained the IIA as an attempt to reconcile various U.S. interests that were in tension with one another. Our goal was an Iraq run not by us or others, he argued, but by Iraqis who would exercise authority in an enlightened way. Paradoxically, he observed, it might be impossible for Iraq to get on the path to *self-government* if we did not, early on, exercise strong influence *from the outside*—to give supporters of democratic principles "a head start in the post-Saddam Iraqi political process." Was this hypocritical? Were we really would-be puppeteers? No, for we actually had *no* interest in controlling Iraq other than helping the country develop a rule of law that could improve life domestically and support international peace and security.

Rumsfeld's paper went on to summarize the dilemma as he saw it:

- **There is tension between our interests in steering the process toward a moderate and free Iraq and our interest in winning immediate broad support in and out of Iraq for our policy.**
- **In other words, there is tension between:**
  - **the *substantive* goal of a free Iraq as envisioned by President Bush and**
  - **the *procedural* goal for the US to be as inclusive, and as "hands off" as possible.**
- **The USG [U.S. government] should not now raise procedural considerations above our substantive goal. An excessively "hands off" approach may produce an antidemocratic result**

(as premature elections in Algeria some years ago, for example, produced a victory for antidemocratic Islamist extremists).

- **It will take time to cultivate a political culture of self-government in Iraq, especially among those who have lived their lives under Saddam's tyranny.**

After discussing the IIA with other agencies and with Iraqi externals, my office had revised our proposal on appointing the executive council, giving a greater voice to internals. But we decided to include the six-person Iraqi Leadership Council elected at the Salahuddin conference,* arguing: "This should help protect us against the charge that the Coalition is arbitrarily selecting the Iraqi leadership. . . . As we have to start somewhere, we should start with Iraqis with whom we are familiar and who have already endorsed principles that the USG supports."

In his regular video teleconferences with Rumsfeld, Abizaid had urged that we find ways to show the Iraqi people that their own countrymen, supported by the United States, were in the process of creating a new government. The idea fit squarely within the IIA concept I had briefed to the President. Abizaid was working with Khalilzad and my staff to implement the idea by organizing what would become the Nasiriyah conference: the first political meeting of Iraqis—internals as well as externals—on newly liberated Iraqi soil.

In an April 1 memo to the President, Rumsfeld argued that it was crucial to our war effort to convince the Iraqi people that the new government in Iraq "is going to be a free Iraqi government, not a US military government." He reported that Franks and Abizaid were pushing to organize a highly visible event *soon* to make this point. The way to do this, Rumsfeld believed, was by announcing the IIA. "Publicly beginning the process of creating the IIA would be a major boost" to our efforts to influence general Iraqi attitudes toward the war, he wrote. Unhappy with Tenet's and Armitage's reluctance to move quickly on the IIA, Rumsfeld wrote:

*The six members of the Iraqi Leadership Council were Iyad Allawi (Shia Arab) of the Iraqi National Accord, Massoud Barzani (Sunni Kurd) of the Kurdistan Democratic Party, Ahmad Chalabi (Shia Arab) of the Iraqi National Congress, Muhammed Bakr al-Hakim (Shia Arab) of the Supreme Council for Islamic Revolution in Iraq, Adnan Pachachi, a former Foreign Minister of Iraq, and Jalal Talabani (Sunni Kurd), of the Patriotic Union of Kurdistan.

> **The implementation plan we distributed may not be perfect, but we've talked with Generals Franks and Abizaid, and others, and I'm convinced the plan is a reasonable one. Outside the National Military Command Center here in the Pentagon hangs a sign that quotes George Patton: "A good plan executed now is better than a perfect plan next week." I'm sure the interagency process could, over time, come up with a lot of good ideas, but we need a good idea cut-off date.**

Frustrated by the resistance from State and CIA, Rumsfeld used language that was pushier than he usually employed with the President: "Unless there is a fundamental objection to what we have proposed, I intend to direct General Franks to coordinate an announcement in Iraq of the formation of an organizing committee to begin implementation of the IIA." Rumsfeld sent a copy of this April 1 memo to his fellow Principals.

Rumsfeld did not like being at odds with Tenet on operational matters—work that Defense and CIA personnel would have to perform together in the field. So he raised our IIA plan with Tenet in an April 2 meeting of only Defense and CIA personnel, including Abizaid (via video connection). Rumsfeld said he wanted to move forward with the IIA in order to help Franks. Tenet repeated the warnings against the ambitions of Chalabi and the externals; though he granted that it would be good to put an Iraqi face forward, Tenet warned against making the internals "feel imposed upon or dispossessed."

Abizaid then laid out his idea of the political conference. His organizing principle, he said, was "don't cut anyone out of the process." At the time, the only liberated Iraqi territory was in the south. This meant the "Sunni heartland" would be underrepresented, Abizaid said, so we would have to find a way to get the Sunnis involved in the IIA.

A CIA official speaking via video from the Persian Gulf region suggested that we should "get Iraqis to stand up—be active" to counter propaganda that the coalition was an occupying force. He urged us to rethink CENTCOM's proposal, which had been to hold the conference far in the south—in the city of Umm Qasr. Coalition forces had enjoyed a positive reception in Najaf, he said; the more northern cities of Najaf or Nasiriyah would be better.

We discussed the mechanics of choosing Iraqis to invite. Wolfowitz said we should start with the six from the Iraqi Leadership Council and then invite more; Tenet said he agreed—finally, a hopeful sign for Defense–CIA cooperation. Declaring that the conference must point toward an IIA, Rumsfeld asked the regional CIA official to work with Abizaid on a plan.

I prepared a draft agenda for a one-day Iraqi political conference in Nasiriyah and sent it around to Tenet, Franks, Abizaid, and others at the CIA and CENTCOM. By April 4 we had general agreement on the location, whom to invite, and points the Iraqis might want to use in a declaration.

Rumsfeld had made clear that he was determined to push forward with the IIA. In line with Powell and Armitage, Tenet and his CIA colleagues had delayed the matter as much as they could. They continued to warn ominously that the internals might resent the externals. Yet Tenet now seemed to understand that he had to shift from overt resistance to a reasonable degree of cooperation, or risk being marginalized.

Like the memoirs of Tenet, Franks, and other insiders, the numerous books and articles about the war in Iraq by outside commentators (such as Woodward, Packer, Ricks, Risen, Gordon and Trainor, Rieff, Fallows, and others) contain scarcely a mention of the Iraqi Interim Authority plan, let alone a discussion of its merits. But the IIA was the official U.S. policy for post-Saddam governance of Iraq, a plan developed through the interagency process and approved by the President.

Powell and Armitage never embraced the IIA. As late as September 15, 2003, Powell still asserted that a power-sharing arrangement between the coalition and the Iraqis was impossible. In interviews with journalists, various State officials have simply ignored the IIA plan. Instead, they maintained that (1) the Pentagon had a plan to make Ahmad Chalabi the head of a new Iraqi government; (2) that State had a better plan (never specified in detail); and (3) that the Pentagon civilian leaders "threw out" the State plan (even though the U.S. never actually appointed Chalabi). The voluminously documented history of the IIA contradicts every element of that widely accepted but fictional account. To date, however, the State officials' narrative—by default—has swept the field.

Coalition forces entered Baghdad on April 5. Four days later, they helped an excited crowd of Iraqis topple the statue of Saddam Hussein in Firdaus Square. The television in my office was on as the statue was being pulled down, and I watched with fascination and happiness—until I saw the exuberant U.S. soldier, who was looping the cable around the statue's neck, take a U.S. flag out of his pocket and drape Saddam's metallic head with it. This was a moment history would remember—an opportunity to proclaim "liberation, not occupation" to the Iraqis and the world—and the U.S. flag was exactly the wrong symbol.

I rarely buzzed the Chairman of the Joint Chiefs on the intercom, but I did so now. Are you watching television? I asked. General Myers turned to the cable news inset on his computer monitor. "That U.S. flag is a big problem," I told him. He immediately understood. "Can you get word to that soldier, *fast*?" I asked. Myers said he would "get on it." A few seconds later, the U.S. soldier pocketed the U.S. flag. Someone had given him an Iraqi flag and he put that over the statue's head. "God bless that soldier," I thought, knowing that even the Chairman could not have worked that quickly. The soldier or one of his buddies must have reasoned the problem through on his own. Myers buzzed me back. "He's a good guy," he said. "I had nothing to do with it."

An hour or so later, I received a phone call from a foreign official. Had he heard that Baghdad had fallen? I asked. "Doug," he answered, "Baghdad didn't fall. It rose."

The twenty-one-day campaign to overthrow the Iraqi regime was a military achievement that brought credit to the men and women of our armed forces, to their coalition comrades in arms, and to General Franks and his staff, who planned and commanded the combat operations.

But Franks's responsibilities did not end with the overthrow of the regime. His duty was to ensure public order once the regime was gone, to provide all basic governmental services for a transition period, and, with the help of Jay Garner's organization (which reported to Franks), to lay the foundation for the new Iraqi government.

As Saddam Hussein's regime collapsed, the looting and violence in the streets of Baghdad resulted in substantial destruction—and the intense news coverage it received badly damaged America's standing in Iraq. Much of the sacking of government buildings appears now to have been purposeful sabotage organized by the ousted Baathists. The systematic destruction was apparently aimed not just at obliterating information about Iraqi weapons programs, but also at sabotaging the effort to create a new government. Whatever Saddam's own doubts that the United States would actually invade, his regime may have planned this scorched-earth campaign as part of a postoverthrow insurgency strategy. If so, the CIA's failure to discover those plans in advance was a serious problem: Such intelligence would have assisted CENTCOM in deciding on the size and type of forces for its stabilization mission. A detailed study would be needed to pin down whether the immediate postoverthrow disorder should be attributed to poor intelligence or a lack of plans on our side, a shortage of coalition troops in Baghdad,* or simply bad decision making.

The unsuppressed violence affected every aspect of the plans the U.S. government had made for reconstructing post-Saddam Iraq. The violence was self-perpetuating: The more violence there was, the less willing the Iraqis were to provide information to allow coalition forces to defeat it. The sackings, shootings, and disorder discouraged Iraqis from cooperating with the coalition across the board. Many refused to accept roles we hoped they would play in the reconstruction of Iraq—as security forces, government officials, and political leaders.

Bush Administration officials had anticipated chaos and violence. Joint Staff and CENTCOM briefings, analyses from my office, CIA assessments, and State Department and National Security Council staff papers all discussed the likelihood of revenge killings, ethnic violence, looting of wealthy neighborhoods in Baghdad, terrorist attacks, violence fomented by Iraq's neighbors, and other types of killing and destruction in the turmoil that would inevitably follow the regime's removal.

What was *not* anticipated—by any office, as far as I know—was the Iraqi regime's ability to conduct a sustained campaign against coalition forces *after it was overthrown.* When the CIA, in August 2002, analyzed how Saddam might attack, surprise, or otherwise foil us in a war, its analysis dealt only with actions Saddam might take while still in power. I never saw a CIA assessment that the Baathists, after their ouster, would be able to organize, recruit for, finance, supply, command, and control an insurgency—let alone in alliance with foreign jihadists. Yet this is the problem that developed during the first year after Saddam's overthrow.

The Administration's postwar plans did anticipate that the environment in Iraq after regime change would be tumultuous and possibly violent. Officials did not assume, however, that the coalition would be reconstructing the economic infrastructure and its political system while the war against the Baathists still raged. The assumption was that the postwar work would be done *post*—after—the war.

By keeping key parts of the country in tumult, the Baathists preserved

---

*Looting—unlike the sabotage campaign—was a major problem mainly in the immediate aftermath of the regime's ouster. The small-force strategy for major combat operations, while it saved American lives, limited the number of forces we had available to deal with looting. Had that been the extent of the post-Saddam disorder, it might be judged a reasonable trade-off, even in retrospect. Whether CENTCOM should have requested a larger U.S. force in Iraq to fight the insurgency as it developed throughout the summer of 2003 and beyond is a different question.

among Iraqis the fear that the old regime might return to power. Even after that statue came down in Baghdad's Firdaus Square, the Iraqis knew that Saddam Hussein and his agents remained at large—and able to strike the coalition and the Iraqis who supported it.

It was an emotional, self-conscious, nervous, and happy collection of approximately eighty Iraqis who gathered in Nasiriyah on April 15 at the political conference organized by Jay Garner and his interagency team. The conference was a way to begin to put an Iraqi face on the liberation of the country. The invitees were mainly internals—notables selected by Garner and his advisers as potential leaders of the new Iraq. For many, this conference was the first opportunity they had had in their lives to join a free, public discussion of political affairs.

Administration officials wanted the conference to serve several purposes. For U.S. officials, it was a chance to learn something about the notables—to hear the internals speak for themselves, without having their thoughts channeled by CIA and State officials as if by séance. We could watch them in action and see how they related to one another, which of them had leadership qualities, and what kind of political principles they espoused. This could help Garner and his team decide whom to support for the IIA. For the Iraqi people, the conference would be a public launch of the political process to create the IIA. It could assure the Iraqi people, as Garner put it, that "our goal is to turn Iraq over to the Iraqi people, but with a government that expresses the free will of the people of Iraq."

Most of the main external organizations sent representatives to the Nasiriyah conference. We made a point, however, of excluding those organizations' *leaders*. We wanted the internals to predominate—to speak up and assume leadership, if they were so inclined—and we thought they might be deferential or keep silent if high-profile externals attended. The external leaders—those on the Leadership Council—all agreed to stay away. After we asked them to do so, however, I received a phone call from Kanan Makiya, the eminent Iraqi expatriate intellectual, who said this was a mistake. He said we could help the cause of democracy more now by including those leaders and bolstering their authority. "What is required to stop chaos and looting are symbols of Iraqi authority," he insisted. I think he was more correct than I and other U.S. officials appreciated at the time.

The conference heard remarks from Garner and representatives of the other coalition countries on the host committee: Australia, Britain, and Poland. The Iraqis crafted political principles for inclusion in a conference declaration. Chris Straub, of my office, attended and reported that the Iraqis roundly cheered a call for elimination of the Baath Party and had a "contentious (but not rancorous) discussion" about whether Iraq should designate itself an Islamic state. The initial speech on the subject was from a Shiite cleric who "endorsed separation of mosque and state as a key prerequisite of democracy." A counterargument was then offered by a lay schoolteacher.

According to Straub, the relationship between internals and externals was "good overall." He observed:

- **A definite "gulf" exists between the two groups, but everyone came together as the event proceeded.**
- **Internals were understandably quieter, but were drawn out by discussion moderators.**
- **No apparent trace of resentment of externals by internals.**

Makiya also attended the Nasiriyah conference and sent me his assessment. Makiya knew a great deal about the Bush Administration's Iraq policy process: He had been active in the Future of Iraq Project at State, and had discussed the issues repeatedly with policy officials in the Pentagon and White House, including the President. He felt qualified and free to criticize Administration policy. After Nasiriyah, he reported that, in his view, the Administration had been too timid about empowering Iraqi leaders. He called the conference "a harmless non-event" that was too much of a public relations exercise, though "a good final statement appeared." Among Makiya's key impressions:

> **The much vaunted inside/outside (internals versus exiles) tensions did not materialize in practice. . . . This is not to say that it might not emerge in the future as time passes. . . .**
>
> **The overwhelming sentiment of the meeting was for a very strict and thorough De-Ba'athification program. . . . There were two notable exceptions [one of whom was a representative of Iyad Allawi's Iraqi National Accord]. . . .**
>
> **It was not my impression that any of the speeches made by non-Iraqis left any deep impression on the Iraqis present, with the exception of Jay Garner. . . . His earnest, genuine, heartfelt devotion to the task of helping Iraqis is worth more than decades of so-called "expertise" on the Middle East.**

> **Participants were terrified at the prospect of anarchy, spread of crime and loss of central authority. . . . The overall impression is that anarchy is in essence breaking out. The vacuum is one of political authority. . . .**

Makiya argued that the IIA concept, as it emerged from the Bush Administration's "deeply debilitating 'interagency process,' " was "overly complicated, theoretical, [and] drawn out." He warned: "Iraqis need a tangible, palpable and simple sense that some Iraqi/Iraqis are in charge. This is non-existent at the moment. The feeling that I am referring to is primal, very basic and goes to the heart of what politics is all about."

Regarding law and order, Makiya said that the only sensible way to solve the problem was to "encourage the rapid growth and training of free Iraqi forces as the Iraqi contingent of the coalition." His sense, though, was that "Centcom is not inclined to go down this road at the moment."

General Pace and I discussed Makiya's critique. Pace undertook to convey it to CENTCOM. I suggested that Rumsfeld meet with Makiya.

On April 16, General Franks issued his "Freedom Message to the Iraqi People." With the removal of the Saddam Hussein regime, Iraq needed an authority to protect lives and property and deliver humanitarian assistance. "Therefore," Franks declared, "I am creating the Coalition Provisional Authority to exercise powers of government temporarily. . . ."

This message had been in the works within the U.S. government for months. The first draft from CENTCOM, which was designated "Proclamation No. 1," had been filled with impenetrable bureaucratic jargon. The title, my staff pointed out, would ring in Iraqi ears as a reminder of past military coups. We rewrote the document, renaming it the "Freedom Message." I handed it to Franks when we were together at a meeting in Rumsfeld's office. He said he would review it with his staff.

A short while later, as we were about to start another meeting with Rumsfeld, Franks told me he liked my rewrite and would propose only one change. The draft he handed back to me had only one sentence crossed out—the statement that the Baath Party "is hereby disestablished."

You're suggesting that you would *not* get rid of the Baath Party? I asked. Franks said that the Baathists were a political party, and if we were going to promote democracy, we shouldn't be banning political parties. At that point, our meeting with Rumsfeld started, so I did not respond.

It was all to the good that I did not have a full exchange with Franks on this point. I might have tried to explain to him that the Baath Party was not a political party in any democratically meaningful sense of the term. The party, rather, had become a synonym for the Iraqi regime, more or less as the Nazi Party *was* the German regime under Adolf Hitler. (Baathism was invented in the 1930s on the model of the European Fascist and Nazi ideologies.) I could not imagine General Dwight Eisenhower thinking he would liberate Germany but not abolish the Nazi political apparatus. I wondered if Franks's CIA advisers were influencing him here: They tended to adopt the Sunni perspective and were inclined to look somewhat benignly on Baathists. If Franks were to insist on preserving the Iraqi Baath Party, I figured it would be better for Rumsfeld, not me, to walk the general through the relevant history and political science.

I mentioned the issue to Rumsfeld. I never heard him discuss it with Franks. When I sent the draft Freedom Message around to the other agencies for their comments, none proposed leaving the Baath Party in existence. The disestablishment language remained in the Freedom Message, as Franks ultimately published it. It never became an issue of great controversy, even when almost every other aspect of U.S. Iraq policy did.

The disestablishment question was separate from the issue of "de-Baathification," which had to do with whether—and which—members of the Baath Party would be allowed to serve in the new Iraqi government and military. Though Franks's April 16 announcement that he was creating (and heading) the Coalition Provisional Authority did disestablish the party, it said nothing specific about the status of *members* of the party. What to do about de-Baathification was still under discussion within the Administration. President Bush had been briefed on the current interagency proposal on de-Baathification by a member of Rice's staff at the March 10 National Security Council meeting, but work on the issue was still under way.

In a paper my office wrote for the Pentagon public affairs office on April 16, we anticipated the question: "What will happen to members of the Ba'ath Party, which General Franks 'disestablished' "? Our proposed answer was:

> **[The party's] property and records will be considered by the CPA as the property of the Iraqi people. Absent exceptional circumstances, top-tier members of the Ba'ath Party will not be eligible to hold any positions of responsibility under the CPA. Lower ranking members of the Ba'ath Party will not necessarily be barred from such employment. No one will be punished**

merely for membership in the Ba'ath Party; however, those party members who committed war crimes or atrocities will be prosecuted in an appropriate forum.

With diplomatic advice from Khalilzad and State's Ryan Crocker, Jay Garner worked to advance the Iraqi political process, aiming to create the IIA as quickly as possible so that national ministries could be put into new Iraqi hands. He was having mixed success. The Nasiriyah conference had gone fairly well; to the extent we could gauge general Iraqi reactions, they seemed mainly positive—better than Makiya's severe assessment.

But the effort to establish an IIA Leadership Council was not going well. Part of the problem was that the Iraqi external leaders selected during February's Salahuddin conference were finding it hard to agree on which internals to recruit to join the organizing committee for the IIA. U.S. officials voiced frustration, but Garner and his team could not solve the problem. Meanwhile, every proposal for breaking the IIA logjam—at another, larger Nasiriyah-type conference, or through a series of regional meetings or otherwise—became the subject of protracted interagency debate in Washington.

During an April 22 meeting with Rumsfeld at the Pentagon, Kanan Makiya sounded an alarm about Islamist influence growing in the south. The problem, he thought, was being aggravated by the coalition's failure to create new Iraqi police, with a new culture symbolized by "wearing new uniforms." The result was that local police were "springing up" in southern cities and "this is creating local militias—dangerous." Makiya asserted that it should be possible to recruit thousands of Iraqis for the Free Iraqi Forces, "but Franks is not doing it yet." They could be used in the cities, he said, and this "would allow U.S. forces to stay out of the cities." He added: "Iraqis will make mistakes, *but they'll be Iraqi mistakes*."

Makiya warned that Iraqi politics would not develop democratically if the United States did not "direct the process." "You're trying so hard not to be imperialists that you're not giving Iraqis a sense that you're in charge," he observed. Regarding the IIA Leadership Council, he said: "You don't want a committee that quarrels among itself. You must pick and choose. Pick people who are with you. Do not be even-handed between those who are with you and those who are against you. Leadership is required—not laissez-faire politically." When Rumsfeld asked for an evaluation of the Iraqi leaders, Makiya responded that Chalabi was the most effective as well as the most controversial; he could be difficult and haughty, but he has "leadership talent." Rumsfeld shared none of his own views at this meeting.

U.S. officials received news and analysis about Iraq from many sources, official and private. I have highlighted here the reports from Makiya because they combined firsthand observation, acute perception, blunt delivery, timeliness, and considerable prescience.

The day after this meeting, as it happened, General Myers sent CENTCOM formal guidance from Rumsfeld on police and civil administration in Iraq. The guidance balanced two major interests: First, to assure the Iraqi people that the Baathists would no longer be allowed to oppress them and, second, to involve Iraqis—including current police forces—as much as possible in establishing law and order. The interplay between these interests was complex. There was an urgent need to employ Iraqi security forces, but using the country's familiar Baathist forces might dishearten, frighten away, and possibly incite to rebellion the vast majority of Iraqis who had suffered badly at the hands of the Baathists (virtually all the Kurds and Shia Arabs, and many of the Sunni Arabs).

Since Franks was responsible for maintaining public order, Myers directed that the CENTCOM commander's first priority should be to "demobilize, to the extent necessary," the particular security units that had served as the Baathist regime's instruments of repression. Franks should also review the operations of the Iraq police, and the Iraqi people's reaction to them, and judge whether they should be retained. Myers wanted Franks to examine the status of local police and civil structures and develop a plan for returning their functions "to the Iraqi people." The plan should address removal of personnel "whose ties to the Ba'athist regime may impede the overall objectives of U.S. policy or who have engaged in or ordered acts in violation of basic human rights." It should also address "reintegration of Iraqis" who could contribute to reform. Under U.S. law it was State, not Defense, that had the authority to train and equip police in such situations, so Franks would have to work with State on these matters.

Garner continued to work to generate momentum for the IIA. In Baghdad on April 28, he convened the second political conference of newly liberated Iraqis. Roughly 250 Iraqis participated—three times the number at the Nasiriyah conference. The participants resolved to create an Iraqi government at their next conference, to be held within four weeks. Garner was encouraged by what he saw as increased interaction between the externals and internals. Also encouraging was the presence at the Baghdad conference of a delegation from the Supreme Council for the Islamic Revolution in Iraq, the Shiite organization that had boycotted the Nasiriyah meeting.

A few days before the Baghdad conference convened, President Bush decided to appoint former Ambassador L. Paul Bremer as the new senior U.S. civilian official in Iraq. My understanding was (and remains) that this was done at Rumsfeld's initiative, with encouragement from Rice.

When I had called Garner in early January 2003 to ask him to organize ORHA, I assured him that his mission would not last more than a few months. I told Garner that, soon after Saddam's removal, Rumsfeld planned to put in place a civilian administrator with a political or diplomatic background. Garner's initial reluctance to accept the ORHA position made it clear that he had no interest in taking on this larger assignment.

In the last week of April, Rumsfeld judged that the work of the top U.S. civilian official in Iraq now had a crucial diplomatic dimension. This required new administrative arrangements.

Before Bremer was appointed to the top civilian job in Iraq, Rumsfeld asked me if I knew him. I said I did, but not well. Rumsfeld told me he was considering Bremer for the Iraq job, and I said I thought he had some good credentials for it. I wasn't in on Rumsfeld's consultations about Bremer with Powell or any of the other Principals—or with the President. Rumsfeld told me that one of his motives in selecting Bremer was to make it easier for Defense and State officials to work together on Iraq. Rumsfeld's recruitment of a former career Foreign Service officer should have discredited the notion that the Defense Department was bent on excluding State from Iraq policy.

Rumsfeld did not view Bremer's appointment as a rejection of Garner. Garner's job had been to create and run ORHA, which became an office within CENTCOM, under Franks. Garner was never the head of the Coalition Provisional Authority; Franks was. Garner's role was to assist Franks in performing the CPA job. After his deployment to the Persian Gulf region, Garner no longer reported directly to Rumsfeld; he reported to Franks (and not even directly to him).

When asked to serve as the new civilian administrator in Iraq, Bremer insisted that the job be elevated. He was *not* interested in stepping into Garner's shoes as head of ORHA. Accordingly, Bremer was hired to replace Franks at the top of the CPA. It was a different and much bigger job that was designed to report directly to Rumsfeld. Bremer's appointment meant that the occupation government of Iraq was now passing from military to civilian hands.

Bremer asked Garner to remain in Iraq and work for him within the

CPA, but Garner refused. He would overlap with Bremer for only a short while. The handling of Bremer's appointment displeased Garner; the news media generally reported that he had been fired, which was obnoxious and unfair. As Garner has stressed in interviews, he was also frustrated by the timing of Bremer's appointment: He believed he was on the verge of a political breakthrough in setting up the IIA, and would have preferred to stay a few months longer to complete some tasks—to "begin to provide the structure of a government":

> **"Really, what I'd like to do is put that off till about July [Garner recalled telling Rumsfeld], because I've got a lot of moving parts here that I think that I can get solidified by July." And [Rumsfeld] said, "Well, I don't have any control over that. . . . I don't think I can give you that." And I said, "Well, then, when [Bremer] gets here, I'll come on home." He says: "I don't want you to come home. I want you to stay there with him a while."**
>
> **I said: "Mr. Secretary, I'm sure that Jerry Bremer and I will get along fine. That's not the problem. . . . The problem is the people below us. You can't have the guy who was in charge staying with the new guy in charge, because the people below you, they don't know where their loyalties are. . . . The best thing that can happen to him and me, really, is for me to leave after he gets here."**

Soon after agreeing to serve, Bremer visited me at the Pentagon. I organized briefings for him about the Pentagon and interagency work done on Iraq over the last year or so. My staff compiled a book for him containing the record on development of the IIA—the "concept for organizing Iraq's postwar political reconstruction." In the cover memo we gave Bremer the following overview of the policy process.

After deciding not to recognize an Iraqi provisional government, we reported, the Administration had first considered giving the Iraqis a highly restricted initial role in reconstruction—a mere "consultative council." In early March 2003, however, the Defense Department's IIA concept was "successfully briefed to the President at the March 10 NSC meeting." The IIA was to be given "significant influence" over Iraq's foreign relations in the immediate postwar period, and also responsibility for drafting a new constitution and the authority to administer government agencies and ministries.

Iraqi political reconstruction was "well under way," we told Bremer, but important questions remained open. We still needed to decide how to select an IIA "in the shortest possible time while maximizing its pro-democratic outlook and legitimacy in the eyes of Iraqis," and to settle the IIA's final structure. The coalition had hoped that the April 28 Baghdad conference would endorse a structure for the IIA and might discuss a timeline. "Both goals were met—and then some." The conference had voted to form an interim "government," a term the Iraqis preferred over "authority." The Iraqis had resolved to hold another meeting within four weeks to choose the government.

In his preparatory meetings at the Pentagon, Bremer heard repeatedly that the President's policy was to form the IIA "as soon as possible after liberation" and to transfer ministries "to full Iraqi control as soon as possible." We discussed the IIA with him at length. We gave him our written work on the subject and the National Security Council meeting summary that recorded the President's approval. Bremer received it all most collegially. As far as we knew, he agreed with the policy and intended to put the IIA plan into practice.

Timeline 3. Iraq: December 2002–December 2003

2002

Dec. 14–16	Iraqi opposition political conference, London

2003

Jan. 20	National Security Presidential Directive 24, creating ORHA (headed by Gen. Garner)
Feb. 24–28	Iraqi opposition political conference, Salahuddin (northern Iraq)
Mar. 19	Start of Operation Iraqi Freedom
Apr. 9	Liberation of Baghdad; toppling of statue
Apr.16	Freedom Message published by General Franks: establishes Coalition Provisional Authority (occupation government headed by Franks)
Apr. 28	Baghdad conference—resolved to create the Iraqi Interim Authority (which never materialized)
May 9	Presidential letter of appointment for Bremer as Special Envoy to Iraq
May 12	Bremer arrives in Baghdad
May 13	Letter from Secretary of Defense naming Bremer the head of CPA (replacing Franks)
May 16	CPA Order No. 1: De-Baathification
May 23	CPA Order No. 2: Dissolution of the Iraqi army
Jul. 13	Iraqi Governing Council created
Aug. 19	Bombing of UN Headquarters, killing Special Representative Vieira de Mello
Aug 28	Bombing of shrine at Najaf, killing Hakim

Sept. 8	**Bremer op-ed appears in Washington Post**
Oct. 26–28	**Meetings in Washington: Rumsfeld, Bremer, Abizaid, et al.**
Nov. 15	**Agreement with Iraqi leadership on terminating CPA and launching Iraqi Interim Government**

14
"FROM LIBERATION TO OCCUPATION"*

L. Paul "Jerry" Bremer said he wanted his arrival in Baghdad to have a theme: The Baathists are not coming back. I met with him on May 9, the day President Bush appointed him Presidential Envoy, just before he left for Baghdad to become the head of the Coalition Provisional Authority.

Bremer had considered his point carefully. Our forces had not yet captured Saddam, and many Iraqis remained fearful of the Baathists—and therefore unwilling to cooperate with U.S. officials—on security, political reconstruction, and other matters. Bremer saw it as his first task to offer assurance: The CPA and coalition military forces would do more than just oust Saddam; they would eliminate his apparatus of tyranny and ensure that his killers would not retake the government. I thought Bremer had selected his "arrival theme" wisely, and I told him so.

My staff had briefed Bremer about the months of interagency work on de-Baathification. Franklin Miller (of Rice's staff) presented a draft policy for President Bush at the March 10 National Security Council meeting. That draft policy concentrated on the top-ranking 1 percent or so of the approximately two million Iraqis in the Baath Party. When President

---

*Iraqi Foreign Minister Hoshyar Zebari: "I think the biggest sin was to change the mission from liberation to occupation. That is the mother of all sins, honestly." Robert L. Pollock, "The Voice of Iraq," *Wall Street Journal*, June 24, 2006, p. A10.

Bush said it was "hard to imagine punishing twenty-five thousand people," Miller clarified that the proposed policy did not call for imprisonment or even fines for people simply because they were members of the party. Baath Party top leaders would be "punished" only by exclusion from government work. No one at that meeting argued that this was draconian, let alone unjust. Even the CIA, which generally made a point of shunning anti-Baathist rhetoric, assessed that some de-Baathification would be required: It would be necessary to dissolve Iraqi military units that were "intimately linked to the regime," and Iraqi ministries should be "purged of Saddam loyalists and restructured to eliminate the Ba'ath party oversight mechanism." And, despite the on-the-one-hand-on-the-other nature of many of the reports in the State Department–sponsored Future of Iraq Project, one unequivocal point made throughout was the necessity for substantial de-Baathification.

After Miller's March 10 briefing, the de-Baathification policy was worked and reworked in interagency meetings, and by early May it had interagency clearance. I was planning to report the policy to Rumsfeld and recommend he send it to Franks for implementation, when Bremer asked me to hold off. Bremer had thoughts of his own on the subject, he said, and wanted to consider the de-Baathification policy carefully. As the new CPA head, he thought *he* should announce and implement the policy himself, to communicate in a memorable way his arrival theme that the Baathists were gone for good. He planned to issue a series of orders soon after his arrival, and he wanted two, in particular, ready for release: De-Baathification as CPA Order No. 1, and the dissolution of the Iraqi army as No. 2.

At this May 9 meeting in my office I was handed a draft of CPA Order No. 2 by Walter Slocombe, whom Rumsfeld had recruited to serve as the Senior Ministry Adviser for the Iraqi Defense Ministry. Slocombe had served as Under Secretary of Defense for Policy for the last seven years of the Clinton Administration. A thoughtful man of wide-ranging experience in national security, he had played a key role in the Bosnia reconstruction effort in the 1990s and worked on arms control in the Carter Administration's Pentagon. Though he also had served on Nixon's National Security Council staff, he generally practiced tax law as a private attorney in the years when the Republicans had the White House.

The draft order Slocombe gave me declared the dissolution of a list of Iraqi military and national security entities, including the following:

- Defense Ministry
- Ministry of Information

- Iraqi Intelligence Service
- Special Security Organization
- Saddam's bodyguards
- Army, air force, navy, and other regular military services
- Republican Guard and Special Republican Guard
- Fedayeen Saddam and other paramilitaries
- Revolutionary Command Council
- Revolutionary, Special, and National Security Courts

It ordered Iraqis to preserve the assets of the dissolved entities and provided that their financial obligations should be paid. It dismissed their employees and provided that those employees (all except senior Baath Party members) would receive a termination payment, to be determined by Bremer. It promised payment of pensions. And it announced the CPA's plans to create a new Iraqi military. I said I would review the draft order and ask Rumsfeld how he wanted to handle it.

Bremer arrived in Iraq on May 12. Four days later, he made news throughout Iraq and the world by issuing CPA Order No. 1, "De-Ba'athification of Iraqi Society."

In later years, as controversy over the war intensified, this de-Baathification order was scorned as excessively severe, a major error of U.S. Iraq policy, and a key cause of Iraq's civil disorder and political upheaval. Others have taken the opposite position—that the coalition did not attack the Baathists quickly, broadly, and strongly enough. Retrospective debates of that kind rarely get resolved. But the debate has left an incorrect impression of the substance of the policy.

The essence of the CPA's de-Baathification policy was as follows:

- Only the top slice of the Baath Party's leadership—approximately 1 percent of the two million–plus party members—would be barred from working for the new Iraqi government. In other words, an Iraqi in the 90th—or even 98th—percentile of high responsibility in the Baath Party would be unaffected by this provision.
- The highest-level officials in government institutions—those at the top three levels of management—could not be Baathists.
- A mechanism would be created to grant exceptions to these two general rules. The rules could be set aside for individuals who did not have blood on their hands and had joined the party not for ideological reasons but simply to keep their jobs and feed their families.

Beyond this, there was no punishment for membership in the Baath Party. (Individuals suspected of atrocities or other specific crimes could, of course, be prosecuted for their personal deeds, as a law enforcement matter.) So the CPA's de-Baathification policy was not extremely extensive or severe. To argue that it affected far too many of the party leaders is to argue that there should have been no de-Baathification at all, beyond the removal of a handful of individuals.

There had been a case for de-Nazification of Germany after World War II, and there was a case for de-Baathification in Iraq—in some respects, perhaps, an even stronger one. The Nazis, after all, had run Germany for a dozen years; the Baathists had tyrannized Iraq for more than thirty. U.S. officials assumed it would be tough under any circumstances to eradicate the totalitarian mentality from the Iraqi government and to achieve proper reform. It would be much tougher—perhaps impossible—if high-level Baathists were allowed to retain power in the ministries and other official institutions.

Moreover, we did not want to aggravate Iraqis' fears and suspicions by appearing to cut a deal with the Baathists in the name of governmental efficiency. Such a deal might generally gratify Sunni Arabs, whose political predominance in Iraq the Baathists ensured. But the other 80 to 85 percent of Iraqis had a compelling interest in eliminating the Baathist domination of Iraq—including not only the Kurds and the Arab Shiites but also Arab Sunnis who opposed the Baathists.

The top Baathists in Iraq were not a sympathetic lot. They had flourished within an organization obsessed with personal loyalty to Saddam. They were the leadership that had launched the Iran-Iraq War, invaded Kuwait, and shot missiles at civilians in Saudi Arabia and Israel. They were responsible for carrying out the Anfal campaign against the Kurds (complete with poison gas attacks against the mothers and infants of Halabja); for the mass graves full of the Shiites massacred after Desert Storm; and for the systematic torture and rape of Iraqis for reasons of policy and personal pleasure. Even so, the U.S. de-Baathification order was moderate and narrowly focused. It was intended to avoid needless harm. It did not impose hardship indiscriminately on all Baath Party members, much less on Sunni Arabs in general.

No agency of the U.S. government had argued in senior-level policy meetings that Iraq needed the Baathist elite to run the government and keep essential services operating, though taking them out of official jobs would clearly cause some disruptions. Bremer was in any case authorized to grant exceptions if administrative necessity required them or if an injustice would otherwise be done to an individual senior party member.

Reports of overzealous de-Baathification are often cited as evidence that the Administration's policy was poorly crafted. I do not doubt that excesses occurred. Many, however, may have been spontaneous actions taken by excited, newly liberated Iraqis, without reference to the CPA-issued policy. I received a number of anecdotal reports from throughout the country that Iraqi Kurds, Shiites, and others took the opportunity to drive away from local schools, police stations, and government offices the party personnel they had long hated as oppressors. I know of no comprehensive data on the subject, but it stands to reason that such actions occurred without anyone seeking a go-ahead or procedural guidance from Ambassador Bremer in his headquarters in Baghdad.

Bremer eventually delegated the de-Baathification process to a committee of Iraqis chaired by Ahmad Chalabi of the INC. Bremer has written that this was an error that gave rise to some valid complaints about overly strict de-Baathification. He said he should have made the delegation to a judicial rather than a political body.

Administration officials were aware, as we debated the de-Baathification policy, that it would please some Iraqis and antagonize others. But we also recognized that if the coalition failed to take serious action against the Baath Party, Iraqis who detested the regime would feel betrayed. Their outrage could give rise to an anti-Baathist bloodbath led by Kurds and Shiites, in defiance of the coalition. In that event, people might now be asking how President Bush could have failed to foresee that soft-pedaling de-Baathification would trigger an uprising by more than 80 percent of the Iraqi population.

At that same May 9 meeting, Bremer and Slocombe told me of their plan to dissolve the Iraqi army. Again, it was necessary to weigh the arguments for and against the policy. Before the war, I had presented to President Bush a plan to use the Iraqi army for reconstruction and then to reform and "downsize" it. That plan, developed by General Garner, assumed that the army would remain largely intact—that we could readily employ its human and material assets, including organization, discipline, technical skills, buildings and facilities, trucks, and other equipment. Given that assumption, the case for Garner's plan was reasonably strong—but even so, there were serious arguments for dissolving the Iraqi army and building a new one from scratch. The army had an absurdly top-heavy structure. Corruption was deeply ingrained. And the officer class (mostly Sunni) brutalized the nonofficers (mostly Shiites). The army had committed large-scale atrocities against the Iraqi Kurds and Shiites. In the eyes of most Iraqis, it would be extremely hard to reform and redeem.

At my March 10 briefing to the President, following Rumsfeld's direction, I had endorsed Garner's plan to use the Iraqi army, reasoning that the pros somewhat outweighed the cons. Now, two months later, the coalition had toppled Saddam's regime—and the Iraqi army had scattered. This was not what U.S. intelligence had told us to expect. The army's organization was in disarray, bordering on nonexistent. Discipline broke down as the mass of Shiite conscripts ran away from their formerly dreaded officers, many of whom had fled to hide from anticipated anti-Baathist retribution. The military's facilities were ransacked and dismantled—tiles pulled off walls, plumbing and electrical fixtures stripped away, vehicles driven off—so all that remained in some places were the concrete slabs on which the buildings had stood.

Under these circumstances, many of the key reasons to *preserve* the army no longer applied, while the arguments for *dissolving* it were still relevant. The March analysis that had supported Garner's plan to use the Iraqi military was now, in May, yielding the opposite conclusion, *because the facts on the ground had changed*. That plan's key assumption—that the Iraqi army would remain mostly intact—had not panned out.

Critics of the Bremer-Slocombe plan have said that the Iraqi army didn't actually dissolve itself, but, rather, the U.S. military encouraged Iraqi soldiers to go home. If the CPA had asked them to return to service, that argument goes, whole units could have been reassembled. As I see it, however, the key issue is not how much of Saddam's army would have returned if asked. It is whether—as a military, political, and economic matter—U.S. officials should have exerted themselves to try to put it back together again. Bremer and Slocombe argued that it would better serve U.S. interests to create an entirely new Iraqi army: Sometimes it is easier to build something new than to refurbish a complex and badly designed structure. In any event, Bremer and Slocombe reasoned, calling the old army back might not succeed—but the attempt could cause grave political problems. As Bremer reported, Kurdish leaders "made it clear" to him that recalling Saddam's army would cause their region to secede from Iraq, "which would have triggered a civil war and tempted Turkey and Iran to invade Iraq to prevent the establishment of an independent Kurdistan." Shiite leaders, he says, would have stopped cooperating with U.S.-led forces and taken up arms against us.

It was obvious that dissolving the army would be a financial blow to its approximately four hundred thousand Iraqi personnel. Accordingly, the Bremer-Slocombe plan provided for payments to the "employees and retirees of the dissolved entities." And the CPA intended to recruit individuals from the old army for the new Iraqi army and for other new security forces.

I encouraged Bremer and Slocombe to discuss their army-dissolution proposal with Rumsfeld. On May 19, a week after arriving in Baghdad, Bremer told Rumsfeld that he proposed to issue the order in "the coming days":

> **The generally positive reaction to the earlier de-Ba'athification order of 16 May 03 leads me to believe this order will generate a good deal of public support, despite its impacting many more people. In any event, it is a critical step in our effort to destroy the underpinnings of the Saddam regime, to demonstrate to the Iraqi people that we have done so, and that neither Saddam nor his gang is coming back.**

I missed some important communications at this time—for example, how Rumsfeld responded to Bremer's May 19 memo on dissolution. I assume he signaled approval, because on May 23 Bremer issued CPA Order No. 2, which dissolved Iraq's military and national security entities.

George Tenet has said he wasn't consulted on CPA Order No. 2. I do not know what discussions the Principals may have had on the subject. From the absence of meeting notes, it appears that I did not bring the matter to the Deputies Committee. (I have tried in vain to recall why; it may be that Rumsfeld instructed me to keep the matter within the Defense Department.) In any event, it would surely have been better if the decision to issue the order had been debated throughout the government. I have no reason to think that the other agencies would have opposed Bremer on the dissolution, but their participation might have improved the crafting or implementation of the policy—and they might have been more inclined to defend it after it was announced.

I thought the CPA's dissolution of the Iraqi army was a sound decision under the circumstances, properly reasoned through by Bremer and Slocombe. I still do. But the decision became associated with a number of unnecessary problems, including the apparent lack of interagency review. Another unnecessary problem was a logistical and political error—a delay in announcing stipends—that would cause serious harm on the ground in Iraq.

The CPA knew it had to arrange payments for the dismissed army personnel: Bremer highlighted the point in his May 19 memo to Rumsfeld. But it wasn't until June 23—a full month after the May 23 dissolution order—that the CPA announced publicly that the out-of-work soldiers would be paid monthly stipends. Of course, it would take some time before the CPA could actually make the payments. It would need accurate rosters and registration and disbursal procedures. But the *intention* to pay the stipends could have been announced along with the army's dissolution. As it was, the first flood of news stories depicted the CPA as cruelly throwing hundreds of thousands of Iraqis out of work with no financial cushion. The CPA was never able to overcome this damaging misimpression.

The initial concept for creating a new army turned out to be another mistake. Bremer's decision to dissolve the Iraqi army rendered irrelevant Garner's plan for restructuring it. CPA officials therefore had to produce a new plan for an army to be built from the ground up. But their plan aimed to create only a small force—forty thousand men over two years—to serve as the core of whatever larger army Iraqi leaders of the future might decide to build.

In his quickly produced outline for the so-called New Iraqi Corps,* Slocombe focused primarily on future needs rather than on the current civil disorder. His June 3 briefing mentioned that the new force could assist with current security problems in limited ways—for example, in protecting fixed sites and convoy escorts. But the briefing's main concern was the development of an Iraqi army that would fit professionally and affordably into a new, democratic Iraqi government. The briefing emphasized de-Baathification and training soldiers to refrain from interference in politics. The Iraqi army would be concerned chiefly with *external* security. The plan was not designed to produce large numbers of Iraqi forces to help immediately to restore law and order inside the country.

CPA officials evidently expected the coalition to handle the problem of political violence in Iraq, rather than give major security responsibilities early on to Iraqis. (As I later understood, this was in line with Bremer's general view that the Iraqis were not ready to assume independent responsibility for their own affairs.) The original concept for a New Iraqi Corps might have made sense if the country's main challenge had been democratic statecraft in circumstances of domestic and regional peace. But the

*The plan was produced too quickly, apparently, to allow time for consultation with any Iraqis: The acronym of the New Iraqi Corps is a particularly foul verb in Arabic (as if a new American entity had been named the Federal United Corps). When the CPA realized the error it renamed the force the New Iraqi Army.

actual problem was to establish security in the face of an incipient and soon metastasizing insurgency.

According to U.S. intelligence at the time, the enemy in Iraq was a mix of former regime officials, foreign jihadists, and common criminals. (For reasons that were never authoritatively established, Saddam had released approximately one hundred thousand criminals from his prisons in October 2002. After Baghdad was liberated, we learned that some of them had been hired to shoot rocket-propelled grenades at coalition forces.) An early sign of administrative trouble was the disjointed U.S. reaction to this new enemy. CENTCOM's focus was on immediate security challenges on the ground, and our commanders were therefore looking for Iraqis who could help them fight the enemy. They had expected to make immediate use of the Iraqi security forces—military and police—but that was clearly not an option. And now they understood that the CPA's New Iraqi Corps would not give them the help they needed: Training would take too long, and the corps's main mission was not internal security. So CENTCOM developed a training program of its own.

CENTCOM's plan to create a local security force became known as the ICDC—the Iraqi Civil Defense Corps. These were Iraqi recruits who, after only a few days of learning basic skills, joined U.S. combat units for on-the-job training, during which they served as interpreters, scouts, guides, and advisers on civil affairs—important functions that we had identified months earlier for the proposed Free Iraqi Forces.

CENTCOM and the CPA thus each pursued its own program to train Iraqi forces. They did not develop a unified concept and plan. When Rumsfeld had proposed, back in October 2002, to take on the responsibility for all aspects of Iraqi reconstruction—civil and military—his idea was to ensure unity of effort through unity of leadership. CENTCOM reported to Rumsfeld; and on paper, the CPA did too. But in fact Bremer resisted requests for reports, and he soon generated multiple chains for sporadic reporting: to the President, Rice, and Powell as well as to Rumsfeld. Although formally there was unity of leadership in Iraq, in practice there was not. And there was not unity of effort between CENTCOM and the CPA.

Before and during Operation Iraqi Freedom, the work my office did on postwar political planning was intended to keep the United States out of the role of military occupier. The capstone of this effort was our plan for the Iraqi Interim Authority (IIA), which became official U.S. policy when it received President Bush's formal endorsement. In the political dimension, the story of post-Saddam Iraq is the painful tale of a missed opportunity to empower an Iraqi authority.

The IIA plan provided for an Iraqi government that would come into being—with limited powers—promptly after the regime's removal. The short lead time was a key argument in favor of the plan, both within the Defense Department and in interagency discussions. The IIA's key concept was power sharing. The plan involved bringing together a reasonably diverse group of Iraqi leaders—including Shiites, Sunnis, and Kurds—to set up a government quickly. This Iraqi authority would have sovereign power in designated areas: foreign relations, justice, and agriculture. In these matters it would not have to get permission from—or account to—any non-Iraqis. The U.S.-led coalition would control other areas (by mutual agreement) for a transitional period. And as the Iraqi government demonstrated its capabilities, the coalition would transfer additional areas to its sovereign control as quickly as possible. The power-sharing and transfer agreement between the IIA and the coalition could be endorsed by the United Nations.

I thought it had been an important success to get President Bush to approve the IIA concept on March 10. I also believed there was a government-wide understanding that such an interim authority was the alternative to a lengthy occupation. State and CIA officials had been as strong as the Defense Department in warning that such an occupation would hurt our interests and likely stimulate an uprising against us. And *no one had developed an option other than the IIA* that would spare the United States having to prolong an occupation.

Yet State and CIA officials had difficulty reconciling their opposition to occupation with their opposition to an early Iraqi government, which would inevitably be dominated by externals. Apparently, despite the President's approval, they never resigned themselves to the IIA concept. In May 2003, Powell once again began advocating a go-slow approach to transferring sovereignty in Iraq. And at that point, it is now clear, the Administration's policy grew dangerously ambiguous. Although the President never reversed his March 10 decision to create the IIA "as soon as possible," neither Rice nor he reaffirmed the policy when Powell denied the need for urgency. Among Garner, Khalilzad, Bremer, Powell, Rumsfeld, and Rice, there was not a common, clear understanding of what the President wanted done.

Though my office had briefed Bremer on the IIA policy approved by the President, Bremer later explained that he developed a different understanding in the days before his departure for Iraq, during meetings with President Bush, Powell, and Rice and in the Principals Committee and National Security Council meetings he attended. Some of those discussions may have convinced him that the interim authority was the plan merely of the "Pentagon's policy office." Bremer relates that he understood that he was free to set the IIA plan aside, because the President wanted him to "Get over there and give us your recommendation."

Bremer's views were crucial. As the man in the field, he was given great latitude to gauge the situation and craft his response. A dozen or so weeks went by before it became clear to Rumsfeld and his team that Bremer's views were at odds with the IIA policy of early transfer of authority. In the end, the CPA lasted a full *fourteen months* as an occupation government, with no Iraqi authority exercising any independent power at all. Those fourteen months proved ample to produce the lasting ill effects of occupation.

How this happened is not entirely clear even today. Key aspects of it did not become clear to me until I read Bremer's book (published in January 2006). Historians will develop a more complete account, but here is what I know now of this story.

At the April 28 public political conference in Baghdad—just two weeks before Bremer's arrival in Iraq—the main topic was creation of the Iraqi Interim Authority. This was the second conference held on newly liberated Iraqi soil, with more than 250 Iraqis attending. The Iraqi delegates resolved to establish the IIA *within one month*. Three days later, in a May 1 meeting with President Bush's envoy Zalmay Khalilzad, key members of the Iraqi Leadership Council endorsed the conference resolution on the IIA, but agreed that "they would not try to form their own interim government, but work with the process we had set up." The Iraqi leaders (according to some reports) believed that Khalilzad had promised a transitional Iraqi "government" near the end of May.

Jay Garner exerted himself to fulfill President Bush's directive to set the IIA up as soon as possible. His top political advisers, officials who had participated in the interagency work on the IIA plan, had presided at the Baghdad conference: Khalilzad (of Rice's staff, named Special Envoy to the Free Iraqi organizations) and Ambassador Ryan Crocker (of the State Department). On May 5, Garner announced to journalists that, by mid-May, "you'll see the beginning of a nucleus of a temporary Iraqi government," and said that the Iraqi leadership was working to try to "form a nucleus of leadership as we enter into June."

In Washington, these reports from Iraq surprised both supporters and opponents of the IIA. There were substantial issues to be resolved before an IIA could come into being. How, and by whom, would delegates be selected for the conference to elect the IIA officials? How should the IIA's executive branch be structured? Moreover, the Iraqi Leadership Council had not accomplished its mission to bring onto the Council more Sunni Arabs and internals, women, and members of minorities such as the Turkomans.

Nor had the Iraqi leaders yet shown decisiveness as a group. To be sure, Khalilzad had a good rapport with them, and his active guidance might give them greater confidence. Nevertheless, it seemed dangerous to raise general expectations of Iraqi government by the end of May.

Rumsfeld told me he was unhappy that the Iraqis were pushing so hard for power before they had expanded their leadership council. He told me he wanted to tap the brakes on the political process. After all, a new person had just been hired to take over the CPA. With Bremer about to take up his duties in Baghdad, Rumsfeld was concerned about reports of Iraqi leaders' indiscipline and worried that they might undermine Bremer's ability to do his job.*

Once again, both Powell and Rumsfeld were talking of slowing down the IIA process, but for different reasons. Powell did so because he opposed setting up an Iraqi government in the coming months. Rumsfeld did so mainly because he didn't want to limit Bremer's flexibility to manage the CPA's relationship with the Iraqi leaders.

Bremer attended the May 8 Principals Committee meeting, where the main topic was the IIA. Khalilzad had drafted the discussion paper, entitled "Next Steps Towards an Iraqi Interim Authority." Some officials had complained that Khalilzad had gone too far too fast with the Iraqis on the IIA, and his paper appeared to react to the criticism. Khalilzad had been following the President's directions in working to set up the IIA quickly, and he may have reasoned that, if his actions were drawing criticism, then perhaps the Principals should reexamine the IIA fundamentals. Khalilzad's paper reopened basic questions—for instance, whether the IIA should be a "fully empowered government" or have "gradually increasing powers" or be merely "technocratic" rather than political in nature—even though the plan President Bush had already approved called for the second of those options: gradually increasing powers.

Neither Rumsfeld nor Wolfowitz was able to attend this May 8 meeting, so I represented the Defense Department as the principal. This was unfortunate. Our views tended to have more clout in the Situation Room

---

*Rumsfeld opposed setting up a full-blown Iraqi government immediately, but this had nothing to do with concerns about the Iraqis' "legitimacy." It reflected his desire to take time to judge the new leaders' competence, integrity, and political acceptability before the coalition gave them sovereign authority over *all* the Iraqi government's ministries and institutions.

when presented by the Pentagon's highest officials. Rice asked me to start the discussion. I explained Rumsfeld's views of the IIA: It would be sovereign from the start in some areas, including foreign affairs, so that Iraqis could represent themselves in foreign capitals and at the UN. Rather than serve as occupier, we could pursue our security and reconstruction missions in Iraq with the IIA's consent and the Security Council's endorsement—much as we did in Afghanistan. I concluded my remarks by saying that Rumsfeld wanted to "move forward promptly" on the IIA.

Powell countered that the President "wants us to take our time." The April 28 Baghdad conference talked of "doing something" on the IIA by the end of May, Powell said, but moving quickly was not our policy. (His remarks ran counter to the President's decision on March 10 that the IIA should be formed "as soon as possible after liberation.") Powell declared that we had to decide if we wanted to "move quickly" or "move like coral"—I assumed that meant slowly—and said that Bremer's "first job out there is to decide which way is best."

Powell asked: "When the IIA is established, what is it?" In answering his own question, he declared: "There can be only one government in Iraq at a time." He was implying that the issue of who would be in charge in Iraq was a simple either-or question—we or they. But the purpose of the IIA plan was to offer an answer that was *not* all or nothing. The Iraqis could be in charge of some things while the coalition (during the transitional period) would be in charge of other things. Powell was ignoring or missing this essential point about the IIA.

Later, after Bremer took over at the CPA, we heard essentially the same either-or comments on Iraqi sovereignty from him. Even after he left the CPA, Bremer continued to discuss this matter as if the only options were either to retain U.S. control over *all* official responsibilities in Iraq or to "hand over sovereignty to the Iraqis." I do not know whether he was ignoring the power-sharing idea behind the IIA plan or had failed to understand it.

Rather than reaffirm the President's policy decision on the IIA, Rice once again sought a kind of middle ground. She floated the suggestion that the IIA might have a "technocratic character"—that is, technical and managerial—but no executive authority. I did not think that would accomplish the IIA's purpose, which was to ensure that the Iraqis would, at least to some extent, be exercising sovereign political power in their own country. Khalilzad showed he understood this point by asking: Are we trying to solve the technocratic problem of having Iraqis manage ministries, or the political problem of letting Iraqis build their own government?

Bremer responded to Rice's suggestion perceptively, saying that the

Iraqi leaders might "choose to stay back and not play" if the IIA were merely technocratic in character. Weeks later, however, as head of the CPA, Bremer designated Iraqis to run ministries while keeping sovereign authority entirely in his own hands. The result was indeed that many Iraqis chose to stay back and not play.

Considering all the circumstances of this May 8 meeting—Khalilzad's paper reopening basic questions about the IIA, the absence of Rumsfeld and Wolfowitz, Powell's declaration that the President "wants us to take our time," and Rice's suggestion to strip the IIA of political authority—it is perhaps understandable that Bremer later felt free to treat the IIA not as a presidentially approved plan but as a mere policy option, one he could implement or reject as he saw fit.

The next day Bremer attended a National Security Council meeting, chaired, as always, by President Bush. My records do not show what, if anything, was said specifically about the IIA. The President provided assurance that he would have patience for the reconstruction work that Bremer would be managing in Iraq. "The message out of this White House is that this will take a long time," the President stated. Bremer could have heard in this comment, too, encouragement to go slow on setting up an IIA.

In his book and in interviews after he left the CPA, Bremer insisted that his instructions before he left Washington for Iraq were straightforward. He heard "very clearly," at that National Security Council meeting, that he was "not to rush" to appoint an Iraqi interim government. But as I review my papers (to be sure, a mere slice of the total record) and the currently available public record, I have been struck by the mixed nature of the signals Bremer received from Administration officials all over town.

At the time, I did not interpret those signals as a reversal or an undoing of the IIA policy. I believed that the President's March 10 approval of the IIA remained in force: The IIA should be formed "as soon as possible after liberation." If top Administration officials made less-than-precise comments on the IIA, well, that is the nature of most discussions—inside and outside the government.

Bremer was processing those comments through a different filter. Although my office had given him the lengthy written record of the government's IIA policy, his understanding developed not from that written record but from what he chose to call the "clear" guidance he received straight from the mouths of the President and the Principals. And, not surprisingly, the thoughts he said were "clear" conformed to his own inclinations. Even before Bremer arrived in Iraq—for the first time in his life—he judged the new Iraqi political leadership incapable of handling an early transfer of power.

In his book *My Year in Iraq*, Bremer refers to Garner's May 5, 2003, public announcement that there would be (in Garner's words) the "beginning of a nucleus of a temporary Iraqi government" by mid-May. Bremer writes that he heard on his car radio that "Garner had announced his intention to *appoint an Iraqi government* [sic] by May 15." Bremer recalls reacting with shock. "I knew it would take careful work to disabuse both the Iraqi and American proponents of this reckless fantasy—what some in the administration were calling 'early transfer' of power," he writes.

Bremer never told me that that was his thinking, so we never discussed the possible risks of an extended occupation government. No one in the Pentagon seemed aware that Bremer had concluded, even before he left Washington, that an early transfer of power to the Iraqis was a "reckless fantasy."

In taking on the CPA job, Bremer made a point of presenting himself as a decisive, bureaucratically clever chief executive—eager to take charge and impatient with what he calls the Defense Department "squirrel cage" and the "bureaucratic hamsters."

Bremer became the highest-ranking U.S. civilian official in Iraq, with a reporting chain that, like Franks's, ran straight to Rumsfeld. (Franks was within weeks of retiring, to be replaced at CENTCOM by Abizaid.) Soon after Bremer arrived in Baghdad, Garner departed and ORHA ceased to be a distinct office; its organization merged into the CPA.

Bremer arranged to obtain two titles. President Bush appointed him Presidential Envoy to Iraq, but specified that he would be "reporting through the Secretary of Defense." Rumsfeld then appointed him to replace Franks as the new head of the CPA. To make clear that Bremer worked for Rumsfeld, the President's appointment letter stated that Bremer was subject to the "authority, direction and control of the Secretary of Defense."

Nonetheless, Bremer chose to think of himself as working not for Rumsfeld, but for the President. In his book he says:

> **As the senior American in Baghdad, I would be President George W. Bush's personal envoy. My chain of command ran through Secretary of Defense Donald Rumsfeld *and straight to the President.* I would be the only *paramount authority figure*—other than dictator Saddam Hussein—that most Iraqis had ever known.**

Bremer describes his first get-together with the President, a private lunch. His opening comment dealt with the need to ensure noninterference from Khalilzad, who was also a Presidential Envoy:

> **First, I noted that my experience in government and the private sector made me a strong proponent of the "unity of command" principle. I could not succeed if there were others in Iraq saying *they too represented the president.***

The private lunch was followed by a National Security Council meeting. "Jerry" Bremer writes:

> **After our lunch, the president led me into the Oval Office and asked the others to join us. As they filed in [Cheney, Powell, Rumsfeld, Rice, and Chief of Staff Andrew Card]—Bush waved me to the chair beside him and joked, "I don't know whether we need this meeting after all. Jerry and I have just had it."**
>
> **His message was clear: I was neither Rumsfeld's nor Powell's man. *I was the president's man.***

Bremer once again considered it "clear" that the President meant what Bremer wanted to hear. Thinking of himself as the "president's man" was not mere vainglory. If Bremer could pull it off, it might mean freedom from close supervision. Officials at the very top of the government tend to be able to absorb only occasional and relatively brief reports from subordinates. As a general proposition, the higher the rank of the supervisor, the less detail one needs to report.

As Bremer started his work in Baghdad, Rumsfeld and Wolfowitz repeatedly discussed how we could best manage our communications with Bremer's CPA and support its work. My staff suggested a daily secure video teleconference with Bremer, led on our side by Rumsfeld twice a week and by me on the other three days. When I proposed the idea to Rumsfeld, I suggested that it would be wise for General Pace to join me in leading the calls on those three days. Rumsfeld, however, rejected the idea of daily reports; Bremer, he thought, had far too much to do to have to confer regularly with anyone at the Pentagon other than Rumsfeld himself.

I revisited this point with Rumsfeld twice over the next few months. We could have a better sense of what was happening at the CPA, I suggested, if Rumsfeld asked Bremer to talk with Pace and me once or twice a week. If our staffs were present for the conference calls, we could discuss matters in reasonable detail and resolve problems. The Secretary, however, remained set against the idea.

Rumsfeld spoke protectively of Bremer's time and status. He wanted the chain of command linking him to Bremer to resemble what he had with his combatant commanders. But, unlike the CPA, General Myers's staff provided a well-established structure for learning what the combatant commands were doing. Nevertheless, Rumsfeld did not want Bremer to think he had to report to any Defense official other than himself. Once Bremer understood Rumsfeld's view, he largely stopped communicating with anyone at the Pentagon other than the Secretary.

Rumsfeld had earned a reputation for exercising tight control over his subordinates, but he did not do this with Bremer. He treated Bremer, in effect, as a field commander, giving him authority and extraordinary freedom of action. Nevertheless, in his book Bremer describes Rumsfeld as a micromanager: He resented the Secretary's request for "a more effective way to measure how we're meeting our goals." Bremer comments: "I didn't want my colleagues to get bogged down writing lots of reports. We needed to keep our focus on getting things done, fast."

For months after Bremer joined the effort in Iraq, Rumsfeld spoke and acted as his admirer and defender. He commented favorably on Bremer's energy. He talked of the hardships of life in Baghdad—the multiplicity of demands on Bremer and his team, the lack of respite and amenities. He admired Bremer's take-charge demeanor. Bremer was spared the kind of grillings and rebukes that Rumsfeld routinely visited on his other subordinates. In drawing up his "first impressions" memo of May 22, 2003, Bremer headed it as follows: "To: The President of the United States/ Through: The Secretary of Defense"—and Rumsfeld did not object to the presumption.

And when Bremer decided that the Administration's IIA policy could not be implemented because the Iraqis lacked the necessary skills and traits, Rumsfeld accepted the judgment as coming from the man "on the ground"—just as he had acquiesced when Bremer insisted on removing Khalilzad as a rival "presidential envoy." Perhaps Rumsfeld looked at Bremer's demands for authority and a free hand as what he himself would have demanded in his position.

On arriving in Iraq, Bremer quickly repudiated the political work Garner and Khalilzad had done. In meetings with Iraqi leaders, he canceled the recent statements by the two of them on setting up an Iraqi government by early June. But he assured Rumsfeld and the President that he was eager to create an Iraqi interim administration, just as quickly as the Iraqis could act to assume responsibility. Though Bremer tended to speak critically, even harshly, about Iraq's political figures, he seemed committed to putting a proper interim administration in place and transferring real power to it promptly.

When Bremer arrived in Baghdad on May 12, 2003, he learned that Garner—committed to getting the IIA up and running—had scheduled him to meet with the Iraqi Leadership Council the following day. Bremer postponed the meeting. He gives three reasons. First, he "wanted to have more time to consult with my political advisers before plunging into delicate discussions about our plans for the interim government." His second and third reasons are revealing: "Also, I wanted to signal to the Iraqi political figures that I was not in a hurry to see them. And finally, I wanted to show everybody that I, not Jay [Garner], was now in charge."

Several days later, Bremer met with the Iraqi leaders for the first time. One of them urged, "[Y]ou *must* hasten the political process" because the " 'street' is waiting for the freedom you promised." Bremer writes, "I would learn that Iraqi politicians love to invoke the mystical 'Arab street' on almost any argument." Bremer's cutting observation was correct in general, but it was not astute here. The spread of civil disorder, the burgeoning of the insurgency, and the increasing unpopularity of the CPA suggest that the warning was well founded.

Chalabi then spoke up, recalling Garner's recent statements on creating a new government within a few weeks. Replying that the process would be "*incremental*" and "must have as its goal a truly representative group," Bremer pointedly told the Council that it was *not* representative. It had only seven members, he explained, and they included only one Sunni Arab and no Turkomans, Christians, or women—and six of the seven were externals. "I was exerting the authority President Bush had granted me, 'putting down the hammer,' " Bremer declares.

Bremer came to Baghdad doubting the ability of Iraq's political leadership to accept early responsibility. Over the months, those doubts crystallized into a sour overall judgment of the quality of those leaders. He made this one of his book's main themes. Iraqi Foreign Minister Hoshyar Zebari later observed that Bremer believed that "one of his tasks was to stop these 'exiles' " and called this reluctance to entrust Iraqis with authority the "biggest mistake" the U.S. government made in Iraq.

Bremer's low regard for the Iraqis had such high importance in the history of the Iraq war that it is worth illustrating the point from his writings. (The context of each quotation can be found in Bremer's book.)

- The Iraqi Leadership Council—also referred to as the Group of Seven, or G-7—had difficulty "making even simple decisions."
- "For two of them, Ahmad Chalabi and Jalal Talabani, their decades of intriguing proved hard to set aside."

- There were "serious issues they need to address instead of fantasizing about which office they will hold. . . ."
- The G-7 "had flunked the test again."
- "From Hakim's bored expression, I might have been discussing obscure mathematical theory, not the future of his party or his country."
- The G-7 spent "many fruitless hours" debating who should speak for them at a meeting: "I instructed our guys to stay out of this food fight. 'Imagine what it will be like,' I said, 'when there are twenty-five of them in the room and they have to decide important matters.' "
- " 'I'm interested in results,' I'd told Dayton, 'not theory or endless debate. I already get too much of that from the Iraqi politicians.' "

Garner and Khalilzad had also sometimes highlighted Iraqi foibles, but they (though not professional diplomats like Bremer) generally conveyed a three-dimensional and understanding picture of the Iraqis they worked with. Bremer rarely spoke a positive word about the Iraqi leaders.

Bremer complained at the time (as he does in his book) that Iraqi leaders failed to attend meetings with him at the CPA. He does not consider that they may have done so because they sensed his low opinion of them. Bremer may have thought he was concealing his lack of regard for them, but few people can manage such a trick.*

We in Washington did not see the problem in Bremer's relations with the Iraqi leaders as sharply as it may have appeared on the scene. In criticizing the Iraqis' competence, Bremer was in fact giving voice to one of Rumsfeld's long-standing concerns; I think it made Rumsfeld sympathetic to Bremer's situation, not suspicious of his refusal to share authority.

Bremer talked of "putting down the hammer" on the Iraqi Leadership Council. His concept of a "truly representative" leadership indeed came down like a hammer on the IIA plan. Those of us who supported the plan understood from recent experience in Afghanistan that the initial leadership could not be as "truly representative" as properly elected officials would eventually be. The first group of officials would have to be a mix, some from the external opposition groups and some newly liberated inter-

---

*In the W. C. Fields movie *My Little Chickadee,* Flower Belle Lee (Mae West), posturing in a courtroom, is asked by the judge, "Are you trying to show contempt for this court?" She answers, "No . . . I'm doin' my best to hide it!"

nals, selected through cooperation between the CPA and those external groups. As Rumsfeld often noted, there would inevitably be objections to the first set of post-Saddam Iraqi leaders and governmental institutions—but those arrangements would be only for the interim. The interim government's main job would be to write a constitution, institute a ratification process, and hold fair elections. Those elections would produce a new Iraqi leadership that *would* be truly representative.

But Bremer's concept of "representative" leadership prevented the IIA plan from getting off the ground. We would later learn that Bremer opposed putting substantial authority into the hands of the Iraqi leaders until he judged them "representative" by his own lights. Indeed, he opposed giving any independent power at all except to a new government elected under a new constitution; in effect, he rejected the interim-authority concept altogether. Meanwhile, the CPA would continue to serve as an occupation government.

Bremer's written reports to Rumsfeld and the President did not have the tone that emerges in his book. While his reports sometimes commented disapprovingly on the Iraqi leaders, they were not contemptuous. And they repeatedly affirmed that Bremer was eager to set up an interim Iraqi authority or administration.*

In his May 22 memo to President Bush, Bremer said that his message to the Iraqis was that "full sovereignty under an Iraqi government can come after democratic elections which themselves must be based on a constitution agreed by all the people." These words set off no alarm bells. He did not say that he would give the Iraqis *no* sovereign control over *anything* until after elections. Meanwhile, he assured the President that he was prepared to move the political process forward as quickly as the Iraqis wanted, provided that it "leads to a representative government." That sounded right to me.

Bremer elaborated on the creation of an Iraqi "Interim Administration" in a memo to Rumsfeld the next day. He criticized the G-7 leaders, noting that "there appears to be paralysis" among them over how to expand their group, but he recommended quickly establishing an interim administration "by invitation." He observed that most Iraqis "believe that Iraq needs an interim administration with an Iraqi face sooner rather than later," and he commented: "I agree."

The interim administration, he said, would appoint people to run ministries. It would also consult with the CPA. Bremer did not explain, however, that it would have no independent power and would be subordinate

---

*Bremer used the terms "authority" and "administration" interchangeably.

to him on all matters. He did not say that all Iraqi officials would continue indefinitely to work *for him*. My office, which wrote the IIA plan, therefore interpreted Bremer's statements as consistent with the IIA plan that President Bush had approved. We recommended that Rumsfeld approve Bremer's approach. He did so.

The CPA staff, meanwhile, was thinking through how the Iraqis could produce a new constitution and organize national elections. It estimated that getting a constitution drafted and ratified and then holding national elections would take *two years*. Some of us thought that sounded longer than necessary, but the estimate in any event vindicated our IIA idea—to give substantial, independent authority to the Iraqis in the interim. It seemed obvious we should not keep Iraq under occupation for that entire period.

As demanding as the political process was, Bremer (like other high-level U.S. officials) had to attend also to a long list of other important tasks. He was concerned with providing water, electricity, and fuel to the Iraqi public despite the decrepitude of the country's infrastructure—which was in far worse shape than U.S. intelligence had thought before the war. And he was overseeing economic reconstruction: getting laws and policies in place, setting priorities for major projects, and deciding how to try to fund them.

On July 13, Bremer created the Iraqi Governing Council. It included the G-7 together with eighteen other Iraqis, whom the CPA had selected through a nationwide search to make the new group diverse. The CPA formally recognized "the formation of the Governing Council as the principal body of the Iraqi interim administration." But even though Bremer called it an "interim administration," the Council had far less power than the IIA was intended to have. Over the coming weeks it became clear that there would be no formal agreement between the Governing Council and the CPA—and thus no power-sharing arrangement—because Bremer had decided to give the Council no authority independent of the CPA.

The Governing Council held a press conference to introduce itself and then sent a delegation to New York to make an appearance at the United Nations. Its first major project was to decide how to organize itself for executive action—a difficult task for statesmen since at least the American Revolution of 1776.* The Governing Council floundered for some

*The leaders of the newly established United States of America did not agree to create a capable executive office under the Articles of Confederation: The national government's leadership was by committee from 1776 until 1789, when the Constitution came into force and George Washington became President.

time. Finally, on July 30, it agreed on an unwieldy arrangement: a nine-person, monthly rotating presidency. As a result, the Governing Council lacked stable, effective leadership.

Bremer later showed that, when he set his mind to it, he could push the Iraqis hard and successfully to agree to measures in their interest and ours—including the November 15, 2003, agreement, the interim constitution, the dissolution of the Governing Council, and the creation of the Iraqi Interim Government. But the Governing Council's rotating presidency—a decision Bremer insists the Iraqis took on their own—made the Council incapable of performing the executive role that was envisioned for the IIA. The Council amounted to little more than an advisory committee to a U.S.-run occupation government. That was not the IIA plan.

Bremer often complained about the Governing Council, which he called "slow to take action on a host of serious issues before it without prodding and handholding by the CPA." He writes of the Governing Council in the same disparaging tone that he applied to externals in general:

- Some officials in Washington "thought we could solve all our problems by simply transferring authority immediately to the Iraqi Governing Council, as if that group could somehow overcome the interconnected security-economic-political problems when we in the CPA could not."
- "Jaafari and his men looked troubled. Governing a country was a complex business. *Cold shower time isn't far off for these guys, I thought. What would have happened if the U.S. government had turned over Iraq to the exiles in May, as some in Washington had wanted.*"
- "I was increasingly frustrated by the inertia that had gripped the Governing Council."
- "The Governing Council's effectiveness was hampered, from the first day to the last, by lax work habits."
- " 'Look,' I said, 'you can't very well hope to run a country of 25 million people without working hard. The Governing Council works fewer hours in a week than the CPA works every day.' "
- To Wolfowitz: " 'Your guys don't seem to understand how ineffective the GC [Governing Council] is turning out to be.' I chose my words, but did not mince them. 'Those people couldn't organize a parade, let alone run a country.' "

Yet aside from the heads of the external groups—who were Iraqi political leaders with their own organizations before the war—all the Governing Council's members owed their new political roles to Bremer. He was the Council's architect, builder, and superintendent. When the Council failed to work well, Bremer criticized the Iraqis, but neither at the time nor in writing his book did he ask whether a body set up differently by the CPA or managed differently—and perhaps given greater dignity and power—might have functioned more effectively.

The Governing Council's next major project was identifying individuals to serve as interim heads of the national ministries. The Council worked on this throughout August. But this important element of political reconstruction was overshadowed by two ominous bombings in the same month.

The first, on August 19, destroyed the UN headquarters in Baghdad, killing UN Special Representative Sergio Vieira de Mello and others. This, together with later attacks, soon led the United Nations and other international organizations to withdraw most of their personnel from Iraq. The second bombing, on August 29, killed Ayatollah Muhammed Bakr al-Hakim, the head of the Supreme Council for the Islamic Revolution in Iraq, and four of his fellow Shiite clerics.

The insurgency had begun.

In August 2003 I traveled to Iraq for the first time. It is valuable for any top policy official to visit the theater of operations. One can never be reminded often enough that national security policy is ultimately about human beings. In this two-day visit, I met with Bremer and with Lieutenant General Ricardo Sanchez (U.S. Army), the commander of coalition military forces in Iraq. I consulted with several members of the Iraqi Governing Council and with Emad Dhia and some of his colleagues on the Iraqi Reconstruction Development Committee—a group of almost two hundred Iraqi Americans that Paul Wolfowitz had organized to advise and assist the CPA. I was also able to spend time with other Iraqis: businessmen, clerics, the new Baghdad City Council, and journalists.

In our meetings, the Iraqis generally spoke with cautious amazement—and occasionally with gratitude—about liberation. They also freely vented their frustration about the general lack of law and order and the problems with distribution of electricity, clean water, gasoline, benzene, and other essential services. At least a dozen times I heard Iraqis say that the United States had landed a man on the moon decades before, so it ought to be able to get electricity distributed quickly throughout Iraq. But a number of Iraqis also commented on the *absence* of disasters that had been widely anticipated before the war: There was no food crisis or environmental disaster, for example, and no major problem of refugees or displaced persons.

In the summer of 2003, sectarian violence by Iraqis against Iraqis had not yet become widespread. There had been systematic sacking of government buildings in the initial episodes of "looting," and there were now daily attacks against coalition forces. Foreign Sunni extremists (such as Abu Musab al-Zarqawi, soon to become the leader of al Qaida in Iraq) were targeting Iraqi Shiites.

In the grim year 2007, commentators wrote as if Iraq had been doomed to sectarian violence—as if Iraqi mutual slaughter between Sunnis and Shiites occurred inevitably and immediately when Saddam was ousted. But such attacks did not become a major phenomenon until February 2006, when the gold-domed mosque in Samarra, an important Shiite shrine, was destroyed.*

For three years after the liberation of Iraq, in fact, the Shiites showed amazing forbearance, responding to the moral leadership of Grand Ayatollah Ali al-Sistani, who called consistently for self-restraint. Sistani deserves more attention from historians than he has received so far. He is a complex figure—an Iranian-born cleric who lived for many years in Iraq and became the single most influential voice among Iraqi Shiites, who compose 60 percent of the country's population. Although he refused ever to meet with Bremer, Sistani played a large and generally constructive role in post-Saddam Iraq. He opposed civil conflict and rejected Iranian-style clerical government. Commentators who have asserted that Shiite political power in Iraq would necessarily translate into a victory for the Iranian clerical regime have tended either to ignore Sistani or to misstate his views.

Among my most memorable experiences during that trip was a visit to a neighborhood in east Baghdad, described as so poor that it made the Sadr City slum seem like the high-rent district. I was shown around by Brigadier General Martin Dempsey (U.S. Army), commander of the 1st Armored Division, on a day with temperatures above 130 degrees. As soon as our group emerged from the Humvees, we were surrounded by small children flashing thumbs-up and saying, "Bush good." We were greeted by a tall U.S. Army major, a reservist in charge of the troops on the scene. When I asked him what he did in civilian life, he told me he practiced law

*The Iraqi government immediately announced its suspicion that Zarqawi was responsible. Even then, Sistani urged restraint. But Shiite advocates of communal violence, such as Moqtada al-Sadr, led a series of retaliatory attacks—against Sunni mosques and the general Sunni population in Baghdad and elsewhere. See Ellen Knickmayer and K. I. Ibrahim, "Bombing Shatters Mosque in Iraq," *Washington Post*, February 23, 2006, p. A1.

in Connecticut. As we talked, a crowd of Iraqi men gathered around, obviously very friendly toward the major, who had arranged for trucks to come to the neighborhood twice a day to deliver water. As one of the trucks unloaded fresh water into a large drum, women and girls—no men or boys—lined up and carried the water off in buckets or plastic containers. It was an image out of the book of Genesis.

The major turned to talk to the crowd of men, through an interpreter. He pleased them by announcing that he would soon install a large underground water tank for the neighborhood, so that people would no longer have to wait for the daily deliveries, with pipes eventually running from the tank to people's homes. The men nodded, then pressed him on when he would bring electricity to their houses. He shook his head and said he was working on one miracle at a time.

This patient, brave, humane, ingenious American lawyer—a veritable Connecticut Yankee in primitive east Baghdad—embodied the extraordinary virtues that are ordinary among U.S. forces doing dangerous work in places like Afghanistan and Iraq. I looked at him in his combat gear, complete with heavy personal armor, as he performed his mission in the hellish heat of that street in Baghdad. Toward him and his colleagues, I felt gratitude, admiration, and affection. Americans have reason to honor the men and women in our armed forces and to take pride in them.

At the same time, this experience dramatized the need for a better way to use the talents of skilled professionals. The United States is full of people who are knowledgeable about municipal water systems. Wouldn't it be better if this soldier were performing tasks for which he was actually trained—and a civilian expert were responsible for the water system? Back in Washington, I began work on this concept with colleagues in my office and on the Joint Staff. We considered how the government could identify American civilians with the skills needed for stabilization and reconstruction work. How could we recruit such people and have them committed to deploy when we needed them? How could we develop doctrine and plans to use them effectively? How could we integrate teams of civilians with our combatant commands so they could perform joint military-civilian operations? These questions gave rise to the idea of creating a U.S. civilian reserve corps, on the model of our military reserve.

While this idea still existed only in broad outline, Rumsfeld asked me to raise it with President Bush, which I did initially in May 2004 and then in greater detail in January 2005. He saw its merits. Our military's Connecticut Yankees should not be the default performers of reconstruction and stabilization missions that are better handled by civilian experts.

Fleshing out the civilian reserve corps idea became, at my urging, a responsibility of the new office for stabilization and reconstruction at the State Department. That office itself was an initiative invented and championed by Rice's staff, General Myers's staff, and my office. At an April 27, 2004, Principals Committee meeting, State's leadership eventually acquiesced in the proposal, though reluctantly. Powell agreed to create the office on the condition that it would be "small scale." He protested that State should not have to take on additional missions without receiving additional personnel and funds. Rumsfeld's view was that this additional mission was important for the future of U.S. national security policy. To free up resources for the task, Rumsfeld argued, State should identify some things it had long been doing that were *less* important and stop doing them.

Just as memorable as that Connecticut reservist was the military crew I flew with during a later trip to Iraq. In Amman, Jordan, my "traveling office" transferred to a C-130 "Hercules" transport plane, capable of maneuvering against missiles. As we taxied toward the runway for takeoff, the crew noticed that we were leaking fuel. (The pilot referred to this as an "uncommanded fuel dump." You have to love the military's way with words.)

We reloaded ourselves onto a substitute Hercules, and the crew invited me to join them in the cockpit for the flight. The pilot was an authoritative, well-spoken air force reserve lieutenant colonel based at Fort Polk, Louisiana. The mother of three children, all under the age of six, she explained that she rotated four months in the Iraq theater, then four at home, and then four back in theater. She missed her kids a lot, she said, but she also had a responsibility for her "boys" in the C-130 squadron.

Her copilot, a captain, mentioned a book he was reading: *The Case for Democracy* by Natan Sharansky. He asked if I had heard of it. I said that my job left little time for nonofficial reading, but that was one of the few books I had managed to read in recent years. I mentioned that President Bush had fairly recently met with Sharansky and urged everyone to read the book. We talked a bit about how democracy relates to security.

The pilot raised a more immediate issue of security: the ground-to-air missile threat. The most dangerous places to land in Iraq, she said, were Baghdad and Balad. The latter was riskier. With our delayed departure, we were heading into Baghdad late, after dusk. With the start of our stomach-churning descent maneuver—a steep corkscrew path designed to minimize exposure to enemy missiles—our cockpit crew broke into song: "Come on people now, smile on your brother/everybody get together, got to love one another right now." Then the engineer, in a mock announcer's voice, intoned: "Welcome to Baghdad. The local time and temperature are twenty-hundred hours and one hundred degrees. We know you have a choice of airlines and we appreciate your choosing us."

But at two thousand feet, already well within missile range, the pilot noticed that the runway lights were out. She stopped the descent. The engineer warned: "It's illegal to land without lights." Baghdad International radioed up that the lights had malfunctioned. After a quick consultation with her crew, the pilot decided to divert—to Balad. There, as we once again began our tactical descent, the crew sang the same chorus. It was a joke in the nature of a prayer—or perhaps a prayer in the nature of a joke.

On September 1, 2003, the Governing Council announced the names of the interim ministers. This would have been a sensible moment to give the Governing Council independent authority over some of the ministries, under an IIA agreement between the Council and the CPA. Within a few days, however, it became clear that Bremer had no thought of implementing the IIA concept.

As the sun was beginning to rise on September 8, I was flipping quickly through the daily papers, turning to the op-ed page of the *Washington Post*. There, under Bremer's byline, was an article headlined "Iraq's Path to Sovereignty."

Bremer's article set out seven steps "on the path to full Iraqi sovereignty," including such formidable and uncertain goals as a ratified constitution and nationwide general elections. The article declared that the CPA would stay in existence—would remain Iraq's occupation government—until the country had achieved *all seven steps*. It was a major policy statement—and one that Bremer had not cleared with anyone in the Pentagon. The piece amazed me, and I soon learned it had a similar startling effect on Rumsfeld and the rest of his team.

CPA officials had told us it would take two years to have a constitution and elected national leaders. What Bremer was outlining in the *Washington Post* was not the Administration's policy of early transfer of authority in Iraq. This timetable corresponded, in fact, to the State Department's original proposal for a transitional civil authority, which was designed to keep authority out of Iraqi hands for several years.

Neither Rumsfeld, Wolfowitz, nor I had realized that Bremer opposed the IIA policy. We were not inclined to judge Bremer's work or attitudes negatively. On the contrary, we knew he had taken on a difficult job, we appreciated his willingness to serve, and we took his assurances at face value. Moreover, we knew that our own understanding of what was happening in Iraq was inevitably incomplete. But Bremer's article shed new light on his thinking.

At his morning Roundtable meeting, Rumsfeld asked if any of us had seen the text of Bremer's article beforehand. After collecting our no's, he remarked that Bremer was promising a long period of U.S. occupation. And what if the Iraqis deadlocked while negotiating the constitution? Did it make sense to say that the United States would remain there indefinitely as the occupier? Understating the point, Rumsfeld said it was "not smart" to tie such a large specific commitment to events we could not control.

Rumsfeld had to rethink his relationship with Bremer. The article, in effect, mocked the idea that Bremer worked for him. (I do not know whether Bremer had sent it to any of the other Principals before publication, but, in any event, he should have sought clearance from Rumsfeld.) Rumsfeld had been supporting Bremer—giving him autonomy and showing deference to his recommendations. He had concurred when Bremer spoke against the CPA's *immediately* turning over "full sovereignty" to the Iraqis. But until this September 8 article appeared, Bremer had never made it clear that he rejected the key premise of the IIA plan: that the United States should move quickly (within weeks, not years) to end the occupation.

Bremer was asserting a philosophically inflexible position. He complained that the Governing Council he had created was not representative, and that it lacked public support. The members, in his view, had no "mandate" to exercise independent power as Iraqi officials.

Bremer's concerns were not entirely unreasonable. Most of the Governing Council's members—the internals—were new to political leadership. (The leaders of the external opposition groups had years of political experience, and Barzani and Talabani, the Kurdish leaders, were actually running elected governments in northern Iraq). And it was true that critics inside and outside Iraq would condemn any government appointed by the CPA—rather than elected by the Iraqi people—as a creature of the U.S. government. These were real problems, but what was the solution?

Bremer's answer was that all political power in Iraq, for the foreseeable future, should be kept in the hands of the American CPA administrator. It was hard to follow the logic. If the Governing Council wasn't sufficiently representative of the Iraqi people, should Iraq be run by someone even *less* representative? If the Iraqi leaders lacked a mandate, did Bremer have that mandate? If the problem with an appointed interim government was that it might look like a U.S. creature, was the solution to have the United States continue to govern Iraq?

Bremer's *Washington Post* article triggered the first—and arguably the only—major intervention by Rumsfeld to overrule Bremer. The result was the President's decision to shut down the CPA by the end of June 2004 and to recognize, at long last, an Iraqi interim government.

Timeline 4. Iraq: January 2004–December 2005

2004

Mar. 4	Iraqi interim constitution (known as Transitional Administrative Law) completed
Mar. 29	Fallujah crisis: murder of four U.S. contractors
Apr. 28	CBS News issues report on detainee abuse at Abu Ghraib prison
May 20	U.S. raid on Chalabi compound in Baghdad
Jun. 2	Iraqi Governing Council dissolves itself
Jun. 28	CPA shuts down; Iraqi Interim Government established (headed by President Sheikh Ghazi al-Yawar and Prime Minister Iyad Allawi)

2005

Jan. 30	Election for Transitional National Assembly, resulting in Iraqi Transitional Government (headed by President Jalal Talabani and Prime Minister Ibrahim al-Jaafari)
Aug. 1	Deadline for drafting permanent constitution
Oct. 15	Referendum on permanent constitution
Dec. 15	Elections to National Assembly, resulting in Iraqi Government (headed by President Jalal Talabani and Prime Minister Nouri al-Maliki)

15
THE TAINT OF OCCUPATION

The United States had gone to war to remove the danger of the Saddam Hussein regime—and the regime was now gone. Major combat operations had ended, and, in the early fall of 2003, the massive disruptions of the insurrection were still in the future.

President Bush urged Iraq to embrace democracy, but the U.S. interest in how the Iraqi people organized their government went only so far. It was important for us that Iraq's new leaders not re-create the problems of the old regime by launching aggression, supporting terrorists, aspiring to catastrophic weapons, or killing its own citizens (as Saddam had done, by the hundreds of thousands). *Those* were our core interests, national and humanitarian. Americans had practical reasons to hope that Iraq would become democratic and help counter political extremism in the Muslim world. But our duty as U.S. officials was to protect U.S. national security. It was not to prolong American control over Iraq in order to compel Iraq's new leaders to do things our way.

Throughout the summer of 2003, Bremer complained that the Iraqi leaders were asking for authority but not giving energetic cooperation: They were slow on decisions about organization, personnel, and reconstruction priorities. His diagnosis was that the Iraqi leaders were not practical, not diligent, not skillful, not dedicated—in sum, not ready to govern.

Bremer's solution was to run Iraq himself—to try to lay a foundation for civil society and Iraqi self-rule and to cultivate new leadership. He intended the Coalition Provisional Authority to remain in power *until Iraq had a new constitution and elections*. Whereas an appointed government might be established in weeks, Bremer's doctrine of legitimacy meant that years of work would be required before Iraqis could run their own administration. Rumsfeld viewed that commitment as open-ended for us, unwelcome to the Iraqis, and unnecessary altogether.

In arguing that the Iraqi leaders' lack of cooperation showed that they were unready for sovereign authority, Bremer contributed to a vicious cycle. The Iraqis had no interest in being seen as mere functionaries in a U.S.-led occupation government of indefinite duration. In addition to the indignity of working under a foreigner, there was the personal danger of appearing to collaborate in perpetuating the occupation. Moreover, cooperation under those circumstances could harm their political careers in post-CPA Iraq. It was one thing for Iraqis to associate with Bremer closely and publicly to bring about a transfer of authority into Iraqi hands. It was another to be seen working for Americans who appeared to be settling in at Saddam's palace for the long haul. Despite State's insistence on the importance of legitimacy, the CPA—run largely by current or former State officials—showed no recognition that Governing Council members might be withholding cooperation from Bremer precisely because serving as junior partners inside the CPA might damage their legitimacy in the eyes of the average Iraqi far more than the fact that they had fled abroad during Saddam's rule.

Some Iraqis reacted to Bremer's *Washington Post* article by demanding immediate sovereign authority for the Governing Council. U.S. officials who still supported the IIA plan urged Bremer to accelerate the transfer of power, even if it fell short of full sovereignty. But Bremer defended his seven-step plan as a matter of principle, insisting on a constitution and elections as steps that had to precede any transfer of sovereign authority.

Bremer was aware that a post-Taliban interim government had recently been appointed in Afghanistan *before* a new constitution or national elections: Hamid Karzai's interim administration had exercised sovereign authority immediately after the Taliban's overthrow. Did anyone contend that the Karzai government was illegitimate? Though the two countries were different in important respects, there was no basis for asserting that an interim government was legitimate in Afghanistan but not in Iraq. Apparently, what the legitimacy argument really boiled down to was that State and CIA officials looked favorably on Karzai but not on the Iraqi externals.

Bremer's *Post* article made plain to Rumsfeld that he and Bremer were fundamentally at odds over Iraq policy (even putting aside Bremer's failure to clear the article with the Secretary). This was a predicament Rumsfeld could not resolve simply by issuing an order. Bremer was not inclined to be deferential, and it would be disruptive and politically costly to fire him (especially because Garner's departure had generally, albeit unfairly, been reported as a firing). And it could harm U.S. war efforts to have Bremer quit in a huff.

To shore up his position on the seven-step plan, Bremer invited Powell to Iraq in mid-September to inform the Governing Council that the plan was the only way forward to Iraqi sovereignty. As Bremer recounts the meeting, Powell declared that it was "absolutely essential" that "governmental legitimacy rest on a constitutional basis leading to elections" and that "giving sovereignty" to the Governing Council was "entirely unacceptable."

Powell and Bremer still refused to grant that there could be any middle ground between giving the Iraqis full sovereignty and retaining all of Iraq's governmental powers for the CPA. They did not acknowledge that the President and his National Security Council had ever seriously discussed the IIA plan for power sharing, or that President Bush had approved it. In his book, Bremer downgrades the IIA plan from a formal policy approved by the President to a mere bureaucratic maneuver promoted by some officials working for Cheney and Rumsfeld. Without mentioning its key feature of allocated powers, he describes the IIA as a " 'sovereignty now' campaign [that] seemed to be centered on Deputy Secretary of Defense Paul Wolfowitz, Under Secretary for Policy Douglas Feith, and John Hannah in the vice president's office."Bremer thus depreciates this "early-power-transfer" or "sovereignty now" policy by associating it with second- and third-tier officials. Elsewhere he suggests it was the position merely of the "Pentagon's policy office"—that is, my organization. But it was President Bush's policy—one that had support throughout the Administration, and not just at subcabinet levels.

Bremer himself gives evidence to support this point, relating that he was continually urged to transfer power more quickly to the Iraqis. In October 2003, for example, Rumsfeld asked Bremer to take steps "to 'migrate' political authority to the Iraqis": "We've got to show some forward motion on the political front, Jerry." Bremer observes, "*That's Feith's Defense policy shop talking.*" Rice asked him later that month, "Can we put together some kind of a provisional government?" Bremer says, "I paused to reflect that now every senior member on the president's foreign policy team—Powell, Rumsfeld, and Rice—had pushed this idea at me over the last three weeks." Despite these and similar stories, Bremer refers repeatedly to the early-power-transfer policy as belonging *to me* (Feith) rather than to the President or the Principals. It's as if he hadn't read his own book.

How to deal with Bremer's seven-step plan occupied Rumsfeld for some weeks. In the interim, he handled the CPA administrator delicately. He knew he had to get rid of the plan while avoiding, if possible, an outright confrontation with Bremer. But the first task for Rumsfeld was to clarify his own thinking about the best way to move forward in Iraq. He decided to convene his top Pentagon advisers, together with Bremer and General John Abizaid, the new CENTCOM commander.

As preparation, Rumsfeld asked me to conduct a review of U.S. Iraq policy. I did so with Lieutenant General Walter "Skip" Sharp (U.S. Army), who served as the Joint Staff's director of strategic plans and policy—a man trained in mathematics, with an unusually rigorous mind and sophisticated judgment on political-military affairs. Our review was a reexamination of basic questions, on the Rumsfeld model: What were we aiming now to accomplish in Iraq? What were our up-to-date key assumptions? What courses of action were most important and most urgent?

Rumsfeld invested a lot of his own time in this project. Unlike his usual ten- or twenty-minute meetings, his October 22 "Iraq Strategic Review" meeting with Wolfowitz, Bill Luti, Sharp, and me was allotted nearly two and a half hours.* The group, joined by General Myers and General Pace, met again the next day for an additional two and a quarter hours—and the next day for another hour and a half. In those sessions, Rumsfeld and the others challenged every element of our prepared briefing. After working the material through from beginning to end several times over those three days, Rumsfeld took ownership of the analysis—he "got conviction," as he liked to put it. He now had a set of strategic concepts honed to his satisfaction—and a plan for his meetings with Bremer.

Rumsfeld and his team formulated the U.S. strategic goal in Iraq in essentially the same terms President Bush had used before the war: We aimed to bring into being an Iraq that would seek peace, remain unified, develop its economy, abandon Saddam's WMD and long-range missile programs, and oppose terrorism. We did not promise to put in place a stable democracy for the Iraqis; rather, we stated the more realistic aim of "a representative government that builds democratic institutions and is respectful of its diverse population." In line with one of the President's key

---

*As shown in Rumsfeld's daily calendar. In attendance were Wolfowitz and I, Bill Luti, Sharp, and one of Sharp's assistants.

themes, we said that an Iraq of this type could serve as a "model of freedom and prosperity in the region."

The review highlighted two observations in particular. The first was that "governance, security, economy, essential services and strategic communications are inter-related."* A proper strategy would involve advancing *simultaneously* on each of those main "tracks." Bremer sometimes claimed that the Iraqis were less concerned about the political process than about improving security and essential services. But that view ignored the fact that political, security, and economic developments all affected one another. While military action would obviously be required to suppress the violence in Iraq, we believed it was equally important to move forward on political reconciliation, the transfer of governmental authority to Iraqis, and visible improvement in the Iraqis' standard of living.

There is a popular notion that military officers tend to view every problem as having a military solution. But, more often than not, an official who declares that a national security problem requires a military solution is looking not to *claim* responsibility but to *shift* it. That is to say, the speaker is likely to be from State rather than Defense. Defense officials—including the senior military—can generally be counted on to highlight the important diplomatic component of any problem.† It was Powell and Bremer, not Rumsfeld or General Myers, who continually spoke as if there were a military solution to the problem of Iraqi instability, when they talked about establishing security as a prerequisite for political progress.

The second major point in our strategic review was that the key to suc-

---

*We hoped to counter the finger-pointing that was already under way: diplomats asserting that political progress was impossible until the military established security, and military personnel contending that security was impossible until there were jobs available to get angry young men off the streets and until diplomats made progress toward an Iraqi government.

†Secretary of Defense Robert Gates made this point succinctly in his confirmation hearing:

> **It was always my experience that, contrary to the conventional wisdom, it was the State Department that most often wanted to use force and the Department of Defense that most often wanted to use diplomacy. And CIA never wanted to use covert action. Everybody wanted everybody else to take the actions.**

Robert Gates, Confirmation Hearing before the U.S. Senate Armed Services Committee, December 5, 2006, available at http://media.washingtonpost.com/wp-srv/politics/documents/rgates_hearing_120506.html. Senior U.S. military officers are taught in war colleges that solving strategic problems requires *all* instruments of national power. They all know better than to believe—or, worse, to say out loud—that a significant problem can be solved by force alone.

cess would be Iraqis acting on their own behalf. The most important task for Americans was not to do things for Iraq, but to "*encourage and enable*" Iraqis to do things for themselves. Iraqi leaders needed to hear two messages from U.S. officials. First, the United States would remain engaged and helpful—not abandon them to chaos. Second, the Iraqis would soon run their own lives. This encourage-and-enable approach was an extension of the "liberation, not occupation" strategy approved by the President in the summer of 2002.

Trying to stabilize Iraq through our own operations should not be the *sole* focus of the U.S. military, we concluded. Iraqis would be better than coalition forces for some internal security missions. High priority should be given to training and equipping Iraqi forces, who would have to maintain order over the long term; and CPA and CENTCOM should integrate their respective efforts to train Iraqi security forces. The coalition should "quickly move Iraqis to greater responsibilities in the security arena with coalition forces moving increasingly to a supporting role." This meant that the coalition "may have to accept some inefficiencies and increased risk."

Along the same lines, we contended that the CPA's principal focus should not be running Iraq, organizing its government and planning its constitution. Rather, it should be "encouraging and enabling Iraqis to assume responsibility for their own affairs—governance, security, and economy." The common Iraqi suspicion that the CPA would remain in power indefinitely—reinforced by Bremer's *Washington Post* article—did *not* encourage leaders to step forward to assume political responsibility. Indeed, it appeared to be having the opposite effect. To remedy this problem, we proposed announcing that the CPA would be terminated on a definite date in the near future. If the Iraqis knew that the CPA was going away soon, they might be more productive in making the arrangements for a proper new Iraqi government. (We did not, however, propose to demoralize the Iraqis by setting a deadline for the withdrawal of U.S. forces.)

Our review therefore recommended a new frame of mind. Bremer tended to prescribe that Americans, not the Iraqi leadership, should solve Iraq's major problems and lay the foundation for Iraq's political reconstruction. Bremer similarly put little stock in the special abilities that Iraqi soldiers and police could bring to suppressing violence—or in the importance of rapidly creating more Iraqi security forces. Instead, he stressed that Iraqi forces needed lengthy training, and he made it one of his personal "red lines" that the Iraqi army *not* be used for internal security. Since his departure from the Bush Administration, Bremer has said that he favored more *American* troops for Iraq. (I am not aware of his having argued that proposition to Rumsfeld at the time.)

These long strategy sessions sharpened Rumsfeld's understanding of the contradictions among the CPA's policies. His next task was to adjust those policies to avoid the default outcome of a prolonged U.S. occupation of Iraq. But Bremer was now committed publicly—in print—to his own position: A constitutionally elected government must precede the transfer of sovereign authority. And, whatever the formal organizational chart showed, Bremer did not consider himself Rumsfeld's subordinate. Rumsfeld understood this and decided to deal with Bremer through negotiation.

The Secretary made a point of showing Bremer consideration. On Sunday evening, October 26, Rumsfeld invited him for a private talk in his home. In the Pentagon over the next two days, Rumsfeld cleared his business calendar to spend nearly the entire time with Bremer. In more than a dozen hours of meetings with his entire strategy team, Rumsfeld walked Bremer through our review of Iraq policy and solicited his views. At no point did Rumsfeld suggest that he was unhappy with Bremer or that he was aiming to overrule him on the seven-step plan. He used the techniques I had seen him use with others—raising fundamental questions, floating broad propositions, resorting to humor, testing the other person's logic, examining his assumptions, probing his facts, and finally—without ever actually butting heads or making a demand—eliciting precisely the recommendation he wanted.

By the time these long deliberations were over, Rumsfeld had secured Bremer's agreement that the CPA should be shut down *before* Iraq had a constitution. As a precondition for an interim government, Bremer conceded, the Governing Council should have to agree only on *key elements* of a constitution—not the full and final text. So Bremer's inflexible principle eventually softened into a practical good idea: Iraq's interim constitution.

Given Bremer's resistance to power sharing, the only way to end the occupation was to shut down the CPA.* But even if he accelerated his work, Bremer argued, he would not be able to shut it down before December 2004. He would need that much time to complete the interim constitution and organize elections, which he insisted were a precondition for a legitimate interim government. Proper elections would take many months

*When Rumsfeld, Wolfowitz, or I used the phrase "end the occupation," Bremer would reply that many Iraqis would still say they were under occupation so long as large numbers of U.S. troops were in their country (*My Year in Iraq*, p. 205). He had a point, but we thought it mattered whether the Iraqi government was run by Americans or Iraqis. There was a difference between occupation as an accusation and occupation as a legal fact.

to organize, given that Iraq lacked a census, a political parties law, voting districts, voter registration regulations, and the like. Rumsfeld realized that the project of creating the interim government could drag on well into the latter half of 2004, and perhaps beyond that.

Deadlines often slip, Rumsfeld said privately to Wolfowitz and me, so we should demand that the CPA be terminated by the end of June 2004. Elections might be possible by then if everyone worked fast. A September 2004 deadline would be easier to achieve, but if the date to end the occupation was bound to "slip to the right," Rumsfeld said, let it slip from June, not September. The earlier the occupation ends, the better.

Wolfowitz and I argued that Bremer was still setting unnecessarily elaborate preconditions for the interim government. We questioned whether elections were necessary *at all* for the interim government. We worried that holding premature elections—before the build-up of civil institutions—could produce anti-democratic results. In any event, we thought there might be procedural shortcuts that would be adequate for electing an interim government. Fully developed election laws could come later, after Iraq had a permanent constitution. We said Bremer should be able to end the occupation before June 2004—even if he insisted on some kind of election beforehand.

Rumsfeld was willing to sustain the CPA through the month of June, but he welcomed the proposal from Wolfowitz and me to make the termination date April 9—the first anniversary of Baghdad's liberation. If the date then became June 30, we joked, Bremer could say he had successfully beaten back the hard-liners.

Papers were written at the Pentagon and the CPA on the pros and cons of the April date as compared to Bremer's timeline, which promised a new interim government (according to CPA staff analysis) "by late 2004, at best." The upshot of these discussions was an agreement among Rumsfeld, Bremer, and Abizaid that the seven-step plan was no longer in effect and that the CPA should be shut down within the coming months—a big step forward. The only thing missing was a consensus on the date, which would have to await Bremer's consultations with the Iraqis.

In the area of security, however, the meetings of October 26–28 were less successful. Both Rumsfeld and Abizaid wanted a stronger force to fight the enemy, and they focused on adding *Iraqi* military and police personnel. The general consistently argued against increasing the size of the American military "footprint" in Iraq.* Abizaid insisted that he did not

---

*With Rumsfeld's support, Abizaid also urged State Department officials to recruit stabilization forces from third countries.

lack U.S. forces to go after the enemy; what he lacked was intelligence about where the enemy was hiding. Increasing the number of American forces in Iraq could aggravate the problem of Iraqis viewing Americans as occupiers—resulting in *less* intelligence. With more U.S. troops on the ground he would have more force protection problems and less ability to find the enemy. What was needed was an effort to encourage and enable the Iraqis to provide security for themselves.

Bremer continued to resist the idea, stressing that the Iraqis were not as well disciplined, trained, equipped, or motivated as the American forces. That was true, of course, but it gave short shrift to other relevant considerations. First and foremost, Iraq belonged to the Iraqis: Success for the United States, by definition, would require Iraqis to become capable of handling their own problems. Moreover, there were important jobs that the Americans could not do as well as Iraqi forces simply because the Iraqis spoke the language, understood the culture, and knew the territory better. Rather than dwell on the Iraqi security forces' inferiority, we wanted to find ways to accelerate their training and expand their role in combating the insurgents. One way to improve the Iraqi forces' motivation and morale was, again, by moving toward a sovereign Iraqi government, giving the Iraqi forces a chain of command with Iraqis, not Americans, at the top.

When the Pentagon sessions with Bremer and Abizaid ended at midday on October 28, the two of them, along with Rumsfeld and Myers, reported first to a Principals Committee meeting and the next day to President Bush, at a National Security Council meeting. (I was not present at those two meetings.) Rumsfeld was pleased that President Bush—apart from the still-open question of timing—supported the key point of the Pentagon review: that the United States should no longer consider a constitution and elections preconditions for establishing an interim government. With the President's support, the CPA could be terminated soon—within months, not years—and the interim government could take its place. Bremer was able to acquiesce—and later claimed that dropping the seven steps was his own idea—because he agreed that an interim constitution was indeed good enough for an interim government. Yet he still insisted that the CPA's shutdown would have to be deferred for four months to create the interim constitution—and another four months to organize elections or caucuses. June 30, he concluded, was the earliest possible date for setting up the interim government.

After the review with Rumsfeld, Bremer left Washington with guidance for a new strategy. In implementing it, he would do his best work in Iraq.

On his return to Baghdad, Bremer talked with the Governing Council. On November 11, he returned to Washington for two days of meetings with the Principals and President Bush, in which the June 30 date was confirmed. He quickly turned around and headed back to Baghdad to get agreement with the Governing Council on a written plan for the adoption of an *interim* constitution and the creation of an *elected* interim government with full sovereign authority.

In Bremer's account of the demise of the seven-step plan, Rumsfeld does not appear to play a key role. Bremer says it was his own idea to kill the plan, attributing his decision to an inflexible demand of Grand Ayatollah Ali al-Sistani. The issue had to do with elections.

Although Sistani was philosophically opposed to government by clerics, he did on important occasions make political pronouncements through fatwas (religious decrees). He issued one of these decrees to declare that delegates to Iraq's constitutional convention must be democratically elected rather than appointed.* Sistani's position was difficult to harmonize with Bremer's seven-step plan, which called for a ratified constitution *before* there could be an interim government. If elections were necessary even to select the drafters of the constitution, the seven steps would take far too long—even from Bremer's point of view.

Sistani had in fact issued his religious decree in June 2003—two months *before* Bremer announced his plan. Did Bremer expect that the Grand Ayatollah, after reading of the seven steps in the *Washington Post*, would say "Never mind" about his fatwa? If Bremer thought the success of the seven steps hinged on whether Sistani would relent on the election of constitutional delegates, he might have gauged the cleric's resolve before publishing his plan in the *Post*.

Bremer now faced another election-related problem. He had an end of June deadline for establishing the interim government, and he had decided that such a government could not be legitimate if it were simply appointed, without a national vote of some kind. But it would be difficult—maybe impossible—to accomplish elections in time. Bremer therefore came up with the idea of using local caucuses throughout Iraq, instead of

---

*Sistani's demand for an elected constitutional convention was not an endorsement of Bremer's view that the CPA should rule the country until Iraq had elections. Sistani was focused specifically on the importance of the constitution: He wanted to ensure that Iraq's Shiites enjoyed the benefits of their 60 percent majority in choosing the writers of the constitution.

national elections, and insisted that these caucuses were the *only* practical approach to elections within the time allotted. Once again Bremer was at odds with Sistani, who had by now expanded his requirement of elections to apply to the legislature as well as to the constitutional convention.

As the Grand Ayatollah was unwilling to give Bremer an audience, the two men never met face-to-face. Instead, they communicated through intermediaries and through the news media. On the issue of elections versus caucuses, they debated—indeed, quarreled—publicly for months, with Bremer in the unenviable position of antagonist to the most widely respected public figure in the country. The American appeared to be an opponent of democratic elections, while Sistani spoke as their champion. If elections had to be held, Wolfowitz and I suggested, simplified preparations might save time while averting a clash with Sistani.* But in spite of Rumsfeld's urging to show some creativity and flexibility on the issue, Bremer stood his ground on caucuses for months. He argued that the caucuses, as an electoral shortcut, would be relatively quick (though not easy) to set up. While caucuses would yield a "less legitimate government" than outright elections, Bremer argued, the results would be legitimate enough for the purpose of an interim government.

At a Principals Committee meeting in Washington on January 16, 2004, several voices around the table advised Bremer to back off from the quarrel with Sistani. I commented that "we don't want to position ourselves as opposed to elections." Rumsfeld said that the word "elections" had more than one definition. A bit later, Cheney observed that Sistani had more legitimacy in the eyes of more Iraqis than anyone else: "We need a strategy that accommodates his legitimate interests." When Bremer countered that Sistani "shifts his bottom line," Powell remarked that, on the point of demanding elections, Sistani had not shifted.

Soon after this meeting, Rumsfeld sent a memo to the other Principals warning of the danger of inflexibility regarding the "plans for moving toward Iraqi sovereignty." "On all but a few key points of strategic importance," Rumsfeld said, "the U.S. has no interest in pushing ideas on the Iraqis [because] Iraq is their country, and the Iraqis should make political arrangements that best suit them." What we needed was an agreed "timetable for early recognition of Iraqi sovereignty, so that the Coalition can shed the 'occupying power' label." The U.S. should not oppose—or appear to oppose—elections.

Bremer's judgments about legitimacy were fundamental to his strat-

---

*For example, by dispensing with a census and simply purpling fingers to prevent double voting.

egy, just as the assertions by State and CIA officials about the legitimacy of the Iraqi externals had for years been central to the policies those agencies promoted. But none of these judgments had any reality outside the subjective thoughts of the officials who asserted them. When Bremer said that elections or caucuses were essential to make the interim government legitimate, he was not stating a self-evident truth or an objective fact or even a finding supported by scientific polling data. He was giving his opinion.

As it happened, Bremer himself demonstrated that his opinion was not correct. It turned out to be impossible to organize either elections or caucuses by June 30, 2004. Instead, when the curtain came down on the CPA, Bremer handed power over to an *appointed* interim government, headed by Prime Minister Iyad Allawi. The main task of that government was to organize the January 2005 national elections, and it fulfilled its responsibility. The elections were held on time and drew widespread support throughout Iraq. The *appointed* administration evidently had enough legitimacy among Iraqis to serve as an interim government with a short life—much as the IIA plan had envisioned.

After his November 11 and 12 meetings in Washington, Bremer returned to Baghdad and met with the Governing Council. By November 15 he reached an agreement with them on the transition to Iraqi self-rule. The Governing Council committed to produce an interim constitution acceptable to the CPA by February 28.* The CPA and the Governing Council promised to enter into a security agreement by March 31 to regulate coalition forces in Iraq. And finally, they agreed that by June 30—after the dissolution of both the Governing Council and the CPA—the coalition would recognize an Iraqi government with "full sovereign powers."

The November 15 agreement was a diplomatic achievement, a turning point in the history of post-Saddam Iraq. It assured Iraqis that the United States would not be running their government for the indefinite future. Bremer showed skill in concluding the agreement so rapidly upon his return to Baghdad. But one of the ways he expedited that work was by not sending the text to Rumsfeld for review.†

When he saw the agreement, Rumsfeld disapproved of one section that called for a negotiated security agreement with the Governing Council.

---

*A CPA staffer later explained that that date should have been February 29, but he had forgotten that 2004 was a leap year.

†Bremer may have cleared the draft with Rice: He recounts that he spoke on the telephone with her as he was completing the agreement. (*My Year in Iraq*, p. 229.)

He anticipated that the Iraqi leaders would want to burnish their nationalist credentials by demanding restrictions on the coalition forces' freedom of action. Once the Iraqis had full sovereign authority, Rumsfeld would be willing to make reasonable accommodations. But he said it made no sense to seek an agreement in March with the outgoing members of the Governing Council—given that, three months later, the incoming members of the interim government would likely want to show their toughness by making stiffer demands. We should rather wait for the interim government to be established and conclude whatever security agreements were necessary with those new officials. Rumsfeld stuck to his guns (as it were), and no security agreement was ever concluded under the November 15 agreement.

Readers may be puzzled or amazed that Bremer did not maintain a tighter connection between himself and Rumsfeld, given that President Bush's appointment letter instructed Bremer to work under the "authority, direction and control of the Secretary of Defense." Bremer, however, had created elbow room for himself. Having been told by Rumsfeld that he could feel free to talk with the other Principals whenever he thought it would be useful, Bremer began making frequent contacts with Rice, which evolved into the daily telephone calls that Bremer refers to repeatedly in his book.

Rice came to play such a major role in managing the Administration's relations with the CPA that she obtained authority from President Bush to create a new apparatus called the Iraq Stabilization Group. In an October 2, 2003, memo (to Cheney, Powell, Rumsfeld, Tenet, Myers, and others), Rice announced that the new group would strengthen interagency support to both the Defense Department and the CPA. Rice's various deputies would chair the Group's "cells" in four areas:

- Politics/governance
- Counterterrorism/jihadist activities
- Economics
- Media/message issues

The *New York Times* described the Iraq Stabilization Group as part of "a major reorganization of American efforts to quell violence in Iraq and Afghanistan and to speed the reconstruction of both countries," through "an effort to assert more direct White House control" over all aspects of U.S. policy there. The article cited a statement by Rice, in a television interview, asserting that the October 2 memo had been devised by herself, Cheney, Powell, and Rumsfeld.

"Inside the State Department and in some offices in the White House," the *Times* article continued, "the decision to create the stabilization group has been interpreted as a direct effort to diminish the authority of the Pentagon and Mr. Rumsfeld in the next phase of the occupation." This was denied by "senior White House officials," one of whom remarked: "Don recognizes that this is not what the Pentagon does best, and he is, in some ways, relieved to give up some of the authority here." This senior official—apparently Rice, one of the few who called Rumsfeld by his first name—then noted that Bremer would still report to the Defense Department.

When the *Times* article was mentioned at Rumsfeld's Roundtable staff meeting that day, the Secretary's reaction was muted. I later learned, however, that he sent a strongly worded memo to the President's Chief of Staff, Andrew Card, contradicting Rice's statement that he had been involved in developing the stabilization group idea. He had been *advised* by the October 2 memo, he said, not consulted. He then recommended that Bremer's "reporting relationship" be transferred from Defense to State rather than to Rice, for her office was not staffed, organized, or capable of handling the task.

Rumsfeld did not mention the "unity of effort/unity of leadership" idea that underlay the original October 2002 decision to put all post-Saddam reconstruction responsibility under the Secretary of Defense. But he reminded Card that everyone had expected that that responsibility would move from Defense to State as the Iraq stabilization effort matured. The CPA's work was now increasingly political and economic in nature, Rumsfeld wrote, and Bremer was already reporting also to Powell, Rice, and the President. He had recently told Bremer he would be happy to have him report to State anytime Bremer thought that would be appropriate and desirable. Many officials there "adamantly felt" that Bremer should report to State, he observed, so a transfer to State might "calm them down and stop them from complaining to the press." The sooner the transfer took place, the better. Rumsfeld was clearly irritated.

Yet Rumsfeld was not able to get the formal chain of command altered. On paper, Bremer continued to work for Rumsfeld, though in fact he never really did, and he did so less and less over time. Bremer came to report directly to a number of people, which meant that he effectively had no boss. This was not how the interagency process was supposed to work.

In the fall of 2003, U.S. officials began to give up on finding chemical or biological weapons stockpiles in Iraq. The investigation was being conducted by the Iraq Survey Group, an organization Rumsfeld had created to investigate the state of Iraq's weapons programs. Although its staff (composed of U.S., British, and Australian military and civilian personnel) worked under the command of Major General Keith Dayton (U.S. Army), the Iraq Survey Group reported not to Defense but to the CIA. George Tenet had appointed David Kay, a former weapons inspector for the UN Special Commission on Iraq (UNSCOM), to serve as the group's first supervisor, from June to December 2003. (Tenet later appointed as Kay's successor Charles Duelfer, another former UNSCOM inspector.)

On October 2, 2003, Kay reported preliminary findings to Congress. Much of his six-thousand-word report supported the Bush Administration's prewar assertions: Saddam Hussein's WMD *history, intentions, capabilities*, and *programs* supported the conclusion that Iraq posed serious threats. These findings were overshadowed, however, by what the Iraq Survey Group did *not* find: the weapons that the CIA said were stockpiled in the country.

The Iraq Survey Group discovered "dozens of WMD-related program activities and significant amounts of equipment that Iraq concealed from the United Nations during the inspections that began in late 2002." In addition to discovering extensive concealment efforts, it was "faced with a systematic sanitization of documentary and computer evidence in a wide range of offices, laboratories, and companies suspected of WMD work." It found that the efforts "to erase evidence—hard drives destroyed, specific files burned, equipment cleaned of all traces of use" were "deliberate, rather than random, acts."

Despite Iraq's denial-and-deception efforts, the Iraq Survey Group found evidence that, after 1996, Iraq had further compartmentalized its biological weapons (BW) program and "focused on maintaining smaller, covert capabilities that could be activated quickly to surge the production of BW agents." When Operation Iraqi Freedom began, Saddam had "a clandestine network of laboratories and facilities within the security service apparatus." This capability was "suitable for preserving BW expertise, BW capable facilities and continuing R&D—all key elements for maintaining a capability for resuming BW production." The Iraqi Intelligence Service (IIS) "played a prominent role in sponsoring students for overseas graduate studies in the biological sciences, according to Iraqi scientists and IIS sources, providing an important avenue for furthering BW-applicable research." This was the "only area of graduate work that the IIS appeared to sponsor."

From interviews with Iraqi scientists, the Iraq Survey Group "uncovered agent R&D work that paired overt work with nonpathogenic organisms serving as surrogates for prohibited investigation with pathogenic agents." The testimony of Iraqi scientists and senior government officials, the Iraq Survey Group further observed, "should clear up any doubts about whether Saddam still wanted to obtain nuclear weapons." They told the Group's investigators that Saddam "remained firmly committed to acquiring nuclear weapons" and that he "would have resumed nuclear weapons development at some future point." Some of the interviewees "indicated a resumption after Iraq was free of sanctions."

Kay stressed that Saddam had preserved the technical cadres for WMD work: "According to documents and testimony of Iraqi scientists, some of the key technical groups from the pre-1991 nuclear weapons program remained largely intact, performing work on nuclear-relevant dual-use technologies within the Military Industrial Commission." Some scientists from the pre-1991 nuclear weapons program testified that "they believed that these working groups were preserved in order to allow a reconstitution of the nuclear weapons program, but none of the scientists could produce official orders or plans to support their belief." One Iraqi scientist stated that "it was a 'common understanding' among the scientists that material was being preserved for reconstitution of nuclear weapons-related work." (Their belief was later confirmed in the Iraq Survey Group's final report, which summarized Saddam's strategy: "Keep nuclear scientists together at IAEC [Iraqi Atomic Energy Commission] in order to pool their skills and have them available when needed.")

In general, the "scientists and other insiders who worked in his military-industrial programs" judged that Saddam "had not given up his aspirations and intentions to continue to acquire weapons of mass destruction." Even those senior officials who claimed no direct knowledge of any ongoing prohibited activities, Kay reported, "readily acknowledge that Saddam intended to resume these programs whenever the external restrictions were removed." Several of them "acknowledge receiving inquiries since 2000 from Saddam or his sons about how long it would take to either restart CW [chemical weapons] production or make available chemical weapons."

The Kay Report explained why fact-finding about Saddam's WMD programs remained difficult. Even in the post-Saddam era, getting to the truth was impeded by fears of Baathist retaliation—and also by the systematic destruction of papers and materiel, as Saddam's regime was being overthrown. Nonetheless, Kay was able to confirm that Saddam posed serious WMD-related threats.

But Kay also reported that coalition investigators had not found the chemical and biological weapons stockpiles that administration officials had believed were in Iraq:

> We have not yet found stocks of weapons, but we are not yet at the point where we can say definitively either that such weapon stocks do not exist or that they existed before the war and our only task is to find where they have gone. We are actively engaged in searching for such weapons based on information being supplied to us by Iraqis.
>
> . . . Our search efforts are being hindered by six principal factors:
>
> 1. From birth all of Iraq's WMD activities were highly compartmentalized within a regime that ruled and kept its secrets through fear and terror and with deception and denial built into each program;
> 2. Deliberate dispersal and destruction of material and documentation related to weapons programs began pre-conflict and ran trans-to-post conflict;
> 3. Post-OIF [Operation Iraqi Freedom] looting destroyed or dispersed important and easily collectable material and forensic evidence concerning Iraq's WMD program. As the report covers in detail, significant elements of this looting were carried out in a systematic and deliberate manner, with the clear aim of concealing pre-OIF activities of Saddam's regime;
> 4. Some WMD personnel crossed borders in the pre/trans conflict period and may have taken evidence and even weapons-related materials with them;
> 5. Any actual WMD weapons or material is likely to be small in relation to the total conventional armaments footprint and difficult to near impossible to identify with normal search procedures. It is important to keep in mind that even the bulkiest materials we are searching for, in the quantities we would expect to find, can be concealed in spaces not much larger than a two car garage;
> 6. The environment in Iraq remains far from permissive for our activities, with many Iraqis that we talk to reporting threats and overt acts of intimidation

> **and our own personnel being the subject of threats and attacks.**

Press stories generally highlighted the discrepancy between Kay's conclusions and what Administration officials had said about Iraqi WMD before the war. David Sanger of the *New York Times* claimed that the Kay Report's "findings support the claims of critics, including Democratic [presidential] candidates, that Mr. Bush used dubious intelligence to justify his decision to go to war." The news media gave little attention to the findings that Iraqi intelligence had destroyed evidence of its laboratory activities and that "dozens of WMD-related program activities" had been concealed from UN inspectors, or to the opportunities for transfer and concealment of materiel that Kay cited.

For obvious reasons, the Administration's political opponents wanted to highlight that Administration officials made errors. Those errors cannot be denied, but they could have been put in perspective. It is remarkable how little the Administration did to distinguish between what the U.S. government got *wrong* about the Iraqi WMD threat and what it got *right*. This failure to address its critics' excesses contributed to a false but by now well-entrenched conventional wisdom.

In fall 2003, President Bush's opponents began to contend that the prewar intelligence errors invalidated the entire rationale for the war. Administration officials should have countered that the rationale for removing Saddam Hussein from power was far broader than the concerns about WMD stockpiles. Indeed, even the WMD part of the rationale wasn't based only on the idea that Saddam possessed stockpiles. Kay's report could have been cited to confirm that even after U.S. intelligence analysts corrected their errors, they found that there *was* a substantial Iraqi WMD threat.

But in the fall of 2003 the Administration failed to make these points. As far as I know, no one at the CIA—or at the White House, for that matter—made a timely, substantial effort to encourage full and accurate news coverage of the Kay Report. No one even assembled a short fact sheet to direct journalists' attention to the report's key points, such as those quoted above. And the news media gave the impression that the report's only major finding was that inspectors discovered no proscribed weapons in Iraq.

The President and his team could have debated their critics. They could have called attention to the infrastructure and personnel that Saddam maintained to preserve his WMD options, and especially the ability to resume production rapidly. Without denying or ignoring the prewar intelligence mistakes, Administration officials could have explained that those mistakes had but a limited effect on the U.S. government's decision to go to war. They could have defended the rationale for the war, despite those mistakes.

The day after the Kay Report was published, President Bush referred to it with a few brief quotes in his remarks at a White House South Lawn press event. Condoleezza Rice, addressing the Council on Foreign Relations in Chicago almost a week after the report was published, quoted three sentences from it. A few days after that—well after the news coverage of the Kay Report had congealed into the simple notion that no WMD were found—Vice President Cheney provided a more substantive treatment of the report in a speech to the Heritage Foundation.

Yet these diffuse and belated efforts by the Administration made little impression. Journalists, members of Congress, and commentators around the world cited the Kay Report countless times as proof that there were no WMD in Iraq at all—and that there was therefore no case for war.

President Bush himself effectively set aside the rationale for the war. Beginning in the fall of 2003, his public remarks on Iraq changed drastically. By and large, he stopped talking about Saddam's brutal record and the threats posed by the Iraqi regime.

Consider the information in Table 2, listing all the President's remarks about Iraq (as posted on the White House website) for the period from September 2002 through September 2004. Shown are the number of paragraphs in each speech that discuss the threat from the Saddam Hussein regime (including its record of aggression and menace) and the number of paragraphs that discuss the prospects for building democracy in Iraq.

Table 2 reveals a stark change in the White House communications strategy. In the first period—beginning on September 12, 2002, when President Bush first brought the Iraq issue before the UN General Assembly—the President explained his focus on Iraq and the rationale for action against Saddam by reference to the Iraqi regime's *record* and the *threats* it posed to international peace and security. After coalition forces overthrew Saddam and failed to find WMD stockpiles, however, the President changed his rhetoric. In the second period—September 2003 to September 2004—he chose to talk virtually not at all about the Baathist regime's history or the danger Saddam represented. Instead, President Bush focused on the current situation—in particular, that Iraq had become a battleground on which we were fighting terrorist insurgents—and he stressed that in Iraq we now had an opportunity to bring *democracy* to the Arab and Muslim worlds.

Table 2. President Bush's Shift of Rhetoric (Number of paragraphs per speech or event)

Speech or Event	*Threat/ Saddam's Record*	*Iraqi Democracy/ Political Future*	*Averages* Threat	Democracy
9–12–02	28	3		
9–14–02	8	0		
10–7-02	30	2		
1–28–03	19	2		
2–6-03	13	0		
2–26–03	6	13		
3–17–03*	13	2		
5–1-03*	5	4		
7–1-03	2	5		
Period I	124	31	13.7	3.4
9–7-03	0	18		
9–23–03	2	10		
10–3-03	4	1		
10–9-03	4	7		
11–6-03	0	3		
11–11–03	0	16		
12–14–03	0	5		
1–20–04	1	5		
3–19–04	0	8		
4–10–04	0	8		
4–13–04	0	22		
5–10–04	0	16		
5–24–04	0	33		
7–12–04	5	0		
9–12–04	1	7		
Period II	17	159	1.1	10.6

*Period of major combat operations.

In the first period, in round numbers, the President's statements on Iraq contained an average of fourteen paragraphs on Saddam's threat and three paragraphs on democracy.* In the second period, the averages were one paragraph on Saddam's threat and eleven on democracy.

I don't know exactly when or how it was decided that the President should change his way of talking about Iraq. The President and his key communications advisers apparently decided that the failure to find WMD stockpiles was such an embarrassment that the President should not even try to explain it or put it in context. Rather, the Administration tried to change the subject.

These calculations were not debated as a change of national security policy in the Deputies or Principals Committee or the National Security Council. Presumably they were considered merely a public affairs matter. But their consequences were strategic.

It is hard to overstate the significance of the mistakes the Administration made in its initial public presentation of the case for war, citing incorrect intelligence as supporting evidence. But these errors were later compounded by the decision that the President's remarks on Iraq should no longer concentrate on history and threats but should rather discuss only current and future challenges and the importance of promoting democracy. This change in rhetoric aggravated the damage to the Administration's credibility. It made the President appear to be shifting his ground—changing the rationale for the war—without forthrightly explaining the change.

Moreover, the President's political opponents quickly came to realize that if they attacked the Administration for its prewar analyses and other prewar work, they would not be refuted. This had the ironic effect of focusing the public debate on the past rather than on the future—the opposite of what White House officials intended. And the emphasis on building a stable democracy in Iraq redefined success in such a way that many Americans stopped believing that success was either possible or worth the sacrifice.

Bremer and his CPA governance team showed energy and skill in helping the Iraqis develop an interim constitution. Bremer's assertiveness served his purposes well here. He pushed the Iraqis to overcome important differences—and they did so. Negotiating the interim constitution

*More than a third of all the "democracy" paragraphs in this first period occurred in a single speech (on February 26, 2003) specifically on the subject of democracy.

required the full period allotted in the November 15 agreement. The Governing Council completed the document, formally entitled the Transitional Administrative Law, on March 8, 2004, only a few days after the deadline.

Moments after it was signed, I caught a glimpse of a news report on a Pentagon television. The American reporter asked one of the Iraqi founding fathers to comment on the achievement. His reply was as incisive as it was succinct: "We actually compromised."

In December 2003, the Secretary and Mrs. Rumsfeld hosted a holiday reception at their home. The gathering was made festive, but at the same time grave, by news we received the previous day, December 13: U.S. forces had captured Saddam Hussein in a makeshift bunker near his hometown of Tikrit. The monstrous egomaniac had humiliated himself both in the way he hid and in the way he surrendered.

President Bush had decided that Iraqi officials should put him on trial. It was gratifying that Saddam had been caught alive, but no civilized process could ever actually achieve justice for the enormities of his tyranny and the terrible consequences of his aggressions and threats. Saddam was eventually tried before the Iraqi Special Tribunal and convicted of crimes against humanity.* He was hanged on December 30, 2005. His notorious two sons, Uday and Qusay, had been killed by U.S. forces in a raid four months before Saddam's capture. The people of Iraq, and the world at large, no longer had to worry about Saddam—or a Saddam Hussein dynasty.

Administration officials were still debating the importance of moving quickly on the Iraqi political process and training Iraqi security forces when the terrorist Abu Musab al-Zarqawi effectively resolved the debate. Zarqawi wrote an extraordinary letter (no date specified) to the top leaders of al Qaida, Usama bin Laden and Ayman al-Zawahiri, which was intercepted by U.S. intelligence and aired publicly for the first time in a February 9, 2004, *New York Times* story.

Zarqawi was the principal foreign jihadist in Iraq. A Sunni extremist from Jordan, Zarqawi had worked for years with Iraq-based terrorists whom the CIA labeled as close affiliates of al Qaida. (In his letter, Zar-

*A separate indictment of Saddam Hussein, on charges of genocide relating to the Anfal campaign against the Kurds, was dropped after his execution.

qawi proposed a formal affiliation between himself and al Qaida.) Later, in October 2004, Zarqawi would pledge fealty to Usama bin Laden and thereafter his group referred to itself as "al Qaida in Mesopotamia" or "al Qaida in Iraq."

Zarqawi argued that Islam's worst enemies were the Shiites, who had "declared a secret war against the people of Islam." He described the Shiites as "the lurking snake, the crafty and malicious scorpion, the spying enemy, and the penetrating venom." To save Iraq from the Shiites, his strategy was to force them into battle. Attacking Shiite political, military, and religious targets, he said, "will provoke them to show the Sunnis their rabies." Zarqawi's major problem, however, was that the Shiites' leaders had cunningly counseled restraint. They "have been able to control the affairs of their sect, so as not to have the battle between them and the Sunnis become an open sectarian war, because they know that they will not succeed in this way."

The letter struck several despairing notes. Because the Shiites weren't fighting back at the moment, the Sunni Iraqis (he said) did not realize how bad the Shiites were. And as the Americans built up the new Iraqi army and police, those forces created splits between Zarqawi's jihadists and the Iraqi Sunnis: The new Iraqi security forces "have been able to come between the Sunni masses and the mujahidin [holy warriors—that is, Zarqawi's own forces]."

After the Americans turned over political and security responsibility to Iraqis, Zarqawi worried, his efforts to prod the Shiites to react violently might lose him the support of the Iraqi people generally. The new Iraqi forces, already deploying in Sunni areas, could link to the inhabitants by "kinship, blood and honor." Fighting those forces would be difficult "because of the gap that will emerge between us and the people of the land [the Iraqi Sunnis]," Zarqawi fretted, asking: "How can we fight their cousins and their sons and under what pretext after the Americans . . . pull back?" He declared his main fear: "Democracy is coming, and *there will be no excuse thereafter.*"

The "excuse" he needed was the open nature of the American occupation. Zarqawi said that America intended to continue to control events even though it "hopes to disappear into its bases secure and at ease and put the battlefields of Iraq into the hands of the foundling government with an army and police." But as the Americans built up the Iraqi government and security forces, the situation was getting worse for Zarqawi's forces: "There is no doubt that the space in which we can move has begun to shrink and that the grip around the throats of the mujahidin has begun to tighten. With the deployment of soldiers and police, the future has become frightening." If a new Iraqi government "extends its control over the country, we will have to pack our bags and break camp for another land," Zarqawi concluded, complaining that he was "racing against time."

The head of the Shiite leadership that was frustrating Zarqawi was Grand Ayatollah Sistani, who urged his flock not to allow Sunni jihadist provocation to trigger a civil war. He was opposed by the young radical Shiite cleric Moqtada al-Sadr, who became the Shiite community's leading voice for violent retaliation against the Sunnis—and for fighting the Americans and other coalition forces, too.

Sadr had been making a violent grab for power within the Shiite community since Saddam's overthrow. The CPA reported that Sadr was guilty of the murder of a Shiite cleric on April 10, 2003, and may have been implicated in the August 29, 2003, car bombing in Najaf that killed Ayatollah Muhammed Bakr al-Hakim, founder of the Supreme Council for the Islamic Revolution in Iraq. In the following months, Sadr's forces attacked other prominent Shiites, assaulting mosques and police stations and "arresting" a number of Iraqi police officers. In January 2004, Sadr tried to set up his own religious law court in the Imam Ali Shrine in Najaf, directly challenging Sistani and the Shiite establishment.

Top U.S. officials in Iraq disagreed on what to do about Sadr. Bremer called repeatedly for U.S. military action to arrest him and destroy his militia, the Mahdi Army. Abizaid counseled caution. He worried that Sadr could win broad sympathy if the United States attacked him personally, especially if U.S. forces had to fight through a mosque or a holy city to get at him. Abizaid warned against "losing" the Shiites, concerned that we had ample problems with the Sunnis already. U.S. forces were clashing with Sadr's militia in various cities, but Abizaid wanted to see if Sistani and the other Shiite leaders could, for the time being, use their own resources to handle the challenge so that our forces wouldn't have to arrest Sadr immediately. Bremer saw the seriousness of Abizaid's concerns, and on occasion agreed that it was inopportune to try to capture Sadr.

On the night of April 2, the CPA arranged for the arrest of Sadr's deputy for the murder of the Shiite cleric. This provided the excuse for Sadr supporters to stage street demonstrations and invade television and radio facilities, police stations, and other civil installations in Najaf, Baghdad, and other cities, sometimes doing battle with coalition or Iraqi security forces.

Meanwhile, the Sunni city of Fallujah had become a tinderbox. On March 31, a mob had grabbed four American contractors out of their cars, murdered and mutilated them on the street, and then ghoulishly displayed their corpses, hanging them from a bridge. U.S. Marines moved on the city in response. Members of the Iraqi Governing Council wanted to obtain custody of the murderers through negotiation with city leaders, heading off a full-scale marine assault on the city. They demanded that Bremer stop the marines in order to permit talks. The Iraqi Interior Minister, a Sunni, resigned to protest marine action against Fallujah. Other Iraqi officials threatened to resign if the marines did not cease fire.

The marines were in a bad position. Having been ordered to attack Fallujah, they had begun offensive operations, but now they were stopped in their tracks. Exposed to enemy fire, they were now told to defend themselves but not to continue their assault on the city until Bremer and Abizaid had a chance to discuss a cease-fire with the President and the National Security Council.

The Iraqi Governing Council saw danger for itself, with just two months until the naming of an Iraqi interim government. Its members didn't want to seem passive in the face of a major U.S. offensive against an Iraqi city of several hundred thousand people. Bremer had been criticizing the Governing Council for not taking initiative. Now some of its members took the initiative—to try to resolve the Fallujah crisis politically.

Bremer feared that several Sunni members of the Governing Council, who had staked out a nationalistic, independent position on Fallujah, might resign if the United States did not give Council members a chance to resolve the problem through negotiations. And Shiite members of the Council had likewise threatened to resign over possible U.S. militia operations against Sadr's militia in southern Iraq. Bremer warned that the Council's chaotic disintegration could endanger the U.S. plan for a smooth transition to an interim government by the end of June.

In a National Security Council meeting on April 9, General Abizaid reviewed the operations both in Fallujah and against Sadr's Mahdi Army. Abizaid projected that the enemy in Fallujah would be "wiped out in three days." He noted, however, that the Iraqi security forces trained by CENTCOM had largely been a disappointment. Many had refused to fight because the operation was viewed not as protecting their country against foreign terrorists but as a battle against Iraqis who opposed the American presence. U.S. commanders on the ground nevertheless highlighted one Iraqi unit that was manning six positions and participating in patrols and raids with "no problems": the 36th battalion of the Iraqi Civil Defense Corps. This particular force had grown out of the Free Iraqi Fighting Force (FIFF), the six hundred Iraqi expatriates organized by

Ahmad Chalabi that Abizaid used in Nasariyah in April 2003. The unit's performance was not perfect, but, given how often its men were maligned, the praise from CENTCOM on this occasion was noteworthy.

Bremer proposed a twenty-four-hour U.S. cease-fire at Fallujah, to work with the Governing Council to achieve a negotiated solution to the Fallujah crisis. If the Council negotiators succeed, Bremer told President Bush, they would be stronger, and that would be good; "if not, then we've tried." They were unlikely, however, to obtain custody of the murderers of the U.S. contractors. President Bush approved the twenty-four-hour cease-fire.

How would we respond if the Iraqis requested an extension of the cease-fire, Rumsfeld asked? Abizaid's answer was equivocal: "I recommend no extension unless there's a strong reason for one." Bremer added: "We'll want to look at that under the circumstances." General Myers warned that an extension could allow the hundreds of enemy fighters to slip out. "They're bad," he commented, "and they'll kill us if they escape."

The meeting then turned to the question of Moqtada al-Sadr. Sadr's forces were in charge of Najaf at the moment, Abizaid observed, and the local police were not acting against them. Meanwhile, U.S. forces were "hurting" Sadr's militia in Baghdad. But "if his stature increases," Abizaid warned, "we'll get an upsurge of problems in Baghdad." Our forces had killed hundreds of Sadr's militia fighters in the last few days, the general reported, but that "creates some sympathy for him." In answer to the President's question about our strategy toward Sadr, Abizaid stressed that U.S. forces would isolate Najaf, and then encourage Iraqis to confront Sadr and his militia and do the "close-in work"—operations in and around holy places.

Rumsfeld asked if we were getting to the edge of a Shiite uprising against us. Acknowledging the importance of the question, Bremer replied: "Our blows against Sadr haven't yet improved his political standing, but they might." Rice commented that we had to keep the Iraqi political process in mind as we chose our battles. She stressed the dangers of storming Najaf, a Shiite holy city. Bremer said he agreed. We've been fighting the Sunnis for a year, he remarked, but "we have a bigger risk of losing the Shia."*

President Bush was worried about our strategy for political transition. "If this all falls apart, we're an occupying power without an end game,"

*Bremer's comments at this meeting were more balanced than the account of the Sadr problem he gives in his book, where he depicts himself as strongly and consistently advocating military action to arrest Sadr.

he noted, adding: "*Transfer of power has been our strategy.*" Powell agreed with the President on giving more time for Fallujah because we would "have no strategy" if we lost the Governing Council. Powell also urged restraint in "trying to pry out Sadr," for fear of the political consequences in Iraq.

Rumsfeld shared the general concern about multiple resignations from the Governing Council, but he rebelled against the idea that the Council members could torpedo the U.S. strategy for Iraqi political reconstruction. He said that Bremer should be thinking about what to do if key Governing Council members did, in fact, resign. If that happened, he asked, what would our three or four options be? Rumsfeld advised Bremer to work on a contingency plan with Rice and Powell in case any resignations occurred quickly. President Bush endorsed Rumsfeld's suggestion and reaffirmed that it was "important to stick with the June 30 date" for establishing the interim government.

Bremer discussed the ambivalence of Iraqis about America's presence in their country. They realized that their security forces weren't up to the job of keeping the peace themselves, he said, which made them more willing to accept a longer stay for U.S. forces. Abizaid was more skeptical, pointing out that the "problem with Iraqi security forces is they don't have a strong leader to fight for" and "*they don't want to fight for Americans.*"

At a National Security Council meeting the next day, April 10, Bremer reported that the Governing Council had had good talks in Fallujah, though he wasn't specific about what they had achieved. Bremer expected the Council to ask to extend the cease-fire, which he called "a good sign" because it might make it possible to "get Fallujah behind us."

Reflecting that the Iraqi political system was "still poisoned by decades of Saddam Hussein's rule," President Bush described the current violence as "a symptom" of that problem. When he asked Abizaid how he planned to handle Fallujah, Abizaid didn't push to resume offensive operations. Rather, he said he wanted to "produce calm" and let the Sunnis on the Governing Council "come up with a success for themselves there." He concluded that we "shouldn't be focused on retaking all of Fallujah." The President worried about the consequences of people thinking that "we've been whipped in Fallujah."

Abizaid argued that the CPA's efforts at outreach to the Sunnis should be a higher priority than launching military efforts to counter Sadr. The general favored easing up on de-Baathification as a way of mollifying the Sunnis. Tenet agreed. As the meeting wound up, Rumsfeld echoed Abizaid's concern that the CPA was too harsh toward the Sunnis and that the de-Baathification policy was perceived as too strict.

Two days later, Rumsfeld wrote to Bremer regarding "outreach" to the Sunnis. Bremer had assured him that the CPA's de-Baathification order was good, though the Governing Council had implemented it too harshly. "Either ensure the Governing Council executes the program properly and promptly acts on waiver requests," Rumsfeld told Bremer, "or return the authority to the CPA." He urged Bremer to energize the process of reconciliation with the Sunnis.

In briefing slides distributed at the April 14 National Security Council meeting, Bremer made three well-stated points on the trade-offs involved in trying to meet the demands of various groups in Iraq. First, he pointed out that the Iraqi "zero-sum mentality" meant that "efforts targeted to specific communities will risk alienating and angering others": Iraqi Shiites would resent outreach initiatives focused on rehabilitating Sunni Arabs and former Baathists, if those initiatives did not adequately address Shiite suffering at the hands of the regime. Second, it was important that we not be seen as rewarding belligerents or sending the message that rebellion pays; we should aim to heal, not deepen, sectarian rifts. And third, the United States should make Sunni-friendly initiatives part of a broader national political strategy.

With the Sadr fight, the stalled Fallujah offensive, the threatened implosion of the Governing Council, and other concerns roiling Iraq, April was a difficult month even before CBS television aired the sickening photos of U.S. soldiers abusing Iraqi detainees at Abu Ghraib prison near Baghdad. When the photos first came to the attention of CENTCOM officers who were not involved in the abuse, they started a criminal investigation and sent a summary report to the Pentagon that made its way to Myers and Rumsfeld. But the Pentagon's leaders were not informed of (and could not have imagined) the nature and extent of the cruel and sexually twisted behavior of the U.S. military prison guards until some of the photos were published by the news media. The reports were deeply shameful for the United States and for the Defense Department in particular. I never saw any news hit Rumsfeld so hard. Though he had no personal culpability, he submitted two letters of resignation over it.

From the outset, Rumsfeld grasped that the scandal could have strategic effects—even if we would learn that it amounted only to the depraved, criminal behavior of an isolated handful of soldiers. Rumsfeld and Myers decided that they personally would work more or less full-time on this issue. This lasted for weeks. At a Roundtable meeting, Rumsfeld told Wolfowitz, Pace, and me to stay away from the matter so that not everyone in the Pentagon leadership would become absorbed in managing the one crisis. Though Rumsfeld often protected his personal reputation by leaving subordinates to defend themselves against allegations and criticism, he stepped forward quickly in this case and became the Department's main spokesman on the scandal.

The publication of the Abu Ghraib photos seems to have been a watershed in the Iraq war. Outrage around the world was instantaneous, intense, and lasting. Much of it was hypocritical, coming from countries that routinely abuse prisoners as a matter of governmental policy, which the United States does not. Nonetheless, the photos did our country severe damage. At home and abroad, they undermined support for America's efforts to reconstruct Iraq and to fight the broader war on terrorism.

The photos had this effect even though the abuse they recorded was, in fact, a matter of personal sadism by a small number of individuals. The abuse had not been inflicted as an interrogation technique. It had not been done on orders from higher authorities. It violated the Defense Department's policies requiring the proper treatment of prisoners. And it violated the Geneva Conventions, which the Administration, without controversy, had from the outset recognized were applicable in Iraq.

The photos depicted domination and powerlessness. They were simple and crude—amateur pornography—and America's enemies displayed them as an allegory that devastatingly reinforced the propaganda of the insurgents in Iraq.

The U.S. Marines remained outside Fallujah for weeks, maintaining their "cessation of offensive operations." At their own local level, they took the initiative to try to solve the Fallujah problem by creating a new Iraqi military unit, to clean out the insurgents so American forces would not have to do it. The new unit, called the Fallujah Brigade, was the brainchild of CIA and Iraqi intelligence officials, who recommended a major general from Saddam's Republican Guard to command it. The general then filled the ranks with soldiers from the old Iraqi army. On April 30, a television report on CNN showed the Fallujah Brigade and its commander—*wearing his Republican Guard uniform*. This news surprised Bremer as well as Washington. The Iraqi general was promptly identified by Iraqis as a participant in atrocities against the Shiites in Karbala in 1991 and had to be replaced within two days of his appointment.

The Fallujah Brigade generated strong complaints from Kurdish and Shiite leaders and proved ineffective—indeed, unwilling even to try to confront the insurgents. Bremer cites the experiment as a cautionary tale of the disaster that might have occurred, if the CPA had tried to recall and use the old Iraqi army from the beginning. He has a point.

In the south, meanwhile, U.S. strikes in April and May against Sadr's militia helped local authorities in Najaf and elsewhere retake control of their cities. Sadr himself remained at large, however, and would build a substantial following over the coming years.

By the time the Fallujah Brigade proved a bust, the transition of power to the interim government was imminent. CENTCOM and the CPA agreed to defer action in Fallujah until after the new Iraqi leaders took office and became ready to address the challenge: The insurgents remained in control of the city for months.

U.S. and Iraqi forces finally retook Fallujah in late November 2004. The Iraqi soldiers performed far better in November than in April, General Abizaid reported, citing two reasons for the improvement: First, CENTCOM had created a new organization in May to train and equip Iraqi security forces—military and police—under the command of Lieutenant General David Petraeus (U.S. Army). And second, Iraqi forces had greater motivation in November, when they were fighting for an Iraqi government, than in April, when their government remained under the control of the CPA.

The political transition continued to absorb much attention, in Iraq and in Washington, as Bremer sought to put together the (appointed) interim government. President Bush was persuaded that if Bremer made the appointments in coordination with a representative of the UN Secretary-General rather than unilaterally, the interim government would command greater respect—greater legitimacy—both inside and outside Iraq.

Robert Blackwill, former U.S. Ambassador to India and a deputy to Rice, persuaded his friend Lakhdar Brahimi to accept the job of UN representative for Iraq. Brahimi was a former Algerian Foreign Minister who had served as chief UN envoy to Afghanistan, managing the Bonn Process. Rice then sent Blackwill himself to Iraq, to work closely with Bremer and Brahimi in compiling a list of interim government appointees who could win support from key Iraqi constituencies.

Brahimi was negative about the leaders of the Iraqi external groups in general, and he was especially antagonistic toward Ahmad Chalabi. Eager to minimize the role of the Governing Council members in the interim government, Brahimi sought a candidate for Prime Minister who did not come from the Council.

The nominee he came up with was Hussein al-Shahristani, a Shiite nuclear physicist who had been imprisoned for years by Saddam, escaped during the Gulf War of 1991, and lived abroad until 2003 running a humanitarian organization. When Bremer brought up Shahristani's name at a May 12 National Security Council meeting, I considered it remarkable that no one in the U.S. government appeared to know anything of substance about him. The CIA was supposed to maintain information on current and potential Iraqi leaders; and the State Department had long been responsible for contact with expatriate Iraqis. But neither CIA nor State had attached much importance to expanding and enriching their ties to that community—with the result that now, when we were presented with a candidate for Prime Minister, no one could give President Bush more than the sketchiest report of who the man was.

After returning from one of his trips to Iraq, Blackwill came to the Pentagon to report to Rumsfeld. He told the Secretary that he found Chalabi far and away the most competent Iraqi official in the country and the most skillful in winning majorities in support of various legislative initiatives within the Governing Council.* Amazed at the relentless attacks on Chalabi by various U.S. officials and others, Blackwill wondered whether they would finally drive one of America's most capable friends into the ranks of our opponents. Knowing Rumsfeld was a fan of the Chicago Bulls basketball team, Blackwill told him: "Chalabi is the Michael Jordan of Iraqi politics. The only question is whether he'll put on a blue [U.S. team] jersey or a red [enemy] jersey."

In early May, *Newsweek* reported that U.S. intelligence agencies were accusing Chalabi of providing Iranian intelligence with sensitive information about U.S. activities in Iraq. A Chalabi aide told the magazine that the allegations were "absolutely false." The story concluded:

---

*Blackwill's evaluation of Chalabi was shared by others. On April 6, 2004, Scott Carpenter, director of the CPA's governance team, told my staff that without Chalabi's help, the CPA would not have achieved many of its successes: the law on direct foreign investment, the flat individual and corporate income tax, the November 15 agreement, or the interim constitution. Carpenter said, "We go to Chalabi on a day-to-day basis to solve problems." Office of Under Secretary of Defense for Policy, Information Paper, "Comments of Scott Carpenter, Director, Governance Team, Coalition Provisional Authority: April 6, 2004," April 8, 2004, 9:00 A.M.

Bremer himself confirmed the point, calling Chalabi "one of the very few Iraqis whom I met in my time there, in government or outside, who actually understands a modern economy. . . . He was very helpful in a number of the major economic steps we took while we were there." "The Lost Year in Iraq," Interview with L. Paul Bremer, *Frontline,* June 26/August 18, 2006, available at http://www.pbs.org/wgbh/pages/frontline/yeariniraq/interviews/bremer.html.

> **Still, the State Department and the CIA are using the intelligence about [Chalabi's] Iran ties to persuade the president to cut him loose once and for all. Officials say that even some of Chalabi's old allies in Washington now see him as a liability. If Chalabi's support in the administration was once an iceberg, says one Bush aide, "it's now an ice cube."**

This attack on Chalabi built on the many news media stories that said State and CIA officials judged the intelligence provided by Chalabi and the INC to be poor (and even dishonest)—inferior to the information provided by other Iraqi groups. Those stories prompted Rumsfeld to ask for an evaluation by the Defense Intelligence Agency, which managed the contract with the INC for its Information Collection Program. (Other Iraqi groups also had agreements with the U.S. government to provide intelligence.) The Defense Intelligence Agency's answer was that the INC's information, like that from most collection programs, was sometimes good and sometimes bad, but on balance was positive, and it recommended that the INC's contract be renewed.

The Secretary also heard from CENTCOM field intelligence officers. The U.S. intelligence chief for coalition forces in Iraq forwarded to the Pentagon (on March 31, 2004) an e-mail from the "G2"—intelligence officer—of a U.S. combat division, reporting that.the information supplied by the INC was "head and shoulders" above anything U.S. forces were receiving from other sources and had been "directly responsible for saving the lives" of numerous soldiers in the division. Rumsfeld referred to these reports on television on April 29, 2004, when he was asked about intelligence from the INC that was "questionable, if not corrupted." "It happens I know an awful lot about this subject," he replied, having spent some time looking into it in recent days. He summarized the reports he had received:

> **One [intelligence customer] in Iraq that is looking at intelligence every day that feels that what they're getting from that organization has been very, very helpful and helps save people's lives in Iraq. Another that was a mixed review and positive on tactical intelligence, less positive on some other things. And a third was a report evaluating the contribution of that organization in terms of the work that is being done in Iraq, and that was positive.**
>
> **Now, it's a mixed bag as most things are in life. There are very few things that are perfect one way or another.**

A few weeks later, a congressman at a House Armed Services Committee hearing confronted General Myers about Chalabi and INC-provided intelligence. The congressman said that Chalabi "may have deliberately misled our nation for months and years." Refusing to comment on the broad allegation, Myers answered: "What I can tell you is that the organization that he is associated with has provided intelligence to our intelligence unit there in Baghdad that has saved soldiers' lives. So I know at least that part of it has been beneficial." He added that "what has been said to me by the intelligence leadership in Baghdad that works for . . . combined Joint Task Force 7 is that intelligence was accurate and useful in many cases."

The harshness of the questions directed at Rumsfeld and Myers reflected the success of Chalabi's detractors in depicting the INC—falsely—as a key prewar supplier of false information about Iraqi WMD. The criticism intensified when the *Los Angeles Times* ran a front-page exposé on how an Iraqi defector code-named "Curveball" misled the CIA about Saddam's biological weapons program. CIA officials had relied heavily on this defector before the war, even though they had no direct access to him and were using interview reports provided by a foreign intelligence service. The CIA later concluded that Curveball's information was wrong—and that he was a fabricator.

The *Los Angeles Times* associated Chalabi indelibly with Curveball by identifying the defector as a brother of one of Chalabi's aides. The Senate Select Committee on Intelligence found, however, that "[t]he CIA believes that Curve Ball's close relative's connection to the INC is coincidental, and is not an explanation for his fabrications." When the bipartisan Silberman-Robb Commission investigated the Curveball matter—and the broader issue of the INC's role in the CIA's prewar errors on Iraqi WMD—it found that Curveball was *not* an INC source and that the INC had *not* significantly influenced U.S. prewar intelligence on Iraq:

> **Despite speculation that Curveball was encouraged to lie by the Iraqi National Congress (INC), the CIA's post-war investigations were unable to uncover any evidence that the INC or any other organization was directing Curveball to feed misleading information to the Intelligence Community. Instead, the post-war investigations concluded that *Curveball's reporting was not influenced by, controlled by, or connected to, the INC.***
>
> **In fact, over all, CIA's post-war investigations revealed that INC-related sources had a *minimal impact on pre-war assessments.***

Shortly after the Iran-related anti-Chalabi accusations were leaked to *Newsweek*, an Iraqi judge issued a warrant for a raid on Chalabi's home. The warrant related to allegations of corruption (which were later dismissed by the Iraqi courts for lack of evidence). Bremer arranged for U.S. forces to participate in the raid, in which Iraqi police seized some files, computer equipment, and weapons. This humiliation of Chalabi received heavy press coverage around the world and was generally interpreted as a sign of irredeemable repudiation by the Bush Administration and as a fatal strike against Chalabi's political ambitions in Iraq.

Although the raid made it easier for Brahimi and Bremer to exclude the INC leadership from the interim government, Chalabi later helped organize the United Iraqi Alliance list for the January 2005 national elections. That list won a plurality (nearly a majority), and Chalabi became Deputy Prime Minister in the resulting government under Prime Minister Ibrahim al-Jaafari. In that capacity, Chalabi was received respectfully in Washington in mid-November 2005 by top-level Bush Administration officials (Vice President Cheney, National Security Adviser Hadley, Secretary of State Rice, Secretary of Defense Rumsfeld, and Treasury Secretary John Snow). I do not know what ultimately became of the accusations that Chalabi was aiding Iranian intelligence, but one supposes that if they were credible, these November 2005 meetings would not have occurred.

The most significant effect of the May 2004 raid on Chalabi's home was that the State and CIA officials who had campaigned against him for years now understood they had won and could relax. From that point forward, one read and heard virtually nothing from either State or the CIA on the distinction between Iraqi externals and internals or about the externals' lack of political legitimacy. For years, those ideas had been the foundation of State and CIA analyses of (and opposition to) Iraq policy initiatives: political conferences of the Iraqi opposition groups, the training of Free Iraqi Forces, recognition of a provisional government, and the creation of an Iraqi Interim Authority. But the concept of the external-internal divide quickly faded away and today plays no role in debates about Iraq policy, within the Administration or in the Congress or news media. Once Chalabi was counted down and out, the notion of the illegitimacy of the former externals evidently lost its reason for being.

In May 2004, the reports from Iraq were mainly negative. The U.S. occupation government was more than a year old. Anti-U.S. and anti-coalition violence was worsening, and Iran and Syria were actively aiding the insurgency. U.S. efforts to train and equip Iraqi security forces had to be rethought and overhauled. Systematic sabotage was undermining economic reconstruction.

The Administration was in danger of losing public patience and support in the United States for the war effort. With the transfer of sovereign authority to the Iraqis imminent, President Bush was scheduled to give a major speech about Iraq on May 24 (at the U.S. Army War College in Carlisle, Pennsylvania). When Rumsfeld received an advance draft, he gave it to me for review.

The President's speeches were usually well conceived and remarkably well written. I considered it ironic that President Bill Clinton, so articulate as an extemporaneous talker, chose to give bland and forgettable prepared speeches, while President Bush—despite his notorious deficiencies in off-the-cuff remarks—generally demanded big thoughts and polished, often elegant, rhetoric in his formal speeches.

In this case, however, I thought the draft speech was off base. In keeping with the recent trend of the President's public comments on Iraq, the draft focused only on the prospects for Iraqi democracy. White House officials understandably preferred affirmative messages about Iraq's future over defensive reexaminations of intelligence embarrassments.

But it was a strategic error for the President to make no effort to defend the arguments that had motivated him before the war. We were in a U.S. presidential election year, and President Bush's political opponents were intent on magnifying the Administration's mistakes regarding WMD in Iraq. On television and radio, in print, and on the Internet, day after day, they repeated the claim that the undiscovered stockpiles were the sum and substance of why the United States went to war against Saddam. At first they argued that the war was based entirely on error. Now critics had escalated to the accusation that the war was based on lies.

Electoral politics aside, I thought it was important for national security reasons that the President refute his critics' misstatements. The CIA assessments of WMD were wrong, but they had originated in the years before he became President. The same intelligence assessments had been accepted by Democratic and Republican members of Congress, as well as UN and other officials around the world. And, in any event, the erroneous intelligence was not the entire rationale for overthrowing Saddam.

On May 22, I gave Rumsfeld a memo he could pass along to Rice and the President's speechwriters. I proposed that the speech "should deal with some basics—in particular, why we went to war in the first place." It would be useful to "make clear the tie-in between Iraq and the broader war on terrorism"—in the following terms: The Saddam Hussein regime "had used WMD, supported various terrorist groups, was hostile to the US and had a record of aggression and of defiance of numerous UN resolutions." In light of 9/11, the "danger that Saddam's regime could provide biological weapons or other WMD to terrorist groups for use against us was too great" to let stand. And other ways of countering the danger—containment, sanctions, inspections, no-fly zones—had proven "unsustainable or inadequate."

I asked, What kind of success can be achieved in Iraq?—and suggested that the President distinguish between the *essential* U.S. interests in Iraq and the *extra* benefits if we could succeed in building democratic institutions there: "A unified Iraq that does not support terrorism or pursue WMD will in and of itself be an important victory in the war on terrorism." Over and above that, helping Iraq to "get on the path to democracy" could "produce an even greater success in the war on terrorism, for it can help transform the Middle East and the broader world of Islam politically and help us counter ideological support for terrorism, which is the key to defeating terrorism in the longer term." I recommended that President Bush quote the Zarqawi letter, to show that the "terrorists know that good government in Iraq will be a disastrous setback for them."

Some of the speech's rhetoric about democracy struck me as a problem: "The draft speech now implies that we went to war in Iraq simply to free the Iraqi people from tyranny and create democracy there," I noted. But that implication "is not accurate and it sets us up for accusations of failure if Iraq does not quickly achieve 'democracy,' an undefined but high standard. . . . [I]t would be better to talk of 'building democratic institutions,' or 'putting the Iraqis on the path to democracy,' rather than 'constructing a stable democracy,' a goal that will not be achievable for many years."

As was typical, the speech went through multiple drafts. Rice's office sent us a new version, and the next day I wrote Rumsfeld another set of comments—without great hope of persuading the speechwriting team. The speech's centerpiece was the set of steps "to help Iraq achieve democracy." One line asserted that we went to Iraq "to make them free," so I dissented:

- **This mixes up our current important goal (i.e., getting Iraq on the path to democratic government) with the strategic rationale for the war, which was to end the danger that Saddam might provide biological or [other] weapons of mass destruction to terrorists for use against us.**
- **There is a widespread misconception that the war's rationale was the existence of Iraqi WMD *stockpiles*. This allows critics**

to say that our failure to find such stockpiles undermines that rationale.

- **If the President ignores this altogether and then implies that the war's rationale was not the terrorism/state sponsorship/ WMD nexus but rather democracy for Iraqis, the critics may say that he is changing the subject or rewriting history.**

Again, I proposed that the President distinguish between achieving our primary goal in Iraq—eliminating a security threat—and aiming for the over-and-above goal of democracy promotion, which may not be readily achievable: "[O]ur objective in the near term is to launch the Iraqis toward democracy; we can't ensure in the near term that they reach the goal of a stable democracy."

Wolfowitz endorsed my memo ("excellent") and sent Rumsfeld a note about it, reiterating that "Iraq must be discussed as part of the war on terrorism." Wolfowitz promised to raise the issue with Steve Hadley and White House speechwriter Michael Gerson, but he also suggested that an "intervention by you" might be necessary to get the speech changed. Rumsfeld says he discussed the matter with the President and the White House speechwriters.

President Bush gave his speech at the Army War College on May 24, as Iraq was entering into the last month of its fourteen-month occupation by the United States. The President declared: "I sent American troops to Iraq to defend our security, not to stay as an occupying power. I sent American troops to Iraq to make its people free, not to make them American. Iraqis will write their own history, and find their own way." I had hoped the President would explain why sending American troops to Iraq had helped defend *our* security, but he did not. The questionable line about sending those troops to make Iraq's people free had remained in the speech. And it was rather late to be promising the Iraqis that we would not stay as an occupying power but rather let them find their own way.

One of Bremer's principal complaints about the Governing Council was that it failed to show initiative while working under him. But the Council did not lack initiative when it came to appointing the interim government. The Council in general reciprocated Lakhdar Brahimi's disapproval: A number of Council members had strong political relationships throughout the country—with provincial officials, religious authorities, tribal sheikhs, and others—so they did not accept the notion that a United Nations official, a *foreigner*, could pick leaders for Iraq who would win more broad-based support than would leaders they selected themselves.

The two most prominent positions in the interim government would be Prime Minister and President. Brahimi had favored Shahristani for the former, and for the presidency he proposed Adnan Pachachi—a Sunni elder statesman who had served as Iraqi Foreign Minister in the early 1960s, had lived for many years in exile, and now served on the Governing Council. My staff noted the irony that the best candidates for these top jobs, according to Brahimi, were both *externals*. I heard no one from State or CIA argue that, as externals, these men lacked legitimacy.

But opposition within the Governing Council undid Brahimi's slate of appointees. The Council eventually lined up behind two of its own members: Iyad Allawi for Prime Minister and Sheikh Ghazi al-Yawar for President. At the end of the day, Allawi and al-Yawar received the endorsement not only of the Governing Council, but of Brahimi, Bremer, and the U.S. government.

Because insurgents might try to disrupt the handover of power, Bremer and General Sanchez recommended that the CPA hand over power to the interim government a little ahead of the June 30 deadline. On June 28, Bremer made the surprise announcement that, as of that day, the interim government had become the new government of Iraq. The President was Sheikh al-Yawar and the Prime Minister was Dr. Allawi. The other top officials, also appointed with the endorsement of Brahimi, Bremer, and the Governing Council, were:

- Ibrahim al-Jaafari as Deputy President
- Rowsch Shaways as Deputy President
- Barham Salih as Deputy Prime Minister
- Hazem Shaalan as Defense Minister
- Adel Abdul Mahdi as Finance Minister
- Hoshyar Zebari as Foreign Minister
- Falah al-Nakib as Interior Minister
- Thamir Abbas Ghadban as Oil Minister

All of these men were externals. The interim government would be led by high-level officials of various external groups: the Iraqi National Accord, the Dawa Party, the Patriotic Union of Kurdistan, the Supreme Council for the Islamic Revolution in Iraq, the Kurdish Democratic Party, and the Iraqi National Movement—but *not* Chalabi's Iraqi National Congress.

In keeping with their argument that the externals would lack political support in post-Saddam Iraq, State and CIA analysts had also predicted that Kurds would not be able to play a significant national role (outside of northern Iraq). But Kurds did, in fact, perform important functions as national leaders, in both appointed and elected governments. The first President was a Kurd: Jalal Talabani (head of the PUK) came into office after Iraq's January 2005 national parliamentary elections and was reelected after his first term. Another Kurd, Hoshyar Zebari, was appointed Foreign Minister in the interim government, was reconfirmed after the first elections in January 2005, and reconfirmed again after the December 2005 elections. The top military officer in Iraq for several years after Saddam's overthrow was Babaker Zabari, a Kurdish general. And Barham Salih, also a Kurd, served first as Deputy Prime Minister of the Iraqi Interim Government, and later as Minister for Planning and Coordination in the elected Transitional Government and as Deputy Prime Minister in Nouri al-Maliki's elected government.

The interim government of Prime Minister Allawi operated on the basis of the interim constitution. Its main responsibility was to organize national elections for a Transitional National Assembly by the end of January 2005, and it accomplished that goal.* The elections were praised around the world as a success in that they involved fair competition among numerous party lists, were reasonably well run, and drew participation from nearly nine million voters—despite harrowing death threats issued by insurgent groups. Pictures of Iraqi voters courageously and jubilantly displaying their purpled fingers drew respectful comment even from many who opposed the Iraq war.

I have never heard anyone anywhere make the case that the Iraqi government performed worse when it was Prime Minister Allawi's interim government than when it was the U.S.–led CPA. The interim government was appointed, not elected. It was dominated by externals, with almost no internals in top positions. Yet it functioned and fulfilled its crucial duty to advance the political process within the specified deadline. The interim government did not lack legitimacy in any practical sense of the term.

---

*This Transitional National Assembly voted into office a government with Ibrahim al-Jaafari as Prime Minister. The Jaafari government's main tasks, as set out in the interim constitution, were to draft a permanent constitution by August 2005, hold a national referendum on the constitution in October 2005, and then hold elections under the new constitution in December 2005. The Jaafari government accomplished all these tasks—and on time. The December 2005 elections would have even greater participation—nearly 12 million voters, including large numbers from Sunni areas where few votes had been cast in the January 2005 elections. International Mission for Iraqi Elections, "Final Report on the December 15, 2005, Iraqi Council of Representatives Elections," April 12, 2006, pp. 19–20, available at http://www.imie.ca/pdf/final_report.pdf.

Why, then, did the United States run Iraq for those first critical fourteen months after liberation, when we could have put the same set of Iraqi leaders in charge of their own government?

What happened to the political reconstruction of Iraq? How did the U.S. government start with a detailed plan for promptly creating an Iraqi Interim Authority and end up with the CPA serving as an occupation government for more than a year? The reason was *not* that President Bush, having approved the IIA plan in March, decided to abandon it two months later.

Bremer at first said he wanted to transfer power *as soon as possible* to the Iraqis. He changed his mind, he said, for purely pragmatic reasons—because the Iraqi leaders were not showing drive and competence. He did not say he opposed the plan; he reported that it would take more time than expected to implement. But his *Washington Post* article showed that he objected philosophically to the plan: He considered it illegitimate to give the Iraqis sovereign authority before there was a new constitution and national elections. His book makes it clear that he had decided, *even before he set foot in Iraq*, that an early transfer of power to the Iraqis was a "reckless fantasy." Bremer had aligned himself with the views prevailing at State and the CIA.

Bremer's policies put the United States on a path that would have prolonged the occupation of Iraq for two years or more. Rumsfeld's intervention in October prevented that outcome. Had Bremer recognized in fall 2003, rather than spring 2004, that elections were *not* actually necessary to give legitimacy to an interim government of short duration, we could have shut down the CPA months earlier than we did. And the proof that those elections were not necessary was that they turned out, in fact, not to be necessary.

Bremer never explained why elections were required for an interim government in Iraq when they had not been required in Afghanistan. He used the terms "representative" and "legitimate," but in essence the issue amounted to disdain for the available candidates.

As for the four months Bremer allowed for negotiation of the interim constitution, that period might have been shorter if the Administration had convened a series of Iraqi opposition political conferences well before the war. If the December 2002 London conference had occurred eight or nine months earlier, followed by two or three additional conferences over the next year or so, the Iraqi leaders might have made substantial political progress—gaining experience working and compromising with each other and with us. It would have been easier for them, later on, to achieve agreement on an interim constitution. This is not to say that the externals could have precooked a new constitution and simply imported it into post-Saddam Iraq. But they might have worked out a number of useful concepts and formulations in advance.

As negotiations on the interim constitution intensified in February 2004, we saw that many of the key players* were in fact the same figures who had participated in the December 2002 political conference in London. And the most important and contentious of their 2004 debates related to topics they had discussed in preliminary fashion at the 2002 conference: protection of individual rights and minority rights, the role of religion, and the way to define and manage federalism. The delay in convening the political conference had wasted an important opportunity to prepare for political reconstruction.†

All in all, the fourteen-month occupation of Iraq was a self-inflicted wound. It was the product of a handful of thoughts that turned out to be wrong.

The occupation was long and, in my view, unnecessary. But was it actually harmful? It appears to have been so. When Bremer first arrived in Iraq, the country had problems of lawlessness, some jihadist terrorism, and a relatively low level of violence against coalition forces. When the CPA dissolved more than a year later, Iraq, by many important measures, was far worse off—afflicted by a formidable insurgency that was bloody and widespread.

Between May 2003 and June 2004, monthly casualties increased tenfold: The number of U.S. troops wounded in action went from 54 to 512 (with a spike in May 2004 of 1,014); Iraqi civilian deaths increased from 23 to 334. Mass-casualty bombings (nonexistent in May 2003) killed 156 people in June 2004. The insurgency had mounted only a few attacks in the early months of the occupation, but in August 2003 there were 470 insurgent attacks on coalition forces—growing to 1,130 in June 2004.

There was going to be resistance to the new Iraq in any event. Baathists and foreign terrorists would be fighting against the coalition and the new

*Mohammed Bahr al-Uloum, Massoud Barzani, Ahmad Chalabi, Abdulaziz al-Hakim, Adel Abdul Mahdi, Adnan Pachachi, Mowaffak al-Rubaie, and Jalal Talabani.

†Another key resource in political reconstruction, similarly disregarded, was the constructive relationship Zalmay Khalilzad of Rice's staff had established with the Iraqi leaders, as President Bush's Special Envoy.

Iraqi government, whether or not the United States ran a protracted occupation. And when Bremer eventually did transfer sovereign authority to the Iraqis, the disorder and violence did not end or even abate. So what was the nature of the harm caused by the occupation?

In the months after the coalition ousted the Saddam Hussein regime, the hard core of the insurgency was able to develop a widening base of support from ordinary Iraqis, who came to believe that the United States was in their country to exploit and dominate them, to control their lives and steal their oil. These Iraqis were not inclined to take risks to help coalition forces find and attack Baathist and jihadist fighters. Coalition forces would have had a better chance of defeating the insurgency *in its early stages*, if those fighters did not swim in a sea of sympathetic countrymen.

Had U.S. officials promptly put Iraqis in charge of Iraq (perhaps working with UN officials, as in the Bonn Process for Afghanistan), the United States might have maintained the image of liberator in Iraq. No one can say that Iraq would have glided smoothly to democracy if only the United States had seized that moment. But whatever problems were inherent in Iraq's emergence from decades of tyrannical stability, the United States aggravated the situation by setting itself up in the Green Zone—in Saddam's own palaces—as an occupying power.

Moreover, with more support early on from the Iraqi people, the coalition might have defeated Zarqawi's Sunni extremists *before* they succeeded in provoking widespread mutual violence between Shiites and Sunnis. Zarqawi's strategy of killing Shiites to create a Sunni-Shiite civil war was effectively stymied for several years by Grand Ayatollah Sistani and other Shiite religious leaders who called for restraint and civil harmony. Their followers showed remarkable forbearance. It wasn't until the destruction of the Shiite shrine at Samarra in February 2006—almost *three years* after Saddam's overthrow—that the al Qaida jihadists managed to trigger substantial indiscriminate retaliation by Shiites against Sunnis.

It is hard to overstate how important it would have been for the United States to win the cooperation of the Iraqi people and defeat the Baathists and the foreign terrorists in the first months after the old regime was overthrown. The occupation was a barrier to cooperation. In fact, it encouraged active opposition.

Over time, the security problems in Iraq would worsen to the point where, in 2007, President Bush and his new Secretary of Defense, Robert Gates, and new military commander in Iraq, General David Petraeus, decided to increase the number of U.S. forces in Iraq. Historians will debate whether, by forgoing a lengthy occupation, accelerating Iraq's transition to self-rule, and rapidly training more Iraqi security forces, U.S.

officials might have prevented the security situation from deteriorating to that point.

The occupation tainted the role of the United States in Iraq, and the taint did not readily fade. Even after the CPA turned power over to the Iraqi interim government, anti-U.S arguments continued to have automatic credibility among many Iraqis, many of whom believed they had to fight us to get us to leave. There were Americans, after all, who believed that President Bush had gone to war in Iraq to exploit that country and plunder its resources. If otherwise rational U.S. citizens could believe that our government was run by thieves, one can only imagine what went through the minds of Iraqis who knew little of the United States, whose sense of national pride was abraded by the U.S. occupation, and who lived in a political culture rife with conspiracy theories.

Again, the standing of the United States among Iraqis contrasted with our position in Afghanistan, where the public generally looked on U.S. forces favorably. There were diverse factors at play in both places, but the people of Afghanistan undoubtedly appreciated our never having subjected them to an occupation government.

Bremer justified setting aside the Iraqi Interim Authority plan and keeping sovereign power out of Iraqi hands on the grounds that it would have been wrong to hand authority over to the externals. He disputed the legitimacy of the Iraqi Leadership Council—the six externals and one internal with whom Garner had worked to try to establish the IIA—and he canceled his first meeting with them partly in order "to signal to the Iraqi political figures that I was not in a hurry to see them."

After he expanded that group into the twenty-five-person Governing Council, he judged that it, too, lacked legitimacy and competence. Some officials in Washington, Bremer writes, "thought we could solve all our problems by simply transferring authority immediately to the Iraqi Governing Council, as if that group could somehow overcome the interconnected security-economic-political problems when we in the CPA could not." Even well after the Iraqis took over from the CPA, Bremer wrote, without irony: *"What would have happened if the U.S. government had turned over Iraq to the exiles in May, as some in Washington had wanted?"*

This is an essential question, but Bremer never analyzes it in his book. It is remarkable that Bremer highlights the matter, even putting it in italics, yet misses the point that the individuals he disparages here are the very same Iraqis to whom he eventually turned over the government. The members of the original Iraqi Leadership Council and their top lieutenants filled almost all the top positions in the Iraqi Interim Government under Prime Minister Allawi and the later elected governments. Historians will indeed want to ask what would have happened if Bremer had made the turnover in May or June or July 2003, rather than in June 2004.

In deciding to eliminate the danger posed by Saddam Hussein and his regime, President Bush launched an enormous and complex enterprise. It involved strategic analysis, diplomacy, a military invasion, and the effort to create a new government in Iraq that could manage the country and not threaten international peace and security.

That enterprise remains grimly incomplete. Almost five years have passed since Saddam's overthrow, and we have still not reached the postwar period. Under the circumstances, every aspect of planning and implementation warrants criticism, including:

- Counterinsurgency strategy
- Coalition building with allies and others
- Cooperation with UN and other international organizations (public and private)
- Funding decisions
- Intelligence collection, analysis, and action
- Developing Iraqi security forces
- Economic reconstruction
- Organization and functioning of the Coalition Provisional Authority
- Strategic communications
- Congressional relations

But the most serious error the United States made in Iraq was, arguably, the mishandling of the political transition: the mechanism for putting governmental power into the hands of a new Iraqi leadership. Rather than implement the Iraqi Interim Authority plan, which would have vested Iraqis with major responsibilities for their own governance and defense, the United States established a protracted occupation regime.

The occupation caused or aggravated important ills. It squandered America's opportunity to relate to the Iraqi people as their liberator. It offended the personal dignity and national pride of many Iraqis, creating opportunities exploitable by hard-core Baathists, sectarian extremists, foreign jihadists, and Iraq's ill-intentioned neighbors.

Ambassador Bremer and his CPA team did much good work under difficult and dangerous circumstances. But the value of that work was outweighed by the harm caused by the fact of occupation. The United States would have been in a far better position to help Iraqis fulfill President Bush's vision of a new, free, and benign Iraq if we had been able to work with them as partners rather than as overlords.

Timeline 5. Global War on Terrorism: Historical Overview

1979	
Throughout year	Islamic Revolution in Iran (Shah forced into exile in January)
Nov.	Seizure of U.S. Embassy and personnel in Tehran
Dec.	Soviet invasion of Afghanistan; jihad begins against Soviets in Afghanistan, eventually assisted by U.S.
1983	
Oct.	U.S. Marine barracks bombing, Beirut, Lebanon
1991	
	Founding of Al Qaida, following Gulf War
1993	
Feb.	World Trade Center bombing
1996	
June	Khobar Towers bombing
Aug.	Bin Laden declares war on U.S.
1998	
Feb.	Bin Laden issues fatwa on jihad against "Jews and Crusaders"
Aug.	U.S. embassies in East Africa bombed
2000	
Oct	Bombing of U.S.S. *Cole*
2001	
Sept. 11	Attack on World Trade Center and Pentagon; downing of United Airlines flight 93

16
LESSONS AND DEBATE

The debate on Iraq remains passionate and divisive as this book goes to print. The news about the war in the past few years has been bad—though in 2007 it turned promising enough to allow the Bush Administration to rebuff congressional pressure for an accelerated withdrawal of U.S. troops. The war has been controversial from the outset, with weighty arguments for and against it. The decision to remove Saddam from power—and to do it in March 2003—was not inevitable. It was an exercise of judgment.

It is fair and proper to ask whether President Bush and his advisers were right or wrong. But the record does not support the now-common accusations that they were either reckless or fraudulent. Rather, it shows that the Saddam Hussein regime was recognized as a serious challenge even before 9/11. Although Saddam was not implicated in that attack, the multifaceted danger he posed appeared more threatening and more pressing after our enemies killed thousands of Americans in New York, Washington, and Pennsylvania, laying bare the vulnerabilities of the American homeland.

The 9/11 attack did not start the war between the United States and the terrorists. It was not the first fatal terrorist operation against an American target; it was not even the first such attack by al Qaida. It became, however, the point at which many Americans concluded that we were at war.

That the jihadists are not a unitary enemy—or even a standard kind of compound enemy, like the Axis powers of World War II—makes it difficult to think about the terrorism problem in conventional terms. We cannot lump them all together and assume that a single approach will counter them adequately.

But the jihadists who target the United States operate within an international network. If we see them as merely a set of disconnected individuals and groups, each with its own grievances, we risk not seeing the forest for the trees. Jihadism is a global phenomenon, a political-religious movement that aims to create a universal polity governed by a severe interpretation of Muslim law. Despite its diversity and internal divisions, its adherents generally are motivated by the belief that they are justified—even duty-bound—to kill ordinary people for religious and political purposes. Americans, and Westerners generally, find it hard to imagine the drive, ruthlessness, and certitude of the Islamist extremists who become terrorist operatives or leaders. There is nothing in the experience of an ordinary American that resembles, even by analogy, the kind of fanaticism that characterizes the Islamist extremists. Americans often use the term "extremist" to apply to people with whom they disagree: about abortion regulations, for example, or how evolution or sex education should be taught in public schools. What special term, then, should be reserved for people who steer commercial airliners into metropolitan office buildings? How should we characterize people who educate young people to blow themselves up in markets to massacre as many ordinary shoppers as possible? How does one conceive of people who cut the throats of writers and soldiers and then broadcast gloating videotapes of their agony?

To discuss this murderous enemy in terms of networks and ideologies may sound abstract, but the network of Islamist extremists is a bloody, down-to-earth reality that has pervasive, practical effects on our lives—on our physical safety, civil liberties, and personal privacy. Beyond the cost in ordinary human life and security, it imposes other direct and indirect costs, from its impact on air travel to deeper alterations of the economic, social, and geopolitical landscape.

Jihadists consider themselves enemies of the United States and every other Western or democratic state. They also see themselves as the enemies of most of the governments in the Muslim world, whom they despise as apostate and corrupt. Jihadist ideologues of varying types have taken over governments in Iran, Sudan, Afghanistan, and the Gaza Strip. They have made serious attempts to take power, start revolutions, or assassinate political leaders in Algeria, Pakistan, the Philippines, Saudi Arabia, Uzbekistan, and elsewhere. They have played important roles in international conflicts: Kashmiri groups against India in Kashmir and beyond, international mujahideen "holy warriors" fighting the Soviet Union in Afghanistan (with U.S. aid), and Hezbollah against Israel in southern Lebanon.

Al Qaida declared in the 1990s that it was at war with the United States, when bin Laden proclaimed to his followers that the United States should be destroyed. Americans may find this notion absurdly ambitious, but Islamist extremists cherish their own grandiose version of history. In the modern era, that narrative might be said to begin with the Islamic Revolution that overthrew the Shah of Iran, a close ally of the United States, in 1978–79. Though carried out by Shiites, Iran's Islamic Revolution thrilled Islamist extremists—Shiite and Sunni—around the world. Their storyline continues in 1983, when jihadists blew up the U.S. Marine barracks in Beirut, killing hundreds of U.S. service members and driving the United States out of Lebanon. It also includes the success of Muslim fighters, local and foreign, in defeating the Soviet Army in Afghanistan. In the jihadist narrative, the significant point is not the irony that the United States supplied weapons to the Muslims, but their belief that their holy war succeeded in destroying the Soviet empire. Jihadists believe (with some justification) that the Soviet Union, one of the two greatest military powers in human history, disintegrated because Muslim holy warriors killed its soldiers, drained its resources, and drove it into a disgraceful retreat from Afghanistan. Bin Laden made his international reputation as a victor over the Soviet forces in Afghanistan.

The Islamists' victories against the Shah and the Soviet Union enormously increased the international appeal of Islamist extremist thought and action—as did the events in Somalia in 1993, in which Somali Muslims killed eighteen U.S. soldiers and marines in Mogadishu, moving President Clinton to withdraw all U.S. forces from the country. Bin Laden cited that retreat as additional proof of America's decadence—and its vulnerability. And when the Shiite "holy warriors" of Hezbollah forced Israel, the major regional power, to withdraw unilaterally from Lebanon in June 2000, Israel's enemies throughout the region—most of them *Sunnis*—celebrated Hezbollah's accomplishment as a brilliant victory. Less than three months later, the so-called "Second *Intifada*" erupted in the West Bank and Gaza territories.

A year later came the 9/11 attack. In its wake, Bin Laden announced that the Muslim faithful could do to America what the holy warriors had done to the Soviet Union. And, like previous blows inflicted on the United States, this new strike was likely to encourage further terrorist attacks by al Qaida and our other enemies.

The Bush Administration's response to 9/11 was different from that of any previous U.S. administration to a terrorist attack. It was based on five major thoughts:

First, the foremost purpose of the U.S. response to the attack was not punishment or retaliation, but *preventing the next attack*—a point that argued for quick action to disrupt ongoing terrorist plans.

Second, we were at war with a global terrorist network of Islamist extremist groups, including state and nonstate sponsors—and the next attack might come not from al Qaida but from some other part of the movement. Our strategy has to target both those groups themselves and their key sources of actual and potential support—operational, logistic, financial, and ideological.

Third, our attackers were bent not on political theater but on *mass destruction*. This highlighted the possibility that terrorists might obtain chemical, biological, or nuclear weapons to maximize the death toll.

Fourth, a series of 9/11-type terrorist attacks on the United States could change the nature of our country. Our national security policy extends beyond simply protecting people or territory. It includes securing our constitutional system, our civil liberties, and the open nature of our society—"our way of life," as President Bush expressed it.

This war aim brought us to the fifth strategic thought: In order to counter this threat successfully, *we could not rely on a defensive strategy alone*. The United States has so many rich targets that it would demand extraordinary measures to secure them individually—and the effort to do so would endanger our free and open society. These considerations necessitated a strategy of initiative and offense—of disrupting the terrorist network abroad.

Taken as a whole, these five thoughts drove the Bush Administration to a strategy that gave weight not just to al Qaida but to terrorists of various stripes—such as Abu Musab al-Zarqawi, who was merely an al Qaida "associate" at that time, and to groups such as Ansar al-Islam and Jemaah Islamiyah, which had trained with al Qaida in Afghanistan, and Hezbollah. And it led to our focus on state supporters—readily locatable targets that gave U.S. officials a means of taking immediate action against the international terrorist network.

In the decades preceding 9/11, various governments had provided support to a range of terrorist groups *without suffering any penalty*. Targeting state supporters—with diplomatic pressure in some cases, and military operations in others—was a way to upset possible attack plans of groups we might otherwise have been unable to reach.

It was also a way of ensuring that potential state sponsors of terrorism would think twice about the consequences of such sponsorship. We anticipated that direct action against some state supporters might help convince others to change their policies. After the overthrow of the Taliban and Saddam Hussein regimes, Libya decided to get out of the WMD business, and Syria withdrew its military forces from Lebanon for the first time in nearly twenty years. The desired effect did not extend, however, to Iran and North Korea; both have continued to pose threats to peace and security. Diplomacy has not persuaded either state to dismantle its nuclear weapons program,* and Iran remains the principal state supporter of both Hezbollah and Hamas.

American efforts in the war on terrorism have been far from painless or cost-free. In Iraq alone, the United States has suffered thousands of fatalities and tens of thousands of casualties. Our coalition partners have also lost lives and limbs. Scores of thousands of Iraqis have been killed—and multiples of those numbers have been injured—mostly as a result of the insurgency.

In his October 15, 2002, memo on the dangers of invading Iraq, Rumsfeld warned that a war could prove longer and costlier than was generally expected. U.S. absorption in Iraq, he warned, could have bad consequences in other arenas. Those were among the risks President Bush had to weigh against the risks of leaving Saddam Hussein in power. U.S. preoccupation in a costly, protracted Iraq effort was one of several predicted "horribles" that in fact materialized. The willingness of Iran and North Korea to defy international pressure regarding their nuclear programs seems to reflect their assessment that U.S. military action against them is not a danger for

---

*According to a summary recently released to the public, a classified National Intelligence Estimate completed in December 2007 reported that Iran decided in 2003 to halt—not dismantle—its military nuclear program. The estimate speculates that that was done as a result of diplomatic pressure on Iran. But any backtracking in the Iranian nuclear program that occurred in 2003 may well have reflected worries among Iranian officials about the dangers of confronting a U.S. government actively engaged militarily just to Iran's east (in Afghanistan) and west (in Iraq). As various commentators have noted, the estimate excluded from its definition of "military nuclear program" the uranium enrichment activities that could assist a nuclear weapons program. Central Intelligence Agency, "Iran: Nuclear Intentions and Capabilities," National Intelligence Estimate, November 2007, available at http://www.dni.gov/press_releases/20071203_release.pdf; Henry Kissinger, "Misreading the Iran Report: Why Spying and Policymaking Don't Mix," *Washington Post*, December 13, 2007, p. A35, available at http://www.washingtonpost.com/wp-dyn/content/article/2007/12/12/AR2007121202331.html.

the foreseeable future. Whether or not they are correct, one can see how the U.S. debate about Iraq could reinforce that conclusion.

On October 16, 2003, Rumsfeld addressed a memo to Wolfowitz, Generals Myers and Pace, and me asking how we should measure our progress in the war on terrorism. Winning in Afghanistan and Iraq, he projected, would be a "long, hard slog." Rumsfeld and I had had several long talks about what I called the main deficiency in the U.S. war effort: opposing pro-terrorist ideologies. Rumsfeld here wondered: "Are we capturing, killing, or deterring and dissuading more terrorists every day than the madrassas [Muslim religious schools] and the radical clerics are recruiting, training and deploying against us?"

This was a good example of the value Rumsfeld brought to the Administration. He wielded a courageous and skeptical intellect. He challenged preconceptions and assumptions—including his own—and drove colleagues as well as subordinates to take a long view and to evaluate honestly whether their work was actually producing results. His ideas and ambitions for the Defense Department and the United States were high-minded, his contributions extensive and influential. But his style of leadership did not always serve his own purposes: He bruised people and made personal enemies, who were eager to strike back at him and try to discredit his work. Losses and disappointments in Iraq gave an opening to those who wanted Rumsfeld out, which led to his resignation in November 2006. At this early remove from the events in question, it would be feckless to venture an overall judgment of his role. But I never ceased to admire him, even when he did not handle matters as I thought best.

I took the lead in responding to Rumsfeld's "long hard slog" memo. As I saw it, the purpose of a Defense Department strategy was to fulfill the *national* strategy—so we had to start with a clear statement of the national strategy. My outline of a national strategy envisioned a multinational effort to deny our terrorist enemies the resources they used "to operate and survive"—that is, to make it as hard as possible for them to operate against us while we worked on the ultimate goal of precluding their survival. We compiled a short list of key enemy resources, organized into categories, including leaders, finances, weapons (especially WMD), foot soldiers, safe havens, communications, movement, access to targets, and ideological support.

Rumsfeld put our strategic review through an elaborate, four-month consultation process that involved the Defense Department's entire civilian and military leadership. He had me brief the review—more than once—to his Senior Level Review Group (a council that included Wolfowitz, the

Joint Chiefs, the secretaries of the military services, the under secretaries of defense, selected assistant secretaries, and others). We reworked the statement of strategy, sent it to all the combatant commanders, and then met with them together with the Senior Level Review Group.

On May 25, 2004, Rumsfeld had me present the resulting strategy in the Oval Office to the President, the Vice President, Powell, Tenet, Rice, and key deputies. Backed up by Rumsfeld, Wolfowitz, Myers, and Pace, I concentrated on one of our key conceptual challenges: *how to fight a war against an enemy located in numerous countries with whom we were not at war.*

When terrorists were based in peaceable sovereign states—the Philippines, Indonesia, Pakistan, Saudi Arabia, Germany, or elsewhere—we could fight them only through cooperation with the local governments. It was in our interest to *encourage* those governments to share our view of the chief terrorist threats. One way to do this was to offer them a regular regimen of briefings and consultations—time-consuming but indispensable. Because our partners often lacked the means to take effective action, another key assignment was to *enable* them to exercise effective control of their territory—by supplying intelligence and resources, including military or law enforcement equipment and training. Some partners, for example, needed help in forensics; others in developing nighttime air assault capability in mountainous terrain.

We handled these tasks largely through our existing assistance programs, developed decades ago. But members of Congress commonly thought of these as giveaway programs—a means to buy (or rent) Cold War allies. Though it would readily approve half a trillion dollars for the Defense Department's role in fighting the war on terrorism, Congress stinted on resources to enable *other countries'* security forces to fight—or to fund educational and other programs overseas that might keep young people from becoming our enemies to begin with.

We are grossly misallocated, I told the President: If Congress gave you an extra billion dollars to fight the war, it would not make sense to put it into the Pentagon. It would be more useful going to State, for such tasks as helping Pakistan draw students away from those *madrassa* schools that indoctrinate young people into murderous extremism. Powell made a show of looking amazed, but he nodded agreement. He found nothing to disagree with in what I was saying, although his own department had never developed a strategic analysis to propose a more active (and better-financed) role for itself.

Besides protecting the homeland and disrupting terrorist networks, I argued, we needed to make progress on a third element of our strategy: countering ideological support for terrorism—an area in which our efforts remained inadequate.

Many Administration officials considered it hopeless to attempt to change people's thinking on such topics as violent jihad and suicide bombing. But history offered some success stories of this kind—from the campaigns against piracy and the slave trade in the nineteenth century to the efforts to anathematize genocide after World War II. In my briefing I touched on the way Britain fought the slave trade by combining the exertions of the Royal Navy and official diplomats with the private efforts of academics, evangelical churchmen, and businessmen. The President responded at length to this point, calling the story a remarkable example of how a high-minded, important effort involving "all instruments of national power," including the private sector, could play an important role in an international ideological battle. In the same vein, I suggested some ways the White House and State Department might encourage private institutions to help counter ideological support for terrorism without compromising their independence.

Powell said the biggest thing the United States could do to counter ideological support for terrorism was to push diplomatically to resolve the Palestinian-Israeli conflict and counter the appearance of U.S. bias toward Israel. I responded that an end to that conflict would obviously be desirable, but it may not soon be achieved—and we needed to counter ideological support for terrorism in any event.

When I finished the briefing, President Bush said he appreciated having a comprehensive and strategic discussion of the war, as opposed to the meetings that dealt with "slices of issues, not the strategic view." He asked that the briefing's main points be incorporated in a National Security Presidential Directive for his signature. But work on that directive was set aside in July, when the 9/11 Commission issued its report and Administration officials debated which of their recommendations to endorse. Then came the fall 2004 presidential election campaign, when (we knew) any new policy document would be dismissed as mere politics.

A few weeks after his reelection President Bush visited the Pentagon, and Rumsfeld used the occasion to revive our war-on-terrorism strategic review. In that January 13, 2005, meeting with the President (including Cheney, Rice, and Hadley), I recapped our May discussion, proposing several "presidential level" initiatives designed to help prosecute the war (and to serve other national security purposes).

First, I recommended a radical idea: terminating the existing U.S. foreign aid and security assistance systems—the complex apparatus grown by accretion during the Cold War—and creating a new set of laws and institutions suitable to current needs. They could be designed to serve multiple purposes, including "building partner capacity" as a principal way to fight the war. I stressed that this would be every bit as important as direct military action by U.S. forces.

The second initiative was the establishment of a civilian reserve corps "on the model of the military reserves." The reserve corps would be made up of volunteers with relevant skills including municipal administration, civil engineering, hospital management, and the organization of legal systems. They would be paid to train and exercise for reconstruction and stabilization missions and obligated, like the military reserves, to deploy as needed. My office invented this idea for two purposes: to handle postconflict rebuilding, as in Afghanistan and Iraq, and to reduce (in the hope of averting conflict) the dangers posed by other ungoverned or ill-governed territories. I believe this briefing was the first time the idea of a civilian reserve corps was presented to the President.

The third major proposed initiative was creating a new agency, similar to the U.S. Information Agency, to spearhead the ideological component of the war on terrorism. This idea had been floated in the public debate for years, especially since 9/11.

Our strategic review encouraged other initiatives, from the technological to the organizational: a new biological-weapons defense program, development of new tools for the remote detection of nuclear fissile material, the reform of interagency policy making, and a system of metrics (that is, benchmarks) to track progress of the various elements of our strategy. When I retired from the Pentagon in August 2005, these ideas, major and minor, were still unfinished business; I regretted that I would not be there to help push and pull them through the bureaucracy.

On several of these points, however, progress has been made. The essence of the strategy I briefed was incorporated into the March 2005 National Military Strategic Plan for the War on Terrorism.* This became the foundation for a new National Security Presidential Directive on the war on terrorism, signed in June 2006. Lieutenant General Walter Sharp and Brigadier General Robert Caslen led an effort within the Joint Staff to develop a broad-ranging set of metrics to measure progress under the strategy. Support for some kind of civilian reserve corps has been growing in the Administration and in Congress. And State has lately been considering major changes to U.S. foreign aid and security assistance—though the changes under discussion fall short of replacing existing programs

---

*General Pace first published this plan in classified form. White House officials inexplicably delayed until February 2006 the publication of an unclassified version, which is available at: http://www.defenselink.mil/qdr/docs/2005–01–25-Strategic-Plan.pdf.

with a wholly new partnership-building apparatus, which the President, the Vice President, and Rumsfeld favored at the January 2005 Pentagon briefing.

But in the fight against terrorism, the effort to counter ideological support remains a gaping deficiency. No one in the Administration, as far as I know, is currently developing and implementing a comprehensive strategy beyond public diplomacy. State officials continue to speak of the matter as a problem of anti-Americanism, though (in my opinion) that is not the heart of it. There are many people around the world who are anti-American and are not terrorists. The challenge is to help credible voices contradict the preaching of extremists that Islam requires the faithful to kill their opponents. Even more important than the dialogue between Westerners and Muslims are the discussions and debates among Muslims themselves. We need to find ways to affect the debate within the Muslim world—whether overtly or covertly, through efforts by our government or by private citizens and institutions. Highlighting this need was one major purpose of both the May 2004 and the January 2005 briefings. President Bush strongly agreed on the importance of countering jihadist terrorist ideology. Yet State has never seized the responsibility, and the President has not forced the assignment onto State or onto any other agency.

Despite the U.S. government's efforts at dissuasion, deterrence, and defense, future terrorist attacks against America remain likely. Al Qaida and other groups appear to remain intent on hitting us, and it is impossible to ensure prevention. With this in mind, U.S. officials have only occasionally and cautiously touted the Administration's success in keeping the United States safe from another large-scale terrorist attack since 2001. Yet that is a remarkable accomplishment: In the days after 9/11, it would have been hard to find an American willing to predict that the United States would not suffer any further attack *for the next six years.* This was one of the main reasons President Bush characterized the terrorism threat as a war: Our goal was not just to render punishment after the fact, but to head off another attack. Officials in the Pentagon and elsewhere in the government took that strategic guidance to heart. It spurred the Administration to develop its comprehensive approach to fighting the international jihadist network.

Yet the Bush Administration has done a better job of strategizing and fighting the war on terrorism than of describing or explaining its actions. Mark Twain made famous a quip about the composer Richard Wagner—that his music is "better than it sounds." Readers and historians will judge whether the Bush Administration's strategy, despite all its setbacks, was better than it sounds.

One sign of the poor job the Administration has done in describing and explaining its actions is that the public debate on Iraq reflects little understanding of the Administration's actual rationale for overthrowing the Saddam Hussein regime. Many believe the war was based solely on the erroneous information about chemical and biological weapons stockpiles. Some maintain, against all logic and evidence, that the war was fought to gain Iraq's oil—as if the U.S. had expected to take money out of Iraq instead of putting billions into the war and reconstruction effort.

Above all, there is little awareness of how Iraq fit into the broader strategy against terrorism. Given Saddam's role as an important problem for the United States—since his rape of Kuwait in 1990—it was clear that Iraq, along with other state supporters of terrorism, would have to be addressed within a comprehensive strategy for the war on terrorism.

Critics naturally highlight the inaccurate CIA assessments about Iraqi WMD. But those assessments, which predated the Bush Administration, were the best information available at the time—consistent with the conclusions of intelligence agencies around the world, and accepted throughout the U.S. government and at the United Nations. In his February 2003 Security Council presentation on Iraq, Colin Powell relied on that intelligence in good faith—as did all the Administration's top officials. Reasonable people can debate whether President Bush would have received public and congressional support for the war if the Administration had presented its case without using any of the bad intelligence. But flogging the flawed intelligence does not dispose of the entire case.

As President George W. Bush started his first term, the Saddam problem was not going away. What *was* going away were the remaining vestiges of the UN Security Council's strategy to contain the Iraqi threat. With economic sanctions eroding, we anticipated that they would soon collapse and Saddam would emerge emboldened by his victory over the United States and the United Nations. Our main concern was *not* that Saddam would then attack the United States out of the blue. We worried rather that, in his effort to dominate the Persian Gulf and the broader Middle East, Saddam would aim to deter outside intervention by developing his conventional and WMD capabilities, along with the prohibited long-range missiles (or, possibly, terrorist alliances) to deliver them.

In some future clash—over Kuwait or some other Iraqi target—Saddam might draw inspiration from 9/11, providing terrorists with anthrax, smallpox, or nerve gas to attack us. Or, if he should one day achieve his goal of possessing a nuclear weapon, he might mobilize yet again to invade Kuwait—this time brandishing such a weapon. Critics around the world would demand to know how President Bush could have been so irresponsible as to allow Saddam to retain his biological and chemical weapons programs, let alone to get a nuclear weapon.

Under those circumstances, who could blame the American people for feeling that their leaders had betrayed their primary obligation—to ensure our national security—by ignoring Saddam's pattern of aggression and provocation? Who could doubt that the same members of Congress who now criticize President Bush for going to war against Saddam would be condemning him for *not* having ousted him before the catastrophe? Many leading antiwar legislators—including Senators Levin and Rockefeller and Representatives Pelosi and Murtha—made hawkish statements about Saddam in the years before the Iraq war. Such critics could cite their own words to show that *they* had had the wisdom to call for tough action, while President Bush had thoughtlessly allowed the Iraqi dictator to remain in power until the inevitable occurred. And they would be right.

President Bush concluded it was too dangerous to wait for such a scenario to unfold before taking action. After weighing the risks of war against the risks of leaving Saddam in power, President Bush decided it was unreasonably risky to allow Saddam to choose the time and place for turning Iraq's ongoing, low-level confrontation with the United States into a high-level conflict.

Operation Iraqi Freedom succeeded in ridding the world of the dangers posed by the Saddam Hussein regime. It paved the way for elections in Iraq that were competitive, fair, and widely supported. If those elections eventually encourage political reform in the Arab and Muslim worlds, that could serve our interests in international peace, security, and prosperity. It could also counter the appeal of Islamist extremism, a crucial mission in the war on terrorism. And the war helped bring about important policy changes in Libya and Syria. All of these benefits—realized and potential—are on the positive side of the war ledger. The negative side contains items that weigh heavily. Foremost among them are the war's dead and wounded.

The setbacks and problems we have faced in this war were aggravated by a number of shortcomings of policy and performance. In my view, two mistaken decisions—along with the intelligence errors that contributed to both of them—were of greatest importance.

As I have described, the chief mistake was maintaining an occupation government in Iraq for over a year—even though the dangers of occupation had been recognized throughout the Bush Administration, and even though the President's policy had called for the early creation of an Iraqi interim authority. The central task of liberation was to bring about political transition in Iraq, but this was impeded, beginning months before Saddam's overthrow, by self-induced anxieties at State and CIA about the externals' presumed lack of "legitimacy."

During his tenure in Baghdad, Ambassador Bremer developed an ambitious program—in line with the State Department version of the transitional civil authority idea developed in the summer of 2002—that would have deferred Iraqi self-rule for at least a couple of years. Due to Rumsfeld's intervention, the occupation formally ended earlier—but it still lasted fourteen months. The protracted occupation did strategic, long-lasting harm. It helped the insurgents win popular support. It seemed to confirm their incendiary propaganda about American domination and exploitation. It demoralized and damaged the standing of the Iraqi democratic opposition, the very people to whom Bremer eventually handed the government. And it turned all the domestic social, political, and other problems of Iraq into *American* problems. The proper U.S. role should have been to provide assistance to a new sovereign Iraqi government from the outside, as we were doing in Afghanistan. Instead, U.S. officials became the rulers of Iraq and got blamed, in Iraq and around the world, for many disasters there—from the blasted economic infrastructure to the poisonous ethnic antagonisms—that would otherwise (and justly) have been understood as the legacy of thirty years of Baathist tyranny.

The second major U.S. mistake in Iraq was failing to organize an adequate security force after Saddam's ouster. It was clear that a sizeable force would be required to establish law and order in Iraq. The only realistic potential sources of large numbers of troops were either the U.S. armed forces or the retrained Iraqi military and police forces. The CPA and CENTCOM had opposing views on this question, and those differences were not promptly resolved.

Abizaid, Myers, and Rumsfeld did not support the idea of bringing in more U.S. troops. They favored quickly training and equipping large numbers of Iraqi soldiers and policemen. If this had been done, and if the United States had also moved quickly to end the occupation, the insurgency might not have grown as it did. (Zarqawi himself, as we saw, believed it would have been severely set back.) We cannot know whether Iraqi forces would have proven more effective—despite their limited training—if they had been working for a sovereign Iraqi government against an insurgency. In any case, Bremer rejected the Abizaid-Myers-Rumsfeld approach on Iraqi forces: It was a principle with Bremer that the Iraqi army should not have responsibility for internal security. Nor did he support CENTCOM's proposal to take on the responsibility for training and equipping *all* Iraqi security forces—police as well as military.

I believed that Abizaid, Myers, and Rumsfeld were correct to keep the U.S. footprint light and to emphasize building Iraqi forces to take responsibility for their own country's security. But whatever one's views of the best approach, our war effort would have benefited from rapid bolstering of our troop strength—with either Iraqi or U.S. forces or both. The CPA-CENTCOM split was costly.

Both of these important, mistaken decisions had their roots in poor intelligence. The political transition was distorted by the CIA's long-standing assessment that there would be a gaping political divide in post-Saddam Iraq between the internals and the externals, and that the former would refuse to vote for the latter. Similarly, CENTCOM's planning on force levels was premised on the CIA's assessments that Iraqi military and police forces would remain largely intact and usable. And before the war, CENTCOM'S resistance to training a military force of Iraqi externals was strengthened by the CIA's overemphasis on external-internal tensions.

The broader intelligence issue was that the CIA actually knew very little about Iraq. To be sure, the CIA's work is difficult and often dangerous. To try to glimpse the closed society of a fearsome tyranny like Saddam's Iraq is a formidable challenge. Nevertheless, the list of important items the CIA got wrong is a long one:

- U.S. intelligence incorrectly assessed that the Iraqi military would remain largely intact and that we could expect whole units to defect to us.
- It incorrectly assessed that the Iraqi police would stay on the job and remain usable after Saddam was overthrown.
- It did not discover before the war the planning Saddam's regime had apparently done to launch guerilla-type fighting in the event of a U.S. invasion.
- It did not predict that the Baathists would be able to promote and sustain an insurgency as they have.
- It wrongly assessed that the secular Baathists would not cooperate strategically with jihadist religious extremists.
- It did not report that Iraq's economic infrastructure was in disastrously bad shape.
- It did not know much about the backgrounds or the views of many Iraqis (internal or external) who had the potential to be leaders in the post-Saddam era.

- It was wrong in insisting that the externals would not be able to win political support among internals.
- For months after Saddam's removal, it persisted in severely underestimating the size of the insurgent forces.
- And, of course, it made the now well-known serious errors regarding WMD.

As the Silberman-Robb Commission noted, the CIA had devoted few resources to Iraq, even though that country should have been a high-priority subject since at least the 1990 invasion of Kuwait. Moreover, the phrasing of CIA reports led policy officials to believe that the Agency had more sources than it actually had.

The CIA's problems in Iraq were an object lesson for *all* national security officials who need information before making important decisions. This story offers lessons for intelligence and policy officials alike. From the perspective of this book, I would highlight a few:

- *Don't pretend to know more than you know.* Don't be categorical when you should be tentative.
- *Seek out important information,* even when it is hard to obtain.
- *Don't scorn information from scholars, exiles, and other open sources.* Don't assume that the only reliable human intelligence comes from foreign officials who betray their governments to intelligence agents for money.
- *Don't be wedded to preconceptions.* Maintain a scholarly or scientific frame of mind—the opposite of that of the ideologue to whom the facts don't matter.
- *Oppose politicization of intelligence,* whether by policy or intelligence officials.
- *Be honorable about government secrets.* Don't leak.
- *Be professional.* Having gotten elected president (which you and I did not), the President has the right to make policy and to expect honest support from all executive branch personnel.

In addition to these errors of policy and intelligence, the Administration's work suffered from sometimes crippling difficulties of coordination, which deserve careful consideration. On key issues we had a *divided government*—and this made it especially hard to maintain clarity of purpose regarding *reconstruction, the use of intelligence,* and *strategic communication.*

Divided government. President Bush crafted a strategy for Iraq, but not a *team.* Large projects—such as war—require cooperation among many government agencies. If a President takes the nation to war, he needs to make a strategy *and* forge a team that will implement it. If he cannot, the various agencies will work at cross purposes.

Top officials in *any* administration owe it to the country to debate important questions vigorously, and within proper channels. A key test of leadership for all involved is whether the members of the National Security Council are committed to frank debate and teamwork, rather than to establishing their positions in the press and shifting blame.

Once the President has decided that a war is necessary, a top official who is unwilling to work to implement that decision should resign. Yes-men are worthless at best, but if the government is to function strategically—that is, act with unity and follow a course set by the chief executive—the top officials have to be willing to work faithfully for the President.* On the crucial issue of Iraq's post-Saddam political transition, however, the officials whose views did not prevail did not line up behind the President to make a success of the Iraqi Interim Authority. Rather, they continued to maneuver in the field (in Baghdad, that is, rather than Washington) for their "transitional civil authority" occupation plan. They prevailed there—with terrible consequences.

Reconstruction. The United States has formidable military capabilities for removing regimes, but our government has nothing comparable for putting new governments in place—even though strategic victory in a war can hinge on a good new government. No civilian office exists to provide the expertise, authorities, doctrine, plans, budgets, or trained teams of officials that such work entails. For decades the United States has had to improvise every time we had a large-scale stabilization and reconstruction mission. In performing these missions, U.S. officials learned lessons. Unlike in the military, however, no civilian office captured and institutionalized these lessons. No one was responsible for incorporating them into strategic guidance, for example, or into the training of personnel for future missions.

When President Bush resolved to oust the Iraqi regime, he had to create a new organization—the Office of Reconstruction and Humanitarian Assistance—to handle the postwar work. A year or so later, the President made the useful decision to tackle this problem institutionally, directing State to set up a new office for reconstruction and stabilization operations. The idea was to create a standing ORHA, as it were, so that the government could do better than the ad hoc-ery that had been our practice for decades.

---

*President Lyndon Johnson spoke grossly, but profoundly, when he declared that it's okay to be inside the tent pissing out, or outside the tent pissing in, but it's not okay to be inside the tent pissing in.

If such an organization had already been in place for a decade or two, the Iraq reconstruction effort would surely have been spared some large problems. It would have been easier to staff the Coalition Provisional Authority. The CPA could have drawn on proven plans and procedures for awarding reconstruction contracts, for setting up the Iraqi judicial system, for training Iraqi police and other tasks. Most important, there might have been a history of cooperation between CENTCOM and the civilian reconstruction officials—facilitating joint military-civilian efforts in Iraq.

But the main problems that confronted U.S. reconstruction efforts in Iraq were not institutional. The first major problem was the fact that the war did not end with Saddam's ouster. Reconstruction operations are always challenging, but the challenges are compounded when the country remains subject every day to bombings, political assassinations, and massive violent sabotage. And the second main problem was the occupation (discussed above).

Use of intelligence. It was a mistake for the Bush Administration to rely so heavily on intelligence community information to make the case for war in Iraq—and not just for the obvious reason that the information contained important errors. It was a mistake because *one did not need secret information* to understand or explain the threat from Saddam. Administration officials thought their arguments would have more clout if they could make use of vivid details, with the dramatic impact of newly revealed intelligence secrets. But what was of greatest importance was not a set of details, but the big picture: that Saddam was an aggressor, a shredder of Security Council resolutions, a tyrant who had used WMD to kill his own citizens as well as his neighbors, and a megalomaniacal enemy of the U.S. That big picture was accessible to anyone who read newspapers or history books. Yielding to the temptation to spice up the government's case with intelligence data was a disastrous move.

It was especially damaging in this case because of the political environment. A number of CIA and other intelligence officials opposed the President politically, specifically disapproving of the Iraq war policy. By making intelligence a key part of the public explanation of his policy, the President gave his detractors in the intelligence community a political opportunity. They seized it by claiming to journalists and members of Congress that Administration officials—including Cheney and the top civilian officials in the Defense Department—had manipulated or politicized the Iraq intelligence.

Though untrue, those accusations have harmed not only the accused individuals but the Administration in general and the credibility of the

United States in the world. The allegations have been the subject of thousands of news stories. When various committees of the House and Senate, and the bipartisan Silberman-Robb WMD Commission, investigated the accusations, none found *even a single case* of improper pressure on an intelligence analyst. Nevertheless, the charges have been repeated and embellished so often, and over so many years, that they are widely assumed to be true.

Politicization of intelligence—the filtering or distorting of information to serve a preconception or a policy preference—is a serious issue. Policy makers should use the best information available, including the best intelligence information. The reason that politicization is stupid and dangerous is that it yields less than the best information available. Commentators generally worry about *policy* officials filtering or distorting the intelligence to bolster their policy arguments, but the issue also arises when *intelligence* officials do the filtering or distorting for their own reasons. Pentagon policy analysts properly criticized CIA officials for doing just that on the subject of the Iraq–al Qaida relationship.

Strategic communication. As we have seen, when U.S. officials began to despair of finding WMD stockpiles in Iraq after Saddam's overthrow, their embarrassment apparently caused a radical shift in Administration rhetoric about Iraq. The President no longer cited Saddam's record or the threats from the Baathist regime as reasons for going to war; rather, he focused almost exclusively on the aim of promoting democracy.

This decision compounded the damage to President Bush's credibility that had already been caused by the CIA's errors on Iraqi WMD. The President was now distancing himself from the actual case he had made for removing Saddam from power. This appeared to confirm his critics' argument that the rationale for the war was (at best) an error. That argument was wrong, but as it congealed into conventional wisdom, the President chose not to challenge it.

The President now talked almost exclusively about Iraq's *future*. His political opponents noticed that if they talked about the *past*—about prewar intelligence and prewar planning for the war and the aftermath—no one in the White House communications effort would contradict them. Opponents could say anything about the prewar period—misstating Saddam's record, the Administration's record, or their own—and their statements would go uncorrected. This was a powerful incentive for them to recriminate about the Administration's prewar work, and congressional Democrats have pressed for one retrospective investigation after another.

But the most damaging effect of this communications strategy was that it changed the definition of success. Before the war, Administration officials said that success would mean an Iraq that no longer threatened important U.S. interests—that did not support terrorism, aspire to WMD, threaten its neighbors, or conduct mass murder. But from the fall of 2003 on, the President publicly defined success as stable democracy in Iraq.

This was a public affairs decision that has had enormous strategic consequences for American support for the war. The new formula fails to connect the Iraq war directly to American interests. It causes many Americans to question why we should be investing so much blood and treasure *for Iraqis.* And many Americans doubt that the new aim is realistic—that stable democracy can be achieved in Iraq in the foreseeable future.

To fight a long war, the president has to ensure he can preserve public and congressional support for the effort. It is not an overstatement to say that the President's shift in rhetoric could cost the United States the war: Victory or defeat can hinge on the President's words as much as on the military plans of his generals or the actions of their troops on the ground.

What should the United States do now in Iraq? Here are some general thoughts on how to approach the question.

***First:* Formulate a realistic goal**—that is, a reasonable definition of success. The achievement of stable democracy is not a sensible goal, because it is not likely to be accomplished in the near term. It may be possible fairly soon, however, for Iraq to reach the point where, despite the inevitable ongoing problems of building a new society, its government can manage its own affairs with only a limited amount of outside help. That is a realistic goal.

The idea is for our military operations and political strategy to beat down the insurgency as we train and equip Iraqi security forces. Iraq's expanded security capabilities may then allow the government to handle the insurgency, with U.S. support confined to rear-area functions like intelligence, training, and medical help. U.S. forces would then no longer be engaged in combat.

If the President can redirect the American people's attention to this sober, limited goal, they might be more willing to maintain support for the war effort. Many would recognize the goal as achievable.

"Stable democracy" would be grand, and Iraq may enjoy it some day. The President talks of democracy in the apparent hope that it will inspire Americans to support the war. But it actually serves to discourage the many Americans who see it as a goal they cannot imagine reaching.

***Second:* Calculate the costs and benefits of pursuing the war in Iraq by looking forward, not backward.** Critics of the war continually attack the Administration for past acts and omissions—for how the war was "sold" or planned or run. Those are important issues, but the current policy question is whether continuing to fight is worth the effort—whether securing the benefits of success, and avoiding the consequences of failure, will be worth the costs yet unpaid.

Third: **Recognize that the main "benefits of success" are not specific or tangible.** The United States went to war in Iraq not to seize territory, oil, or military bases, but to end the threat the Iraqi regime posed to the region, the United States, and the world. If this fundamental goal is achieved—if that regime is replaced with a reasonably stable government that poses no such threats—it would make the United States safer and improve international security. Above and beyond this, if Iraq should one day build stable democratic institutions, it might spur political reform in the Muslim world—an even more valuable accomplishment that could help curtail the appeal of Islamist extremism. Success in Iraq would also demonstrate that the United States is capable of persevering in a costly effort to defend its interests. This would increase American credibility, making it easier in the future to win cooperation from other countries.

But the largest benefit of success is avoiding the horrific costs of failure. Preventing calamities is one of the most important and least appreciated functions of government. When an evil is averted—perhaps as a result of insight, intensive effort, and administrative skill—the result is that *nothing happens*. It is easy, after the fact, for critics to ignore or deprecate the accomplishment. Political opponents may scoff at the effort as unnecessary, citing the absence of disaster as proof that the problem could not have been very serious to begin with. After the Cold War, some commentators argued that the West's victory was no big deal because the Soviet Union's demise proved that the communist empire wasn't much of a power after all. Likewise, because the United States has not suffered another large-scale terrorist attack since 9/11, some commentators have belittled the challenge of jihadist terrorism as overblown and ridiculed the description of it as "war." And now that Saddam has been overthrown, there are critics who speak dismissively of the danger he posed.

Such criticism is understandable as politics, but it is bad history. It is *not* true that the Soviets, the jihadist extremists, or Saddam and his Baathist regime were actually benign or minor phenomena that produced security concerns only in the overheated imaginations of "hard-liners." When there are no longer political motives to say such things, no serious person will say them.

If and when new major terrorist attacks occur in the United States, the public will reexamine the Bush Administration's strategy for the war on terrorism. The likely criticism then will not be that the President was too tough on the jihadists, the Baathists, and other state supporters of terrorism, but that the Administration might have fought the terrorist network even more intensely and comprehensively.

No dereliction of statesmanship is as unpardonable as a failure to protect the nation's security. If the head of government underreacts when the country is threatened, history is not likely to excuse him on the grounds that his excessive caution enjoyed bipartisan support. British Prime Minister Neville Chamberlain's name has become a byword for irresponsibility, though his appeasement policy toward the Nazis in the 1930s enjoyed broad support among his countrymen at the time.

***Fourth*: Recognize that the costs of failure in Iraq would be great.** If jihadists or Baathists or both were to overrun the new Iraqi government, the result could be a bloodbath far worse than the current insurgency and civil strife. Iraqis who worked with the United States would likely be murdered by the tens of thousands. Americans would bear the moral burden for this—and we would pay a practical price, as our allies and partners in the world discounted the value of cooperation with us.

The collapse of the new Iraqi government would pressure and tempt Iraq's neighbors to intervene. The result could be wars among the Iraqis, Iranians, Turks, Syrians, Jordanians, and Saudis. Victory by the insurgents would make Iraq once again a base and safe haven for enemies of the United States, including terrorists, and energize anti-American forces globally. Islamist extremists would turn our rout into a vehicle for recruitment and indoctrination into their movement. Success in Iraq would spur rather than satisfy the jihadists' ambitions: In Shakespeare's phrase, their increase of appetite would grow by what it feeds on.

Some critics of the Iraq war seem to think that America could withdraw and escape direct consequences at home, as we did when we withdrew from Vietnam. Setting aside the humanitarian catastrophe and other consequences of the U.S. defeat in Southeast Asia, they focus only on what they consider the comforting fact that America's enemies there did not follow us across the Pacific. But that is cold comfort in the case of Iraq.

Our enemies in the Middle East—al Qaida and the other jihadists in particular—have the desire and ability to attack us globally. They are exhilarated by success, seeing it as a reward and encouragement from God. If they drive us out of Iraq, we can expect them to exploit success by launching further attacks against an America in retreat. Americans should not suppose that our enemies in Iraq will leave us alone if we flee from them. If al Qaida should acquire a comfortable base in Iraq, a future president might conclude he has to send American troops once again to remove the regime.

At every stage, the Iraq war debate has turned on variations of the question, How do we weigh various kinds of risk? These calculations cannot be objective. Reasonable people differ on the type and extent of acceptable risk.

As a general proposition, American "hawks" ascribe a lot of weight to threats from aggressive, violent, and hostile powers. To counter such threats, hawks tend to favor early and sustained action, which might range from diplomatic denunciations through economic sanctions and military pressure to all-out war. "Doves," on the other hand, tend to discount the threats. They resist moving up the ladder of confrontation, preferring to wait and see how threats develop. In a war, doves are more inclined to quit, in the belief that the consequences of doing so would be less bad than persisting in the fight. Hawks reject dovish policies as too risky. And doves denounce hawks for being too ready to run the risks (and pay the costs) of confrontation and war.

Hawks have grounds to worry that dovish policies can increase the *likelihood* of war and its dangers. In recent decades, U.S. policies—intended to show prudence and self-restraint in the face of affronts and attacks—were viewed by bin Laden and Saddam Hussein as evidence of weakness and cowardice. Rather than promote peace, those cautious policies emboldened our enemies to defy and attack the United States. The consequences of avoiding confrontation can be grave, even fatal. The French lost their country in 1940 because they waited too long to confront Hitler.

But in emphasizing the risks of war, doves, too, make a weighty point. Wars debilitate all sides and can produce unanticipated results, sometimes the opposite of those intended even by the side that wins.*

As noted, the President's main job in national security affairs is to weigh risks. In dealing with the threat from Saddam Hussein, President Bush understood that he was responsible for calculating the risks of *inaction* as well as the risks of *action*. In the prewar deliberations on Iraq, he discussed both types of risk. The decision to go to war was controversial, and he knew he would be damned if he did and damned if he didn't. He

*I would reject, however, the unthinking implication of some critics that war is *never* necessary.

had to choose the course of action for which he would rather be damned by his contemporaries and by history.

Sitting in the Situation Room and listening to the participants in National Security Council meetings discuss al Qaida, Saddam Hussein, Kim Jong Il, and Iran, I frequently thought of the perils of over- and under-reaction to threats. What happens if the President decides that a threat is unacceptable? Few things could be worse than launching an unnecessary war, in which soldiers and civilians would die for no reason. On the other hand, what if the President decides that a threat does not require a strong U.S. response—and he turns out to be wrong? America could then suffer deadly attacks that might have been prevented. Thousands or even millions of Americans could pay the price for that error. The effects could be catastrophic, undermining our civil liberties and even endangering the survival of our constitutional system.

With all its imperfections, the United States is a thing of beauty, one of the greatest achievements in world history. For hundreds of millions of people over a span of more than two centuries, it has made possible a humane existence, a life of opportunity, with the dignity of self-government. America's founders had the amazing ambition to light a flame to brighten lives at home and inspire people to seek freedom around the world. I do not think I ever attended a National Security Council meeting without a conscious thought of the awesome stakes of the decisions being made there.

As this book makes clear, President Bush did not handle every matter as I hoped he might. But I saw that he approached his national security responsibilities with solemnity, awe, and love for the Constitution. He faced grave problems and made difficult decisions with strategic insight and nonpartisan concern for the best interests of the country.

In particular, I believe the President decided correctly to treat the jihadist terrorist challenge as a war. And I believe he was right to decide that the world had exhausted all reasonable options short of war to contain the dangers of the Saddam Hussein regime.

The Iraq war—in its planning stages, in the major combat phase, and since Saddam's overthrow—has entailed countless decisions and actions, many of which can properly be criticized and regretted. That is true in varying degrees of all wars. The Administration made errors, including some large ones that are dissected in this book. But the decision to oust Saddam's regime should not be regretted. The President, with the support of Congress, launched the war for sound reasons. Neither Iraq, nor America, nor the world in general would be better off if Saddam Hussein remained in power. As in Afghanistan, the U.S. and other coalition forces that have prosecuted the war in Iraq have done an important service. To claim that they have fought and sacrificed for a mistake, let alone for a lie, is both cruel and untrue.

To a large extent, America owes its good fortune as a nation to the fact that its domestic political battles are fought within a relatively narrow slice of the political spectrum. There are large practical benefits to preserving a sense of community with our political opponents even as we contend with them in debates and elections. Within a healthy community, there are shared principles and a general assumption that the other members of the community are operating in good faith. It is divisive—destructive of a sense of community—when political partisans make no assumption of good faith in the other side, implying that their rivals are scoundrels, liars, thieves, cowards, idiots, or traitors.

In recent years, technology has both improved and debased our public discourse. Cable television and the Internet have made libraries full of useful information instantly available to millions of people in their homes and offices. But the new media have also affected manners and social and intellectual fashions, creating incentives for coarse and outrageous language and instantaneous judgments. The blogosphere is rife with errors, echoes of errors, conspiracy-mongering, and the passionate intensity of ill-informed people of uncharitable sentiment. Although public debates can now draw on better information than in the past, our debates often reflect the worst traits of cable television news and the Internet: ad hominem arguments, vicious accusations, and disdain for accuracy and precision. These are sins committed across the political spectrum.

The war on terrorism—including the campaigns in Afghanistan and Iraq—involves many difficult and debatable judgments. Do we have the right understanding of the enemy? Do we have the right global strategy and are we implementing it properly? What are the costs and benefits of maintaining the effort in Iraq—and what is the relationship of Iraq to the broader terrorism problem?

Public debate among citizens is the proper means to get the best answers—and the broadest possible support for those answers. Is the debate in America as serious and civil as it should be? Is it worthy of the stakes in this war, worthy of the reason we are fighting, to preserve the free and open nature of our society? And is it worthy of the men and women in our armed forces, who are bearing the brunt of this fight? Our military forces are performing skillfully and courageously. Their sacrifices are securing our lives and liberty. We owe them gratitude, and we honor them when we aspire to fulfill our duties as citizens at home as nobly as they fulfill their duties as warriors abroad.

ACKNOWLEDGMENTS

Completing a book is an occasion for thanks, and I am happy to give gratitude to my colleagues at the Pentagon and those who helped me produce this book. As Under Secretary of Defense, I was supported by a large team of national security professionals—patriotic, intelligent, energetic officials who helped me run the Policy organization: Robert Andrews, Marshall Billingslea, Lisa Bronson, Steve Cambone, J. D. Crouch, Ken deGraffenreid, Peter Flory, Dan Gallington, Ryan Henry, Paul McHale, Richard Lawless, William Luti, Tom O'Connell, Mira Ricardel, Peter Rodman, David Trachtenberg, and Peter Verga. I want to thank all the men and women in the Policy organization who worked hard and well with me to safeguard the United States: preserving, protecting, and defending our Constitution.

Long hours were routine for my front office, which admirably processed huge quantities of work under pressure-cooker conditions for years at a time. I gratefully commend my military assistants: Colonel George Gagnon (U.S. Air Force), Rear Admiral Bruce Grooms (U.S. Navy), Colonel Chris King (U.S. Army), Colonel Kathy Pivarsky (U.S. Air Force), Captain Riqui Saez (U.S. Navy, retired), Colonel James Tubbs (U.S. Air Force, retired), and Brigadier General Ronald Yaggi (U.S. Air Force, retired)—and my secretaries: Cassandra ("CB") Lee and the late Maggie Souleyret. Special thanks are due to Lauren Haber, my special assistant, whose high-quality work reflected dedication of superhuman intensity.

As I wrote this book, I received important assistance from a number of people who read and commented on all or some of the chapters, supported my research, or otherwise helped me bring the work forward. For this assistance, I thank: Leonard Abramson, Graham Allison, my literary agent Mel Berger (of the William Morris Agency), Ken Bialkin, Brad and Terrie Bloom, Danny J. Boggs, Victoria Coates, Colonel Joseph Collins (U.S. Army, retired), Evan Daar, Larry DiRita, Lieutenant General Mike Dunn (U.S. Air Force, retired), Daniel J. Feith, David Feith, Donald Feith, Mark B. Feldman, Peter Flory, Richard Fox, Robert Gallucci, Admiral Ed Giambastiani (U.S. Navy, retired), Roger Hertog, Fred Iklé, the late Herb Katz, Mary Beth Long, William Luti, Michael Mobbs, General Richard Myers (U.S. Air Force, retired), Jeffrey Nadaner, General Peter Pace (U.S. Marines, retired), Richard Perle, Michael Poliner, Peter Rodman, Donald Rumsfeld, Mel Sembler, Lieutenant General Walter ("Skip") Sharp (U.S. Army), Abram Shulsky, Robert Sloan, Marin Strmecki, Bruce Toll, Debbie Tye, the late Cary Tye, and Brooks Washington. I am grateful to Mark Langerman of the Defense Department for supervising the security review of my manuscript.

Research assistants provided me valuable help. I appreciate the contributions of Rania Adwan (Georgetown University) Jacob Boyars (Georgetown), Ensign Will Kelly (U.S. Navy, Harvard University), Anastasia Moro (Georgetown), David Post (Georgetown), and John Ward (Harvard). I owe particular thanks to Pratik Chougule (Brown University), 2d Lieutenant Bethany Kauffman (U.S. Marines, Georgetown), Matthew Larssen (Georgetown), and Lance Lauchengco (Harvard).

Each interaction I had with Calvert Morgan of HarperCollins Publishers demonstrated the value of an astute, professional editor. He improved this book greatly.

With appreciation for the valor and sacrifice of the men and women of the U.S. Armed Forces, I have donated all of my revenues from this book to a charitable foundation that will use the funds exclusively for the benefit of veterans and their families.

APPENDIX 1

U.S. Government national security organization: Key members of top committees

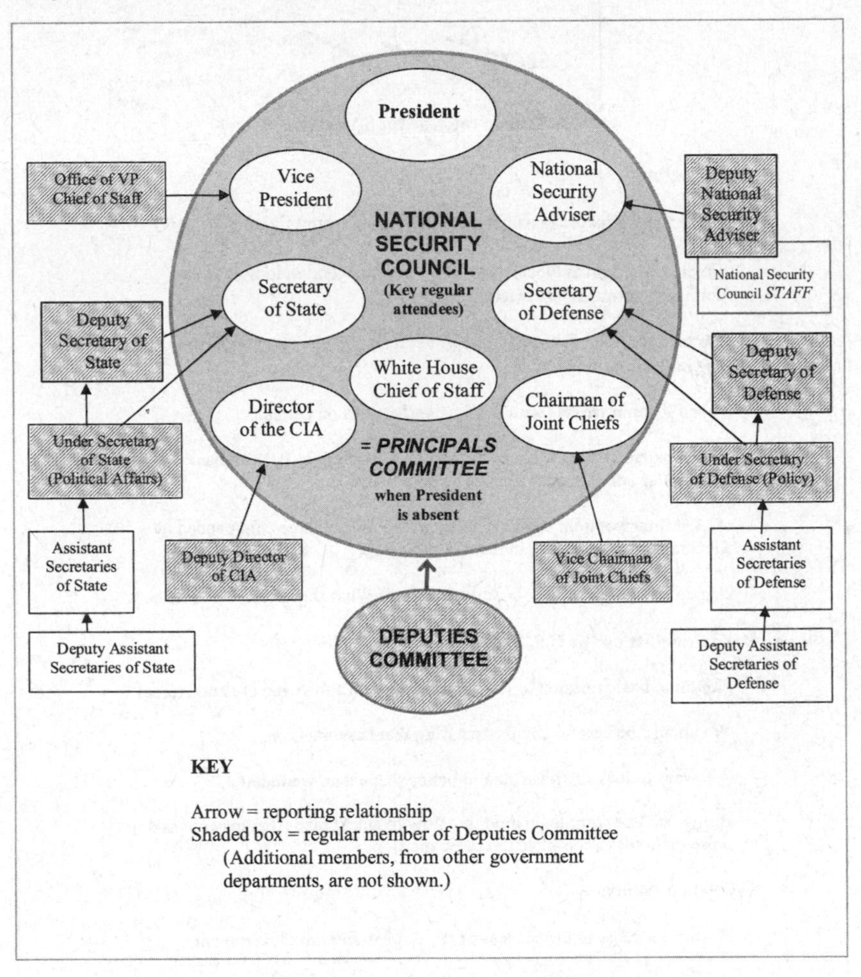

APPENDIX 2

U.S. Role in the Gardez Situation

Memo, May 6, 2002

SECRET CLOSE HOLD

6 May, 2002
3:00PM

U.S. Role in the Gardez Situation

- **Scene Setting:**
  - Gardez and Khwost remain a tangle of intra-Pashtun fighting.
  - No clearly dominant local "warlord" (order is good in locales where dominant commanders exist).
  - Karzai appointed Pacha Khan as governor of Gardez; appointment rejected by Gardez Shura (council).
  - Pacha Khan retaliates with shelling and attacks on Gardez.
  - AIA Chairman Karzai issues (30 April) ultimatum to Pacha Khan: "surrender and leave the area or be annihilated."
  - AIA military option: dispatch 1,200 man Pashtun force commanded by General Shir Alam. Still in the planning stage.
  - Karzai has, more or less, boxed himself in. What should the U.S. role be?
- **Basic thoughts on the U.S. Role:**
  - Continue basic mission to root out remaining Taliban and al-Qaida forces.
  - We should be careful about expanding that basic mission.
  - We want to leave Afghanistan in better shape than we found it.
  - But we do not want to do anything now to antagonize Afghans and make it more difficult to complete the basic mission.
- **Key Policy Points:**
  - We have a stake in the success of the Afghan Interim Government.
  - So what's the best way to help them out while serving the broader U.S. interest?

Classified by: Dr. William J. Luti, DASD NESA
Reason: 1.5 (d)
Declassify on: 6 may, 2012

Declassified By
USDP Declass Team
10 May 2007
IAW EO 12958

(2)

SECRET CLOSE HOLD

This memo from my office presented Rumsfeld's (successful) argument against using U.S. troops to help President Karzai against an Afghan warlord challenger (Chapter 5).

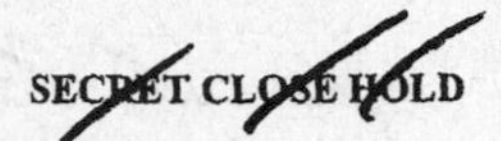

SECRET CLOSE HOLD

- Tough love: say to Karzai:
    - " We can not tell you whether to settle the Pacha Khan problem politically (e.g., with money, concessions) or by force.
    - "That's a judgment you [Karzai] will have to make."
    - "We can advise that if you use force, it's best to do it right."
    - "But do not count on us to bail you out militarily."

- **Why not use U.S. forces?**
    - Would divert limited resources from our main mission to root out remaining terrorists.
    - Would foster dependency on the U.S. making it difficult for U.S. to withdraw from Afghanistan without the country falling back into internecine war.
    - Better for Karzai to use his own resources (wisely) and to prove his mettle.
    - If we throw American power around between Afghan factions:
        - We will likely be viewed as an invading force.
        - Find it more difficult to achieve our basic mission.

- **Proposed U.S. Role/Mission:**
    - Make it clear we are not Karzai's enforcer.
    - But put U.S. SOF and Civil Affairs team with Fahim's force. Purpose:
        - Maintain situational awareness.
        - Provide humanitarian assistance.
        - Consult with Fahim on his plan. If poor plan, help make it better.
        - Not perform military mission or provide advice on how to fight.

Declassified by
USDP Declass Team
10 May 2007
IAW EO 12958

SECRET CLOSE HOLD

SECRET CLOSE HOLD

- **Final Analysis:**
  - If we do it once (intervene in internecine Afghan fights), we will find ourselves doing it again and again.
  - Will be a major expansion of the U.S. mission (mission leap, not mission creep).
  - Will create a dependency on the U.S., setting the U.S. up for the blame if Afghanistan falls apart after we leave.
  - Will antagonize the Afghans making it difficult to complete the basic U.S mission.

Declassified by
USDP Declass Team
10 May 2007
IAW EO 12958

SECRET CLOSE HOLD

APPENDIX 3

Memo on Iraq

Rumsfeld Memo, July 27, 2001

SECRET/NOFORN
CLOSE HOLD
Working Paper

July 27, 2001
4:47 PM

TO: Honorable Condoleezza Rice

CC: Vice President Richard B. Cheney
Honorable Colin Powell

FROM: Donald Rumsfeld

SUBJECT: Iraq

I recommend we have a Principals Committee meeting on Iraq, to be followed by a National Security Council meeting.

Background

We have discussed Iraq on a number of occasions. The discussions have been inconclusive. Several things have evolved in the intervening period:

— Sanctions are being limited in a way that cannot weaken Saddam Hussein. He undid the UN inspections in the 1990s and is working now to further undo the sanctions and the no-fly zones. He appears to believe he is getting stronger. His general behavior and relationships with his neighbors suggest he is riding higher than a year ago.

— The routes into and out of Iraq seem to be increasing. One has to assume the volume and mix of materials he desires are increasing.

— We have had a series of coalition air incidents, which, thus far, have not resulted in the shooting down of a coalition plane, but this is an increasingly likely danger. The recent firings demonstrate two things:

- a greater degree of Iraqi aggressiveness; and, even more important,
- what appears to be significantly improved Iraqi air defense capability, coupled with a reduction in U.S. ability to know what they are doing—partly because of their improved fiber optic linkages.

Working Paper
CLOSE HOLD
SECRET/NOFORN

Declassified by
USDP Declass Team
10 May 2007
IAW EO 12958

In this pre-9/11 memo, Rumsfeld called attention to the risk in continuing no-fly-zone patrols. Weapons inspections had long since ended, and the economic sanctions were in tatters; the patrols were the third element of the eroding strategy to contain Saddam Hussein (Chapter 6).

Proposal

We have a number of options with respect to the northern and southern no-fly zones. They include:

— Continue current U.S. course, with the distinct possibility that a coalition plane will be shot down and the crew either killed or captured in the period immediately ahead. If some important U.S. interest is being accomplished by the flights, it is well worth the risk. If not, it isn't.

— Undertake a fairly significant U.S. strike against Iraq's fiber optic links, radars, SAM sites and perhaps some asymmetrical strategic assets that would impose a more-than-tit-for-tat cost on Saddam for his endangerment of our pilots. A number of the currently proposed targets are near Baghdad. Hitting them would result in a great deal of attention on CNN, accusations that Iraqi civilians were killed and strong—potentially explosive—public expressions of consternation from our moderate Arab friends in the region, even more so than was the case during the last major strike in February.

— Finally, the U.S. could either discontinue or significantly reduce the number of flights in the northern and southern zones. However, if we seek to limit the risk to coalition aircraft by cutting back on the number and/or locations of patrols, Iraqi air defenses will continue to improve, which will further add to the risk and create increased pressure to limit the patrols still further or to stop them altogether.

The Broader Context

While it is important, indeed necessary, that we confront the no-fly zone issues, the NFZs are only a piece of a set of broader Iraqi policy issues. It is the broader subject of Iraq that merits the attention of the Administration.

There are people in the Administration who can come up with a variety of more nuanced options. However, for the sake of beginning the discussion, here are some possibilities:

— The U.S. can roll up its tents and end the no-fly zones before someone is killed or captured. We can try to figure out a way to keep an eye on Saddam Hussein's aggressiveness against his neighbors from a distance.

2

Working Paper
CLOSE HOLD
SECRET/NOFORN

Declassified by
USDP Declass Team
10 May 2007
IAW EO 12958

Working Paper

We can publicly acknowledge that sanctions don't work over extended periods and stop the pretense of having a policy that is keeping Saddam "in the box," when we know he has crawled a good distance out of the box and is currently doing the things that will ultimately be harmful to his neighbors in the region and to U.S. interests—namely developing WMD and the means to deliver them and increasing his strength at home and in the region month-by-month. Within a few years the U.S. will undoubtedly have to confront a Saddam armed with nuclear weapons.

— A second option would be to go to our moderate Arab friends, have a reappraisal and see whether they are willing to engage in a more robust policy. We would have to assert strong leadership and convince them that we will see the project through and not leave them later to face a provoked, but still incumbent, Saddam. The risks of a serious regime-change policy must be weighed against the certainty of the danger of an increasingly bold and nuclear-armed Saddam in the near future.

— A third possibility perhaps is to take a crack at initiating contact with Saddam Hussein. He has his own interests. It may be that, for whatever reason, at his stage in life he might prefer to not have the hostility of the United States and the West and might be willing to make some accommodation. Opening a dialogue with Saddam would be an astonishing departure for the USG, although I did it for President Reagan the mid-1980s. It would win praise from certain quarters, but might cause friends, especially those in the region, to question our strength, steadiness and judgment. And the likelihood of Saddam making and respecting an acceptable accommodation of our interests over a long period may be small.

— There ought to be a way for the U.S. to not be at loggerheads with both of the two most powerful nations in the Gulf—Iran and Iraq—when the two of them do not like each other, are firing at each other and have groups in their respective countries that are hostile to the other side. The particularly unfortunate circumstances of Iraq being governed by Saddam and Iran being governed by the clerics have suspended the standard rule that "my enemy's enemy is my friend." If Saddam's regime were ousted, we would have a much-improved position in the region and elsewhere.

3

Working Paper
CLOSE HOLD
SECRET/NOFORN

Declassified by
USDP Declass Team
10 May 2007
IAW EO 12958

Closing Thoughts

Two problems coming down the road are the following:

— Iran will almost certainly have a nuclear weapon sometime within the next five years, and that will change the balance in the region notably.

— Somebody, whether Iran, Iraq, or Usama Bin Laden, could take out the royal family in one or more of the Gulf states and change the regime and the balance, perhaps inviting Iranian or Iraqi troops in to protect them.

Clearly, the Arab-Israeli situation makes it more difficult to take strong action, but it is at least questionable to assume that our ability to act will improve by waiting. It is possible that Saddam's options will increase with time, while ours could decrease. We certainly need to consider the effects of the Arab-Israeli situation on U.S. Iraq policy. We also need to consider the reverse effects. A major success with Iraq would enhance U.S. credibility and influence throughout the region.

Why don't we get some smart people to take this memo, rip it apart and refashion it into an appropriate paper for discussion at an early Principals Committee meeting?

DHR/dh
072601-1C

4

Working Paper
CLOSE HOLD
SECRET/NOFORN

Declassified by
USDP Declass Team
10 May 2007
IAW EO 12958

APPENDIX 4

Amnesty and Regime Change

Memo, August 23, 2002

~~SECRET~~

DRT
Feb 05

23 Aug 02

Amnesty and Regime Change

"We can do this the easy way, or we can do it the hard way"

Concept

- Regime change does not necessarily equal war – there are other ways to change the regime.

- Aside from a coup or internal collapse of the regime, it might be possible to induce Saddam and his inner circle to give up.

- Even if it is a long shot, it may be worthwhile trying. In any case, it shows that we are trying to avoid military conflict.

Proposal

- We announce that our overriding goal is to rid Iraq of a regime that
    - threatens us,
    - threatens Iraq's neighbors, and
    - oppresses its people.

- Toward this end, we announce that general amnesty of all officials, military and civilian, of the regime, under the following conditions:

- Saddam and a small number of his inner circle (perhaps 12 people in all) will be amnestied if they surrender power and leave Iraq within ____ days.
    - We will help them find a place of exile.

- All other regime members will be amnestied if they:
    - Do not commit any war crimes or atrocities after the date of the announcement.
    - Do not resist efforts by the U.S. or the Iraqi people to get rid of the Ba'athist regime and replace it by a broad-based, representative government.

~~SECRET~~

This document, produced by the Defense Department's Policy office, was an early outline of the "ultimatum strategy" that culminated in President Bush's public ultimatum to Saddam Hussein on March 17, 2003.

- Cooperate fully with any South Africa-style "Truth and Reconciliation" commission, or similar body, that may be established by the new Iraqi government.

- We would have to decide how to broach this proposal to the opposition, and whether we would give them a veto over it.

Assessment:

- Unlikely that Saddam and his closest cronies would accept such an offer:
  - More interested in power than money and comfort.
  - Wouldn't believe that they could be safe outside Iraq and out of power.
- Pros and cons, below, assume that offer will not be accepted by Saddam.
  - Some lower-level officials might abide by conditions.

Pro:

- Demonstrate our desire to avoid conflict.
- Make clear that our motive is not hatred of Saddam.
- Sow distrust among regime officials, if some show an interest in obtaining amnesty.
  - Encourage lower-level officials to find creative ways to sit out the war.

Con:

- Could demoralize members of the opposition.
  - Would antagonize them if they disagreed with it, and we proceeded to make the offer anyway.
- Going to such lengths to avoid conflict could sow doubts about our resolve and ultimate willingness to use force.
- Might not be able to deliver, if the opposition or Iraqi populace were determined to exact revenge on Ba'athist officials.

APPENDIX 5

Iraq: Goals, Objectives, Strategy

Rice Memo, October 29, 2002

FROM WHITE HOUSE SITUATION ROOM 8A (TUE)10. 29' 02 19:05/ST. 19:01/NO. 3760645968 P 2

8688

THE WHITE HOUSE

WASHINGTON

October 29, 2002

MEMORANDUM FOR THE VICE PRESIDENT
THE SECRETARY OF STATE
THE SECRETARY OF DEFENSE
CHIEF OF STAFF TO THE PRESIDENT
DIRECTOR OF CENTRAL INTELLIGENCE
CHAIRMAN OF THE JOINT CHIEFS OF STAFF

SUBJECT: Principals' Committee Review of Iraq Policy Paper

Attached at Tab A is a draft unclassified paper that defines our goals, objectives, and strategy for Iraq. Such a document was very useful in explaining our policy in Afghanistan. A previous version of the attached document was reviewed by Principals in August, and has been modified to reflect policy developments and advances in our thinking on post-Saddam Iraq. **Please provide your comments to the NSC by close of business, Friday, November 1, 2002.**

Condoleezza Rice
Assistant to the President
for National Security Affairs

Attachment
Tab A Iraq: Goals, Objectives, and Strategy

This memo from National Security Adviser Condoleezza Rice went through multiple versions in the months before the Iraq war. Rumsfeld and his team continually argued against making grand statements about Americans creating democracy in Iraq. This version used more sober language than that of the August versions (Chapters 9 and 10).

8688

Iraq: Goals, Objectives, Strategy

U.S. Goals:

- An Iraq that:
  - Does not threaten its neighbors;
  - Renounces support for, and sponsorship of, international terrorism;
  - Continues to be a single, unitary state;
  - Is free of weapons of mass destruction (WMD), their means of delivery, and associated programs;
  - No longer oppresses or tyrannizes its people;
  - Respects the basic rights of all Iraqis--including women and minorities;
  - Adheres to the rule of law and respects fundamental human rights, including freedom of speech and worship; and
  - Encourages the building of democratic institutions.

U.S. Objectives

- To achieve this goal in a way that:
- Minimizes the risk of a WMD attack against the United States, U.S. fielded forces, our allies or friends;
- Does not contribute to regional instability;
- Minimizes the chance of internal instability, fragmentation, and the loss of control of WMD within Iraq;
- Improves the conditions of life for the Iraqi population;
- Ends Iraq as a safe haven for terrorists.

Strategy

- Employ all instruments of U.S. national power in a coordinated fashion.
- Pursue our goals and objectives with a coalition of committed countries.
- Secure UNSC approval if possible.
- Work with the Iraqis opposed to the regime that share our vision for Iraq.
- Demonstrate that the U.S. and coalition partners are prepared to play a sustained role in providing security, humanitarian assistance, and reconstruction aid in support of this vision with contributions from, and participation by, the International Community that:

- establishes an interim administration in Iraq that prepares for the transition to an elected Iraqi government as quickly as practicable;
- immediately helps to provide for external and internal security;
- rapidly starts the country's political, economic, and security reconstruction;
- provides immediate humanitarian assistance to those in need;
- substantially preserves but reforms the current Iraqi bureaucracy;
- brings war criminals to justice;
- reforms the Iraqi military, security, and law enforcement institutions; and
- transitions to an elected Iraqi government.

APPENDIX 6

Transitional Authority in Iraq

Joint Staff Briefing, October 2002

These charts were part of a briefing given to the President at a National Security Council meeting.

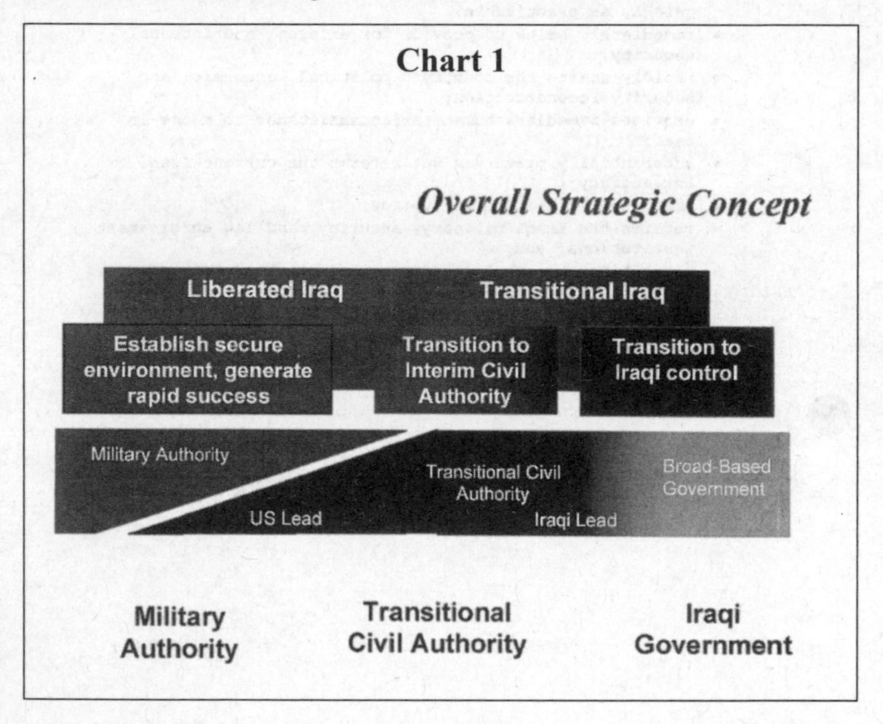

Chart 1 outlines the transition from military to civilian authority and from foreign to Iraqi governance. The transitional civil authority concept had yet to be defined. The competing models were State's concept of a multi-year occupation (often called simply the Transitional Civil Authority), the Defense Department's initial proposal of an Iraqi Provisional Government, and the eventual proposal by the Defense Department of an Iraqi Interim Authority, which President Bush approved on March 10, 2003.

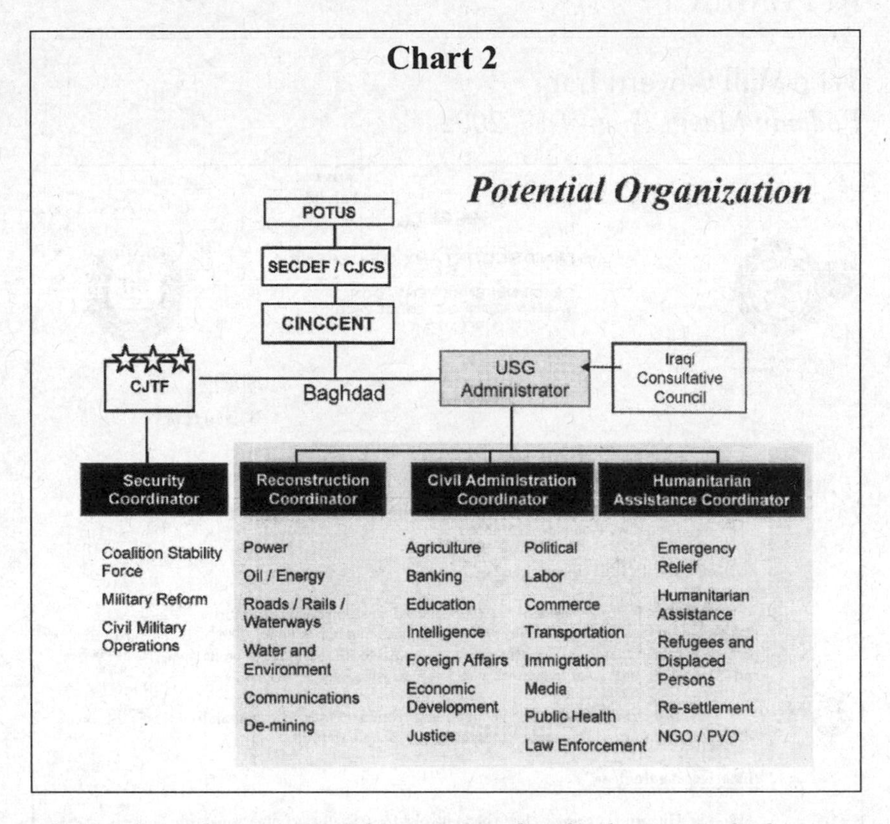

Chart 2 shows the top U.S. military and civilian leaders in Iraq both reporting to the Commander in Chief of CENTCOM, General Tommy Franks. These were the U.S. government adminstrator (that is, the head of ORHA) and the Commander of the Combined Joint Task Force (the coalition military force in Iraq), Lieutenant General Ricardo Sanchez.

POTUS = President of the United States
CJCS = Chairman, Joint Chiefs of Staff
CINCCENT = Commander in Chief, CENTCOM
CJTF = Combined Joint Task Force (i.e., multinational and interservice)
NGO = nongovernmental organization
PVO = private voluntary organization

APPENDIX 7

Who Will Govern Iraq?
Rodman Memo, August 15, 2002

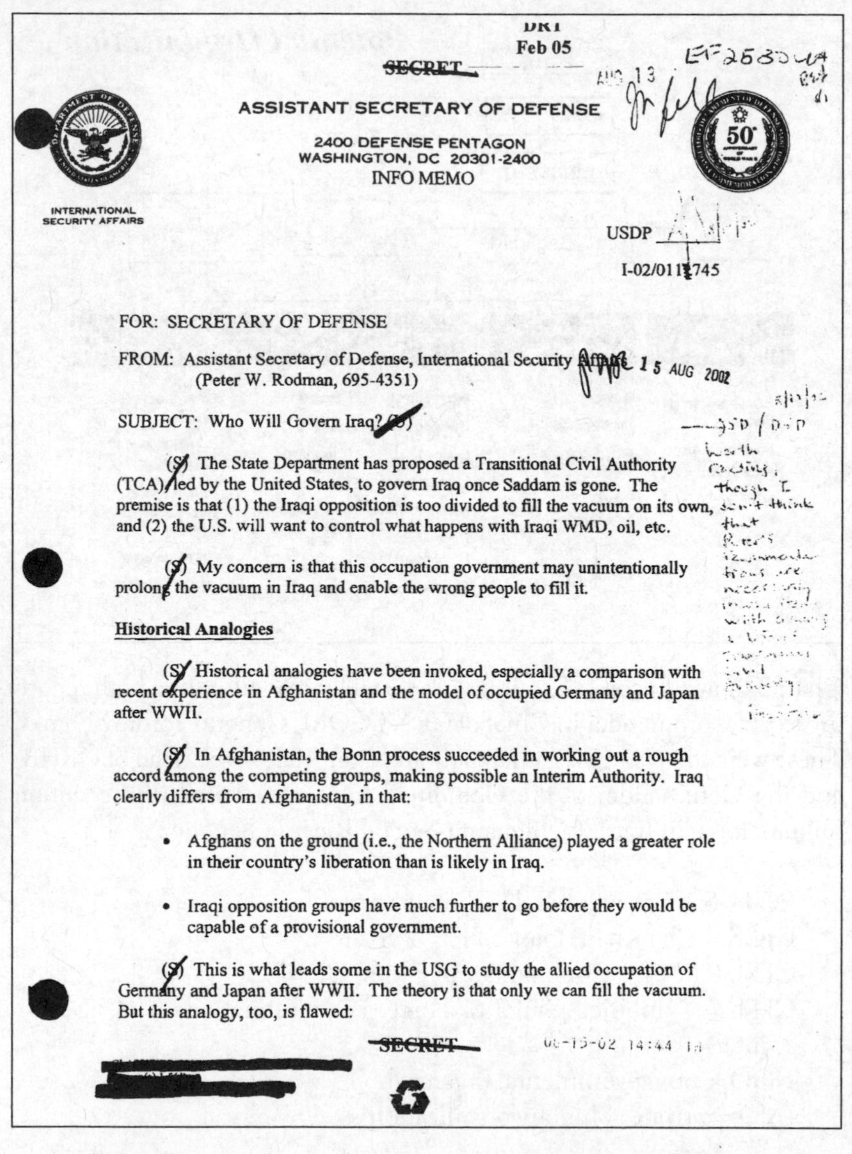

DR1
Feb 05

~~SECRET~~

ASSISTANT SECRETARY OF DEFENSE

2400 DEFENSE PENTAGON
WASHINGTON, DC 20301-2400

INFO MEMO

INTERNATIONAL SECURITY AFFAIRS

USDP

I-02/011745

FOR: SECRETARY OF DEFENSE

FROM: Assistant Secretary of Defense, International Security Affairs 15 AUG 2002
(Peter W. Rodman, 695-4351)

SUBJECT: Who Will Govern Iraq? (S)

(S) The State Department has proposed a Transitional Civil Authority (TCA), led by the United States, to govern Iraq once Saddam is gone. The premise is that (1) the Iraqi opposition is too divided to fill the vacuum on its own, and (2) the U.S. will want to control what happens with Iraqi WMD, oil, etc.

(S) My concern is that this occupation government may unintentionally prolong the vacuum in Iraq and enable the wrong people to fill it.

Historical Analogies

(S) Historical analogies have been invoked, especially a comparison with recent experience in Afghanistan and the model of occupied Germany and Japan after WWII.

(S) In Afghanistan, the Bonn process succeeded in working out a rough accord among the competing groups, making possible an Interim Authority. Iraq clearly differs from Afghanistan, in that:

- Afghans on the ground (i.e., the Northern Alliance) played a greater role in their country's liberation than is likely in Iraq.
- Iraqi opposition groups have much further to go before they would be capable of a provisional government.

(S) This is what leads some in the USG to study the allied occupation of Germany and Japan after WWII. The theory is that only we can fill the vacuum. But this analogy, too, is flawed:

~~SECRET~~

08-15-02 14:44 IN

This Defense Department memo argues for working with the Iraqi opposition. It invokes the history of France in World War II—even though "Iraq has no DeGaulle"—and argues against creating a government of occupation (Chapter 8).

- We will have nowhere near the total control in Iraq that we had in Germany and Japan.
- There is already a lively Iraqi opposition, which, despite its current disunity, will be essential for adding legitimacy to a U.S. military action.

(S) A more interesting analogy is with postwar France:

- FDR and Churchill planned an Allied Military Government for France, the same as for Germany. They did not take deGaulle seriously; only after millions turned out to greet him on his return after D-Day did they conclude that he represented Free France as he claimed.
- Had an occupation government been imposed on France, the Communists – who dominated the Resistance – would have taken over the countryside while the allies sat in Paris imagining that they were running the country. Meanwhile, the occupation government would have neutered the Gaullists.
- As it happened, deGaulle in power (1944-46) built up his own movement as a counterweight to the Communists and neutralized them.

The Iraq Case

(S) While Iraq has no deGaulle, the French experience seems to me more instructive than that of Germany and Japan:

- There are bad guys all over Iraq – radical Shia, Communists, Wahhabis, al-Qaeda – who will strive to fill the political vacuum.
- An occupation government will only delay the process of unifying the moderate forces.
- The best hope for filling the vacuum is to prepare Iraqis to do it.

(S) Thus, I see Afghanistan as the model to be emulated, even if the Iraqis are not yet ready for their Bonn process. **We should accelerate the process of unifying the opposition** – more or less the six organizations that were represented in Washington on 9-10 August – into a coherent political force:

- First, they should agree on a common program.

- Using our considerable leverage, we should then press them to form an umbrella group, with the aim of setting up a Provisional Government in the near term.

- The sooner they work out their mutual relations and allocate power among themselves, the better.

- The U.S. has enough leverage to reach firm understandings with this umbrella group or Provisional Government on issues that concern us (e.g., oil; WMD; relations with Turkey, Kuwait, Jordan; Kurdish autonomy).

P[redacted]

APPENDIX 8

Pros and Cons of a Provisional Government

Memo, October 10, 2002

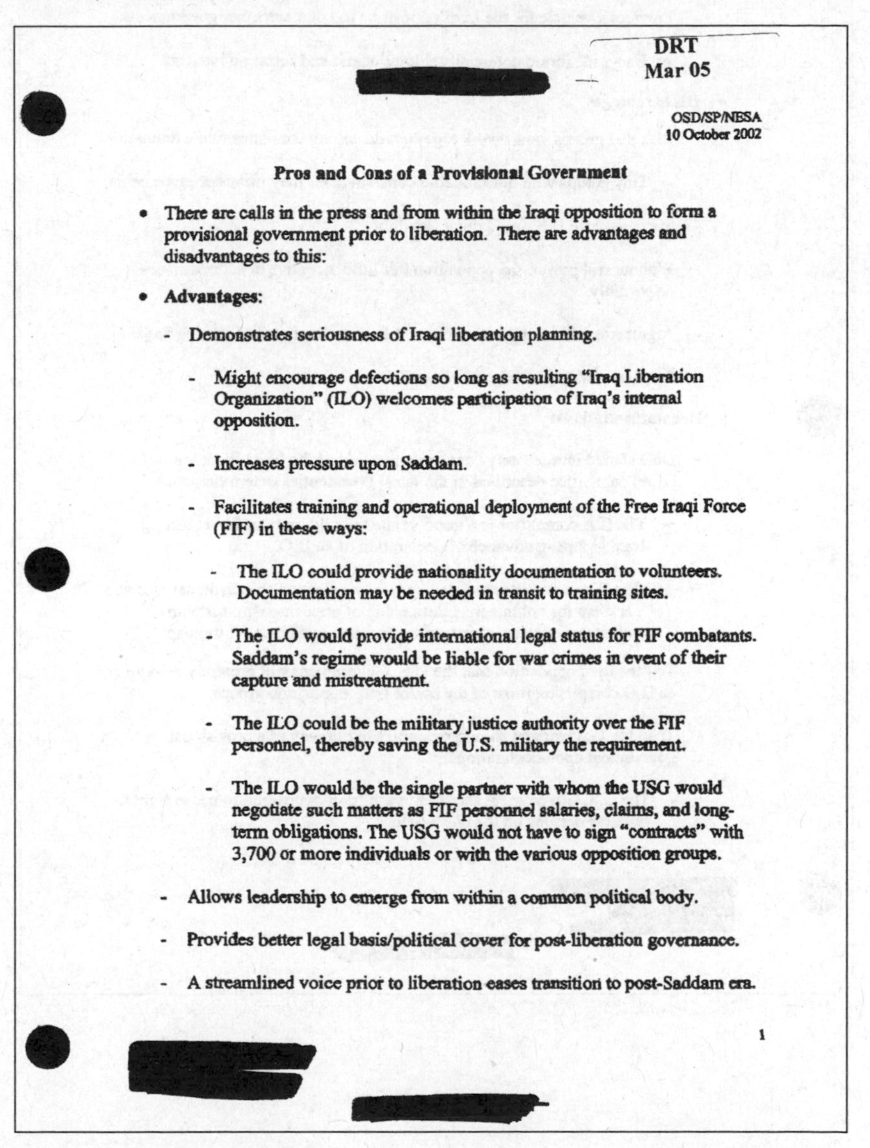

DRT
Mar 05

OSD/SP/NESA
10 October 2002

Pros and Cons of a Provisional Government

- There are calls in the press and from within the Iraqi opposition to form a provisional government prior to liberation. There are advantages and disadvantages to this:

- **Advantages:**

  - Demonstrates seriousness of Iraqi liberation planning.

    - Might encourage defections so long as resulting "Iraq Liberation Organization" (ILO) welcomes participation of Iraq's internal opposition.

    - Increases pressure upon Saddam.

    - Facilitates training and operational deployment of the Free Iraqi Force (FIF) in these ways:

      - The ILO could provide nationality documentation to volunteers. Documentation may be needed in transit to training sites.

      - The ILO would provide international legal status for FIF combatants. Saddam's regime would be liable for war crimes in event of their capture and mistreatment.

      - The ILO could be the military justice authority over the FIF personnel, thereby saving the U.S. military the requirement.

      - The ILO would be the single partner with whom the USG would negotiate such matters as FIF personnel salaries, claims, and long-term obligations. The USG would not have to sign "contracts" with 3,700 or more individuals or with the various opposition groups.

  - Allows leadership to emerge from within a common political body.

  - Provides better legal basis/political cover for post-liberation governance.

  - A streamlined voice prior to liberation eases transition to post-Saddam era.

1

This internal Defense Department memo, generated by my Policy organization, presents the pros and cons of creating an "Iraqi Liberation Organization" that could eventually declare itself the provisional government of Iraq. The Iraqi Interim Authority proposal was eventually developed for this initial concept (Chapters 6 and 7).

OSD/SP/NESA
10 October 2002

- Provides a vehicle for the Iraqi opposition to approach other governments.

- An Iraq-wide forum potentially dilutes ethnic and sectarian interests.

- **Disadvantages:**

  - Risk that groups won't work together, damaging the opposition's reputation.

    - Tiny groups with questionable constituencies may filibuster agreements.

  - May constrain U.S. Iraq policy flexibility.

  - Without real power, the opposition has little incentive to address issues responsibly.

  - Arguments within opposition distract from the end goal of ousting Saddam.

  - Practical problem of where to host ILO.

- **Recommendations:**

  - DoD should immediately convene a meeting of the Iraq Liberation Act (ILA) committee described in the latest Presidential Determination.

    - The ILA committee is a good venue to build unity and trust among Iraqi groups in advance of declaration of an ILO.

    - The ILA committee can decide: leader selection standards, salaries and per diem for volunteers, relationship of opposition groups with volunteers once training begins, and date and place for training.

  - Tell the Iraqi opposition that the U.S. Government will promptly recognize an ILO comprising most of the major Iraqi opposition groups.

  - The U.S. Government should recognize legitimacy of a provisional government upon declaration.

    - The U.S. Government should not ask Iraqi opposition forces to fight as stateless persons on the battlefield.

2

OSD/SP/NESA
10 October 2002

- **The ILO will not dispense ministries or hierarchical leadership, but will open offices in important capitals.**
  - **This avoids squabbling over ministries and positions.**
  - **Representation offices allow the Iraqi opposition to dispense patronage.**
  - **Such offices can gather support for US efforts on behalf of the ILO.**
  - **After liberation, such offices can coordinate donor assistance.**
  - **Such offices can merge with (and absorb) the Kurdistan Regional Government representations.**
- **ILO can make agreements with the U.S. relating to aid and governance in the post-Liberation period.**

3

DRT = Declassification Review Team
OSD/SP/NESA = Office of the Secretary of Defense/Special Plans/Near East South Asia

APPENDIX 9

Iraq Interim Authority Implementation Plan

Office of the Under Secretary of Defense for Policy Memo, April 29, 2003

DRAFT/ FOR OFFICIAL USE ONLY

OSD Policy
29 April 2003
8:00pm EST

Iraqi Interim Authority (IIA)
Implementation Plan

IIA Overview

- The Iraqi Interim Authority (IIA) would serve as the instrument of Iraqi national leadership in the period before the ratification of a new Iraqi Constitution and the free election of a new Iraqi government.
- The IIA might have a number of major components:
  - Leadership Council (12-25 members): This might include an interim chief executive, who might be required to agree not to run for office for a period of years. The Council would take the lead in liaising with ORHA, foreign governments, and international institutions. It would assume responsibility for administering Iraqi government functions (including running ministries) as determined by ORHA. It could also set up subordinate commissions, perhaps including:
    - Economic Reform Commission: Responsible for advising on issues of trade, national finance, privatization, monetary/fiscal policy, and embracing free-market practices.
    - External Affairs Commission: Responsible for representing Iraqi views to the world, and advocating for the normalization of Iraq's status in the international system.
  - Constitutional Commission (150-225 members): Responsible for drafting new Iraqi Constitution and Bill of Rights, in addition to devising process for constitutional ratification. Independent of Leadership Council.
  - Legal Reform Commission (9-15 members): Responsible for advising the Coalition on eliminating Ba'athist elements were eliminated from the legal code. It might also consider issues of transitional justice. Independent of Leadership Council.
- All members of the IIA would be required to live in Iraq.
- The specific relationship between the IIA and the Coalition will be established in an agreement to be signed as soon as the IIA Leadership Council is selected.

DRAFT/ FOR OFFICIAL USE ONLY 1

This paper, generated by my Policy organization, outlines a plan for implementing the Iraqi Interim Authority proposal approved by President Bush on March 10, 2003. It identifies major issues but purposely leaves key decisions to be made by U.S. authorities in Iraq, in consultation with Iraqi leaders.

OSD Policy
29 April 2003
8:00pm EST

IIA Road Map

- Central Iraq meeting (April 28) agreed that a subsequent nationwide conference should be held within four weeks to select the IIA.
- IIA Conference could include total of 300-350 Iraqis.
  - 150-225 internal Iraqis, distributed proportionally by province. Selected by the Coalition or elected by local town hall meetings.
  - 65-person Iraqi Opposition Committee from London.
  - 50-100 additional Iraqis chosen by Coalition. Selected by the interagency, in conjunction with the British.
- IIA Conference, guided by Coalition consultation, could select an Organizing Committee (10-15 members), which would choose IIA Leadership Council.
- IIA Conference/Organizing Committee could either select members of Constitutional Commission and Legal Reform Commission, or agree upon a process for doing so.

Action Items

- Determine a mechanism by which each governorate would be represented at IIA Conference.
  - If they are to be chosen by local meetings, immediately establish talks with local Iraqis from Nasiriyah/Central Iraq meetings and the Opposition Leadership Committee to organize.
  - If they are to be selected by Coalition, prepare list of candidates and devise process by which list can gain popular legitimacy.
- Plan the IIA Conference.
- Draft an agreement to govern relations between the IIA and the Coalition. Informally discuss with prominent Iraqis likely to play leading roles in IIA.
- Determine whether Iraqi Interim "Authority" should be modified to be an Iraqi Interim "Government," as voted on in the April 28 Central Iraq meeting.

DRAFT/ FOR OFFICIAL USE ONLY

OSD Policy
29 April 2003
8:00pm EST

Key Outstanding Questions

- What decision-making powers should the IIA have?
  - What veto powers should the Coalition have?
- Should the IIA have a legislative assembly?
  - Should there be any legislative function at all in the IIA?
- What should be the relationship between the various components of the IIA?
  - Should there be independence for the Constitutional and Legal Reform Commissions?
  - Should Economic Reform and/or External Affairs Commissions be independent of Leadership Council, or subordinate to it?
- Who chooses the IIA Leadership Council?
- Who chooses the IIA Legislative Assembly, if there is one?
- Who chooses members of the additional IIA commissions?
- How, if at all, should existing Iraqi Opposition structures/organizations be utilized in selecting the IIA?
- How should the Coalition ensure that religious/ethnic minorities and women are represented in the IIA?
- Should the Coalition have veto power over individuals selected by Iraqis to join the IIA?
- What regional and/or national political meetings, organized by Iraqis and/or the Coalition, should take place before any final conference to choose the IIA?

DRAFT/ FOR OFFICIAL USE ONLY 3

NOTE: "Central Iraq meeting (April 28)" refers to the Baghdad Conference, discussed in Chapter 13.
OSD Policy = the Policy organization in the Office of the Secretary of Defense.

APPENDIX 10

Action Plan to Train and Equip the Iraqi Opposition

Briefing, August 20, 2002

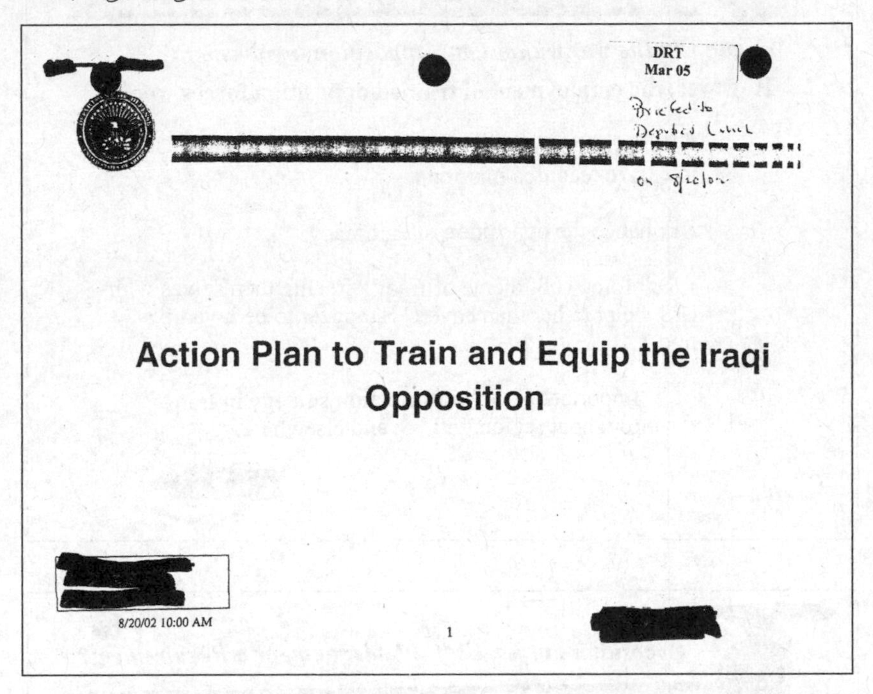
DRT
Mar 05

Briefed to
Deputies Lunch
on 8/20/02

Action Plan to Train and Equip the Iraqi Opposition

8/20/02 10:00 AM

1

This Policy organization briefing sets out the rationale for military training of Iraqi exiles. This idea was the foundation for the Free Iraqi Forces program, which produced disappointing results (Chapter 12).

CMO = civilian-military operations
DCI = Director of Central Intelligence
DOD = Department of Defense
DRT = Declassification Review Team
ILA = Iraq Liberation Act of 1998
JCS = Joint Chiefs of Staff
LOCs = lines of communication
NGOs = nongovernmental organizations
PC = Principals Committee
SecDef = Secretary of Defense
USDP = Under Secretary of Defense for Policy

Handwritten note: "Briefed to Deputies Lunch on 8/20/02"

Opposition Force: Useful Addendum, or a Requirement?

We can win the war without any opposition involvement

However, the employment of trained opposition forces would:

- Relieve CENTCOM combat forces of manpower-intensive rear area missions.
- Enhance the opposition's legitimacy.
- Reinforce U.S. theme of Iraqi's freeing themselves with U.S. help, rather than have U.S. appear to be invading Iraq.
  - Important to U.S. information strategy in Iraq, throughout region, in U.S. and elsewhere.

8/20/02 10:00 AM

2

Opposition Force: Useful Addendum, or a Requirement?

How the Opposition Could Support CENTCOM

During the war:

- Govern and provide security and essential services.
- Secure Lines of Communication
- Sort and guard POW's.
- Assume command of defecting units.
- Maintain liaison with NGO's
- Maintain liaison with coalition forces.
- Advise senior coalition leaders; form Iraq fusion cell.
- Provide interpreters.
- Provide scouts for combat units.
- Contract for indigenous logistics support.

Estimated force size: 1,500-2,000.

3

Key Opposition Positions and Units

- **Senior advisor to combatant commander**
  Leads an Iraqi fusion center
  Provides Iraqi information and views to commander.

- **Liaison officers**
  Assigned to ground forces, brigade and above.
  Report to assigned commander and to Iraqi Senior Advisor.
  Former military preferable.
  Interpreter skills required.

- **Commanders of Defecting Units**
  Move defecting unit to safe location.
  Arrange for water, rations, medical support.
  Former military preferable.

8/20/02 10:00 AM

4

SECR FORN

Key Opposition Positions and Units

Civil military operations (CMO) teams

- **Team leader acts as governor, district chief, or mayor.**

- **The team:**
  encompasses main CMO skills.
  is ethnically harmonious with governed region.
  recruits key local providers: power, water, medical, police.
  prepares to contract for local labor: truck drivers, food distribution.
  establishes liaison with NGO's.

8/20/02 10:00 AM

5

Key Opposition Positions and Units

Military police units

- **Estimate two battalions: commanders and staff.**

- **Unit tasks:**

  Secure LOC's.
  Sort and guard POW's.
  Maintain local order.
  Vet and command existing police.
  Investigate war crimes and humanitarian offenses.

8/20/02 10:00 AM

6

Key Opposition Positions and Units

Scouts

- **Iraqis with local area knowledge to assist ground forces.**

  Several for each battalion/cavalry squadron.
  Former military preferable.
  Could also function as interpreters.

Interpreters

One per battalion and higher level unit.
One per CMO team.
Ten-person interpreter reserve located at Iraqi fusion center.

8/20/02 10:00 AM

7

Opposition Force: Useful Addendum, or a Requirement?

How the Opposition Could Support CENTCOM

After the war:

- CMO Teams become temporary local and regional government, aid the transition to democratic government.

- Former officers take charge of training new Iraqi military.
  Supported by MP units, interpreters.

- MP units facilitate opposition and U.S. investigation of regime war crimes and humanitarian offenses.

8/20/02 10:00 AM

8

Action Plan: Tasks Underway

- **Task 1:** Determine functions and size of opposition force.
  Status: Underway at CENTCOM.

✓ **Task 2:** Intelligence support to trainers:
  - Vet trainees for war crimes, anti-Americanism.
  - Recruit trainees as independent information sources.

  Status: USDP has requested DIA plan. DIA ready to start when names are received.

✓ **Task 3:** Convene meeting of the top five opposition leaders. Build unity. If timing is appropriate, ask for volunteers for training.
  Status: State and Defense co-hosted meeting 9-10 August

8/20/02 10:00 AM

9

Action Plan: Task Requiring Secretary's Approval

✓ **Task 4:** Ask Chairman, Joint Chiefs of Staff, for a plan to train, organize, and equip the Iraqi opposition. This request

- determines and warns the command which will train the Iraqis.
- formalizes the CENTCOM planning on roles for the opposition.

Drives equipment, duration, and location decisions tuned to operational plan.

Status: SecDef has requested plan with options for combat as well as combat support forces. Planning underway.

8/20/02 10:00 AM

10

Action Plan: Tasks Requiring Presidential Approval

• **Task 5:** Authorize full use of the Iraq Liberation Act (ILA)drawdown authority, including lethal training and equipment.

- Recommend Secretary brief Principals' on DoD's plans to use the opposition.
- ✓ - Briefing would also seek approval to request Iraqi volunteers, and for a foreign venue for training and equipping if required.

Status: Secretary has asked National Security Advisor for Principals' Committee discussion of full use of the ILA's authority. With Secretary's approval, OSD has asked the opposition for volunteers to be trained under the ILA.

8/20/02 10:00 AM

11

Opposition Training Timeline

Month 0	*Month 1*	*Month 2*	*Month 3*	*Month 4*	*Month 5*
Presidential approval of full ILA drawdown and lethality.	Principals approve request for volunteers.	Training, equipping underway	Training, equipping underway.	Equipping complete	Training complete
	Principals approve foreign training location				
	Opposition leaders supply names.				
	Vetting begins.				
	Courses and standards approved				

8/20/02 10:00 AM

12

DoD Opposition Training: What We Have Done

- **Opposition met 9-10 Aug with VP, Sec State, Sec Def, Deputy DCI, Under Secretaries of State and Defense.**
- **On 9 Aug 02, Sec Def asked Chairman, JCS for plan to train and employ opposition force by 23 Aug 02.**
  - **Requested combat as well as combat support options.**
- **On 9 Aug 02, Sec Def asked Nat'l Security Advisor to schedule discussion of full use of ILA at next Iraq PC.**
  - **Need:**
    - **Full $97 million in draw down.**
    - **Lethality.**
- **On 17 Aug 02, opposition received first request for trainees under ILA.**
  - **DIA ready to start vetting, with FBI and CIA help.**
- **DoD is assuming sponsorship of Information Collection Program**

8/20/02 10:00 AM

1B

APPENDIX 11

Iraq Security Force
Feith Memo, June 27, 2003

CONFIDENTIAL

OSD Policy 27 Jun 03

MEMORANDUM FOR THE DEPUTY SECRETARY OF DEFENSE

FROM: Douglas J. Feith 6/27/03

SUBJECT: Iraqi Security Force

- Iraq's internal security situation would be improved by the presence of a security force composed of Iraqis.
  - This force could replace U.S. forces required for internal security missions and would thereby reduce the risks faced by U.S. forces.
  - An Iraqi force would also reduce the possibility of confrontation between U.S. personnel and Iraqis.
- Plans to restructure the police and create a New Iraqi Army will not produce additional forces in the near term. In addition to these longer-range projects, it would be desirable to have a large Iraqi security force on the streets of major cities within weeks.
- The Iraqi security force would have the following characteristics:
  - An Iraqi force, organized initially into a brigade of 2,000 personnel.
  - Ethnically mixed units.
  - Continuous CENTCOM control.
  - Capable of urban security patrols, response to crimes in progress, and security of fixed installations.
  - Vetted for association with the former regime.
  - Trained to the basic military training level.
  - Armed with assault rifles and pistols.
- One way to quickly assemble this force would be to ask the former opposition ("G-7") to ask local leaders to provide personnel for such a force.

Derived from multiple sources
Reason: 1.5 c
Declassify on 27 Jun 13
Declassified by
USDP Declass Team
10 May 2007
IAW EO 12958

CONFIDENTIAL

After the liberation of Iraq, I wanted to encourage a rapid training progam for an Iraqi force to assist CENTCOM with maintaining order in urban areas. This memo proposed starting *small* in order to start *fast* (Chapter 16).

CONFIDENTIAL

OSD Policy 27 Jun 03

- Local leaders who know the Baathis in their communities would vet the personnel provided.

- The personnel would be armed, trained, and led by CENTCOM Special Operations Forces. Initial training would be no longer than one week and would build on basic military skills already possessed by the recruits.

- Security force salaries and equipment costs would be a CENTCOM responsibility.

- Once personnel report for service in the Security Force, they would have no further contact with the leader or political party that nominated them.

- On demobilization (date and circumstances to be determined by the Commander, CENTCOM) security force personnel who had served honorably would be eligible for transfer to the New Iraqi Army or for preferential consideration for civil service positions.

* SOF WOULD BE IN CHARGE 24 HOURS A DAY FOR TEAM BUILDING, "CARE AND FEEDING" OF THE FORCE.

Derived from multiple sources
Reason: 1.5 c
Declassify on: 27 Jun 13

Declassified by
USDP Declass Team
10 May 2007
IAW EO 12958

CONFIDENTIAL

G-7 = Group of Seven (the initial Iraqi leadership council)
SOF = Special Operations Forces

APPENDIX 12

Global Conflict Strategy
Rumsfeld Memo, July 30, 2004

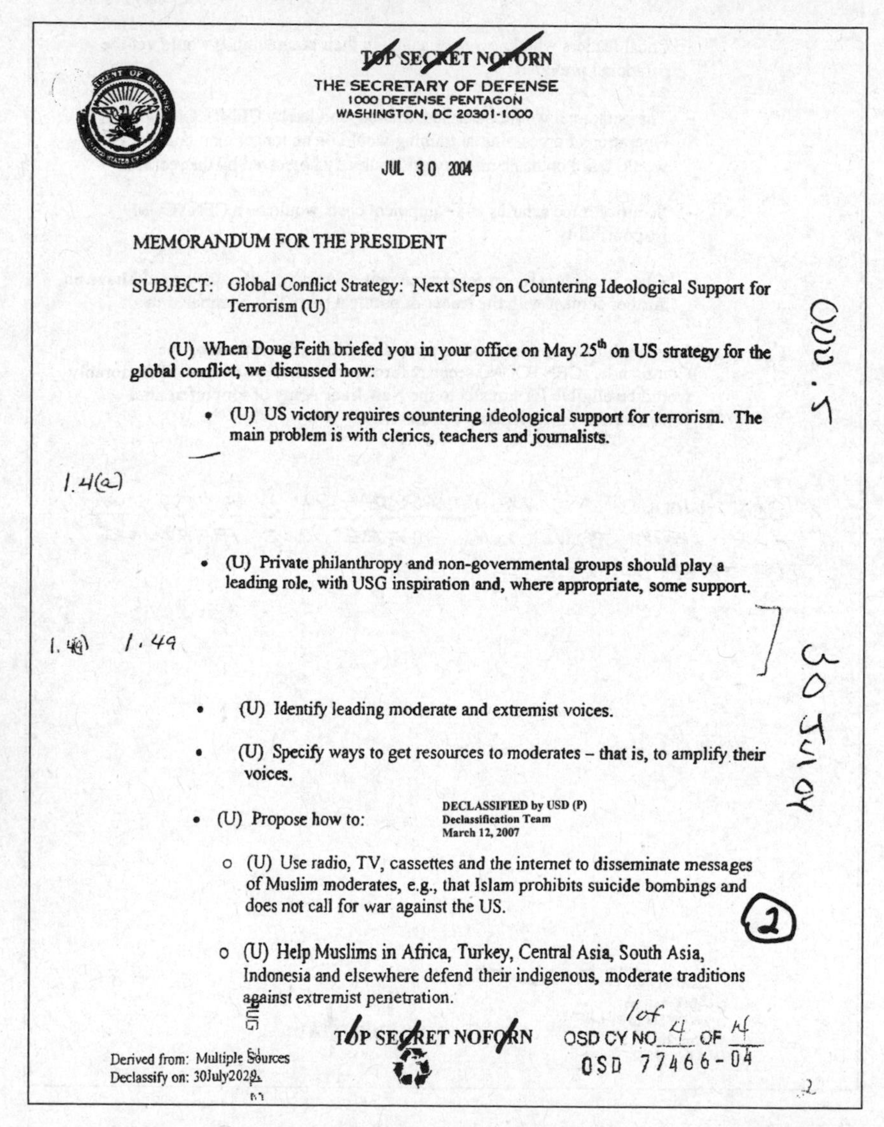

~~TOP SECRET NOFORN~~

THE SECRETARY OF DEFENSE
1000 DEFENSE PENTAGON
WASHINGTON, DC 20301-1000

JUL 30 2004

MEMORANDUM FOR THE PRESIDENT

SUBJECT: Global Conflict Strategy: Next Steps on Countering Ideological Support for Terrorism (U)

(U) When Doug Feith briefed you in your office on May 25th on US strategy for the global conflict, we discussed how:

- (U) US victory requires countering ideological support for terrorism. The main problem is with clerics, teachers and journalists.

1.4(a)

- (U) Private philanthropy and non-governmental groups should play a leading role, with USG inspiration and, where appropriate, some support.

1.4(a) 1.4a

- (U) Identify leading moderate and extremist voices.
- (U) Specify ways to get resources to moderates – that is, to amplify their voices.
- (U) Propose how to:
  - (U) Use radio, TV, cassettes and the internet to disseminate messages of Muslim moderates, e.g., that Islam prohibits suicide bombings and does not call for war against the US.
  - (U) Help Muslims in Africa, Turkey, Central Asia, South Asia, Indonesia and elsewhere defend their indigenous, moderate traditions against extremist penetration.

DECLASSIFIED by USD (P)
Declassification Team
March 12, 2007

OSD 5

30 Jul 04

2

~~TOP SECRET NOFORN~~ OSD CY NO 4 OF 4
1 of

OSD 77466-04

Derived from: Multiple Sources
Declassify on: 30July2029

This memo (redacted for security reasons) followed up on the briefing on the GWOT strategy I presented to President Bush on May 25, 2004. It focused on the "single biggest deficiency" noted in that briefing: the inadequate effort to counter ideological support for terrorist organizations (Chapter 5).

TOP SECRET NOFORN

- (U) Expand US support for moderate education.
- (U) Mobilize NGOs, think tanks, universities and private philanthropy here and abroad in the effort.

• (U) Develop metrics to track USG progress in this campaign.

(U) I know the interagency has done some good work on this subject, but using a department led task force may expedite the effort.

1.4g

(U) I look forward to discussing this with you.

SIGNED

cc: Vice President
Secretary of State (by hand)
White House Chief of Staff
Assistant to the President for National Security Affairs
Acting Director of Central Intelligence

DECLASSIFIED by USD (P)
Declassification Team
March 12, 2007

TOP SECRET NOFORN

ENDNOTES

All web links cited here (and in the footnotes accompanying body text) were active as of 2/15/2008. For the convenience of readers, the website addresses provided in the endnotes may be accessed by hyperlink at www.waranddecision.com. In addition, those government documents that are already declassified are available on the website in PDF format.

CHAPTER 1: THIS MEANS WAR

2 starting a new arms race: President Bush's optimism on U.S.-Russian relations had several sources. The two nations had common interests: regional stability, trade and investment, nonproliferation of WMD, opposition to Islamist extremism, and the nonthreatening growth of China. Systematic antagonism against the United States would be expensive for Russia. And the attitude of America's leaders—and the American people—toward Russia was benign and forward-leaning. President Bush managed to free the United States from the ABM Treaty, begin deploying missile defenses, and enlarge NATO—including even the Soviet Union's former Baltic republics—without triggering the deterioration in relations that his critics feared. As time went on, Putin proved himself less enlightened than we had hoped. High world oil prices—a bonanza for Russia—reduced the economic pressure he felt. U.S.-Russian relations did not improve as President Bush and his team wanted them to do.

3 "Terrorism against our nation will not stand.": "Remarks by the President after Two Planes Crash into World Trade Center," Emma Booker Elementary School, Sarasota, Florida, September 11, 2001, 9:30 A.M., available at http://www.whitehouse.gov/news/releases/2001/09/20010911-3.html.

3 "this aggression against Kuwait": "Remarks and an Exchange with Reporters on the Iraqi Invasion of Kuwait," George Bush Presidential Library and Museum Archives, August 5, 1990, available at http://bushlibrary.tamu.edu/research/public_papers.php?id=2138&year=1990&month.

3 protection against ballistic missiles: The *Times* was intensely negative about missile defense and often used the 9/11 attack as a debating point. On September 12,

2001, it ran no fewer than four pieces—two news stories, one op-ed article, and one editorial—saying that the attacks may and should "undercut Mr. Bush's campaign for a missile defense shield. . . ." R. W. Apple Jr., "A Day of Terror; Awaiting the Aftershocks," *New York Times*, September 12, 2001, p. A1. See also Patrick E. Tyler, "Bush Aides Say Attacks Don't Recast Shield Debate," *New York Times*, September 12, 2001, p. A24; Anthony Lewis, "Abroad at Home; A Different World," *New York Times*, September 12, 2001, p. A27; "The War Against America; The National Defense," *New York Times*, p. A26.

3 **"some type of fire at the Pentagon":** Public Affairs Office, U.S. Embassy Moscow, informal transcript of press conference by Douglas J. Feith and J. D. Crouch, September 11, 2001.

4 **"committed by a pirate or a slaver":** Feith memo to Rumsfeld, "Response to Terror Attacks," September 11, 2001 (cable from U.S. Defense Attaché's Office, Moscow, Russia).

6 **viewed the previous day's attack as "war":** "Remarks by the President in Photo Opportunity with the National Security Team," Cabinet Room, White House, September 12, 2001, 10:53 A.M., available at http://www.whitehouse.gov/news/releases/2001/09/20010912–4.html.

7 **but as a network:** "The fact that there is such a thing as an international terrorist circuit, or network, or fraternity—that a multitude of disparate terrorist groups have been helping one another out and getting help from not altogether disinterested outsiders—is hardly classified information anymore." The Soviet Union "took an avuncular interest in terrorist 'adventurers' of every alarming shade. Nothing was too good for armed 'national liberation movements,' however improbable in geography or politics, even if dominated by visceral anti-Stalinists—or worse, by Trotskyites, long regarded in conformist Communist circles as ritually impure if not certifiably insane. Practically every other sort of armed guerilla group bent on destroying the vital centers of multinational imperialism has been able since to count on a discreetly sympathetic ear in Moscow." Claire Sterling, *The Terror Network* (New York: Holt, Rinehart and Winston, 1981), pp. 10, 13.

7 **invoked to explain their actions:** See, e.g., Blaine Harden, "Terrorism . . . Are the Reasons for It as Simple as Ronald Reagan, Alexander Haig and Claire Sterling Would Have Us Believe?" *Washington Post Magazine*, March 15, 1981, p. 15; Diana Johnston, "Terrorism's Terror—It's Fascinating," *Los Angeles Times*, April 24, 1981, p. 7. The difference in approach is well described in Robert M. Gates, "The CIA and American Foreign Policy," *Foreign Affairs* 66, No. 2 (Fall/Winter 1987/88), pp. 215–230.

8 **cutting off their means of support:** This argument was made long before 9/11. See, e.g., N. C. Livingstone, "Taming Terrorism: In Search of a New U.S. Policy," *International Security Review*, Vol. VII, No. 1 (Spring 1982), p. 31:

> **Nations should present international claims against states which fail to prevent terrorist attacks launched from their territory, or which aid and abet international terrorists by means of training and the supply of weapons and money.**

and Martha Crenshaw, "Incentives for Terrorism," *Outthinking the Terrorism: An International Challenge*, Proceedings of the 10th Annual Symposium on the Role of Behavioral Science in Physical Security, 23–24 April 1985, Springfield, Virginia, pp. 21–22:

> If deterrence is a recommended policy against terrorist organizations, it should be doubly applicable to states that sponsor terrorists. States have a wider range of values that are easier to identify. For states, supporting terrorists is not likely to be a benefit that would outweigh any cost, whereas the terrorist may feel that no cost is great enough to justify abandoning the struggle. Theoretically, it should be easier to alter a state's cost-benefit calculation.

9 coining the term "war on terror": President Bush was using the terms "war on terrorism" and "war on terror" in his public statements by September 16, 2001. "Remarks by the President Upon Arrival," South Lawn, White House, September 16, 2001, available at http://www.whitehouse.gov/news/releases/2001/09/20010916-2.html.

16 injured more than four thousand others: See "African Embassy Bombings," Online NewsHour Special Report, Online NewsHour, updated October 18, 2001, available at http://www.pbs.org/newshour/bb/africa/embassy_bombing.

16 he had directed the 9/11 attack: In late November 2001, U.S. forces in Jalalabad, Afghanistan, found the video of Usama bin Laden and an unidentified sheikh, believed to have been taped in Kandahar in mid-November. The Defense Department released the tape and a translation of the transcript on December 13, 2001, which contained the following comments by bin Laden:

> ... we calculated in advance the number of casualties from the enemy, who would be killed based on the position of the tower. We calculated that the floors that would be hit would be three or four floors. I was the most optimistic of them all. *(Inaudible)* due to my experience in this field, I was thinking that the fire from the gas in the plane would melt the iron structure of the building and collapse the area where the plane hit and all the floors above it only. This is all that we had hoped for.
>
> ———
>
> The brothers, who conducted the operation, all they knew was that they have a martyrdom operation and we asked each of them to go to America but they didn't know anything about the operation, not even one letter. But they were trained and we did not reveal the operation to them until they are there and just before they boarded the planes.

U.S. Department of Defense, "Transcript of Usama Bin Laden Video Tape," December 13, 2001, available at http://www.defenselink.mil/news/Dec2001/d20011213ubl.pdf. See U.S. Department of Defense, News Release, "U.S. Releases Videotape of

Osama Bin Laden," December 13, 2001, available at http://www.defenselink.mil/releases/release.aspx?releaseid=3184.

20 flexible enough to handle: U.S. Department of Defense, *Quadrennial Defense Review Report,* September 30, 2001, available at http://www.dod.mil/pubs/qdr2001.pdf

CHAPTER 2: PERSONAL TRAJECTORY

24 "marginal advantage" over each other: See Strategic Arms Limitations Agreements: Hearings before the Committee on Foreign Relations, U.S. Senate, 92nd Congress, 2nd Session (Washington, 1972), pp. 393–398, 400–402, available at http://www.state.gov/r/pa/ho/frus/nixon/i/20706.htm.

27 sailors' beards, motorcycles, and civilian garb: Elmo R. Zumwalt Jr., *On Watch: A Memoir* (New York: Quadrangle/New York Times Book Co., 1976), Chapters 8 and 9.

31 a series of articles: See, e.g., Douglas J. Feith, "The Oil Weapon De-Mystified," *Policy Review,* Winter 1981; Douglas J. Feith, "Saudi Production Cutback: An Empty Threat," *Wall Street Journal,* March 30, 1981.

34 ". . . standing of the State Department within the Government": Dean Acheson, *Present at the Creation* (New York: W.W. Norton & Company Inc., 1969), p. 157.

34 "he disagrees is really clear-cut": Henry Kissinger, *White House Years* (Boston: Little, Brown and Company, 1979), p. 27.

39 "their right of self-determination": Protocol Additional to the Geneva Conventions of August 12, 1949, and relating to the Protection of Victims of International Armed Conflicts (Protocol 1) (opened for signature in 1977), Articles 1(4) and 44(3); available at http://www.icrc.org/ihl.nsf/FULL/470?OpenDocument.

39 "The Strange Case of the Additional Protocol": Douglas J. Feith, "Law in the Service of Terror: The Strange Case of the Additional Protocol," *The National Interest* 1 (Fall 1985), pp. 36–47.

40 "legitimacy as international actors": Ronald Reagan, *Message from the President of the United States Transmitting the Protocol II Additional to the Geneva Conventions of August 12, 1949, and Relating to the Protection of Victims of Noninternational Armed Conflicts, Concluding at Geneva on June 10, 1977* (U.S. Government Printing Office, Senate Treaty Doc. 100–2, January 29, 1987), p. iv.

40 "have read that as legitimizing terrorists": Editorial, "Denied: A Shield for Terrorists," *New York Times,* February 17, 1987, p. A22.

40 "for progress in humanitarian law": Editorial, "Hijacking the Geneva Conventions," *Washington Post,* February 18, 1987, p. A18.

41 sing a different tune: Nicholas D. Kristof, "Let Them Be P.O.W.'s," *New York Times,* January 29, 2002, A21; Editorial, "Bending the Geneva Rules," *Washington Post,* February 10, 2002, p. B06.

44 a law firm, which I managed for the next fifteen years: In 1989, I created an affiliate of my law firm to represent the Government of Turkey in Washington to the Congress and to the Executive Branch. It did so until 1994.

44 cut off support for al Qaida: In an August 24, 2001, memo from my office to Wolfowitz, we summarized our thoughts on Afghanistan as follows:

> **The Taliban regime presents several threats to US national interests in the Middle East, South Asia, Central Asia and beyond:**
>
> - **Harboring and supporting Usama bin Laden;**
> - **Sponsoring insurgency in Uzbekistan;**
> - **Opium production and trafficking;**
> - **Condoning or perpetuating widespread human, ethnic, religious and gender abuses;**
> - **Serving as a model for discontented populations of other Islamic states; and**
> - **Impeding the advancement of a negotiated settlement to Afghanistan's own civil war.**
>
> **Options include maintaining the status quo, working to install a US- or coalition-backed government, backing the Northern Alliance, or recognizing the Taliban. All would require substantial regional support and entail significant diplomatic initiative.**

44 pay for the operation: See National Commission on Terrorist Attacks Upon the United States, *The 9/11 Commission Report: Final Report of the National Commission on Terrorist Attacks Upon the United States*, July 22, 2004, pp. 210–212, available at http://www.9-11commission.gov. Later published as *The 9/11 Commission Report* (New York: W.W. Norton & Company, 2004).

46 wants Russia to succeed: Donald H. Rumsfeld, informal notes on "Discussions with Russia," July 12, 2001, 12:08 P.M.

CHAPTER 3: CHANGE THE WAY WE LIVE, OR CHANGE THE WAY THEY LIVE

48 "to eliminate Iraqi threat": [National Security Council staff], briefing slides for September 15–16, 2001, Camp David meetings (first slide entitled "Agenda"), undated, received on September 13, 2001.

50 "state support for that terrorism": [Principal drafters: Peter W. Rodman and Douglas J. Feith], discussion paper on "War on Terrorism: Strategic Concept," September 14, 2001, 2:15 P.M. (prepared for Rumsfeld and Wolfowitz). Note: In all quotations from written documents I have retained the spelling of names such as "Qaeda" or "Taleban" as used in the original. Such words were spelled variously throughout the U.S. government.

52 We identified Libya and Syria: Following the U.S.-led military actions against the Taliban and Saddam Hussein regimes, Libya renounced its nuclear and chemical weapons programs and Syria submitted to demands to remove its military forces (at least for the time being) from Lebanon.

52 to defer such action against Iraq: See National Commission on Terrorist Attacks Upon the United States, *The 9/11 Commission Report*, pp. 332–335.

55 than they otherwise might have: Rumsfeld memo to Shelton, "Some Thoughts for CINCs as They Prepare Plans," September 19, 2001, 3:56 P.M.

56 In another memo he drafted that day: Rumsfeld memo to Tenet, Libby, Hughes, [No subject line or title], September 19, 2001, 3:13 P.M.

62 clashes between Powell and Rumsfeld: A "clash of style and politics, between the soldier and the conservative ideologue, that almost came to blows after a shouting match beneath the colonnades of the White House" ("The Day the World Changed Forever," *The Observer*, March 16, 2003); "[T]he grudge match between Powell and Rummy is one of the few dependable leitmotivs of the second Bush presidency" (Michael Duffy and Massimo Calabresi, "Clash of the Administration Titans," *Time*, April 5, 2003).

62 mysteriously or conspiratorially achieved sway over the President: See, e.g., Daniel Benjamin and Steven Simon, *The Next Attack* (New York: Henry Holt and Company, 2005); Glenn Kessler, "U.S. Decision on Iraq Has Puzzling Past," *Washington Post*, January 12, 2003, p. A01, available at http://www.washingtonpost.com/ac2/wp-dyn/A43909–2003Jan11?language=printer.

63 set down his thoughts about Franks's briefing: Feith Draft Memo to Rumsfeld, "Briefing President on Operational Plan," September 20, 2001, 8:50 P.M.

63 "three key limitations": Ibid.

64 "waste of time that neither the Secretary nor I could spare": General Tommy Franks with Malcolm McConnell, *American Soldier* (New York: ReganBooks, 2004), pp. 274–278.

64 "not like the Joint Chiefs of Staff": "Title ten" is a reference to the volume of the United States Code that sets out the service chiefs' duties to recruit, train, and equip the personnel within their own services. In interviews I conducted after I resigned as Under Secretary, General Jones and Admiral Clark each told me that the story related in Franks's book about his rebuke of them on September 21 never occurred.

64 "visibly annoyed" with the Chiefs' criticism: General Tommy Franks with Malcolm McConnell, *American Soldier* (New York: ReganBooks, 2004), pp. 274–278.

64 "not likely produce impressive results": Feith Draft Memo to Rumsfeld, "Briefing President on Operational Plan," September 20, 2001, 8:50 P.M.

65 no POWs there when we got there: Ibid.

65 war against terror and state support for terror: Ibid.

66 better intelligence than I've seen so far: Ibid. All other quotations on this page are also from the same source.

67 The 9/11 Commission Report referred to this September 20 memo: National Commission on Terrorist Attacks Upon the United States, *The 9/11 Commission Report*, p. 559, note 75 to Chapter 10.

67 **"didn't seem to get it":** David Ignatius, "The Book on Terror," *Washington Post Book World,* August 1, 2004, p. T5.

67 **calling attention to the conflict's global nature:** See Douglas J. Feith, "A War Plan That Cast a Wide Net," *Washington Post,* August 7, 2004, p. A21.

67 **first major speech following the 9/11 attack:** George W. Bush, "Address to a Joint Session of Congress and the American People," U.S. Capitol, Washington, D.C., September 20, 2001, available at http://www.whitehouse.gov/news/releases/2001/09/print/20010920–8.html.

68 **his speech received bipartisan approval:** Both the *Wall Street Journal* and *New York Times* praised the speech in editorials. See "Rallying the country," *Wall Street Journal,* September 21, 2001; "Mr. Bush's Most Important Speech," *New York Times,* September 21, 2001, p. A34. See also Dan Balz, "A resolute and focused call to arms," *Washington Post,* September 21, 2001, p. A1; David E. Rosenbaum, "Congress Joins in Support of President," *New York Times,* September 21, 2001, p. B6. A rare critical voice was that of Representative Barney Franks (D-Massachusetts), who objected to the statement "God is not neutral." Doyle McManus, "Bush Vows Firm 'Justice,'" *Los Angeles Times,* September 21, 2001.

70 **but throughout the country:** This discussion of the stakes in the war on terrorism and the tension between civil liberties and fears for public safety draws on a March 3, 2005, speech I gave at the Kennedy School of Government at Harvard University, available at http://www.defenselink.mil/policy/sections/public_statements/speeches/archive/former_usdp/feith/2005/march_03_05.html.

75 **". . . on 'Our Side' of the Line":** Wolfowitz Memo to Rumsfeld, "Using Special Forces on 'Our Side' of the Line," September 23, 2001.

79 **military partnership with the Northern Alliance "will backfire":** Milton Bearden, "Afghanistan, Graveyard of Empires," *Foreign Affairs* 80, No. 6 (November/December 2001), pp. 17–30.

79 **properly classified and should not have been leaked:** As for my book—the one you are reading now—I submitted it to the appropriate authorities to ensure that I am not disclosing any currently classified information, and the manuscript was cleared for publication.

80 **Originally published anonymously:** Michael Scheuer ("Anonymous"), *Imperial Hubris: Why the West Is Losing the War on Terror* (Dulles, Virginia: Potomac Books, 2004).

80 **"failure of the bureaucracy to support policymakers":** Dana Priest, "CIA Officer Criticizes Agency's Handling of Bin Laden," *Washington Post,* November 9, 2004, p. A28.

81 **sent it to President Bush on September 30:** Rumsfeld Memo to Bush, "Strategic Thoughts," September 30, 2001.

83 **"Very important aspect":** Abizaid Memo to Myers, "Wolfowitz/Feith Memo of 9/29/01," September 29, 2001. General Myers sent this memo to me with a note he penned on it as follows: "Doug—J5 [Abizaid] thoughts on your paper, with my edits."

84 **Rumsfeld approved the Strategic Guidance on October 3:** Rumsfeld

memo to Wolfowitz, Secretaries of the Military Departments, and others, "Strategic Guidance for the Campaign Against Terrorism," October 3, 2001. This memo had attached to it the October 2, 2001, briefing slides, written by Lieutenant General Abizaid and me, entitled "CAMPAIGN AGAINST TERRORISM: Strategic Guidance for the US Department of Defense."

CHAPTER 4: STEADY IN AFGHANISTAN

88 never exceeded four thousand troops: Interview with Rear Admiral William Sullivan, Deputy Director, J-5, Joint Staff, June 15, 2006.

90 contributed personnel, equipment, or services to the fight: A May 29, 2002, U.S. Department of Defense Office of Public Affairs fact sheet, "International Contributions to the War Against Terrorism," highlighted the following countries in what was labeled a "partial list" of military contributions to date: Australia, Belgium, Bulgaria, Canada, Czech Republic, Denmark, Egypt, Estonia, Finland, France, Germany, Greece, India, Italy, Japan, Jordan, Kuwait, Latvia, Lithuania, Malaysia, Netherlands, New Zealand, Norway, Pakistan, Philippines, Poland, Portugal, Republic of Korea, Romania, Russia, Slovakia, Spain, Sweden, Turkey, United Arab Emirates, United Kingdom, Uzbekistan.

90 a go-it-alone approach to world affairs: See, e.g., Peter Ford, "Coalition Allies Lament: It's Still 'America First,'" *Christian Science Monitor,* December 27, 2001; Ivo H. Daalder and James M. Lindsay, "Unilateralism Is Alive and Well in Washington," *International Herald Tribune,* December 21, 2001.

100 as long as they do it "not openly": Paul Pillar, "Intelligence, Policy, and the War in Iraq," *Foreign Affairs* 85, No. 2 (March/April 2006), pp. 16–17 (emphasis added). Pillar served at the CIA as National Intelligence Officer for the Near East and South Asia from 2000 to 2005, and in the 1990s he was the top analyst at the CIA's CounterTerrorism Center. Just months before 9/11, he published an analysis concluding that fighting terrorism "is not accurately represented by the metaphor of a war." Paul Pillar, *Terrorism and U.S. Foreign Policy* (Washington D.C.: Brookings Institution Press, 2001), p. 217.

100 Principals Committee meeting on Afghanistan: Feith memo to Rumsfeld, "Afghanistan Strategy," October 11, 2001.

104 entitled "Military Strategy in Afghanistan": [Wolfowitz, Feith, Pace, Newbold] draft for discussion, "Military Strategy in Afghanistan," October 15, 2001, 10:23 P.M.

106 disrupt terrorist operations around the world: See "Intelligence from Afghanistan Breaks Singapore Plot," CNN.com, January 11, 2002, available at http://archives.cnn.com/2002/US/01/11/ret.singapore.plot/index.html.

106 suggest that he "select another commander": Franks, *American Soldier,* p. 300.

107 "or better support our friends": Feith Memo to Rumsfeld, "Humanitarian Assistance: The Way Ahead," October 13, 2001.

113 "to drive the people responsible for producing actionable ideas": Rumsfeld

Memo to Myers and Pace, "What Will Be the Military Role in the War on Terrorism," October 10, 2001.

113 Proliferation Security Initiative launched by President Bush: President Bush announced the Proliferation Security Initiative in a speech: George W. Bush, "Remarks by the President to the People of Poland," Wawel Royal Castle, Krakow, Poland, May 31, 2003, available at www.whitehouse.gov/news/releases/2003/05/20030531–3.html.

116 cite as their sources current or former intelligence officials: See, e.g., James Risen, "How Pair's Finding on Terror Led to Clash on Shaping Intelligence," *New York Times,* April 28, 2004, p. A1; Eric Schmidt and Thom Shanker, "Threats and Responses: A CIA Rival: Pentagon Sets Up Intelligence Unit," *New York Times,* October 24, 2002, p. A1.

116 "intelligence analyses provided by the CIA": Murray Waas, "Key Bush Intelligence Briefing Kept from Hill Panel," *National Journal,* November 22, 2005, available at http://nationaljournal.com/about/njweekly/stories/2005/1122nj1.htm.

116 Hersh garbled his reporting on the PCTEG: Seymour Hersh, "Selective Intelligence," *The New Yorker,* May 12, 2003.

118 the Policy Counter Terrorism Evaluation Group: Feith memo to Admiral Tom Wilson, "Request for Support," February 2, 2002. The explanation of the request read as follows:

> **We are establishing an ad hoc Policy Counter Terrorism Evaluation Group (PCTEG) to take an independent look at Al-Qaida's worldwide organization and linkages. In addition to cataloging suppliers and analyzing Al-Qaida's relations with states and their supply networks, this group will seek to identify 'chokepoints' of cooperation and coordination, identify vulnerabilities, and recommend strategies to render the terrorist networks ineffective. We need the support of the intelligence community for this project to go forward.**

121 "with a greater sense of urgency": The Feith-Pace-Dunn first draft was completed within the five-hour deadline. In a series of discussions and editorial sessions with Rumsfeld, Wolfowitz, and Myers, it was revised many times over the next week. The quotations here are from a draft dated November 6, 2001. Feith, Pace, and Dunn, "Afghanistan Strategy—Moving Forward," with cover note from Feith to Rumsfeld dated November 6, 2001.

124 disparaging United States airpower: David Rohde, "Anti-Taliban Forces Say Light U.S. Strikes Lift Foes' Morale," *New York Times,* October 26, 2001, p. B3.

124 "it may be a quagmire": Musharraf answered: "If the military objectives are such that their attainment is causing difficulty, their identification is causing difficulty, their locations are causing difficulty, then yes, it may be a quagmire." Pervez Musharraf, Interview with Peter Jennings, *World News Tonight,* ABC News, October 26, 2001.

124 "getting bogged down over there": Maureen Dowd, "Can Bush Bushkazi?" *New York Times,* October 26, 2001, section 4, p. 13.

124 "A Military Quagmire Remembered: Afghanistan as Vietnam": R. W. Apple Jr., "A Military Quagmire Remembered: Afghanistan as Vietnam," *New York Times,* October 31, 2001, p. B1.

125 "That could be a quagmire": Francine Kiefer, "Is America losing the war on terrorism?" *Christian Science Monitor,* November 2, 2001, p. 2.

125 "but we do expect candor": Richard Cohen, "War Behind Schedule," *Washington Post,* November 6, 2001, p. A23.

126 "as the Pentagon attempts to massage the news": Jacob Heilbrunn, "Opinion: The Powell Doctrine: Pinpricks Still Won't Work," *Los Angeles Times,* November 4, 2001, Part M, p. 2.

128 closely identified with the Taliban: Douglas Jehl, "A Nation Challenged: Pakistan to Cut Islamists' Links to Spy Agency," *New York Times,* February 20, 2002, available at http://query.nytimes.com/gst/fullpage.html?res=9B05EFD7173EF933A15751C0A9649C8B63&sec=&spon=&pagewanted=all#.

132 The pantyhose saved the day: Michael DeLong with Noah Lukeman, *Inside CENTCOM: The Unvarnished Truth about the Wars in Afghanistan and Iraq* (Washington, DC: Regnery Publishing, Inc., 2004), p. 46.

132 the Northern Alliance would make its own decision: Fox News Sunday, November 11, 2001, transcript available at http://www.defenselink.mil/Transcripts/Transcript.aspx?Transcript ID=2363.

134 a resolution blessing the agreement reached at Bonn: United Nations, Security Council, Resolution 1383, December 6, 2001, available at http://www.un.org/Docs/scres/2001/sc2001.htm.

135 " 'That's wrong' ": Presidential election debate, Coral Gables, Florida, September 30, 2004, transcript available at http://www.washingtonpost.com/wp-srv/politics/debatereferee/debate_0930.html.

137 a good indication of that: General Wesley Clark interview with Jonathan Karl, CNN Live Event/Special 22:00, December 30, 2001, transcript #123002CN.V54 available at http://transcripts.cnn.com/TRANSCRIPTS/0112/30/se.02.html.

Chapter 5: Easier to Topple Than Rebuild

141 "Karzai has no power": "Afghan warlord rejects Kabul's ultimatum to end rebellion," *Deutsche Presse-Agentur,* August 5, 2002. See also "Eastern Warlord Rejects Afghan Government's Warning," *BBC Worldwide Monitoring,* August 5, 2002.

141 a Deputies Committee teleconference: It was rare for General Franks to participate, by telephone or otherwise, in a meeting of the Deputies Committee. The other participants in the teleconference, beside Franks and Khalilzad, included Hadley, Wolfowitz, Pace, Armitage, McLaughlin, and me.

142 second teleconference later that day: On this second teleconference with

Khalilzad were Deputies Committee regulars Hadley, Wolfowitz, Pace, Eric Edelman of Cheney's office, Armitage, McLaughlin, and I, together with General Franks.

143 "antagoniz[ing] the Afghans": Point paper on "U.S. Role in the Gardez Situation," prepared by Office of the Secretary of Defense, Near East and South Asia office, May 6, 2002, which Rumsfeld distributed at the May 9, 2002, Principals Committee meeting.

148 were ignored in the field: This point—that a government's strategy can be ignored in the field by the people responsible for implementing it—was a theme of an essay I wrote on Winston Churchill's tenure as colonial secretary. See Douglas J. Feith, "Palestine and Zionism: 1904—1922," in James W. Muller (ed.), *Churchill As Peacemaker* (New York: Woodrow Wilson Center Press and Cambridge University Press, 1997), pp. 210–262.

149 "We're not going to repeat that mistake": George W. Bush, "President Outlines War Effort: Remarks by the President to the George C. Marshall ROTC Award Seminar on National Security," Virginia Military Institute, Lexington, Virginia, April 17, 2002, available at http://www.whitehouse.gov/news/releases/2002/04/print/20020417–1.html.

151 from the recipient country: For restrictions on security assistance, see "United States Arms Transfers Eligibility Criteria" at http://www.fas.org/asmp/campaigns/legislation.html. Eligible countries are those whose security "will strengthen the security of the United States and promote world peace" and that cannot maintain their own security (Section 503 FAA); recipient countries must agree to such provisions as "guaranteeing 'substantially the same degree' of security that the U.S. provides its own articles and services" (Section 505(a) FAA) (http://www.ciponline.org/facts/eligib.htm#1a).

153 retained high popularity among the Afghan people: According to a 2005 ABC News poll, 87 percent of Afghans polled considered the overthrow of the Taliban "good for their country," and 83 percent expressed a "favorable opinion of the United States." Gary Langer, "Poll: Four Years After the Fall of the Taliban, Afghans Optimistic About the Future," ABC News, December 7, 2005, available at http://abcnews.go.com/International/PollVault/story?id=1363276.

154 including combat against al Qaida and the Taliban: The British organized their special operations forces as we in the United States did—that is, SOF "owned" the mission to train foreign security forces. That made sense, given that SOF also had the unconventional warfare mission. Training tasks also helped the SOF stay busy during peacetime. Now that the war on terrorism was under way, however, British SOF were in demand for higher-end missions, such as combat. The same problem existed for U.S. SOF. Rumsfeld saw training foreign security forces as a key to prosecuting the war on terrorism, so he leaned on the services—mainly the army and marines—to teach non-SOF personnel how to train foreign forces. The British may someday do the same.

157 blamed for opposing it: See Mike Jendrzejczyk, "Afghanistan: A Major U-Turn in U.S. Policy on Peacekeeping," *International Herald Tribune*, September 7, 2002; Ivo H. Daalder or James M. Lindsay, "US Must Work to Keep Victory from Unraveling," *Baltimore Sun*, March 1, 2002.

157 "as a substitute for ISAF": Rodman memo to Rumsfeld, "Brahimi Idea of a 'UN ISAF,'" March 27, 2002.

157 *funds to make it possible*: See, e.g., June 26, 2002, hearings on "Building Stability, Avoiding Chaos" of U.S. Senate Foreign Relations Committee, at which the witnesses included Deputy Secretary of State Armitage and Deputy Secretary of Defense Wolfowitz (http://frwebgate.access.gpo.gov/cgi-bin/getdoc.cgi?dbname=107_senate_hearings&docid=f:82115.wais).

158 appropriated annually to Defense: Office of Management and Budget, *2003 Report to Congress on Combating Terrorism,* September 2003, p. 9, available at http://www.whitehouse.gov/omb/inforeg/2003_combat_terr.pdf.

159 greater flexibility for military commanders: For example, in 2003, Congress gave commanders Commander's Emergency Response Program funds that they can use to fund urgent humanitarian and reconstruction assistance. Also in 2003, Congress approved my office's proposal for a "small rewards" program that allows combatant commanders to pay rewards for items such as improvised explosive devices (IEDs) and weapons caches or for information for force protection. (Emergency Supplemental Appropriations for Defense and for the Reconstruction of Iraq and Afghanistan, 2004, Public Law No. 108-106, Section 1110, 117 Statute. 1209 (2003), available at http://www.export.gov/iraq/pdf/public_law_108-116.pdf.)

162 wrote up some talking points: Douglas J. Feith, "Points for 2/4/02 NSC Meeting on Geneva Convention," February 3, 2002. I quoted this memo at length in a newspaper article I wrote after the Abu Ghraib prison scandal broke. See Douglas J. Feith, "Conventional Warfare," *Wall Street Journal*, May 24, 2004, p. A14.

164 the President's position on the Third Geneva Convention: Ari Fleischer, "Statement by the Press Secretary on the Geneva Convention," February 7, 2002, available at http://www.state.gov/s/l/38727.htm.

165 to head the problems off: Critics of the Bush Administration have claimed wrongly that the President's decision not to give prisoner-of-war treatment to the detainees at Guantanamo signaled hostility to the Geneva Conventions. A *New York Times* editorial asserted that the Abu Ghraib abuses in Iraq "grew out of President Bush's decision to ignore the Geneva Conventions" ("Abu Ghraib Swept Under the Carpet," *New York Times,* August 30, 2007, p. A22). In the first place, there was never any doubt that the Geneva Conventions applied in Iraq. Second, even those detainees who were judged not covered by the Geneva Conventions—the al Qaida in Afghanistan—were nevertheless supposed to be accorded humane treatment. That decision was respectful of the letter and the spirit of the Conventions. (See Chapter 2 for a discussion of the "laws of war" requirements of the Geneva Conventions in relation to terrorist fighters.) The abuses at Abu Ghraib were abuses of U.S. policy as well as of international law.

165 the Assistant Secretary of Defense for Homeland Defense: See Bob Stump National Defense Authorization Act for Fiscal Year 2003, U.S. Public Law 314, 107th Congress, 2nd Session (December 2, 2002), Statute 116.2485.

166 the department's homeland defense strategy: See U.S. Department of Defense, *Strategy of Homeland Defense and Civil Support,* June 2005, available at http://www.defenselink.mil/news/Jun2005/d20050630homeland.pdf#search=%22 Strategy%20of%20Homeland%20Defense%20and%20Civil%20Support%22.

166 were assigned in our government: For this reason, the Defense Department's Homeland Defense Strategy highlighted what the department was and was not responsible for: **"It is the primary mission of the Department of Homeland Security to prevent terrorist attacks within the United States. The Attorney General leads our Nation's law enforcement effort to detect, prevent, and investigate terrorist activity within the United States."** Defense, it continued, is not responsible for stopping terrorists from entering the country, preventing them from hijacking aircraft inside or outside the United States, or seeking out and arresting terrorists in the United States"—responsibilities that belonged to the Departments of Homeland Security and Defense respectively. Ibid., p. 5 (boldface in original).

167 "the momentum of freedom": "President Delivers State of the Union Address," Office of the Press Secretary, White House, January 29, 2002, available at http://www.whitehouse.gov/news/releases/2002/01/20020129-11.html.

169 the sovereignty of God: Mary Haback gives a detailed account:

> **The entire concept of democracy comes in for special condemnation by jihadists. Unlike Islamists, who agree that there should be no separation between religion and politics but who do not necessarily reject democratic governance, jihadis want nothing to do with "man-made" laws or men legislating according to their own choices and desires. . . . Jihadis today have made a critique of democracy the centerpiece of their ideology.**

Mary Habeck, *Knowing the Enemy: Jihadist Ideology and the War on Terror* (New Haven, CT: Yale University Press, 2006), pp. 72–74 (references omitted). See also Mary Habeck, "Islamist Extremism in Europe," Statement to Committee on Foreign Relations, U.S. Senate, April 5, 2006, available at http://www.senate.gov/~foreign/testimony/2006/HabeckTestimony060405.pdf#search=%22habeck%20Islam%20and %20democracy%22.

174 "the Office of the General Counsel reported": "[Defense Department Office of the General Counsel,] "Department of Defense Responses to Senator Carl Levin . . . in his letter of 22 February 2002 to the Secretary of Defense Regarding the Office of Strategic Influence," April 15, 2002, sent under cover letter from Douglas J. Feith to Levin, April 6, 2002.

175 "to the foreign press or any press": Donald Rumsfeld, "Secretary Rumsfeld Media Availability in Utah," February 20, 2002, available at http://www.defenselink.mil/Transcripts/Transcript.aspx?TranscriptID=2722. When the public controversy about OSI arose, Rumsfeld alluded to military deception as an integral part of warfare, but he also declared that Defense Department officials do not lie. He was not being inconsistent. Military deception does not require lying to the public. Misleading the enemy about combat plans has been a venerable military practice since at least the days of the Trojan horse; General Patton's 1944 decoy invasion force, which appeared to be readying to land at the Pas de Calais rather than Normandy, is just one modern example. As both Odysseus and Patton demonstrated, one does not actually have to lie to the public—or even say anything false to anyone—to deceive an enemy for strategic purposes. That can be accomplished through actions—for example, visible actions that reinforce the enemy's inaccurate assumptions.

175 "nor the domestic public, nor to the press": Douglas J. Feith, "Under Secretary Feith Breakfast with Defense Writers Group," Transcript of breakfast meeting in Washington, D.C., with the Defense Writers Group, published by U.S. Department of Defense, February 20, 2002, available at http://www.defenselink.mil/transcripts/2002/t02232002_t0220dwg.html.

176 was behind OSI's demise: Franklin Foer, "Flacks Americana," *The New Republic Online*, May 14, 2002, available at http://www.prfirms.org/resources/news/redon051402.asp; Paul M. Rodriguez, "Disinformation dustup shrouded in secrecy—political notebook—Department of Defense—Brief Article," *Insight on the News*, May 6, 2002, available at http://www.findarticles.com/p/articles/mi_m1571/is_16_18/ai_85523463; David E. Kaplan, "How Rocket Scientists Got Into the Hearts-and-Minds Game," *U.S. News & World Report*, April 25, 2005, available at http://www.usnews.com/usnews/news/articles/050425/25roots.b1.htm.

177 as of American foreign policy: See Scheuer ("Anonymous"), *Imperial Hubris*, p. x: "Bin Laden has been precise in telling Americans the reasons he is waging war on us. None of the reasons have anything to do with our freedoms, liberty, and democracy, but have everything to do with U.S. policies and actions in the Muslim world."

178 this is where we'll find it: Douglas J. Feith, "The War on Terrorism—America's War and Israel's War," Speech to American-Israel Public Affairs Committee, Washington, D.C., April 21, 2002, available at http://www.dod.mil/policy/sections/public_statements/speeches/archive/former_usdp/feith/2002/april_21_02.html.

CHAPTER 6: WHY IRAQ?

182 to replace that regime: Iraq Liberation Act of 1998, H.R. 4655, Public Law No. 105-338 (October 31, 1998), Section 3, available at http://thomas.loc.gov/cgi-bin/query/z?c105:H.R.4655.ENR:.

182 "Kerry . . . and others had sent a letter to President Clinton": Letter of the Senate Armed Services Committee to President Clinton, October 9, 1998, available at http://cornyn.senate.gov/public/index.cfm?FuseAction=ForPress.NewsReleases&ContentRecord_id=bdf1fbab-bfd4–4b50-b7fa-7204db679bf2&Region_id=&Issue_id=3d67782c-17b8–4d84-bb21-dab2240d6850&IsTextOnly=True&IsPrint=true.

182 if compliance is not achieved: Carl Levin, "Concern Over Recent Developments in Iraq," *Congressional Record*, U.S. Senate, October 9, 1998, p. S12240, available at http://frwebgate.access.gpo.gov/cgi-bin/getpage.cgi?position=all&page=S12240&dbname=1998 record.

182 rebuilding its weapons of mass destruction: Editorial, "Facing Up to Iraq," *Washington Post*, January 29, 2001, p. A18.

182 one *Times* editorial said: Editorial, "Eliminating Hidden Weapons; Illusory Inspections in Iraq," *New York Times*, August 28, 1998, p. A24.

182 "eager to ease inspections and sanctions": Editorial, "Drifting to a New Iraq Policy," *New York Times*, August 12, 1998, p. A18.

182 "is destined to be weak": Editorial, "No Illusions About Iraq," *New York Times*, December 27, 1998, p. A18.

183 for their purged party colleagues: See Samir al-Khalil (pseudonym of Kanan Makiya), *Republic of Fear* (Berkeley and Los Angeles: University of California Press, 1989), pp. 71–72; see also Judith Miller and Laurie Mylroie, *Saddam Hussein and the Crisis in the Gulf* (New York: Times Books, 1990), pp. 42–46.

184 used chemical weapons against Iran: In the note to the UN Security Council by UN Secretary-General Javier Perez de Cuellar accompanying the report of the special mission, the secretary-general confirmed that Iraq did use chemical weapons against Iran and, in doing so, violated the 1925 Geneva Protocol (on the Prohibition of the Use in War of Asphyxiating, Poisonous or Other Gases, and of Bacteriological Methods of Warfare). See paragraph 14 of UN Security Council document S/17911 ("Report of the mission dispatched by the Secretary-General to investigate allegations of the use of chemical weapons in the conflict between the Islamic Republic of Iran and Iraq S/17911," March 12, 1986, available at http://www.iranwatch.org/international/UNSC/unsc-s17911-cwusewar-031286.pdf). For the observation that the Iraqi regime was the first in history to make such use of nerve gas, see U.S. Central Intelligence Agency, *Intelligence Update: Chemical Warfare Agent Issues During the Persian Gulf War*, April 2002, available at http://www.cia.gov/library/reports/general-reports-1/gulfwar/cwagents/index.htm.

184 meaning "booty" or spoils of war: Regarding definition of "Anfal," see Kanan Makiya, *Cruelty and Silence: War, Tyranny, Uprising and the Arab World* (New York: W. W. Norton & Company, Inc., 1993), pp. 156–158.

184 put it at more than 100,000: Ibid., p. 22. An Iraqi official flew into a rage when Kurdish leaders claimed a figure of 182,000 deaths. "It couldn't have been more than one hundred thousand," he shouted. See *Iraq's Crime of Genocide: The Anfal Campaign Against the Kurds*, Human Rights Watch, 1994, pp. 14, 230.

184 disappeared in the Anfal campaign: Makiya, *Cruelty and Silence*, p. 17.

185 its nonglorious, negotiated end in 1988: Ibid., p. 19. As a result of this and other reported poison gas attacks, the commander of the Anfal campaign, Saddam's cousin, Ali Hassan al-Majid, acquired the nickname "Chemical Ali."

185 to pour into the Persian Gulf: See "Saddam Hussein: Crimes and Human Rights Abuses," United Kingdom Foreign and Commonwealth Office, London, November 2002, pp. 18–22, 29, available at http://image.guardian.co.uk/sys-files/Guardian/documents/2002/12/02/hrdossierenglish.pdf; Timothy J. Feighery, "Conference Papers: 3. The Impact on the Economic and Social Fabric Assessing the Costs of Iraq's 1990 Invasion and Occupation of Kuwait—The United Nations Compensation Commission," *Refugee Survey Quarterly* 22 (December 2003), pp. 88, 94; The Economic and Environmental Impact of the Gulf War on Kuwait and the Persian Gulf, The Trade & Environment Database, available at http://www.american.edu/TED/kuwait.htm.

186 "that threatened the regime's survival": Kevin M. Woods, with Michael

R. Pease, Mark E. Stout, Williamson Murray, and James G. Lacey, *Iraqi Perspectives Project: A View of Operation Iraqi Freedom from Saddam's Senior Leadership*, Joint Center for Operational Analysis, U.S. Joint Forces Command March 2006, pp. viii, 14–16, available at http://www.jfcom.mil/newslink/storyarchive/2006/ipp.pdf.

186 humanitarian needs (mainly food and medicine): United Nations Security Council, Security Council Resolution 687, April 3, 1991, available at http://www.un.org/Docs/scres/1991/scres91.htm, cited January 12, 2007.

186 culture of the "marsh Arabs": See CIA, "Facts on Iraq's Humanitarian Situation," July 17, 1998, p. 19.

186 another resolution, directing Iraq to cease oppressing its own civilians: United Nations Security Council, Security Council Resolution 688, April 5, 1991, available at http://daccessdds.un.org/doc/RESOLUTION/GEN/NR0/596/24/IMG/NR059624.pdf?OpenElement.

187 with a car bomb: The Kuwaitis caught the team of failed assassins, which was led by Iraqi nationals. See White House, "Decade of Defiance," September 12, 2002, p. 18, available at http://www.whitehouse.gov/news/releases/2002/09/iraqdecade.pdf.

187 "a long history of supporting terrorism": CIA, *Iraqi Support for Terrorism*, September 2002, as summarized in U.S. Senate, Select Committee on Intelligence, *Report on the U.S. Intelligence Community's Prewar Intelligence Assessments on Iraq*, July 7, 2004, p. 314, available at http://intelligence.senate.gov/108301.pdf. (Hereafter, *SSCI Report on Iraq Prewar Intelligence*.) See Chapter 8.

187 families of Palestinian suicide bombers: In 2002, he pledged $25,000 per family to the families of Palestinian suicide bombers: "The rules for rewarding suicide/homicide bombers are strict and insist that only someone who blows himself up with a belt of explosives gets the full payment." White House, "Decade of Defiance," September 12, 2002, p. 18, available at http://www.whitehouse.gov/news/releases/2002/09/iraqdecade.pdf.

> **Saddam paid the families of Palestinian suicide bombers to encourage Palestinian terrorism, channeling $25,000 since March through the ALF alone to families of suicide bombers in Gaza and the West Bank. Public testimonials by Palestinian civilians and officials and cancelled checks captured by Israel in the West Bank verify the transfer of a considerable amount of Iraqi money.**

U.S. Department of State, "Patterns of Global Terrorism 2002," April 30, 2003, available at http://www.state.gov/s/ct/rls/crt/2002/html/19988.htm. See also "Jenin Families Pocket Iraqi Cash," *Washington Times, London Daily Telegraph*, May 31, 2002.

187 including many Americans: *Iraq: Weapons Threat, Compliance, Sanctions, and U.S. Policy*: CRS Report to Congress Updated December 10, 2002, available at http://fpc.state.gov/documents/organization/16172.pdf.

187 bombing of the World Trade Center in 1993: Yasin was imprisoned by Saddam after the first year while the regime attempted to negotiate the conditions of his transfer to U.S. custody, according to a CBS News interview conducted in the Iraqi prison. "The Yasin Interview: A 60 Minutes Exclusive," *60 Minutes*, CBS News, June 2, 2002, available at www.cbsnews.com/stories/2002/06/02/60minutes/main 510847.shtml.

187 **Leon Klinghoffer, an elderly American:** Abbas was captured outside Baghdad by U.S. Special Forces in April 2003. "U.S. captures mastermind of Achille Lauro hijacking," CNN, April 16, 2003, available at http://www.cnn.com/2003/WORLD/ meast/04/15/sprj.irq.abbas.arrested/.

187 **Arab Liberation Front (ALF):** See U.S. Department of State, "Patterns of Global Terrorism 2001," May 2002, p. 65, available at http://www.state.gov/s/ct/ rls/crt/2001/pdf/; White House, "Decade of Defiance," September 12, 2002, p. 18, available at http://www.whitehouse.gov/news/releases/2002/09/iraqdecade.pdf.

188 **Saddam brought Arab volunteers. . . to those camps for training:** Woods, et al., *Iraqi Perspectives Project*, p. 54 (endnotes omitted), available at http://www .jfcom.mil/newslink/storyarchive/2006/ipp.pdf. The cited Iraqi regime document was dated October 7, 2000, and was entitled "Correspondence from Presidential Office to Secretary General of the Fedayeen Saddam Regarding Foreign Arab Volunteers." Ibid., note 54, p. 68.

188 **"test various chemicals and poisons":** Charles Duelfer, *Comprehensive Report of the Special Advisor to the DCI on Iraq's Weapons of Mass Destruction*, September 30, 2004, Vol. IIIB, "Biological Warfare," p. 15, available at http://news. findlaw.com/hdocs/docs/iraq/cia93004wmdrpt.html. (Hereafter, Duelfer Report.) Ibid., Vol. IIIA, "Chemical Warfare," p. 3.

188 **"enhance its military capability in southern Iraq":** United Nations Security Council, Security Council Resolution 949, October 15, 1992, available at http:// www.un.org/docs/scres/1994/scres94.htm.

188 **of southern Iraq's no-fly zone:** U.S. Department of State, "Timeline of UN-Iraq-Coalition Activity," December 31, 2002, available at http://www.state.gov/p/ nea/rls/17912.htm.

188 **"deployed biological weapons for combat use":** United Nations Special Commission (UNSCOM), "Report on Status of Disarmament and Monitoring," January 29, 1999, available at http://www.un.org/Depts/unscom/s99–94.htm. (Hereafter, *UNSCOM Report*.)

188 **"a surrogate for smallpox research":** Duelfer Report, Vol. IIIB, "Biological Warfare," p. 27 (in original, the quoted words were all in italics).

188 ***before* Desert Storm:** Ibid., p. 28.

189 **under the cover of civilian research:** Ibid., p. 11, 13 (in original, the quoted words were all in italics).

189 **"an overarching Regime objective":** Ibid., p. 15.

189 **under the auspices of the Iraqi Intelligence Service:** Ibid. (in original, the quoted words were all in italics).

189 **"When I pardon, I mean it":** Ibid., Vol. IA ("Regime Strategic Intent"), pp. 45–46.

190 **replacing the Saddam Hussein regime with a democratic government:** See

Ahmad Chalabi, "A Democratic Future for Iraq," *Wall Street Journal*, February 27, 1991, p. A10.

190 "as its very center the armed forces": John Lancaster and David B. Ottaway, "With CIA's Help, Group in Jordan Targets Saddam; U.S. Funds Support Campaign to Topple Iraqi Leader from Afar," *Washington Post*, June 23, 1996, p. A1. In June 2004, Allawi became Prime Minister of the first post-Saddam Iraqi government.

190 "acts of revenge or chaos": Ibid.

190 denounced the CIA for incompetence: See Robert Baer, *See No Evil* (New York: Crown Publishers, 2002), pp. 200–205; David Ignatius, "The CIA and the Coup That Wasn't," *Washington Post*, May 16, 2003.

190 burning his bridges with the CIA: The CIA's intense antagonism toward Chalabi was recorded in the U.S. Senate Intelligence Committee's September 2006 report, "Use by the Intelligence Community of Information Provided by the Iraqi National Congress." That lengthy report included several pages of tendentious and controversial conclusions that were approved by a committee vote largely along party lines. But the bulk of the report—factual background material reflecting sober, non-polemical work by the committee's bipartisan staff—was accepted without partisan dispute among the senators. This account draws from that material.

190 "not a U.S. intelligence asset": U.S. Senate Select Committee on Intelligence, *Report on the Use by the Intelligence Community of Information Provided by the Iraqi National Congress together with Additional Views*, September 8, 2006, p. 7, available at http://intelligence.senate.gov/phaseiiinc.pdf. (Hereafter, *SSCI Report on the Chalabi Group*.)

191 "which Iraqi opposition members to support": Ibid., p. 8.

191 including from Iranian officials: Ibid., p. 14.

191 "a firestorm in the National Security Council": Ibid., p. 15.

191 "from some groups in the CIA": Ibid., p. 20.

191 "the plan had U.S. support": Ibid., p. 21 (emphasis added).

191 had uncovered this new plan: Ibid.

191 reminiscent of the 1961 Bay of Pigs fiasco: Both Speaker of the U.S. House of Representatives Newt Gingrich and former Under Secretary of Defense for Policy Paul Wolfowitz invoked the Bay of Pigs in their criticism of the CIA's failure in northern Iraq. See Newt Gingrich, "In the Absence of Clarity and Consistency," *Washington Times*, September 23, 1996, p. A17; Testimony of Paul Wolfowitz before the Near Eastern and South Asian Affairs Subcommittee of the U.S. Senate Foreign Relations Committee, September 19, 1996, available through http://www.nexis.com; *Nightline*, ABC News, September 10, 1996 (transcript #3992–1).

192 ". . . CIA asset's three children": Ibid., p. 24. A former CIA official summarizes the story this way:

> One of the principal reasons the clandestine service's Near East Division loathes Chalabi is that he tried to warn [CIA headquarters] that its coup d'état plans with the Iraqi National Accord . . . had been thoroughly pene-

trated by Saddam. . . . When Saddam tore the INA scheme apart, Chalabi became one of [the CIA's] least favorite people.

Reuel Marc Gerecht, "Liberate Iraq," *Weekly Standard*, May 14, 2001, p. 23. See also David Ignatius, "The CIA and the Coup that Wasn't," *Washington Post*, May 16, 2003.

192 negotiated the Oil-for-Food (OFF) Program with Iraq: The Oil-for-Food resolution, passed almost a year earlier, was initially rejected by Iraq. The program was finally implemented with a Memorandum of Understanding that gave Iraq some authority over its administration. UNSCR 986 of April 14, 1995, UN Security Council, available at: http://www2.unog.ch/uncc/resolutio/res0986.pdf. See also President William J. Clinton, *Report to the Congress of the United States on the National Emergency in Iraq*, February 4, 1998, available at http://clinton6.nara.gov/1998/02/1998–02–04-transmittal-to-congress-on-national-emergency-iraq.html.

192 including militarily relevant goods: As far back as September 25, 1996, CIA Director John Deutch told a congressional committee: "Saddam's family profits from covert sales of Iraqi oil and dominance of the black market, where many of the donated medicines and food end up." Testimony of John Deutch before the House Permanent Select Committee on Intelligence, September 25, 1996, available through http://www.nexis.com. Such covert sales were only one of a number of ways that Saddam undermined the Oil-for-Food program. See Claudia Rossett, "Oil, Food and a Whole Lot of Questions," *New York Times*, April 18, 2003, available at http://query.nytimes.com/gst/fullpage.html?res=9401E3DE173AF93BA25757C0A9659C8B63.

192 described the pattern of abuse: Charles Duelfer, Special Advisor to the DCI for Iraqi Weapons of Mass Destruction, Testimony before the Senate Armed Services Committee, October 6, 2004, p. 3, available at http://armed-services.senate.gov/statemnt/2004/October/Duelfer%2010–06–04.pdf. (Hereafter, Duelfer Testimony.)

193 "resolutions passed by the Security Council": Duelfer Testimony, p. 3. See also Woods, et al., *Iraqi Perspectives Project*, pp. 28–29; Claudia Rosett, "What's 'Illegal'?" *Wall Street Journal*, September 22, 2004, available at http://www.opinionjournal.com/columnists/cRosett/?id=110005652; Claudia Rosett, "Oil-for-Terror?" *National Review Online*, April 18, 2004, available at http://www.nationalreview.com/comment/rosett200404182336.asp.

193 "by the end of 1999": Duelfer Report, Vol. I, "Regime Intent": Key Findings.

193 crimped his military supply lines: See Woods, et al., *Iraqi Perspectives Project*, p. 41, available at http://www.jfcom.mil/newslink/storyarchive/2006/ipp.pdf.

194 "while the inspectors were forced to wait": Hans Blix, *Disarming Iraq* (New York: Pantheon, 2004), p. 33.

194 "predict the Commission's inspection activities": The report also cites "outright lying, evasiveness, intimidation, forging of documents, misrepresentation of sites and personnel, the denial of access to individuals and the issue of successive [accounts] that were fraudulent"—as well as "direct evidence of Mukhabarat involvement." United Nations Special Commission (UNSCOM), "Report on Status of Disarmament and Monitoring," January 29, 1999, available at http://www.un.org/Depts/unscom/s99–94.htm.

194 But Saddam was determined to prevent the inspectors: See Woods, et al., *Iraqi Perspectives Project*, pp. 91–95, available at http://www.jfcom.mil/newslink/storyarchive/2006/ipp.pdf.

195 letter to President Clinton signed by eighteen individuals: Project for a New American Century, Open Letter to President Clinton, January 26, 1998, available at http://www.newamericancentury.org/iraqclintonletter.htm. The signers were Elliott Abrams, Richard L. Armitage, William J. Bennett, Jeffrey Bergner, John Bolton, Paula Dobriansky, Francis Fukuyama, Robert Kagan, Zalmay Khalilzad, William Kristol, Richard Perle, Peter W. Rodman, Donald Rumsfeld, William Schneider Jr., Vin Weber, Paul Wolfowitz, R. James Woolsey, and Robert B. Zoellick.

195 another open letter to President Clinton: Committee for Peace and Security in the Gulf, Open Letter to President Clinton, February 19, 1998, available at http://www.iraqwatch.org/perspectives/rumsfeld-openletter.htm.

196 cochaired the sponsoring group: The letter listed the signers as follows: **Hon. Stephen Solarz**, Former Member, Foreign Affairs Committee, U.S. House of Representatives; **Hon. Richard Perle**, Resident Fellow, American Enterprise Institute; Former Assistant Secretary of Defense; **Hon. Elliot Abrams**, President, Ethics & Public Policy Center; Former Assistant Secretary of State; **Richard V. Allen**, Former National Security Advisor; **Hon. Richard Armitage**, President, Armitage Associates, L.C.; Former Assistant Secretary of Defense; **Jeffrey T. Bergner**, President, Bergner, Bockorny, Clough & Brain; Former Staff Director, Senate Foreign Relations Committee; **Hon. John Bolton**, Senior Vice President, American Enterprise Institute; Former Assistant Secretary of State; **Stephen Bryen**, Former Deputy Assistant Secretary of Defense; **Hon. Richard Burt**, Chairman, IEP Advisors, Inc.; Former U.S. Ambassador to Germany; Former Assistant Secretary of State for European Affairs; **Hon. Frank Carlucci**, Former Secretary of Defense; **Hon. Judge William Clark**, Former National Security Advisor; **Paula J. Dobriansky**, Vice President, Director of Washington Office, Council on Foreign Relations; Former Member, National Security Council; **Doug Feith**, Managing Attorney, Feith & Zell P.C.; Former Deputy Assistant Secretary of Defense for Negotiations Policy; **Frank Gaffney**, Director, Center for Security Policy; Former Deputy Assistant Secretary of Defense for Nuclear Forces; **Jeffrey Gedmin**, Executive Director, New Atlantic Initiative; Research Fellow, American Enterprise Institute; **Hon. Fred C. Ikle**, Former Undersecretary of Defense; **Robert Kagan**, Senior Associate, Carnegie Endowment for International Peace; **Zalmay M. Khalilzad**, Director, Strategy and Doctrine, RAND Corporation; **Sven F. Kraemer**, Former Director of Arms Control, National Security Council; **William Kristol**, Editor, The Weekly Standard; **Michael Ledeen**, Resident Scholar, American Enterprise Institute; Former Special Advisor to the Secretary of State; **Bernard Lewis**, Professor Emeritus of Middle Eastern and Ottoman Studies, Princeton University; **R. Admiral Frederick L. Lewis**, U.S. Navy, Retired; **Maj. Gen. Jarvis Lynch**, U.S. Marine Corps, Retired; **Hon. Robert C. McFarlane**, Former National Security Advisor; **Joshua Muravchik**, Resident Scholar, American Enterprise Institute; **Robert A. Pastor**, Former Special Assistant to President Carter for Inter-American Affairs; **Martin Peretz**, Editor-in-Chief, The New Republic; **Roger Robinson**, Former Senior Director of International Economic Affairs, National Security Council; **Peter Rodman**, Director of National Security Programs, Nixon Center for Peace and Freedom; Former Director, Policy Planning Staff, U.S. Department of State; **Hon. Peter Rosenblatt**, Former Ambassador to the Trust Territories of the Pacific; **Hon. Donald Rumsfeld**, Former Secretary of Defense; **Gary Schmitt**, Executive Director, Project for the New American Century; Former Executive Director, President's Foreign Intelligence Advisory Board; **Max Singer**, President, The Potomac Organization; Former President, The Hudson Institute; **Hon. Helmut Sonnenfeldt**, Guest Scholar, The Brookings Institution; Former Counsellor, U.S. Department of State; **Hon. Caspar Weinberger**, Former Secretary of Defense; **Leon Wieseltier**, Literary Editor, The New Republic; **Hon. Paul Wolfowitz**, Dean, Johns Hopkins SAIS; Former Undersecretary of Defense; **David Wurmser**, Director, Middle East Program, AEI; Research Fellow, American Enterprise Institute; **Dov S. Zakheim**, Former Deputy Undersecretary of Defense.

196 $97 million worth of military education and training: Iraq Liberation Act of 1998.

196 "are U.S. policy": *Congressional Record*, 105th Congress, 2nd Session (October 7, 1998), 144 Cong. Rec. Sect. 11812 (emphasis added).

197 "under the current Iraq leadership": Statement by President Clinton on the Iraq Liberation Act, October 31, 1998, White House, available at http://www.clintonfoundation.org/legacy/103198-presidential-statement-on-iraq-liberation-act-of.htm.

197 Chalabi championed the measure on Capitol Hill: See James Risen and Barbara Crossette, "Even U.S. Sees Iraq Opposition as Faint Hope," *New York Times*, November 19, 1998, p. A1.

197 the respect his organization had won: See, e.g.:

- Senator Trent Lott (R-Mississippi): "I have repeatedly stated that the Iraqi National Congress has been effective in the past and can be effective in the future. They represent the broadest possible base of the opposition." Senator Jesse Helms (R-North Carolina): "The bill requires the President to designate an Iraqi opposition group or groups to receive military drawdown assistance. The President need not look far; the Iraqi National Congress once flourished as an umbrella organization for Kurds, Shi'ites and Sunni Muslims. It should flourish again, but it needs our help." "Establishing a Program to Support a Transition to Democracy in Iraq," *Congressional Record*, U.S. Senate, October 7, 1998, pp. S11811–S11812.
- "It is for Iraqis, not Americans to organize themselves to put Saddam Hussein out of power, just as it will be for Iraqis to choose their leaders in a democratic Iraq. This bill will help the Administration encourage and

support Iraqis to make their revolution." Senator Robert Kerrey, http://fas.org/irp/congress/1998_cr/s981007-iraq.htm.

- "The overt support for political activities and broadcasting by opposition forces can have a significant impact inside Iraq. In addition, the committee of conference notes that disparate Kurdish, Shiite, and Sunni groups have in the past been willing to set aside their differences and unite under the umbrella of the Iraqi National Congress (INC) to effectively challenge Saddam Hussein. The committee of conference recommends supporting efforts to reunite these disparate groups under a unified umbrella, whether it be the INC or another opposition group, to present a solid, pro-democracy, Iraqi front against Saddam Hussein." Conference Report, 105th Congress, 2nd Session, 105–432, U.S. House of Representatives, "Foreign Affairs Reform and Restructuring Act," Joint Explanatory Statement of the Committee of Conference, Sec. 1813 Support for Democratic Opposition in Iraq.
- "The managers expect that a significant portion of the support for the democratic opposition should go to the Iraqi National Congress, a group that has demonstrated the capacity to effectively challenge the Saddam Hussein regime with representation from Sunni, Shia, and Kurdish elements in Iraq." Conference Report (to accompany H.R. 3579), 105th Congress, 2nd Session, 105–504, U.S. House of Representatives, "Making Emergency Supplemental Appropriations for the Fiscal Year Ending September 30, 1998, and for Other Purposes," Joint Explanatory Statement of the Committee of Conference, Sec. 10008 Support for Democratic Opposition in Iraq.
- ". . . not less than $8,000,000 shall be made available only for assistance to the Iraqi democratic opposition for such activities as organization, training, communication and dissemination of information, and developing and implementing agreements among opposition groups; . . . Provided further, that of this amount not less than $3,000,000 should be made available as a grant to the Iraqi National Congress, to be administered by its Executive Committee for the benefit of all constituent groups of the Iraqi National Congress. . . ." Conference Report (to accompany H.R. 4328), 105th Congress, 2nd Session, 105–825, U.S. House of Representatives, "Making Omnibus Consolidated and Emergency Supplemental Appropriations for Fiscal Year 1999," Title IV, Sec. 590 Iraq Opposition.

197 the UN Security Council adopted: See United Nations Security Council, Security Council Resolution 1194, September 9, 1998, available at http://www.un.org/Depts/unscom/Keyresolutions/sres98-1194.htm. This resolution unanimously condemned Iraq's decision to suspend cooperation with UNSCOM and called Iraq's actions a totally unacceptable contravention of Iraq's obligations and United

Nations Security Council. Resolution 1205 unanimously condemned Iraq's actions and demanded that Iraq rescind immediately and unconditionally its decision not to cooperate with UNSCOM. (Security Council Resolution 1205, November 5, 1998, available at http://www.un.org/Depts/unscom/Keyresolutions/sres98-1205.htm.) Regarding UNSCOM's withdrawal of its staff from Iraq on December 16, 1998, see United Nations Special Commission, "UNSCOM: Chronology of Main Events," December 1999, available at http://www.un.org/Depts/unscom/Chronology/chronologyframe.htm.

197 "made a mockery of the weapons inspection process": Representative Nancy Pelosi (D-California), "Statement on U.S. Led Military Strike Against Iraq," U.S. House of Representatives, December 16, 1998, available at www.house.gov/pelosi/priraq1.htm. Similar statements were made by other Democratic leaders:

"Iraq is a long way from [here], but what happens there matters a great deal here. For the risks that the leaders of a rogue state will use nuclear, chemical or biological weapons against us or our allies is the greatest security threat we face." Remarks by Secretary of State Madeleine K. Albright at Town Hall Meeting, Ohio State University, February 18, 1998.

"He will use those weapons of mass destruction again, as he has ten times since 1983." Sandy Berger, Clinton National Security Adviser, February 18, 1998.

197 the United Nations Monitoring Verification and Inspection Commission (UNMOVIC): See United Nations Security Council, Security Council Resolution 1284, December 17, 1999, available at http://www.un.org/Depts/unscom/Keyresolutions/sres99-1284.htm. This resolution replaced UNSCOM with UNMOVIC.

198 Iraq's northern and southern no-fly zones: General Myers testified in September 2002 that the aircraft had been fired on 2,300 times in two and a half years. Statement of General Richard B. Myers, Chairman, Joint Chiefs of Staff, "United States Policy Toward Iraq," Hearing before the Committee on Armed Services, U.S. House of Representatives, September 18, 2002, at http://commdocs.house.gov/committees/security/has261000.000/has261000_0f.htm. Aerial inspections also served to uphold UN Resolutions 687, 688, and 949.

199 "that moment cannot come too soon": Gerald Butt, "Saddam Hussein Profile," BBC News, January 4, 2001, available at http://news.bbc.co.uk/1/hi/world/middle_east/1100529.stm.

199 "and were eroding": Blix, *Disarming Iraq*, p. 54.

200 on which the Security Council built its containment strategy: In his September 2002 speech to the UN, President Bush underlined the challenge to the UN itself:

> **The conduct of the Iraqi regime is a threat to the authority of the United Nations, and a threat to peace. Iraq has answered a decade of UN demands with a decade of defiance. All the world now faces a test, and the United Nations a difficult and defining moment. Are Security Council resolutions to be honored and enforced, or cast aside without**

> **consequence? Will the United Nations serve the purpose of its founding, or will it be irrelevant?**

George W. Bush, Speech to United Nations General Assembly, September 12, 2002, available at http://www.whitehouse.gov/news/releases/2002/09/200200912–1.html.

200 for whom CIA officials had particular admiration: George Tenet was one of Allawi's fans:

> **Iyad Allawi was and remains far too independent to be anyone's puppet. He knew his country, he knew the challenges, and he had perhaps the best chance of bringing order out of the chaos that had become Iraq. In the end he had to fight various sectarian opponents to achieve success. The fight proved too hard; to my mind, it was a loss. But that can be said about Iraq in general, too.**

George Tenet with Bill Harlow, *At the Center of the Storm* (New York: HarperCollins, 2007), p. 444.

210 our own memo, which we sent him on July 26: Feith memo to Rumsfeld, "Moving Ahead on Iraq," July 26, 2001, which included a draft memo from Wolfowitz to Hadley with the same title (emphasis in original).

210 July 27, Rumsfeld signed it out to Rice, Powell, and Cheney: Rumsfeld memo to Rice on "Iraq," July 27, 2001. Reproduced at Appendix 3.

210 "but [I]f not, it isn't": Rumsfeld wanted to force a government-wide reassessment of the no-fly zones—the Defense Department's element of the broader strategy of containment. Unlike the State Department, which continued to support its eroding economic sanctions policy, Defense was unwilling to prolong an exercise that was elaborate, costly, and dangerous but not actually consequential.

CHAPTER 7: RISKS OF ACTION AND INACTION

215 No one I know of believed Saddam was part of the 9/11 plot: The Administration did not claim that Iraq had sponsored or supported the attacks of 9/11. Both Tenet and Cheney called attention to the record of Saddam's interaction with al Qaida as signaling *potential future collaboration*. According to Cheney:

> **We learned more and more that there was a relationship between Iraq and al-Qaeda that stretched back through most of the decade of the '90s, that it involved training, for example, on BW and CW, that al-Qaeda sent personnel to Baghdad to get trained on the systems that are involved. The Iraqis providing bomb-making expertise and advice to the al-Qaeda organization.**
>
> **We know, for example, in connection with the original World Trade Center bombing in '93 that one of the bombers was Iraqi, returned to Iraq after the attack of '93. And we've learned subsequent to that, since**

> **we went into Baghdad and got into the intelligence files, that this individual probably also received financing from the Iraqi government as well as safe haven.**
>
> **. . . The Czechs alleged that Mohamed Atta, the lead attacker, met in Prague with a senior Iraqi intelligence official five months before the attack, but we've never been able to develop anymore of that yet either in terms of confirming it or discrediting it. We just don't know.**

Tim Russert interview with Dick Cheney, *Meet the Press*, September 14, 2003, available at: http://www.msnbc.msn.com/id/3080244/. Historians will be hard-pressed to find substantial support for the current widespread belief that Cheney (or other Administration officials) hammered on the Iraq–al Qaida connection. Tenet told the U.S. Senate:

> **Iraq is harboring senior members of a terrorist network led by Abu Musab al-Zarqawi, a close associate of al Qaeda. . . . Iraq has in the past provided training in document forgery and bomb-making to al Qaeda. It has also provided training in poisons and gases to two al Qaeda associates. One of these associates characterized the relationship he forged with Iraqi officials as successful. . . . I know that part of this—and part of this Zarqawi network in Baghdad are two dozen Egyptian Islamic jihad which is indistinguishable from al Qaeda—operatives who are aiding the Zarqawi network, and two senior planners who have been in Baghdad since last May. Now, whether there is a base or whether there is not a base, they are operating freely, supporting the Zarqawi network that is supporting the poisons network in Europe and around the world. . . . And it is inconceivable to us that the Iraqi intelligence service doesn't know that they live there or what they're doing.**

George Tenet, Testimony before Senate Select Committee on Intelligence, February 11, 2003.

215 dealing with terrorists and terrorist organizations: The Fedayeen Saddam opened camps in 1994 to train thousands of volunteers, "graduating more than 7,200 . . . in the first year." Beginning in 1998, the Fedayeen also trained "Arab volunteers from Egypt, Palestine, Jordan, 'the Gulf,' and Syria" (quotation from a captured Iraqi regime document). Where the Arab volunteers went after their training remains unclear. The Fedayeen had assistance from the Iraqi Intelligence Service, whose Division 27 "supplied the Fedayeen Saddam with silencers, equipment for booby-trapping vehicles, special training on the use of certain explosive devices, special molds for explosives, and a variety of explosive timers. . . . The only apparent use for all of this Division 27 equipment was to conduct commando or terrorist operations." Woods, et al., *The Iraqi Perspectives Project*, p. 54, available at http://www.jfcom.mil/newslink/storyarchive/2006/ipp.pdf.

216 expectation of further major terrorist attacks remained widespread: See

Karlyn Bowman, *AEI Studies in Public Opinion: America and the War on Terrorism,* updated November 29, 2007, available at www.aei.org/publications/pubID.22819/pub_detail.asp.

217 "dire consequences of a BW attack" : "Dark Winter—Bioterrorism Simulation Exercise," developed and produced by Center for Strategic and International Studies, Washington, D.C., Johns Hopkins Center for Civilian Biodefense Studies, ANSER Institute for Homeland Security, conducted June 22–23, 2001. Among the participants: former senator Sam Nunn (D-Georgia), former Governor of Oklahoma Frank Keating, former CIA Director James Woolsey, former FBI Director William Sessions, and former Deputy Secretary of Defense John White. Report available at http://www.upmc-biosecurity.org/website/events/2001_darkwinter/index.html (italics in original).

217 We knew Saddam's weapons scientists had been researching: "ISG concludes that Iraq intended to develop smallpox . . . as potential BW weapons. . . . ISG assesses that Iraq maintained the capability in its personnel and basic equipment to conduct R&D into viral agents including smallpox." Duelfer Report, Vol. IIIB, "Biological Warfare," available at http://www.cia.gov/library/reports/general-reports-1/iraq_wmd_2004/chap6.html. (Hereafter Duelfer Report, IIIB.)

218 had done work on anthrax: Duelfer Report, IIIB, pp. 5, 10. The FBI initially asserted that the anthrax spores had been produced in a U.S. government laboratory, but in September 2006 the FBI investigation was extended to include international and nongovernment sources. Allan Lengel and Joby Warrick, "FBI Is Casting a Wider Net in Anthrax Attacks," *Washington Post,* September 25, 2006, available at http://www.washingtonpost.com/wp-dyn/content/article/2006/09/24/AR2006092401014_pf.html.

219 for Iraqi democratic opposition groups: Feith Memo to Rumsfeld, Action Plan for Next Steps on Possible Moves on Iraq, November 8, 2001.

220 gave the Secretary a set of rough notes: Typewritten notes by Feith labeled "Iraq war planning focus on WMD," November 27, 2001, annotated in pen by Rumsfeld. Rumsfeld's annotations borrowed points from an earlier Wolfowitz markup of this draft. This was typical of way ideas were exchanged within Rumsfeld's inner circle.

222 had generally agreed since the mid-1990s: The following are representative examples:

- "There is no doubt that . . . Saddam Hussein has invigorated his weapons programs. Reports indicate that biological, chemical and nuclear programs continue apace and may be back to pre-Gulf War status." Letter to President Bush, signed by Senator Bob Graham (D-Florida) and others, December 5, 2001.
- "We begin with the common belief that Saddam Hussein is a tyrant and a threat to the peace and stability of the region. He has ignored the mandate of the United Nations and is building weapons of mass destruction and the means of delivering them." Senator Carl Levin (D-Michigan), September 19, 2002.

- "Iraq's search for weapons of mass destruction has proven impossible to deter and we should assume that it will continue for as long as Saddam is in power." Al Gore, September 23, 2002, speech before the Commonwealth Club of San Francisco, available at http://www.washingtonpost.com/wp-srv/politics/transcripts/gore_text092302.html.
- "We have known for many years that Saddam Hussein is seeking and developing weapons of mass destruction." Senator Ted Kennedy (D-Massachusetts), September 27, 2002.
- "According to the CIA's report, all U.S. intelligence experts agree that Iraq is seeking nuclear weapons. There is little question that Saddam Hussein wants to develop nuclear weapons." Senator John Kerry (D-Massachusetts), *Congressional Record,* October 9, 2002, pp. S10172–S10173.

223 shooting at the patrol aircraft almost every day: General Myers reported that the patrol aircraft had been fired on 2,300 times in two and a half years. "United States Policy Toward Iraq," Hearing before the Committee on Armed Services, U.S. House of Representatives, September 18, 2002, available at http://commdocs.house.gov/committees/security/has261000.000/has261000_0f.htm.)

224 "the rationale for this work was not given": The Iraq Survey Group determined that camel pox research was "a surrogate for smallpox research." Duelfer Report, Biological Warfare.

224 produce his own fissile material domestically: U.S. Central Intelligence Agency, National Intelligence Estimate, "Iraq's Continuing Programs for Mass Destruction," October 2002, p. 5 (approved for release April 2004), available at http://www.dni.gov/nic/special_keyjudgements.html. (Hereafter, National Intelligence Estimate, October 2002.)

226 "decided to do so": *UNSCOM Report,* paragraph 41.

226 "if Iraq has done so": U.S. Central Intelligence Agency, "Unclassified Report to Congress on the Acquisition of Technology Relating to Weapons of Mass Destruction and Advanced Conventional Munitions, 1 July through 31 December 1999," available at https://www.cia.gov/library/reports/archived-reports-1/july_dec1999.htm. The CIA website http://www.odci.gov/cia/2000wn_archive.html gives its publication date as August 9, 2000.

226 "*at any time, if needed*": U.S. Central Intelligence Agency, "Unclassified Report to Congress on the Acquisition of Technology Relating to Weapons of Mass Destruction and Advanced Conventional Munitions, 1 January through 30 June 2000" (emphasis added), https://www.cia.gov/library/reports/archived-reports-1/jan_jun2000.htm. The CIA website http://www.odci.gov/cia/2001wn_archive.html gives its publication date as February 23, 2001.

226 "no evidence Iraq used this capability for BW production": Duelfer Report, IIIB, p. 38, available at https://www.cia.gov/library/reports/general-reports-1/iraq_wmd_2004/index.html.

226 "4 to 5 weeks after the decision to do so": Ibid.

227 "2 to 3 weeks after the decision to do so": Ibid., p. 42. The Iraqi Perspectives Project concluded: "Even when viewed through the post-war lens, documentary evidence of messages are consistent with the Iraqi Survey Group's conclusion that Saddam was at least keeping a WMD program primed for a quick re-start the moment the UN Security Council lifted sanctions." Woods, et al., *Iraqi Perspectives Project*, p. 95, available at http://www.jfcom.mil/newslink/storyarchive/2006/ipp.pdf.)

227 "lay the foundations of a BW program": Duelfer Report, IIIB, pp. 2, 5 (italics in original).

227 active rather than dormant: "We judge that all key aspects—R&D, production, and weaponization—of Iraq's offensive BW program are active and that most elements are larger and more advanced than they were before the Gulf War. We judge Iraq has some lethal and incapacitating BW agents and is capable of quickly producing and weaponizing a variety of such agents, including anthrax, for delivery by bombs, missiles, aerial sprayers, and covert operatives. . . . Saddam probably has stocked at least 100 metric tons (MT) and possibly as much as 500 MT of CW agents—much of it added in the last year." *NIE October* 2002, p. 6.

228 Silberman-Robb Commission criticized the CIA: See Commission on the Intelligence Capabilities of the United States Regarding Weapons of Mass Destruction, *Report to the President of the United States*, March 31, 2005 (Washington, D.C.: Government Printing Office, 2005), p. 158, available at http://www.wmd.gov/report/. (Hereafter, Silberman-Robb Commission.)

CHAPTER 8: DISCORD IN WASHINGTON

232 North Korea or another outside source: Iran had already bought ballistic missiles from North Korea. See Lionel Beehner, "The Impact of North Korea's Nuclear Test on Iran Crisis," Council on Foreign Relations, October 13, 2006, available at http://www.cfr.org/publication/11712/impact_of_north_koreas_nuclear_test_on_iran_crisis.html#7.

232 killed more Americans than any other terrorist group: See U.S. Department of State, Bureau of Near Eastern Affairs, "Background Note: Lebanon," August 2005, available at http://www.state.gov/r/pa/ei/bgn/35833.htm. See also Office of the Coordinator for Counterterrorism, U.S. Department of State, *Country Reports on Terrorism 2005*, April 2006, p. 198, available at http://www.state.gov/documents/organization/65463.pdf.

233 independent of U.S. pressure: President Bush was willing to proclaim America's sympathy for Iranians aspiring to freedom, but he was sensitive to the danger of making the Iranian people's dislike appear to be a movement created or fed by support from the United States.

234 spread democracy by the sword: See, e.g., Gerard Baker, "Bush's vision of free world will keep the neocon faith alive," *The Times* (London), November 6, 2004; Francis Fukuyama, *America at the Crossroads: Democracy, Power, and the Neoconservative Legacy* (New Haven: Yale University Press), 2007.

235 that are not both democratic: There is a grand debate among scholars over democratic war theory. It seems to me that much of the debate involves taking issue with overstatements. One such overstatement is that democracies never fight each other. Another, the converse, is that war is no less likely among democracies than among nondemocracies.

238 No one asserted that the risks of leaving Saddam in power: See Richard Armitage interview, *Charlie Rose,* December 10, 2004, available at http://www.state.gov/s/d/former/armitage/remarks/39973.htm.

238 general rationale for regime change in Iraq: The accompanying quotes may be found in *Congressional Record,* 107th Congress, 2nd Session, Vol. 148, No. 133 (October 10, 2002), available at http://frwebgate.access.gpo.gov/cgi-bin/getpage.cgi?dbname=2002_record&page=S10233&position=all.

238 a dangerous force in the world: Ibid.

239 a terrible danger to the people of the United States: Ibid.

239 This much is undisputed: Senator Hillary Clinton, "October 10, 2002, Floor Speech of Senator Hillary Rodham Clinton on S.J. Res. 45, A Resolution to Authorize the Use of United States Armed Forces Against Iraq," available at http://clinton.senate.gov/speeches/iraq_101002.html.

240 as supporters of Chalabi: Chalabi's support within the Pentagon was, in fact, rather restrained. His main champion was Richard Perle, who chaired the Defense Advisory Board but was not involved in official interagency policy deliberations or decisions. I had met Chalabi half a dozen times at most, both before and after I became Under Secretary, and I respected his intellect and his advocacy of freedom for Iraq. Wolfowitz had known Chalabi since the mid-1990s and admired his talents. But neither Wolfowitz (as far as I know) nor I ever argued for naming him the ruler of Iraq. Rumsfeld recalls meeting Chalabi briefly at a conference in the 1990s. According to Pentagon office records, he did not meet with him for a conversation until January 2004—nine months after Saddam's overthrow—at a one-hour lunch he hosted for a number of Iraqi leaders including Adnan Pachachi, Abdulaziz al-Hakim, Hoshyar Zebari, Jalal Talabani, and Chalabi. The only other meeting between Rumsfeld and Chalabi was on November 14, 2005, and it lasted thirty minutes. Chalabi was on good terms with officials at the National Security Council staff and the office of the Vice President.

240 who had fallen out with Saddam: See Congressional Research Service, "Iraq: U.S. Regime Change Efforts and Post-War Governance," October 10, 2003, available at http://fpc.state.gov/documents/organization/25433.pdf:

> The INA, originally founded in 1990 with Saudi support, consists of military and security defectors who were perceived as having ties to disgruntled officials currently serving within their former organizations. It is headed by Dr. Iyad Alawi, former president of the Iraqi Student Union in Europe and a physician by training. He is a secular Shiite Muslim, but most of the members of the INA are Sunni Muslims.

240 Congress had recognized the INC as a coordinating body: See note "the respect his organization had won" for p. 197.

244 to review the INC's finances: See U.S. Department of State and the Broadcasting Board of Governors Office of Inspector General, *Follow Up Review of Iraqi National Congress Support Foundation*, Report Number AUD/CG-02–44, September 2002, p. 4, available at http://oig.state.gov/documents/organization/15006.pdf#search=%22follow%20up%20review%20of%20iraqi%20national%20congress%20support%20foundation%22.

244 recommendations to resolve the problems: See U.S. Department of State and the Broadcasting Board of Governors Office of Inspector General, *Review of Awards to Iraqi National Congress Support Foundation*, Report Number 01-FMA-R-092, September 2001, pp. 1–2, 12, available at http://oig.state.gov/documents/organization/7508.pdf#search=%22follow%20up%20review%20of%20iraqi%20national%20congress%20support%20foundation%22.

245 Powell came to be seen . . . as opposing regime change: One article claims that Powell, on the eve of his UN speech, "had argued against the war for months." Bryan Burrough, Evgenia Peretz, David Rose, and David Wise, "The Path to War," *Vanity Fair*, May 2004, p. 230. Another asserts that "inside the foreign-policy, defense and intelligence agencies, nearly the whole rank and file, along with many senior officials, are opposed to invading Iraq. But because the less than two dozen neoconservatives leading the war party have the support of Vice President Dick Cheney and Secretary of Defense Donald Rumsfeld, they are able to marginalize that opposition." Robert Dreyfuss, "The Pentagon Muzzles the CIA: Devising bad intelligence to promote bad policy," *The American Prospect*, December 16, 2002, p. 26. Regarding assertions of CIA opposition to the war, see John B. Judis and Spencer Ackerman, "Selling of the Iraq War: The First Casualty," *The New Republic*, June 30, 2003.

246 a solution other than war: For example: "Secretary of State Colin Powell, the most dovish member of the Bush Cabinet." Barbara Slavin and Bill Nichols, "U.S. Says Omissions Put Iraq in 'Material Breach,'" *USA Today*, December 20, 2002.

246 urgency of the threat: Powell, as Secretary of State, had his own intelligence office, known as the Bureau of Intelligence and Research, which did not dispute the basic intelligence community consensus that Iraq had chemical and biological weapons stockpiles. (That bureau did, however, dispute the view of the CIA and others that the famous interdicted aluminum tubes were for uranium enrichment.) See National Intelligence Estimate, October 2002.

246 "a good time to begin the attack": Michael R. Gordon and General Bernard E. Trainor, *Cobra II: The Inside Story of the Invasion and Occupation of Iraq* (New York: Pantheon, 2006), p. 72.

247 chemical and biological weapons stockpiles: See Armitage interview, *Charlie Rose*, December 10 2004, available at http://www.state.gov/s/d/former/armitage/remarks/39973.htm:

MR. ROSE: Did you have reservations about Iraq?

DEPUTY SECRETARY ARMITAGE: Not about the need to take down Saddam Hussein. To the extent I had any questions, it was only about the timing, but not about the proposition.

MR. ROSE: You might have preferred a delay for a while to let inspections continue?

DEPUTY SECRETARY ARMITAGE: I was one who thought that there would be weapons of mass destruction, like everyone else . . .

247 not a fully invested member of the President's team: Rick Atkinson, *Crusade: The Untold Story of the Persian Gulf War* (New York: Houghton Mifflin, 1993), p. 122.

247 as reluctant warrior in the George W. Bush Administration: Senator Robert Byrd summarized Powell's role as "being a good soldier." "Interview with Robert Byrd," *Larry King Live,* CNN, March 7, 2003, available at http://transcripts.cnn.com/TRANSCRIPTS/0303/07/lkl.00.html.

248 had been too timid: Bob Woodward, *Plan of Attack* (New York: Simon and Schuster, 2004), p. 151.

248 "and becoming the occupiers": Sarah Baxter, "Powell tried to talk Bush out of war," *Sunday Times* (London), July 8, 2007, available at http://www.timesonline.co.uk/tol/news/world/us_and_americas/article2042072.ece.

248 "My job is to be strategic": Woodward, *Plan of Attack,* p. 152.

249 the World Economic Forum in Davos, Switzerland: See U.S. Department of State website listing of Powell's foreign travels, available at http://www.state.gov/secretary/former/powell/travels/index.htm.

249 George Shultz's State Department: See George Bush and Brent Scowcroft, *A World Transformed* (New York: Alfred A. Knopf, Inc., 1998), pp. 18–19.

250 leaking their criticisms of the President: Examples of anonymous State Department and CIA criticisms abound: See, e.g., Glenn Kessler, "U.S. Decision on Iraq Has Puzzling Past: Opponents of War Wonder When, How Policy was Set," *Washington Post,* January 12, 2003, p. A1; Gerard Baker and Stephen Fidler, "The best-laid plans? How turf battles and mistakes in Washington dragged down the reconstruction of Iraq," *Financial Times,* August 4, 2003, p. 15; Anonymous, "The State Department's Extreme Makeover," Salon.com, October 4, 2004, available at http://dir.salon.com/story/opinion/feature/2004/10/04/foggybottom/index_np.html; Seymour M. Hersh, "Manhunt," *The New Yorker,* December 23, 2002, p. 66; Bryan Burrough, "The Path to War," *Vanity Fair,* May 2004, p. 228.

252 to "avoid a political vacuum" in Iraq: Rodman memo to Rumsfeld, "Support for Iraqi Opposition," May 9, 2002.

253 and perhaps violent resistance: The likelihood that a prolonged occupation government would engender violent resistance was recognized by everyone. It was a theme of another State Department paper ("Diplomatic Plan for the Day After," [undated], discussed in Chapter 9), and it was flagged (though not emphasized as a key finding) in the CIA's intelligence summary, "Principal Challenges in Post-

Saddam Iraq," reprinted in U.S. Senate, Select Committee on Intelligence, *Report on the U.S. Intelligence Community's Prewar Intelligence Assessments on Iraq*, July 7, 2004, as Appendix B: National Intelligence Council, "Principal Challenges in Post-Saddam Iraq," January 2003. CENTCOM included the point prominently, as the third and last "Don't" of its Phase IV planning: "Don't . . . Create any appearance of occupying Iraq." United States Central Command, Phase IV IPB, as of March 1, 2003, p. 60 (cited in *SSCI Report on Prewar Intelligence on Postwar Iraq*, May 2007, p. 97).

253 "and effectively neutralize the Communists": Rumsfeld Memo to Cheney, Powell, Tenet, and Rice, "Supporting the Iraqi Opposition," July 1, 2002.

254 "*only the I.N.C. can lead the opposition*": Seymour M. Hersh, "The Debate Within," *The New Yorker*, March 4, 2002 (emphasis added), available at http://www.newyorker.com/fact/content/articles/020311fa_FACT.

254 "efforts to put Chalabi in charge": Tenet, *At the Center of the Storm*, p. 419. Despite a career of sifting and weighing evidence, Tenet provides no supporting evidence for this claim.

254 whether Chalabi or anyone else: "Asked about the status of Ahmad Chalabi, the leader of the Iraqi National Congress, who is often seen as a political favorite of Wolfowitz and other neoconservatives, the Pentagon official said this: 'We ought to be supporting everyone who can do something useful. I think the decision has been made to support democracy and a big tent.'" David Ignatius, "'Wolfowitz's War': Not Over Yet," *Washington Post*, May 13, 2003. A remarkable aspect of the "anoint-Chalabi" myth is the credence it received throughout the media, in spite of the lack of evidence. The explanation may be that the source was someone whose word was taken as sufficient authority, with no need of corroboration.

255 selecting particular leaders for Iraq: Contemporary news stories quoted Rumsfeld, Wolfowitz, and me on this question: "Mr Rumsfeld denied he had ever endorsed Mr Chalabi. 'If anyone has attributed anything to me about that, it's inaccurate,' he said. . . . 'The Iraqi people are going to sort out what their Iraqi government ought to look like.' " Guy Dinmore, "Opposition leader's role 'no guarantee of power'" *Financial Times*, April 8, 2003, p. 7.

Alan Beattie and Roula Khalaf ("U.S. 'aims for a legitimate Iraqi government'," *Financial Times*, April 7, 2003, p. 4) reports that Wolfowitz emphasized that the Iraqis should choose their own leaders. Peter Slevin ("U.S. Won't Install Iraqi Expatriates; Inclusive Interim Authority Is Pledged," *Washington Post*, April 5, 2003, p. A28) quotes me as saying, "Our intention is not to be picking and choosing among Iraqis but arranging a platform on which Iraqi leaders can emerge by some natural process."

255 "every one of the opposition leaders": Interview with General Jay Garner, in "Truth, War and Consequences," *Frontline*, Public Broadcasting System, July 17, 2003, available at http://www-c.pbs.org/wgbh/pages/frontline/shows/truth/interviews/garner.html. Curiously, Garner elsewhere mentions, as a generally known fact, that Chalabi was a favored candidate of Wolfowitz and me—though he does not claim that Wolfowitz or I, or anyone else, ever tried to get Garner to favor him. Interview with General Jay Garner, in "The Lost Year in Iraq," *Frontline*, Public Broadcasting System, August 11, 2006, available at http://www-c.pbs.org/wgbh/pages/frontline/yeariniraq/interviews/garner.html.)

255 working on a pro-Chalabi plot: The absence of any such direction to Garner was noted, but quickly discounted, in one journalist's account:

> **Rumsfeld, Wolfowitz, and Doug Feith did not tell Garner how to manage the political transition. Garner assumed that all three favored a dominant role for exiled leaders, particularly Chalabi, in a transitional government. But the Pentagon trio worried that an order to Garner to hand over authority to the exiles would have made its way back to the State Department and sparked a new debate within the Bush Administration.**

Rajiv Chandrasekaran, *Imperial Life in the Emerald City* (New York: Alfred A. Knopf, 2006), pp. 51–52.

256 "crawling their way back": Hersh, "The Debate Within."

256 "contributing to liberating their country": State Department paper, "The Iraqi Opposition," [undated], distributed at a Deputies Lunch meeting on June 6, 2002.

258 tap some of the remaining funds: The $97 million was to be used for defense articles, defense services, and military education and training for "Iraqi democratic opposition organizations." President Clinton limited the training to "non-lethal" skills. See William J. Clinton, "Memorandum on Assistance to the Iraqi National Congress," October 29, 1999, Presidential Determination No. 2000–05, available at: http://frwebgate1.access.gpo.gov/cgi-bin/waisgate.cgi?WAISdocID=72534987701+3+0+0&WAISaction=retrieve; Secretary of Defense William Cohen Memorandum for Secretaries of the Military Departments and Directors of the Defense Agencies, May 2, 2000, "Support for the Implementation of the Iraq Liberation Act."

259 "the consequences of which are hard to judge": Acheson, *Present at the Creation: My Years in the State Department*, p. 22.

260 devoted to WMD-related matters: "After 1998, the CIA had no dedicated unilateral sources in Iraq reporting on Iraq's nuclear, biological, and chemical program; indeed, the CIA had only a handful of Iraqi assets in total as of 2001." See also U.S. Senate, Select Committee on Intelligence, *Report on the U.S. Intelligence Community's Prewar Intelligence Assessments on Iraq*, July 7, 2004, p. 263, available at http://intelligence.senate.gov/108301.pdf. (Hereafter, *SSCI Report on Iraq Prewar Intelligence*.) ("Committee staff asked why the CIA had not considered placing a CIA officer in the years before Operation Iraqi Freedom to investigate Iraq's WMD programs. A CIA officer said, 'because it's very hard to sustain. . . .'")

260 "one of the United States' top intelligence priorities": Silberman-Robb Commission, p. 157.

260 would not cooperate with al Qaida: The Silberman-Robb report specifically faults the CIA's reporting on Iraq's BW program for creating the impression that its assessment was "more broadly based than was in fact the case" (see discussion in Chapter 10).

260 styled in his own handwriting: See U.S. Central Intelligence Agency, *The World Factbook,* available at https://www.cia.gov/cia/publications/factbook/flags/iz-flag.html. See also Sonni Efron and Sebastian Rotella, "Saddam profile," in *Los Angeles Times,* available at http://ktla.trb.com/sports/sns-iraqprofile-hussein-lat,0,677490.story. The profile cites former CIA Director James Woolsey's observation that the inscription on the Iraq flag was in Saddam Hussein's handwriting.

260 in a *Foreign Affairs* article: Pillar, "Intelligence, Policy, and the War in Iraq," p. 15.

261 even chemical and biological weapons, into Afghanistan: Jeffrey Goldberg, "The Great Terror: In northern Iraq, there is new evidence of Saddam Hussein's genocidal war on the Kurds—and of his possible ties to Al Qaeda," *The New Yorker,* March 25, 2002, p. 52.

262 by the CIA's own analysts: An account of the intelligence gathered in northern Iraq was given to Bob Woodward for his book *Plan of Attack.* Woodward notes that the CIA confirmed the connection between Ansar and al Qaida, but he does not mention that the debriefings also supported the PUK's initial charges that the *Iraqi regime* cooperated with Ansar al-Islam, an al Qaida affiliate. Nor does he mention that the CIA had resisted the mission for months. Woodward, *Plan of Attack,* p. 141.

262 CIA in fact had very few American personnel at all in Iraq: The *SSCI Report on Iraq Prewar Intelligence* states (p. 25):

> **Intelligence Community HUMINT efforts against a closed society like Iraq prior to Operation Iraqi Freedom were hobbled by the Intelligence Community's dependence on having an official U.S. presence in-country to mount clandestine HUMINT collection efforts.**
>
> **When UN inspectors departed Iraq, the placement of HUMINT agents and the development of unilateral sources inside Iraq were not top priorities for the Intelligence Community. The Intelligence Community did not have a single HUMINT source collecting against Iraq's weapons of mass destruction programs in Iraq after 1998. The Intelligence Community appears to have decided that the difficulty and risks inherent in developing sources or inserting operations officers into Iraq outweighed the potential benefits.**

The Silberman-Robb Commission notes (pp. 157–158):

> **We had precious little human intelligence, and virtually no useful signals intelligence, on a target that was one of the United States' top intelligence priorities. The preceding sections, which have focused on the Intelligence Community's assessments on particular aspects of Iraq's weapons programs, have tended to reflect shortcomings in what is com-**

monly referred to as "tradecraft"; the focus has been on questions such as whether a critical human source was properly validated, or whether analysts drew unduly sweeping inferences from limited or dubious intelligence. But it should not be forgotten why these tradecraft failures took on such extraordinary importance. They were important because of how little additional information our collection agencies managed to provide on Iraq's weapons programs.

This was a problem the Intelligence Community saw coming. As early as September 1998, the Community recognized its limited collection on Iraq. The National Intelligence Council noted these limits in 1998, the specifics of which cannot be discussed in an unclassified forum. Yet the Intelligence Community was still unwilling—or unable—to take steps necessary to improve its capabilities after late 1998. In short, as one senior policy maker described it, the Intelligence Community after 1998 "was running on fumes," depending on "inference and assumptions rather than hard data."

262 impression that diligent efforts had been made to uncover such evidence: See, e.g., James Risen and David Johnston, "Split at C.I.A. and F.B.I. on Iraqi Ties to Al Qaeda," *New York Times*, February 2, 2003, p. 13.

263 The CIA officials . . . overstated or erred about other political and military matters before the Iraq war: The CIA failed to warn (for example) that Baathists would remain a significant factor after Saddam's overthrow. A CIA report stated that "we expect the Ba'th Party to collapse with the regime. . . . [It] lacks ideological coherence or organizational autonomy." CIA, *Iraq: The Day After*, October 18, 2002, p. 1 (cited in *SSCI Report on Prewar Intelligence on Postwar Iraq*, May 2007, p. 100).

263 CIA officials reacted to criticism by going on the offensive: See David Brooks, "The C.I.A. versus Bush," *New York Times*, November 13, 2004; Douglas Jehl, "C.I.A-White House Tensions Are Unusually Public," *New York Times*, October 2, 2004.

264 members of Congress persist in asserting it: See, e.g., Peter Spiegel, "Report outlines Pentagon effort to link Iraq, al Qaeda. Declassified memo shows how officials shaped intelligence," *San Francisco Chronicle*, April 6, 2007. See also Senator Carl Levin's comments that Pentagon "intelligence" work "which was wrong, which was distorted, which was inappropriate . . . is something which is highly disturbing." Robert Burns, "Levin: Investigation says Pentagon Manipulated Intelligence," *Chicago Tribune*, February 9, 2007.

264 My office initiated a project: This project was the brainchild of Kenneth deGraffenreid, whom I had hired as my deputy to run the office that served as liaison with the intelligence community.

264 "playing into the hands of people like Wolfowitz": Eric Edelman, "Comments by the Office of the Under Secretary of Defense on a Draft of a Proposed

Report by the DOD Office of Inspector General Project no. D2006DINTOl-0077.000 Review of Pre-Iraqi War Activities of the Office of the Under Secretary of Defense for Policy," January 16, 2007, available at http://www.dod.mil/policy/downloads/OUSDP_Comments_on_Official_Draft_OIG_Review.pdf.

265 a disturbingly unprofessional comment: The analyst's comment, while unprofessional, is not unprecedented. Former CIA Director (and current Secretary of Defense) Robert Gates described the phenomenon almost twenty years ago—in circumstances remarkably similar to those of the debates over the Iraq–al Qaida relationship:

> It is no surprise that few policymakers welcome CIA information or analysis that directly or by implication challenges the adequacy of their chosen policies or the accuracy of their pronouncements. . . . On the other hand, I concede that on more than a few occasions, policymakers have analyzed or forecast developments better than intelligence analysts. And, truth be known, analysts have sometimes gone overboard to prove a policymaker wrong. When Secretary of State Alexander Haig asserted that the Soviets were behind international terrorism, intelligence analysts initially set out, not to address the issue in all its aspects, but rather to prove the secretary wrong—to prove simply that the Soviets do not orchestrate all international terrorism. But in so doing they went too far themselves and failed in early drafts to describe extensive and well-documented indirect Soviet support for terrorist groups and their sponsors. Far from kowtowing to policymakers, there is sometimes a strong impulse on the part of intelligence officers to show that a policy or decision is misguided or wrong, to poke an analytical finger in the policy eye. Policymakers know this and understandably resent it.

Gates, "The CIA and American Foreign Policy," p. 221.

265 such nonrigorous, prejudicial terminology: For Shelton's summary of methods used by intelligence officials to discount the credibility of the 1990s reporting on the Iraq–al Qaida relationship, see Christina Shelton, "Iraq, al-Qaeda and Tenet's Equivocation," *Washington Post,* June 30, 2007, p. A21.

267 Shelton and Carney spoke well: Conflicting versions of this briefing may be found in Tenet, *At the Center of the Storm,* pp. 346–349, and Christina Shelton, "Iraq, al-Qaeda, and Tenet's Equivocation," p. A21.

267 dating from the early 1990s: *SSCI Report on Iraq Prewar Intelligence,* p. 314. The report went on to describe the underlying information:

> . . . The CIA provided 78 reports, from multiple sources, [] documenting instances in which the Iraqi regime either trained operatives for attacks or dispatched them to carry out attacks. Each of the reports provided by the CIA was accurately reflected in *Iraqi Support for Terrorism*

> **and the majority of them were summarized as examples to support the CIA's assessment.**

Ibid., p. 315.

Tenet testified on February 11, 2003, about training provided by Iraqi intelligence for al Qaida associates:

> **Iraq has in the past provided training in document forgery and bomb-making to al-Qaida. It has also provided training in poisons and gases to two al-Qaida associates. One of these associates characterized the relationship he forged with Iraqi officials as successful.**

Ibid., p. 329.

268 **trying to politicize the intelligence:** See, e.g., James Risen, "Prewar Views of Iraq Threat Are Under Review by CIA," *New York Times*, May 22, 2003, p. A1; Walter Pincus and Dana Priest, "Some Iraq Analysts Felt Pressure from Cheney Visits," *Washington Post*, June 5, 2003, p. A1; Pillar, "Intelligence, Policy, and the War in Iraq."

269 **did *not* pressure intelligence officials to politicize the intelligence:** The *SSCI Report on Iraq Prewar Intelligence* notes:

> **The Committee did not find any evidence that Administration officials attempted to coerce, influence or pressure analysts to change their judgements related to Iraq's weapons of mass destruction capabilities (p. 284).**
>
> **Committee staff also conducted interviews with IC analysts regarding their interaction with staffers from the Office of the Under Secretary of Defense for Policy (OUSDP), particularly in the coordination of the September 2002 version of *Iraqi Support for Terrorism*. . . . Although IC analysts considered the attendance of OUSDP staffers at the meeting unusual, all of the meeting attendees interviewed by the Committee staff (eight of the twelve individuals) agreed that the OUSDP staffers were not given special treatment and their attendance contributed to a frank exchange of opinions. . . . Each analyst, as well as the meeting's chairman, indicated the OUSDP staffer "played by IC rules" in terms of their participation. In other words, each point that was raised was discussed, debated, and incorporated only if there was agreement around the table (pp. 361–363).**
>
> **Conclusion 102. The Committee found that none of the analysts or other people interviewed by the Committee said that they were pressured to change their conclusions related to Iraq's links to terrorism. . . . All of the participants in the August 2002 coordination meeting on the September 2002 version of *Iraqi Support for Terrorism* interviewed by the Committee agreed that while some changes were made to the paper as a result of the participation of two Office of the Under Secretary of**

> **Defense for Policy staffers, their presence did not result in changes to their analytical judgments (p. 363).**

269 stories about pressure to come forward: Regarding the Committee's advertising for analysts to come forward with any information they had about politicization or improper pressure, see *SSCI Report on Iraq Prewar Intelligence*, pp. 357–358.

269 "related to Iraq's links to terrorism": Ibid., p. 363.

269 "*improved the Central Intelligence Agency's (CIA) products*": Ibid., p. 34 (emphasis added).

269 "are entirely legitimate": Silberman-Robb Commission, p. 189. The report also stated:

> **The Commission also found no evidence of "politicization" even under the broader definition used by the CIA's Ombudsman for Politicization, which is not limited solely to the case in which a policymaker applies overt pressure on an analyst to change an assessment. The definition adopted by the CIA is broader, and includes any "unprofessional manipulation of information and judgments" by intelligence officers to please what those officers perceive to be policymakers' preferences** (p. 188).
>
> **There is also the issue of interaction between policymakers and other customers on the one hand and analysts on the other. According to some analysts, senior decisionmakers continually probed to assess the strength of the Intelligence Community's analysis, but did not press for changes in the Intelligence Community's analytical judgments. We conclude that good-faith efforts by intelligence consumers to understand the bases for analytic judgments, far from constituting "politicization," are entirely legitimate. This is the case even if policymakers raise questions because they do not like the conclusions or are seeking evidence to support policy preferences. Those who must use intelligence are entitled to insist that they be fully informed as to both the evidence and the analysis** (p. 189; footnote omitted).

270 had not interviewed either Hadley or Libby on this matter: Gimble stated incorrectly in his testimony that he had interviewed Hadley. In response to questioning, he corrected the statement: He had requested that interview and had been denied. He had not requested an interview with Libby. U.S. Senate Armed Services Committee, Hearing on the Defense Department Inspector General's Report on the Activities of the Office of Special Plans Prior to the War in Iraq, February 9, 2007, pp. 41, 82, transcript available at http://dougfeith.com/docs/SASC.pdf.

271 "prepared in the first place": Douglas J. Feith, "Tough Questions We Were Right to Ask," *Washington Post*, February 14, 2007.

271 "on another point beggars belief": Michael Barone, "Doug Feith Talks Back," Barone Blog, *U.S. News and World Report*, February 14, 2007, 0600 P.M.

ET, available at http://www.usnews.com/blogs/barone/2007/2/14/rudy-takes-the-lead.html.

271 a cover story in the *Weekly Standard*: See Stephen Hayes, "Case Closed," *Weekly Standard,* November 24, 2003, pp. 20–25. This article quoted at length from a purported leak of my list. I do not know who gave the magazine the information they published. My list was extremely highly classified—Top Secret Codeword. When Hayes's article first appeared, I helped draft the Defense Department's public statement, which described the publication of purportedly classified information as "reprehensible." I use the word "purportedly" because the government has never confirmed whether the material published in the *Weekly Standard* was in fact an accurate leak of classified information. The Justice Department investigated the matter, but brought no charges against anyone.

272 *after* Saddam had been overthrown: The author of the *Weekly Standard* article, Stephen Hayes, went on to do impressive investigative work on the issue of Iraq–al Qaida linkages and the downplaying of those linkages by some intelligence community officials.

273 a fixture of the public discussion of Iraq: Examples are cited in endnote to p. 250 (leaking their criticisms of the President).

Chapter 9: Iraq Planning–The Who and the Why

275 would be joyous and trouble-free: See, e.g., Joseph L. Galloway, Jonathan S. Landay, Warren P. Strobel, and John Walcott, "Postwar planning for Iraq 'ignored'; Insiders say the White House failed to develop a realistic strategy for winning the peace. Lack of plan to rebuild undermines Iraq effort," *Philadelphia Inquirer,* October 17, 2004, p. A1.

276 Casey created an interagency group: See Joint Staff Briefing, "Iraq Pol-Mil Cell: Concept, Mission, and Tasks," July 10, 2002.

276 efforts tucked in under the Executive Steering Group: The Humanitarian Reconstruction Group was cochaired by Elliott Abrams of the NSC staff and Robin Cleveland of the Office of Management and Budget; it also included members from State, Defense, the CIA, the Office of the Vice President, Treasury, Justice, and the U.S. Agency for International Development. The Energy Infrastructure Working Group, chaired by Michael Mobbs of my Policy organization, included members from State, the Joint Staff, the CIA, and Energy. The Coalition Working Group included members from State and Defense. See "Pre-war Planning for Post-war Iraq," Defenselink, http://www.defenselink.mil/policy/sections/policy_offices/isa/nesa/postwar_iraq.html; Joshua B. Bolten, Director, Office of Management and Budget, Testimony before the Senate Foreign Relations Committee on Reconstruction in Iraq, July 29, 2003, available at http://www.whitehouse.gov/omb/legislative/testimony/director/072903bolten.pdf.

277 claimed that my office served as "Chalabi's handler": See, e.g., the especially inaccurate article by a former DIA official: W. Patrick Lang, "Drinking the

Kool-Aid," *Middle East Policy*, Vol. XI, No. 2 (Summer 2004), available at http://www.mepc.org/journal_vol11/0406_lang.asp.

277 "Diplomatic Plan for the Day After": State Department policy paper, "Diplomatic Plan for the Day After," [undated], distributed by Richard Armitage at Deputies Lunch, July 25, 2002.

277 the Administration's strategy for Iraq: In some of its assessments, the CIA, too, warned against an extended occupation:

> Iraq's history of foreign occupation . . . has left Iraqis with a deep dislike of occupiers. An indefinite foreign military occupation, with ultimate power in the hands of a non-Iraqi officer, would be widely unacceptable.

National Intelligence Council, "Principal Challenges in Post-Saddam Iraq," January 2003, p. 10. Redacted and reproduced as Appendix B of *Report of the Senate Select Committee on Intelligence on Prewar Intelligence Assessments about Postwar Iraq*, [undated], released May 25, 2007. (Hereafter, *2007 SSCI Report on Prewar Intelligence on Postwar Iraq*.)

277 Armitage's other paper: This second State Department policy paper was entitled "The Future of Iraq." Undated, it was distributed by Richard Armitage at the Deputies Lunch on July 25, 2002. It was a three-page paper and should not be confused with the voluminous set of concept papers later produced at State with the same overall title. (Emphasis added in quoted text.)

279 proposal for military training of Iraqi oppositionists: Office of the Secretary of Defense, Near East and South Asia Affairs Office, Briefing entitled "Action Plan to Train and Equip the Iraqi Opposition in Support of Military Operations to Liberate Iraq," July 26, 2002.

281 opposition conferences held in the 1990s: See *SSCI Report on Chalabi Group*, p. 6.

282 demonstrate teamwork and productivity: See Bremer, *My Year in Iraq*, pp.123–124, 167–168, 189.

283 Political-Military Strategic Plan for Iraq: Joint Staff Briefing, "Iraq: Political-Military Strategic Plan," June 28, 2002.

283 at the August 6 Principals Committee meeting: [National Security Council Staff], "Liberation Strategy for Iraq," August 5, 2002, distributed by Condoleezza Rice for August 6, 2002, Principals Committee meeting, four pages.

285 "perceive U.S. actions as a new colonial occupation": Ibid. (emphasis added).

288 "based on moderation, pluralism, and democracy": [National Security Council Staff], "Iraq: Goals, Objectives, Strategy," August 14, 2002.

290 lacked conviction about the idea: Franks made a sharp distinction between advice that came from Rumsfeld and that from other Defense Department officials—especially me. See Franks, *American Soldier*, p. 330.

291 having relevance to his operational concerns: Ibid.

291 before the start of Operation Enduring Freedom: See Chapter 3.

292 ***"immediately promote civil order"***: Iraq Political-Military Cell, "Post-War Strategy," Briefing for Principals Meeting, October 23, 2002.

292 **and other basic services in liberated areas:** A U.S. Army handbook gives this definition of "civil affairs" operations:

> Civil affairs units help military commanders by working with civil authorities and civilian populations in the commander's area of operations to lessen the impact of military operations on them during peace, contingency operations and declared war. Civil Affairs forces support activities of both conventional and special operations forces, and are capable of assisting and supporting the civil administration in the area of operations.

292 **initiated *as early as possible* in the planning process:** General Richard B. Myers, Planning Order for General Tommy Franks, Commander, U.S. Central Command, July 9, 2002 (emphasis added). The Planning Order was written in all capital letters. For ease of reading, I have presented it with capitals and lowercase letters.

292 **"and strategic military objectives":** Iraq Political-Military Cell, Joint Staff J-5 Directorate, "Review of CENTCOM 'Hybrid Start' CONPLAN," Information Paper, September 6, 2002.

292 **"complex Phase IV requirements":** Joint Staff, "Prominent Hammer II Initial Insights," September 26, 2002.

292 **"refine planning for Phase IV operations":** General Richard B. Myers, Planning Order for General Tommy Franks, Commander, U.S. Central Command, December 19, 2002 (emphasis added). The Planning Order was written in all capital letters. For ease of reading, I have presented it with capitals and lowercase letters.

293 **Myers's December 19 instruction:** Ibid.

293 **for all aspects of governing Iraq:** CENTCOM's comprehensive responsibility for post-Saddam Iraq was reiterated in various contexts. I made the point in congressional testimony (Douglas J. Feith, "Post-War Planning," Statement to the Senate Committee on Foreign Relations, February 11, 2003; available at http://www.defenselink.mil/policy/sections/public_statements/speeches/archive/former_usdp/feith/2003/february_11_03.html).

293 **On January 10, 2003, Rumsfeld directed Giambastiani:** General Richard B. Myers, Execute Order, January 10, 2003.

294 **"consumer, rather than producer, of intelligence":** Douglas J. Feith Letter to Senator John Warner, Chair of Senate Armed Services Committee, June 21, 2003. The letter clarified:

> [T]he team had nothing to do with the "Intelligence Collection Program" (ICP), which was transferred from the State Department to the Defense Humint Service.
>
> [The Office of] Special Plans was created in October 2002 by expanding the Near East and South Asia Bureau's Northern Gulf section, in order

to provide enough manpower to handle policy issues with respect to Iran, Iraq and the Global War on Terrorism.

298 a greater threat from hostile neighbors: These paragraphs are drawn verbatim from that August 2002 paper. Office of the Under Secretary of Defense for Policy, "Sovereignty and Anticipatory Self-Defense," August 24, 2002, four pages (emphasis in original).

CHAPTER 10: UNITED NATIONS BOUND

300 ". . . policies and behaviour by Iraq": *UNSCOM Report.*

302 unsatisfactory deal with the UN on inspections: Rumsfeld Memo to the Vice President, "Enforcing Iraqi Disarmament," August 6, 2002 (emphasis in original).

302 Declaratory Policy on UN WMD Inspections in Iraq: As defined in a briefing by my office, "'declaratory policy' refers to all messages that elements of the U.S. government transmit: either publicly or privately; to a government, an entire society, a segment of society, or selected individuals. It includes messages transmitted by diplomacy, mass media, the Internet, mail, and individual contacts." Office of the Under Secretary of Defense for Policy, " 'Declaratory Policy' Themes for Key Audiences," February 5, 2003.

302 compliance with its UN obligations: National Security Council staff, "Declaratory Policy on UN WMD Inspections in Iraq," faxed to the Defense Department and other U.S. government agencies on August 8, 2002.

303 Saddam's abdication and exile: New information raises interesting questions about whether there was a real possibility of persuading Saddam that we posed a credible military threat to him. On one hand, a study of detention interviews of Saddam and other top Iraqi military and civilian officials revealed that Saddam had persuaded himself that the United States was unwilling to go to Baghdad to overthrow him. Woods, et al., *Iraqi Perspectives Project,* p. 15, available at http://www.jfcom.mil/newslink/storyarchive/2006/ipp.pdf. On the other hand, recent news articles report that President Bush told Spanish President Jose Maria Aznar that Saddam had discussed with Egyptian officials the possibility of accepting a deal for going into exile to avoid overthrow. Jason Webb, "Bush thought Saddam was prepared to flee: report," Reuters, September 26, 2007, available at http://www.reuters.com/article/newsOne/idUSL2683831120070926.

303 Dr. Mohammed made the point: See Chapter 4.

304 and a draft UN resolution: Office of the Under Secretary of Defense for Policy, "Ultimatum Strategy—Exile and Asylum as an Alternative to War," March 4, 2003.

304 "WMD and the Three Ts": An NSC staff paper entitled "Ultimatum to Saddam Hussein and the Iraqi Regime," circulated for August 30, 2002, Deputies Committee meeting, summarized the problem posed by Iraq:

> **The history of the Iraqi regime is a litany of violations of international law and norms that has made it impossible to extend it the presumption of good faith.**
>
> **In 1980 it invaded Iran and during the course of the war used chemical weapons and ballistic missiles against civilian populations.**
>
> **In 1990 it invaded Kuwait and has continued to threaten Kuwait throughout the decade.**
>
> **It agreed to end the war on the basis of UNSC Resolutions 686, 687, 688 that called for it to eliminate its weapons of mass destruction (UNSC resolution 687), end support for terror (UNSC resolution 687), cease the repression of the Iraqi people (UNSC resolution 688), and to account for missing Kuwaiti personnel (UNSC resolutions 686 and 687). It has failed to do so for 11 years.**
>
> **Its reprehensible pattern of "cheat and retreat" with the UNSCOM inspectors made a mockery of the notion of verification. Eventually the Baghdad regime expelled the inspectors.**
>
> **The regime has repeatedly menaced not only its neighbors but inflicted horrendous crimes on its own people, including use of CBW.**
>
> **Any Iraq government that wanted to implement its international obligations would have this dismal history to overcome.**
>
> **We have concluded that only a government concerned with bettering the life of its own people, through a pluralistic, democratic, representative government can be counted on to meet the concerns we have outlined. The Iraqi people could bring such a government about, Saddam could leave the country to facilitate such a government, or the United States can assist the process. What is the ultimate path to this outcome is still an open question.**

304 "The answer is no": Nicholas Lemann, "After Iraq: The Plan to Remake the Middle East," *The New Yorker*, February 17, 2003, p. 70. Wolfowitz, too, is on record stating that the rationale for the invasion of Iraq went beyond the question of WMD: "[T]here have always been three fundamental concerns. One is weapons of mass destruction, the second is support for terrorism, the third is the criminal treatment of the Iraqi people." Transcript of Wolfowitz interview conducted by Sam Tanenhaus, May 9–10, 2003, available at http://www.defenselink.mil/transcripts/transcript.aspx?transcriptid=2594.

305 sent back to Rumsfeld at the time: Feith report to Rumsfeld. "3–4 Sep Policy Quad Talks in Berlin: Discussion on Iraq," September 4, 2002.

306 a useful role for the United Nations: Feith Memo to Rumsfeld, "UN Participation in the Iraq Debate," September 5, 2002, 7:30 A.M.

307 to use WMD not to do so: Office of Under Secretary of Defense for Policy (drafted by Abram Shulsky), "Declaratory Policy on WMD," August 1, 2002 (emphasis in original). I faxed this paper to Hadley on August 5, 2002.

307 *against* going to war with Saddam: Brent Scowcroft, "Don't Attack Saddam," *Wall Street Journal*, August 15, 2002, p. A12. For reasons presented in Chapters 6 and 8, I believed (and continue to believe) that Scowcroft had his facts wrong on Saddam's ties to terrorist groups and hostility to the United States. I also thought he oversold the risk that countries opposing our Iraq policy would withhold cooperation from us in other areas. In fact, such countries, by and large, did not refuse to work with us on intelligence, law enforcement, financial, and other counterterrorism projects.

308 only a five-vote margin: Senate Joint Resolution 2, "A joint resolution to authorize the use of United States Armed Forces pursuant to United Nations Security Council Resolution 678," January 12, 1991. The resolution passed, 52–47. *Congressional Record,* 102nd Congress, 1st Session, Vol. 137 (12 January 1991), pp. S1018–S1019.

308 "had acquired nuclear-weapons capability": Scowcroft, "Don't Attack Saddam," p. A12 (emphasis added).

309 what he would say: This raises the question of what exactly "policy" is. President Reagan would sometimes make statements about Middle East policy—for example, sympathizing with Israel's June 1981 strike at Iraq's Osirak nuclear reactor or rejecting the long-standing State Department position on the illegality of Israeli settlements in the territories—that were not supported by the relevant officials at State or Defense, who effectively ignored the President's words. It was unclear what was U.S. policy. Was it what the President said? Was it what the State Department wrote in its talking points that it cabled for use by our diplomats abroad? In a variation on Bishop Berkeley's famous question about the tree falling in the uninhabited forest, I wondered: If a President makes a statement but no one in his cabinet is inclined to implement it, does it qualify as policy? It is the job of the National Security Adviser to try to discipline the government to implement the President's views, but this is difficult to do if the head of an agency is politically formidable and recalcitrant.

309 one day after the anniversary of 9/11: George W. Bush, "President's Remarks at the United Nations General Assembly," September 12, 2002, available at http://www.whitehouse.gov/news/releases/2002/09/20020912–1.html.

313 "widely accepted intelligence findings": Greg Miller and Bob Drogin, "Debate on Iraq: Bush Makes Tough Statement but Pulls His Punches," *Los Angeles Times*, September 13, 2002, p. A9.

313 "and all support for terrorists": Karen DeYoung, "Bush Tells United Nations It Must Stand Up to Hussein, or U.S. Will," *Washington Post*, September 13, 2002, p. A1.

313 On October 5, Rumsfeld sent the President a memo: Rumsfeld Memo to President Bush, "UN Security Council Resolution on Iraq," October 5, 2002.

314 fail to approve the second resolution: The chances of the Security Council's approving a second resolution authorizing force seemed remote. I recalled that in 1989, when a UN team confirmed that Iraq had used chemical weapons against Iran—thus violating the Geneva Protocol, perhaps the most significant multilateral legal convention after the UN Charter itself—the international meeting to address the violation was unable even to agree to a condemning resolution that would name Iraq as the violator. Indeed, the press representative for the Arab nations was Iraq's Foreign Minister, Tariq Aziz:

> Aziz, who also is deputy prime minister, rebuffed questions about Iraq's use of chemical weapons in the war with Iran and against rebellious Kurds in Iraq, saying, "The past is past." These incidents, which precipitated the concern in the United States and elsewhere that led to the Paris conference, were strongly condemned, but without naming Iraq, by participating nations.

Edward Cody, "149 Countries Vow to Shun Poison Gas; Paris Talks Close with Compromise," *Washington Post*, January 12, 1989, p. A1.

315 October 14 memo to President: Rumsfeld Memo to President Bush, "UN Inspections of Iraq," October 14, 2002.

314 it would allow UN inspectors back: "Iraq agrees to unconditional return of UN weapons inspectors—Annan," UN News Centre, September 16, 2002, available at http://www.un.org/apps/news/storyAr.asp?NewsID=4733&Cr=iraq&Cr1=.

314 Rumsfeld's follow-up memo observed: Rumsfeld Memo to President Bush, "UN Inspections of Iraq," October 14, 2002.

315 "Russians and French will work to save him": U.S. intelligence later confirmed that Saddam perceived the situation much as Wolfowitz had predicted. See Woods, et al., *Iraqi Perspectives Project*, pp. 28–29, available at http://www.jfcom.mil/newslink/storyarchive/2006/ipp.pdf.

315 Rumsfeld noted in his October 14 memo: Rumsfeld Memo to President Bush, "UN Inspections of Iraq," October 14, 2002.

318 "We just dodged a big bullet": Bob Woodward, *State of Denial: Bush at War, Part III* (New York: Simon & Schuster, 2006), p. 91.

318 many other journalists had misreported: See, e.g., Chris Suellentrop, "Douglas Feith; What has the Pentagon's third man done wrong? Everything," *Slate*, May 20, 2004; Jonathan S. Landay and Warren P. Strobel, "Plan B for postwar Iraq didn't exist," *Philadelphia Inquirer*, July 13, 2003, p. A1, which states, "Responsibility for post-war preparations lay with senior officials supervising the Office of Special Plans."

319 goals and objectives for Iraq: See Rice Memo to Cheney, Powell, Rumsfeld, Card, Tenet, and Myers, "Principals' Committee Review of Iraq Policy Paper," October 29, 2002, attaching "Iraq: Goals, Objectives, and Strategy" (reproduced as Appendix 5).

322 Tenet released an unclassified letter: George Tenet Letter to Senator Bob

Graham, Chairman, Senate Select Committee on Intelligence, October 7, 2002, reproduced in *Congressional Record*, 107th Congress, 2nd Session, Vol. 148, No. 132 (October 9, 2002), p. S10154 (emphasis added; hereafter, Tenet Letter). The 2006 *SSCI Report on Prewar Intelligence* (not unanimous) raised questions about some of the material in this letter, though it did not specifically cite the letter. While it is unclear whether all the statements in the Tenet letter remain consistent with our best information in 2008, that letter did represent bedrock on this issue for me and others in the Administration in the period leading up to the start of Operation Iraqi Freedom.

323 most other high-level Administration officials: As Rumsfeld put it in an interview, "I [used the] unclassified version of George Tenet's testimony in a press briefing. Condi Rice used the same piece of paper and that was the government's position. Not complicated." Interview with Donald Rumsfeld by Chris Matthews, *Hardball*, MSNBC, April 29, 2004, available at http://www.defenselink.mil/utility/printitem.aspx?print=http://www.defenselink.mil/transcripts/transcript.aspx?transcriptid=2555. Cheney continued to make reference to the disputed intelligence report of a 2001 meeting between 9/11 hijacker Mohammed Atta and an Iraq intelligence officer in Prague, saying that it was "credible" but "unconfirmed." See Stephen F. Hayes, *Cheney: The Untold Story of America's Most Powerful and Controversial Vice-President* (New York: HarperCollins, 2007), pp. 440–445. That report, however, played no significant role in the Administration's decision to oust the Saddam Hussein regime.

323 critics implied that the Iraq–al Qaida relationship was a major reason: See, e.g., Hersh, "Selective Intelligence," *The New Yorker*, May 12, 2003.

324 confidential discussions within the government: Writers with an axe to grind can usually find some remark in the record and assert that it was crucial to the debate, whether or not it played a significant role. If future historians conduct a rigorous review of the Administration's prewar debate on Iraq, I suspect it would show that comments by Administration officials about the al Qaida connection amounted to a drop in the bucket.

324 "no collaborative operational relationship": *The 9/11 Commission Report*, p. 66, available at http://www.gpoaccess.gov/911/pdf/fullreport.pdf.

324 commentators slipped quickly and sloppily: For example:

> Representative Jack Murtha: "There was no connection with al-Qaida, there was no connection with terrorism in Iraq itself." Jack Murtha on *Meet the Press with Tim Russert*, NBC, March 19, 2003, available at http://www.msnbc.msn.com/id/11823851/page/5/.
>
> Al Gore: "[T]he evidence now shows clearly that Saddam did not want to work with Osama bin Laden at all. . . ." Al Gore, "Remarks to Moveon.org," New York University, August 7, 2003, available at http://www.moveon.org/gore-speech.html.

Senator Ron Wyden: "There was no connection between Hussein and Al Qaeda." Ron Wyden on *Charlie Rose*, PBS, February 16, 2007, available at http://www.charlierose.com.

324 news headlines that simplified the issue: See, e.g.:

Walter Pincus and Dana Milbank, "Al Qaeda-Hussein Link Is Dismissed," *Washington Post*, June 17, 2004, p. A1, available at http://www.washingtonpost.com/wp-dyn/articles/A47812–2004Jun16.html.

MSNBC staff and news service reports, "9/11 panel sees no link between Iraq, al-Qaida," MSNBC.com, June 16, 2004, available at http://www.msnbc.msn.com/id/5223932/.

CBS/AP, "9/11 Panel: No Qaeda-Iraq Link," CBSNEWS.com, June 16, 2004, available at http://www.cbsnews.com/stories/2004/06/16/terror/main623504.shtml.

324 had trained thousands of non-Iraqi terrorists: See Woods, et al., *Iraqi Perspectives Project*, pp. 53–55, available at http://www.jfcom.mil/newslink/storyarchive/2006/ipp.pdf.

325 National Intelligence Estimate (NIE) of October 2002: U.S. Central Intelligence Agency, National Intelligence Estimate: *Iraq's Continuing Programs for Weapons of Mass Destruction* (emphasis added), available at www.dni.gov/nic/special_keyjudgements.html.

326 in 1998, the inspector's final report: *UNSCOM Report.*

326 documentation related to weapons programs: David Kay, Statement on the Interim Progress Report on the Activities of the Iraq Survey Group (ISG), Joint Hearing of House Permanent Select Committee on Intelligence, House Committee on Appropriations Subcommittee on Defense, and Senate Select Committee on Intelligence, October 2, 2003, available at https://www.cia.gov/news-information/speeches-testimony/2003/david_kay_10022003.html (emphasis added).

326 *active* rather than dormant: "We judge that all key aspects—R&D, production, and weaponization—of Iraq's offensive BW program are active and that most elements are larger and more advanced than they were before the Gulf War. We judge Iraq has some lethal and incapacitating BW agents and is capable of quickly producing and weaponizing a variety of such agents, including anthrax, for delivery by bombs, missiles, aerial sprayers, and covert operatives." "Saddam probably has stocked at least 100 metric tons (MT) and possibly as much as 500 MT of CW agents—much of it added in the last year," National Intelligence Estimate, October 2002.

326 The Duelfer Report (presenting the findings of the Iraq Survey Group) gives this snapshot: Duelfer Report, Vol. IA, p. 1; Vol. IIIB, p. 18 (emphasis added). The Iraq Survey Group concluded:

> Saddam Husayn so dominated the Iraqi Regime that its strategic intent was his alone. He wanted to end sanctions while preserving the capability to reconstitute his weapons of mass destruction (WMD) when sanctions were lifted. (Duelfer Report, Vol. IA, p. 1.)

327 **primarily for intelligence operations:** Ibid., Vol. IIIA, p. 3.

327 **once UN sanctions ended:** Ibid., Vol. IIB, p. 1.

327 **components of Saddam's future WMD force:** Ibid., Vol. IA, p. 44.

327 **leaving either their jobs or Iraq:** Ibid., Vol. IIB, p, 2.

328 **invested in numerous new projects:** Ibid., Vol. IA, p. 59.

329 **within several months to a year:** National Intelligence Estimate, October 2002.

329 **could produce a nuclear bomb in less than a year:** Graham Allison, *Nuclear Terrorism* (New York: Times Books, 2004), pp. 92, 213.

329 **including North Korea:** Duelfer Report, Vol. I, pp. 116–142.

329 **". . . members of the UNSC [UN Security Council]":** Ibid., p. 116.

329 **"nothing was found":** For example: John Diamond, "Final report: Iraq had no WMD," *USA Today*, October 7, 2004, Thursday, p. 1A; Editorial, "Weapons That Weren't There," *Washington Post*, October 7, 2004, p. A38; Thomas Catan and Mark Huband, "Iraq WMD report counters claims by Bush and Blair," *Financial Times*, October 7, 2004, p. 14; Christopher Adams, Thomas Catan, Stephen Fidler, and Mark Huband, "Report confirms Iraq had no weapons of mass destruction," *Financial Times*, October 7, 2004, p. 1; Editorial, "Iraq Survey Group: Definitive and Deadly," *The Guardian* (Comment & Analysis), October 8, 2004, p. 29.

329 **"to help put down a Shia rebellion" in southern Iraq:** Duelfer Report, Vol. IIIA, p. 5.

329 **causing them to walk out altogether:** Kay reported findings of concealed programs, including the following details regarding chemical and biological weapons:

- "We have discovered dozens of WMD-related program activities and significant amounts of equipment that Iraq concealed from the United Nations during the inspections that began in late 2002. . . .
- "A clandestine network of laboratories and safehouses within the Iraqi Intelligence Service that contained equipment subject to UN monitoring and suitable for continuing CBW research.
- "A prison laboratory complex, possibly used in human testing of BW agents, that Iraqi officials working to prepare for UN inspections were explicitly ordered not to declare to the UN.
- "Reference strains of biological organisms concealed in a scientist's home, one of which can be used to produce biological weapons."

Statement by David Kay on the Interim Progress Report on the Activities of the Iraq Survey Group (ISG) before the House Permanent Select Committee on Intelligence and the House Committee on Appropriations, Subcommittee on Defense and the

Senate Select Committee on Intelligence, October 2, 2003, available at https://www.cia.gov/news-information/speeches-testimony/2003/david_kay_10022003.html.

329 had retained his weapons programs: Silberman-Robb Commission, p. 156.

329 Even Iraqi generals believed he did: See Woods, et al., *Iraqi Perspectives Project*, p. 92.

329 "mustard gas is not like . . . marmalade": Blix, *Disarming Iraq*, p. 95.

330 "Iraq retained some BW-related seed stocks *until their discovery after Operation Iraqi Freedom* (OIF)": Duelfer Report, Vol. IIIB, p. 2 (emphasis added).

331 the primary threats to his rule: "Saddam walked a tightrope with WMD because as he often reminded his close advisors, they lived in a very dangerous global neighborhood where even the perception of weakness drew wolves. For him, there were real dividends to be gained by letting his enemies believe he possessed WMD whether it was true or not. . . . When it came to WMD, Saddam was simultaneously attempting to deceive one audience that they were gone and another that Iraq still had them." Woods, et al., *Iraqi Perspectives Project*, p. 91.

331 (and especially in a march to Baghdad): "Through the distortions of his ideological perceptions, Saddam simply could not take the Americans seriously. . . . [T]he Americans could not possibly launch a ground invasion that would seriously threaten his regime. . . . Like the First World War generals, Saddam's conception of military effectiveness revolved around the number of casualties that an army suffered." Woods, et al., *Iraqi Perspectives Project*, pp. viii–ix.

331 not a single instance of improper pressure occurred: See Silberman-Robb Commission, pp. 188–189. That bipartisan report concluded:

> **The Commission has found no evidence of "politicization" of the Intelligence Community's assessments concerning Iraq's reported WMD programs. No analytical judgments were changed in response to political pressure to reach a particular conclusion. The Commission has investigated this issue closely, querying in detail those analysts involved in formulating pre-war judgments about Iraq's WMD programs.** (p. 188.)
>
> **These analysts universally assert that in no instance did political pressure cause them to change any of their analytical judgments . . .** (p. 188.)
>
> **[A]ll of the Iraqi WMD analysts interviewed by the Commission staff stated that they reached their conclusions about Iraq's pursuit of WMD independently of policymaker pressure, based on the evidence at hand.** (p. 189.)

The *SSCI Report on Prewar Intelligence* reached a similar conclusion:

> **Conclusion 83. The Committee did not find any evidence that Administration officials attempted to coerce, influence or pressure analysts to change their judgments related to Iraq's weapons of mass destruction capabilities.** (p. 284 [italics in original].)
>
> **Conclusion 102. The Committee found that none of the analysts or**

> **other people interviewed by the Committee said that they were pressured to change their conclusions related to Iraq's links to terrorism. . . . All of the participants in the August 2002 coordination meeting on the September 2002 version of *Iraqi Support for Terrorism* interviewed by the Committee agreed that while some changes were made to the paper as a result of the participations of two Office of the Under Secretary of Defense for Policy staffers, their presence did not result in changes to their analytical judgments.** (p. 363 [italics in original].)

333 "ultimate version of the Parade of Horribles memo": [Donald H. Rumsfeld], "Iraq: An Illustrative List of Potential Problems," October 15, 2002, 07:45 A.M.

334 any warning I saw from State or the CIA: The CIA issued a paper on August 12, 2002, entitled "Iraq: Saddam's Options in a Conflict with the US." It listed many possible actions that the Iraqi regime could take to damage the United States or our coalition partners in the event of war. The actions involved diplomacy, influence operations, Iraqi domestic options, economic measures, and military options. Nothing in this CIA paper anticipated that the Baathist regime leaders might be able to continue to operate against us after the regime fell. CIA officials did not assess that Saddam and his top officials might be able to promote, finance, and command an insurgency after they were overthrown. For CIA prewar analysis, see Senate Select Committee on Intelligence, *Prewar Intelligence Assessments about Postwar Iraq*, released May 2007, available at http://intelligence.senate.gov/prewar.pdf.

334 that we "cherry-picked" intelligence: For example: "[Paul Pillar,] the former CIA official who coordinated U.S. intelligence on the Middle East until last year has accused the Bush administration of 'cherry-picking' intelligence on Iraq to justify a decision it had already reached to go to war, and of ignoring warnings that the country could easily fall into violence and chaos after an invasion to overthrow Saddam Hussein." Walter Pincus, "Ex-CIA Official Faults Use of Data on Iraq," *Washington Post*, February 10, 2006, p. A1.

335 "Some Potential Post-War Challenges": Joint Staff briefing, "Immediate Post-War Concerns," January 16, 2003.

335 unanimously adopted Resolution 1441: UN Security Council Resolution 1441, November 8, 2002, available at http://www.un.org/News/Press/docs/2002/SC7564.doc.htm.

336 Administration officials praised its strong rhetoric: For details regarding the resolution, see U.S. Department of State, "UN Security Council Resolution 1441," Fact Sheet, Bureau of International Organizations Affairs, February 25, 2003, available at http://www.state.gov/p/io/rls/fs/2003/17926.htm.

CHAPTER 11: LOSING GROUND ON THE DIPLOMATIC FRONT

338 intent on averting war: In his memoir, Blix reproduced his diary entry of December 31, 2002: "The inspection path must be and must be seen as an alternative, not a prelude to armed action." Blix, *Disarming Iraq*, pp. 109–110.

338 didn't take our military preparations seriously: Woods, et al., *Iraqi Perspectives Project,* pp. vii–viii, 15–16, available at http://www.jfcom.mil/newslink/story archive/2006/ipp.pdf.

343 the *New York Times* reported in some detail: Eric Schmitt and Julia Preston, "Threats and Responses: The Inspections," *New York Times,* December 19, 2002, A16.

344 he offered an assessment of the Iraqi declaration's inadequacies: The State Department supported Powell's press conference presentation with a fact sheet listing "illustrative omissions" in eight categories. State Department, "Illustrative Examples of Omissions from the Iraqi Declaration to the United Nations Security Council," December 19, 2002, available at http://www.state.gov/r/pa/prs/ps/2002/16118.htm.

344 "*constitute another material breach*": Colin L. Powell, Press Conference on Iraq Declaration, December 16, 2002 (emphasis added), available at http://www.state.gov/secretary/former/powell/remarks/2002/16123.htm.

344 "with the will of the international community": Ibid.

345 in South Africa, Ukraine, Kazakhstan, and elsewhere: A White House summary offered three criteria that indicate good-faith disarmament:

- **The decision to disarm is made at the highest political level.**
- **The regime puts in place national initiatives to dismantle weapons and infrastructure.**
- **The regime fully cooperates with international efforts to implement and verify disarmament; its behavior is transparent, not secretive.**

The White House, "What Does Disarmament Look Like?" January 2003, available at http://www.whitehouse.gov/infocus/iraq/disarmament/disarmament.pdf. See also the Nuclear Threat Initiative's profiles of South Africa, Kazakhstan, Ukraine, and Libya's weapons of mass destruction programs, available at http://www.nti.org/e_research/profiles/index.html.

345 the strategic decision to rid itself of WMD: Office of Under Secretary of Defense for Policy, "Read Ahead for Secretary Rumsfeld Dealing with Iraq's WMD Declaration," December 2, 2002.

349 Bush signed the charter for the office: See National Security Presidential Directive 24, January 20, 2003. Its key points can be summarized and paraphrased as follows:

- If the United States liberates Iraq, it will want to meet the humanitarian, reconstruction, and administration challenges. Immediate responsibility will fall on CENTCOM, but overall success will require a national effort.
- The Defense Department shall establish a Postwar Planning Office to conduct detailed planning on such issues as:
  - Humanitarian relief
  - Dismantling WMD

- Defeating and exploiting terrorist networks
- Protecting natural resources
- Reconstruction
- Key civilian services, such as food, water, electricity, and health care
- Reshaping the Iraqi military and other security institutions
- Supporting the transition to Iraqi-led authority over time

- The Planning Office will draw on the existing interagency work. It will receive policy guidance and direction from the Executive Steering Group, the Deputies Committee, and the Principals Committee, as appropriate.
- The Planning Office will build links to United Nations, nongovernmental organizations, and Free Iraqi forces. It will invite coalition partners to participate in its efforts.
- The Planning Office shall be deployed to Iraq to form the nucleus of the administrative apparatus that will assist in administering Iraq for a limited period of time.
- The Planning Office will require the full-time services of employees of a number of federal departments and agencies. The relevant agencies shall provide such employees as detailees to the Planning Office.

349 Bremer explained ORHA incorrectly: Bremer, *My Year in Iraq*, p. 24.

349 not to supplant it in any way: This was consistent with the briefing on post-Saddam Iraq that I gave the Principals Committee in October 2002 (prepared by the Joint Staff and my office, and based on interagency work). The briefing foresaw that after Saddam there would be a military administration of Iraq run by Franks. (This became the Coalition Provisional Authority; Franks was its first head.) That administration would transition to a not-yet-defined "transitional civil authority," which State officials said would be run by either the United States or the United Nations. Governmental authority in Iraq would then transition into the hands of Iraqis.

Charts from that briefing, showing the transitions of authority and the relationship between ORHA and CENTCOM, are reproduced in Appendix [6]. Garner's position, as head of what became ORHA, was designated in those charts as the "U.S. government administrator." He reported to the Commander in Chief of CENTCOM, General Franks, who would run the post-Saddam government of Iraq—that is, the CPA. Garner was never the head of that government. Only months later, with the appointment of Ambassador Bremer in May 2003, did we have a civilian official in Iraq who reported directly to Rumsfeld rather than Franks.

351 Iraq's BW programs actually was: Silberman-Robb Commission, p. 93.

352 Hans Blix delivered his report: Hans Blix, Executive Chairman of UNMOVIC, "An Update on Inspection," UN Security Council, January 27, 2003, available at http://www.un.org/Depts/unmovic/Bx27.htm. That same day, Mohammed El Baradei, Director General of the International Atomic Energy Agency, gave the Security Council his assessment of the nuclear-weapons-related portion of the Iraqi weapons declaration. He reported that the IAEA was "not able to reach any conclusion about Iraq's compliance with its Security Council obligations in the nuclear field after December 1998," when Saddam effectively expelled the IAEA inspectors. He said Iraq was cooperating to some extent with current inspections, but he noted that Iraq had an unmet burden of proof: "The international community will not be satisfied when questions remain open with regard to weapons of mass destruction. The world is asking for a high level of assurance that Iraq is completely free from all such weapons, and is already impatient to receive it." He called it "urgent and essential" that Iraq "on its own initiative, identify and provide any additional evidence that would assist the inspectors in carrying out their mandate." Mohammed El Baradei, "The Status of Nuclear Inspections in Iraq," UN Security Council, January 27, 2003, available at http://www.iaea.org/NewsCenter/Statements/2003/ebsp2003n003.shtml.

352 "a grim 15-page catalogue": Julia Preston, "Threats and Responses: Report to Council; U.N. Inspector Says Iraq Falls Short on Cooperation," *New York Times*, January 28, 2003, p. A1.

353 "is fast coming to an end": Colin L. Powell, "Briefing on the Iraq Weapons Inspectors' 60-Day Report: Iraqi Non-cooperation and Defiance of the UN," Washington, D.C., January 27, 2003, available at http://www.state.gov/secretary/former/powell/remarks/2003/16921.htm.

353 Powell made his memorable presentation to the UN Security Council: Colin L. Powell, "Remarks to the United Nations Security Council," New York City, February 5, 2003, available at http://www.state.gov/secretary/former/powell/remarks/2003/17300.htm.

353 "as set out in UNSCR 1441": Straw presented his own list of key omissions and violations, based on Blix's report to the UN:

- **Why is Iraq refusing to allow UNMOVIC to use a U-2 plane to conduct aerial imagery and surveillance operations?**
- **When will Iraq account for the 6,500 bombs which could carry up to 1,000 tonnes of chemical agent?**
- **How will Iraq justify having a prohibited chemical precursor for mustard gas?**
- **And how will Iraq explain the concealment of nuclear documents and the development of a missile programme in clear contravention of UN resolutions?**

"Straw's Response: Full Text," February 5, 2003, available at http://www.guardian.co.uk/politics/2003/feb/05/foreignpolicy.iraq.

355 a problem President Clinton had called attention to: President Bill Clinton, statement at the Pentagon, February 17, 1998, reported in "Standoff with Iraq: In

Clinton's Words: Containing the 'Predators of the 21st Century,'" *New York Times*, February 18, 1998, p. A9.

356 through defiance of the Security Council: Administration officials knew there were important things they did not know about Iraq's WMD capabilities. In testimony before the House Armed Services Committee on September 18, 2002, Rumsfeld discussed his thoughts on how to deal with the gaps in our information:

> If someone is waiting for a so-called smoking gun, it's certain that we will have waited too long. But the question raises another issue that's useful to discuss, and that's what kind of evidence ought we to consider is appropriate to act in the 21st century? In our country, it's been customary to seek evidence that would prove guilty beyond a reasonable doubt in a court of law. That approach, of course, is appropriate when the objective is to protect the rights of the accused, but in the age of weapons of mass destruction, the objective is not to protect the rights of a Saddam Hussein. It is to protect the lives of the American people and our friends and allies, and when there is that risk and we are trying to defend against closed societies and shadowy terrorist networks, expecting to find that standard of evidence before such a weapon has been used is really not realistic, and after such a weapon has been used it is too late.
>
> I suggest that any who insist on perfect evidence really are thinking back in the 20th century in a pre-9/11 context. . . .
>
> We will not have, we do not have and cannot know everything that is going on in the world at any time. Over the years, despite the very best efforts of enormously expensive and talented intelligence capabilities, we have repeatedly underestimated the weapons capabilities in a variety of countries of major concern to us. We have had numerous gaps of two, four, six, eight, ten—and in one case more—years between the time a country developed the capability and the time that the United States of America became aware of it.

Donald H. Rumsfeld, Secretary of Defense, "United States Policy Toward Iraq," Statement before the House Committee on Armed Services, September 18, 2002, available at http://commdocs.house.gov/committees/security/has261000/has261000_0f.htm.

356 "*and alone if we must*": Senator Joseph R. Biden Jr., Floor Statement: "Iraq," *Congressional Record*, U.S. Senate, January 28, 2003, pp. S1506–S1509 (emphasis added), available at http://frwebgate.access.gpo.gov/cgi-bin/getpage.cgi?dbname=2003_record&page=S1506&position=all.

356 "it is the world's problem": At a January 30, 2003, Senate Foreign Relations Committee hearing, Biden elaborated on his distinction between law enforcement and preemption:

> **I am so frustrated by some other parts of this Administration of injecting into this debate a notion relating to preemption that has not a damn thing to do with whether or not we move against Saddam Hussein. . . . We are not acting as if we act preemptively. We are enforcing a surrender document.**
>
> **Saddam Hussein invaded another country. The world responded. If this were 1930 he would have signed a peace agreement. It's not. We have a United Nations. [I]n return for his ability to stay in power, he made a commitment to the world, several commitments. Enforcing that if necessary is not preemption—is not preemption—whatever the hell that doctrine is supposed to mean.**
>
> **And so, I would respectively suggest that when you talk about this, do not further confuse the devil out of the rest of the world and make us sound like a bunch of cowboys that we're going to be out there preemptively imposing our view. This is an enforcement of a binding international legal commitment that a man made to save his skin and stay in power.**

Senator Joseph R. Biden Jr., "Senate Foreign Relations Committee Holds Hearing on UN Weapons Inspectors' Report," U.S. Senate, January 30, 2003, available at http://www.iraqwatch.org/government/US/HearingsPreparedstatements/sfrc-013003.htm.

357 Administration officials who advocated war against Saddam: Senator John Kerry asserted: "The very worst that Members of Congress can be accused of is trusting the intelligence we were selectively given by this Administration, and taking the President at his word. But unlike this Administration, there is absolutely no suggestion that we intentionally went beyond what we were told were the facts." Office of Senator John Kerry, "Kerry Responds to Bush Attacks: White House Misleading Public on Prewar Iraq Intelligence," Press Release, November 14, 2005, available at http://kerry.senate.gov/v3/cfm/record.cfm?id=248761. See also Office of Senator Carl Levin, "The CIA Director Misled Congress," Press Release, February 23, 2004, available at http://www.senate.gov/~levin/newsroom/release.cfm?id=218281; Office of Representative Dennis J. Kucinich, "Administration Capitalized on Fear of Americans Misled Congress and the American People," Press Release, June 12, 2003, available at http://kucinich.house.gov/News/DocumentSingle.aspx?DocumentID=28150.

357 essential points in the CIA's threat assessments: A 1998 CIA report on "Iraq's Weapons of Mass Destruction" included these assessments:

> **Without effective UN monitoring, Baghdad could probably begin production [of BW] within a few days. For example, Iraq can convert production of biopesticides to anthrax simply by changing seed material. . . . In the absence of UNSCOM inspectors, Iraq could restart limited mustard agent production within a few weeks, full-scale produc-**

> **tion of sarin within a few months, and pre-Gulf war production levels—including [nerve agent] VX—within two or three years.**

CIA, *Iraq's Weapons of Mass Destruction*, February 13, 1998, pp. 5, 7.

357 Al Gore warned: Gore called attention to the danger of Iraq's pursuit of WMD, saying that the United States needed to assemble a coalition of countries to stop Saddam's WMD programs, but he did not call for war. He did not explain why he thought we could succeed in stopping those programs without war when the United Nations had tried to do so unsuccessfully for nearly a dozen years. Al Gore, Speech at Commonwealth Club, September 23, 2002, available at http://www.washingtonpost.com/wp-srv/politics/transcripts/gore_text092302.html.

357 John Kerry asserted: Statement of Senator John Kerry on the Senate Floor on the Iraq Resolution, October 9, 2002, *Congressional Record*, 107th Congress, 2nd Session, Vol. 148, No. 132, S10170–S10175 (October 10, 2002), available in pdf at http://frwebgate.access.gpo.gov/cgi-bin/getpage.cgi?dbname=2002_record&page=S10137&position=all.

357 Senator Jay Rockefeller: Rockefeller's remarks are worth quoting more fully, given his position at the time as the ranking Democrat on the Senate Intelligence Committee:

> **There is unmistakable evidence that Saddam Hussein is working aggressively to develop nuclear weapons and will likely have nuclear weapons within the next five years. And that may happen sooner if he can obtain access to enriched uranium from foreign sources—something that is not that difficult in the current world. We also should remember we have always underestimated the progress Saddam has made in development of weapons of mass destruction.**
>
> ---
>
> **Americans will return to a situation like that we faced in the Cold War, waking each morning knowing we are at risk from nuclear blackmail by a dictatorship that has declared itself to be our enemy.**
>
> **The global community—in the form of the United Nations—has declared repeatedly, through multiple resolutions, that the frightening prospect of a nuclear-armed Saddam cannot come to pass. But the UN has been unable to enforce those resolutions. We must eliminate that threat now, before it is too late.**
>
> **But this isn't just a future threat. Saddam's existing biological and chemical weapons capabilities pose a very real threat to America, now. Saddam has used chemical weapons before, both against Iraq's enemies and against his own people. He is working to develop delivery systems like missiles and unmanned aerial vehicles that could bring these deadly weapons against U.S. forces and U.S. facilities in the Middle East.**
>
> **And he could make those weapons available to many terrorist groups**

which have contact with his government, and those groups could bring those weapons into the U.S. and unleash a devastating attack against our citizens. I fear that greatly.

Saddam has misjudged what he can get away with, and how the United States and the world will respond, many times before. At the end of the day, we cannot let the security of American citizens rest in the hands of someone whose track record gives us every reason to fear that he is prepared to use the weapons he has against his enemies.

As the attacks of September 11 demonstrated, the immense destructiveness of modern technology means we can no longer afford to wait around for a smoking gun. September 11 demonstrated that the fact that an attack on our homeland has not yet occurred cannot give us any false sense of security that one will not occur in the future. We no longer have that luxury.

Statement of Senator John D. Rockefeller IV on the Senate Floor on the Iraq Resolution, October 10, 2002, *Congressional Record*, 107th Congress, 2nd Session, Vol. 148, No. 133 (October 10, 2002), available at http://frwebgate.access.gpo.gov/cgi-bin/getpage.cgi?dbname=2002_record&page=S10233&position=all.

357 "there was, you know, an imminent threat": Senator John D. Rockefeller, quoted in James Risen and Judith Miller, "The Struggle for Iraq: The Search; No Illicit Arms Found in Iraq, U.S. Inspector Tells Congress," *New York Times*, October 3, 2003, p. A1.

358 "you want everything to be accounted for": Bill Clinton, "His Side of the Story," *Time*, June 28, 2004.

358 Bush had won a vote in Congress: Authorization for Use of Military Force Against Iraq Resolution of 2002, Public Law 107–243 (October 16, 2002), 116 Statute 1498, H.J. Res. 114, available at http://frwebgate.access.gpo.gov/cgi-bin/getdoc.cgi?dbname=107_cong_public_laws&docid=f:publ243.107.pdf. For House and Senate votes, see http://thomas.loc.gov/cgi-bin/bdquery/z?d107:HJ00114:@@@R.

359 focused narrowly on the issues of WMD stockpiles and inspections: The resolution of Congress authorizing military force, while it emphasized the danger of WMD production and use, also set forth the full range of considerations:

including the development of weapons of mass destruction and refusal or obstruction of United Nations weapons inspections in violation of United Nations Security Council Resolution 687 (1991), repression of its civilian population in violation of United Nations Security Council Resolution 688 (1991), and threatening its neighbors or United Nations operations in Iraq in violation of United Nations Security Council Resolution 949 (1994).

Ibid.

Chapter 12: Final Preparations for War and Its Aftermath

361 new lists of possible challenges, pitfalls, and disasters: Planning addressed a variety of possible operational difficulties, including (for example) the "human shields" problem of whether and how to evacuate civilians, including diplomats, from Baghdad; the protection and repair of dams, waterworks, and oil fields; and organizing humanitarian assistance. Plans were developed to recover Captain Michael Scott Speicher (USN) and other missing coalition forces from Operation Desert Storm, to secure and destroy Iraqi WMD, and to manage and translate captured Iraqi documents.

Officials expected that, after Saddam's overthrow, we would need mechanisms to control heavy weapons, vet Iraqi civilian and military officials, prosecute war crimes, and help friends in the region handle economic and other effects of the war. Interagency teams developed plans accordingly. In the nine months or so before the war started, State, CIA, Defense, and NSC staff officials produced versions of plans for the governance of post-Saddam Iraq and reconstruction of the country's security forces and economy.

361 might be aggravated by Iraq's neighbors: See, e.g., briefing on "Immediate Post-War Concerns" for January 16, 2003, Principals Committee meeting, which had a Joint Staff–produced slide entitled "Some Potential Post-War Challenges" warning of (among other items):

- **Internal clash between Arabs and Kurds**
- **Not all WMD accounted for**
- **Unclear status and location of regime leadership**
- **Flood damage and oil-field fires**
- **Tribal maneuvering and settling of old scores**
- **Sunni Officer Corps flees Southern Iraq and consolidates in Sunni heartland**
- **Regional neighbors seeking to influence**
- **Internal and expatriate opposition competing for leadership roles**

This briefing called attention to the danger of the "fracturing of Iraq or threats to its territorial integrity."

361 A December 19, 2002, modification of the war-planning order: Richard B. Myers, "Planning Order (PLANORD) For Possible Military Operations in Iraq II PLANORD Modification (MOD) 006," December 19, 2002.

362 "cannot be met by local manpower": Feith Memo to Paul Williams [counsel to Bosnian Muslim delegation], "IFOR and Police," November 16, 1995.

363 "maintaining public order" in Iraq: Office of Deputy Assistant Secretary of Defense for Resources and Plans [Christopher Lamb], "Action Memo: Maintaining Public Order during Combat Operations in Iraq," February 9, 2003.

363 briefed it to the Deputies Committee at least twice: The basic argument appeared also in the NIC summary of principal challenges: "Local police and the

Regular Army are less tainted [than other agencies] by association with Saddam's rule and could assist in law enforcement." National Intelligence Council, *Principal Challenges in Post-Saddam Iraq*, January 2003, p. 20 (reprinted as Appendix B of *SSCI Report on Prewar Intelligence on Postwar Iraq*, May 2007). CENTCOM's planning drew on this guidance: "Leverage well-rooted police and judiciary systems, which could promote good governance once stripped of their Ba'athist leadership." United States Central Command, Phase IV IPB, as of March 1, 2003, p 57 (cited in *SSCI Report on Prewar Intelligence on Postwar Iraq*, p. 96).

363 **"CENTCOM planners relied on the CIA's assessment in calculating troop levels"**: See Gordon and Trainor, *Cobra II*, p. 105.

364 **detract from the success of the operation:** Office of Deputy Assistant Secretary of Defense for Resources and Plans, "Action Memo: Maintaining Public Order during Combat Operations in Iraq," February 9, 2003.

365 **rejoice when liberated from Saddam's tyranny:** See, e.g., Jonathan S. Landay and Warren P. Strobel, "U.S. Lacked Plan B in Iraq," *Philadelphia Inquirer*, July 13, 2003, p. A01; David Rieff, "Blueprint for a Mess," *New York Times*, November 2, 2003, p. A28; Gerard Baker and Stephen Fidler, "The best-laid plans? How turf battles and mistakes in Washington dragged down the reconstruction of Iraq," *Financial Times*, August 4, 2003, p. A15.

365 **received suggestions more tolerantly from Myers and Pace than from civilians:** It was a standing joke in my office that whenever CENTCOM asked for policy guidance, it meant they didn't like the guidance they had been given. When Franks was faced with a task he wanted to do, he did it on his own authority. For tasks he disagreed with—taking custody of Mujahadin al-Khalk (MEK) terrorists, fighting the Kurdish terrorists of the PKK, training the Free Iraqi Force—he would send us repeated requests for "guidance." In each case, he already had clear guidance. The message from the field was, essentially, "not interested."

When I received an official briefing from Lieutenant General Ricardo Sanchez during my trip to Iraq in August 2003, one of the first slides included the item "MEK," with a notation along the lines of "awaiting policy guidance." I interrupted the briefing to say that CENTCOM *had* guidance—I had written it myself. Sure enough, one of the officers at the table retrieved the guidance from a file, at which point General Sanchez explained that he disagreed with the guidance. I told him I had no problem discussing the disagreement, but the briefing slide should not have said that CENTCOM was without guidance.

366 **"Stuff happens"**: Department of Defense News Briefing—Secretary Rumsfeld and General Myers, April 11, 2003, transcript available at http://www.defenselink.mil/Transcripts/Transcript.aspx?TranscriptID=2367.

366 **"a plan for rebuilding the Iraqi military"**: Office of Near East and South Asia Affairs, Office of the Under Secretary of Defense for Policy, Briefing, "Rebuilding the Iraqi Military," January 21, 2003.

367 **Garner's plan at the March 10, 2003, National Security Council meeting:** Office of Reconstruction and Humanitarian Assistance, Briefing for National Security Council, "Reshaping the Iraqi Military," February 26, 2003 (briefed at March 10, 2003, meeting).

368 Strategic victory was a larger and more challenging goal: The October 29, 2002, "Goals, Objectives, and Strategy" paper by National Security Adviser Condoleezza Rice listed the following goals:
An Iraq that:

- **Does not threaten its neighbors;**
- **Renounces support for, and sponsorship of international terrorism;**
- **Continues to be a single, unitary state;**
- **Is free of weapons of mass destruction (WMD), their means of delivery, and associated programs;**
- **No longer oppresses or tyrannizes its people;**
- **Respects the basic rights of all Iraqis—including women and minorities;**
- **Adheres to the rule of law and respects fundamental human rights, including freedom of speech and worship; and**
- **Encourages the building of democratic institutions.**

These goals were reproduced as strategic guidance in CENTCOM and Joint Staff planning documents.

368 inviting guerilla warfare, terrorism, and political instability: Papers from State and NSC are discussed in Chapter 9. See State Department policy paper, "Diplomatic Plan for the Day After," [undated], distributed by Richard Armitage at Deputies Lunch, July 25, 2002; [National Security Council Staff], "Liberation Strategy for Iraq," August 5, 2002, distributed by Rice for August 6, 2002, Principals Committee meeting. In a January 2003 paper, the CIA also warned of the dangers of occupation (though the warning was omitted from the report's Key Findings), saying that "Iraq's history of foreign occupation . . . has left Iraqis with a deep dislike of occupiers. An indefinite foreign military occupation, with ultimate power in the hands of a non-Iraqi officer, would be widely unacceptable." National Intelligence Council, "Principal Challenges in Post-Saddam Iraq," January 2003, p. 10, excerpted as Appendix B of the *Report of the Senate Select Committee on Intelligence on Prewar Intelligence Assessments about Postwar Iraq*, [undated], released May 25, 2007.

369 testimony to the Senate Foreign Relations Committee: Douglas J. Feith, "Post-War Planning," Statement to the Senate Committee on Foreign Relations, February 11, 2003.

370 Armitage had argued since at least the early summer: "Diplomatic Plan for the Day After," State Department Policy Paper, [undated], distributed to Deputies on July 25, 2002.

371 political commissars at our headquarters: Michael Gordon and Bernard Trainor recount the following story indicating the difficulty of close collaboration between policy and operations:

> **After Franks endured a particularly difficult grilling from Rumsfeld the [CENTCOM] planners suspected that Feith's aides were feeding tough**

> **questions to Washington in advance. Dealing with Rumsfeld was hard enough without the boys from Feith's office tipping the secretary to their every move. The two Defense aides were told they would not be welcome if they were going to function as moles for the Pentagon, and they stopped working in the trailer. . . . They were no longer part of the planning team.**

Gordon and Trainor, *Cobra II*, p. 45.

372 pros and cons of an Iraqi provisional government: Department of Defense (Office of the Secretary of Defense/Near East and South Asia Affairs), Briefing Slides on "A Provisional Government for Iraq?" February 14, 2003, 7:28 P.M.

373 participate fully in any structures: Office of Under Secretary of Defense for Policy, Office of Near East and South Asia Affairs, Briefing Paper, "Iraqi Opposition Strategy," January 31, 2003.

375 Final Report on the Transition to Democracy in Iraq: Conference of the Iraqi Opposition and Democratic Principles Work Group, "Final Report on the Transition to Democracy in Iraq," November 2002.

375 the scholar Kanan Makiya: See Kanan Makiya, *Republic of Fear: The Politics of Modern Iraq*, updated ed. (Berkeley: University of California Press, 1998); Kanan Makiya, *Cruelty and Silence: War, Tyranny, Uprising, and the Arab World* (New York: W.W. Norton and Company, 1993).

375 Most of the groups produced a report: The final reports were Transitional Justice, Democratic Principles and Procedures, Water, Agriculture and Environment, Public Health and Humanitarian Needs, Defense Policy and Institutions, Local Government, Economy and Infrastructure (Public Finance), Civil Society Capacity Building, Transparency and Anti-Corruption Measures, Education, Free Media, Oil and Energy, available at http://www.gwu.edu/~nsarchiv/NSAEBB/NSAEBB198/index.htm.

375 ordered Jay Garner and ORHA to ignore it: For example: "An ambitious, yearlong State Department planning effort predicted many of the postwar troubles and advised how to resolve them. But the man who oversaw that effort was kept out of Iraq by the Pentagon, and most of his plans were shelved." Mark Fineman, Robin Wright, and Doyle McManus, "Preparing for War, Stumbling to Peace—U.S. Is Paying the Price for Missteps Made on Iraq," *Los Angeles Times*, July 18, 2003. See also Rieff, "Blueprint for a Mess," p. A28; Gerard Baker and Stephen Fidler, "The best-laid plans? How turf battles and mistakes in Washington dragged down the reconstruction of Iraq," *Financial Times*, August 4, 2003, p. A15; George Packer, *The Assassins' Gate: America in Iraq* (New York: Farrar, Straus and Giroux, 2005), pp. 124–126.

376 journalists and members of Congress could invoke it without feeling obliged to cite details or sources: Kerry stated, "They left the planning of the State Department in the State Department desks." Presidential debate, September 30, 2004, available at http://edition.cnn.com/TRANSCRIPTS/0409/30/se.01.html. For journalists' accounts, see, e.g., Mike Allen, "Rumsfeld to Remain at Pentagon," *Washington Post*, December 4, 2004, p. A1; Jonathan S. Landay and Warren P.

Strobel, "Pentagon civilians' lack of planning contributed to chaos in Iraq," Knight Ridder/Tribune News Service, July 13, 2003. Landay and Strobel assert:

> **Pentagon planners ignored an eight-month-long effort led by the State Department to prepare for the day when Saddam's dictatorship was gone. The 'Future of Iraq' project, which involved dozens of exiled Iraqi professionals and 17 U.S. agencies, including the Pentagon, prepared strategies for everything from drawing up a new Iraqi judicial code to restoring the unique ecosystem of Iraq's southern marshes, which Saddam's regime had drained. Virtually none of the 'Future of Iraq' project's work was used once Saddam fell.**

> Similar inaccurate accusations were made in Congress as well:

> ***Rep. Van Hollen:*** **. . . But the fact of the matter is, at least at the State Department, there was a plan that had been put together to try to address some of those issues. But that plan was thrown out of the window by Secretary Rumsfeld. And they decided that they were going to do it their own way, rather than abide by that plan.**

Remarks of Representative Chris Van Hollen (D-Maryland), Hearing of the National Security, Emerging Threats and International Relations Subcommittee of the House Government Reform Committee on the Evolving National Strategy for Victory in Iraq, July 11, 2006, available at http://frwebgate.access.gpo.gov/cgi-bin/getdoc.cgi?dbname=109_house_hearings&docid=f:34545.wais.

376 **"read the fifteen volume study, I agreed":** L. Paul Bremer III, *My Year in Iraq*, p. 25.

377 **they were never intended to be one:** John B. Taylor, Under Secretary of the Treasury for the first four years of the George W. Bush Administration, has praised the Future of Iraq Project's financial report as "helpful in pulling together information and in making initial contacts with people who might be interested in going to Iraq if there were to be a regime change." But he noted that, "unlike some have claimed, it was by no means a post-war financial plan for Iraq, and I assume that is how it was in other areas." John B. Taylor, *Global Financial Warriors: The Untold Story of International Finance in the Post-9/11 World* (New York: W.W. Norton & Co., 2007), pp. 202–203. Gordon and Trainor provide a similar picture:

> **[David] Kay, who read the study, summed it up: "It was unimplementable. It was a series of essays to describe what the future could be. It was not a plan to hand to a task force and say 'go implement.' If it had been carried out it would not have made a difference." [Paul] Hughes agreed. "There is a real lack of planning capacity at the Department of State, hence, just about any study gets labeled a plan," he said. "While it produced some useful background information it had no chance of**

really influencing the post-Saddam phase of the war." Even so, the study was eventually conveyed to the U.S. officials who administered Iraq.

Gordon and Trainor, *Cobra II*, p. 159.

377 **on his return to the Pentagon:** In a work generally sympathetic to Warrick's views, George Packer writes that "Warrick warned 'his' Iraqis not to work with the Pentagon." See Packer, *The Assassins' Gate*, p. 125.

378 **no one did the latter:** In a July 2003 interview, Garner did say that Rumsfeld told him "we're not going to bring Tom Warrick *or his work* on the team." Interview with General Garner, *Frontline*, PBS, July 17, 2003, available at http://www-c.pbs.org/wgbh/pages/frontline/shows/truth/interviews/garner.html (emphasis added). Garner sometimes spoke imprecisely, however, and I believe the phrase "or his work" here is not accurate, for the reasons I have explained.

378 **as one of its key sources:** Office of Reconstruction and Humanitarian Assistance (Post-Conflict Planning Group), Briefing Slides on "Civil Administration Section, Justice/Law Enforcement," [undated; declassified—DRT March 20, 2005].

378 **the Powell-Armitage view:** Ironically, one of the more important effects of the Future of Iraq Project was to help my office appreciate the case for giving governmental responsibility early to a new Iraqi leadership. We drew on the project when we considered a prewar Iraqi provisional authority, and later for the plan to create an Iraqi Interim Authority after Saddam's overthrow.

378 **meetings that Grossman and I cochaired:** See "Political Statement of the Iraqi Opposition Conference in London 14–16 December 2002," available at http://home.cogeco.ca/~konews/20-12-02-political-statement-london-conference.html.

381 **"The terrible 'ifs' accumulate":** Winston S. Churchill, *The World Crisis: 1911–1914* (New York: Charles Scribner's Sons, 1930), p. 274.

381 **more aggressively than in this paper:** See the account of Luti's briefing and Myers's comments in Chapter 9.

382 **vet Iraqis for jobs in the new government:** Vetting the Iraqi officials had been a Policy concern for many months, as highlighted in my congressional testimony in February 2003 (Douglas J. Feith, "Post-War Planning," Statement to the Senate Committee on Foreign Relations, February 11, 2003, available at http://www.defenselink.mil/policy/sections/public_statements/speeches/archive/former_usdp/feith/2003/february_11_03.html). Eventually a "fusion cell" was created as a clearinghouse for submitting background information, involving FBI, CIA, DIA, CENTCOM, and State. It did not work as planned, and some senior Baathists were hired inadvertently.

383 **"scrap the idea of a fighting force of Iraqi exiles":** Tenet, *At the Center of the Storm*, p. 398.

383 **work so closely with the externals:** See ibid., pp. 419–420 ("it was as though Defense and the Vice President's staff wanted to invite comparison with the Soviet invasion of Afghanistan, when Russian troops deposed the existing government and installed Babrak Karmal, whom they had brought with them from Moscow.")

383 **favoring him over other externals:** Rumsfeld made clear to Jay Garner that he

did not favor Chalabi. When a PBS journalist asked Garner, as former ORHA director, about "a plan to move Chalabi in to start up a government," Garner replied that he knew of no such plan and did not believe there was one. He said that some Pentagon officials were "pro-Chalabi" as other U.S. officials were "pro" other Iraqi opposition leaders. But Garner understood Rumsfeld's position to be "No, Chalabi's a candidate, but I don't have a candidate." Interview with Garner, *Frontline*, July 17, 2003.

384 everything that could go wrong did: My discussion of what went wrong with the Free Iraqi Forces program is drawn largely from my interviews in 2006 and 2007 with Chris Straub, who worked on the program in my Near East and South Asia Affairs office under William Luti.

384 President didn't sign the necessary funding authorization until December 9: President Bush Memo to Powell and Rumsfeld, "Presidential Determination on Authorization to Furnish Drawdown Assistance to the Iraqi Opposition Under the Iraq Liberation Act of 1998," Dec. 9, 2002, available at http://www.state.gov/p/nea/rls/15857.htm.

385 "a waste of time and energy for us": Lieutenant General Michael DeLong with Noah Lukeman, *Inside CentCom: The Unvarnished Truth About the Wars in Afghanistan and Iraq* (Washington, DC: Regnery Publishing, Inc., 2004), p. 78.

385 Tenet likewise writes contemptuously: See Tenet, *At the Center of the Storm*, pp. 398–399.

387 By late February, Garner later said: Interview with Garner, *Frontline*, July 17, 2003.

388 phraseology characteristic of Richard Armitage: See Hersh, "The Debate Within," p. 34.

Other observers have remarked that many quotes by anonymous State Department officials resemble Armitage's speaking style: See Jack Schafer, "Who's wearing a bag on his head in today's *New York Times*?," *Slate*, April 19, 2004. A *New York Times* article notes that "Richard Armitage looks—and often talks—more like a barroom bouncer than the nation's second-ranking diplomat." Barbara Slavin and Bill Nichols, "State Dept.'s No. 2 has flair for blunt diplomacy," *New York Times*, February 12, 2002, p. A7.

CHAPTER 13: SADDAM'S REGIME FALLS

391 television broadcast from the White House: George W. Bush, "President says Saddam Hussein Must Leave Iraq Within 48 Hours," March 17, 2003, available at http://www.whitehouse.gov/news/releases/2003/03/20030317-7.html.

391 "not dealing with peaceful men": In an interview with Bob Woodward, the President said he spoke with Karen Hughes, his communications director, who had recently resigned, about the decision to go to war: "'She said if you go to war, exhaust all opportunities to achieve [regime change] peacefully. And she was right. She actually captured my own sentiments.'" Woodward, *Plan of Attack*, p. 252 (bracketed words in the original). In his March 17, 2003, broadcast announcing the ultimatum to Saddam Hussein and his sons, President Bush said: "Should Saddam Hussein choose confrontation, the American people can know that every measure has been taken to avoid war. . . ."

392 "speed kills": Garner also discussed the value of speed in a retrospective interview:

> **I thought there would be a lot of refugees and displaced people, because I thought [Saddam] would use chemicals. In my heart of hearts, I'll always believe he intended to. But because of the speed of the military operation, and the fact they went after him the first night, he wasn't able to do that. They cut all his communications the first night. So he was never able to execute that.**
>
> **My second fear was he'd torch all the oil fields. We knew he intended to do that, because they were wired with explosives. But the military got in there so fast.**

Interview with General Garner, *Frontline*, July 17, 2003.

392 Saddam knew we were coming: After Saddam's overthrow, we learned that we had had a measure of strategic surprise after all: Saddam thought that France's and Russia's UN Security Council efforts would prevent the United States from going to war. See Woods, et al., *Iraqi Perspectives Project*, p. 28. Saddam thought he could avoid a war by admitting UN weapons inspectors and by refusing to take the provocative actions advised by his son—mining the Persian Gulf, destroying Iraq's oil infrastructure, and preemptively attacking Kuwait. Ibid., p. 29.

> **Through the distortions of his ideological perceptions, Saddam simply could not take the Americans seriously. . . . [T]he Americans could not possibly launch a ground invasion that would seriously threaten his regime. . . . Like the First World War generals, Saddam's conception of military effectiveness revolved around the number of casualties that an army suffered.**

Ibid. pp. viii–ix, 28.

All these points suggest that Administration officials overestimated the difficulty of achieving surprise. Even in mid-March 2003, Saddam thought he could avert war. Ibid., p. 113. Note that, even if these reports had been available before the war, they might not have been given great weight. Military planners would rightly have been reluctant to make plans on the rosy assumption that our enemy would behave foolishly.

393 "simultaneous air and ground attack": Woods, et al., *Iraqi Perspectives Project*, p. 125 (footnote omitted).

394 shouldn't be micromanaged from Washington: General Tommy Franks explains in his book that the decision on troop levels was his, and lays out his reasons for a smaller, faster force. Franks, *American Soldier*, pp. 367–368, 393–397. Though

Franks was usually persuaded by Rumsfeld's reasoning, he was willing to buck the Secretary's views on occasion—when he was more strongly against an idea than the Secretary favored it. An example was when Franks resisted training Iraqi exiles for the Free Iraqi Forces, as discussed later in this chapter.

394 "there was never a push inside the Joint Chiefs of Staff for more forces": See General Richard Myers, Testimony before the Senate Armed Services Committee, June 25, 2004, available at http://www.defenselink.mil/speeches/speech.aspx?speechid=134.

394 the Turkish parliament failed: See Dexter Filkins, "Turkish Parliament Refuses to Accept G.I.'s in Blow to Bush," *New York Times*, March 1, 2003, p. A1. The Turkish government led by Prime Minister Recep Erdogan had endorsed the measure allowing U.S. access, urged the parliament to vote favorably on it, and expected approval. The final vote was 264 to 251 in favor of allowing U.S. access, with 19 abstentions—but that majority was not sufficient under Turkish law to grant approval.

395 perhaps eventually from Turkey: Bob Woodward relates Franks's claim that this gambit—keeping the 4th Infantry Division sailing around in the Mediterranean Sea—tied down a large number of Iraqi forces because CENTCOM led Saddam to believe that the division would indeed eventually enter through Turkey. According to Woodward, Powell dismissed Franks's claim as "bullsh—." See Woodward, *Plan of Attack*, p. 325.

395 historian Victor Davis Hanson has asked: Victor David Hanson, "Refighting the War," *Commentary*, June 7, 2006, available at http://www.victorhanson.com/articles/hanson060706.html.

396 eventually ran to thirty countries: As of January 2003, thirty countries were playing a role in the coalition: Twenty-five were providing access, basing, and overflight, and three were providing military forces, while several others were discussing possible participation. Feith Memo to Rumsfeld, "Iraq Coalition Update," January 30, 2003.

396 among the bloodiest in history: See, e.g., Simon Jenkins, "Baghdad will be near impossible to conquer," *The Times* (London), March 28, 2003; Robert Fisk, "Saddam Using Stalin's Tactics," *Toronto Star*, March 25, 2006, p. A06; Walter Shapiro, "U.S. Should Pay Heed to Iraq's History," *USA Today*, March 28, 2003, p. 11A.

397 predicted that we would see helpful uprisings: See also Gordon and Trainor, *Cobra II*, p. 137.

397 "put an Iraqi face": Memo of conversation with Lieutenant General John Abizaid by Chris Straub, March 26, 2003.

397 "a military component like the Kurdish parties": Memo from Feith to Wolfowitz, "CENTCOM Military Liaison Officers Assigned to Democratic Iraqi Opposition Groups," March 3, 2003.

398 Probably closer to seven hundred: See Gordon and Trainor, *Cobra II*, p. 315.

398 helped cripple the program: George Tenet recounts that, in the fall of 2002, CIA "officers suggested to DOD [Department of Defense] that they scrap the idea of a fighting force of Iraqi exiles. . . ." See Tenet, *At the Center of the Storm*, p. 398.

In *Cobra II*, Gordon and Trainor reported that a CIA official tried at the last minute to block CENTCOM's deployment into combat of a Chalabi-led expatriate force in April 2003. See Gordon and Trainor, *Cobra II*, p. 316; see also discussion of the FIFF in Chapter 15.

399 subplot in the anoint-Chalabi myth: Tenet, for example, retails this inaccurate account (*At the Center of the Storm*, pp. 398–399, 419): "Long after I left office I heard that Chalabi had been lobbying senior Central Command generals to transport him and his supporters into the war zone so that they could legitimize themselves. Senior CENTCOM officials turned down this request on the night of April 4. When they woke up April 5, they found that their orders had apparently been countermanded by Paul Wolfowitz at the Pentagon." See also Packer, *The Assassins' Gate*, pp. 140–141: "The Pentagon was still trying. Without informing the White House or military commanders, it had flown Chalabi and seven hundred followers—with American uniforms and weapons—from northern Iraq down to the desert outside Nasiriya. The idea was to give Chalabi a head start in the race to power."

399 "to recruit from all eligible groups": [Near East and South Asia Affairs office], Office of the Secretary of Defense/Policy Briefing Paper, "Objections Raised by CENTCOM to Ahmed Chalabi's Participation in Southern Iraq Operation," April 6, 2003.

399 would have preferred that Chalabi stay behind: Interview with William Luti.

400 who cheered and chanted celebratory slogans: The French wire service reported ten thousand people in the crowd. See Agence France Presse, "Baath party must be uprooted forever: Iraqi opposition chief," April 9, 2003. Another account described it as "an ecstatic crowd of several thousand." See David Rose, "Focus: The Battle for Iraq: The Succession: Exile Takes Centre Stage," *The Observer*, April 13, 2003, p. 17.

400 getting supplies for themselves through looting: Information on what happened to the Free Iraqi Fighting Force once they were flown to Tallil Air Base comes from interviews with William Luti and Chris Straub. See also Gordon and Trainor, *Cobra II*, p. 317.

401 directed chiefly against Chalabi: Tenet says that "while you could tell that one name was on the minds of many in the room, no one would utter it," and that "you had the impression" that representatives of the Office of the Vice President and of the Defense Department had a "schoolgirl crush" on Chalabi. Tenet, *At the Center of the Storm*, p. 440. He cites no evidence to support any of this.

402 Iraqis complained publicly about this U.S. policy: See Ahmad Chalabi, "Iraq for the Iraqis," *Wall Street Journal*, February 19, 2003; Kanan Makiya, "Our Hopes Betrayed," *The Observer*, February 16, 2003; Kanan Makiya, "War Diary," The New Republic Online, March 19, 2003, was available through www.tnr.com at time of article's original publication.

404 papers we wrote for the Principals' March 7 meeting: [Office of the Under Secretary of Defense for Policy], Briefing Paper for Rumsfeld, "Iraqi Interim Authority," March 6, 2003, 12:30 P.M. (emphasis added).

404 continued to assert that the IIA was designed to make Chalabi the new leader of Iraq: See, e.g., Tenet, *At the Center of the Storm,* pp. 418–420.

405 In our draft proposed agreement . . .: See [Office of the Under Secretary of Defense for Policy], Briefing paper for Rumsfeld, "Draft Agreement between USG and 'Iraqi Interim Authority' (IIA)," March 6, 2003, 9:20 A.M.

407 Tenet seems to be referring to the proposal: Tenet, *At the Center of the Storm,* p. 419.

408 The meeting's official summary of conclusions: National Security Council, "Summary of Conclusions NSC Meeting on Regional Issues," March 11, 2003. Though this document shows March 11 as the date of the meeting, my notes show it should be March 10.

409 easy to set up a democratic government in post-Saddam Iraq: See, e.g., Francis Fukuyama, *America at the Crossroads: Democracy, Power, and the Neoconservative Legacy* (New Haven: Yale University Press, 2006), pp. 114–118. Fukuyama asserts that "neoconservatives seemed to have assumed that the institutions [in Iraq] would somehow take care of themselves once the United States had done the heavy lifting of coercive regime change" (pp. 117–118), but he offers no quotations from any Administration neoconservatives to support this inaccurate assertion.

410 For a March 31 Principals Committee meeting, Rumsfeld sent: Office of Under Secretary of Defense for Policy, "Iraqi Interim Authority Implementation Concept—Summary," March 30, 2003.

411 "endorsed principles that the USG supports": Ibid.

411 In an April 1 memo to the President: Rumsfeld Memo to President Bush, "Iraqi Interim Authority," April 1, 2003.

413 By April 4 we had general agreement: The *Washington Post* account reported on this phase of the IIA process:

> "We will work with Iraqis, our coalition partners and international organizations to rebuild Iraq," Rice said in a briefing arranged on short notice before she left for the presidential retreat at Camp David. "We will leave Iraq completely in the hands of Iraqis as quickly as possible."
>
> Although established exile politicians would appear to have an organizational edge, Rice said coalition troops have begun to identify Iraqis inside the country who can advise U.S. occupation forces. She said the timing for the establishment of an Iraqi interim authority has not been set, but it may precede the end of hostilities.
>
> "We're watching how events are unfolding on the ground," Rice said. "We're watching the development of potential leaders—local people, for instance—who are coming out. The most important is events on the ground, but it's also the emergence of leadership." . . .
>
> "Decision-making will be done in a consultative process, and Iraqis will be deciding a lot among themselves," said Douglas J. Feith, the Pentagon's policy director. "Our intention is not to be picking and

choosing among Iraqis but arranging a platform on which Iraqi leaders can emerge by some natural process."

Peter Slevin, "U.S. Won't Install Iraqi Expatriates; Inclusive Interim Authority Is Pledged," *Washington Post*, April 5, 2003, p. A28.

413 As late as September 15, 2003, Powell still asserted: In a press conference in Kuwait, Powell emphasized that sovereignty entails a full transfer of governing authority. Colin Powell, Press Briefing at the Kuwait International Airport, Sept. 15, 2003; available at: http://www.state.gov/secretary/former/powell/remarks/2003/24896.htm.

414 sabotage organized by the ousted Baathists: In Baghdad, Jay Garner observed, "not only did they take everything out of the buildings, but then they pulled all the wiring out of the buildings, they pulled all of the plumbing out of the buildings, and they set it on fire. . . . 17 of the 23 ministries were gone when we got to Baghdad." Interview with General Garner, *Frontline*, July 17, 2003. David Kay similarly reported on the "intentional" and "unparalleled" destruction, "designed by the security services to cover the tracks of the Iraq WMD program and their other programs as well." Testimony of David Kay, former Head of Iraq Survey Group, "Iraqi Weapons of Mass Destruction Programs," Hearing of the Senate Armed Services Committee, January 28, 2004, available at http://www.cnn.com/2004/US/01/28/kay.transcript/.

415 When the CIA, in August 2002 . . .: Several years after the fact, news reports generated by the Senate Intelligence Committee called attention to a prewar CIA paper that mentioned that "guerrilla warfare" might occur after Saddam's overthrow. That mention was in a thirty-eight-page National Intelligence Council assessment: "[R]ogue ex-regime elements could forge an alliance with existing terrorist organizations or act independently to wage guerilla warfare against the new government of Coalition forces." National Intelligence Council, "Principal Challenges in Post-Saddam Iraq," January 2003, p. 38.

While the analyst responsible for that sentence deserves some credit, the point was not a major part of the CIA's message to the Administration about post-Saddam Iraq. The observation appeared at the tail end of the report and was not mentioned in the summary of key points at the front of the paper. The fact that such a sentence appeared among the thousands of pages of material on Iraq produced by the CIA in the year or two before the war does not mean that the Agency duly warned CENTCOM or the Administration generally to prepare for the kind of insurgency coalition forces actually faced. (Despite its lack of prominence in the original report, critics of the Administration on the Senate Intelligence Committee highlighted that sentence in the lead paragraph of the "Terrorism" section of a report they published in July 2004 *SSCI Report on Prewar Intelligence*, p. 7.)

George Tenet had the good grace in his book to point out that it is misleading to mine for nuggets of this kind in voluminous intelligence materials and then claim that a nugget proves the CIA was on the top of a matter: "It's tempting to cite this information and say, 'See. We predicted many of the difficulties that later ensued'—but doing so would be disingenuous. . . . Had we felt strongly that these were likely outcomes, we should have shouted our conclusions." George Tenet, *At the Center of the Storm*, p. 318.

416 expresses the free will of the people of Iraq: Lawrence Morahan, "Officials Foresee Role for Regular Iraqi Army in Reconstruction," CNSNEWS.com, March 11, 2003, available at www.cnsnews.com/ViewPentagon.asp?Page=%5cPentagon.%5carchive%5c200303%5cPEN20030311b.html.

ORHA's "A Unified Plan for Post-Hostilities Iraq," with an introduction by Jay Garner, states:

> ***A rapid and orderly transfer of authority from the international mission to the host nation is of the essence.*** **The process of transformation is driven by the indigenous people and is fuelled by their desire to build a self sustaining peace. An important role for the military is to assist the civil authorities in empowering existing legitimate organizations and dismantling separate or parallel power structures in order to create the basis for Iraqi self-government. Parallel, not sequential, deconstruction and reconstruction underpins transition and transformation. The goal is to set the conditions to enable the rapid transfer of government to the Iraqi people.**

A draft copy of the paper, obtained by PBS, is available at http://www.pbs.org/wgbh/pages/frontline/yeariniraq/documents/orha.html (emphasis added).

417 inclusion in a conference declaration: The Nasiriyah conference of April 15, 2003, published the following declaration:

1. Iraq must be democratic.
2. A future government should not be based on communal identity.
3. A future government should be organized as a democratic federal system, but on the basis of countrywide consultation.
4. The rule of law must be paramount.
5. That Iraq must be built on respect for diversity including respect for the role of women.
6. The meeting discussed the role of religion in state and society.
7. The meeting discussed the principle that Iraqis must choose their leaders, not have them imposed from outside.
8. That political violence must be rejected, and that Iraqis must immediately organize themselves for the task of reconstruction at both the local and national levels.
9. That Iraqis and the coalition must work together to tackle the immediate issues of restoring security and basic services.
10. That the Ba'ath party must be dissolved and its effect on society must be eliminated.

11. That there should be an open dialogue with all national political groups to bring them into the process.
12. That the meeting condemns the looting that has taken place and the destruction of documents.
13. The Iraqi participation in the Nasiriyah meeting voted that there should be another meeting in 10 days in a location to be determined with additional Iraqi participants and to discuss procedures for developing an Iraqi interim authority.

Associated Press Worldstream, April 15, 2003. The declarations were formally announced by Wolfowitz. Paul Wolfowitz, Foreign Press Center Briefing on Iraqi Interim Authority, Washington, D.C., April 25, 2003, available at http://www.defenselink.mil/speeches/speech.aspx?speechid=373.

417 Chris Straub, of my office, attended and reported: Straub's report was contained in a memo from Luti to Wolfowitz, "Nasariyah Meeting," April 15, 2003.

417 Makiya also attended the Nasariyah conference: Kanan Makiya, "Memorandum on My Trip to Iraq and Kuwait," April 18, 2003.

419 In a paper my office wrote for the Pentagon public affairs office on April 16: Office of Under Secretary of Defense for Policy, "Freedom Message Statement and Q&A," April 16, 2003 (marked "Draft").

421 General Myers sent CENTCOM formal guidance from Rumsfeld: General Richard Myers message to CENTCOM, "Implementing Guidance Related to Police and Civil Administration," April 23, 2003.

421 the participants resolved to create an Iraqi government: See "Coalition, Factions Discuss Iraq's Political Future," PBS Online NewsHour, April 28, 2003, available at http://www.pbs.org/newshour/updates/meeting_04-28-03.html.

422 President Bush decided to appoint Ambassador L. Paul Bremer: Various commentators at the time (and since) have called Bremer's appointment a victory by State over Defense in the interagency contest for influence over U.S. Iraq policy. See, e.g., Michael Hirsh, "The State Dept. Wins One," *Newsweek* (Newsweek Web Exclusive), April 30, 2003, available at http://www.newsweek.com/id/58325.

422 the notion that the Defense Department was bent on excluding State from Iraq policy: In his book, Bremer relates the following conversation with Powell:

> "You know," Powell said smiling, "Don Rumsfeld called me in early May before the president announced your appointment."
>
> "Well," I answered as the big, frigidly air-conditioned SUV crawled down the twisting escarpment road through the heat mirage, "he told me he was going to bounce my name off you, Condi, George Tenet, and the vice president before going to the president."
>
> "I tried to keep my voice lukewarm on the phone," Colin admitted. "But when I hung up, I flat-out whooped with joy." He pumped

> **his arm to emulate his gesture. "The people in my outer office thought I had just won the lottery."**

Bremer, *My Year in Iraq*, p. 76.

422 government of Iraq was now passing from military to civilian hands: The official announcement specified the responsibilities and reporting relationships of the new role:

> **Ambassador Bremer will serve as the senior Coalition official in Iraq. In his capacity as Presidential Envoy, he will oversee Coalition reconstruction efforts and the process by which the Iraqi people build the institutions and governing structures that will guide their future. General Tommy Franks will maintain command over Coalition military personnel in the theater. Ambassador Bremer will report to Secretary of Defense Rumsfeld and will advise the President, through the Secretary, on policies designed to achieve American and Coalition goals for Iraq.**

Statement by the Press Secretary, "President Names Envoy to Iraq, May 6, 2003, available at http://www.whitehouse.gov/news/releases/2003/05/20030506–5.html.

423 "best thing. . . is for me to leave after he gets here": "I think if I'd had 120 days," Garner continued, "I could have gotten a hell of a lot of stuff done. . . . We would at least have an opportunity to have a different outcome. . . . We could have been very involved and started [the constitutional process]. Instead, we shifted from the Iraqi perception of us being liberators to the Iraqi perception of us being occupiers, and they resented that. The Iraqis are good people, and they're nice people, but they're fiercely independent, probably more so than we are. So I don't think you can take on the mantle of an occupier and last very long." Interview with General Garner, "The Lost Year in Iraq," *Frontline*, PBS, August 11, 2006, http://www.pbs.org/wgbh/pages/frontline/yeariniraq/interviews/garner.html.

423 In the cover memo we gave Bremer: Office of Under Secretary of Defense for Policy, "Iraqi Interim Authority Overview," April 28, 2003.

424 The Iraqis had resolved to hold another meeting within four weeks: "Coalition, Factions Discuss Iraq's Political Future," PBS Online NewsHour, April 28, 2003, available at http://www.pbs.org/newshour/updates/meeting_04–28–03.html.

CHAPTER 14: "FROM LIBERATION TO OCCUPATION"

427 head of the Coalition Provisional Authority: President Bush appointed L. Paul Bremer as Presidential Envoy to Iraq. See Statement by the Press Secretary, "President Names Envoy to Iraq," White House, May 6, 2006, available at http://www.whitehouse.gov/news/releases/2003/05/20030506–5.html. Rumsfeld then designated Bremer "as the head of the Coalition Provisional Authority, with the title of

Administrator." See Rumsfeld Memo to Bremer, "Designation as Administrator of the Coalition Provisional Authority," May 13, 2003.

427 **Bush at the March 10 National Security Council meeting:** Tenet's claim that "there was no NSC Principals meeting to debate [de-Baathification]" is incorrect (Tenet, *In the Center of the Storm*, p. 427). At the March 10, 2003, National Security Council meeting at which that policy was discussed, Tenet was present, according to the official Summary of Conclusions of the meeting.

428 **"intimately linked to the regime":** U.S. Central Intelligence Agency, *Iraq: The Day After*, October 18, 2002, p. 1, cited in U.S. Senate Select Committee on Intelligence, *Prewar Intelligence Assessments About Postwar Iraq Together with Additional Views*, [undated, publicly released on May 25, 2007], pp. 100–101 of 226, available at http://intelligence.senate.gov/prewar.pdf.

428 **"eliminate the Ba'ath party oversight mechanism":** U.S. Central Intelligence Agency, *The Iraqi Ba'th Party: Inexorably Tied to Saddam*, October 31, 2002, p. 2, cited in U.S. Senate Select Committee on Intelligence, *Prewar Intelligence Assessments About Postwar Iraq Together with Additional Views*, p. 101 of 226.

428 **the necessity for substantial de-Baathification:** U.S. Department of State, *Future of Iraq Project* [2005], available at http://www.gwu.edu/~nsarchiv/NSAEBB/NSAEBB198/index.htm. (The Future of Iraq meetings were held June 2002–April 2003.) The Democratic Principles and Procedures Working Group states in its report that the tasks of the transitional government should include "De-Ba'athification of the institutions of government." It goes on to state that "the liberation of Iraq from a regime which is totalitarian in its nature will not be complete or effective without dismantling the structures of control exercised by the Ba'ath Party, as an institution as well as an ideology, over Iraqi society. A program of de-Ba'athification of all facets of Iraqi life has therefore to be put into effect, aiming towards a disengagement of the party presence and control from all institutions of Iraqi society."

429 **issuing CPA Order No. 1, "De-Ba'athification of Iraqi Society":** See Coalition Provisional Authority Order No. 1, "De-Ba'athification of Iraqi Society," May 16, 2003, available at http://www.iraqcoalition.org/regulations/20030516_CPAORD_1_De-Ba_athification_of_Iraqi_Society_.pdf.

429 **this de-Baathification order was scorned:** See David Rieff, "Blueprint for a Mess"; Thomas Ricks, "In Iraq, Military Forgot Lessons of Vietnam," *Washington Post*, July 23, 2006, p. A01; General Anthony Zinni (USMC, retired), "Equal Time: Restore regular Iraqi army to assist with reconstruction," *Atlanta Journal-Constitution*, February 5, 2004, p. 15A.

429 **Others have taken the opposite position:** See, e.g., Reuel Marc Gerecht, "On Democracy in Iraq," *The Weekly Standard*, April 30, 2007; Victor Davis Hanson, "Stasis or Victory?," *National Review Online*, January 5, 2007, available at http://www.victorhanson.com/articles/hanson010507.html; Interview with Sam Spector by Kanan Mikiya, January 26, 2005, published in the *Middle East Quarterly*, Spring 2005, available at http://www.meforum.org/article/718.

431 **had long hated as oppressors:** See Bremer, *My Year in Iraq*, p. 261: "We had

reports from our provincial offices and military commanders that many more people were being subjected to de-Baathification than foreseen in my initial order."

431 Bremer eventually delegated the de-Baathification process: See Coalition Provisional Authority Memorandum No. 7, "Delegation of Authority Under De-Baathification Order No. 1," November 4, 2003, available at http://www.iraqcoalition.org/regulations/20031104_CPAMEM0_7_Delegation_of_Authority.pdf.

431 Bremer has written that this was an error: See L. Paul Bremer III, "What We Got Right in Iraq," *Washington Post*, May 13, 2007, p. B1; Interview with L. Paul Bremer, "The Lost Year in Iraq," *Frontline*, PBS, conducted on June 26 and August 18, 2006, transcript available at http://www.pbs.org/wgbh/pages/frontline/yeariniraq/interviews/bremer.html.

431 would feel betrayed: Brian Bennett, "Sorting the Bad from the Not-So-Bad," *Time*, May 11, 2003, available at http://www.time.com/time/magazine/article/0,9171,450991-1,00.html.

431 the case for Garner's plan was reasonably strong: See Chapter 12 for a discussion of my briefing to the President of the Garner plan for using the Iraqi army in the postwar period.

432 whole units could have been reassembled: See Tenet, *At the Center of the Storm*, pp. 428–430; Rieff, "Blueprint for a Mess."

432 Shiite leaders, he says, would have stopped cooperating: Bremer, "What We Got Right in Iraq," p. B1. See also Interview with Bremer, "The Lost Year in Iraq," *Frontline*.

432 "employees and retirees of the dissolved entities": Bremer Memo to Rumsfeld, "Dissolution of the Ministry of Defense and Related Entities," May 19, 2003.

433 in "the coming days": Ibid.

433 neither Saddam nor his gang is coming back: Ibid.

433 Bremer issued CPA Order No. 2: See Coalition Provisional Authority Order No. 2, "Dissolution of Entities," May 23, 2003, available at http://www.iraqcoalition.org/regulations/20030823_CPAORD_2_Dissolution_of_Entities_with_Annex_A.pdf. I have no record of Rumsfeld's response to Bremer's May 19 memo on dissolution. (The official CPA website (http://www.cpa-iraq.org/) gives August 23, 2003, as the date of CPA Order No. 2. The order itself, however, shows the date as May 23, 2003. The error may reflect a misreading of Bremer's handwritten date on the document: The "5," representing the month of May, looks like an "8.")

433 wasn't consulted on CPA Order No. 2: Tenet, *At the Center of the Storm*, p. 428.

433 more inclined to defend it after it was announced: My meeting notes from May 2003 show that Bremer circulated the army dissolution order to my office, the Joint Staff, and the office of the Defense Department General Counsel before it was finalized and published. Bremer writes that Slocombe consulted CENTCOM in advance and "Lieutenant General David McKiernan, Abizaid's commander on the ground, had been fully consulted, too." Bremer, *My Year in Iraq*, pp. 223–224.

433 properly reasoned through by Bremer and Slocombe: See Bremer, "What

We Got Right in Iraq," p. B1; Bremer, *My Year in Iraq*, pp. 53–59; Walter B. Slocombe, "To Build an Army," *Washington Post*, November 5, 2003, p. A29; Interview with Bremer, "The Lost Year in Iraq," *Frontline*.

434 would be paid monthly stipends: Coalition Provisional Authority, Press Release, "Good News for Iraqi Soldiers," June 23, 2003, available at http://www.iraqcoalition.org/pressreleases/23June03PR6_good_news.pdf.

434 protecting fixed sites and convoy escorts: Coalition Provisional Authority, Briefing Slides, "New Iraqi Corps (NIC) Concept," June 3, 2003.

435 did not develop a unified concept and plan: Even as late as October 2003, Bremer resented CENTCOM's desire to get the new Iraqi army "more involved in internal security." He reports having said at the time that one of his "red lines" about Iraq was that "we must not have an army involved in internal affairs." Bremer, *My Year in Iraq*, p. 203. This became an issue with Abizaid, who favored a U.S. military role in training Iraqi police. Ibid., pp. 198–199.

435 out of the role of military occupier: In his book, *Imperial Life in the Emerald City: Inside Iraq's Green Zone, Washington Post* reporter Rajiv Chandrasekaran argues that the occupation was a mistake and criticizes the Administration for ignoring the advice of experienced State Department Middle East experts. Dan Senor, a CPA official, responded: The argument that the Administration should have moved quickly "to empower a full, sovereign Iraqi government" was "precisely the policy that was vociferously opposed by the State Department's Middle East experts." Indeed, Senor points out, "the approach Chandrasekaran now claims to prefer has much more in common with the rapid political transition plan backed by the very Pentagon neoconservatives he disparages throughout his account." Dan Senor, "The Realities of Trying to Rebuild Iraq," *Washington Post*, October 10, 2006, p. A21.

436 within a month or two of the regime's removal: See OSD Policy, "Iraq Interim Authority Implementation Plan," April 29, 2003.

437 "give us your recommendation": See Interview with Bremer, "The Lost Year in Iraq," *Frontline*: "My impressions from my meetings in Washington in early May, and very clearly from a meeting at the NSC [National Security Council], was that we were to take our time and put the Iraqis on a path to democracy, and that this would take time. We were not to rush to [appoint an] interim government."

437 "work with the process we had set up": David Sedney [assistant to Zalmay Khalilzad] Fax to McLaughlin, Wolfowitz, Pace, and Armitage, "Khalilzad/Baghdad Meeting," May 1, 2003. The principal Iraqi leaders at that meeting were Iyad Allawi of the Iraqi National Accord, Massoud Barzani of the Kurdish Democratic Party, Ahmad Chalabi of the Iraqi National Congress, Abdulaziz el-Hakim of the Supreme Council for Islamic Revolution in Iraq, and Jalal Talabani of the Patriotic Union of Kurdistan.

437 transitional Iraqi "government" near the end of May: Office of Under Secretary of Defense for Policy, Briefing Paper for Rumsfeld, "Read Ahead for PC [Principals Committee meeting] on IIA [Iraqi Interim Authority]," May 3, 2003.

437 On May 5, Garner announced to journalists: See Carol Morello, "'Nucleus' of Iraqi Leaders Emerges; Occupation Chief Outlines Plan for Interim Authority,"

Washington Post, May 6, 2003, p. A1 (emphasis added); Patrick E. Tyler, "Aftereffects: Postwar Rule; Opposition Groups to Help to Create Assembly in Iraq," *New York Times*, May 6, 2003, p. 1.

439 "hand over sovereignty to the Iraqis": Interview with Bremer, "The Lost Year in Iraq," *Frontline*.

440 to appoint an Iraqi interim government: Ibid.

441 "reckless fantasy": Bremer, *My Year in Iraq*, p. 12 (emphasis added).

441 "bureaucratic hamsters": Ibid., pp. 81, 192.

441 President Bush appointed him Presidential Envoy: President Bush letter to Bremer, [no subject line], May 9, 2003.

441 as the new head of the CPA: Rumsfeld Memo to Bremer, "Designation as Administrator of the Coalition Provisional Authority," May 13, 2003 (unclassified).

441 "that most Iraqis had ever known": Bremer, *My Year in Iraq*, p. 4 (emphasis added).

442 "saying they too represented the President": Ibid., p. 11 (emphasis added).

442 "I was the President's man": Ibid., p. 12 (emphasis added).

442 my staff suggested a daily secure video: Office of the Under Secretary of Defense for Policy, Briefing Paper, "Support for the Presidential Envoy to Iraq," May 13, 2003.

443 "getting things done, fast": Bremer, *My Year in Iraq*, pp. 156, 208.

443 his "first impressions" memo of May 22, 2003: Bremer Memo to President Bush, [no title], May 22, 2003, reprinted on nytimes.com, available at http://www.nytimes.com/ref/washington/04bremer-text1.html. The memo has the May 22 date at the top but a May 20, 2003, date under Bremer's signature block.

443 he canceled the recent statements by the two of them: Bremer, *My Year in Iraq*, p. 44.

444 "was now in charge": Ibid., p. 43.

444 "on almost any argument": Ibid., pp. 48–49.

444 "putting down the hammer": Bremer declares: Ibid., p. 49 (emphasis in original).

444 Zebari later observed: Robert L. Pollock, "The Voice of Iraq," *Wall Street Journal*, June 24, 2006, p. A10.

444 "making even simple decisions": Bremer, *My Year in Iraq*, p. 49.

444 "intriguing proved hard to set aside": Ibid., p. 82.

445 "about which office they will hold": Ibid., p. 86.

445 "had flunked the test again": Ibid.

445 "not the future of his party or his country": Ibid., p. 88.

445 "to decide important matters": Ibid., p. 100.

445 "from the Iraqi politicians": Ibid., p. 115.

445 Iraqi leaders failed to attend meetings with him at the CPA: Ibid., p. 194.

446 "agreed by all the people": Bremer Memo to President Bush, [no title], May 22, 2003.

446 in a memo to Rumsfeld the next day: Bremer Memo to Rumsfeld, "The 'Fast-Slow' Approach to the Creation of an Interim Administration," May 23, 2003.

447 holding national elections would take *two years*: Chris Straub Memo to William Luti, "Coalition Provisional Authority's (CPA's) Plans for Iraqi Governance," June 2, 2003 (FOUO).

447 deciding how to try to fund them: The problem of funding made every problem more difficult. I argued for an approach that would frontload the reconstruction budget, on the assumption that the initial needs would be disproportionately large. [Office of the Under Secretary of Defense for Policy] briefing, "'Jump Up,' Don't 'Ramp Up,'" July 19, 2003.

447 "principal body of the Iraqi interim administration": See Coalition Provisional Authority Regulation No. 6, "Governing Council of Iraq," July 13, 2003, available at http://www.iraqcoalition.org/regulations/20030713_CPAREG_6_Governing_Council_of_Iraq_.pdf. The regulation describes the process in these terms: The Governing Council "met and announced its formation."

448 a nine-person, monthly rotating presidency: The nine members elected to the rotational leadership group were: Jaafari, Chalabi, Allawi, Talabani, Hakim, Pachachi, Hamid, Bahr al-Uloum, and Barzani. See Bremer Memo to Rumsfeld, "CPA Issues," July 30, 2003.

448 role that was envisioned for the IIA: See Bremer, *My Year in Iraq*, pp. 123–124.

448 "without prodding and handholding by the CPA": Ibid., p. 143.

448 "when we in the CPA could not": Ibid., p. 117.

448 "*as some in Washington had wanted*": Ibid., p. 121 (emphasis in original).

448 "had gripped the Governing Council": Ibid., p. 122.

448 "by lax work habits": Ibid., p. 123.

448 "than the CPA works every day": Ibid.

448 "let alone run a country": Ibid., p. 171.

453 "Iraq's Path to Sovereignty": L. Paul Bremer III, "Iraq's Path to Sovereignty," *Washington Post*, September 8, 2003, p. A21.

CHAPTER 15: THE TAINT OF OCCUPATION

457 compel Iraq's new leaders to do things our way: Our public statements stressed U.S. respect for Iraqi sovereignty and promised that the CPA and U.S. forces would depart as soon as their missions were done. See, e.g., Douglas J. Feith, "Post-War Planning," Testimony before the Senate Committee on Foreign Relations, February 11, 2003, available at http://www.defenselink.mil/policy/sections/public_statements/speeches/archive/former_usdp/feith/2003/february_11_03.html; Douglas Feith, "Remarks to the Center for Strategic and International Studies," Washington, D.C., July 7, 2003, available at http://www.defenselink.mil/transcripts/2003/tr20030707–0362.html: "We are not interested in staying any longer than is required. We have no ambitions to control or dominate Iraq and will be very happy when our work is done and we can depart."

458 run largely by current or former State officials: The leadership of the CPA was composed almost entirely of current or former State Department officials. For the list, see L. Paul Bremer III, "These Are Not Ideologues: The top officials during my time at the Coalition Provisional Authority," *Wall Street Journal* OpinionJournal (For the Record), November 2, 2006, available at http://www.opinionjournal.com/extra/?id=110009179.

458 fell short of full sovereignty: See Bremer, *My Year in Iraq*, pp. 163–168.

459 was "entirely unacceptable": Ibid., p. 164. Bremer writes of telling Rumsfeld: "The Governing Council has no mandate to rule Iraq. Its members, however capable as individuals, have little support. They lack credibility in large sectors of the population. As yet, they have hesitated in making important policy decisions unless pushed and prodded by the CPA." Ibid., pp. 167–168.

459 "John Hannah in the vice president's office": Ibid., p. 167. Noting that France was urging UN Secretary-General Kofi Annan to work directly with the Iraqi Governing Council (which would tend to delegitimate the U.S. role in Iraq), Bremer conflates his critics as some sort of Franco-neocon axis: "factions were forming at Washington and at the United Nations that shared the goal of granting sovereignty prematurely to Iraq." Ibid., p. 167.

459 that is, my organization: Ibid., pp. 217.

459 "*That's Feith's Defense policy shop talking*": Ibid., p. 183 (emphasis in original).

459 "every senior member on the president's foreign policy team": Ibid., p. 188.

459 Despite these and similar stories: Some similar stories from Bremer:

- In November 2003, Rice pressed Bremer again on "handing sovereignty to an appointed government"; "earlier is better." Bremer, *My Year in Iraq*, p. 218.
- At a National Security Council meeting, General Peter Pace observed, "The most important military strategy is to accelerate the governance track." Bremer read that as advocating that the United States "slap together an Iraqi government, grant it sovereignty, and end the occupation." Ibid., p. 223.
- Also in November, Cheney suggested, "Maybe the Governing Council should just choose an executive body that we could recognize as the transitional government." Ibid., p. 225.

460 handled the CPA administrator delicately: Bremer recounts that in a September 13, 2003, conversation, Rumsfeld made him "uneasy" by expressing "enthusiasm for the concept of granting sovereignty as soon as possible to the Council or some other group of Iraqis." Bremer writes that he "told him bluntly that I disagreed" and sent Rumsfeld a memo that argued: "The Council is a leaky vessel. To grant them sovereignty before a constitution and elections not only mocks our avowed commitment to a constitutional process, it risks failure of that process. Left to their own devices with only the 'guiding hand' of the UN, it is entirely possible that the GC would dissolve itself, or worse, be dominated by one or two individuals." He also reports that Rumsfeld, in a note, said that he agreed with Bremer. Ibid., pp. 167–168. If the story is accurate, it appears that Rumsfeld had decided to keep his misgivings about Bremer's seven-step plan to himself for the time being.

460 He now had a set of strategic concepts: [Douglas J. Feith and Lieutenant General Walter L. Sharp (principal drafters)], "Strategic Review: Stay the Course—Faster," October 28, 2003, 12:15 P.M.

461 improving security and essential services: See Bremer, *My Year in Iraq*, pp. 115–116, for a discussion of the CPA's strategic priorities. Bremer states that "the plan identified security as our top priority," and goes on to discuss economic and basic services goals. At the end of that discussion he introduces the political tasks: "Finally, we would prepare the ground for representative government." Bremer reports that "Powell noted that the real problem in Iraq was security" and that "nothing we did [on the political front] would matter if we didn't solve the security problem." Ibid., p. 207. Again, Bremer stresses the failures of others rather than the interconnectedness of the political, military, and economic missions.

461 a prerequisite for political progress: Ibid., p. 209: "I said [to President Bush] that I agreed with Powell's comment that we had to fix the security problem or none of the other areas—governance, reconstruction—could succeed."

462 "governance, security, and economy": Feith and Sharp, "Stay the Course—Faster."

462 *not* be used for internal security: See Bremer, *My Year in Iraq*, p. 203: "we must not have an army involved in internal affairs." Also (in mid-July 2003): "'In my view,' I'd told [Rice], 'the Coalition's got about *half* the number of soldiers we need here" (p. 106, emphasis in original). In mid-September 2003, Bremer reacted to Abizaid's proposal that the U.S. military take responsibility for training Iraqi police: "Pushing tens of thousands of Iraqi police recruits through truncated training courses in order to replace American troops didn't appear to me to be a sensible long-term approach to the country's security" (p. 168).

463 a practical good idea: Iraq's interim constitution: I saw Bremer's idea of an interim constitution as a variation—and an improvement—on the aspect of the original IIA plan that envisioned an agreement between the IIA and the U.S. government on a bill of rights for later inclusion in the Iraqi constitution. See Office of Under Secretary of Defense for Policy, "Draft Agreement between the USG and 'Iraqi Interim Authority' (IIA)," March 6, 2003, 9:20 A.M.

464 "by late 2004, at best": Meghan O'Sullivan and Roman Martinez Memo to Bremer on "Overview of Changing Timeline Proposals," October 28, 2003.

466 an inflexible demand of Grand Ayatollah Ali al-Sistani: See Bremer, *My Year in Iraq*, p. 167: Referring to the seven-step plan, he writes that Sistani's "inflexible position would prove to be the undoing of our first plan for Iraq's political process."

466 even from Bremer's point of view: Ibid., pp. 211–212.

467 caucuses were the *only* practical approach: Ibid., pp. 226–227.

467 while Sistani spoke as their champion: Ibid., pp. 163–167. A theme of Bremer's tenure in Iraq was "we have to show that we're not going to be pushed around by Ayatollah Sistani." Ibid., p. 281.

467 yield a "less legitimate government": Bremer, *My Year in Iraq*, p. 225.

467 or appear to oppose—elections: Rumsfeld Memo to Cheney, Powell, Tenet, Card, and Rice, "Quick thoughts following the January 16 meeting on Iraq," January 18, 2004.

468 By November 15 he reached an agreement: The November 15 Agreement between the Iraq Governing Council and the Coalition Provisional Authority, available at http://www.memri.org/bin/articles.cgi?Page=archives&Area=ia&ID=IA15703#_edn1.

469 "authority, direction and control of the Secretary of Defense": President Bush Letter to Bremer, May 9, 2003.

469 repeatedly in his book: See Bremer, *My Year in Iraq*, pp. 247, 271.

469 In an October 2, 2003 memo . . .: Rice Memo to Cheney, Powell, Snow, Rumsfeld, Card, Bolten, Tenet, and Myers, "Iraq Stabilization Group," October 2, 2003.

469 The *New York Times* described the Iraq Stabilization Group: David E. Sanger, "White House to Overhaul Iraq and Afghan Missions," *New York Times*, October 6, 2003.

470 Strongly worded memo to the President's Chief of Staff: Rumsfeld Memo to Card, "Iraq Stabilization Phase Reporting Relationship," October 6, 2003.

471 another former UNSCOM inspector: Iraq Survey Group, *Comprehensive Report of the Special Advisor to the DCI on Iraq's Weapons of Mass Destruction*, September 30, 2004, Vol. 1, "Scope Note," pp. 1—2, available at https://www.cia.gov/library/reports/general-reports-1/iraq_wmd_2004/index.html. (Hereafter, Duelfer Report.)

471 Kay reported preliminary findings to Congress: David Kay, "Statement on the Interim Progress Report on the Activities of the Iraq Survey Group (ISG) before the House Permanent Select Committee on Intelligence, the House Committee on Appropriations, Subcommittee on Defense, and the Senate Select Committee on Intelligence," October 2, 2003 (emphasis in original), available at https://www.cia.gov/news-information/speeches-testimony/2003/david_kay_10022003.html. (Hereafter, Kay Report.)

471 "deliberate, rather than random, acts": Ibid.

471 "a capability for resuming BW production": Ibid. The final Duelfer Report confirms the point:

> **Depending on its scale, Iraq could have re-established an elementary BW program within a few weeks to a few months of a decision to do so, but ISG discovered no indications that the Regime was pursuing such a course.**

Duelfer Report, Vol. III, "Biological Warfare", p. 2 (emphasis in original).

471 "avenue for furthering BW-applicable research": Kay Report.

471 "that the IIS appeared to sponsor": Ibid.

472 "after Iraq was free of sanctions": Ibid.

472 "reconstitution of nuclear weapons–related work": Ibid.

472 "have them available when needed": Duelfer Report, Vol. II, "Nuclear," p. 132.

472 "or make available chemical weapons": Kay Report.

474 "the subject of threats and attacks": Ibid.

474 "justify his decision to go to war": David E. Sanger, "The Struggle for Iraq: Assessment; A Reckoning: Iraq Arms Report Poses Test for Bush," *New York Times*, October 3, 2003, p. A13. The *Washington Post* story on Kay's report was headlined: "Search in Iraq Finds No Banned Weapons" (Dana Priest and Walter Pincus, *Washington Post*, October 3, 2003, p. A1). Similar headlines ran throughout the United States and around the world. See, e.g., "US team finds no Iraq WMD," BBC News, October 3, 2003. http://news.bbc.co.uk/1/hi/world/middle_east/3157246.stm; "CIA Chief Weapons Inspector: No WMD Found," CNN *American Morning*, October 3, 2003, http://transcripts.cnn.com/TRANSCRIPTS/0310/03/ltm.13.html. The misleading headlines helped create the common misimpression that the Kay Report simply confirmed that prewar fears of Saddam's WMD capabilities were groundless.

474 broader than the concerns about WMD stockpiles: The Congressional Resolution of October 10, 2002, authorized military action against Iraq. Of its eighteen substantive clauses, six focused on WMD and twelve discussed a range of issues (sometimes including WMD). ("Joint Resolution to Authorize the Use of United States Armed Forces Against Iraq," available at http://www.whitehouse.gov/news/releases/2002/10/20021002–2.html.)

474 wasn't based only on the idea that Saddam possessed stockpiles: As noted, Administration officials discussed the Iraqi WMD threat as a matter of Saddam's history of WMD development and use, his intentions, facilities, programs, and capabilities—and not just stockpiles. Examples of this argument abound. In October 2002, President Bush stated: "By its past and present actions, by its technological capabilities, by the merciless nature of its regime, Iraq is unique. As a former chief weapons inspector of the U.N. has said, 'The fundamental problem with Iraq remains the nature of the regime, itself. Saddam Hussein is a homicidal dictator who is addicted to weapons of mass destruction.' . . . If the Iraqi regime is able to produce, buy, or steal an amount of highly enriched uranium a little larger than a single softball, it could have a nuclear weapon in less than a year. And if we allow that to happen, a terrible line would be crossed. Saddam Hussein would be in a position to blackmail anyone who opposes his aggression." Remarks by President Bush on Iraq at the Cincinnati Museum Center—Cincinnati Union Terminal, Cincinnati, Ohio, October 10, 2002, available at http://www.whitehouse.gov/news/releases/2002/10/20021007-8.html. See also Vice President Richard Cheney, Remarks to the Veterans of Foreign Wars 103rd National Convention, August 26, 2002, available at http://www.whitehouse.gov/news/releases/2002/08/20020826.html.

475 at a White House South Lawn press event: President George W. Bush, "President Bush, Police Commissioner Kerik Discuss Police Force in Iraq," October 3, 2003, available at http://www.whitehouse.gov/news/releases/2003/10/20031003–2.html.

475 Rice, addressing the Council on Foreign Relations: Condoleezza Rice, "Dr. Condoleezza Rice Discusses Iraq in Chicago," October 8, 2003, available at http://www.whitehouse.gov/news/releases/2003/10/20031008-4.html.

475 Cheney provided a more substantive treatment: Richard Cheney, "Remarks by the Vice President to the Heritage Foundation," October 10, 2003, available at http://www.whitehouse.gov/news/releases/2003/10/print/20031010-1.html.

478 Zarqawi wrote an extraordinary letter: Abu Musab al-Zarqawi, Letter obtained by United States Government in Iraq, February 2004 Coalition Provisional Authority English translation, available at http://www.state.gov/p/nea/rls/31694.htm.

478 in a February 9, 2004, *New York Times* story: Dexter Filkins, "The Struggle for Iraq: Intelligence; U.S. Says Files Seek Qaeda Aid in Iraq Conflict," *New York Times*, February 9, 2004, p. A1.

478 as close affiliates of al Qaida: In his February 5, 2003, speech to the UN Security Council, Powell said:

> Iraq today harbors a deadly terrorist network, headed by Abu Musaab al-Zarqawi, an associate and collaborator of Osama bin Laden and his Al Qaeda lieutenants.
>
> Zarqawi, a Palestinian born in Jordan, fought in the Afghan War more than a decade ago. Returning to Afghanistan in 2000, he oversaw a terrorist training camp. One of his specialties and one of the specialties of this camp is poisons.
>
> When our coalition ousted the Taliban, the Zarqawi network helped establish another poison and explosive training center camp, and this camp is located in Northeastern Iraq. . . .
>
> ---
>
> Those helping to run this camp are Zarqawi lieutenants operating in northern Kurdish areas outside Saddam Hussein's controlled Iraq, but Baghdad has an agent in the most senior levels of the radical organization Ansar al-Islam, that controls this corner of Iraq. In 2000, this agent offered Al Qaeda safe haven in the region. After we swept Al Qaeda from Afghanistan, some of its members accepted this safe haven. They remain there today.
>
> Zarqawi's activities are not confined to this small corner of northeast Iraq. He traveled to Baghdad in May 2002 for medical treatment, staying in the capital of Iraq for two months while he recuperated to fight another day. During this stay, nearly two dozen extremists converged on Baghdad and established a base of operations there. These Al Qaeda affiliates, based in Baghdad, now coordinate the movement of people, money and supplies into and throughout Iraq for his network, and they've now been operating freely in the capital for more than eight months.
>
> Iraqi officials deny accusations of ties with Al Qaeda. These deni-

als are simply not credible. Last year, an Al Qaeda associate bragged that the situation in Iraq was "good," that Baghdad could be transited quickly. . . .

From his terrorist network in Iraq, Zarqawi can direct his network in the Middle East and beyond. We in the United States, all of us at the State Department, and the Agency for International Development, we all lost a dear friend with the cold-blooded murder of Mr. Lawrence Foley in Amman, Jordan, last October. . . .

Iraqi officials protest that they are not aware of the whereabouts of Zarqawi or of any of his associates. Again, these protests are not credible. We know of Zarqawi's activities in Baghdad. I described them earlier. And now, let me add one other fact. We asked a friendly security service to approach Baghdad about extraditing Zarqawi and providing information about him and his close associates. This service contacted Iraqi officials twice, and we passed details that should have made it easy to find Zarqawi. The network remains in Baghdad; Zarqawi still remains at large to come and go.

Colin L. Powell, "Remarks to the United Nations Security Council," New York City, February 5, 2003, available at http://www.state.gov/secretary/former/powell/remarks/2003/17300.htm.

479 **or "al Qaida in Iraq"**: See U.S. State Department, Office of the Coordinator for Counterterrorism, *Country Reports on Terrorism*, April 28, 2006, Chapter 8: "Foreign Terrorist Organizations," section on Al-Qaida in Iraq, available at http://www.state.gov/s/ct/rls/crt/2005/65275.htm.

480 **"the CPA reported that Sadr was guilty"**: See Office of Political Adviser, Coalition Provisional Authority office in Najaf, Iraq, "Muqtada Sadr Chronology," Information Paper, [undated], circulated to the Principals and others by Frank Miller of National Security Council staff for March 11, 2004 Principals Committee meeting.

480 **to try to capture Sadr:** On August 18, 2003, Bremer told Rumsfeld during a regular video teleconference that an Iraqi judge might be issuing an arrest warrant for Sadr the next day. Rumsfeld asked how the arrest would be executed and where Sadr would be held—would that be done by Iraqi police or U.S. forces? Bremer did not give Rumsfeld confidence that the potentially large political effects of the arrest had been thought through. After the teleconference, Rumsfeld dictated a list of questions for me to fax to Bremer, emphasizing that he wanted answers "before an operation to detain Sadr is initiated." Among the questions:

- **"Who would detain Sadr and where? What is the process thereafter—how long before trial, then what, etc.?"**
- **"What is your plan to inform and guide Iraqi opinion about the arrest? International opinion?"**
- **"Have you consulted with the Shi'a clerical leadership in the Howza**

(seminary) in an-Najaf? As you know, Ayatollah Sistani and the Howza are monitoring Sadr's behavior."

- **"What would be the role—if any—of the Governing Council?"**
- **"Is this something that must be done now? Or can it wait for the results of your campaign to inform Shi'a opinion?"**
- **"How do you plan to consult with the UK?"**

Feith Memo to Bremer, "Muqtada al-Sadr," August 18, 2003.

According to Bremer, these questions stymied the arrest operation. He gives a fractured account of the story in his book, making no mention of the teleconference and saying that "out of the blue" he received word from Rumsfeld not to arrest Sadr "until further notice." (I doubt that Rumsfeld ever sent such word to Bremer.) Bremer quotes only one of the questions and says they "repeated the same points that we had already answered many times." But Bremer had not answered these questions—and, even if he thought he had, Rumsfeld was not satisfied that the CPA was on top of the matter.

No one at the Pentagon wanted to be accused—in the standard terminology—of trying to wield a five-thousand-mile-long screwdriver to fine-tune operations in the field. But if the CPA botched Sadr's arrest and provoked a Shiite uprising, Rumsfeld would be held accountable: He had the obligation to ensure that Bremer was being careful. Bremer had a difficult job, but it would have gone better if he were not so easily exasperated. See Bremer, *My Year in Iraq*, pp. 135–136.

481 the 36th battalion of the Iraqi Civil Defense Corps: CENTCOM Briefing Slides, distributed at April 9, 2004, National Security Council meeting.

485 surprised Bremer as well as Washington: See Bremer, *My Year in Iraq*, p. 344.

486 use the old Iraqi army from the beginning: Ibid., pp. 345–346.

486 Brahimi was negative about the leaders: Ibid., p. 348: Brahimi "envisioned replacing almost all the ministers in the existing Iraqi government, and excluding members of the Governing Council from the new cabinet, even making them ineligible to run for election in January [2005]."

486 antagonistic toward Ahmad Chalabi: My staff, in a read-ahead memo for Rumsfeld for a Principals Committee meeting, observed that "Brahimi appears determined to get rid of some GC [Governing Council] members, most notably Ahmed Chalabi." Office of Under Secretary of Defense for Policy, "Read Ahead on Ambassador Brahimi's Mission," April 20, 2004, 11:00 A.M.

487 intelligence agencies were accusing Chalabi: Mark Hosenball, "Intelligence: A Double Game," *Newsweek*, May 10, 2004, p. 30.

488 "are perfect one way or another": Interview with Donald Rumsfeld, *Hardball with Chris Matthews*, MSNBC, April 29, 2004, transcript available at http://www.defenselink.mil/transcripts/transcript.aspx?transcriptid=2555.

489 "that intelligence was accurate and useful in many cases": General Richard Myers, "Operations and Reconstruction Efforts in Iraq," Testimony before the House

Armed Services Committee, May 21, 2004, transcript available at http://commdocs.house.gov/committees/security/has142000.000/has142000_0f.htm.

489 *Los Angeles Times* ran a front-page exposé: See Bob Drogin and Greg Miller, "Iraqi Defector's Tales Bolstered U.S. Case for War: Colin Powell presented the U.N. with details on mobile germ factories, which came from a now-discredited source known as 'Curveball,'" *Los Angeles Times,* March 28, 2004, p. A1.

489 "not an explanation for his fabrications": *SSCI Report on the Chalabi Group,* p. 108.

489 "*minimal impact on pre-war assessments*": Silberman-Robb Report, p. 108, (emphasis added [citations omitted]).

490 later dismissed by the Iraqi courts for lack of evidence: See Rajiv Chandrasekaran, "Iraqi Judge Dismisses Chalabi Case," *Washington Post,* September 28, 2004, p. A22.

490 seized some files, computer equipment, and weapons: See Bremer, *My Year in Iraq,* p. 364.

490 fatal strike against Chalabi's political ambitions in Iraq: See, e.g., Barbara Slavin, "*Former exile's U.S. supporters seem to have cut him loose,*" *USA Today,* May 21, 2004, p. A4; Jim Hoagland, "Cutting off Chalabi," *Washington Post,* May 21, 2004, p. A25; Luke Harding and Julian Borger, "*Pentagon protege humiliated as US and Iraqi police raid Baghdad villa: Defiant fall from grace,*" *The Guardian,* May 21, 2004, p. 4.

490 November 2005 meetings would not have occurred: For the December 2005 national elections, Chalabi broke away from the main Shiite party and formed his own party, but failed to win any parliamentary seats. The government of Prime Minister Nouri al-Maliki nevertheless asked him to perform some official assignments, and it appears that Chalabi intends to remain active in Iraqi politics. See, e.g., Melik Kaylan, "Survivor: The Weekend Interview," *Wall Street Journal,* July 7, 2007, available at http://www.opinionjournal.com/editorial/feature.html?id=110010305.

491 On May 22, I gave Rumsfeld a memo: Douglas J. Feith Memo to Rumsfeld, "President's Speech on Iraq," May 22, 2004.

492 the next day I wrote Rumsfeld another set of comments: Douglas J. Feith Memo to Rumsfeld, "Comments on Draft #8 of President's Speech on Iraq," May 23, 2004.

493 Wolfowitz endorsed my memo: Paul Wolfowitz E-mail to Feith, "Re: Speech Memo," May 23, 2004, 11:46 A.M., containing a memo from Wolfowitz to Rumsfeld, "Presidential Speech."

493 Rumsfeld says he discussed the matter: I clarified this with Rumsfeld in an exchange on January 30, 2008.

495 respectful comment even from many who opposed the Iraq war: See, e.g., Editorial, "Message from Iraq," *New York Times,* January 31, 2005, p. A22:

> **Courageous Iraqis turned out to vote yesterday in numbers that may have exceeded even the most optimistic predictions. Participation varied by region, and the impressive national percentages should not**

obscure the fact that the country's large Sunni Arab minority remained broadly disenfranchised—due to alienation or terror or both. But even in some predominantly Sunni areas, turnout was higher than expected. And in an impressive range of mainly Shiite and Kurdish cities, a long silenced majority of ordinary Iraqis defied threats of deadly mayhem to cast votes for a new, and hopefully democratic, political order.

This page has not hesitated to criticize the Bush administration over its policies in Iraq, and we continue to have grave doubts about the overall direction of American strategy there. Yet today, along with other Americans, whether supporters or critics of the war, we rejoice in a heartening advance by the Iraqi people. For now at least, the multiple political failures that marked the run-up to the voting stand eclipsed by a remarkably successful election day.

497 growing to 1,130 in June 2004: Michael O'Hanlon and Adriana Lins de Albuquerque, *Iraq Index: Tracking Variables of Reconstruction and Security in Post-Saddam Iraq,* Brookings Institution, August 13, 2004, available at http://www3.brookings.edu/fp/saban/iraq/index20040813.pdf.

498 and steal their oil: An April 2004 Gallup Poll in Iraq found that nationwide, 71 percent of Iraqis viewed coalition forces as "occupiers" rather than "liberators," compared to 43 percent at the time of the invasion. ("Key findings: Nationwide survey of 3,500 Iraqis," April 28, 2004, available at http://www.usatoday.com/news/world/iraq/2004–04–28-gallup-iraq-findings.htm.)

499 looked on U.S. forces favorably: A 2005 ABC News poll in Afghanistan found that 83 percent of Afghans had a favorable view of the United States and 87 percent believed that the Taliban's ouster was a "good thing"; despite the many challenges facing Afghanistan, 77 percent of Afghans felt their country was moving in the right direction. Gary Langer, "2005 Poll: Four Years After the Fall of the Taliban, Afghans Optimistic About the Future," ABC News Online, December 7, 2005, available at http://abcnews.go.com/International/PollVault/story?id=1363276.

499 "in a hurry to see them": Bremer, *My Year in Iraq,* p. 43.

499 "when we in the CPA could not": Ibid., p. 117.

499 "*as some in Washington had wanted?*": Ibid., p. 121 (emphasis in original).

Chapter 16: Lessons and Debate

506 Bin Laden cited that retreat: Bin Laden called Somalia "your most disgraceful case":

> [W]hen tens of your soldiers were killed in minor battles and one American pilot was dragged in the streets of Mogadishu you left the area carry-

ing disappointment, humiliation, defeat and your dead with you. Clinton appeared in front of the whole world threatening and promising revenge, but these threats were merely a preparation for withdrawal.

Usama bin Laden, "Declaration of War against the Americans Occupying the Land of the Two Holy Places," *Al Quds al Arabi*, August 1996, available at http://www.pbs.org/newshour/terrorism/international/fatwa_1996.html.

508 of both Hezbollah and Hamas: It is unclear how the Iraq war will ultimately affect Iran's position in the world. Some commentators argue that Iraqi Shiite political power necessarily redounds to Iran's benefit. If and when the insurgency diminishes, however, Iraq's development under a freely elected, Shiite-led government could aggravate the vulnerabilities of Iran's clerical regime. It could energize Iran's pro-democracy forces, as Iranians ask why Iraqi Shiites have a greater voice in governing themselves than Iran's Shiites do. In other words, the notion that a successful Iraq necessarily strengthens the clerical regime in Teheran is far from certain and may be backward. Indeed, the Iranian government does not appear to accept that notion, given its efforts to foment chaos in Iraq.

509 On October 16, 2003, Rumsfeld addressed a memo: Rumsfeld Memo to Wolfowitz, Myers, Pace, and Feith, "Global War on Terrorism," October 16, 2003. The memo was leaked to *USA Today*, which published it in full. See Dave Moniz and Tom Squitieri, "Defense memo: A grim outlook," *USA Today*, October 22, 2003, p. 1A.

509 a clear statement of the national strategy: In February 2003, the White House published a document called *National Strategy for Combating Terrorism*. It had a peculiar status within the government, not having emerged through any standard interagency process: It was produced the way the White House generated press releases, not strategy documents. I saw it for the first time when the National Security Council staff sent it to my office for comment, though there had been no discussion of it in either the Deputies Committee or the Principals Committee. As far as I know, it was published without the Principals ever having met to discuss it, let alone approve it. Rumsfeld never read it at all. The *National Strategy* never served the essential purpose of a strategy document, which is to guide the policies and actions of the various agencies. When my colleagues and I drafted the war on terrorism strategy to answer Rumsfeld's October 2003 memo, we did not use the February 2003 document as the foundation. And when we eventually presented our strategy to President Bush and the National Security Council in May 2004 and January 2005, *no one* made any reference to the February 2003 document.

510 On May 25, 2004, Rumsfeld had me present the resulting strategy: See [Office of the Under Secretary of Defense for Policy], "The Nature of the Conflict and a Long-Term USG Strategy for Addressing It," May 25, 2004 3:55 P.M. [labeled "Draft Working Papers," though this was the briefing presented to the President].

511 In that January 13, 2005, meeting: See [Office of the Under Secretary of Defense for Policy], "New Initiatives in the Global War on Terrorism," January 13,

2005 8:13 A.M. [labeled "Draft Working Papers," though this was the briefing presented to the President].

513 impossible to ensure prevention: U.S. Central Intelligence Agency, "The Terrorist Threat to the US Homeland," Office of the Director of National Security, National Intelligence Estimate, July 2007, p. 6, available at http://www.dni.gov/press_releases/20070202_release.pdf.

520 A number of CIA and other intelligence officials opposed the President: See, e.g., Paul R. Pillar, "Intelligence, Policy, and the War in Iraq," *Foreign Affairs*, March/April 2006; Michael Scheuer ("Anonymous"), *Imperial Hubris* (Dulles, Virginia: Potomac Books, 2004).

INDEX